Algorithm Design and Applications

Michael T. Goodrich
Department of Information and Computer Science
University of California, Irvine

Roberto Tamassia
Department of Computer Science
Brown University

Algorithm Design and Applications

Michael T. Goodrich
Department of Information and Computer Science
University of California, Irvine

Roberto Tamassia
Department of Computer Science
Brown University

WILEY

VICE PRESIDENT & PUBLISHER	Don Fowley
EXECUTIVE EDITOR	Beth Lang Golub
EDITORIAL ASSISTANT	Jayne Ziemba
ASSISTANT MARKETING MANAGER	Debbie Martin
ASSOCIATE PRODUCTION MANAGER	Joyce Poh
PRODUCTION EDITOR	Wanqian Ye
COVER CREDIT	© Ansel Adams/U.S. National Archives and Records Administration

This book was set by the authors and printed and bound by Quad/Graphics.

This book is printed on acid free paper. ∞

Founded in 1807, John Wiley & Sons, Inc. has been a valued source of knowledge and understanding for more than 200 years, helping people around the world meet their needs and fulfill their aspirations. Our company is built on a foundation of principles that include responsibility to the communities we serve and where we live and work. In 2008, we launched a Corporate Citizenship Initiative, a global effort to address the environmental, social, economic, and ethical challenges we face in our business. Among the issues we are addressing are carbon impact, paper specifications and procurement, ethical conduct within our business and among our vendors, and community and charitable support. For more information, please visit our website: www.wiley.com/go/citizenship.

Library of Congress Cataloging in Publication Data:

Goodrich, Michael T., author.
Algorithm design and applications / Michael T. Goodrich, Department of Information and Computer Science, University of California, Irvine, Roberto Tamassia, Department of Computer Science, Brown University.
    pages cm
Includes bibliographical references and index.
ISBN 978-1-118-33591-8 (hardback)
1. Computer algorithms. 2. Data structures (Computer science) I. Tamassia, Roberto, 1960- author. II. Title.
QA76.9.A43G668 2014
005.7'3--dc23
                        2014021534

Printed in the United States of America

SKY10032430_010722

To Karen, Paul, Anna, and Jack
– *Michael T. Goodrich*

To Isabel
– *Roberto Tamassia*

Contents

Preface   xi

1 Algorithm Analysis   1
  1.1 Analyzing Algorithms   3
  1.2 A Quick Mathematical Review 19
  1.3 A Case Study in Algorithm Analysis 29
  1.4 Amortization 34
  1.5 Exercises 42

Part I: Data Structures

2 Basic Data Structures   51
  2.1 Stacks and Queues 53
  2.2 Lists 60
  2.3 Trees 68
  2.4 Exercises 84

3 Binary Search Trees   89
  3.1 Searches and Updates 91
  3.2 Range Queries 101
  3.3 Index-Based Searching 104
  3.4 Randomly Constructed Search Trees 107
  3.5 Exercises 110

4 Balanced Binary Search Trees   115
  4.1 Ranks and Rotations 117
  4.2 AVL Trees 120
  4.3 Red-Black Trees 126
  4.4 Weak AVL Trees 130
  4.5 Splay Trees 139
  4.6 Exercises 149

5 Priority Queues and Heaps   155
  5.1 Priority Queues 157
  5.2 PQ-Sort, Selection-Sort, and Insertion-Sort 158
  5.3 Heaps 163
  5.4 Heap-Sort 174
  5.5 Extending Priority Queues 179
  5.6 Exercises 182

6 Hash Tables   **187**
  6.1 Maps 189
  6.2 Hash Functions 192
  6.3 Handling Collisions and Rehashing 198
  6.4 Cuckoo Hashing 206
  6.5 Universal Hashing 212
  6.6 Exercises 215

7 Union-Find Structures   **219**
  7.1 Union-Find and Its Applications 221
  7.2 A List-Based Implementation 225
  7.3 A Tree-Based Implementation 228
  7.4 Exercises 236

Part II: Sorting and Selection

8 Merge-Sort and Quick-Sort   **241**
  8.1 Merge-Sort 243
  8.2 Quick-Sort 250
  8.3 A Lower Bound on Comparison-Based Sorting 257
  8.4 Exercises 259

9 Fast Sorting and Selection   **265**
  9.1 Bucket-Sort and Radix-Sort 267
  9.2 Selection 270
  9.3 Weighted Medians 276
  9.4 Exercises 279

Part III: Fundamental Techniques

10 The Greedy Method   **283**
  10.1 The Fractional Knapsack Problem 286
  10.2 Task Scheduling 289
  10.3 Text Compression and Huffman Coding 292
  10.4 Exercises 298

11 Divide-and-Conquer   **303**
  11.1 Recurrences and the Master Theorem 305
  11.2 Integer Multiplication 313
  11.3 Matrix Multiplication 315
  11.4 The Maxima-Set Problem 317
  11.5 Exercises 319

12 Dynamic Programming **323**
   12.1 Matrix Chain-Products 325
   12.2 The General Technique 329
   12.3 Telescope Scheduling 331
   12.4 Game Strategies 334
   12.5 The Longest Common Subsequence Problem 339
   12.6 The 0-1 Knapsack Problem 343
   12.7 Exercises 346

Part IV: Graph Algorithms

13 Graphs and Traversals **353**
   13.1 Graph Terminology and Representations 355
   13.2 Depth-First Search 365
   13.3 Breadth-First Search 370
   13.4 Directed Graphs 373
   13.5 Biconnected Components 386
   13.6 Exercises 392

14 Shortest Paths **397**
   14.1 Single-Source Shortest Paths 399
   14.2 Dijkstra's Algorithm 400
   14.3 The Bellman-Ford Algorithm 407
   14.4 Shortest Paths in Directed Acyclic Graphs 410
   14.5 All-Pairs Shortest Paths 412
   14.6 Exercises 418

15 Minimum Spanning Trees **423**
   15.1 Properties of Minimum Spanning Trees 425
   15.2 Kruskal's Algorithm 428
   15.3 The Prim-Jarník Algorithm 433
   15.4 Barůvka's Algorithm 436
   15.5 Exercises 439

16 Network Flow and Matching **443**
   16.1 Flows and Cuts 445
   16.2 Maximum Flow Algorithms 452
   16.3 Maximum Bipartite Matching 458
   16.4 Baseball Elimination 460
   16.5 Minimum-Cost Flow 462
   16.6 Exercises 469

Part V: Computational Intractability

17 *NP*-Completeness   **473**
   17.1 *P* and *NP* 476
   17.2 *NP*-Completeness 483
   17.3 CNF-SAT and 3SAT 489
   17.4 VERTEX-COVER, CLIQUE, and SET-COVER 492
   17.5 SUBSET-SUM and KNAPSACK 496
   17.6 HAMILTONIAN-CYCLE and TSP 499
   17.7 Exercises 502

18 Approximation Algorithms   **507**
   18.1 The Metric Traveling Salesperson Problem 511
   18.2 Approximations for Covering Problems 515
   18.3 Polynomial-Time Approximation Schemes 518
   18.4 Backtracking and Branch-and-Bound 521
   18.5 Exercises 525

Part VI: Additional Topics

19 Randomized Algorithms   **529**
   19.1 Generating Random Permutations 531
   19.2 Stable Marriages and Coupon Collecting 534
   19.3 Minimum Cuts 539
   19.4 Finding Prime Numbers 546
   19.5 Chernoff Bounds 551
   19.6 Skip Lists 557
   19.7 Exercises 563

20 B-Trees and External Memory   **569**
   20.1 External Memory 571
   20.2 (2,4) Trees and B-Trees 574
   20.3 External-Memory Sorting 590
   20.4 Online Caching Algorithms 593
   20.5 Exercises 600

21 Multidimensional Searching   **603**
   21.1 Range Trees 605
   21.2 Priority Search Trees 609
   21.3 Quadtrees and k-d Trees 614
   21.4 Exercises 618

22 Computational Geometry   623
   22.1 Operations on Geometric Objects 625
   22.2 Convex Hulls 630
   22.3 Segment Intersection 638
   22.4 Finding a Closest Pair of Points 642
   22.5 Exercises 646

23 String Algorithms   651
   23.1 String Operations 653
   23.2 The Boyer-Moore Algorithm 656
   23.3 The Knuth-Morris-Pratt Algorithm 660
   23.4 Hash-Based Lexicon Matching 664
   23.5 Tries 669
   23.6 Exercises 680

24 Cryptography   685
   24.1 Greatest Common Divisors (GCD) 687
   24.2 Modular Arithmetic 691
   24.3 Cryptographic Operations 699
   24.4 The RSA Cryptosystem 703
   24.5 The El Gamal Cryptosystem 706
   24.6 Exercises 708

25 The Fast Fourier Transform   711
   25.1 Convolution 713
   25.2 Primitive Roots of Unity 715
   25.3 The Discrete Fourier Transform 717
   25.4 The Fast Fourier Transform Algorithm 721
   25.5 Exercises 727

26 Linear Programming   731
   26.1 Formulating the Problem 734
   26.2 The Simplex Method 739
   26.3 Duality 746
   26.4 Applications of Linear Programming 750
   26.5 Exercises 753

A Useful Mathematical Facts   761
Bibliography   765
Index   774

Preface

This book is designed to provide a comprehensive introduction to the design and analysis of computer algorithms and data structures. We have made each chapter to be relatively independent of other chapters so as to provide instructors and readers greater flexibility with respect to which chapters to explore. Moreover, the extensive collection of topics we include provides coverage of both classic and emerging algorithmic methods, including the following:

- *Mathematics for asymptotic analysis*, including amortization and randomization
- *General algorithm design techniques*, including the greedy method, divide-and-conquer, and dynamic programming
- *Data structures*, including lists, trees, heaps, search trees, B-trees, hash tables, skip lists, union-find structures, and multidimensional trees
- *Algorithmic frameworks*, including *NP*-completeness, approximation algorithms, and external-memory algorithms
- *Fundamental algorithms*, including sorting, graph algorithms, computational geometry, numerical algorithms, cryptography, Fast Fourier Transform (FFT), and linear programming.

Application-Motivated Approach

This is an exciting time for computer science. Computers have moved beyond their early uses as computational engines to now be used as information processors, with applications to every other discipline. Moreover, the expansion of the Internet has brought about new paradigms and modalities for computer applications to society and commerce. For instance, computers can be used to store and retrieve large amounts of data, and they are used in many other application areas, such as sports, video games, biology, medicine, social networking, engineering, and science. Thus, we feel that algorithms should be taught to emphasize not only their mathematical analysis but also their practical applications.

To fulfill this need, we have written each chapter to begin with a brief discussion of an application that motivates the topic of that chapter. In some cases, this application comes from a real-world use of the topic discussed in the chapter, and in other cases it is a contrived application that highlights how the topic of the chapter could be used in practice. Our intent in providing this motivation is to give readers a conceptual context and practical justification to accompany their reading of each chapter. In addition to this application-based motivation we include also detailed pseudocode descriptions and complete mathematical analysis. Indeed, we feel that mathematical rigor should not simply be for its own sake, but also for its pragmatic implications.

For the Instructor

This book is structured to allow an instructor a great deal of freedom in how to organize and present material. The dependence between chapters is relatively minimal, which allows the instructor to cover topics in her preferred sequence. Moreover, each chapter is designed so that it can be covered in 1–3 lectures, depending on the depth of coverage.

Example Courses

This book has several possible uses as a textbook. It can be used, for instance, for a core Algorithms course, which is classically known as CS7. Alternatively, it could be used for an upper-division/graduate data structures course, an upper-division/graduate algorithms course, or a two-course sequence on these topics. To highlight these alternatives, we give an example syllabus for each of these possible courses below.

Example syllabus for a core Algorithms (CS7) course:

1. Algorithm Analysis
   (Skip, skim, or review Chapters 2–4 on fundamental data structures)[1]
5. Priority Queues and Heaps
6. Hash Tables
7. Union-Find Structures
8. Merge-Sort and Quick-Sort
9. Fast Sorting and Selection (if time permits)
10. The Greedy Method
11. Divide-and-Conquer
12. Dynamic Programming
13. Graphs and Traversals
14. Shortest Paths
15. Minimum Spanning Trees
16. Network Flow and Matching (if time permits)
17. *NP*-Completeness
18. Approximation Algorithms
    Optional choices from Chapters 19–26, as time permits

The optional choices from Chapters 19–26 that could be covered at the end of the course include randomized algorithms, computational geometry, string algorithms, cryptography, Fast Fourier Transform (FFT), and linear programming.

---

[1]These topics, and possibly even the topics of Chapters 5 and 6, are typically covered to at least a basic level in a Data Structures course that could be a prerequisite to this course.

Example syllabus for an upper-division/graduate Data Structures course:

1. Algorithm Analysis
2. Basic Data Structures
3. Binary Search Trees
4. Balanced Binary Search Trees
5. Priority Queues and Heaps
6. Hash Tables
7. Union-Find Structures
8. Merge-Sort and Quick-Sort
13. Graphs and Traversals
14. Shortest Paths
15. Minimum Spanning Trees
20. B-Trees and External-Memory
21. Multi-Dimensional Searching

Example syllabus for an upper-division/graduate Algorithms course:

(Skip, skim, or review Chapters 1–8)
9. Fast Sorting and Selection
10. The Greedy Method
11. Divide-and-Conquer
12. Dynamic Programming
16. Network Flow and Matching
17. *NP*-Completeness
18. Approximation Algorithms
19. Randomized Algorithms
22. Computational Geometry
23. String Algorithms
24. Cryptography
25. The Fast Fourier Transform (FFT)
26. Linear Programming

This course could be taught either as a stand-alone course or in conjunction with an upper-division Data Structures course, such as that given above.

Of course, other options are also possible. Let us not belabor this point, however, leaving such creative arrangements to instructors.

Three Kinds of Exercises

This book contains many exercises—over 800—which are divided between the following three categories:

- *reinforcement* exercises, which test comprehension of chapter topics
- *creativity* exercises, which test creative utilization of techniques from the chapter
- *application* exercises, which test uses of the topics of the chapter for real-world or contrived applications

The exercises are distributed so that roughly 35% are reinforcement exercises, 40% are creativity exercises, and 25% are application exercises.

Web Added-Value Education

This book comes accompanied by an extensive website:

http://www.wiley.com/college/goodrich/

This site includes an extensive collection of educational aids that augment the topics of this book. Specifically for *students* we include the following:

- Presentation handouts in PDF format for most topics in this book
- Hints on selected exercises.

The hints should be of particular interest for creativity and application problems that may be quite challenging for some students.

For *instructors* using this book, there is a dedicated portion of the site just for them, which includes the following additional *teaching aids*:

- Solutions to selected exercises in this book
- Editable presentations in PowerPoint format for most topics in this book.

Prerequisites

We have written this book assuming that the reader comes to it with certain knowledge. In particular, we assume that the reader has a basic understanding of elementary data structures, such as arrays and linked lists, and is at least vaguely familiar with a high-level programming language, such as C, C++, Java, or Python. Thus, all algorithms are described in a high-level "pseudocode," which avoids some details, such as error condition testing, but is suitable for a knowledgeable reader to convert algorithm descriptions into working code.

In terms of mathematical background, we assume the reader is familiar with exponents, logarithms, summations, limits, and elementary probability. Even so, we review many of these concepts in Chapter 1, and we give a summary of other useful mathematical facts, including elementary probability, in Appendix A.

About the Authors

Professors Goodrich and Tamassia are well-recognized researchers in algorithms and data structures, having published many papers in this field, with applications to computer security, cryptography, Internet computing, information visualization, and geometric computing. They have served as principal investigators in several joint projects sponsored by the National Science Foundation, the Army Research Office, and the Defense Advanced Research Projects Agency. They are also active in educational technology research.

Michael Goodrich received his Ph.D. in Computer Sciences from Purdue University in 1987. He is a Chancellor's Professor in the Department of Computer Science at University of California, Irvine. Previously, he was a professor at Johns Hopkins University. His research interests include analysis, design, and implementation of algorithms, data security, cloud computing, graph drawing, and computational geometry. He is a Fulbright scholar and a fellow of the American Association for the Advancement of Science (AAAS), Association for Computing Machinery (ACM), and Institute of Electrical and Electronics Engineers (IEEE). He is a recipient of the IEEE Computer Society Technical Achievement Award, the ACM Recognition of Service Award, and the Pond Award for Excellence in Undergraduate Teaching. He serves on the advisory boards of the *International Journal of Computational Geometry & Applications* (IJCGA) and of the *Journal of Graph Algorithms and Applications* (JGAA).

Roberto Tamassia received his Ph.D. in Electrical and Computer Engineering from the University of Illinois at Urbana-Champaign in 1988. He is the Plastech Professor of Computer Science in the Department of Computer Science at Brown University. He is also the Director of Brown's Center for Geometric Computing. His research interests include data security, applied cryptography, cloud computing, analysis, design, and implementation of algorithms, graph drawing and computational geometry. He is a fellow of the American Association for the Advancement of Science (AAAS), Association for Computing Machinery (ACM), and Institute for Electrical and Electronic Engineers (IEEE). He is also a recipient of the Technical Achievement Award from the IEEE Computer Society. He co-founded the *Journal of Graph Algorithms and Applications* (JGAA) and the Symposium on Graph Drawing. He serves as co-editor-in-chief of JGAA.

Acknowledgments

There are a number of individuals with whom we have collaborated on research and educational projects about algorithms. Working with them helped us refine the vision and content of this book. Specifically, we thank Jeff Achter, Vesselin Arnaudov, James Baker, Ryan Baker, Benjamin Boer, John Boreiko, Devin Borland, Lubomir Bourdev, Ulrik Brandes, Stina Bridgeman, Bryan Cantrill, Yi-Jen Chiang,

Robert Cohen, David Ellis, David Emory, Jody Fanto, Ben Finkel, Peter Fröhlich, Ashim Garg, David Ginat, Natasha Gelfand, Esha Ghosh, Michael Goldwasser, Mark Handy, Michael Horn, Greg Howard, Benoît Hudson, Jovanna Ignatowicz, James Kelley, Evgenios Kornaropoulos, Giuseppe Liotta, David Mount, Jeremy Mullendore, Olga Ohrimenko, Seth Padowitz, Bernardo Palazzi, Charalampos Papamanthou, James Piechota, Daniel Polivy, Seth Proctor, Susannah Raub, Haru Sakai, John Schultz, Andrew Schwerin, Michael Shapiro, Michael Shim, Michael Shin, Galina Shubina, Amy Simpson, Christian Straub, Ye Sun, Nikos Triandopoulos, Luca Vismara, Danfeng Yao, Jason Ye, and Eric Zamore.

We are grateful to our editor, Beth Golub, for her enthusiastic support of this project. The production team at Wiley has been great. Many thanks go to people who helped us with the book development, including Jayne Ziemba, Jennifer Welter, Debbie Martin, Chris Ruel, Julie Kennedy, Wanqian Ye, Joyce Poh, and Janis Soo.

We are especially grateful to Michael Bannister, Jenny Lam, and Joseph Simons for their contributions to the chapter on linear programming. We would like to thank Siddhartha Sen and Robert Tarjan for an illuminating discussion about balanced search trees.

We are truly indebted to the outside reviewers, and especially to Jack Snoeyink, for detailed comments and constructive criticism, which were extremely useful. These other outside reviewers included John Donald, Hui Yang, Nicholas Tran, John Black, My Thai, Dana Randall, Ming-Yang Kao, Qiang Cheng, Ravi Janarden, Fikret Ercal, Jack Snoeyink, S. Muthukrishnan, Elliot Anshelevich, Mukkai Krishnamoorthy, Roxanne Canosa, Michael Cutler, Roger Crawfis, Glencora Borradaile, and Jennifer Welch.

This manuscript was prepared primarily with LaTeX for the text and Microsoft PowerPoint®, Visio®, and Adobe FrameMaker® for the figures.

Finally, we warmly thank Isabel Cruz, Karen Goodrich, Giuseppe Di Battista, Franco Preparata, Ioannis Tollis, and our parents for providing advice, encouragement, and support at various stages of the preparation of this book. We also thank them for reminding us that there are things in life beyond writing books.

Michael T. Goodrich
Roberto Tamassia

Chapter

1

Algorithm Analysis

Microscope: U.S. government image, from the N.I.H. Medical Instrument Gallery, DeWitt Stetten, Jr., Museum of Medical Research. Hubble Space Telescope: U.S. government image, from NASA, STS-125 Crew, May 25, 2009.

Contents

1.1 Analyzing Algorithms 3

1.2 A Quick Mathematical Review 19

1.3 A Case Study in Algorithm Analysis 29

1.4 Amortization 34

1.5 Exercises 42

Scientists often have to deal with differences in scale, from the microscopically small to the astronomically large, and they have developed a wide range of tools for dealing with the differences in scale in the objects they study. Similarly, computer scientists must also deal with scale, but they deal with it primarily in terms of data volume rather than physical object size. In the world of information technology, *scalability* refers to the ability of a system to gracefully accommodate growing sizes of inputs or amounts of workload. Being able to achieve scalability for a computer system can mean the difference between a technological solution that can succeed in the marketplace or scientific application and one that becomes effectively unusable as data volumes increase. In this book, we are therefore interested in the design of scalable algorithms and data structures.

Simply put, an *algorithm* is a step-by-step procedure for performing some task in a finite amount of time, and a *data structure* is a systematic way of organizing and accessing data. These concepts are central to computing, and this book is dedicated to the discussion of paradigms and principles for the design and implementation of correct and efficient data structures and algorithms. But to be able to determine the degree to which algorithms and data structures are scalable, we must have precise ways of analyzing them.

The primary analysis tool we use in this book is to characterize the *running time* of an algorithm or data structure operation, with *space usage* also being of interest. Running time is a natural measure for the purposes of scalability, since time is a precious resource. It is an important consideration in economic and scientific applications, since everyone expects computer applications to run as fast as possible.

We begin this chapter by describing the basic framework needed for analyzing algorithms, which includes the language for describing algorithms, the computational model that language is intended for, and the main factors we count when considering running time. We also include a brief discussion of how recursive algorithms are analyzed. In Section 1.1.5, we present the main notation we use to characterize running times—the so-called "big-Oh" notation. These tools comprise the main theoretical tools for designing and analyzing algorithms.

In Section 1.2, we take a short break from our development of the framework for algorithm analysis to review some important mathematical facts, including discussions of summations, logarithms, proof techniques, and basic probability. Given this background and our notation for algorithm analysis, we present a case study on algorithm analysis in Section 1.3, focusing on a problem often used as a test question during job interviews. We follow this case study in Section 1.4 by presenting an interesting analysis technique, known as amortization, which allows us to account for the group behavior of many individual operations. Finally, we conclude the chapter with some exercises that include several problems inspired by questions commonly asked during job interviews at major software and Internet companies.

1.1 Analyzing Algorithms

The running time of an algorithm or data structure operation typically depends on a number of factors, so what should be the proper way of measuring it? If an algorithm has been implemented, we can study its running time by executing it on various test inputs and recording the actual time spent in each execution. Such measurements can be taken in an accurate manner by using system calls that are built into the language or operating system for which the algorithm is written. In general, we are interested in determining the dependency of the running time on the size of the input. In order to determine this, we can perform several experiments on many different test inputs of various sizes. We can then visualize the results of such experiments by plotting the performance of each run of the algorithm as a point with x-coordinate equal to the input size, n, and y-coordinate equal to the running time, t. (See Figure 1.1.) To be meaningful, this analysis requires that we choose good sample inputs and test enough of them to be able to make sound statistical claims about the algorithm.

In general, the running time of an algorithm or data structure method increases with the input size, although it may also vary for distinct inputs of the same size. Also, the running time is affected by the hardware environment (processor, clock rate, memory, disk, etc.) and software environment (operating system, programming language, compiler, interpreter, etc.) in which the algorithm is implemented, compiled, and executed. All other factors being equal, the running time of the same algorithm on the same input data will be smaller if the computer has, say, a much faster processor or if the implementation is done in a program compiled into native machine code instead of an interpreted implementation run on a virtual machine.

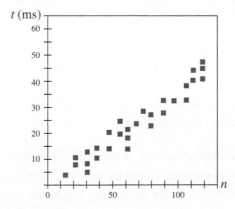

Figure 1.1: Results of an experimental study on the running time of an algorithm. A dot with coordinates (n, t) indicates that on an input of size n, the running time of the algorithm is t milliseconds (ms).

Requirements for a General Analysis Methodology

Experimental studies on running times are useful, but they have some limitations:

- Experiments can be done only on a limited set of test inputs, and care must be taken to make sure these are representative.
- It is difficult to compare the efficiency of two algorithms unless experiments on their running times have been performed in the same hardware and software environments.
- It is necessary to implement and execute an algorithm in order to study its running time experimentally.

Thus, while experimentation has an important role to play in algorithm analysis, it alone is not sufficient. Therefore, in addition to experimentation, we desire an analytic framework that

- Takes into account all possible inputs
- Allows us to evaluate the relative efficiency of any two algorithms in a way that is independent from the hardware and software environment
- Can be performed by studying a high-level description of the algorithm without actually implementing it or running experiments on it.

This methodology aims at associating with each algorithm a function $f(n)$ that characterizes the running time of the algorithm in terms of the input size n. Typical functions that will be encountered include n and n^2. For example, we will write statements of the type "Algorithm A runs in time proportional to n," meaning that if we were to perform experiments, we would find that the actual running time of algorithm A on **any** input of size n never exceeds cn, where c is a constant that depends on the hardware and software environment used in the experiment. Given two algorithms A and B, where A runs in time proportional to n and B runs in time proportional to n^2, we will prefer A to B, since the function n grows at a smaller rate than the function n^2.

We are now ready to "roll up our sleeves" and start developing our methodology for algorithm analysis. There are several components to this methodology, including the following:

- A language for describing algorithms
- A computational model that algorithms execute within
- A metric for measuring algorithm running time
- An approach for characterizing running times, including those for recursive algorithms.

We describe these components in more detail in the remainder of this section.

1.1.1 Pseudo-Code

Programmers are often asked to describe algorithms in a way that is intended for human eyes only. Such descriptions are not computer programs, but are more structured than usual prose. They also facilitate the high-level analysis of a data structure or algorithm. We call these descriptions ***pseudocode***.

An Example of Pseudo-Code

The array-maximum problem is the simple problem of finding the maximum element in an array A storing n integers. To solve this problem, we can use an algorithm called arrayMax, which scans through the elements of A using a **for** loop.

The pseudocode description of algorithm arrayMax is shown in Algorithm 1.2.

Algorithm arrayMax(A, n):
   Input: An array A storing $n \geq 1$ integers.
   Output: The maximum element in A.
   currentMax $\leftarrow A[0]$
   for $i \leftarrow 1$ **to** $n - 1$ **do**
      if *currentMax* $< A[i]$ **then**
         currentMax $\leftarrow A[i]$
   return *currentMax*

Algorithm 1.2: Algorithm arrayMax.

Note that the pseudocode is more compact than an equivalent actual software code fragment would be. In addition, the pseudocode is easier to read and understand.

Using Pseudo-Code to Prove Algorithm Correctness

By inspecting the pseudocode, we can argue about the correctness of algorithm arrayMax with a simple argument. Variable *currentMax* starts out being equal to the first element of A. We claim that at the beginning of the ith iteration of the loop, *currentMax* is equal to the maximum of the first i elements in A. Since we compare *currentMax* to $A[i]$ in iteration i, if this claim is true before this iteration, it will be true after it for $i + 1$ (which is the next value of counter i). Thus, after $n - 1$ iterations, *currentMax* will equal the maximum element in A. As with this example, we want our pseudocode descriptions to always be detailed enough to fully justify the correctness of the algorithm they describe, while being simple enough for human readers to understand.

What Is Pseudo-Code?

Pseudo-code is a mixture of natural language and high-level programming constructs that describe the main ideas behind a generic implementation of a data structure or algorithm. There really is no precise definition of the *pseudocode* language, however, because of its reliance on natural language. At the same time, to help achieve clarity, pseudocode mixes natural language with standard programming language constructs. The programming language constructs we choose are those consistent with modern high-level languages such as Python, C++, and Java. These constructs include the following:

- *Expressions:* We use standard mathematical symbols to express numeric and Boolean expressions. We use the left arrow sign ($\leftarrow$) as the assignment operator in assignment statements (equivalent to the $=$ operator in C, C++, and Java) and we use the equal sign ($=$) as the equality relation in Boolean expressions (equivalent to the "$==$" relation in C, C++, and Java).
- *Method declarations:* **Algorithm** name($param1, param2, \ldots$) declares a new method "name" and its parameters.
- *Decision structures:* **if** condition **then** true-actions [**else** false-actions]. We use indentation to indicate what actions should be included in the true-actions and false-actions, and we assume Boolean operators allow for short-circuit evaluation.
- *While-loops:* **while** condition **do** actions. We use indentation to indicate what actions should be included in the loop actions.
- *Repeat-loops:* **repeat** actions **until** condition. We use indentation to indicate what actions should be included in the loop actions.
- *For-loops:* **for** variable-increment-definition **do** actions. We use indentation to indicate what actions should be included among the loop actions.
- *Array indexing:* $A[i]$ represents the ith cell in the array A. We usually index the cells of an array A of size n from 1 to n, as in mathematics, but sometimes we instead such an array from 0 to $n - 1$, consistent with C, C++, and Java.
- *Method calls:* object.method(args) (object is optional if it is understood).
- *Method returns:* **return** value. This operation returns the value specified to the method that called this one.

When we write pseudocode, we must keep in mind that we are writing for a human reader, not a computer. Thus, we should strive to communicate high-level ideas, not low-level implementation details. At the same time, we should not gloss over important steps. Like many forms of human communication, finding the right balance is an important skill that is refined through practice.

Now that we have developed a high-level way of describing algorithms, let us next discuss how we can analytically characterize algorithms written in pseudocode.

1.1.2   The Random Access Machine (RAM) Model

As we noted above, experimental analysis is valuable, but it has its limitations. If we wish to analyze a particular algorithm without performing experiments on its running time, we can take the following more analytic approach directly on the high-level code or pseudocode. We define a set of high-level ***primitive operations*** that are largely independent from the programming language used and can be identified also in the pseudocode. Primitive operations include the following:

- Assigning a value to a variable
- Calling a method
- Performing an arithmetic operation (for example, adding two numbers)
- Comparing two numbers
- Indexing into an array
- Following an object reference
- Returning from a method.

Specifically, a primitive operation corresponds to a low-level instruction with an execution time that depends on the hardware and software environment but is nevertheless constant. Instead of trying to determine the specific execution time of each primitive operation, we will simply ***count*** how many primitive operations are executed, and use this number t as a high-level estimate of the running time of the algorithm. This operation count will correlate to an actual running time in a specific hardware and software environment, for each primitive operation corresponds to a constant-time instruction, and there are only a fixed number of primitive operations. The implicit assumption in this approach is that the running times of different primitive operations will be fairly similar. Thus, the number, t, of primitive operations an algorithm performs will be proportional to the actual running time of that algorithm.

RAM Machine Model Definition

This approach of simply counting primitive operations gives rise to a computational model called the ***Random Access Machine*** (RAM). This model, which should not be confused with "random access memory," views a computer simply as a CPU connected to a bank of memory cells. Each memory cell stores a word, which can be a number, a character string, or an address—that is, the value of a base type. The term "random access" refers to the ability of the CPU to access an arbitrary memory cell with one primitive operation. To keep the model simple, we do not place any specific limits on the size of numbers that can be stored in words of memory. We assume the CPU in the RAM model can perform any primitive operation in a constant number of steps, which do not depend on the size of the input. Thus, an accurate bound on the number of primitive operations an algorithm performs corresponds directly to the running time of that algorithm in the RAM model.

1.1.3   Counting Primitive Operations

We now show how to count the number of primitive operations executed by an algorithm, using as an example algorithm arrayMax, whose pseudocode was given back in Algorithm 1.2. We do this analysis by focusing on each step of the algorithm and counting the primitive operations that it takes, taking into consideration that some operations are repeated, because they are enclosed in the body of a loop.

- Initializing the variable *currentMax* to $A[0]$ corresponds to two primitive operations (indexing into an array and assigning a value to a variable) and is executed only once at the beginning of the algorithm. Thus, it contributes two units to the count.
- At the beginning of the for loop, counter i is initialized to 1. This action corresponds to executing one primitive operation (assigning a value to a variable).
- Before entering the body of the for loop, condition $i < n$ is verified. This action corresponds to executing one primitive instruction (comparing two numbers). Since counter i starts at 1 and is incremented by 1 at the end of each iteration of the loop, the comparison $i < n$ is performed n times. Thus, it contributes n units to the count.
- The body of the for loop is executed $n - 1$ times (for values $1, 2, \ldots, n - 1$ of the counter). At each iteration, $A[i]$ is compared with *currentMax* (two primitive operations, indexing and comparing), $A[i]$ is possibly assigned to *currentMax* (two primitive operations, indexing and assigning), and the counter i is incremented (two primitive operations, summing and assigning). Hence, at each iteration of the loop, either four or six primitive operations are performed, depending on whether $A[i] \leq \text{currentMax}$ or $A[i] > \text{currentMax}$. Therefore, the body of the loop contributes between $4(n - 1)$ and $6(n - 1)$ units to the count.
- Returning the value of variable *currentMax* corresponds to one primitive operation, and is executed only once.

To summarize, the number of primitive operations $t(n)$ executed by algorithm arrayMax is at least

$$2 + 1 + n + 4(n - 1) + 1 = 5n$$

and at most

$$2 + 1 + n + 6(n - 1) + 1 = 7n - 2.$$

The best case ($t(n) = 5n$) occurs when $A[0]$ is the maximum element, so that variable *currentMax* is never reassigned. The worst case ($t(n) = 7n - 2$) occurs when the elements are sorted in increasing order, so that variable *currentMax* is reassigned at each iteration of the for loop.

Average-Case and Worst-Case Analysis

Like the arrayMax method, an algorithm may run faster on some inputs than it does on others. In such cases we may wish to express the running time of such an algorithm as an average taken over all possible inputs. Although such an ***average case*** analysis would often be valuable, it is typically quite challenging. It requires us to define a probability distribution on the set of inputs, which is typically a difficult task. Figure 1.3 schematically shows how, depending on the input distribution, the running time of an algorithm can be anywhere between the worst-case time and the best-case time. For example, what if inputs are really only of types "A" or "D"?

An average-case analysis also typically requires that we calculate expected running times based on a given input distribution. Such an analysis often requires heavy mathematics and probability theory.

Therefore, except for experimental studies or the analysis of algorithms that are themselves randomized, we will, for the remainder of this book, typically characterize running times in terms of the ***worst case***. We say, for example, that algorithm arrayMax executes $t(n) = 7n - 2$ primitive operations ***in the worst case***, meaning that the maximum number of primitive operations executed by the algorithm, taken over all inputs of size n, is $7n - 2$.

This type of analysis is much easier than an average-case analysis, as it does not require probability theory; it just requires the ability to identify the worst-case input, which is often straightforward. In addition, taking a worst-case approach can actually lead to better algorithms. Making the standard of success that of having an algorithm perform well in the worst case necessarily requires that it perform well on ***every*** input. That is, designing for the worst case can lead to stronger algorithmic "muscles," much like a track star who always practices by running uphill.

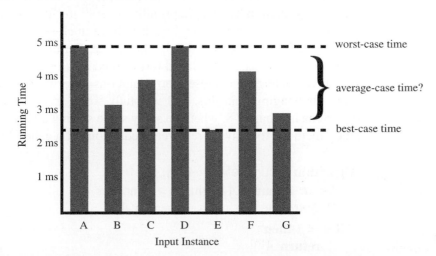

Figure 1.3: The difference between best-case and worst-case time. Each bar represents the running time of some algorithm on a different possible input.

1.1.4   Analyzing Recursive Algorithms

Iteration is not the only interesting way of solving a problem. Another useful technique, which is employed by many algorithms, is to use **recursion**. In this technique, we define a procedure P that is allowed to make calls to itself as a subroutine, provided those calls to P are for solving subproblems of smaller size. The subroutine calls to P on smaller instances are called "recursive calls." A recursive procedure should always define a **base case**, which is small enough that the algorithm can solve it directly without using recursion.

We give a recursive solution to the array maximum problem in Algorithm 1.4. This algorithm first checks if the array contains just a single item, which in this case must be the maximum; hence, in this simple base case we can immediately solve the problem. Otherwise, the algorithm recursively computes the maximum of the first $n - 1$ elements in the array and then returns the maximum of this value and the last element in the array.

As with this example, recursive algorithms are often quite elegant. Analyzing the running time of a recursive algorithm takes a bit of additional work, however. In particular, to analyze such a running time, we use a **recurrence equation**, which defines mathematical statements that the running time of a recursive algorithm must satisfy. We introduce a function $T(n)$ that denotes the running time of the algorithm on an input of size n, and we write equations that $T(n)$ must satisfy. For example, we can characterize the running time, $T(n)$, of the recursiveMax algorithm as

$$T(n) = \begin{cases} 3 & \text{if } n = 1 \\ T(n-1) + 7 & \text{otherwise,} \end{cases}$$

assuming that we count each comparison, array reference, recursive call, max calculation, or **return** as a single primitive operation. Ideally, we would like to characterize a recurrence equation like that above in **closed form**, where no references to the function T appear on the righthand side. For the recursiveMax algorithm, it isn't too hard to see that a closed form would be $T(n) = 7(n-1) + 3 = 7n - 4$. In general, determining closed form solutions to recurrence equations can be much more challenging than this, and we study some specific examples of recurrence equations in Chapter 8, when we study some sorting and selection algorithms. We study methods for solving recurrence equations of a general form in Section 11.1.

Algorithm recursiveMax(A, n):
> **Input:** An array A storing $n \geq 1$ integers.
> **Output:** The maximum element in A.

> **if** $n = 1$ **then**
> > **return** $A[0]$
> **return** $\max\{$recursiveMax$(A, n-1),\ A[n-1]\}$

Algorithm 1.4: Algorithm recursiveMax.

1.1.5   Asymptotic Notation

We have clearly gone into laborious detail for evaluating the running time of such a simple algorithm as arrayMax and its recursive cousin, recursiveMax. Such an approach would clearly prove cumbersome if we had to perform it for more complicated algorithms. In general, each step in a pseudocode description and each statement in a high-level language implementation tends to correspond to a small number of primitive operations that does not depend on the input size. Thus, we can perform a simplified analysis that estimates the number of primitive operations executed up to a constant factor, by counting the steps of the pseudocode or the statements of the high-level language executed. Fortunately, there is a notation that allows us to characterize the main factors affecting an algorithm's running time without going into all the details of exactly how many primitive operations are performed for each constant-time set of instructions.

The "Big-Oh" Notation

Let $f(n)$ and $g(n)$ be functions mapping nonnegative integers to real numbers. We say that $f(n)$ is $O(g(n))$ if there is a real constant $c > 0$ and an integer constant $n_0 \geq 1$ such that $f(n) \leq cg(n)$ for every integer $n \geq n_0$. This definition is often pronounced as "$f(n)$ is **big-Oh** of $g(n)$" or "$f(n)$ is **order** $g(n)$." (See Figure 1.5.)

Example 1.1: *$7n - 2$ is $O(n)$.*

Proof: *We need a real constant $c > 0$ and an integer constant $n_0 \geq 1$ such that $7n - 2 \leq cn$ for every integer $n \geq n_0$. It is easy to see that a possible choice is $c = 7$ and $n_0 = 1$, but there are other possibilities as well.* ∎

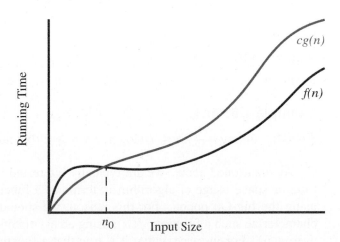

Figure 1.5: The function $f(n)$ is $O(g(n))$, for $f(n) \leq c \cdot g(n)$ when $n \geq n_0$.

The big-Oh notation allows us to say that a function of n is "less than or equal to" another function (by the inequality "$\leq$" in the definition), up to a constant factor (by the constant c in the definition) and in the **asymptotic** sense as n grows toward infinity (by the statement "$n \geq n_0$" in the definition).

The big-Oh notation is used widely to characterize running times and space bounds of algorithm in terms of a parameter, n, which represents the "size" of the problem. For example, if we are interested in finding the largest element in an array of integers (see arrayMax given in Algorithm 1.2), it would be most natural to let n denote the number of elements of the array. For example, we can write the following precise statement on the running time of algorithm arrayMax from Algorithm 1.2.

Theorem 1.2: *The running time of algorithm* arrayMax *for computing the maximum element in an array of n integers is $O(n)$.*

Proof: As shown in Section 1.1.3, the number of primitive operations executed by algorithm arrayMax is at most $7n - 2$. We may therefore apply the big-Oh definition with $c = 7$ and $n_0 = 1$ and conclude that the running time of algorithm arrayMax is $O(n)$. ∎

Let us consider a few additional examples that illustrate the big-Oh notation.

Example 1.3: $20n^3 + 10n \log n + 5$ *is $O(n^3)$.*

Proof: $20n^3 + 10n \log n + 5 \leq 35n^3$, *for $n \geq 1$.* ∎

In fact, any polynomial, $a_k n^k + a_{k-1} n^{k-1} + \cdots + a_0$, will always be $O(n^k)$.

Example 1.4: $3 \log n + \log \log n$ *is $O(\log n)$.*

Proof: $3 \log n + \log \log n \leq 4 \log n$, *for $n \geq 2$. Note that $\log \log n$ is not even defined for $n = 1$, but $\log \log n < \log n$, for $n \geq 2$. That is why we use $n \geq 2$.* ∎

Example 1.5: 2^{100} *is $O(1)$.*

Proof: $2^{100} \leq 2^{100} \cdot 1$, *for $n \geq 1$. Note that variable n does not appear in the inequality, since we are dealing with constant-valued functions.* ∎

Example 1.6: $5n \log n + 2n$ *is $O(n \log n)$.*

Proof: $5n \log n + 2n \leq 7n \log n$, *for $n \geq 2$ (but not for $n = 1$).* ∎

As mentioned above, we are typically interested in characterizing the running time or space usage of algorithm in terms of a function, $f(n)$, which we bound using the big-Oh notion. For this reason, we should use the big-Oh notation to characterize such a function, $f(n)$, using an asymptotically small and simple function, $g(n)$. For instance, while it is true that a function, $f(n) = 4n^3 + 3n^{4/3}$, is $O(n^5)$, it is more informative to say that such an $f(n)$ is $O(n^3)$. Moreover, it is often difficult or cumbersome to characterize the running time or space usage of algorithm exactly, whereas characterizing such measures using the big-Oh notion is typically easier.

Instead of always applying the big-Oh definition directly to obtain a big-Oh characterization, we can often use the following rules to simplify our task of figuring out the simplest characterization.

Theorem 1.7: *Let $d(n)$, $e(n)$, $f(n)$, and $g(n)$ be functions mapping nonnegative integers to nonnegative reals.*

1. *If $d(n)$ is $O(f(n))$, then $ad(n)$ is $O(f(n))$, for any constant $a > 0$.*
2. *If $d(n)$ is $O(f(n))$ and $e(n)$ is $O(g(n))$, then $d(n)+e(n)$ is $O(f(n)+g(n))$.*
3. *If $d(n)$ is $O(f(n))$ and $e(n)$ is $O(g(n))$, then $d(n)e(n)$ is $O(f(n)g(n))$.*
4. *If $d(n)$ is $O(f(n))$ and $f(n)$ is $O(g(n))$, then $d(n)$ is $O(g(n))$.*
5. *If $f(n)$ is a polynomial of degree d (that is, $f(n) = a_0 + a_1 n + \cdots + a_d n^d$), then $f(n)$ is $O(n^d)$.*
6. *n^x is $O(a^n)$ for any fixed $x > 0$ and $a > 1$.*
7. *$\log n^x$ is $O(\log n)$ for any fixed $x > 0$.*
8. *$\log^x n$ is $O(n^y)$ for any fixed constants $x > 0$ and $y > 0$.*

It is considered poor taste to include constant factors and lower order terms in the big-Oh notation. For example, it is not fashionable to say that the function $2n^2$ is $O(4n^2 + 6n \log n)$, although this is completely correct. We should strive instead to describe the function in the big-Oh in ***simplest terms***.

Example 1.8: $2n^3 + 4n^2 \log n$ is $O(n^3)$.

Proof: *We can apply the rules of Theorem 1.7 as follows:*

- *$\log n$ is $O(n)$ (Rule 8).*
- *$4n^2 \log n$ is $O(4n^3)$ (Rule 3).*
- *$2n^3 + 4n^2 \log n$ is $O(2n^3 + 4n^3)$ (Rule 2).*
- *$2n^3 + 4n^3$ is $O(n^3)$ (Rule 5 or Rule 1).*
- *$2n^3 + 4n^2 \log n$ is $O(n^3)$ (Rule 4).*

Some functions appear often in the analysis of algorithms and data structures, and we often use special terms to refer to them. Table 1.6 shows some terms commonly used in algorithm analysis.

logarithmic	linear	quadratic	polynomial	exponential
$O(\log n)$	$O(n)$	$O(n^2)$	$O(n^k)$ $(k \geq 1)$	$O(a^n)$ $(a > 1)$

Table 1.6: Terminology for classes of functions.

Using the Big-Oh Notation

It is considered poor taste, in general, to say "$f(n) \leq O(g(n))$," since the big-Oh already denotes the "less-than-or-equal-to" concept. Likewise, although common, it is not completely correct to say "$f(n) = O(g(n))$" (with the usual understanding of the "$=$" relation), and it is actually incorrect to say "$f(n) \geq O(g(n))$" or "$f(n) > O(g(n))$." It is best to say "$f(n)$ *is* $O(g(n))$." For the more mathematically inclined, it is also correct to say,

$$\text{"}f(n) \in O(g(n)),\text{"}$$

for the big-Oh notation is, technically speaking, denoting a whole collection of functions.

Even with this interpretation, there is considerable freedom in how we can use arithmetic operations with the big-Oh notation, provided the connection to the definition of the big-Oh is clear. For instance, we can say,

$$\text{"}f(n) \text{ is } g(n) + O(h(n)),\text{"}$$

which would mean that there are constants $c > 0$ and $n_0 \geq 1$ such that $f(n) \leq g(n) + ch(n)$ for $n \geq n_0$. As in this example, we may sometimes wish to give the exact leading term in an asymptotic characterization. In that case, we would say that "$f(n)$ is $g(n) + O(h(n))$," where $h(n)$ grows slower than $g(n)$. For example, we could say that $2n \log n + 4n + 10\sqrt{n}$ is $2n \log n + O(n)$.

Big-Omega and Big-Theta

Just as the big-Oh notation provides an asymptotic way of saying that a function is "less than or equal to" another function, there are other notations that provide asymptotic ways of making other types of comparisons.

Let $f(n)$ and $g(n)$ be functions mapping integers to real numbers. We say that $f(n)$ is $\Omega(g(n))$ (pronounced "$f(n)$ is big-Omega of $g(n)$") if $g(n)$ is $O(f(n))$; that is, there is a real constant $c > 0$ and an integer constant $n_0 \geq 1$ such that $f(n) \geq cg(n)$, for $n \geq n_0$. This definition allows us to say asymptotically that one function is greater than or equal to another, up to a constant factor. Likewise, we say that $f(n)$ is $\Theta(g(n))$ (pronounced "$f(n)$ is big-Theta of $g(n)$") if $f(n)$ is $O(g(n))$ and $f(n)$ is $\Omega(g(n))$; that is, there are real constants $c' > 0$ and $c'' > 0$, and an integer constant $n_0 \geq 1$ such that $c'g(n) \leq f(n) \leq c''g(n)$, for $n \geq n_0$.

The big-Theta allows us to say that two functions are asymptotically equal, up to a constant factor. We consider some examples of these notations below.

Example 1.9: $3 \log n + \log \log n$ *is* $\Omega(\log n)$.

Proof: $3 \log n + \log \log n \geq 3 \log n$, *for* $n \geq 2$. ■

This example shows that lower-order terms are not dominant in establishing lower bounds with the big-Omega notation. Thus, as the next example sums up, lower-order terms are not dominant in the big-Theta notation either.

Example 1.10: $3 \log n + \log \log n$ *is* $\Theta(\log n)$.

Proof: *This follows from Examples 1.4 and 1.9.* ■

Some Words of Caution

A few words of caution about asymptotic notation are in order at this point. First, note that the use of the big-Oh and related notations can be somewhat misleading should the constant factors they "hide" be very large. For example, while it is true that the function $10^{100}n$ is $\Theta(n)$, if this is the running time of an algorithm being compared to one whose running time is $10n \log n$, we should prefer the $\Theta(n \log n)$-time algorithm, even though the linear-time algorithm is asymptotically faster. This preference is because the constant factor, 10^{100}, which is called "one googol," is believed by many astronomers to be an upper bound on the number of atoms in the observable universe. So we are unlikely to ever have a real-world problem that has this number as its input size. Thus, even when using the big-Oh notation, we should at least be somewhat mindful of the constant factors and lower order terms we are "hiding."

The above observation raises the issue of what constitutes a "fast" algorithm. Generally speaking, any algorithm running in $O(n \log n)$ time (with a reasonable constant factor) should be considered efficient. Even an $O(n^2)$-time method may be fast enough in some contexts—that is, when n is small. But an algorithm running in $\Theta(2^n)$ time should never be considered efficient. This fact is illustrated by a famous story about the inventor of the game of chess. He asked only that his king pay him 1 grain of rice for the first square on the board, 2 grains for the second, 4 grains for the third, 8 for the fourth, and so on. But try to imagine the sight of 2^{64} grains stacked on the last square! In fact, this number cannot even be represented as a standard long integer in most programming languages.

Therefore, if we must draw a line between efficient and inefficient algorithms, it is natural to make this distinction be that between those algorithms running in polynomial time and those requiring exponential time. That is, make the distinction between algorithms with a running time that is $O(n^k)$, for some constant $k \geq 1$, and those with a running time that is $\Theta(c^n)$, for some constant $c > 1$. Like so many notions we have discussed in this section, this too should be taken with a "grain of salt," for an algorithm running in $\Theta(n^{100})$ time should probably not be considered "efficient." Even so, the distinction between polynomial-time and exponential-time algorithms is considered a robust measure of tractability.

Little-Oh and Little-Omega

There are also some ways of saying that one function is strictly less than or strictly greater than another asymptotically, but these are not used as often as the big-Oh, big-Omega, and big-Theta. Nevertheless, for the sake of completeness, we give their definitions as well.

Let $f(n)$ and $g(n)$ be functions mapping integers to real numbers. We say that $f(n)$ is $o(g(n))$ (pronounced "$f(n)$ is little-oh of $g(n)$") if, for any constant $c > 0$, there is a constant $n_0 > 0$ such that $f(n) \leq cg(n)$ for $n \geq n_0$. Likewise, we say that $f(n)$ is $\omega(g(n))$ (pronounced "$f(n)$ is little-omega of $g(n)$") if $g(n)$ is $o(f(n))$, that is, if, for any constant $c > 0$, there is a constant $n_0 > 0$ such that $g(n) \leq cf(n)$ for $n \geq n_0$. Intuitively, $o(\cdot)$ is analogous to "less than" in an asymptotic sense, and $\omega(\cdot)$ is analogous to "greater than" in an asymptotic sense.

Example 1.11: *The function $f(n) = 12n^2 + 6n$ is $o(n^3)$ and $\omega(n)$.*

Proof: *Let us first show that $f(n)$ is $o(n^3)$. Let $c > 0$ be any constant. If we take $n_0 = (12 + 6)/c = 18/c$, then $18 \leq cn$, for $n \geq n_0$. Thus, if $n \geq n_0$,*

$$f(n) = 12n^2 + 6n \leq 12n^2 + 6n^2 = 18n^2 \leq cn^3.$$

Thus, $f(n)$ is $o(n^3)$.

To show that $f(n)$ is $\omega(n)$, let $c > 0$ again be any constant. If we take $n_0 = c/12$, then, for $n \geq n_0$, $12n \geq c$. Thus, if $n \geq n_0$,

$$f(n) = 12n^2 + 6n \geq 12n^2 \geq cn.$$

Thus, $f(n)$ is $\omega(n)$. ∎

For the reader familiar with limits, we note that $f(n)$ is $o(g(n))$ if and only if

$$\lim_{n \to \infty} \frac{f(n)}{g(n)} = 0,$$

provided this limit exists. The main difference between the little-oh and big-Oh notions is that $f(n)$ is $O(g(n))$ if *there exist* constants $c > 0$ and $n_0 \geq 1$ such that $f(n) \leq cg(n)$, for $n \geq n_0$; whereas $f(n)$ is $o(g(n))$ if *for all* constants $c > 0$ there is a constant n_0 such that $f(n) \leq cg(n)$, for $n \geq n_0$. Intuitively, $f(n)$ is $o(g(n))$ if $f(n)$ becomes insignificant compared to $g(n)$ as n grows toward infinity. As previously mentioned, asymptotic notation is useful because it allows us to concentrate on the main factor determining a function's growth.

To summarize, the asymptotic notations of big-Oh, big-Omega, and big-Theta, as well as little-oh and little-omega, provide a convenient language for us to analyze data structures and algorithms. As mentioned earlier, these notations provide convenience because they let us concentrate on the "big picture" rather than low-level details.

1.1.6   The Importance of Asymptotic Notation

Asymptotic notation has many important benefits, which might not be immediately obvious. Specifically, we illustrate one important aspect of the asymptotic viewpoint in Table 1.7. This table explores the maximum size allowed for an input instance for various running times to be solved in 1 second, 1 minute, and 1 hour, assuming each operation can be processed in 1 microsecond (1 μs). It also shows the importance of algorithm design, because an algorithm with an asymptotically slow running time (for example, one that is $O(n^2)$) is beaten in the long run by an algorithm with an asymptotically faster running time (for example, one that is $O(n \log n)$), even if the constant factor for the faster algorithm is worse.

Running Time	Maximum Problem Size (n)		
	1 second	1 minute	1 hour
$400n$	2,500	150,000	9,000,000
$20n\lceil \log n \rceil$	4,096	166,666	7,826,087
$2n^2$	707	5,477	42,426
n^4	31	88	244
2^n	19	25	31

Table 1.7: Maximum size of a problem that can be solved in one second, one minute, and one hour, for various running times measured in microseconds.

The importance of good algorithm design goes beyond just what can be solved effectively on a given computer, however. As shown in Table 1.8, even if we achieve a dramatic speedup in hardware, we still cannot overcome the handicap of an asymptotically slow algorithm. This table shows the new maximum problem size achievable for any fixed amount of time, assuming algorithms with the given running times are now run on a computer 256 times faster than the previous one.

Running Time	New Maximum Problem Size
$400n$	$256m$
$20n\lceil \log n \rceil$	approx. $256((\log m)/(7 + \log m))m$
$2n^2$	$16m$
n^4	$4m$
2^n	$m + 8$

Table 1.8: Increase in the maximum size of a problem that can be solved in a certain fixed amount of time, by using a computer that is 256 times faster than the previous one, for various running times of the algorithm. Each entry is given as a function of m, the previous maximum problem size.

Ordering Functions by Their Growth Rates

Suppose two algorithms solving the same problem are available: an algorithm A, which has a running time of $\Theta(n)$, and an algorithm B, which has a running time of $\Theta(n^2)$. Which one is better? The little-oh notation says that n is $o(n^2)$, which implies that algorithm A is **asymptotically better** than algorithm B, although for a given (small) value of n, it is possible for algorithm B to have lower running time than algorithm A. Still, in the long run, as shown in the above tables, the benefits of algorithm A over algorithm B will become clear.

In general, we can use the little-oh notation to order functions by asymptotic growth rate, as we show in Table 1.9.

Some Functions Ordered by Growth Rate	Common Name
$\log n$	logarithmic
$\log^2 n$	polylogarithmic
$\sqrt{n}$	square root
n	linear
$n \log n$	linearithmic
n^2	quadratic
n^3	cubic
2^n	exponential

Table 1.9: An ordered list of simple functions such that if a function $f(n)$ precedes a function $g(n)$ in the list, then $f(n)$ is $o(g(n))$. Using common terminology, the function, $\log^c n$, for any $c > 0$, is also polylogarithmic, and the functions, n^2 and n^3, are also polynomial.

In Table 1.10, we illustrate the difference in the growth rate of the functions shown in Table 1.9.

n	$\log n$	$\log^2 n$	$\sqrt{n}$	$n \log n$	n^2	n^3	2^n
4	2	4	2	8	16	64	16
16	4	16	4	64	256	4,096	65,536
64	6	36	8	384	4,096	262,144	1.84×10^{19}
256	8	64	16	2,048	65,536	16,777,216	1.15×10^{77}
1,024	10	100	32	10,240	1,048,576	1.07×10^9	1.79×10^{308}
4,096	12	144	64	49,152	16,777,216	6.87×10^{10}	10^{1233}
16,384	14	196	128	229,376	268,435,456	4.4×10^{12}	10^{4932}
65,536	16	256	256	1,048,576	4.29×10^9	2.81×10^{14}	10^{19728}
262,144	18	324	512	4,718,592	6.87×10^{10}	1.8×10^{16}	10^{78913}

Table 1.10: Growth rates of several functions. Note the point at which the function $\sqrt{n}$ dominates $\log^2 n$.

1.2 A Quick Mathematical Review

In this section, we briefly review some of the fundamental concepts from discrete mathematics that will arise in several of our discussions. In addition to these fundamental concepts, Appendix A includes a list of other useful mathematical facts that apply in the context of data structure and algorithm analysis.

1.2.1 Summations

A notation that appears again and again in the analysis of data structures and algorithms is the **summation**, which is defined as

$$\sum_{i=a}^{b} f(i) = f(a) + f(a+1) + f(a+2) + \cdots + f(b).$$

Summations arise in data structure and algorithm analysis because the running times of loops naturally give rise to summations. For example, a summation that often arises in data structure and algorithm analysis is the geometric summation.

Theorem 1.12: *For any integer* $n \geq 0$ *and any real number* $0 < a \neq 1$, *consider*

$$\sum_{i=0}^{n} a^i = 1 + a + a^2 + \cdots + a^n$$

(remembering that $a^0 = 1$ *if* $a > 0$). *This summation is equal to*

$$\frac{1 - a^{n+1}}{1 - a}.$$

Summations as shown in Theorem 1.12 are called **geometric** summations, because each term is geometrically larger than the previous one if $a > 1$. That is, the terms in such a geometric summation exhibit exponential growth. For example, everyone working in computing should know that

$$1 + 2 + 4 + 8 + \cdots + 2^{n-1} = 2^n - 1,$$

for this is the largest integer that can be represented in binary notation using n bits.

Another summation that arises in several contexts is

$$\sum_{i=1}^{n} i = 1 + 2 + 3 + \cdots + (n-2) + (n-1) + n.$$

This summation often arises in the analysis of loops in cases where the number of operations performed inside the loop increases by a fixed, constant amount with each iteration. This summation also has an interesting history. In 1787, a German elementary schoolteacher decided to keep his 9- and 10-year-old pupils occupied with the task of adding up all the numbers from 1 to 100. But almost immediately after giving this assignment, one of the children claimed to have the answer—5,050.

That elementary school student was none other than Carl Gauss, who would grow up to be one of the greatest mathematicians of the 19th century. It is widely suspected that young Gauss derived the answer to his teacher's assignment using the following identity.

Theorem 1.13: *For any integer $n \geq 1$, we have*

$$\sum_{i=1}^{n} i = \frac{n(n+1)}{2}.$$

Proof: We give two "visual" justifications of Theorem 1.13 in Figure 1.11, both of which are based on computing the area of a collection of rectangles representing the numbers 1 through n. In Figure 1.11a we draw a big triangle over an ordering of the rectangles, noting that the area of the rectangles is the same as that of the big triangle ($n^2/2$) plus that of n small triangles, each of area $1/2$. In Figure 1.11b, which applies when n is even, we note that 1 plus n is $n + 1$, as is 2 plus $n - 1$, 3 plus $n - 2$, and so on. There are $n/2$ such pairings. ∎

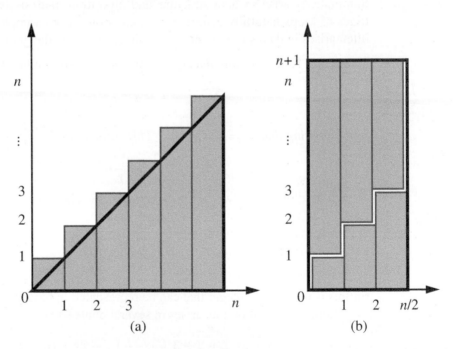

(a)   (b)

Figure 1.11: Visual justifications of Theorem 1.13. Both illustrations visualize the identity in terms of the total area covered by n unit-width rectangles with heights $1, 2, \ldots, n$. In (a) the rectangles are shown to cover a big triangle of area $n^2/2$ (base n and height n) plus n small triangles of area $1/2$ each (base 1 and height 1). In (b), which applies only when n is even, the rectangles are shown to cover a big rectangle of base $n/2$ and height $n + 1$.

1.2.2 Logarithms and Exponents

One of the interesting and sometimes even surprising aspects of the analysis of data structures and algorithms is the ubiquitous presence of logarithms and exponents, where we say

$$\log_b a = c \qquad \text{if} \qquad a = b^c.$$

As is the custom in the computing literature, we omit writing the base b of the logarithm when $b = 2$. For example, $\log 1024 = 10$.

There are a number of important rules for logarithms and exponents, including the following:

Theorem 1.14: *Let a, b, and c be positive real numbers. We have*

1. $\log_b ac = \log_b a + \log_b c$
2. $\log_b a/c = \log_b a - \log_b c$
3. $\log_b a^c = c \log_b a$
4. $\log_b a = (\log_c a)/\log_c b$
5. $b^{\log_c a} = a^{\log_c b}$
6. $(b^a)^c = b^{ac}$
7. $b^a b^c = b^{a+c}$
8. $b^a/b^c = b^{a-c}.$

Also, as a notational shorthand, we use $\log^c n$ to denote the function $(\log n)^c$ and we use $\log \log n$ to denote $\log(\log n)$. Rather than show how we could derive each of the above identities, which all follow from the definition of logarithms and exponents, let us instead illustrate these identities with a few examples of their usefulness.

Example 1.15: *We illustrate some interesting cases when the base of a logarithm or exponent is 2. The rules cited refer to Theorem 1.14.*

- $\log(2n \log n) = 1 + \log n + \log \log n$, *by Rule 1 (twice)*
- $\log(n/2) = \log n - \log 2 = \log n - 1$, *by Rule 2*
- $\log \sqrt{n} = \log(n)^{1/2} = (\log n)/2$, *by Rule 3*
- $\log \log \sqrt{n} = \log(\log n)/2 = \log \log n - 1$, *by Rules 2 and 3*
- $\log_4 n = (\log n)/\log 4 = (\log n)/2$, *by Rule 4*
- $\log 2^n = n$, *by Rule 3*
- $2^{\log n} = n$, *by Rule 5*
- $2^{2 \log n} = (2^{\log n})^2 = n^2$, *by Rules 5 and 6*
- $4^n = (2^2)^n = 2^{2n}$, *by Rule 6*
- $n^2 2^{3 \log n} = n^2 \cdot n^3 = n^5$, *by Rules 5, 6, and 7*
- $4^n/2^n = 2^{2n}/2^n = 2^{2n-n} = 2^n$, *by Rules 6 and 8*

The Floor and Ceiling Functions

One additional comment concerning logarithms is in order. The value of a logarithm is typically not an integer, yet the running time of an algorithm is typically expressed by means of an integer quantity, such as the number of operations performed. Thus, an algorithm analysis may sometimes involve the use of the so-called "floor" and "ceiling" functions, which are defined respectively as follows:

- $\lfloor x \rfloor$ = the largest integer less than or equal to x
- $\lceil x \rceil$ = the smallest integer greater than or equal to x.

These functions give us a way to convert real-valued functions into integer-valued functions. Even so, functions used to analyze data structures and algorithms are often expressed simply as real-valued functions (for example, $n \log n$ or $n^{3/2}$). We should read such a running time as having a "big" ceiling function surrounding it.[1]

1.2.3 Simple Justification Techniques

We will sometimes wish to make strong claims about a certain data structure or algorithm. We may, for example, wish to show that our algorithm is correct or that it runs fast. In order to rigorously make such claims, we must use mathematical language, and in order to back up such claims, we must justify or ***prove*** our statements. Fortunately, there are several simple ways to do this.

By Example

Some claims are of the generic form, "There is an element x in a set S that has property P." To justify such a claim, we need only produce a particular $x \in S$ that has property P. Likewise, some hard-to-believe claims are of the generic form, "Every element x in a set S has property P." To justify that such a claim is false, we need to only produce a particular x from S that does not have property P. Such an instance is called a ***counterexample***.

Example 1.16: *A certain Professor Amongus claims that every number of the form $2^i - 1$ is a prime, when i is an integer greater than 1. Professor Amongus is wrong.*

Proof: *To prove Professor Amongus is wrong, we need to find a counterexample. Fortunately, we need not look too far, for $2^4 - 1 = 15 = 3 \cdot 5$.* ∎

---

[1] Real-valued running-time functions are almost always used in conjunction with the asymptotic notation described in Section 1.1.5, for which the use of the ceiling function would usually be redundant anyway. (See Exercise R-1.25.)

Contrapositives and Contradiction

Another set of justification techniques involves the use of the negative. The two primary such methods are the use of the **contrapositive** and the **contradiction**. To justify the statement "if p is true, then q is true," we instead establish that "if q is not true, then p is not true." Logically, these two statements are the same, but the latter, which is called the **contrapositive** of the first, may be easier to think about.

Example 1.17: *If ab is odd, then a is odd and b is odd.*

Proof: *To justify this claim, let us prove the contrapositive, "If a is even or b is even, then ab is even." So, suppose $a = 2i$ or $b = 2i$, for some integer i. Then we have $ab = (2i)b = 2ib$, or we have $ab = a(2i) = 2ai$; hence, in either case, ab is even. Since this establishes the contrapositive, it proves the original statement.* ∎

Besides showing a use of the contrapositive proof technique, the above example also contains an application of **DeMorgan's law**. This law helps us deal with negations, for it states that the negation of a statement, "p or q," is "not p and not q," and that the negation of a statement, "p and q," is "not p or not q."

Another justification technique is proof by **contradiction**, which also often involves using DeMorgan's law. In applying the proof by contradiction technique, we establish that a statement q is true by first supposing that q is false and then showing that this assumption leads to a contradiction (such as $2 \neq 2$ or $1 > 3$). By reaching such a contradiction, we show that no consistent situation exists with q being false, so q must be true. Of course, in order to reach this conclusion, we must be sure our situation is consistent before we assume q is false.

Example 1.18: *If ab is even, then a is even or b is even.*

Proof: *Let ab be even. We wish to show that a is even or b is even. So, with the hope of leading to a contradiction, let us assume the opposite, namely, suppose a is odd and b is odd. Then $a = 2i + 1$ and $b = 2j + 1$, for some integers i and j. Hence, $ab = (2i + 1)(2j + 1) = 4ij + 2i + 2j + 1 = 2(2ij + i + j) + 1$; that is, ab is odd. But this is a contradiction: ab cannot simultaneously be odd and even. Therefore, a is even or b is even.* ∎

Induction

Most of the claims we make about a running time or a space bound involve an integer parameter n (usually denoting an intuitive notion of the "size" of the problem). Moreover, most of these claims are equivalent to saying some statement $q(n)$ is true "for all $n \geq 1$." Since this is making a claim about an infinite set of numbers, we cannot justify this exhaustively in a direct fashion.

We can often justify claims such as those above as true, however, by using the technique of **induction**. This technique amounts to showing that, for any particular

$n \geq 1$, there is a finite sequence of implications that starts with something known to be true and ultimately leads to showing that $q(n)$ is true. Specifically, we begin a proof by induction by showing that $q(n)$ is true for $n = 1$ (and possibly some other values $n = 2, 3, \ldots, k$, for some constant k). Then we justify that the inductive "step" is true for $n > k$, namely, we show "if $q(i)$ is true for $i < n$, then $q(n)$ is true." The combination of these two pieces completes the proof by induction.

Example 1.19: *Consider the Fibonacci sequence:* $F(1) = 1$, $F(2) = 2$, *and* $F(n) = F(n-1) + F(n-2)$ *for* $n > 2$. *We claim that* $F(n) < 2^n$.

Proof: *We will show our claim is right by induction.*
Base cases: *($n \leq 2$).* $F(1) = 1 < 2 = 2^1$ *and* $F(2) = 2 < 4 = 2^2$.
Induction step: *($n > 2$).* *Suppose our claim is true for* $n' < n$. *Consider* $F(n)$. *Since* $n > 2$, $F(n) = F(n-1) + F(n-2)$. *Moreover, since* $n - 1 < n$ *and* $n - 2 < n$, *we can apply the inductive assumption (sometimes called the "inductive hypothesis") to imply that* $F(n) < 2^{n-1} + 2^{n-2}$. *In addition,*

$$2^{n-1} + 2^{n-2} < 2^{n-1} + 2^{n-1} = 2 \cdot 2^{n-1} = 2^n.$$

∎

Let us do another inductive argument, this time for a fact we have seen before.

Theorem 1.20:   *(which is the same as Theorem 1.13)*

$$\sum_{i=1}^{n} i = \frac{n(n+1)}{2}.$$

Proof: We will justify this equality by induction.
Base case: $n = 1$. Trivial, for $1 = n(n+1)/2$, if $n = 1$.
Induction step: $n \geq 2$. Assume the claim is true for $n' < n$. Consider n.

$$\sum_{i=1}^{n} i = n + \sum_{i=1}^{n-1} i.$$

By the induction hypothesis, then

$$\sum_{i=1}^{n} i = n + \frac{(n-1)n}{2},$$

which we can simplify as

$$n + \frac{(n-1)n}{2} = \frac{2n + n^2 - n}{2} = \frac{n^2 + n}{2} = \frac{n(n+1)}{2}.$$

∎

It is useful to think about the concreteness of the inductive technique. It shows that, for any particular n, there is a finite step-by-step sequence of implications that starts with something true and leads to the truth about n. In short, the inductive argument is a formula for building a sequence of direct proofs.

Loop Invariants

The final justification technique we discuss in this section is the ***loop invariant***.

To prove some statement S about a loop is correct, define S in terms of a series of smaller statements $S_0, S_1, \ldots, S_k$, where

1. The ***initial*** claim, S_0, is true before the loop begins.
2. If S_{i-1} is true before iteration i begins, then one can show that S_i will be true after iteration i is over.
3. The final statement, S_k, implies the statement S that we wish to justify as being true.

We have, in fact, already seen the loop-invariant justification technique at work in Section 1.1.1 (for the correctness of arrayMax), but let us nevertheless give one more example here. In particular, let us consider applying the loop invariant method to justify the correctness of Algorithm arrayFind, shown in Algorithm 1.12, which searches for an element x in an array A.

To show arrayFind to be correct, we use a loop invariant argument. That is, we inductively define statements, S_i, for $i = 0, 1, \ldots, n$, that lead to the correctness of arrayFind. Specifically, we claim the following to be true at the beginning of iteration i:

S_i: x is not equal to any of the first i elements of A.

This claim is true at the beginning of the first iteration of the loop, since there are no elements among the first 0 in A (this kind of a trivially-true claim is said to hold ***vacuously***). In iteration i, we compare element x to element $A[i]$ and return the index i if these two elements are equal, which is clearly correct. If the two elements x and $A[i]$ are not equal, then we have found one more element not equal to x and we increment the index i. Thus, the claim S_i will be true for this new value of i, for the beginning of the next iteration. If the while-loop terminates without ever returning an index in A, then S_n is true—there are no elements of A equal to x. Therefore, the algorithm is correct to return the nonindex value -1, as required.

Algorithm arrayFind(x, A):

    Input: An element x and an n-element array, A.

    Output: The index i such that $x = A[i]$ or -1 if no element of A is equal to x.

    $i \leftarrow 0$

    while $i < n$ **do**

        if $x = A[i]$ **then**

            return i

        else

            $i \leftarrow i + 1$

    return -1

Algorithm 1.12: Algorithm arrayFind.

1.2.4 Basic Probability

When we analyze algorithms that use randomization or if we wish to analyze the average-case performance of an algorithm, then we need to use some basic facts from probability theory. The most basic is that any statement about a probability is defined upon a **sample space** S, which is defined as the set of all possible outcomes from some experiment. We leave the terms "outcomes" and "experiment" undefined in any formal sense, however.

Example 1.21: *Consider an experiment that consists of the outcome from flipping a coin five times. This sample space has 2^5 different outcomes, one for each different ordering of possible flips that can occur.*

Sample spaces can also be infinite, as the following example illustrates.

Example 1.22: *Consider an experiment that consists of flipping a coin until it comes up heads. This sample space is infinite, with each outcome being a sequence of i tails followed by a single flip that comes up heads, for $i \in \{0, 1, 2, 3, \ldots\}$.*

A **probability space** is a sample space S together with a probability function, Pr, that maps subsets of S to real numbers in the interval $[0, 1]$. It captures mathematically the notion of the probability of certain "events" occurring. Formally, each subset A of S is called an **event**, and the probability function Pr is assumed to possess the following basic properties with respect to events defined from S:

1. $\Pr(\emptyset) = 0$.
2. $\Pr(S) = 1$.
3. $0 \leq \Pr(A) \leq 1$, for any $A \subseteq S$.
4. If $A, B \subseteq S$ and $A \cap B = \emptyset$, then $\Pr(A \cup B) = \Pr(A) + \Pr(B)$.

Independence

Two events A and B are **independent** if

$$\Pr(A \cap B) = \Pr(A) \cdot \Pr(B).$$

A collection of events $\{A_1, A_2, \ldots, A_n\}$ is **mutually independent** if

$$\Pr(A_{i_1} \cap A_{i_2} \cap \cdots \cap A_{i_k}) = \Pr(A_{i_1})\Pr(A_{i_2}) \cdots \Pr(A_{i_k}),$$

for any subset $\{A_{i_1}, A_{i_2}, \ldots, A_{i_k}\}$.

Example 1.23: *Let A be the event that the roll of a die is a 6, let B be the event that the roll of a second die is a 3, and let C be the event that the sum of these two dice is a 10. Then A and B are independent events, but C is not independent with either A or B.*

Conditional Probability

The ***conditional probability*** that an event A occurs, given an event B, is denoted as $\Pr(A|B)$, and is defined as

$$\Pr(A|B) = \frac{\Pr(A \cap B)}{\Pr(B)},$$

assuming that $\Pr(B) > 0$.

Example 1.24: *Let A be the event that a roll of two dice sums to 10, and let B be the event that the roll of the first die is a 6. Note that $\Pr(B) = 1/6$ and that $\Pr(A \cap B) = 1/36$, for there is only one way two dice can sum to 10 if the first one is a 6 (namely, if the second is a 4). Thus, $\Pr(A|B) = (1/36)/(1/6) = 1/6$.*

Random Variables and Expectation

An elegant way for dealing with events is in terms of ***random variables***. Intuitively, random variables are variables whose values depend upon the outcome of some experiment. Formally, a ***random variable*** is a function X that maps outcomes from some sample space S to real numbers. An ***indicator random variable*** is a random variable that maps outcomes to the set $\{0,1\}$. Often in algorithm analysis we use a random variable X that has a discrete set of possible outcomes to characterize the running time of a randomized algorithm. In this case, the sample space S is defined by all possible outcomes of the random sources used in the algorithm. We are usually most interested in the typical, average, or "expected" value of such a random variable. The ***expected value*** of a discrete random variable X is defined as

$$E(X) = \sum_x x \Pr(X = x),$$

where the summation is defined over the range of X.

Theorem 1.25 (The Linearity of Expectation): *Let X and Y be two arbitrary random variables. Then $E(X + Y) = E(X) + E(Y)$.*

Proof:

$$
\begin{aligned}
E(X + Y) &= \sum_x \sum_y (x + y) \Pr(X = x \cap Y = y) \\
&= \sum_x \sum_y x \Pr(X = x \cap Y = y) + \sum_x \sum_y y \Pr(X = x \cap Y = y) \\
&= \sum_x \sum_y x \Pr(X = x \cap Y = y) + \sum_y \sum_x y \Pr(Y = y \cap X = x) \\
&= \sum_x x \Pr(X = x) + \sum_y y \Pr(Y = y) \\
&= E(X) + E(Y).
\end{aligned}
$$

Note that this proof does not depend on any independence assumptions about the events when X and Y take on their respective values. ∎

Example 1.26: *Let X be a random variable that assigns the outcome of the roll of two fair dice to the sum of the number of dots showing. Then $E(X) = 7$.*

Proof: *To justify this claim, let X_1 and X_2 be random variables corresponding to the number of dots on each die, respectively. Thus, $X_1 = X_2$ (that is, they are two instances of the same function) and $E(X) = E(X_1 + X_2) = E(X_1) + E(X_2)$. Each outcome of the roll of a fair die occurs with probability $1/6$. Thus*

$$E(X_i) = \frac{1}{6} + \frac{2}{6} + \frac{3}{6} + \frac{4}{6} + \frac{5}{6} + \frac{6}{6} = \frac{7}{2},$$

for $i = 1, 2$. Therefore, $E(X) = 7$. ∎

Two random variables X and Y are **independent** if

$$\Pr(X = x | Y = y) = \Pr(X = x),$$

for all real numbers x and y.

Theorem 1.27: *If two random variables X and Y are independent, then*

$$E(XY) = E(X)E(Y).$$

Example 1.28: *Let X be a random variable that assigns the outcome of a roll of two fair dice to the product of the number of dots showing. Then $E(X) = 49/4$.*

Proof: *Let X_1 and X_2 be random variables denoting the number of dots on each die. The variables X_1 and X_2 are clearly independent; hence*

$$E(X) = E(X_1 X_2) = E(X_1)E(X_2) = (7/2)^2 = 49/4.$$

∎

Chernoff Bounds

It is often necessary in the analysis of randomized algorithms to bound the sum of a set of random variables. One set of inequalities that makes this tractable is the set of Chernoff Bounds. Let $X_1, X_2, \ldots, X_n$ be a set of mutually independent indicator random variables, such that each X_i is 1 with some probability $p_i > 0$ and 0 otherwise. Let $X = \sum_{i=1}^{n} X_i$ be the sum of these random variables, and let μ denote the mean of X, that is, $\mu = E(X) = \sum_{i=1}^{n} p_i$. We prove the following later in this book (Section 19.5).

Theorem 1.29: *Let X be as above. Then, for $\delta > 0$,*

$$\Pr(X > (1 + \delta)\mu) < \left[\frac{e^{\delta}}{(1 + \delta)^{(1+\delta)}} \right]^{\mu},$$

and, for $0 < \delta \leq 1$,

$$\Pr(X < (1 - \delta)\mu) < e^{-\mu\delta^2/2}.$$

1.3 A Case Study in Algorithm Analysis

Having presented the general framework for describing and analyzing algorithms, we now present a case study in algorithm analysis to make this discussion more concrete. Specifically, we show how to use the big-Oh notation to analyze three algorithms that solve the same problem but have different running times.

The problem we focus on is one that is reportedly often used as a job interview question by major software and Internet companies—the ***maximum subarray problem***. Here, we are given an array of integers and asked to find the subarray whose elements have the largest sum. See the example of Figure 1.13. That is, given array $A = [a_1, a_2, \ldots, a_n]$, find indices j and k that maximize the sum

$$s_{j,k} = a_j + a_{j+1} + \cdots + a_k = \sum_{i=j}^{k} a_i.$$

Note that each element of the array could have a positive, negative, or zero value. Thus, in the special case where all array elements are negative, the solution is an empty subarray of conventional zero sum.

To define the problem more formally, we conventionally define the special array element $A[0] = 0$ and let $A[j : k]$ denote the sequence of elements of A from index j to index k ($0 \le j \le k \le n$). The maximum subarray problem consists of finding the sequence $A[j : k]$ ($0 \le j \le k \le n$) that maximizes $s_{j,k}$, the sum of its values. Such a maximum sum is referred to as the ***maximum subarray sum*** of array A.

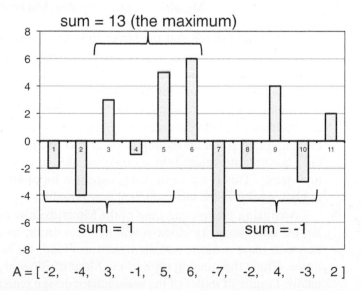

Figure 1.13: An instance of the maximum subarray problem. In this case, the maximum subarray is $A[3 : 6]$, that is, the maximum sum is $s_{3,6} = 13$.

In addition to being a good problem for testing the thinking skills of prospective employees, the maximum subarray problem also has applications in pattern analysis in digitized images.

1.3.1 A First Solution to the Maximum Subarray Problem

Our first algorithm for the maximum subarray problem, which we call Maxsub-Slow, is shown in Algorithm 1.14. It computes the maximum of every possible subarray summation, $s_{j,k}$, of A separately.

Algorithm MaxsubSlow(A):

    Input: An n-element array A of numbers, indexed from 1 to n.
    Output: The maximum subarray sum of array A.

    $m \leftarrow 0$ // the maximum found so far
    for $j \leftarrow 1$ **to** n **do**
        for $k \leftarrow j$ **to** n **do**
            $s \leftarrow 0$ // the next partial sum we are computing
            for $i \leftarrow j$ **to** k **do**
                $s \leftarrow s + A[i]$
            if $s > m$ **then**
                $m \leftarrow s$
    return m

Algorithm 1.14: Algorithm MaxsubSlow.

It isn't hard to see that the MaxsubSlow algorithm is correct. This algorithm calculates the partial sum, $s_{j,k}$, of every possible subarray, by adding up the values in the subarray $A[j : k]$. Moreover, for every such subarray sum, it compares that sum to a running maximum and if the new value is greater than the old, it updates that maximum to the new value. In the end, this will be maximum subarray sum.

Incidentally, both the calculating of subarray summations and the computing of the maximum so far are examples of an ***accumulator*** pattern, where we incrementally accumulate values into a single variable to compute a sum or maximum (or minimum). This is a pattern that is used in a lot of algorithms, but in this case it is not being used in the most efficient way possible.

Analyzing the running time of the MaxsubSlow algorithm is easy. In particular, the outer loop, for index j, will iterate n times, its inner loop, for index k, will iterate at most n times, and the inner-most loop, for index i, will iterate at most n times. Thus, the running time of the MaxsubSlow algorithm is $O(n^3)$. Unfortunately, in spite of its use of the accumulator design pattern, giving the MaxsubSlow algorithm as a solution to the maximum subarray problem would be a bad idea during a job interview. This is a slow algorithm for the maximum subarray problem.

1.3.2 An Improved Maximum Subarray Algorithm

We can design an improved algorithm for the maximum subarray problem by observing that we are wasting a lot of time by recomputing all the subarray summations from scratch in the inner loop of the MaxsubSlow algorithm. There is a much more efficient way to calculate these summations. The crucial insight is to consider all the **prefix sums**, which are the sums of the first t integers in A for $t = 1, 2, \ldots, n$. That is, consider each prefix sum, S_t, which is defined as

$$S_t = a_1 + a_2 + \cdots + a_t = \sum_{i=1}^{t} a_i.$$

If we are given all such prefix sums, then we can compute any subarray summation, $s_{j,k}$, in constant time using the formula

$$s_{j,k} = S_k - S_{j-1},$$

where we use the notational convention that $S_0 = 0$. To see this, note that

$$S_k - S_{j-1} = \sum_{i=1}^{k} a_i - \sum_{i=1}^{j-1} a_i$$

$$= \sum_{i=j}^{k} a_i = s_{j,k},$$

where we use the notational convention that $\sum_{i=1}^{0} a_i = 0$. We can incorporate the above observations into an improved algorithm for the maximum subarray problem, called MaxsubFaster, which we show in Algorithm 1.15.

Algorithm MaxsubFaster(A):

    Input: An n-element array A of numbers, indexed from 1 to n.
    Output: The maximum subarray sum of array A.

    $S_0 \leftarrow 0$ // the initial prefix sum
    for $i \leftarrow 1$ **to** n **do**
        $S_i \leftarrow S_{i-1} + A[i]$
    $m \leftarrow 0$ // the maximum found so far
    for $j \leftarrow 1$ **to** n **do**
        for $k \leftarrow j$ **to** n **do**
            $s = S_k - S_{j-1}$
            if $s > m$ **then**
                $m \leftarrow s$
    return m

Algorithm 1.15: Algorithm MaxsubFaster.

Analyzing the MaxsubFaster Algorithm

The correctness of the MaxsubFaster algorithm follows along the same arguments as for the MaxsubSlow algorithm, but it is much faster. In particular, the outer loop, for index j, will iterate n times, its inner loop, for index k, will iterate at most n times, and the steps inside that loop will only take $O(1)$ time in each iteration. Thus, the total running time of the MaxsubFaster algorithm is $O(n^2)$, which improves the running time of the MaxsubSlow algorithm by a linear factor.

True story: A former student of one of the authors gave this very algorithm during a job interview for a major software company, when asked about the maximum subarray problem, correctly observing that this algorithm beats the running time of the naive $O(n^3)$-time algorithm by a linear factor. Sadly, this student did not get a job offer, however, and one reason could have been because there is an even better solution to the maximum subarray problem, which the student didn't give.

1.3.3   A Linear-Time Maximum Subarray Algorithm

We can improve the running time for solving the maximum subarray further by applying the intuition behind the prefix sums idea to the computation of the maximum itself. Recall our notation of letting $s_{j,k}$ denote the partial sum of the values in $A[j : k]$. Instead of computing prefix sum $S_t = s_{1,t}$, what if, we compute a ***maximum suffix sum***, M_t, which is the maximum of $s_{j,t}$ for $j = 1, \cdots, t$?

Such a definition is an interesting idea, but it is not quite right, because it doesn't include the boundary case where we wouldn't want any subarray that ends at t, in the event that all such subarrays sum up to a negative number. Instead, let us define

$$M_t = \max\{0, \max_{j=1,\cdots,t}\{s_{j,t}\}\}.$$

In other words, M_t is the maximum of 0 and the maximum $s_{j,k}$ value where we restrict k to equal t. For example, in the array shown in Figure 1.13, we have $M_2 = 0$, $M_3 = 3$, and $M_4 = 2$.

This definition implies that if $M_t > 0$, then it is the summation value for a maximum subarray that ends at t, and if $M_t = 0$, then we can safely ignore any subarray that ends at t.

Note that if we know all the M_t values, for $t = 1, 2, \ldots, n$, then the solution to the maximum subarray problem would simply be the maximum of all these values. So let us consider how we could compute these M_t values.

The crucial observation is that, for $t \geq 2$, if we have a maximum subarray that ends at t, and it has a positive sum, then it is either $A[t : t]$ or it is made up of the maximum subarray that ends at $t - 1$ plus $A[t]$. If this were not the case, then we could make a subarray of even larger sum by swapping out the one we chose to end at $t - 1$ with the maximum one that ends at $t - 1$, which would contradict the fact that we have the maximum subarray that ends at t. In addition, if taking the value of maximum subarray that ends at $t-1$ and adding $A[t]$ makes this sum no longer be positive, then $M_t = 0$, for there is no subarray that ends at t with a positive summation. In other words, we can define $M_0 = 0$ as a boundary condition, and use the following formula to compute M_t, for $t = 1, 2, \ldots, n$:

$$M_t = \max\{0,\ M_{t-1} + A[t]\}.$$

Therefore, we can solve the maximum subarray problem using the algorithm, MaxsubFastest, shown in Algorithm 1.16.

Algorithm MaxsubFastest(A):
    Input: An n-element array A of numbers, indexed from 1 to n.
    Output: The maximum subarray sum of array A.
  $M_0 \leftarrow 0$ // the initial prefix maximum
  for $t \leftarrow 1$ **to** n **do**
      $M_t \leftarrow \max\{0,\ M_{t-1} + A[t]\}$
  $m \leftarrow 0$ // the maximum found so far
  for $t \leftarrow 1$ **to** n **do**
      $m \leftarrow \max\{m,\ M_t\}$
  return m

Algorithm 1.16: Algorithm MaxsubFastest.

Analyzing the MaxsubFastest Algorithm

The MaxsubFastest algorithm consists of two loops, which each iterate exactly n times and take $O(1)$ time in each iteration. Thus, the total running time of the MaxsubFastest algorithm is $O(n)$. Incidentally, in addition to using the accumulator pattern, to calculate the M_t and m variables based on previous values of these variables, it also can be viewed as a simple application of the ***dynamic programming*** technique, which we discuss in Chapter 12.

Given all these positive aspects of this algorithm, even though we can't guarantee that a prospective employee will get a job offer by describing the MaxsubFastest algorithm when asked about the maximum subarray problem, we can at least guarantee that this is the way to nail this question. Still, we are nonetheless leaving one small detail as an exercise (C-1.1), which is to modify the description of the MaxsubFastest algorithm so that, in addition to the value of the maximum subarray summation, it also outputs the indices j and k that identify the maximum subarray $A[j:k]$.

1.4 Amortization

An important analysis tool useful for understanding the running times of algorithms that have steps with widely varying performance is ***amortization***. The term "amortization" itself comes from the field of accounting, which provides an intuitive monetary metaphor for algorithm analysis, as we shall see in this section.

The typical data structure usually supports a wide variety of different methods for accessing and updating the elements it stores. Likewise, some algorithms operate iteratively, with each iteration performing a varying amount of work. In some cases, we can effectively analyze the performance of these data structures and algorithms on the basis of the worst-case running time of each individual operation. Amortization takes a different viewpoint. Rather than focusing on each operation separately, it considers the interactions between all the operations by studying the running time of a series of these operations.

The Clearable Table Data Structure

As an example of amortized analysis, let us introduce a simple data structure, the ***clearable table***. This structure stores a table of elements, which can be accessed by their indices in the table. In addition, the clearable table supports the following two methods:

> add(e): Add the element e to the next available cell in the table.
>
> clear(): Empty the table by removing all its elements.

Let S be a clearable table with n elements implemented by means of an array, with a fixed upper bound, N, on its size. Operation clear takes $\Theta(n)$ time, since we should dereference all the elements in the table in order to really empty it.

Now consider a series of n operations on an initially empty clearable table S. If we take a worst-case viewpoint, we may say that the running time of this series of operations is $O(n^2)$, since the worst case of a single clear operation in the series is $O(n)$, and there may be as many as $O(n)$ clear operations in this series. While this analysis is correct, it is also an overstatement, since an analysis that takes into account the interactions between the operations shows that the running time of the entire series is actually $O(n)$.

Theorem 1.30: *A series of n operations on an initially empty clearable table implemented with an array takes $O(n)$ time.*

Proof: Let $M_0, \ldots, M_{n-1}$ be the series of operations performed on S, and let $M_{i_0}, \ldots, M_{i_{k-1}}$ be the k clear operations within the series. We have

$$0 \le i_0 < \ldots < i_{k-1} \le n - 1.$$

Let us also define $i_{-1} = -1$. The running time of operation M_{i_j} (a clear operation) is $O(i_j - i_{j-1})$, because at most $i_j - i_{j-1} - 1$ elements could have been added into the table (using the add operation) since the previous clear operation $M_{i_{j-1}}$ or since the beginning of the series. Thus, the running time for the clear operations is

$$O\left(\sum_{j=0}^{k-1}(i_j - i_{j-1})\right).$$

A summation such as this is known as a ***telescoping sum***, for all terms other than the first and last cancel each other out. That is, this summation is $O(i_{k-1} - i_{-1})$, which is $O(n)$. All the remaining operations of the series take $O(1)$ time each. Thus, we conclude that a series of n operations performed on an initially empty clearable table takes $O(n)$ time. ∎

Theorem 1.30 indicates that the average running time of any operation on a clearable table is $O(1)$, where the average is taken over an arbitrary series of operations, starting with an initially empty clearable table.

Amortizing an Algorithm's Running Time

The above example provides a motivation for the amortization technique, which gives us a worst-case way of performing an average-case analysis. Formally, we define the ***amortized running time*** of an operation within a series of operations as the worst-case running time of the series of operations divided by the number of operations. When the series of operations is not specified, it is usually assumed to be a series of operations from the repertoire of a certain data structure, starting from an empty structure. Thus, by Theorem 1.30, we can say that the amortized running time of each operation for a clearable table structure is $O(1)$ when we implement that clearable table with an array. Note that the actual running time of an operation may be much higher than its amortized running time (for example, a particular clear operation may take $O(n)$ time).

The advantage of using amortization is that it gives us a way to do a robust average-case analysis without using any probability. It simply requires that we have some way of characterizing the worst-case running time for performing a series of operations. We can even extend the notion of amortized running time so as to assign each individual operation in a series of operations its own amortized running time, provided the total actual time taken to process the entire series of operations is no more than the sum of amortized bounds given to the individual operations.

There are several ways of doing an amortized analysis. The most obvious way is to use a direct argument to derive bounds on the total time needed to perform a series of operations, which is what we did in the proof of Theorem 1.30. While direct arguments can often be found for a simple series of operations, performing an amortized analysis of a nontrivial series of operations is often easier using special techniques for amortized analysis.

1.4.1   Amortization Techniques

There are two fundamental techniques for performing an amortized analysis, one based on a financial model—the accounting method—and the other based on an energy model—the potential function method.

The Accounting Method

The ***accounting method*** for performing an amortized analysis is to use a scheme of credits and debits for keeping track of the running time of the different operations in the series. The basis of the accounting method is simple. We view the computer as a coin-operated appliance that requires the payment of 1 ***cyber-dollar*** for a constant amount of computing time. We also view an operation as a sequence of constant time ***primitive operations***, which each cost 1 ***cyber-dollar*** to be executed. When an operation is executed, we should have enough cyber-dollars available to pay for its running time. Of course, the most obvious approach is to charge an operation a number of cyber-dollars equal to the number of primitive operations performed. However, the interesting aspect of using the accounting method is that we do not have to be fair in the way we charge the operations. Namely, we can overcharge some operations that execute few primitive operations and use the profit made on them to help out other operations that execute many primitive operations. This mechanism may allow us to charge the same amount a of cyber-dollars to each operation in the series, without ever running out of cyber-dollars to pay for the computer time. Hence, if we can set up such a scheme, called an ***amortization scheme***, we can say that each operation in the series has an amortized running time that is $O(a)$. When designing an amortization scheme, it is often convenient to think of the unspent cyber-dollars as being "stored" in certain places of the data structure, for example, at the elements of a table.

An alternative amortization scheme charges different amounts to the various operations. In this case, the amortized running time of an operation is proportional to the total charges made divided by the number of operations.

We now go back to the clearable table example and present an amortization scheme for it that yields an alternative proof of Theorem 1.30. Let us assume that one cyber-dollar is enough to pay for the execution of operation of an index access or an add operation, and for the time spent by operation clear to dereference one element. We shall charge each operation 2 cyber-dollars. This means undercharging operation clear and overcharging all the other operations by 1 cyber-dollar. The cyber-dollar profited in an add operation will be stored at the element inserted by the operation. (See Figure 1.17.) When a clear operation is executed, the cyber-dollar stored at each element in the table is used to pay for the time spent dereferencing it. Hence, we have a valid amortization scheme, where each operation is charged 2 cyber-dollars, and all the computing time is paid for. This simple amortization scheme implies the result of Theorem 1.30.

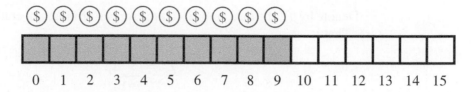

Figure 1.17: Cyber-dollars stored at the elements of a clearable table S in the amortized analysis of a series of operations on S.

Notice that the worst case for the running time occurs for a series of **add** operations followed by a single **clear** operation. In other cases, at the end of the series of operations, we may end up with some unspent cyber-dollars, which are those profited from index access operations and those stored at the elements still in the sequence. Indeed, the computing time for executing a series of n operations can be paid for with the amount of cyber-dollars between n and $2n$. Our amortization scheme accounts for the worst case by always charging 2 cyber-dollars per operation.

At this point, we should stress that the accounting method is simply an analysis tool. It does not require that we modify a data structure or the execution of an algorithm in any way. In particular, it does not require that we add objects for keeping track of the cyber-dollars spent.

Potential Functions

Another useful technique for performing an amortized analysis is based on an energy model. In this approach, we associate with our structure a value, Φ, which represents the current energy state of our system. Each operation that we perform will contribute some additional amount, known as the amortized time, to Φ, but then also extracts value from Φ in proportion to the amount of time actually spent. Formally, we let $\Phi_0 \geq 0$ denote the initial value of Φ, before we perform any operations, and we use Φ_i to denote the value of the potential function, Φ, after we perform the ith operation. The main idea of using the potential function argument is to use the change in potential for the ith operation, $\Phi_i - \Phi_{i-1}$, to characterize the amortized time needed for that operation.

Let us focus more closely on the action of the ith operation, letting t_i denote its actual running time. We define the amortized running time of the ith operation as

$$t_i' = t_i + \Phi_i - \Phi_{i-1}.$$

That is, the amortized cost of the ith operation is the actual running time plus the net change in potential that operation causes (which may be positive or negative). Or, put another way,

$$t_i = t_i' + \Phi_{i-1} - \Phi_i,$$

that is, the actual time spent is the amortized cost plus the net drop in potential.

Denote by T' the total amortized time for performing n operations on our structure. That is,

$$T' = \sum_{i=1}^{n} t_i'.$$

Then the total actual time, T, taken by our n operations can be bounded as

$$
\begin{aligned}
T &= \sum_{i=1}^{n} t_i \\
  &= \sum_{i=1}^{n} \left(t_i' + \Phi_{i-1} - \Phi_i \right) \\
  &= \sum_{i=1}^{n} t_i' + \sum_{i=1}^{n} \left(\Phi_{i-1} - \Phi_i \right) \\
  &= T' + \sum_{i=1}^{n} \left(\Phi_{i-1} - \Phi_i \right) \\
  &= T' + \Phi_0 - \Phi_n,
\end{aligned}
$$

since the second term above forms a telescoping sum. In other words, the total actual time spent is equal to the total amortized time plus the net drop in potential over the entire sequence of operations. Thus, so long as $\Phi_n \geq \Phi_0$, then $T \leq T'$, the actual time spent is no more than the amortized time.

To make this concept more concrete, let us repeat our analysis of the clearable table using a potential argument. In this case, we choose the potential Φ of our system to be the actual number of elements in our clearable table. We claim that the amortized time for any operation is 2, that is, $t_i' = 2$, for $i = 1, \ldots, n$. To justify this, let us consider the two possible methods for the ith operation.

- add(e): inserting the element e into the table increases Φ by 1 and the actual time needed is 1 unit of time. So, in this case,
  $$1 = t_i = t_i' + \Phi_{i-1} - \Phi_i = 2 - 1,$$
  which is clearly true.
- clear(): removing all m elements from the table requires no more than $m+2$ units of time—m units to do the removal plus at most 2 units for the method call and its overhead. But this operation also drops the potential Φ of our system from m to 0 (we even allow for $m = 0$). So, in this case
  $$m + 2 = t_i = t_i' + \Phi_{i-1} - \Phi_i = 2 + m,$$
  which clearly holds.

Therefore, the amortized time to perform any operation on a clearable table is $O(1)$. Moreover, since $\Phi_i \geq \Phi_0$, for any $i \geq 1$, the actual time, T, to perform n operations on an initially empty clearable table is $O(n)$.

1.4.2 Analyzing an Extendable Array Implementation

A major weakness of the simple array implementation for a clearable table given above is that it requires advance specification of a fixed capacity, N, for the total number of elements that may be stored in the table. If the actual number of elements, n, of the table is much smaller than N, then this implementation will waste space. Worse, if n increases past N, then this implementation will crash.

Let us provide a means to grow the array A that stores the elements of a table S. Of course, in any conventional programming language, such as C, C++, and Java, we cannot actually grow the array A; its capacity is fixed at some number N. Instead, when an **overflow** occurs, that is, when $n = N$ and method add is called, we perform the following steps:

1. Allocate a new array B of capacity $2N$.
2. Copy $A[i]$ to $B[i]$, for $i = 0, \dots, N - 1$.
3. Let $A = B$, that is, we use B as the array supporting S.

This array replacement strategy is known as an **extendable array**. (See Figure 1.18.) Intuitively, this strategy is much like that of the hermit crab, which moves into a larger shell when it outgrows its previous one.

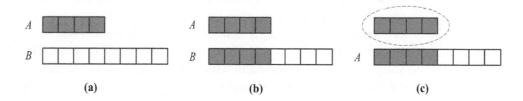

Figure 1.18: An illustration of the three steps for "growing" an extendable array: (a) create new array B; (b) copy elements from A to B; (c) reassign reference A to the new array. Not shown is the future garbage collection of the old array.

In terms of efficiency, this array replacement strategy might at first seem slow, for performing a single array replacement of size n required by some element insertion takes $\Theta(n)$ time. Still, notice that after we perform an array replacement, our new array allows us to add n new elements to the table before the array must be replaced again. This simple fact allows us to show that the running time of a series of operations performed on an initially empty extendable table is actually quite efficient. As a shorthand notation, let us refer to the insertion of an element to be the last element in a vector as an "add" operation. Using **amortization**, we can show that performing a sequence of such add operations on a table implemented with an extendable array is actually quite efficient.

Theorem 1.31: *Let S be a table implemented by means of an extendable array A, as described above. The total time to perform a series of n add operations in S, starting from S being empty and A having size $N = 1$, is $O(n)$.*

Proof: We justify this theorem using the accounting method for ***amortization***. To perform this analysis, we again view the computer as a coin-operated appliance that requires the payment of 1 ***cyber-dollar*** for a constant amount of computing time. When an operation is executed, we should have enough cyber-dollars available in our current "bank account" to pay for that operation's running time. Thus, the total amount of cyber-dollars spent for any computation will be proportional to the total time spent on that computation. The beauty of this analysis is that we can over charge some operations to save up cyber-dollars to pay for others.

Let us assume that 1 cyber-dollar is enough to pay for the execution of each add operation in S, excluding the time for growing the array. Also, let us assume that growing the array from size k to size $2k$ requires k cyber-dollars for the time spent copying the elements. We shall charge each add operation 3 cyber-dollars. Thus, we over charge each add operation not causing an overflow by 2 cyber-dollars. Think of the 2 cyber-dollars profited in an insertion that does not grow the array as being "stored" at the element inserted. An overflow occurs when the table S has 2^i elements, for some integer $i \geq 0$, and the size of the array used by S is 2^i. Thus, doubling the size of the array will require 2^i cyber-dollars. Fortunately, these cyber-dollars can be found at the elements stored in cells 2^{i-1} through $2^i - 1$. (See Figure 1.19.) Note that the previous overflow occurred when the number of elements became larger than 2^{i-1} for the first time, and thus the cyber-dollars stored in cells 2^{i-1} through $2^i - 1$ were not previously spent. Therefore, we have a valid amortization scheme in which each operation is charged 3 cyber-dollars and all the computing time is paid for. That is, we can pay for the execution of n add operations using $3n$ cyber-dollars.   ∎

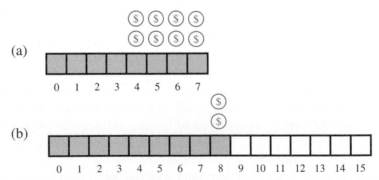

Figure 1.19: A costly add operation: (a) a full 8-cell with 2 cyber-dollars for cells 4 through 7; (b) an add doubles the capacity. Copying elements spends the cyber-dollars in the table, inserting the new element spends 1 cyber-dollar charged to the add, and 2 cyber-dollars "of profit" are stored at cell 8.

A table can be doubled in size with each extension, as we have described it, or we can specify an explicit capacityIncrement parameter that determines the fixed amount an array should grow with each expansion. That is, this parameter is set to a value, k, then the array adds k new cells when it grows. We must utilize such a parameter with caution, however. For most applications, doubling in size is the right choice, as the following theorem shows.

Theorem 1.32: *If we create an initially empty table with a fixed positive* capacityIncrement *value, then performing a series of n* add *operations on this vector takes $\Omega(n^2)$ time.*

Proof: Let $c > 0$ be the capacityIncrement value, and let $c_0 > 0$ denote the initial size of the array. An overflow will be caused by an add operation when the current number of elements in the table is $c_0 + ic$, for $i = 0, \ldots, m - 1$, where $m = \lfloor (n - c_0)/c \rfloor$. Hence, by Theorem 1.13, the total time for handling the overflows is proportional to

$$\sum_{i=0}^{m-1} (c_0 + ci) = c_0 m + c \sum_{i=0}^{m-1} i = c_0 m + c \frac{m(m-1)}{2},$$

which is $\Omega(n^2)$. Thus, performing the n add operations takes $\Omega(n^2)$ time. ∎

Figure 1.20 compares the running times of a series of add operations on an initially empty table, for two initial values of capacityIncrement.

We discuss applications of amortization further when we discuss splay trees (Section 4.5) and a tree structure for set partitions (Section 7.1).

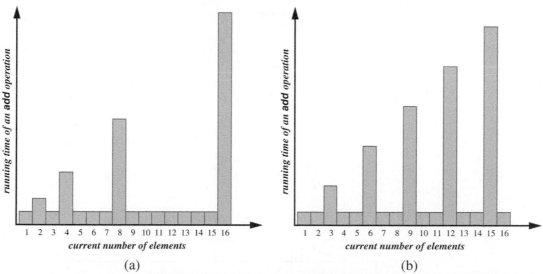

Figure 1.20: Running times of a series of add operations on an extendable table. In (a) the size is doubled with each expansion, and in (b) it is simply incremented by capacityIncrement $= 3$.

1.5 Exercises

Reinforcement

R-1.1 Graph the functions $12n$, $6n \log n$, n^2, n^3, and 2^n using a logarithmic scale for the x- and y-axes; that is, if the function value $f(n)$ is y, plot this as a point with x-coordinate at $\log n$ and y-coordinate at $\log y$.

R-1.2 Show that the MaxsubSlow algorithm runs in $\Omega(n^3)$ time.

R-1.3 Algorithm A uses $10n \log n$ operations, while algorithm B uses n^2 operations. Determine the value n_0 such that A is better than B for $n \geq n_0$.

R-1.4 Repeat the previous problem assuming B uses $n\sqrt{n}$ operations.

R-1.5 Show that $\log^3 n$ is $o(n^{1/3})$.

R-1.6 Show that the following two statements are equivalent:

(a) The running time of algorithm A is always $O(f(n))$.

(b) In the worst case, the running time of algorithm A is $O(f(n))$.

R-1.7 Order the following list of functions by the big-Oh notation. Group together (for example, by underlining) those functions that are big-Theta of one another.

$$
\begin{array}{ccccc}
6n \log n & 2^{100} & \log\log n & \log^2 n & 2^{\log n} \\
2^{2^n} & \lceil \sqrt{n} \rceil & n^{0.01} & 1/n & 4n^{3/2} \\
3n^{0.5} & 5n & \lfloor 2n \log^2 n \rfloor & 2^n & n \log_4 n \\
4^n & n^3 & n^2 \log n & 4^{\log n} & \sqrt{\log n}
\end{array}
$$

Hint: When in doubt about two functions $f(n)$ and $g(n)$, consider $\log f(n)$ and $\log g(n)$ or $2^{f(n)}$ and $2^{g(n)}$.

R-1.8 For each function $f(n)$ and time t in the following table, determine the largest size n of a problem that can be solved in time t assuming that the algorithm to solve the problem takes $f(n)$ microseconds. Recall that $\log n$ denotes the logarithm in base 2 of n. Some entries have already been completed to get you started.

	1 Second	1 Hour	1 Month	1 Century
$\log n$	$\approx 10^{300000}$			
$\sqrt{n}$				
n				
$n \log n$				
n^2				
n^3				
2^n				
$n!$		12		

R-1.9 Bill has an algorithm, find2D, to find an element x in an $n \times n$ array A. The algorithm find2D iterates over the rows of A and calls the algorithm arrayFind, of Algorithm 1.12, on each one, until x is found or it has searched all rows of A. What is the worst-case running time of find2D in terms of n? Is this a linear-time algorithm? Why or why not?

R-1.10 Consider the following recurrence equation, defining $T(n)$, as

$$T(n) = \begin{cases} 4 & \text{if } n = 1 \\ T(n-1) + 4 & \text{otherwise.} \end{cases}$$

Show, by induction, that $T(n) = 4n$.

R-1.11 Give a big-Oh characterization, in terms of n, of the running time of the Loop1 method shown in Algorithm 1.21.

R-1.12 Perform a similar analysis for method Loop2 shown in Algorithm 1.21.

R-1.13 Perform a similar analysis for method Loop3 shown in Algorithm 1.21.

R-1.14 Perform a similar analysis for method Loop4 shown in Algorithm 1.21.

R-1.15 Perform a similar analysis for method Loop5 shown in Algorithm 1.21.

Algorithm Loop1(n):
  $s \leftarrow 0$
  for $i \leftarrow 1$ **to** n **do**
    $s \leftarrow s + i$

Algorithm Loop2(n):
  $p \leftarrow 1$
  for $i \leftarrow 1$ **to** $2n$ **do**
    $p \leftarrow p \cdot i$

Algorithm Loop3(n):
  $p \leftarrow 1$
  for $i \leftarrow 1$ **to** n^2 **do**
    $p \leftarrow p \cdot i$

Algorithm Loop4(n):
  $s \leftarrow 0$
  for $i \leftarrow 1$ **to** $2n$ **do**
    for $j \leftarrow 1$ **to** i **do**
      $s \leftarrow s + i$

Algorithm Loop5(n):
  $s \leftarrow 0$
  for $i \leftarrow 1$ **to** n^2 **do**
    for $j \leftarrow 1$ **to** i **do**
      $s \leftarrow s + i$

Algorithm 1.21: A collection of loop methods.

R-1.16 Show that if $f(n)$ is $O(g(n))$ and $d(n)$ is $O(h(n))$, then the summation $f(n) + d(n)$ is $O(g(n) + h(n))$.

R-1.17 Show that $O(\max\{f(n), g(n)\}) = O(f(n) + g(n))$.

R-1.18 Show that $f(n)$ is $O(g(n))$ if and only if $g(n)$ is $\Omega(f(n))$.

R-1.19 Show that if $p(n)$ is a polynomial in n, then $\log p(n)$ is $O(\log n)$.

R-1.20 Show that $(n + 1)^5$ is $O(n^5)$.

R-1.21 Show that 2^{n+1} is $O(2^n)$.

R-1.22 Show that n is $o(n \log n)$.

R-1.23 Show that n^2 is $\omega(n)$.

R-1.24 Show that $n^3 \log n$ is $\Omega(n^3)$.

R-1.25 Show that $\lceil f(n) \rceil$ is $O(f(n))$ if $f(n)$ is a positive nondecreasing function that is always greater than 1.

R-1.26 Justify the fact that if $d(n)$ is $O(f(n))$ and $e(n)$ is $O(g(n))$, then the product $d(n)e(n)$ is $O(f(n)g(n))$.

R-1.27 Given the values of the maximum suffix sums, M_t ($t = 1, \cdots, 11$), for the array $A = [-2, -4, 3, -1, 5, 6, -7, -2, 4, -3, 2]$.

R-1.28 What is the amortized running time of an operation in a series of n add operations on an initially empty extendable table implemented with an array such that the capacityIncrement parameter is always maintained to be $\lceil \log(m+1) \rceil$, where m is the number of elements of the stack? That is, each time the table is expanded by $\lceil \log(m + 1) \rceil$ cells, its capacityIncrement is reset to $\lceil \log(m' + 1) \rceil$ cells, where m is the old size of the table and m' is the new size (in terms of actual elements present).

R-1.29 Describe a recursive algorithm for finding both the minimum and the maximum elements in an array A of n elements. Your method should return a pair (a, b), where a is the minimum element and b is the maximum. What is the running time of your method?

R-1.30 Suppose you have an array of n numbers and you select each one independently with probability $1/n^{1/2}$. Use the Chernoff bound to determine an upper bound on the probability that you would have more than $4n^{1/2}$ elements in this random sample.

R-1.31 Rewrite the proof of Theorem 1.31 under the assumption that the cost of growing the array from size k to size $2k$ is $3k$ cyber-dollars. How much should each add operation be charged to make the amortization work?

R-1.32 Suppose we have a set of n balls and we choose each one independently with probability $1/n^{1/2}$ to go into a basket. Derive an upper bound on the probability that there are more than $3n^{1/2}$ balls in the basket.

Creativity

C-1.1 Describe how to modify the description of the MaxsubFastest algorithm so that, in addition to the value of the maximum subarray summation, it also outputs the indices j and k that identify the maximum subarray $A[j : k]$.

C-1.2 Describe how to modify the MaxsubFastest algorithm so that it uses just a single loop and, instead of computing $n + 1$ different M_t values, it maintains just a single variable M.

C-1.3 What is the amortized running time of the operations in a sequence of n operations $P = p_1 p_2 \ldots p_n$ if the running time of p_i is $\Theta(i)$ if i is a multiple of 3, and is constant otherwise?

C-1.4 What is the total running time of counting from 1 to n in binary if the time needed to add 1 to the current number i is proportional to the number of bits in the binary expansion of i that must change in going from i to $i + 1$?

C-1.5 Consider the following recurrence equation, defining a function $T(n)$:

$$T(n) = \begin{cases} 1 & \text{if } n = 1 \\ T(n-1) + n & \text{otherwise,} \end{cases}$$

Show, by induction, that $T(n) = n(n+1)/2$.

C-1.6 Consider the following recurrence equation, defining a function $T(n)$:

$$T(n) = \begin{cases} 1 & \text{if } n = 0 \\ T(n-1) + 2^n & \text{otherwise,} \end{cases}$$

Show, by induction, that $T(n) = 2^{n+1} - 1$.

C-1.7 Consider the following recurrence equation, defining a function $T(n)$:

$$T(n) = \begin{cases} 1 & \text{if } n = 0 \\ 2T(n-1) & \text{otherwise,} \end{cases}$$

Show, by induction, that $T(n) = 2^n$.

C-1.8 Al and Bill are arguing about the performance of their sorting algorithms. Al claims that his $O(n \log n)$-time algorithm is *always* faster than Bill's $O(n^2)$-time algorithm. To settle the issue, they implement and run the two algorithms on many randomly generated data sets. To Al's dismay, they find that if $n < 100$, the $O(n^2)$-time algorithm actually runs faster, and only when $n \geq 100$ is the $O(n \log n)$-time algorithm better. Explain why this scenario is possible. You may give numerical examples.

C-1.9 Give an example of a positive function $f(n)$ such that $f(n)$ is neither $O(n)$ nor $\Omega(n)$.

C-1.10 Show that $\sum_{i=1}^{n} i^2$ is $O(n^3)$.

C-1.11 Show that $\sum_{i=1}^{n} i/2^i < 2$.

Hint: Try to bound this sum term by term with a geometric progression.

C-1.12 Show that $\log_b f(n)$ is $\Theta(\log f(n))$ if $b > 1$ is a constant.

C-1.13 Describe a method for finding both the minimum and maximum of n numbers using fewer than $3n/2$ comparisons.

Hint: First construct a group of candidate minimums and a group of candidate maximums.

C-1.14 An n-degree ***polynomial*** $p(x)$ is an equation of the form

$$p(x) = \sum_{i=0}^{n} a_i x^i,$$

where x is a real number and each a_i is a constant.

    a. Describe a simple $O(n^2)$-time method for computing $p(x)$ for a particular value of x.

    b. Consider now a rewriting of $p(x)$ as

$$p(x) = a_0 + x(a_1 + x(a_2 + x(a_3 + \cdots + x(a_{n-1} + xa_n)\cdots))),$$

    which is known as ***Horner's method***. Using the big-Oh notation, characterize the number of multiplications and additions this method of evaluation uses.

C-1.15 Consider the following induction "proof" that all sheep in a flock are the same color:

Base case: One sheep. It is clearly the same color as itself.

Induction step: A flock of n sheep. Take a sheep, a, out of the flock. The remaining $n - 1$ are all the same color by induction. Now put sheep a back in the flock, and take out a different sheep, b. By induction, the $n - 1$ sheep (now with a in their group) are all the same color. Therefore, a is the same color as all the other sheep; hence, all the sheep in the flock are the same color.

What is wrong with this "proof"?

C-1.16 Consider the following "proof" that the Fibonacci function, $F(n)$, defined as $F(1) = 1$, $F(2) = 2$, $F(n) = F(n-1) + F(n-2)$, is $O(n)$:

Base case ($n \le 2$): $F(1) = 1$, which is $O(1)$, and $F(2) = 2$, which is $O(2)$.

Induction step ($n > 2$): Assume the claim is true for $n' < n$. Consider n. $F(n) = F(n-1) + F(n-2)$. By induction, $F(n-1)$ is $O(n-1)$ and $F(n-2)$ is $O(n-2)$. Then, $F(n)$ is $O((n-1) + (n-2))$, by the identity presented in Exercise R-1.16. Therefore, $F(n)$ is $O(n)$, since $O((n-1) + (n-2))$ is $O(n)$. What is wrong with this "proof"?

C-1.17 Consider the Fibonacci function, $F(n)$, from the previous exercise. Show by induction that $F(n)$ is $\Omega((3/2)^n)$.

C-1.18 Draw a visual justification of Theorem 1.13 analogous to that of Figure 1.11b for the case when n is odd.

C-1.19 An array A contains $n - 1$ unique integers in the range $[0, n-1]$; that is, there is one number from this range that is not in A. Design an $O(n)$-time algorithm for finding that number. You are allowed to use only $O(1)$ additional space besides the array A itself.

C-1.20 Show that the summation $\sum_{i=1}^{n} \lceil \log_2 i \rceil$ is $O(n \log n)$.

C-1.21 Show that the summation $\sum_{i=1}^{n} \lceil \log_2 i \rceil$ is $\Omega(n \log n)$.

C-1.22 Show that the summation $\sum_{i=1}^{n} \lceil \log_2(n/i) \rceil$ is $O(n)$. You may assume that n is a power of 2.

Hint: Use induction to reduce the problem to that for $n/2$.

C-1.23 Let S be a set of n lines such that no two are parallel and no three meet in the same point. Show by induction that the lines in S determine $\Theta(n^2)$ intersection points.

C-1.24 Suppose that each row of an $n \times n$ array A consists of 1's and 0's such that, in any row of A, all the 1's come before any 0's in that row. Assuming A is already in memory, describe a method running in $O(n)$ time (not $O(n^2)$ time) for finding the row of A that contains the most 1's.

C-1.25 Suppose that each row of an $n \times n$ array A consists of 1's and 0's such that, in any row i of A, all the 1's come before any 0's in that row. Suppose further that the number of 1's in row i is at least the number in row $i + 1$, for $i = 0, 1, \ldots, n - 2$. Assuming A is already in memory, describe a method running in $O(n)$ time (not $O(n^2)$ time) for counting the number of 1's in the array A.

C-1.26 Describe, using pseudocode, a method for multiplying an $n \times m$ matrix A and an $m \times p$ matrix B. Recall that the product $C = AB$ is defined so that $C[i][j] = \sum_{k=1}^{m} A[i][k] \cdot B[k][j]$. What is the running time of your method?

C-1.27 Give a recursive algorithm to compute the product of two positive integers m and n using only addition.

C-1.28 Give complete pseudocode for a new class, ShrinkingTable, that performs the add method of the extendable table, as well as methods, remove(), which removes the last (actual) element of the table, and shrinkToFit(), which replaces the underlying array with an array whose capacity is exactly equal to the number of elements currently in the table.

C-1.29 Consider an extendable table that supports both add and remove methods, as defined in the previous exercise. Moreover, suppose we grow the underlying array implementing the table by doubling its capacity any time we need to increase the size of this array, and we shrink the underlying array by half any time the number of (actual) elements in the table dips below $N/4$, where N is the current capacity of the array. Show that a sequence of n add and remove methods, starting from an array with capacity $N = 1$, takes $O(n)$ time.

C-1.30 Consider an implementation of the extendable table, but instead of copying the elements of the table into an array of double the size (that is, from N to $2N$) when its capacity is reached, we copy the elements into an array with $\lceil \sqrt{N} \rceil$ additional cells, going from capacity N to $N + \lceil \sqrt{N} \rceil$. Show that performing a sequence of n add operations (that is, insertions at the end) runs in $\Theta(n^{3/2})$ time in this case.

Applications

A-1.1 Communication security is extremely important in computer networks, and one way many network protocols achieve security is to encrypt messages. Typical *cryptographic* schemes for the secure transmission of messages over such networks are based on the fact that no efficient algorithms are known for factoring large integers. Hence, if we can represent a secret message by a large prime number p, we can transmit over the network the number $r = p \cdot q$, where $q > p$ is another large prime number that acts as the *encryption key*. An eavesdropper who obtains the transmitted number r on the network would have to factor r in order to figure out the secret message p.

Using factoring to figure out a message is very difficult without knowing the encryption key q. To understand why, consider the following naive factoring algorithm:

> For every integer p such that $1 < p < r$, check whether p divides r.
> If so, print "The secret message is p!" and stop; if not, continue.

   a. Suppose that the eavesdropper uses the above algorithm and has a computer that can carry out in 1 microsecond (1 millionth of a second) a division between two integers of up to 100 bits each. Give an estimate of the time that it will take in the worst case to decipher the secret message if r has 100 bits.

   b. What is the worst-case time complexity of the above algorithm? Since the input to the algorithm is just one large number r, assume that the input size n is the number of bytes needed to store r, that is, $n = (\log_2 r)/8$, and that each division takes time $O(n)$.

A-1.2 Program the three algorithms given in the chapter for the maximum subarray problem, from Section 1.3, and perform a careful experimental analysis of their running times. Plot their running times as a function of their input sizes as scatter plots on both a linear-linear scale and a log-log scale. Choose representative values of the size n, and run at least five tests for each size value n in your tests. Note that the slope of a line plotted on a log-log scale is based on the exponent of a function, since $\log n^c = c \log n$.

A-1.3 Implement an extendable table using arrays that can increase in size as elements are added. Perform an experimental analysis of each of the running times for performing a sequence of n **add** methods, assuming the array size is increased from N to the following possible values:

   a. $2N$
   b. $N + \lceil \sqrt{N} \rceil$
   c. $N + \lceil \log N \rceil$
   d. $N + 100$.

A-1.4 An evil king has a cellar containing n bottles of expensive wine, and his guards have just caught a spy trying to poison the king's wine. Fortunately, the guards caught the spy after he succeeded in poisoning only one bottle. Unfortunately, they don't know which one. To make matters worse, the poison the spy used was very deadly; just one drop diluted even a billion to one will still kill someone. Even so, the poison works slowly; it takes a full month for the person to die. Design a scheme that allows the evil king to determine exactly which one of his wine bottles was poisoned in just one month's time while expending at most $O(\log n)$ of his taste testers.

Note: **All the remaining problems are inspired by questions reported to have been asked in job interviews for major software and Internet companies.**

A-1.5 Suppose you are given a set of small boxes, numbered 1 to n, identical in every respect except that each of the first i contain a pearl whereas the remaining $n - i$ are empty. You also have two magic wands that can each test whether a box is empty or not in a single touch, except that a wand disappears if you test it on an empty box. Show that, without knowing the value of i, you can use the two wands to determine all the boxes containing pearls using at most $o(n)$ wand touches. Express, as a function of n, the asymptotic number of wand touches needed.

A-1.6 Repeat the previous problem assuming that you now have k magic wands, with $k > 2$ and $k < \log n$. Express, as a function of n and k, the asymptotic number of wand touches needed to identify all the magic boxes containing pearls.

A-1.7 Suppose you are given an integer c and an array, A, indexed from 1 to n, of n integers in the range from 1 to $5n$ (possibly with duplicates). Describe an efficient algorithm for determining if there are two integers, $A[i]$ and $A[j]$, in A that sum to c, that is, such that $c = A[i] + A[j]$, for $1 \le i < j \le n$. What is the running time of your algorithm?

A-1.8 Given an array, A, describe an efficient algorithm for reversing A. For example, if $A = [3, 4, 1, 5]$, then its reversal is $A = [5, 1, 4, 3]$. You can only use $O(1)$ memory in addition to that used by A itself. What is the running time of your algorithm?

A-1.9 Given a string, S, of n digits in the range from 0 to 9, describe an efficient algorithm for converting S into the integer it represents. What is the running time of your algorithm?

A-1.10 Given an array, A, of n integers, find the longest subarray of A such that all the numbers in that subarray are in sorted order. What is the running time of your method?

A-1.11 Given an array, A, of n positive integers, each of which appears in A exactly twice, except for one integer, x, describe an $O(n)$-time method for finding x using only a single variable besides A.

A-1.12 Given an array, A, of $n - 2$ unique integers in the range from 1 to n, describe an $O(n)$-time method for finding the two integers in the range from 1 to n that are not in A. You may use only $O(1)$ space in addition to the space used by A.

A-1.13 Suppose you are writing a simulator for a single-elimination sports tournament (like in NCAA Division-1 basketball). There are n teams at the beginning of the tournament and in each round of the tournament teams are paired up and the games for each pair are simulated. Winners progress to the next round and losers are sent home. This continues until a grand champion team is the final winner.

Suppose your simulator takes $O(\log n)$ time to process each game. How much time does your simulator take in total?

A-1.14 Suppose you are given an array, A, of n positive integers. Describe an $O(n)$ algorithm for removing all the even numbers from A. That is, if A has m odd numbers, then, after you are done, these odd numbers should occupy the first m cells of A in the same relative order they were in originally.

A-1.15 Given an integer $k > 0$ and an array, A, of n bits, describe an efficient algorithm for finding the shortest subarray of A that contains k 1's. What is the running time of your method?

A-1.16 A certain town has exactly n married heterosexual couples. Every wife knows whether every other wife's husband is cheating on his wife or not, but no wife knows if her own husband is cheating or not. In fact, if a wife ever learns that her husband is cheating on her, then she will poison him that very night. So no husband will ever confess that he is cheating. One day, the mayor (who is not married) announces that there is at least one cheating husband in the town. What happens next?

A-1.17 Imagine that a magician has just given you a biased coin. It looks just like a normal coin, with a "heads" side and a "tails" side, but each time this coin is flipped, it is more likely to come up heads than tails. How can you use this coin to generate an unbiased sequence of independent random bits, that is, a random sequence of 0's and 1's where each bit has an independent equal probability of being a 0 or 1?

A-1.18 Suppose you are processing a stream of bytes, one at a time, but you don't know in advance how many there will be, as the last byte is a special EOF character. You only get to consider each byte once. Describe a scheme for choosing a byte in this stream at random so that every byte in the stream has an equal chance of being chosen. You may use only an $O(1)$ amount of space.

Chapter Notes

The big-Oh notation has prompted several discussions over its proper use [36, 95, 128]. Knuth [129, 128], for example, defines it using the notation $f(n) = O(g(n))$, but refers to this "equality" as being only "one way." We have chosen to take a more standard view of equality and view the big-Oh notation as a set, following Brassard [36]. The linear-time algorithm we gave for the maximum subarray problem is due to Kadane [26]. For more information on amortization, please see Tarjan [207, 208]. We include a number of useful mathematical facts in Appendix A. The reader interested in further study into the analysis of algorithms is referred to the books by Graham, Knuth, and Patashnik [93], and Sedgewick and Flajolet [190]. Finally, for more information about using experimentation to estimate the running time of algorithms, we refer the interested reader to papers by McGeoch and coauthors [151, 152, 153].

Chapter

2

Basic Data Structures

An astronaut recording a video of a Hubble Space Telescope servicing mission in 1997. U.S. government image. NASA.

Contents

2.1 Stacks and Queues 53
2.2 Lists 60
2.3 Trees 68
2.4 Exercises 84

The Internet is designed to route information in discrete packets, which are at most 1500 bytes in length. Because of this design, any time a video stream is transmitted on the Internet, it must be subdivided into packets and these packets must each be individually routed to their destination. In the case of a stored video file, it is desirable to send packets using the Transmission Control Protocol (TCP), since this protocol guarantees that all the packets will arrive at their destination in the correct order. Nevertheless, because of vagaries and errors, the time it takes for these packets to arrive at their destination can be highly variable. Thus, we need a way of "smoothing out" these variations in order to avoid long pauses if someone wants to watch a video at the same time it is being transmitted.

This smoothing is typically achieved is by using a *buffer*, which is a portion of computer memory that is used to temporarily store items, as they are being produced by one computational process and consumed by another. For example, in this case of video packets arriving via TCP, the networking process is producing the packets and the playback process is consuming them. Thus, ignoring any rewinding, this *producer-consumer model* is enforcing a first-in, first-out (FIFO) protocol for the packets, in that the consumer process is always retrieving the packet that has been in the buffer the longest. (See Figure 2.1.)

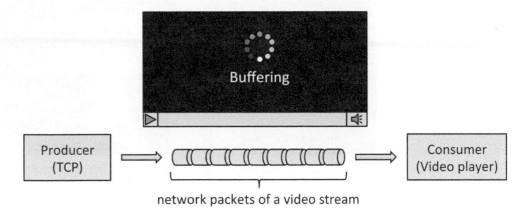

network packets of a video stream

Figure 2.1: Using a buffer to smooth video transmission over the Internet.

Network packets are produced by the TCP process, which inserts packets in the correct order into the buffer, but does so at a variable rate. Packets are consumed by the video player process, which removes packets from the buffer at a constant speed according to the video standard it is using. The buffer enforces a first-in, first-out (FIFO) protocol and, if it is big enough, it should smooth out the packet production and consumption so that packets can be processed at the average transmission rate without annoying pauses. In this chapter, we explore how to implement such a buffer using a *queue* data structure, which itself can be implemented with either an array or a linked list. We also study several other basic data structures, including stacks, lists, and trees, along with applications of these structures.

2.1 Stacks and Queues

2.1.1 Stacks

A *stack* is a container of objects that are inserted and removed according to the *last-in first-out* (*LIFO*) principle. Objects can be inserted into a stack at any time, but only the most-recently inserted (that is, "last") object can be removed at any time. The name "stack" is derived from the metaphor of a stack of plates in a spring-loaded cafeteria plate dispenser. In this case, the fundamental operations involve the "pushing" and "popping" of plates on the stack.

Example 2.1: *Internet web browsers store the addresses of recently visited sites on a stack. Each time a user visits a new site, that site's address is "pushed" onto the stack of addresses. The browser then allows the user to "pop" back to previously visited sites using the "back" button.*

Viewed abstractly, a *stack*, S, is a container that supports the following two methods:

push(o): Insert object o at the top of the stack.

pop(): Remove from the stack and return the top object on the stack, that is, the most recently inserted element still in the stack; an error occurs if the stack is empty.

A Simple Array-Based Implementation

A stack is easily implemented with an N-element array S, with elements stored from $S[0]$ to $S[t]$, where t is an integer that gives the index of the top element in S. Note that one of the important details of such an implementation is that we must specify some maximum size N for our stack, say, $N = 1,000$. (See Figure 2.2.)

S

0 1 2 t N–1

Figure 2.2: Implementing a stack with an array S. The top element is in cell $S[t]$.

If we use the convention that arrays begin at index 0, then we would initialize t to -1 (for an initially empty stack), and we can use this value to also test if a stack is empty. In addition, we can use this variable to determine the number of elements in a stack ($t+1$). In this array-based implementation of a stack, we also must signal an error condition that arises if we try to insert a new element and the array S is full. Given this error condition, we can then implement the main methods of a stack as described in Algorithm 2.3.

Algorithm push(o):
    if $t + 1 = N$ **then**
        return that a stack-full error has occurred
    $t \leftarrow t + 1$
    $S[t] \leftarrow o$
    return

Algorithm pop():
    if $t < 0$ **then**
        return that a stack-empty error has occurred
    $e \leftarrow S[t]$
    $S[t] \leftarrow$ **null**
    $t \leftarrow t - 1$
    return e

Algorithm 2.3: Implementing a stack with an array.

Turning to the analysis of this array-based implementation of a stack, it should be clear that each of the stack methods, push and pop, runs in a constant amount of time. This is because they only involve a constant number of simple arithmetic operations, comparisons, and assignment statements. That is, in this array-based implementation of the stack, each method runs in $O(1)$ time.

The array implementation of a stack is both simple and efficient, and is widely used in a variety of computing applications. Nevertheless, this implementation has one negative aspect; it must assume a fixed upper bound N on the ultimate size of the stack. An application may actually need much less space than this, in which case we would be wasting memory. Alternatively, an application may need more space than this, in which case our stack implementation may "crash" the application with an error as soon as it tries to push its $(N + 1)$st object on the stack. Thus, even with its simplicity and efficiency, the array-based stack implementation is not always ideal.

Fortunately, there is another implementation, which is to use a linked list, discussed later in this chapter. Such an implementation would not have a size limitation (other than that imposed by the total amount of memory on our computer) and it would use an amount of space proportional to the actual number of elements stored in the stack. Alternatively, we could also use an extendable table, as discussed in Section 1.4.2, which could grow in size as the stack grows. In cases where we have a good estimate on the number of items needing to go in the stack, however, the array-based implementation is hard to beat, because they achieve $O(1)$-time performance for the push and pop operations. Stacks serve a vital role in a number of computing applications, so it is helpful to have a fast stack implementation, such as the simple array-based implementation.

Using Stacks for Procedure Calls and Recursion

Stacks have an important application in the runtime environments of programming languages, such as C, C++, Java, and Python. Each thread in a running program written in one of these languages has a private stack, called the ***method stack***, which is used to keep track of local variables and other important information on methods, as they are invoked during execution. (See Figure 2.4.)

More specifically, during the execution of a program thread, the runtime environment maintains a stack whose elements are descriptors of the currently active (that is, nonterminated) invocations of methods. These descriptors are called ***frames***. A frame for some invocation of method cool stores the current values of the local variables and parameters of method cool, as well as information on the method that called cool and on what needs to be returned to this method.

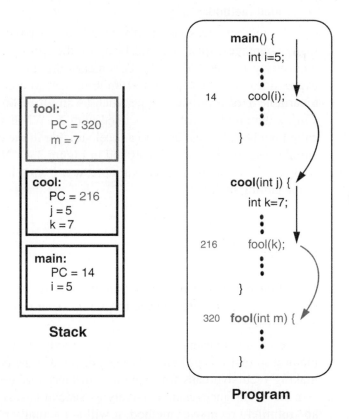

Figure 2.4: An example of a method stack: Method fool has just been called by method cool, which itself was previously called by method main. Note the values of the program counter, parameters, and local variables stored in the stack frames. When the invocation of method fool terminates, the invocation of method cool will resume its execution at instruction 217, which is obtained by incrementing the value of the program counter stored in the stack frame.

The runtime environment keeps the address of the statement the thread is currently executing in the program in a special register, called the ***program counter***. When a method, cool, invokes another method, fool, the current value of the program counter is recorded in the frame of the current invocation of cool (so the computer will "know" where to return to when method fool is done).

At the top of the method stack is the frame of the ***running method***—that is, the method that currently has control of the execution. The remaining elements of the stack are frames of the ***suspended methods***—that is, methods that have invoked another method and are currently waiting for it to return control to them upon its termination. The order of the elements in the stack corresponds to the chain of invocations of the currently active methods. When a new method is invoked, a frame for this method is pushed onto the stack. When it terminates, its frame is popped from the stack and the computer resumes the processing of the previously suspended method.

The method stack also performs parameter passing to methods. Specifically, many languages, such as C and Java, use the ***call-by-value*** parameter passing protocol using the method stack. This means that the current ***value*** of a variable (or expression) is what is passed as an argument to a called method. In the case of a variable x of a primitive type, such as an int or float, the current value of x is simply the number that is associated with x. When such a value is passed to the called method, it is assigned to a local variable in the called method's frame. (This simple assignment is also illustrated in Figure 2.4.) Note that if the called method changes the value of this local variable, it will ***not*** change the value of the variable in the calling method.

Recursion

One of the benefits of using a stack to implement method invocation is that it allows programs to use ***recursion*** (Section 1.1.4). That is, it allows a method to call itself as a subroutine.

Recall that in using this technique correctly, we must always design a recursive method so that it is guaranteed to terminate at some point (for example, by always making recursive calls for "smaller" instances of the problem and handling the "smallest" instances nonrecursively as special cases). We note that if we design an "infinitely recursive" method, it will not actually run forever. It will instead, at some point, use up all the memory available for the method stack and generate an out-of-memory or stack-overflow error. If we use recursion with care, however, the method stack will implement recursive methods without any trouble. Each call of the same method will be associated with a different frame, complete with its own values for local variables. Recursion can be very powerful, as it often allows us to design simple and efficient programs for fairly difficult problems.

2.1.2 Queues

Another basic data structure is the *queue*. It is a close "cousin" of the stack, as a queue is a container of objects that are inserted and removed according to the *first-in first-out* (**FIFO**) principle, as in the video buffering application discussed at the beginning of this chapter. That is, elements can be inserted at any time, but only the element that has been in the queue the longest can be removed at any time. We usually say that elements enter the queue at the *rear* and are removed from the *front*.

Queue Definition

Viewed abstractly, a queue keeps objects in a sequence, where element access and deletion are restricted to the first element in the sequence, which is called the *front* of the queue, and element insertion is restricted to the end of the sequence, which is called the *rear* of the queue. Thus, we enforce the rule that items are inserted and removed according to the FIFO principle. A *queue* supports the following two fundamental methods:

enqueue(o): Insert object o at the rear of the queue.

dequeue(): Remove and return from the queue the object at the front; an error occurs if the queue is empty.

A Simple Array-Based Implementation

As with a stack, we can implement a queue with an array, but the details are slightly more complicated. In this case, we use an array, Q, with capacity N, for storing its elements. Since the main rule for a queue is that we insert and delete objects according to the FIFO principle, we must decide how we are going to keep track of the front and rear of the queue.

To avoid moving objects once they are placed in Q, we define two variables f and r, which have the following meanings:

- f is an index to the cell of Q storing the first element of the queue (which is the next candidate to be removed by a dequeue operation), unless the queue is empty (in which case $f = r$).
- r is an index to the next available array cell in Q.

Initially, we assign $f = r = 0$, and we indicate that the queue is empty by the condition $f = r$. Now, when we remove an element from the front of the queue, we can simply increment f to index the next cell. Likewise, when we add an element, we can simply increment r to index the next available cell in Q. We have to be a little careful not to overflow the end of the array, however. Consider, for example, what happens if we repeatedly enqueue and dequeue a single element N different times. We would have $f = r = N$. If we were then to try to insert the element just one more time, we would get an array-out-of-bounds error (since the N valid locations in Q are from $Q[0]$ to $Q[N-1]$), even though there is plenty of room in the queue in this case. To avoid this problem and be able to utilize all of the array Q, we let the f and r indices "wrap around" the end of Q. That is, we now view Q as a "circular array" that goes from $Q[0]$ to $Q[N-1]$ and then immediately back to $Q[0]$ again. (See Figure 2.5.)

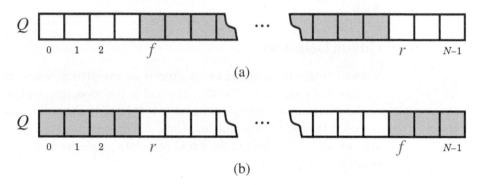

(a)

(b)

Figure 2.5: Implementing a queue using an array Q in a circular fashion: (a) the "normal" configuration with $f \leq r$; (b) the "wrapped around" configuration with $r < f$. The cells storing queue elements are highlighted.

Implementing this circular view of Q is pretty easy. Each time we increment f or r, we simply compute this increment as "$(f+1) \bmod N$" or "$(r+1) \bmod N$," respectively. Recall here that the operator "mod" is the *modulo* operator, which is computed by taking the remainder after an integral division, so that, if y is nonzero, then

$$x \bmod y = x - \lfloor x/y \rfloor y.$$

Consider now the situation that occurs if we enqueue N objects without dequeuing them. We would have $f = r$, which is the same condition as when the queue is empty. Hence, we would not be able to tell the difference between a full queue and an empty one in this case. Fortunately, this is not a big problem, and a number of ways for dealing with it exist. For example, we can simply insist that Q can never hold more than $N-1$ objects. The above simple rule for handling a full queue takes care of the final problem with our implementation, and leads to the pseudocoded descriptions of the main queue methods given in Algorithm 2.6. Note that we may compute the size of the queue by means of the expression $(N - f + r) \bmod N$, which gives the correct result both in the "normal" configuration (when $f \leq r$) and in the "wrapped around" configuration (when $r < f$).

Algorithm dequeue():

   if $f = r$ **then**

      return an error condition that the queue is empty

   $temp \leftarrow Q[f]$

   $Q[f] \leftarrow$ **null**

   $f \leftarrow (f + 1) \bmod N$

   return $temp$

Algorithm enqueue(o):

   if $(N - f + r) \bmod N = N - 1$ **then**

      return an error condition that the queue is full

   $Q[r] \leftarrow o$

   $r \leftarrow (r + 1) \bmod N$

   return

Algorithm 2.6: Implementing a queue with an array, which is viewed circularly.

Analysis and Applications of Queues

As with our array-based stack implementation, it should be clear that each of the above queue methods based on implementing the queue with an array executes in a constant number of statements involving arithmetic operations, comparisons, and assignments. Thus, each method in this array-based queue implementation runs in $O(1)$ time.

We have already discussed the application of queues to the problem of buffering video as it is streamed on the Internet. There are several other applications of queues, as well. For instance, a queue is an ideal data structure for processing online ticketing requests. Likewise, a queue is typically used to manage a ***printer spooler***, which is a process that manages documents that are sent to be output by a printer.

As with the array-based stack implementation, the only real disadvantage of the array-based queue implementation is that we artificially set the capacity of the queue to be some number N. In a real application, we may actually need more or less queue capacity than this, but if we have a good estimate of the number of elements that will be in the queue at the same time, then the array-based implementation is quite efficient. If we don't have a good estimate, however, then we can implement a queue using a linked list, which is a data structure we discuss in the next section.

2.2   Lists

Stacks and queues store elements according to a linear sequence determined by update operations that act on the "ends" of the sequence. Lists, on the other hand, which we discuss in this section, maintain linear orders while allowing for accesses and updates in the "middle."

2.2.1   Index-Based Lists

Suppose we are given a linear sequence, S, that contains n elements. We can uniquely refer to each element e of S using an integer in the range $[0, n-1]$ that is equal to the number of elements of S that precede e in S. In particular, we define the **index** (or **rank**) of an element e in S to be the number of elements that are before e in S. Hence, the first element in a sequence is at index 0 and the last element is at index $n-1$.

Note that this notion of "index" is different from indices of cells in an array, since array cells are static. This notion of index in a list of elements implies that the index of an element can change depending on whether elements before it are inserted or removed in its list. Such an index in a list is therefore dynamic and depends on the operations that are performed on the list. For instance, if we insert a new element at the beginning of such a list, the index of each of the other elements increases by one. This definition is consistent, for example, with the ArrayList class in Java.

We refer to a linear sequence that supports access to its elements by their indices in this way as an **index-based list**.

An index-based list, S, storing n elements supports the following methods:

> get(r): Return the element of S with index r; an error condition occurs if $r < 0$ or $r > n-1$.

> set(r, e): Replace with e the element at index r and return it; an error condition occurs if $r < 0$ or $r > n-1$.

> add(r, e): Insert a new element e into S to have index r; an error condition occurs if $r < 0$ or $r > n$.

> remove(r): Remove from S the element at index r; an error condition occurs if $r < 0$ or $r > n-1$.

An obvious choice for implementing an index-based list is to use an array A, where $A[i]$ stores (a reference to) the element with index i. We choose the size N of array A to be sufficiently large, and we maintain in an instance variable the actual number $n < N$ of elements in the list. The details of the implementation of the methods of index-based list are reasonably simple. To implement the get(r)

operation, for example, we just return $A[r]$. Implementations of methods $\mathrm{add}(r, e)$ and $\mathrm{remove}(r)$ are given in Algorithm 2.7.

Algorithm $\mathrm{add}(r, e)$:

   if $n = N$ **then**

      return "Array is full."

   if $r < n$ **then**

      for $i \leftarrow n - 1, n - 2, \ldots, r$ **do**

         $A[i + 1] \leftarrow A[i]$ // make room for the new element

   $A[r] \leftarrow e$

   $n \leftarrow n + 1$

Algorithm $\mathrm{remove}(r)$:

   $e \leftarrow A[r]$ // e is a temporary variable

   if $r < n - 1$ **then**

      for $i \leftarrow r, r + 1, \ldots, n - 2$ **do**

         $A[i] \leftarrow A[i + 1]$ // fill in for the removed element

   $n \leftarrow n - 1$

   return e

Algorithm 2.7: Methods in an array implementation of an index-based list.

An important (and time-consuming) part of this implementation involves the shifting of elements up or down to keep the occupied cells in the array contiguous. That is, in inserting a new element at rank r we must shift up by 1 the places where all elements previously of index r and higher are stored. Likewise, in removing an element at rank r we must shift down by 1 the places where all elements previously of index $r + 1$ and higher are stored. These shifting operations are required to maintain our rule of always storing an element of rank i at index i in A. (See Figure 2.8 and also Exercise C-2.8.)

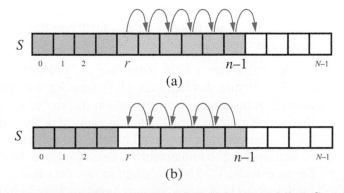

Figure 2.8: Array-based implementation of an index-based list, S: (a) shifting up for an insertion at index r; (b) shifting down for a removal at index r.

Analysis of an Array Implementation of an Index-Based List

Table 2.9 shows the running times of the methods of an index-based list implemented with an array. Note that the insertion and removal methods can take time much longer than $O(1)$. In particular, $\mathsf{add}(r, e)$ runs in time $\Theta(n)$ in the worst case. Indeed, the worst case for this operation occurs when $r = 0$, since all the existing n elements have to be shifted over. A similar argument applies to the method $\mathsf{remove}(r)$, which runs in $O(n)$ time, because we have to shift $n-1$ elements in the worst case ($r = 0$). In fact, assuming that each possible index is equally likely to be passed as an argument to these operations, their average running time is $\Theta(n)$, since we would have to shift $n/2$ elements on average.

Method	Time
$\mathsf{get}(r)$	$O(1)$
$\mathsf{set}(r, e)$	$O(1)$
$\mathsf{add}(r, e)$	$O(n)$
$\mathsf{remove}(r)$	$O(n)$

Table 2.9: Worst-case performance of an index-based list with n elements implemented with an array. The space usage is $O(N)$, where N is the size of the array.

Looking more closely at $\mathsf{add}(r, e)$ and $\mathsf{remove}(r)$, we note that they each run in time $O(n-r+1)$, for only those elements at rank r and higher have to be shifted up or down. Thus, inserting or removing an item at the end of a list, using the methods $\mathsf{add}(n, e)$ and $\mathsf{remove}(n-1)$, respectively take $O(1)$ time each. That is, inserting or removing an element at the end of an index-based list takes constant time, as would inserting or removing an element within a constant number of cells from the end. Still, with the above implementation, inserting or removing an element at the beginning of a list requires shifting every other element by one; hence, it takes $\Theta(n)$ time. Thus, there is an asymmetry to this implementation—updates at the end are fast, whereas updates at the beginning are slow.

Actually, with a little effort, we can produce an array-based implementation of this structure that achieves $O(1)$ time for insertions and removals at index 0, as well as insertions and removals at the end of the list. Achieving this requires that we give up on our rule that an element at list-index i is stored in the array at index i, however, as we would have to use a circular array approach like we used in Section 2.1.2 to implement a queue. We leave the details of this implementation for an exercise (C-2.8). In addition, we note that an index-based list can also be implemented to achieve constant-time amortized insertion and removal operations at the end of a list, by using an extendable table (Section 1.4.2), which, in fact, is the default implementation of the ArrayList class in Java.

2.2.2   Linked Lists

Using an index is not the only way to refer to elements in a list. We could alternatively implement a list S so that each element is stored in a special ***node*** object with references (that is, pointers) to the nodes before and after it in the list. In this case, it could be more natural and efficient to use a node instead of an index to identify where to access and update a list. In this section, we explore such a way of using nodes to represent "places" in a list.

To abstract a way of storing elements in a list, we introduce the concept of ***position*** in a list, which formalizes the intuitive notion of "node" that is storing an element relative to others in the list. In this framework, we view a ***linked list*** as a container of elements that stores each element at a node position and that keeps these positions arranged in a linear order relative to one another. A position is itself an object that supports the following simple method:

element(): Return the element stored at this position.

A position (or node) is always defined ***relatively***, that is, in terms of its neighbors. In a list, a position p will always be "after" some position q and "before" some position s (unless p is the first or last position). A position p, which is associated with some element e in a list S, does not change, even if the rank of e changes in S, unless we explicitly remove e (and, hence, destroy position p). Moreover, the position p does not change even if we replace or swap the element e stored at p with another element. These facts about positions allow us to define a set of position-based list methods that take position objects as parameters and also provide position objects as return values.

Using the concept of position to encapsulate the idea of "node" in a list, we can define a linked list. This structure supports the following methods for a list, S:

first(): Return the position of the first element of S; an error occurs if S is empty.

last(): Return the position of the last element of S; an error occurs if S is empty.

before(p): Return the position of the element of S preceding the one at position p; an error occurs if p is the first position.

after(p): Return the position of the element of S following the one at position p; an error occurs if p is the last position.

The above methods allow us to refer to relative positions in a list, starting at the beginning or end, and to be able to move incrementally up or down the list. As mentioned above, these positions can be thought of as nodes in the list, but note that there are no specific references to pointers or links to previous or next nodes in these methods.

We can also include the following update methods for a linked list.

insertBefore(p, e): Insert a new element e into S before position p in S.

insertAfter(p, e): Insert a new element e into S after position p in S.

remove(p): Remove from S the element at position p.

This approach allows us to view an ordered collection of objects in terms of their places, without worrying about the exact way those places are represented. In addition, this structure, with its built-in notion of position, is useful in a number of settings. For example, a simple text editor embeds the notion of positional insertion and removal, since such editors typically perform all updates relative to a *cursor*, which represents the current position in a list of characters being edited.

We can use node objects to implement a *linked list*, so that a great variety of operations, including insertion and removal at various places, can run in $O(1)$ time. A node in a *singly linked* list stores in a *next* link a reference to the next node in the list. Thus, a singly linked list can only be traversed in one direction—from the head to the tail. A node in a *doubly linked* list, on the other hand, stores two references—a *next* link, which points to the next node in the list, and a *prev* link, which points to the previous node in the list. Therefore, a doubly linked list can be traversed in either direction. Being able to determine the previous and next node from any given node in a list greatly simplifies list implementation; so let us assume we are using such doubly linked nodes to implement a linked list.

To simplify updates and searching, it is convenient to add special nodes at both ends of the list: a *header* node just before the head of the list, and a *trailer* node just after the tail of the list. These "dummy" or *sentinel* nodes do not store any element, but their ubiquitous existence allows us to avoid worrying about special cases for inserting and removing elements at the beginning or end of a list. The header has a valid *next* reference but a null *prev* reference, while the trailer has a valid *prev* reference but a null *next* reference. A doubly linked list with these sentinels is shown in Figure 2.10. Note that a linked list object would simply need to store these two sentinels and a size counter that keeps track of the number of elements (not counting sentinels) in the list.

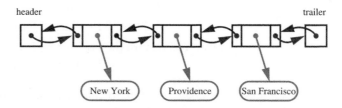

Figure 2.10: A doubly linked list with sentinels, header and trailer, marking the ends of the list. An empty list would have these sentinels pointing to each other.

We can simply make the nodes of the linked list implement the position concept, defining a method element(), which returns the element stored at the node. Thus, the nodes themselves act as positions.

Consider how we might implement the insertAfter(p, e) method, for inserting an element e after position p. We create a new node v to hold the element e, link v into its place in the list, and then update the next and prev references of v's two new neighbors. This method is given in pseudocode in Algorithm 2.11 and is illustrated in Figure 2.12.

Algorithm insertAfter(p, e):
    Create a new node v
    v.element $\leftarrow e$
    v.prev $\leftarrow p$ // link v to its predecessor
    v.next $\leftarrow p$.next   // link v to its successor
    (p.next).prev $\leftarrow v$ // link p's old successor to v
    p.next $\leftarrow v$ // link p to its new successor, v
    return v // the position for the element e

Algorithm 2.11: Inserting an element e after a position p in a linked list.

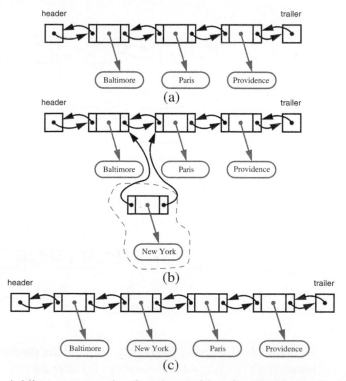

Figure 2.12: Adding a new node after the position for "Baltimore": (a) before the insertion; (b) creating node v and linking it in; (c) after the insertion.

The algorithms for methods insertBefore, insertFirst, and insertLast are similar to that for method insertAfter; we leave their details as an exercise (R-2.3). Next, consider the remove(p) method, which removes the element e stored at position p. To perform this operation, we link the two neighbors of p to refer to one another as new neighbors—linking out p. Note that after p is linked out, no nodes will be pointing to p; hence, a garbage collector can reclaim the space for p. This algorithm is given in Algorithm 2.13 and is illustrated in Figure 2.14. Recalling our use of sentinels, note that this algorithm works even if p is the first, last, or only real position in the list.

Algorithm remove(p):
    $t \leftarrow p$.element   // a temporary variable to hold the return value
    (p.prev).next $\leftarrow p$.next   // linking out p
    (p.next).prev $\leftarrow p$.prev
    p.prev $\leftarrow$ **null**   // invalidating the position p
    p.next $\leftarrow$ **null**
    return t

Algorithm 2.13: Removing an element e stored at a position p in a linked list.

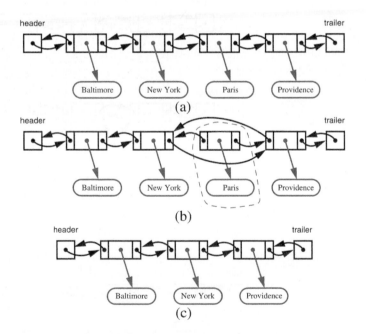

Figure 2.14: Removing the object stored at the position for "Paris": (a) before the removal; (b) linking out the old node; (c) after the removal (and garbage collection).

Analyzing List Implementations

Let us consider the performance of the above node-based linked list implementation. It should not be too difficult to see that all of the methods for a linked list can be implemented to run in $O(1)$ time using a node-based approach. That is, we can perform the methods for a linked list to have running times as shown in Table 2.15.

Method	Time
first()	$O(1)$
last()	$O(1)$
before(p)	$O(1)$
after(p)	$O(1)$
insertBefore(p, e)	$O(1)$
insertAfter(p, e)	$O(1)$
remove(p)	$O(1)$

Table 2.15: Worst-case performance of a node-based linked list with n elements. The space usage is $O(n)$, where n is the number of elements in the list.

Thinking generally about accessing elements by either indices or nodes, we can compare the performance of a linked list to that of an array-based list implementation. If we need to be accessing elements by their ranks or indices, clearly an array-based list is more efficient than a linked list, since the only way to determine the rank of an element e in a linked list is to follow the sequence of pointers from the node storing e to the end or beginning of its list. Thus, using a linked list for index-based operations would require $O(n)$ time for each such operation. Regarding update operations, the linked-list implementation beats the array-based implementation in the position-based update operations, since it can insert or remove elements in the "middle" of a list in constant time, whereas an array-based implementation takes $O(n)$ time (to keep the list contiguous in the array).

Considering space usage, note that an array requires $O(N)$ space, where N is the size of the array (unless we utilize an extendable array), while a doubly linked list uses $O(n)$ space, where n is the number of elements in the sequence. If n is much less than N, this implies that the asymptotic space usage of a linked-list implementation is better than that of a fixed-size array, although there is a small constant factor overhead that is larger for linked lists, since arrays do not need links to maintain the ordering of their cells.

Array-based and linked-list implementations of lists each have advantages and disadvantages, therefore. The correct one for a particular application depends on the operations that are to be performed and the memory space available.

2.3 Trees

Viewed abstractly, a ***tree*** is a data structure that stores elements hierarchically. With the exception of the top element, each element in a tree has a ***parent*** element and zero or more ***children*** elements. A tree is usually visualized by placing elements inside ovals or rectangles, and by drawing the connections between parents and children with straight lines. (See Figure 2.16.) We typically call the top element the ***root*** of the tree, but it is drawn as the highest element, with the other elements being connected below (just the opposite of a botanical tree).

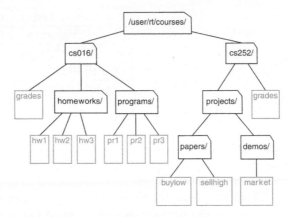

Figure 2.16: A tree representing a portion of a file system.

A ***tree*** T is a set of ***nodes*** storing elements in a ***parent-child*** relationship with the following properties:

- T has a special node r, called the ***root*** of T, with no ***parent*** node.
- Each node v of T different from r has a unique ***parent*** node u.

Note that according to the above definition, a tree cannot be empty, since it must have at least one node, the root. One could also allow the definition to include empty trees, but we adopt the convention that a tree always has a root so as to keep our presentation simple and to avoid having to always deal with the special case of an empty tree in our algorithms.

If node u is the parent of node v, then we say that v is a ***child*** of u. Two nodes that are children of the same parent are ***siblings***. A node is ***external*** if it has no children, and it is ***internal*** if it has one or more children. External nodes are also known as ***leaves***. The ***subtree*** of T ***rooted*** at a node v is the tree consisting of all the descendants of v in T (including v itself). An ***ancestor*** of a node is either the node itself, its parent, or an ancestor of its parent. Conversely, we say that a node v is a ***descendant*** of a node u if u is an ancestor of v.

Example 2.2: *In most operating systems, files are organized hierarchically into nested directories (also called folders), which are presented to the user in the form of a tree. (See Figure 2.16.) More specifically, the internal nodes of the tree are associated with directories and the external nodes are associated with regular files. In Unix-like operating systems, the root of the tree is appropriately called the "root directory," and is represented by the symbol "/." It is the ancestor of all directories and files in such a file system.*

A tree is **ordered** if there is a linear ordering defined for the children of each node; that is, we can identify children of a node as being the first, second, third, and so on. Ordered trees typically indicate the linear order relationship existing between siblings by listing them in the correct order.

Example 2.3: *A structured document, such as a book, is hierarchically organized as a tree whose internal nodes are chapters, sections, and subsections, and whose external nodes are paragraphs, tables, figures, the bibliography, and so on. (See Figure 2.17.) We could in fact consider expanding the tree further to show paragraphs consisting of sentences, sentences consisting of words, and words consisting of characters. In any case, such a tree is an example of an ordered tree, because there is a well-defined ordering among the children of each node.*

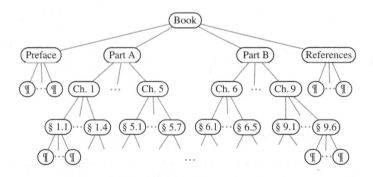

Figure 2.17: A tree associated with a book.

A **binary tree** is an ordered tree in which every node has at most two children. A binary tree is **proper** if each internal node has two children. For each internal node in a binary tree, we label each child as either being a **left child** or a **right child**. These children are ordered so that a left child comes before a right child. The subtree rooted at a left or right child of an internal node v is called a **left subtree** or **right subtree**, respectively, of v. Of course, even an improper binary tree is still a general tree, with the property that each internal node has at most two children. Binary trees have a number of useful applications, including the following.

Example 2.4: *An arithmetic expression can be represented by a tree whose external nodes are associated with variables or constants, and whose internal nodes are associated with one of the operators $+$, $-$, $\times$, and $/$. (See Figure 2.18.) Each node in such a tree has a value associated with it.*

- *If a node is external, then its value is that of its variable or constant.*
- *If a node is internal, then its value is defined by applying its operation to the values of its children.*

Such an arithmetic expression tree is a proper binary tree, since each of the operators $+$, $-$, $\times$, and $/$ take exactly two operands. Of course, if we were to allow for unary operators, like negation $(-)$, as in "$-x$," then we could have an improper binary tree.

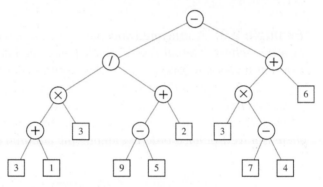

Figure 2.18: A binary tree representing an arithmetic expression. This tree represents the expression $((((3 + 1) \times 3)/((9 - 5) + 2)) - ((3 \times (7 - 4)) + 6))$. The value associated with the internal node labeled "$/$" is 2.

2.3.1 A Tree Definition

Viewed abstractly, a tree stores elements at positions, which, as with positions in a list, are defined relative to neighboring positions. The ***positions*** in a tree are its ***nodes***, and neighboring positions satisfy the parent-child relationships that define a valid tree. Therefore, we use the terms "position" and "node" interchangeably for trees. As with a list position, a position object for a tree supports the element() method, which returns the object at this position. The real power of node positions in a tree, however, comes from the following ***accessor methods*** for a tree:

root(): Return the root of the tree.

parent(v): Return the parent of node v; an error occurs if v is root.

children(v): Return a set containing the children of node v.

If a tree T is ordered, then the children(v) operation returns the children of v in order. If v is an external node, then children(v) is an empty set.

In addition, we also include the following *query methods*:

isInternal(v): Test whether node v is internal.

isExternal(v): Test whether node v is external.

isRoot(v): Test whether node v is the root.

There are also a number of methods a tree should support that are not necessarily related to its tree structure. Such *generic methods* include the following:

size$()$: Return the number of nodes in the tree.

elements$()$: Return a set containing all the elements stored at nodes of the tree.

positions$()$: Return a set containing all the nodes of the tree.

swapElements(v, w): Swap the elements stored at the nodes v and w.

replaceElement(v, e): Replace with e and return the element stored at node v.

We do not define any specialized update methods for a tree here. Instead, let us reserve the potential to define different tree update methods in conjunction with specific tree applications.

2.3.2 Tree Traversal

In this section, we present algorithms for performing some important *traversal* operations on a tree.

Assumptions

In order to analyze the running time of tree-based algorithms, we make the following assumptions on the running times of various methods for a tree:

- The accessor methods root$()$ and parent(v) take $O(1)$ time.
- The query methods isInternal(v), isExternal(v), and isRoot(v) take $O(1)$ time, as well.
- The accessor method children(v) takes $O(c_v)$ time, where c_v is the number of children of v.
- The generic methods swapElements(v, w) and replaceElement(v, e) take $O(1)$ time.
- The generic methods elements$()$ and positions$()$, which return sets, take $O(n)$ time, where n is the number of nodes in the tree.

In Section 2.3.4, we present data structures for trees that satisfy the above assumptions. Before we describe how to implement a tree using a concrete data structure, however, let us describe how we can use the methods for an abstract tree structure to solve some interesting problems for trees.

Depth and Height

Let v be a node of a tree T. The **depth** of v is the number of ancestors of v, excluding v itself. Note that this definition implies that the depth of the root of T is 0. The depth of a node v can also be recursively defined as follows:

- If v is the root, then the depth of v is 0.
- Otherwise, the depth of v is one plus the depth of the parent of v.

Based on the above definition, the recursive algorithm depth, shown in Algorithm 2.19, computes the depth of a node v of T by calling itself recursively on the parent of v, and adding 1 to the value returned.

Algorithm depth(T, v):
  if T.isRoot(v) **then**
      return 0
  else
      return $1 +$ depth$(T, T$.parent$(v))$

Algorithm 2.19: Algorithm depth for computing the depth of a node v in a tree T.

The running time of algorithm depth(T, v) is $O(1 + d_v)$, where d_v denotes the depth of the node v in the tree T, because the algorithm performs a constant-time recursive step for each ancestor of v. Thus, in the worst case, the depth algorithm runs in $O(n)$ time, where n is the total number of nodes in the tree T, since some nodes may have nearly this depth in T. Although such a running time is a function of the input size, it is more accurate to characterize the running time in terms of the parameter d_v, since this will often be much smaller than n.

The **height** of a tree T is equal to the maximum depth of an external node of T. While this definition is correct, it does not lead to an efficient algorithm. Indeed, if we were to apply the above depth-finding algorithm to each node in the tree T, we would derive an $O(n^2)$-time algorithm to compute the height of T. We can do much better, however, using the following recursive definition of the **height** of a node v in a tree T:

- If v is an external node, then the height of v is 0.
- Otherwise, the height of v is one plus the maximum height of a child of v.

The **height** of a tree T is the height of the root of T.

Algorithm height, shown in Algorithm 2.20 computes the height of tree T in an efficient manner by using the above recursive definition of height. The algorithm is expressed by a recursive method $\text{height}(T, v)$ that computes the height of the subtree of T rooted at a node v. The height of tree T is obtained by calling $\text{height}(T, T.\text{root}())$.

Algorithm $\text{height}(T, v)$:
  if $T.\text{isExternal}(v)$ **then**
    return 0
  else
    $h = 0$
    for each $w \in T.\text{children}(v)$ **do**
      $h = \max(h, \text{height}(T, w))$
    return $1 + h$

Algorithm 2.20: Algorithm height for computing the height of the subtree of tree T rooted at a node v.

The height algorithm is recursive, and if it is initially called on the root of T, it will eventually be called once on each node of T. Thus, we can determine the running time of this method by an amortization argument where we first determine the amount of time spent at each node (on the nonrecursive part), and then sum this time bound over all the nodes. The computation of a set returned by $\text{children}(v)$ takes $O(c_v)$ time, where c_v denotes the number of children of node v. Also, the **for** loop has c_v iterations, and each iteration of the loop takes $O(1)$ time plus the time for the recursive call on a child of v. Thus, the algorithm height spends $O(1 + c_v)$ time at each node v, and its running time is $O(\sum_{v \in T}(1 + c_v))$. In order to complete the analysis, we make use of the following property.

Theorem 2.5: *Let T be a tree with n nodes, and let c_v denote the number of children of a node v of T. Then*

$$\sum_{v \in T} c_v = n - 1.$$

Proof: Each node of T, with the exception of the root, is a child of another node, and thus contributes one unit to the summation $\sum_{v \in T} c_v$. ∎

By Theorem 2.5, the running time of Algorithm height when called on the root of T is $O(n)$, where n is the number of nodes of T.

A *traversal* of a tree T is a systematic way of accessing, or "visiting," all the nodes of T. We next present basic traversal schemes for trees, called preorder and postorder traversals.

Preorder Traversal

In a ***preorder*** traversal of a tree T, the root of T is visited first and then the subtrees rooted at its children are traversed recursively. If the tree is ordered, then the subtrees are traversed according to the order of the children. The specific action associated with the "visit" of a node v depends on the application of this traversal, and could involve anything from incrementing a counter to performing some complex computation for v. The pseudocode for the preorder traversal of the subtree rooted at a node v is shown in Algorithm 2.21. We initially call this routine as preorder(T, T.root()).

Algorithm preorder(T, v):
    perform the "visit" action for node v
    for each child w of v **do**
        recursively traverse the subtree rooted at w by calling preorder(T, w)

Algorithm 2.21: Algorithm preorder.

The preorder traversal algorithm is useful for producing a linear ordering of the nodes of a tree where parents must always come before their children in the ordering. Such orderings have several different applications; we explore a simple instance of such an application in the next example.

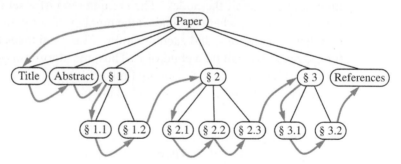

Figure 2.22: Preorder traversal of an ordered tree.

Example 2.6: *The preorder traversal of the tree associated with a document, as in Example 2.3, examines an entire document sequentially, from beginning to end. If the external nodes are removed before the traversal, then the traversal examines the table of contents of the document. (See Figure 2.22.)*

The analysis of preorder traversal is actually similar to that of algorithm height given above. At each node v, the nonrecursive part of the preorder traversal algorithm requires time $O(1 + c_v)$, where c_v is the number of children of v. Thus, by Theorem 2.5, the overall running time of the preorder traversal of T is $O(n)$.

Postorder Traversal

Another important tree traversal algorithm is the ***postorder*** traversal. This algorithm can be viewed as the opposite of the preorder traversal, because it recursively traverses the subtrees rooted at the children of the root first, and then visits the root. It is similar to the preorder traversal, however, in that we use it to solve a particular problem by specializing an action associated with the "visit" of a node v. Still, as with the preorder traversal, if the tree is ordered, we make recursive calls for the children of a node v according to their specified order. Pseudo-code for the postorder traversal is given in Algorithm 2.23.

Algorithm postorder(T, v):
    for each child w of v **do**
        recursively traverse the subtree rooted at w by calling postorder(T, w)
    perform the "visit" action for node v

Algorithm 2.23: Method postorder.

The name of the postorder traversal comes from the fact that this traversal method will visit a node v after it has visited all the other nodes in the subtree rooted at v. (See Figure 2.24.)

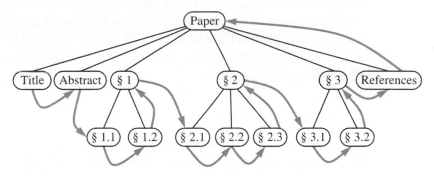

Figure 2.24: Postorder traversal of the ordered tree of Figure 2.22.

The analysis of the running time of a postorder traversal is analogous to that of a preorder traversal. The total time spent in the nonrecursive portions of the algorithm is proportional to the time spent visiting the children of each node in the tree. Thus, a postorder traversal of a tree T with n nodes takes $O(n)$ time, assuming that visiting each node takes $O(1)$ time. That is, the postorder traversal runs in linear time.

The postorder traversal method is useful for solving problems where we wish to compute some property for each node v in a tree, but computing that property for v requires that we have already computed that same property for v's children.

2.3.3   Binary Trees

One kind of tree that is of particular interest is the binary tree. As we mentioned in Section 2.3, a proper *binary tree* is an ordered tree in which each internal node has exactly two children. We make the convention that, unless otherwise stated, binary trees are assumed to be proper. Note that our convention for binary trees is made without loss of generality, for we can easily convert any improper binary tree into a proper one, as we explore in Exercise C-2.16. Even without such a conversion, we can consider an improper binary tree as proper, simply by viewing missing external nodes as "null nodes" or place holders that still count as nodes.

Viewed abstractly, a binary tree is a specialization of a tree that supports three additional accessor methods:

> leftChild(v): Return the left child of v; an error condition occurs if v is an external node.

> rightChild(v): Return the right child of v; an error condition occurs if v is an external node.

> sibling(v): Return the sibling of node v; an error condition occurs if v is the root.

Note that these methods must have additional error conditions if we are dealing with improper binary trees. For example, in an improper binary tree, an internal node may not have the left child or right child. We do not include here any methods for updating a binary tree, for such methods can be created as required in the context of specific needs.

Properties of Binary Trees

We denote the set of all nodes of a tree T at the same depth d as the *level* d of T. In a binary tree, level 0 has one node (the root), level 1 has at most two nodes (the children of the root), level 2 has at most four nodes, and so on. (See Figure 2.25.) In general, level d has at most 2^d nodes, which implies the following theorem (whose proof is left to Exercise R-2.6).

Theorem 2.7: *Let T be a proper binary tree with n nodes, and let h denote the height of T. Then T has the following properties:*

1. *The number of external nodes in T is at least $h + 1$ and at most 2^h.*
2. *The number of internal nodes in T is at least h and at most $2^h - 1$.*
3. *The total number of nodes in T is at least $2h + 1$ and at most $2^{h+1} - 1$.*
4. *The height of T is at least $\log(n + 1) - 1$ and at most $(n - 1)/2$, that is,*
   $$\log(n + 1) - 1 \leq h \leq (n - 1)/2.$$

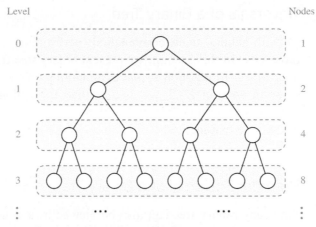

Figure 2.25: Maximum number of nodes in the levels of a binary tree.

In addition, we also have the following.

Theorem 2.8: *In a proper binary tree T, the number of external nodes is 1 more than the number of internal nodes.*

Proof: The proof is by induction. If T itself has only one node v, then v is external, and the proposition clearly holds. Otherwise, we remove from T an (arbitrary) external node w and its parent v, which is an internal node. If v has a parent u, then we reconnect u with the former sibling z of w, as shown in Figure 2.26. This operation, which we call removeAboveExternal(w), removes one internal node and one external node, and it leaves the tree being a proper binary tree. Thus, by the inductive hypothesis, the number of external nodes in this tree is one more than the number of internal nodes. Since we removed one internal and one external node to reduce T to this smaller tree, this same property must hold for T. ∎

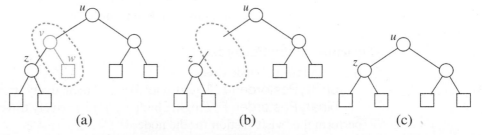

Figure 2.26: Operation removeAboveExternal(w), which removes an external node and its parent node, used in the justification of Theorem 2.8.

Note that the above relationship does not hold, in general, for nonbinary trees.

In subsequent chapters, we explore some important applications of the above facts. Before we can discuss such applications, however, we should first understand more about how binary trees are traversed and represented.

Traversals of a Binary Tree

As with general trees, computations performed on binary trees often involve tree traversals. In this section, we present binary tree traversal algorithms. As for running times, in addition to the assumptions on the running time for tree methods made in Section 2.3.2, we assume that, for a binary tree, the children(v) operation takes $O(1)$ time, because each node has either zero or two children. Likewise, we assume that methods leftChild(v), rightChild(v), and sibling(v) each take $O(1)$ time.

Preorder Traversal of a Binary Tree

Since any binary tree can also be viewed as a general tree, the preorder traversal for general trees (Code Fragment 2.21) can be applied to any binary tree. We can simplify the pseudocode in the case of a binary tree traversal, however, as we show in Algorithm 2.27.

Algorithm binaryPreorder(T, v):
    perform the "visit" action for node v
    if v is an internal node **then**
        binaryPreorder$(T, T.\text{leftChild}(v))$ // recursively traverse left subtree
        binaryPreorder$(T, T.\text{rightChild}(v))$ // recursively traverse right subtree

Algorithm 2.27: Algorithm binaryPreorder that performs the preorder traversal of the subtree of a binary tree T rooted at node v.

Postorder Traversal of a Binary Tree

Analogously, the postorder traversal for general trees (Algorithm 2.23) can be specialized for binary trees, as shown in Algorithm 2.28.

Algorithm binaryPostorder(T, v):
    if v is an internal node **then**
        binaryPostorder$(T, T.\text{leftChild}(v))$ // recursively traverse left subtree
        binaryPostorder$(T, T.\text{rightChild}(v))$ // recursively traverse right subtree
    perform the "visit" action for the node v

Algorithm 2.28: Algorithm binaryPostorder for performing the postorder traversal of the subtree of a binary tree T rooted at v.

Interestingly, the specialization of the general preorder and postorder traversal methods to binary trees suggests a third traversal in a binary tree that is different from both the preorder and postorder traversals.

Inorder Traversal of a Binary Tree

An additional traversal method for a binary tree is the ***inorder*** traversal. In this traversal, we visit a node between the recursive traversals of its left and right subtrees, as shown in Algorithm 2.29.

Algorithm inorder(T, v):
    if v is an internal node **then**
        inorder(T, T.leftChild(v))   // recursively traverse left subtree
    perform the "visit" action for node v
    if v is an internal node **then**
        inorder(T, T.rightChild(v))   // recursively traverse right subtree

Algorithm 2.29: Algorithm inorder for performing the inorder traversal of the subtree of a binary tree T rooted at a node v.

The inorder traversal of a binary tree T can be informally viewed as visiting the nodes of T "from left to right." Indeed, for every node v, the inorder traversal visits v after all the nodes in the left subtree of v and before all the nodes in the right subtree of v. (See Figure 2.30.)

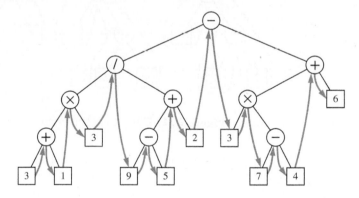

Figure 2.30: Inorder traversal of a binary tree.

A Unified Tree Traversal Framework

Each traversal visits the nodes of a tree in a certain order and is guaranteed to visit each node exactly once. We can unify the tree-traversal algorithms given above into a single framework, however, by relaxing the requirement that each node be visited exactly once. The resulting traversal method is called the ***Euler tour traversal***, which we study next. The advantage of this traversal is that it allows for more general kinds of algorithms to be expressed easily.

The Euler Tour Traversal of a Binary Tree

The Euler tour traversal of a binary tree T can be informally defined as a "walk" around T, where we start by going from the root toward its left child, viewing the edges of T as being "walls" that we always keep to our left. (See Figure 2.31.) Each node v of T is encountered three times by the Euler tour:

- "On the left" (before the Euler tour of v's left subtree)
- "From below" (between the Euler tours of v's two subtrees)
- "On the right" (after the Euler tour of v's right subtree).

If v is external, then these three "visits" actually all happen at the same time.

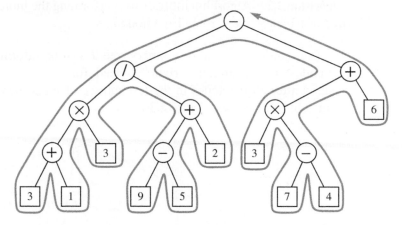

Figure 2.31: Euler tour traversal of a binary tree.

We give pseudocode for the Euler tour of the subtree rooted at a node v in Algorithm 2.32.

Algorithm eulerTour(T, v):

   perform the action for visiting node v on the left
   if v is an internal node **then**
       recursively tour the left subtree of v by calling eulerTour(T, T.leftChild(v))
   perform the action for visiting node v from below
   if v is an internal node **then**
       recursively   tour   the   right   subtree   of v by   calling
       eulerTour(T, T.rightChild(v))
   perform the action for visiting node v on the right

Algorithm 2.32: Algorithm eulerTour for computing the Euler tour traversal of the subtree of a binary tree T rooted at a node v.

The preorder traversal of a binary tree is equivalent to an Euler tour traversal such that each node has an associated "visit" action occur only when it is encountered on the left. Likewise, the inorder and postorder traversals of a binary tree are equivalent to an Euler tour such that each node has an associated "visit" action occur only when it is encountered from below or on the right, respectively.

The Euler tour traversal extends the preorder, inorder, and postorder traversals, but it can also perform other kinds of traversals. For example, suppose we wish to compute the number of descendants of each node v in an n node binary tree T. We start an Euler tour by initializing a counter to 0, and then increment the counter each time we visit a node on the left. To determine the number of descendants of a node v, we compute the difference between the values of the counter when v is visited on the left and when it is visited on the right, and add 1. This simple rule gives us the number of descendants of v, because each node in the subtree rooted at v is counted between v's visit on the left and v's visit on the right. Therefore, we have an $O(n)$-time method for computing the number of descendants of each node in T.

The running time of the Euler tour traversal is easy to analyze, assuming visiting a node takes $O(1)$ time. Namely, in each traversal, we spend a constant amount of time at each node of the tree during the traversal, so the overall running time is $O(n)$ for an n node tree.

Another application of the Euler tour traversal is to print a fully parenthesized arithmetic expression from its expression tree (Example 2.4). The method printExpression, shown in Algorithm 2.33, accomplishes this task by performing the following actions in an Euler tour:

- "On the left" action: if the node is internal, print "("
- "From below" action: print the value or operator stored at the node
- "On the right" action: if the node is internal, print ")."

Algorithm printExpression(T, v):

  if T.isExternal(v) **then**

      print the value stored at v

  else

      print "("

      printExpression(T, T.leftChild(v))

      print the operator stored at v

      printExpression(T, T.rightChild(v))

      print ")"

Algorithm 2.33: An algorithm for printing the arithmetic expression associated with the subtree of an arithmetic expression tree T rooted at v.

Having presented these pseudocode examples, we now describe a number of efficient ways of realizing the tree abstraction by concrete data structures, such as arrays and linked structures.

2.3.4   Data Structures for Representing Trees

In this section, we describe concrete data structures for representing trees.

A Linked Structure for Binary Trees

A natural way to implement a binary tree T is to use a ***linked structure***. In this approach we represent each node v of T by an object with references to the element stored at v and the positions associated with the children and parent of v. We show a linked structure representation of a binary tree in Figure 2.34.

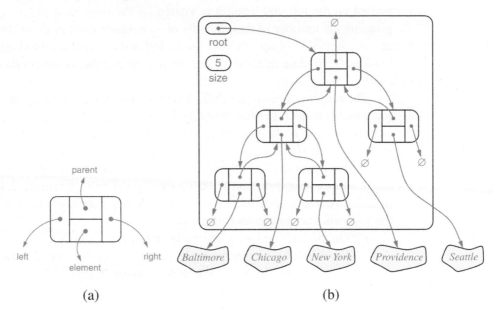

(a)   (b)

Figure 2.34: An example linked data structure for representing a binary tree: (a) object associated with a node; (b) a structure for a binary tree with five nodes.

If v is the root of T, then the reference to the parent node is null, and if v is an external node, then the references to the children of v are null. If we wish to save space for cases when external nodes are empty, then we can have references to empty external nodes be null. That is, we can allow a reference from an internal node to an external node child to be null. In addition, it is fairly straightforward to implement each of the methods size(), isEmpty(), swapElements(v, w), and replaceElement(v, e) in $O(1)$ time. Moreover, the method positions() can be implemented by performing an inorder traversal, and implementing the method elements() is similar. Thus, methods positions() and elements() take $O(n)$ time each. Considering the space used by this data structure, note that there is a constant-sized object for every node of tree T. Thus, the overall space used is $O(n)$.

A Linked Structure for General Trees

We can extend the linked structure for binary trees to represent general trees. Since there is no limit on the number of children that a node v in a general tree can have, we use a container (for example, a list or array) to store the children of v, instead of using instance variables. This structure is schematically illustrated in Figure 2.35, assuming we implement the container for a node as a list.

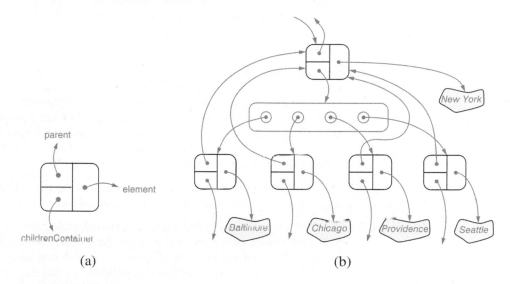

(a)   (b)

Figure 2.35: The linked structure for a tree: (a) the object associated with a node; (b) the portion of the data structure associated with a node and its children.

We note that the performance of a linked implementation of a tree, shown in Table 2.36, is similar to that of the linked implementation of a binary tree. The main difference is that in the implementation of a tree we use an efficient container, such as a list or array, to store the children of each node v, instead of direct links to exactly two children.

Operation	Time
size, isEmpty	$O(1)$
positions, elements	$O(n)$
swapElements, replaceElement	$O(1)$
root, parent	$O(1)$
children(v)	$O(c_v)$
isInternal, isExternal, isRoot	$O(1)$

Table 2.36: Running times of the methods of an n-node tree implemented with a linked structure. We let c_v denote the number of children of a node v.

2.4 Exercises

Reinforcement

R-2.1 Suppose you are given an array, A, containing n numbers in order. Describe in pseudocode an efficient algorithm for reversing the order of the numbers in A using a single for-loop that indexes through the cells of A, to insert each element into a stack, and then another for-loop that removes the elements from the stack and puts them back into A in reverse order. What is the running time of this algorithm?

R-2.2 Solve the previous exercise using a queue instead of stack. That is, suppose you are given an array, A, containing n numbers in order, as in the previous exercise. Describe in pseudocode an efficient algorithm for reversing the order of the numbers in A using a single for-loop that indexes through the cells of A, to insert each element into a queue, and then another for-loop that removes the elements from the queue and puts them back into A in reverse order. What is the running time of this algorithm?

R-2.3 Describe, using pseudocode, an implementation of the method insertBefore(p, e), for a linked list, assuming the list is implemented using a doubly linked list.

R-2.4 Draw an expression tree that has four external nodes, storing the numbers 1, 5, 6, and 7 (with each number stored one per external node but not necessarily in this order), and has three internal nodes, each storing an operation from the set $\{+, -, \times, /\}$ of binary arithmetic operators, so that the value of the root is 21. The operators are assumed to return rational numbers (not integers), and an operator may be used more than once (but we only store one operator per internal node).

R-2.5 Let T be an ordered tree with more than one node. Is it possible that the preorder traversal of T visits the nodes in the same order as the postorder traversal of T? If so, give an example; otherwise, argue why this cannot occur. Likewise, is it possible that the preorder traversal of T visits the nodes in the reverse order of the postorder traversal of T? If so, give an example; otherwise, argue why this cannot occur.

R-2.6 Answer the following questions so as to justify Theorem 2.7.

    a. Draw a binary tree with height 7 and maximum number of external nodes.

    b. What is the minimum number of external nodes for a binary tree with height h? Justify your answer.

    c. What is the maximum number of external nodes for a binary tree with height h? Justify your answer.

    d. Let T be a binary tree with height h and n nodes. Show that

$$\log(n + 1) - 1 \le h \le (n - 1)/2.$$

    e. For which values of n and h can the above lower and upper bounds on h be attained with equality?

R-2.7 Let T be a binary tree such that all the external nodes have the same depth. Let D_e be the sum of the depths of all the external nodes of T, and let D_i be the sum of the depths of all the internal nodes of T. Find constants a and b such that

$$D_e + 1 = aD_i + bn,$$

where n is the number of nodes of T.

R-2.8 Let T be a binary tree with n nodes, and let p be the level numbering of the nodes of T, so that the root, r, is numbered as $p(r) = 1$, and a node v has left child numbered $2p(v)$ and right child numbered $2p(v) + 1$, if they exist.

    a. Show that, for every node v of T, $p(v) \leq 2^{(n+1)/2} - 1$.

    b. Show an example of a binary tree with at least five nodes that attains the above upper bound on the maximum value of $p(v)$ for some node v.

Creativity

C-2.1 A *double-ended queue*, or *deque*, is a list that allows for insertions and removals at either its head or its tail. Describe a way to implement a deque using a doubly linked list, so that every operation runs in $O(1)$ time.

C-2.2 Suppose that a friend has implemented a deque, as defined in the previous exercise, using a singly linked list, but hasn't given you the details, for example, of whether the links go forward or backward in the list or whether sentinel nodes are used. Nevertheless, show that one of the insertion or removal methods must take $\Omega(n)$ time, where n is the number of elements in the deque.

C-2.3 Describe, in pseudocode, a link-hopping method for finding the middle node of a doubly linked list with header and trailer sentinels, and an odd number of real nodes between them. (Note: This method must only use link hopping; it cannot use a counter.) What is the running time of this method?

C-2.4 Describe how to implement a queue using two stacks, so that the amortized running time for dequeue and enqueue is $O(1)$, assuming that the stacks support constant-time push, pop, and size methods. What is the worst-case running time of the enqueue() and dequeue() methods in this case?

C-2.5 Describe how to implement a stack using two queues. What is the running time of the push() and pop() methods in this case?

C-2.6 Describe a recursive algorithm for enumerating all permutations of the numbers $\{1, 2, \ldots, n\}$. What is the running time of your method?

C-2.7 Show that a stack and a queue can be used to realize any permutation. That is, suppose you are given an empty stack, S, and the numbers, $1, 2, \ldots, n$, in this order, initially stored in a queue, Q. Show how to use only these two structures, and at most a constant number of additional registers, to result in any given permutation, π, of the numbers, $1, 2, \ldots, n$, stored in the Q in the order specified by π. What is the running time of your algorithm?

C-2.8 Describe the structure and pseudocode for an array-based implementation of an index-based list that achieves $O(1)$ time for insertions and removals at index 0, as well as insertions and removals at the end of the list. Your implementation should also provide for a constant-time get method.

C-2.9 Using an array-based list, describe an efficient way of putting a sequence representing a deck of n cards into random order. Use the function randomInt(n), which returns a random number between 0 and $n - 1$, inclusive. Your method should guarantee that every possible ordering is equally likely. What is the running time of your method?

C-2.10 Design an algorithm for drawing a binary tree, using quantities computed in a tree traversal.

C-2.11 Design algorithms for the following operations for a node v in a binary tree T:

- preorderNext(v): return the node visited after v in a preorder traversal of T
- inorderNext(v): return the node visited after v in an inorder traversal of T
- postorderNext(v): return the node visited after v in a postorder traversal of T.

What are the worst-case running times of your algorithms?

C-2.12 Give an $O(n)$-time algorithm for computing the depth of all the nodes of a tree T, where n is the number of nodes of T.

C-2.13 The *balance factor* of an internal node v of a binary tree is the difference between the heights of the right and left subtrees of v. Show how to specialize the Euler tour traversal to print the balance factors of all the nodes of a binary tree.

C-2.14 Two ordered trees T' and T'' are said to be *isomorphic* if one of the following holds:

- Both T' and T'' consist of a single node
- Both T' and T'' have the same number k of subtrees, and the ith subtree of T' is isomorphic to the ith subtree of T'', for $i = 1, \ldots, k$.

Design an algorithm that tests whether two given ordered trees are isomorphic. What is the running time of your algorithm?

C-2.15 Let a visit action in the Euler tour traversal be denoted by a pair (v, a), where v is the visited node and a is one of *left*, *below*, or *right*. Design an algorithm for performing operation tourNext(v, a), which returns the visit action (w, b) following (v, a). What is the worst-case running time of your algorithm?

C-2.16 Show how to represent an improper binary tree by means of a proper one.

C-2.17 Let T be a binary tree with n nodes. Define a *Roman node* to be a node v in T, such that the number of descendants in v's left subtree differ from the number of descendants in v's right subtree by at most 5. Describe a linear-time method for finding each node v of T, such that v is not a Roman node, but all of v's descendants are Roman nodes.

C-2.18 Describe in pseudocode a nonrecursive method for performing an Euler tour traversal of a binary tree that runs in linear time and does not use a stack.

Hint: You can tell which visit action to perform at a node by taking note of where you are coming from.

C-2.19 Describe in pseudocode a nonrecursive method for performing an inorder traversal of a binary tree in linear time.

C-2.20 Let T be a binary tree with n nodes. Give a linear-time method that uses the methods of the BinaryTree interface to traverse the nodes of T by increasing values of the level numbering function p given in Exercise R-2.8. This traversal is known as the *level order traversal*.

C-2.21 The *path length* of a tree T is the sum of the depths of all the nodes in T. Describe a linear-time method for computing the path length of a tree T (which is not necessarily binary).

C-2.22 Define the *internal path length*, $I(T)$, of a tree T to be the sum of the depths of all the internal nodes in T. Likewise, define the *external path length*, $E(T)$, of a tree T to be the sum of the depths of all the external nodes in T. Show that if T is a binary tree with n internal nodes, then $E(T) = I(T) + 2n$.

Applications

A-2.1 In the children's game "hot potato," a group of n children sit in a circle passing an object, called the "potato," around the circle (say in a clockwise direction). The children continue passing the potato until a leader rings a bell, at which point the child holding the potato must leave the game, and the other children close up the circle. This process is then continued until there is only one child remaining, who is declared the winner. Using a list, describe an efficient method for implementing this game. Suppose the leader always rings the bell immediately after the potato has been passed k times. (Determining the last child remaining in this variation of hot potato is known as the *Josephus problem*.) What is the running time of your method in terms of n and k, assuming the list is implemented with a doubly linked list? What if the list is implemented with an array?

A-2.2 Suppose you work for a company, iPuritan.com, that has strict rules for when two employees, x and y, may date one another, requiring approval from their lowest-level common supervisor. The employees at iPuritan.com are organized in a tree, T, such that each node in T corresponds to an employee and each employee, z, is considered a supervisor for all of the employees in the subtree of T rooted at z (including z itself). The lowest-level common supervisor for x and y is the employee lowest in the organizational chart, T, that is a supervisor for both x and y. Thus, to find a lowest-level common supervisor for the two employees, x and y, you need to find the *lowest common ancestor* (LCA) between the two nodes for x and y, which is the lowest node in T that has both x and y as descendants (where we allow a node to be a descendant of itself). Given the nodes corresponding to the two employees x and y, describe an efficient algorithm for finding the supervisor who may approve whether x and y may date each other, that is, the LCA of x and y in T. What is the running time of your method?

A-2.3 Suppose you work for a company, iPilgrim.com, whose n employees are organized in a tree T, so that each node is associated with an employee and each employee is considered a supervisor for all the employees (including themselves) in his or her subtree in T, as in the previous exercise. Furthermore, suppose that communication in iPilgrim is done the "old fashioned" way, where, for an employee, x, to send a message to an employee, y, x must route this message up to a lowest-level common supervisor of x and y, who then routes this message down to y. The problem is to design an algorithm for finding the length of a longest route that any message must travel in iPilgrim.com. That is, for any node v in T, let d_v denote the depth of v in T. The **distance** between two nodes v and w in T is $d_v + d_w - 2d_u$, where u is the LCA u of v and w (as defined in the previous exercise). The **diameter** of T is the maximum distance between two nodes in T. Thus, the length of a longest route that any message must travel in iPilgrim.com is equal to the diameter of T. Describe an efficient algorithm for finding the diameter of T. What is the running time of your method?

Chapter Notes

The basic data structures of stacks, queues, and linked lists discussed in this chapter belong to the folklore of computer science. They were first chronicled by Knuth in his seminal book on *Fundamental Algorithms* [129]. In this chapter, we have taken the approach of defining basic data structures first abstractly in terms of their methods and then in terms of concrete implementations. This approach to data structure specification and implementation is an outgrowth of software engineering advances brought on by the object-oriented design approach, and is now considered a standard approach for teaching data structures. We were introduced to this approach to data structure design by the classic books by Aho, Hopcroft, and Ullman on data structures and algorithms [8, 9].

Sequences and lists are pervasive concepts in the C++ Standard Template Library (STL) [163], and they play fundamental roles in Java as well. Lists are also discussed in the book by Arnold and Gosling [14]) and others, including Aho, Hopcroft, and Ullman [9], who introduce the "position" abstraction, and Wood [217], who defines a list abstraction similar to ours. Implementations of sequences via arrays and linked lists are discussed in Knuth's seminal book, *Fundamental Algorithms* [129].

The concept of viewing data structures as containers (and other principles of object-oriented design) can be found in object-oriented design books by Booch [33] and Budd [40]. The concept also exists under the name "collection class" in books by Golberg and Robson [83] and Liskov and Guttag [144]. Our use of the "position" abstraction for tree nodes derives from the "position" and "node" abstractions introduced by Aho, Hopcroft, and Ullman [9]. Discussions of the classic preorder, inorder, and postorder tree traversal methods can be found in Knuth's *Fundamental Algorithms* book [129]. The Euler tour traversal technique comes from the parallel algorithms community, as it is introduced by Tarjan and Vishkin [204] and is discussed by JáJá [110] and by Karp and Ramachandran [124]. The algorithm for drawing a tree is part of the "folklore" of graph drawing algorithms. The reader interested in graph drawing is referred to the handbook edited by Tamassia [203] and the book by Di Battista, Eades, Tamassia and Tollis [55]. The puzzler in Exercise R-2.4 was communicated by Micha Sharir.

Chapter

3

Binary Search Trees

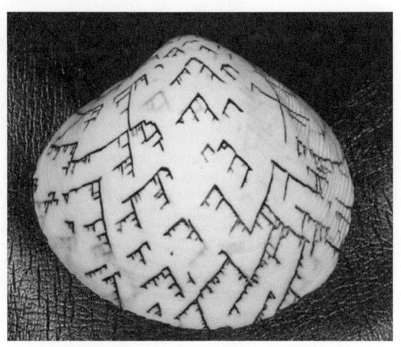

Lioconcha castrensis shell, 2005. Michael T. Goodrich. Used with permission.

Contents

3.1	Searches and Updates	91
3.2	Range Queries	101
3.3	Index-Based Searching	104
3.4	Randomly Constructed Search Trees	107
3.5	Exercises	110

Figure 3.1: A three-dimensional virtual environment. U.S. Army photo.

In three-dimensional video games and virtual environments, it is important to be able to locate objects relative to the other objects in their environment. For example, if the system is modeling a player driving a simulated vehicle through a virtual war zone, it is useful to know where that vehicle is relative to various obstacles and other players. Such nearby objects are useful for the sake of rendering a scene or identifying targets, for example. (See Figure 3.1.)

Of course, one way to do such a reference check for some object, x, relative to a virtual environment is to compare x to every other object in the environment. For an environment made up of n objects, such a search would require $O(n)$ object-object comparisons for x; hence, doing such a search for every object, x, would take $O(n^2)$ time, which is expensive. Such a computation for a given object x is not taking advantage of the fact that it is likely that there are potentially large groups of objects far from x. It would be nice to quickly dismiss such groups as being of low interest, rather than comparing each one to x individually.

For such reasons, many three-dimensional video games and virtual environments, including the earliest versions of the game ***Doom***, create a partitioning of space using a binary tree, by applying a technique known as ***binary space partitioning***. To create such a partitioning, we identify a plane, P, that divides the set of objects into two groups of roughly equal size—those objects to the left of P and those objects to the right of P. Then, for each group, we recursively subdivide them with other separating planes until the number of objects in each subgroup is small enough to handle as individuals. Given such a binary space partition (or BSP) tree, we can then locate any object in the environment simply by locating it relative to P, and then recursively locating it with respect to the objects that fall on the same side of P as it does. Such BSP tree partitions represent a three-dimensional environment using the data structure we discuss in this chapter, the ***binary search tree***, in that a BSP tree is a binary tree that stores objects at its nodes in a way that allows us to perform searches by making left-or-right decisions at each of its nodes.

3.1 Searches and Updates

Suppose we are given an ordered set, S, of objects, represented as key-value pairs, for which we would like to locate query objects, x, relative to the objects in this set. That is, we would like to identify the nearest neighbors of x in S, namely, the smallest object greater than x in S and the largest object smaller than x in S, if these objects exist. One of the simplest ways of storing S in this way is to store the elements of S in order in an array A. Such a representation would allow us, for example, to identify the ith smallest key, simply by looking up the key of the item stored in cell $A[i]$. In other words, if we needed a method, $\mathsf{key}(i)$, for accessing the key of the ith smallest key-value pair, or $\mathsf{elem}(i)$, the element that is associated with this key, then we could implement these methods in constant time given the representation of S in sorted order in the array A. In addition, if we store the elements of S in such a sorted array, A, then we know that the item at index i has a key no smaller than keys of the items at indices less than i and no larger than keys of the items at indices larger than i.

The Binary Search Algorithm

This observation allows us to quickly "home in" on a search key k using a variant of the children's game "high-low." We call an item I of S a **candidate** if, at the current stage of the search, we cannot rule out that I has key equal to k. The algorithm that results from this strategy is known as **binary search**.

There are several ways to implement this strategy. The method we describe here maintains two parameters, low and high, such that all the candidate items have index at least low and at most high in S. Initially, $\mathsf{low} = 1$ and $\mathsf{high} = n$, and we let $\mathsf{key}(i)$ denote the key at index i, which has $\mathsf{elem}(i)$ as its element. We then compare k to the key of the median candidate, that is, the item with index

$$\mathsf{mid} = \lfloor (\mathsf{low} + \mathsf{high})/2 \rfloor.$$

We consider three cases:

- If $k = \mathsf{key}(\mathsf{mid})$, then we have found the item we were looking for, and the search terminates successfully returning $\mathsf{elem}(\mathsf{mid})$.
- If $k < \mathsf{key}(\mathsf{mid})$, then we recur on the first half of the vector, that is, on the range of indices from low to $\mathsf{mid} - 1$.
- If $k > \mathsf{key}(\mathsf{mid})$, we recursively search the range of indices from $\mathsf{mid} + 1$ to high.

This **binary search** method is given in detail in Algorithm 3.2. To initiate a search for key k on an n-item sorted array, A, indexed from 1 to n, we call $\mathsf{BinarySearch}(A, k, 1, n)$.

Algorithm BinarySearch($A, k,$ low, high):

> *Input:* An ordered array, A, storing n items, whose keys are accessed with
> method key(i) and whose elements are accessed with method elem(i); a
> search key k; and integers low and high
> *Output:* An element of A with key k and index between low and high, if such
> an element exists, and otherwise the special element *null*

if low > high **then**
> **return** *null*

else
> mid ← $\lfloor$(low + high)/2$\rfloor$
> **if** $k = $ key(mid) **then**
> > **return** elem(mid)
>
> **else if** $k < $ key(mid) **then**
> > **return** BinarySearch($A, k,$ low, mid − 1)
>
> **else**
> > **return** BinarySearch($A, k,$ mid + 1, high)

Algorithm 3.2: Binary search in an ordered array.

We illustrate the binary search algorithm in Figure 3.3.

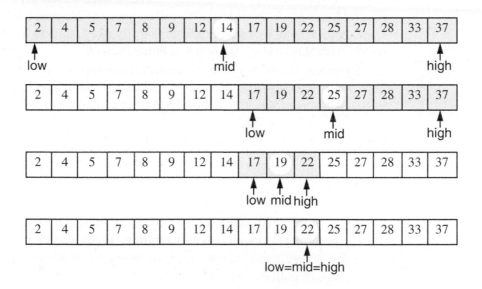

Figure 3.3: Example of a binary search to search for an element with key 22 in a
sorted array. For simplicity, we show the keys but not the elements.

Analyzing the Binary Search Algorithm

Considering the running time of binary search, we observe that a constant number of operations are executed at each recursive call. Hence, the running time is proportional to the number of recursive calls performed. A crucial fact is that, with each recursive call, the number of candidate items still to be searched in the array A is given by the value $\text{high} - \text{low} + 1$. Moreover, the number of remaining candidates is reduced by at least one half with each recursive call. Specifically, from the definition of mid, the number of remaining candidates is either

$$(\text{mid} - 1) - \text{low} + 1 = \left\lfloor \frac{\text{low} + \text{high}}{2} \right\rfloor - \text{low} \leq \frac{\text{high} - \text{low} + 1}{2}$$

or

$$\text{high} - (\text{mid} + 1) + 1 = \text{high} - \left\lfloor \frac{\text{low} + \text{high}}{2} \right\rfloor \leq \frac{\text{high} - \text{low} + 1}{2}.$$

Initially, the number of candidate is n; after the first call to BinarySearch, it is at most $n/2$; after the second call, it is at most $n/4$; and so on. That is, if we let a function, $T(n)$, represent the running time of this method, then we can characterize the running time of the recursive binary search algorithm as follows:

$$T(n) \leq \begin{cases} b & \text{if } n < 2 \\ T(n/2) + b & \text{else,} \end{cases}$$

where b is a constant. In general, this recurrence equation shows that the number of candidate items remaining after each recursive call is at most $n/2^i$. (We discuss recurrence equations like this one in more detail in Section 11.1.) In the worst case (unsuccessful search), the recursive calls stop when there are no more candidate items. Hence, the maximum number of recursive calls performed is the smallest integer m such that $n/2^m < 1$. In other words (recalling that we omit a logarithm's base when it is 2), $m > \log n$. Thus, we have $m = \lfloor \log n \rfloor + 1$, which implies that BinarySearch$(A, k, 1, n)$ runs in $O(\log n)$ time.

The space requirement of this solution is $\Theta(n)$, which is optimal, since we have to store the n objects somewhere. This solution is only efficient if the set S is static, however, that is, we don't want to insert or delete any key-value pairs in S. In the dynamic case, where we want to perform insertions and deletions, then such updates take $O(n)$ time. The reason for this poor performance in an insertion, for instance, is due to our need to move elements in A greater than the insertion key in order to keep all the elements in A in sorted order, similar to the methods described in Section 2.2.1. Thus, using an ordered array to store elements to support fast searching only makes sense for the sake of efficiency if we don't need to perform insertions or deletions.

3.1.1   Binary Search Tree Definition

The data structure we discuss in this section, the binary search tree, applies the motivation of the binary search procedure to a tree-based data structure, to support update operations more efficiently. We define a binary search tree to be a binary tree in which each internal node v stores an element e such that the elements stored in the left subtree of v are less than or equal to e, and the elements stored in the right subtree of v are greater than or equal to e. Furthermore, let us assume that external nodes store no elements; hence, they could in fact be **null** or references to a special NULL_NODE object.

An inorder traversal of a binary search tree visits the elements stored in such a tree in nondecreasing order. A binary search tree supports searching, where the question asked at each internal node is whether the element at that node is less than, equal to, or larger than the element being searched for.

We can use a binary search tree T to locate an element with a certain value x by traversing down the tree T. At each internal node we compare the value of the current node to our search element x. If the answer to the question is "smaller," then the search continues in the left subtree. If the answer is "equal," then the search terminates successfully. If the answer is "greater," then the search continues in the right subtree. Finally, if we reach an external node (which is empty), then the search terminates unsuccessfully. (See Figure 3.4.)

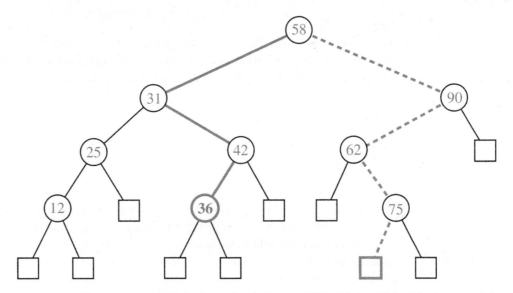

Figure 3.4: A binary search tree storing integers. The thick solid path drawn with thick lines is traversed when searching (successfully) for 36. The thick dashed path is traversed when searching (unsuccessfully) for 70.

3.1.2 Searching in a Binary Search Tree

Formally, a **binary search tree** is a binary tree, T, in which each internal node v of T stores a key-value pair, (k, e), such that keys stored at nodes in the left subtree of v are less than or equal to k, while keys stored at nodes in the right subtree of v are greater than or equal to k.

In Algorithm 3.5, we give a recursive method TreeSearch, based on the above strategy for searching in a binary search tree T. Given a search key k and a node v of T, method TreeSearch returns a node (position) w of the subtree $T(v)$ of T rooted at v, such that one of the following two cases occurs:

- w is an internal node of $T(v)$ that stores key k.
- w is an external node of $T(v)$. All the internal nodes of $T(v)$ that precede w in the inorder traversal have keys smaller than k, and all the internal nodes of $T(v)$ that follow w in the inorder traversal have keys greater than k.

Thus, a method find(k), which returns the element associated with the key k, can be performed on a set of key-value pairs stored in a binary search tree, T, by calling the method TreeSearch$(k, T.\text{root}())$ on T. Let w be the node of T returned by this call of the TreeSearch method. If node w is internal, we return the element stored at w; otherwise, if w is external, then we return ***null***.

Algorithm TreeSearch(k, v):
  Input: A search key k, and a node v of a binary search tree T
  Output: A node w of the subtree $T(v)$ of T rooted at v, such that either w is an internal node storing key k or w is the external node where an item with key k would belong if it existed

  if v is an external node **then**
      return v
  if $k = \text{key}(v)$ **then**
      return v
  else if $k < \text{key}(v)$ **then**
      return TreeSearch$(k, T.\text{leftChild}(v))$
  else
      return TreeSearch$(k, T.\text{rightChild}(v))$

Algorithm 3.5: Recursive search in a binary search tree.

The analysis of the running time of this algorithm is simple. The binary tree search algorithm executes a constant number of primitive operations for each node it traverses in the tree. Each new step in the traversal is made on a child of the previous node. That is, the binary tree search algorithm is performed on the nodes of a path of T that starts from the root and goes down one level at a time. Thus, the number of such nodes is bounded by $h + 1$, where h is the height of T. In other words, since we spend $O(1)$ time per node encountered, the search method runs in $O(h)$ time, where h is the height of the binary search tree T. (See Figure 3.6.)

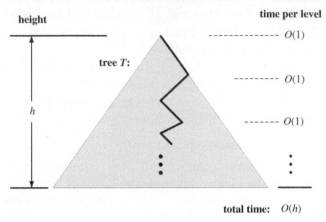

Figure 3.6: Illustrating the running time of searching in a binary search tree. The figure uses standard visualization shortcuts of viewing a binary search tree as a big triangle and a path from the root as a zig-zag line.

Admittedly, the height h of T can be as large as n, but we expect that it is usually much smaller. The best we can do for the height, h, is $\lceil \log(n + 1) \rceil$ (see Exercise C-3.5), and we would hope that in most cases h would in fact be $O(\log n)$. For instance, we show below, in Section 3.4, that a randomly constructed binary search tree will have height $O(\log n)$ with high probability. For now, though, consider a binary search tree, T, storing n items, such that, for each node v in T, each of v's children store at most three-quarters as many items in their subtrees as v does. Lots of binary search trees could have this property, and, for any such tree, its height, $H(n)$, would satisfy the following recurrence equation:

$$H(n) \leq \begin{cases} 1 & \text{if } n < 2 \\ H(3n/4) + 1 & \text{else.} \end{cases}$$

In other words, a child of the root stores at most $(3/4)n$ items in its subtree, any of its children store at most $(3/4)^2 n$ items in their subtrees, any of their children store at most $(3/4)^3 n$ items in their subtrees, and so on. Thus, since multiplying by $3/4$ is the same as dividing by $4/3$, this implies that $H(n)$ is at most $\lceil \log_{4/3} n \rceil$, which is $O(\log n)$. Intuitively, the reason we achieve a logarithmic height for T in this case is that the subtrees rooted at each child of a node in T have roughly "balanced" sizes.

We show in the next chapter how to maintain an upper bound of $O(\log n)$ on the height of a search tree T, by maintaining similar notions of balance, even while performing insertions and deletions. Before we describe such schemes, however, let us describe how to do insertions and deletions in a standard binary search tree.

3.1.3 Insertion in a Binary Search Tree

Binary search trees allow implementations of the insert and remove operations using algorithms that are fairly straightforward, but not trivial. To perform the operation insert(k, e) in a binary search tree T, to insert a key-value pair, (k, e), we perform the following algorithm (which works even if the tree holds multiple key-value pairs with the same key):

Let $w \leftarrow$ TreeSearch$(k, T.\text{root}())$
while w is an internal node **do**
    // There is item with key equal to k in T in this case
    Let $w \leftarrow$ TreeSearch$(k, T.\text{leftChild}(w))$
Expand w into an internal node with two external-node children
Store (k, e) at w

The above insertion algorithm eventually traces a path from the root of T down to an external node, w, which is the appropriate place to insert an item with key k based on the ordering of the items stored in T. This node then gets replaced with a new internal node accommodating the new item. Hence, an insertion adds the new item at the "bottom" of the search tree T. An example of insertion into a binary search tree is shown in Figure 3.7.

The analysis of the insertion algorithm is analogous to that for searching. The number of nodes visited is proportional to the height h of T in the worst case, since we spend $O(1)$ time at each node visited. Thus, the above implementation of the method insert runs in $O(h)$ time.

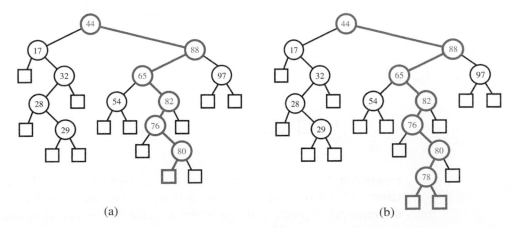

(a)   (b)

Figure 3.7: Insertion of an item with key 78 into a binary search tree. Finding the position to insert is shown in (a), and the resulting tree is shown in (b).

3.1.4   Deletion in a Binary Search Tree

Performing a remove(k) operation, to remove an item with key k from a binary search tree T is a bit more complex than the insertion algorithm, since we do not wish to create any "holes" in the tree T. Such a hole, where an internal node would not store an element, would make it difficult if not impossible for us to correctly perform searches in the binary search tree. Indeed, if we have many removals that do not restructure the tree T, then there could be a large section of internal nodes that store no elements, which would confuse any future searches. Thus, we must implement item deletion to avoid this situation.

The removal operation starts out simple enough, since we begin by executing algorithm TreeSearch(k, T.root()) on T to find a node storing key k. If TreeSearch returns an external node, then there is no element with key k in T, and we return the special element ***null*** and are done. If TreeSearch returns an internal node w instead, then w stores an item we wish to remove.

We distinguish two cases (of increasing difficulty) of how to proceed based on whether w is a node that is easily removed:

- If one of the children of node w is an external node, say node z, we simply remove w and z from T, and replace w with the sibling of z (which is an operation called removeAboveExternal(z) in Section 2.3.4).

This case is illustrated in Figure 3.8.

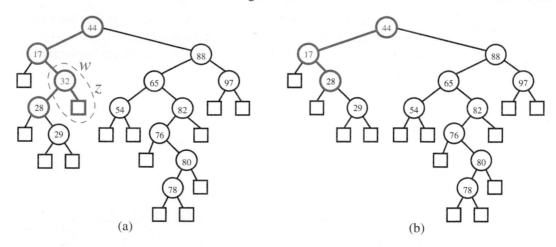

(a)   (b)

Figure 3.8: Deletion from the binary search tree of Figure 3.7b, where the key to remove (32) is stored at a node (w) with an external child: (a) shows the tree before the removal, together with the nodes affected by the operation that removes the external node, z, and its parent, w, replacing w with the sibling of z; (b) shows the tree T after the removal.

- If both children of node w are internal nodes, we cannot simply remove the node w from T, since this would create a "hole" in T. Instead, we proceed as follows (see Figure 3.9):

  1. We find the first internal node y that follows w in an inorder traversal of T. Node y is the left-most internal node in the right subtree of w, and is found by going first to the right child of w and then down T from there, following left children. Also, the left child x of y is the external node that immediately follows node w in the inorder traversal of T.

  2. We save the element stored at w in a temporary variable t, and move the item of y into w. This action has the effect of removing the former item stored at w.

  3. We remove x and y from T by replacing y with x's sibling, and removing both x and y from T (which is equivalent to operation removeAboveExternal(x) on T, using the terminology of Section 2.3.4).

  4. We return the element previously stored at w, which we had saved in the temporary variable t.

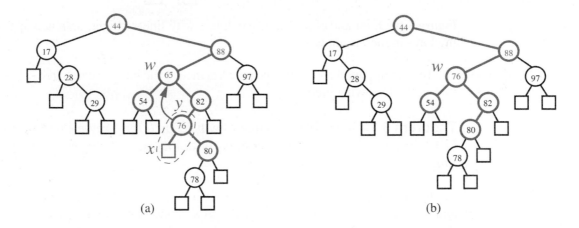

Figure 3.9: Deletion from the binary search tree of Figure 3.7b, where the key to remove (65) is stored at a node whose children are both internal: (a) before the removal; (b) after the removal.

Note that in Step 1 above, we could have selected y as the right-most internal node in the left subtree of w.

The analysis of the removal algorithm is analogous to that of the insertion and search algorithms. We spend $O(1)$ time at each node visited, and, in the worst case, the number of nodes visited is proportional to the height h of T. Thus, in a binary search tree, T, the remove method runs in $O(h)$ time, where h is the height of T.

3.1.5   The Performance of Binary Search Trees

A binary search tree T is an efficient implementation of an ordered set of n key-value pairs but only if the height of T is small. For instance, if T is balanced so that it has height $O(\log n)$, then we get logarithmic-time performance for the search and update operations described above. In the worst case, however, T could have height as large as n; hence, it would perform like an ordered linked list in this case. Such a worst-case configuration arises, for example, if we insert a set of keys in increasing order. (See Figure 3.10.)

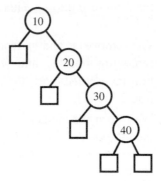

Figure 3.10: Example of a binary search tree with linear height, obtained by inserting keys in increasing order.

To sum up, we characterize the performance of the binary search tree data structure in the following theorem.

Theorem 3.1: *A binary search tree T with height h for n key-element items uses $O(n)$ space and executes the operations* find, insert, *and* remove *each in $O(h)$ time.*

Ideally, of course, we would like our binary search tree to have height $O(\log n)$, and there are several ways to achieve this goal, including several that we explore in the next chapter. For instance, as we explore in this chapter (in Section 3.4), if we construct a binary search tree, T, by inserting a set of n items in random order, then the height of T will be $O(\log n)$ with high probability. Alternatively, if we have our entire set, S, of n items available, then we can sort S and build a binary search tree, T, with height $O(\log n)$ from the sorted listing of S (see Exercise A-3.2). In addition, if we already have a binary search tree, T, of $O(\log n)$ height, and thereafter only perform deletions from T, then each of those deletion operations will run in $O(\log n)$ time (although interspersing insertions and deletions can lead to poor performance if we don't have some way to maintain balance). There are a number of other interesting operations that can be done using binary search trees, however, besides simple searches and insertions and deletions.

3.2 Range Queries

Besides the operations mentioned above, there are other interesting operations that can be performed using a binary search tree. One such operation is the ***range query*** operation, where, we are given an ordered set, S, of key-value pairs, stored in a binary search tree, T, and are asked to perform the following query:

findAllInRange(k_1, k_2): Return all the elements stored in T with key k such that $k_1 \leq k \leq k_2$.

Such an operation would be useful, for example, to find all cars within a given price range in a set of cars for sale. Suppose, then, that we have a binary search tree T representing S. To perform the findAllInRange(k_1, k_2) operation, we use a recursive method, RangeQuery, that takes as arguments, k_1 and k_2, and a node v in T. If node v is external, we are done. If node v is internal, we have three cases, depending on the value of key(v), the key of the item stored at node v:

- key(v) $< k_1$: We recursively search the right child of v.
- $k_1 \leq$ key(v) $\leq k_2$: We report element(v) and recursively search both children of v.
- key(v) $> k_2$: We recursively search the left child of v.

We describe the details of this search procedure in Algorithm 3.11 and we illustrate it in Figure 3.12. We perform operation findAllInRange(k_1, k_2) by calling RangeQuery(k_1, k_2, T.root()).

Algorithm RangeQuery(k_1, k_2, v):
    Input: Search keys k_1 and k_2, and a node v of a binary search tree T
    Output: The elements stored in the subtree of T rooted at v whose keys are in the range $[k_1, k_2]$

    if T.isExternal(v) **then**
        return $\emptyset$
    if $k_1 \leq$ key(v) $\leq k_2$ **then**
        $L \leftarrow$ RangeQuery(k_1, k_2, T.leftChild(v))
        $R \leftarrow$ RangeQuery(k_1, k_2, T.rightChild(v))
        return $L \cup \{$element(v)$\} \cup R$
    else if key(v) $< k_1$ **then**
        return RangeQuery(k_1, k_2, T.rightChild(v))
    else if $k_2 <$ key(v) **then**
        return RangeQuery(k_1, k_2, T.leftChild(v))

Algorithm 3.11: The method for performing a range query in a binary search tree.

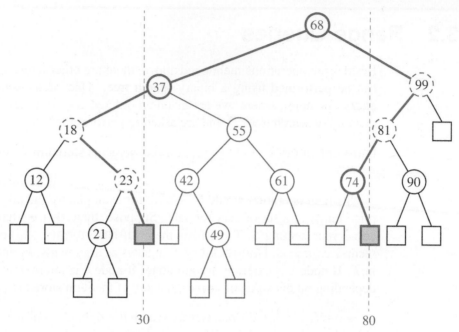

Figure 3.12: A range query using a binary search tree for the keys $k_1 = 30$ and $k_2 = 80$. Paths P_1 and P_2 of boundary nodes are drawn with thick lines. The boundary nodes storing items with key outside the interval $[k_1, k_2]$ are drawn with dashed lines. There are four internal inside nodes.

Intuitively, the method RangeQuery is a modification of the standard binary-tree search method (Algorithm 3.5) to search for the keys between k_1 and k_2, inclusive. For the sake of simplifying our analysis, however, let us assume that T does not contain items with key k_1 or k_2.

Let P_1 be the search path traversed when performing a search in tree T for key k_1. Path P_1 starts at the root of T and ends at an external node of T. Define a path P_2 similarly with respect to k_2. We identify each node v of T as belonging to one of following three groups (see Figure 3.12):

- Node v is a ***boundary node*** if v belongs to P_1 or P_2; a boundary node stores an item whose key may be inside or outside the interval $[k_1, k_2]$.

- Node v is an ***inside node*** if v is not a boundary node and v belongs to a subtree rooted at a right child of a node of P_1 or at a left child of a node of P_2; an internal inside node stores an item whose key is inside the interval $[k_1, k_2]$.

- Node v is an ***outside node*** if v is not a boundary node and v belongs to a subtree rooted at a left child of a node of P_1 or at a right child of a node of P_2; an internal outside node stores an item whose key is outside the interval $[k_1, k_2]$.

Analysis of the Range Query Operation

Consider an execution of the algorithm RangeQuery(k_1, k_2, r), where r is the root of T. We traverse a path of boundary nodes, calling the algorithm recursively either on the left or on the right child, until we reach either an external node or an internal node w (which may be the root) with key in the range $[k_1, k_2]$. In the first case (we reach an external node), the algorithm terminates returning the empty set. In the second case, the execution continues by calling the algorithm recursively at both of w's children. We know that node w is the bottommost node common to paths P_1 and P_2. For each boundary node v visited from this point on, we either make a single call at a child of v, which is also a boundary node, or we make a call at one child of v that is a boundary node and the other child that is an inside node. Once we visit an inside node, we will visit all of its (inside node) descendants.

Since we spend a constant amount of work per node visited by the algorithm, the running time of the algorithm is proportional to the number of nodes visited. We count the nodes visited as follows:

- We visit no outside nodes.
- We visit at most $2h + 1$ boundary nodes, where h is the height of T, since boundary nodes are on the search paths P_1 and P_2 and they share at least one node (the root of T).
- Each time we visit an inside node v, we also visit the entire subtree T_v of T rooted at v and we add all the elements stored at internal nodes of T_v to the reported set. If T_v holds s_v items, then it has $2s_v + 1$ nodes. The inside nodes can be partitioned into j disjoint subtrees $T_1, \ldots, T_j$ rooted at children of boundary nodes, where $j \leq 2h$. Denoting with s_i the number of items stored in tree T_i, we have that the total number of inside nodes visited is equal to

$$\sum_{i=1}^{j} (2s_i + 1) = 2s + j \leq 2s + 2h.$$

Therefore, at most $2s + 4h + 1$ nodes of T are visited and the operation findAllInRange runs in $O(h + s)$ time. We summarize:

Theorem 3.2: *A binary search tree of height h storing n items supports range query operations with the following performance:*

- *The space used is $O(n)$.*
- *Operation* findAllInRange *takes $O(h + s)$ time, where s is the number of elements reported.*
- *Operations* insert *and* remove *each take $O(h)$ time.*

3.3   Index-Based Searching

We began this chapter by discussing how to search in a sorted array, A, which allows us to quickly identify the ith smallest item in the array simply by indexing the cell $A[i]$. As we mentioned, a weakness of this array representation is that it doesn't support efficient updates, whereas a binary search tree allows for efficient insertions and deletions. But when we switched to a binary search tree, we lost the ability to quickly find the ith smallest item in our set. In this section, we show how to regain that ability with a binary search tree.

Suppose, then, that we wish to support the following operation on a binary search tree, T, storing n key-value pairs:

> select(i): Return the item with ith smallest key, for $1 \le i \le n$.

For example, if $i = 1$, then we would return the minimum item, if $i = n$, then we would return the maximum, and if $i = \lceil n/2 \rceil$, then we would return the median (assuming n is odd).

The main idea for a simple way to support this method is to ***augment*** each node, v, in T so as to add a new field, n_v, to that node, where

- n_v is the number of items stored in the subtree of T rooted at v.

For instance, see Figure 3.13.

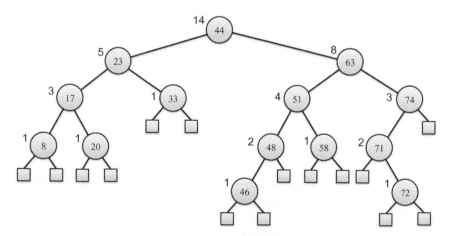

Figure 3.13: A binary search tree augmented so that each node, v, stores a count, n_v, of the number of items stored in the subtree rooted at v. We show the key for each node inside that node and the n_v value of each node next to the node, except for external nodes, which each have an n_v count of 0.

Searching and Updating Augmented Binary Search Trees

Having defined the n_v count for each node in a binary search tree, T, we need to maintain it during updates to T. Fortunately, such updates are easy.

First, note that the n_v count for any external node is 0, so we don't even need to store an actual n_v field for external nodes (especially if they are **null** objects). To keep the n_v counts for internal nodes up to date, we simply need to modify the insertion and deletion methods as follows:

- If we are doing an insertion at a node, w, in T (which was previously an external node), then we set $n_w = 1$ and we increment the n_v count for each node v that is an ancestor of w, that is, on the path from w to the root of T.

- If we are doing a deletion at a node, w, in T, then we decrement the n_v count for each node v that is on the path from w's parent to the root of T.

In either the insertion or deletion case, the additional work needed to perform the updates to n_v counts takes $O(h)$ time, where h is the height of T. This updating takes an additional amount of time that is $O(h)$, where h is the height of T, because we spend an additional amount of $O(1)$ time for each node from w to the root of T in either case. (See Figure 3.14.)

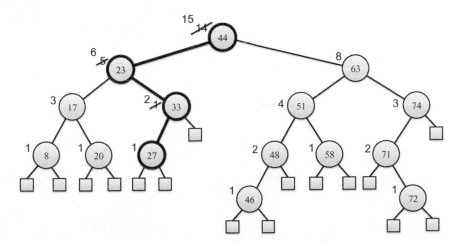

Figure 3.14: A update in an a binary search tree augmented so that each node, v, stores a count, n_v, of the number of items stored in the subtree rooted at v. We show the path taken, along with n_v updates, during this update, which is an insertion of a node with key 27 in the tree from Figure 3.13.

Let us consider how to perform method **select**(i) on a tree, T, augmented as described above. The main idea is to search down the tree, T, while maintaining the value of i so that we are looking for the ith smallest key in the subtree we are still searching in. We do this by calling the **TreeSelect**(i, r, T), shown in Algorithm 3.15, where r is the root of T. Note that this algorithm assumes that the n_v count for any external node is 0. (See Figure 3.16.)

Algorithm TreeSelect(i, v, T):
    Input: Search index i and a node v of a binary search tree T
    Output: The item with ith smallest key stored in the subtree of T rooted at v
    Let $w \leftarrow T.\mathsf{leftChild}(v)$
    if $i \leq n_w$ **then**
        return TreeSelect(i, w, T)
    else if $i = n_w + 1$ **then**
        return $(\mathsf{key}(v), \mathsf{element}(v))$
    else
        return TreeSelect$(i - n_w - 1, T.\mathsf{rightChild}(v), T)$

Algorithm 3.15: The TreeSelect algorithm.

The correctness of this algorithm follows from the fact that we are always maintaining i to be the index of the ith smallest item in the subtree we are searching in, so that the item returned will be the correct index. In particular, note that when we recursively search in a right subtree, we first subtract the count of the number of items stored in the left subtree and the parent. The running time for performing this query is $O(h)$, where h is the height of T, since we spend $O(1)$ time per level of T in our search to the node storing the ith smallest key.

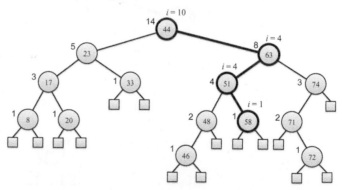

Figure 3.16: A search for the 10th smallest item in a binary search tree augmented so that each node, v, stores a count, n_v, of the number of items stored in the subtree rooted at v. We show the path taken during this search, along with the value, i, that is maintained during this search.

3.4 Randomly Constructed Search Trees

Suppose we construct a binary search tree, T, by a sequence of insertions of n distinct, random keys. Since the only thing that impacts the structure of T is the relative order of the keys, we can assume, without loss of generality, that the keys involved are the integers from 1 to n. That is, we can assume that we are given a random permutation, P, of the keys in the set $\{1, 2, \ldots, n\}$, where all permutations are equally likely, and are asked to build the binary search tree, T, by inserting the keys in P in the given order.

Let v_j denote the node in T that holds the item with key j, and let $D(v_j)$ denote the depth of v_j in T. Note that $D(v_j)$ is a random variable, since T is constructed at random (based on P). Define $X_{i,j}$ to be a 0-1 indicator random variable that is equal to 1 if and only if v_i is an ancestor of v_j, where, for the sake of this analysis, we consider a node to be an ancestor of itself. That is, $X_{i,i} = 1$. We can write

$$D(v_j) = \sum_{i=1}^{n} X_{i,j} - 1,$$

since the depth of a node is equal to the number of its proper ancestors. Thus, to derive a bound on the expected value of $D(v_j)$, we need to determine the probability that $X_{i,j}$ is 1.

Lemma 3.3: *The node v_i is an ancestor of the node v_j in T if and only if i appears earliest in P of any integer in $R_{i,j}$, the range of integers between i and j, inclusive.*

Proof: If i appears earliest in P of any integer in $R_{i,j}$, then, by definition, it is inserted into T before any of these integers. Thus, at the time when j is inserted into T, and we perform j in T, we must encounter the node v_i as our depth $D(v_i)$ comparison, since there is no other element from $R_{i,j}$ at a higher level in T.

Suppose, on the other hand, that i appears earliest in P of any integer in $R_{i,j}$. Then i is inserted into T before any item with a key in this range; hence, for the search for j, we will encounter v_i at some point along the way, since j has to be located into this interval and, at the depth of v_i, there is no other element from $R_{i,j}$ to use as a comparison key. ∎

This fact allows us to then derive the probability that any $X_{i,j}$ is 1, as follows.

Lemma 3.4: *Let $X_{i,j}$ be defined as above. Then $\Pr(X_{i,j} = 1) = 1/(|i-j|+1)$.*

Proof: There are $|i - j| + 1$ items in the range from i to j, inclusive, and the probability that i appears earliest in P of all of them is 1 over this number, since all the numbers in this range have an equal and independent probability of being earliest in P. The proof follows, then, from this fact and Lemma 3.3. ∎

An Analysis Based on Harmonic Numbers

In addition to the above lemmas, our analysis of a randomly constructed binary search tree also involves harmonic numbers. For any integer $n \geq 1$, we define the nth **harmonic number**, H_n, as

$$H_n = \sum_{i=1}^{n} \frac{1}{i},$$

for which it is well known that H_n is $O(\log n)$. In fact,

$$\ln n \leq H_n \leq 1 + \ln n,$$

as we explore in Exercise C-3.11.

Harmonic numbers are important in our analysis, because of the following.

Lemma 3.5:

$$E[D(v_j)] \quad \leq \quad H_j + H_{n-j+1} - 1.$$

Proof: To see this relationship, note that, by the linearity of expectation,

$$
\begin{aligned}
E[D(v_j)] &= \sum_{i=1}^{n} E[X_{i,j}] - 1 \\
&= \sum_{i=1}^{j} E[X_{i,j}] + \sum_{i=j+1}^{n} E[X_{i,j}] - 1 \\
&= \sum_{i=1}^{j} \frac{1}{j-i+1} + \sum_{i=j+1}^{n} \frac{1}{i-j+1} - 1 \\
&\leq \sum_{k=1}^{j} \frac{1}{k} + \sum_{k=1}^{n-j+1} \frac{1}{k} - 1 \\
&= H_j + H_{n-j+1} - 1.
\end{aligned}
$$

∎

So, in other words, the expected depth of any node in a randomly constructed binary search tree with n nodes is $O(\log n)$. Or, put another way, the average depth of the nodes in a randomly constructed binary search tree is $O(\log n)$.

Bounding the Overall Height with High Probability

In addition to the above bound for the average depth of a randomly constructed binary search tree, we might also be interested in bounding the overall height of such a tree, T, which is equal to the maximum depth of any node in T. In order to analyze this maximum depth of a node in T, let us utilize the following Chernoff bound (see Exercise C-19.14).

Let $X_1, X_2, \ldots, X_n$ be a set of mutually independent indicator random variables, such that each X_i is 1 with some probability $p_i > 0$ and 0 otherwise. Let $X = \sum_{i=1}^{n} X_i$ be the sum of these random variables, and let μ' denote an upper bound on the mean of X, that is, $E(X) \leq \mu'$. Then, for $\delta > 0$,

$$\Pr(X > (1+\delta)\mu') < \left[\frac{e^\delta}{(1+\delta)^{(1+\delta)}}\right]^{\mu'}.$$

Using this bound, we can derive the following theorem.

Theorem 3.6: *If T is a randomly constructed binary search tree with $n > 4$ nodes, then the height of T is $O(\log n)$ with probability at least $1 - 1/n$.*

Proof: Recall that $D(v_j) = \sum_{i=1}^{n} X_{i,j} - 1$. Let $L_j = \sum_{i=1}^{j-1} X_{i,j}$ denote the "left" part of this sum and $R_j = \sum_{i=j+1}^{n} X_{i,j}$ denote the "right" part, with both leaving off the term $X_{j,j}$. Then $D(v_j) = L_j + R_j$. So, by symmetry, it is sufficient for us to bound R_j, since a similar bound will hold for L_j. The important observation is that all of the $X_{i,j}$ terms in the definition of R_j are independent 0-1 random variables. This independence is due to the fact that whether i is chosen first in P from $\{j, j+1, \ldots, i\}$ has no bearing on whether $i + 1$ is chosen first in P from $\{j, j+1, \ldots, i, i+1\}$. Moreover, $E[R_j] = H_{n-j+1} \leq H_n$. Thus, by the above Chernoff bound, for $n > 4$,

$$\Pr(R_j > 4H_n) < \left[\frac{e^3}{4^4}\right]^{H_n} \leq \frac{1}{n^{2.5}},$$

since $H_n \geq \ln n$. Therefore, $\Pr(D(v_j) > 8H_n) \leq 2/n^{2.5}$, which implies that the probability that *any* node in T has depth more than $8H_n$ is at most $2n/n^{2.5} = 2/n^{1.5}$. Since $n > 4$ and H_n is $O(\log n)$, this establishes the theorem. ∎

So, if we construct a binary search tree, T, by inserting a set of n distinct items in random order, then, with high probability, the height of T will be $O(\log n)$.

The Problem with Deletions

Unfortunately, if we intersperse random insertions with random deletions, using the standard insertion and deletion algorithms given above, then the expected height of the resulting tree is $\Theta(n^{1/2})$, not $O(\log n)$. Indeed, it has been reported that a major database company experienced poor performance of one its products because of an issue with maintaining the height of a binary search tree to be $O(\log n)$ even while allowing for deletions. Thus, if we are hoping to achieve $O(\log n)$ depth for the nodes in a binary search tree that is subject to both insertions and deletions, even if these operations are for random keys, then we need to do more than simply performing the above standard insertion and deletion operations. For example, we could use one of the balanced search tree strategies discussed in the next chapter.

3.5   Exercises

Reinforcement

R-3.1 Suppose you are given the array $A = [1, 2, 3, 4, 5, 6, 7, 8, 9, 10, 11, 12]$, and you then perform the binary search algorithm given in this chapter to find the number 8. Which numbers in the array A are compared against the number 8?

R-3.2 Insert items with the following keys (in the given order) into an initially empty binary search tree: 30, 40, 50, 24, 8, 58, 48, 26, 11, 13. Draw the tree that results.

R-3.3 Suppose you have a binary search tree, T, storing numbers in the range from 1 to 500, and you do a search for the integer 250. Which of the following sequences are possible sequences of numbers that were encountered in this search. For the ones that are possible, draw the search path, and, for the ones that are impossible, say why.

a. (2, 276, 264, 270, 250)

b. (100, 285, 156, 203, 275, 250)

c. (475, 360, 248, 249, 251, 250)

d. (450, 262, 248, 249, 270, 250)

R-3.4 Suppose T is a binary search tree of height 4 (including the external nodes) that is storing all the integers in the range from 1 to 15, inclusive. Suppose further that you do a search for the number 11. Explain why it is impossible for the sequence of numbers you encounter in this search to be $(9, 12, 10, 11)$.

R-3.5 Draw the binary search trees of minimum and maximum heights that store all the integers in the range from 1 to 7, inclusive.

R-3.6 Give a pseudocode description of an algorithm to find the element with smallest key in a binary search tree. What is the running time of your method?

R-3.7 Draw the binary search tree that results from deleting items with keys 17, 28, 54, and 65, in this order, from the tree shown in Figure 3.7b.

R-3.8 A certain Professor Amongus claims that the order in which a fixed set of elements is inserted into a binary search tree does not matter—the same tree results every time. Give a small example that proves Professor Amongus wrong.

R-3.9 Suppose you are given a sorted set, S, of n items, stored in a binary search tree. How many different range queries can be done where both of the values, k_1 and k_2, in the query range $[k_1, k_2]$ are members of S?

R-3.10 Suppose that a binary search tree, T, is constructed by inserting the integers from 1 to n in this order. Give a big-Oh characterization of the number of comparisons that were done to construct T.

R-3.11 Suppose you are given a binary search tree, T, which is constructed by inserting the integers in the set $\{1, 2, \ldots, n\}$ in a random order into T, where all permutations of this set are equally likely. What is the average running time of then performing a select(i) operation on T?

R-3.12 If one has a set, S, of n items, where n is even, then the median item in S is the average of the ith and $(i+1)$st smallest elements in S, where $i = n/2$. Describe an efficient algorithm for computing the median of such a set S that is stored in a binary search tree, T, where each node, v, in T is augmented with a count, n_v, which stores the number of items stored in the subtree of T rooted at v.

R-3.13 What is H_5, the 5th harmonic number?

Creativity

C-3.1 Suppose you are given a sorted array, A, of n distinct integers in the range from 1 to $n + 1$, so there is exactly one integer in this range missing from A. Describe an $O(\log n)$-time algorithm for finding the integer in this range that is not in A.

C-3.2 Let S and T be two ordered arrays, each with n items. Describe an $O(\log n)$-time algorithm for finding the kth smallest key in the union of the keys from S and T (assuming no duplicates).

C-3.3 Describe how to perform the operation findAllElements(k), which returns every element with a key equal to k (allowing for duplicates) in an ordered set of n key-value pairs stored in an ordered array, and show that it runs in time $O(\log n + s)$, where s is the number of elements returned.

C-3.4 Describe how to perform the operation findAllElements(k), as defined in the previous exercise, in an ordered set of key-value pairs implemented with a binary search tree T, and show that it runs in time $O(h + s)$, where h is the height of T and s is the number of items returned.

C-3.5 Prove, by induction, that the height of a binary search tree containing n items is at least $\lceil \log(n + 1) \rceil$.

C-3.6 Describe how to perform an operation removeAllElements(k), which removes all key-value pairs in a binary search tree T that have a key equal to k, and show that this method runs in time $O(h + s)$, where h is the height of T and s is the number of items returned.

C-3.7 Let S be an ordered set of n items stored in a binary search tree, T, of height h. Show how to perform the following method for S in $O(h)$ time:

countAllInRange(k_1, k_2): Compute and return the number of items in S with key k such that $k_1 \leq k \leq k_2$.

C-3.8 Describe the structure of a binary search tree, T, storing n items, such that T has height $\Omega(n^{1/2})$ yet the average depth of the nodes in T is $O(\log n)$.

C-3.9 Suppose n key-value pairs all have the same key, k, and they are inserted into an initially empty binary search tree using the algorithm described in Section 3.1.3. Show that the height of the resulting tree is $\Theta(n)$. Also, describe a modification to that algorithm based on the use of random choices and show that your modification results in the binary search tree having height $O(\log n)$ with high probability.

C-3.10 Suppose that each row of an $n \times n$ array A consists of 1's and 0's such that, in any row of A, all the 1's come before any 0's in that row. Assuming A is already in memory, describe a method running in $O(n \log n)$ time (not $O(n^2)$ time!) for counting the number of 1's in A.

C-3.11 (For readers familiar with calculus): Use the fact that, for a decreasing integrable function, f,

$$\int_{x=a}^{b+1} f(x)dx \ \leq \ \sum_{i=a}^{b} f(i) \ \leq \ \int_{x=a-1}^{b} f(x)dx,$$

to show that, for the nth harmonic number, H_n,

$$\ln n \ \leq \ H_n \ \leq \ 1 + \ln n.$$

C-3.12 Without using calculus (as in the previous exercise), show that, if n is a power of 2 greater than 1, then, for H_n, the nth harmonic number,

$$H_n \leq 1 + H_{n/2}.$$

Use this fact to conclude that $H_n \leq 1 + \lceil \log n \rceil$, for any $n \geq 1$.

Applications

A-3.1 Suppose you are asked to automate the prescription fulfillment system for a pharmacy, MailDrugs. When an order comes in, it is given as a sequence of requests, "x_1 ml of drug y_1," "x_2 ml of drug y_2," "x_3 ml of drug y_3," and so on, where $x_1 < x_2 < x_3 < \cdots < x_k$. MailDrugs has a practically unlimited supply of n distinctly sized empty drug bottles, each specified by its capacity in milliliters (such 150 ml or 325 ml). To process a drug order, as specified above, you need to match each request, "x_i ml of drug y_i," with the size of the smallest bottle in the inventory than can hold x_i milliliters. Describe how to process such a drug order of k requests so that it can be fulfilled in $O(k \log(n/k))$ time, assuming the bottle sizes are stored in an array, T, ordered by their capacities in milliliters.

A-3.2 Imagine that you work for a database company, which has a popular system for maintaining sorted sets. After a negative review in an influential technology website, the company has decided it needs to convert all of its indexing software from using sorted arrays to an indexing strategy based on using binary search trees, so as to be able to support insertions and deletions more efficiently. Your job is to write a program that can take a sorted array, A, of n elements, and construct a binary search tree, T, storing these same elements, so that doing a binary search for any element in T will run in $O(\log n)$ time. Describe an $O(n)$-time algorithm for doing this conversion.

A-3.3 Suppose you work for a computer game company, which is designing a first person shooting game. In this game, players stand just outside of a circular playing field and shoot at targets inside the circle. There are a lot of players and targets, however, so, for any given player, it only makes sense to display the targets that are close by that player. Thus, whenever a new target, t, appears, the game should only make it visible to the players that are in the same "zone" as t. In order to support the fast processing of such queries, you offer to build a binary space partitioning (BSP) tree, T, for use in the game engine. You are given the (x, y) coordinates of all n players, which are in no particular order, but are constrained to all lie at different locations on a circle, C. Your job is to design an efficient algorithm for building such a BSP tree, T, so that its height is $O(\log n)$. Thus, the root, r, of T is associated with a line, L, that divides the set of players into two groups of roughly equal size. Then, it should recursively partition each group into two groups of roughly equal size. Describe an $O(n \log n)$-time algorithm for constructing such a tree T. (See Figure 3.17.)

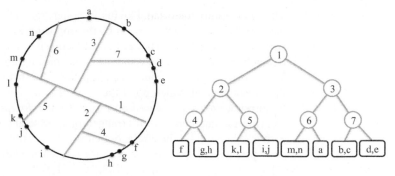

Figure 3.17: A circular environment for a first-person shooter game, where players are represented as points (labeled with letters), together with a two-dimensional BSP tree for this configuration, where dividing lines and nodes are similarly numbered.

A-3.4 It is sometimes necessary to send a description of a binary search tree in text form, such as in an email or text message. Since it is a significant challenge to draw a binary search tree using text symbols, it is useful to have a completely textural way of representing a binary search tree. Fortunately, the structure of a binary search tree is uniquely determined by labeling each node with its preorder and postorder numbers. Thus, we can build a textural representation of a binary search tree T by listing its nodes sorted according to their preorder labels, and listing each node in terms of its contents and its postorder label. For example, the tree of Figure 3.10 would be represented as the string,
$$[(10, 9), (\emptyset, 1), (20, 8), (\emptyset, 2), (30, 7), (\emptyset, 3), (40, 6), (\emptyset, 5), (\emptyset, 6)].$$
Describe an $O(n)$ time method for converting an n-node binary search tree, T, into such a textural representation.

A-3.5 Consider the reversal of the problem from the previous exercise. Now you are the recipient of such a message, containing a textural representation of a binary search tree as described in the previous exercise. Describe an algorithm running in $O(n \log n)$ time, or better, for reconstructing the binary search tree, T, that is represented in this message.

A-3.6 Suppose you are building a first-person shooter game, where virtual zombies are climbing up a wall while the player, who is moving left and right in front of the wall, is trying to knock them down using various weapons. The position of each zombie is represented with a pair, (x, y), where x is the horizontal position of the zombie and y is its height on the wall. The player's position is specified with just a horizontal value, x_p. One of the weapons that a player can use is a bomb, which kills the zombie that is highest on the wall from all those zombies within a given horizontal distance, r, of x_p. Suppose the zombies are stored in a binary search tree, T, of height h, ordered in terms of their horizontal positions. Describe a method for augmenting T so as to answer maximum-zombie queries in $O(h)$ time, where such a query is given by a range $[x_p - r, x_p + r]$ and you need to return the coordinates of the zombie with maximum y-value whose horizontal position, x, is in this range. Describe the operations that must be done for inserting and deleting zombies as well as performing maximum-zombie queries.

A-3.7 The first-century historian, Flavius Josephus, recounts the story of how, when his band of 41 soldiers was trapped by the opposing Roman army, they chose group suicide over surrender. They collected themselves into a circle and repeatedly put to death every third man around the circle, closing up the circle after every death. This process repeated around the circle until the only ones left were Josephus and one other man, at which point they took a new vote of their group and decided to surrender after all. Based on this story, the ***Josephus problem*** involves considering the numbers 1 to n arranged in a circle and repeatedly removing every mth number around the circle, outputting the resulting sequence of numbers. For example, with $n = 10$ and $m = 4$, the sequence would be

$$4, 8, 2, 7, 3, 10, 9, 1, 6, 5.$$

Given values for n and m, describe an algorithm for outputting the sequence resulting from this instance of the Josephus problem in $O(n \log n)$ time.

Chapter Notes

Interestingly, the binary search algorithm was first published in 1946, but was not published in a fully correct form until 1962. For some lessons to be learned from this history, please see the related discussions in Knuth's book [131] and the papers by Bentley [28] and Levisse [142]. Another excellent source for additional material about binary search trees is the book by Mehlhorn in [157]. In addition, the handbook by Gonnet and Baeza-Yates [85] contains a number of theoretical and experimental comparisons among binary search tree implementations. Additional reading can be found in the book by Tarjan [207], and the chapter by Mehlhorn and Tsakalidis [160].

Our analysis of randomly constructed binary search trees is based on the analysis of randomized search trees by Seidel and Aragon [191]. The analysis that a random sequence of insertions and deletions in a standard binary search tree can lead to it having $\Theta(n^{1/2})$ depth is due to Culberson and Munro [53]. The report of a database company that experienced poor performance of one of its products due to an issue with how to maintain a balanced binary search tree subject to insertions and deletions is included in a paper by Sen and Tarjan [193].

Chapter

4

Balanced Binary Search Trees

U.S. Navy Blue Angels, performing their delta formation during the Blues on the Bay Air Show at Marine Corps Base Hawaii in 2007. U.S. government photo by Petty Officer 2nd Class Michael Hight, U.S. Navy.

Contents

4.1 Ranks and Rotations 117

4.2 AVL Trees 120

4.3 Red-Black Trees 126

4.4 Weak AVL Trees 130

4.5 Splay Trees 139

4.6 Exercises 149

Real-time systems are computational platforms that have real-time constraints, where computations must complete in a given amount of time. Examples include antilock braking systems on cars, video and audio processing systems, operating systems kernels, and web applications. In these real-time applications, if a software component takes too much time to finish, then the entire system can crash (sometimes literally).

Suppose, then, that you are designing a real-time web application for users to find A-list celebrities who are closest to them in age. In other words, your system should maintain a set of celebrities, sorted by their birth dates. In addition, it should allow for celebrities to be added to your set (namely, when they become popular enough to be added to the A-list) and removed from your set (say, when they fall off the A-list).

Most importantly, your system should support a *nearest-neighbor query*, where a user specifies their birth date and your system then returns the ten A-list stars closest in age to the user. The real-time constraint for your system is that it has to respond in at most a few hundred milliseconds or users will notice the delay and go to your competitor. Of course, if users would simply be looking up celebrities with a specific birth date, you could use a lookup table, indexed by birth date, to implement your database. But such schemes don't support fast nearest neighbor queries.

Note that a binary search tree, T, provides almost everything you need in order to implement your system, since it can maintain a sorted set of items so as to perform insertions and removals based on their keys (which in this case are birth dates). It also supports nearest-neighbor queries, in that, for any key k, we can perform a search in T for the smallest key that is greater than or equal to k, or, alternatively, for the largest key that is less than or equal to k. Given either of the nodes in T storing such a key, we can then perform a forward or backward inorder traversal of T starting from that point to list neighboring smaller or larger keys.

The problem is that without some way of limiting the height of T, the worst-case running time for performing searches and updates in T can be linear in the number of items it stores. Indeed, this worst-case behavior occurs if we insert and delete keys in T in a somewhat sorted order, which is likely for your database, since celebrities are typically added to the A-list when they are in their mid-twenties and removed when they are in their mid-fifties. Without a way to restructure T while you are using it, this kind of updating will result in T becoming unbalanced, which will result in poor performance for searches and updates in your system.

Fortunately, there is a solution. Namely, as we discuss in this chapter, there are ways of restructuring a binary search tree while it is being used so that it can guarantee logarithmic-time performance for searches and updates. These restructuring methods result in a class of data structures known as *balanced binary search trees*.

4.1 Ranks and Rotations

Recall that a binary search tree stores elements at the internal nodes of a proper binary tree so that the key at each left child is not greater than its parent's key and the key at each right child is not less than its parent's key. Searching in a binary search tree can be described as a recursive procedure, as we did in the previous chapter (in Algorithm 3.5), or as an iterative method, as we show in Algorithm 4.1.

Algorithm IterativeTreeSearch(k, T):

> **Input:** A search key k and a binary search tree, T
>
> **Output:** A node in T that is either an internal node storing key k or the external node where an item with key k would belong in T if it existed

> $v \leftarrow T.\text{root}()$
> **while** v is not an external node **do**
> > **if** $k = \text{key}(v)$ **then**
> > > **return** v
> > **else if** $k < \text{key}(v)$ **then**
> > > $v \leftarrow T.\text{leftChild}(v)$
> > **else**
> > > $v \leftarrow T.\text{rightChild}(v)$
> **return** v

Algorithm 4.1: Searching a binary search tree iteratively.

As mentioned above, the worst-case performance of searching in a binary search tree can be as bad as linear time, since the time to perform a search is proportional to the height of the search tree. Such a performance is no better than that of looking through all the elements in a set to find an item of interest. In order to avoid this poor performance, we need ways of maintaining the height of a search tree to be logarithmic in the number of nodes it has.

Balanced Binary Search Trees

The primary way to achieve logarithmic running times for search and update operations in a binary search tree, T, is to perform restructuring actions on T based on specific rules that maintain some notion of "balance" between sibling subtrees in T. We refer to a binary search tree that can maintain a height of $O(\log n)$ through such balancing rules and actions as a ***balanced binary search tree***. Intuitively, the reason balance is so important is that when a binary search tree T is balanced, the number of nodes in the tree increases exponentially as one moves down the levels of T. Such an exponential increase in size implies that if T stores n items, then it will have height $O(\log n)$.

In this chapter, we discuss several kinds of balanced binary search trees. Three of these search trees—AVL trees, red-black trees, and weak AVL trees—are ***rank-balanced trees***, where we define an integer ***rank***, $r(v)$, for each node, v, in a binary search tree, T, where $r(v)$ is either the height of v or a value related to the height of v. Balance in such a tree, T, is enforced by maintaining certain rules on the relative ranks of children and sibling nodes in T. These three rank-balanced trees have slightly different rules guaranteeing that the height of a binary search tree satisfying these rules has logarithmic height. The final type of balanced binary search tree we discuss in this chapter is the splay tree, which achieves its balance in an amortized way by blindly performing a certain kind of restructuring action, called splaying, after every access and update operation.

One restructuring operation, which is used in all of the balanced binary search trees we discuss is known as a ***rotation***, of which there are four types. Here, we describe a unified restructuring operation, called ***trinode restructuring***, which combines the four types of rotations into one action. The trinode restructuring operation involves a node, x, which has a parent, y, and a grandparent, z. This operation, $\mathsf{restructure}(x)$, is described in detail in Algorithm 4.2 and illustrated in Figure 4.3. At a high level, a trinode restructure temporarily renames the nodes x, y, and z as a, b, and c, so that a precedes b and b precedes c in an inorder traversal of T. There are four possible ways of mapping x, y, and z to a, b, and c, as shown in Figure 4.3, which are unified into one case by our relabeling. The trinode restructure then replaces z with the node called b, makes the children of this node be a and c, and makes the children of a and c be the four previous children of x, y, and z (other than x and y) while maintaining the inorder relationships of all the nodes in T.

Algorithm $\mathsf{restructure}(x)$:

> ***Input:*** A node x of a binary search tree T that has both a parent y and a grandparent z
>
> ***Output:*** Tree T after a trinode restructuring (which corresponds to a single or double rotation) involving nodes x, y, and z

1: Let (a, b, c) be a left-to-right (inorder) listing of the nodes x, y, and z, and let (T_0, T_1, T_2, T_3) be a left-to-right (inorder) listing of the four subtrees of x, y, and z that are not rooted at x, y, or z.
2: Replace the subtree rooted at z with a new subtree rooted at b.
3: Let a be the left child of b and let T_0 and T_1 be the left and right subtrees of a, respectively.
4: Let c be the right child of b and let T_2 and T_3 be the left and right subtrees of c, respectively.
5: Recalculate the heights of a, b, and c, (or a "standin" function for height), from the corresponding values stored at their children, and return b.

Algorithm 4.2: The trinode restructure operation for a binary search tree.

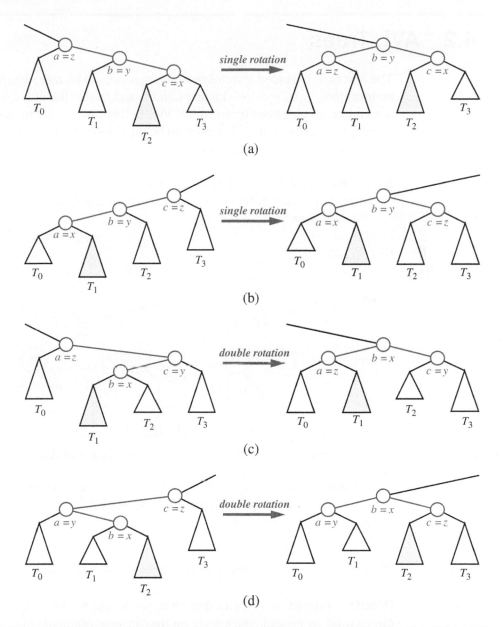

Figure 4.3: Schematic illustration of a trinode restructure operation (Algorithm 4.2). Parts (a) and (b) show a single rotation, and parts (c) and (d) show a double rotation.

The modification of a tree T caused by a trinode restructure operation is often called a ***rotation***, because of the geometric way we can visualize the way it changes T. If $b = y$ (see Algorithm 4.2), the trinode restructure method is called a ***single rotation***, for it can be visualized as "rotating" y over z. (See Figure 4.3a and b.) Otherwise, if $b = x$, the trinode restructure operation is a ***double rotation***, for it can be visualized as first "rotating" x over y and then over z. (See Figure 4.3c and d.)

4.2   AVL Trees

The first rank-balanced search tree we discuss is the ***AVL tree***, which is named after
its inventors, Adel'son-Vel'skii and Landis, and is also the oldest known balanced
search tree, having been invented in 1962. In this case, we define the rank, $r(v)$, of
a node, v, in a binary tree, T, simply to be the height of v in T. The rank-balancing
rule for AVL trees is then defined as follows:

Height-balance Property: For every internal node, v, in T, the heights of the children of v may differ by at most 1. That is, if a node, v, in T has children, x
and y, then $|r(x) - r(y)| \leq 1$.

(See Figure 4.4.)

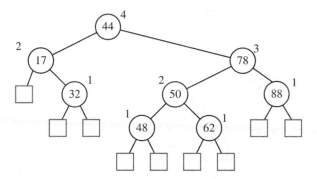

Figure 4.4: An AVL tree. Heights are shown next to the nodes.

An immediate consequence of the height-balance property is that any subtree
of an AVL tree is itself an AVL tree. The height-balance property has also the important consequence of keeping the height small, as shown in the following proposition.

Theorem 4.1: *The height of an AVL tree, T, storing n items is $O(\log n)$.*

Proof: Instead of trying to find an upper bound for the height of an AVL tree
directly, let us instead concentrate on the "inverse problem" of characterizing the
minimum number of internal nodes, n_h, of an AVL tree with height h. As base
cases for a recursive definition, notice that $n_1 = 1$, because an AVL tree of height
1 must have at least one internal node, and $n_2 = 2$, because an AVL tree of height
2 must have at least two internal nodes. Now, for the general case of an AVL tree,
T, with the minimum number of nodes for height, h, note that the root of such a
tree will have as its children's subtrees an AVL tree with the minimum number of
nodes for height $h - 1$ and an AVL tree with the minimum number of nodes for
height $h - 2$. Taking the root itself into account, we obtain the following formula

for the general case, $h \geq 3$:

$$n_h = 1 + n_{h-1} + n_{h-2}.$$

This formula implies that the n_h values are strictly increasing as h increases, in a way that corresponds to the Fibonacci sequence (e.g., see Exercise C-4.3). In other words, $n_{h-1} > n_{h-2}$, for $h \geq 3$, which allows us to simplify the above formula as

$$n_h > 2n_{h-2}.$$

This simplified formula shows that n_h at least doubles each time h increases by 2, which intuitively means that n_h grows exponentially. Formally, this simplified formula implies that

$$n_h \ > \ 2^{\frac{h}{2}-1}. \tag{4.1}$$

By taking logarithms of both sides of Equation (4.1), we obtain

$$\log n_h \ > \ \frac{h}{2} - 1,$$

from which we get

$$h \ < \ 2\log n_h + 2, \tag{4.2}$$

which implies that an AVL tree storing n keys has height at most $2 \log n + 2$. ■

In fact, the bound of $2 \log n + 2$, from Equation (4.2), for the height of an AVL tree is an overestimate. It is possible, for instance, to show that the height of an AVL tree storing n items is at most $1.441 \log (n + 1)$, as is explored, for instance, in Exercise C-4.4. In any case, by Theorem 4.1 and the analysis of binary search trees given in Section 3.1.1, searching in an AVL tree runs in $O(\log n)$ time. The important issue remaining is to show how to maintain the height-balance property of an AVL tree after an insertion or removal.

Insertion

An insertion in an AVL tree T begins as in an insert operation described in Section 3.1.3 for a (simple) binary search tree. Recall that this operation always inserts the new item at a node w in T that was previously an external node, and it makes w become an internal node with operation expandExternal. That is, it adds two external-node children to w. This action may violate the height-balance property, however, for some nodes increase their heights by one. In particular, node w, and possibly some of its ancestors, increase their heights by one. Therefore, let us describe how to restructure T to restore its height balance.

In the AVL tree approach to achieving balance, given a binary search tree, T, we say that a node v of T is **balanced** if the absolute value of the difference between the heights of the children of v is at most 1, and we say that it is **unbalanced** otherwise. Thus, the height-balance property characterizing AVL trees is equivalent to saying that every internal node is balanced.

Suppose that T satisfies the height-balance property, and hence is an AVL tree, prior to our inserting the new item. As we have mentioned, after performing the operation expandExternal(w) on T, the heights of some nodes of T, including w, increase. All such nodes are on the path of T from w to the root of T, and these are the only nodes of T that may have just become unbalanced. (See Figure 4.5a.) Of course, if this happens, then T is no longer an AVL tree; hence, we need a mechanism to fix the "unbalance" that we have just caused.

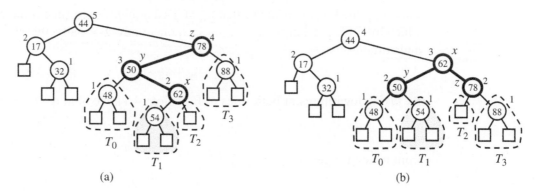

Figure 4.5: An example insertion of an element with key 54 in the AVL tree of Figure 4.4: (a) after adding a new node for key 54, the nodes storing keys 78 and 44 become unbalanced; (b) a trinode restructuring restores the height-balance property. We show the heights of nodes next to them, and we identify the nodes x, y, and z.

We restore the balance of the nodes in the binary search tree T by a simple "search-and-repair" strategy. In particular, let z be the first node we encounter in going up from w toward the root of T such that z is unbalanced. (See Figure 4.5a.) Also, let y denote the child of z with higher height (and note that y must be an ancestor of w). Finally, let x be the child of y with higher height (and if there is a tie, choose x to be an ancestor of w). Note that node x could be equal to w and x is a grandchild of z. Since z became unbalanced because of an insertion in the subtree rooted at its child y, the height of y is 2 greater than its sibling. We now rebalance the subtree rooted at z by calling the ***trinode restructuring*** method, restructure(x), described in Algorithm 4.2. (See Figure 4.5b.)

Thus, we restore the height-balance property ***locally*** at the nodes x, y, and z. In addition, since after performing the new item insertion the subtree rooted at b replaces the one formerly rooted at z, which was taller by one unit, all the ancestors of z that were formerly unbalanced become balanced. (The justification of this fact is left as Exercise C-4.9.) Therefore, this one restructuring also restores the height-balance property ***globally***. That is, one rotation (single or double) is sufficient to restore the height-balance in an AVL tree after an insertion. Of course, we may have to update the height values (ranks) of $O(\log n)$ nodes after an insertion, but the amount of structural changes after an insertion in an AVL tree is $O(1)$.

Removal

We begin the implementation of the remove operation on an AVL tree T as in a regular binary search tree. We may have some additional work, however, if this update violates the height-balance property.

In particular, after removing an internal node with operation removeAboveExternal and elevating one of its children into its place, there may be an unbalanced node in T on the path from the parent w of the previously removed node to the root of T. (See Figure 4.6a.) In fact, there can be one such unbalanced node at most. (The justification of this fact is left as Exercise C-4.8.)

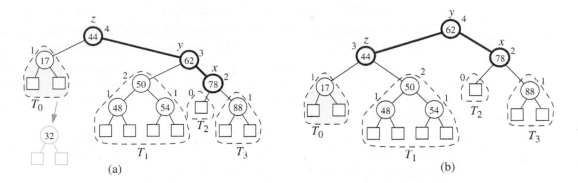

(a)   (b)

Figure 4.6: Removal of the element with key 32 from the AVL tree of Figure 4.4: (a) after removing the node storing key 32, the root becomes unbalanced; (b) a (single) rotation restores the height-balance property.

As with insertion, we use trinode restructuring to restore balance in the tree T. In particular, let z be the first unbalanced node encountered going up from w toward the root of T. Also, let y be the child of z with larger height (note that node y is the child of z that is not an ancestor of w). Finally, let x be the child of y defined as follows:

- if one of the children of y is taller than the other, let x be the taller child of y;
- else (both children of y have the same height), let x be the child of y on the same side as y (that is, if y is a left child, let x be the left child of y, else let x be the right child of y).

In any case, we then perform a restructure(x) operation, which restores the height-balance property *locally*, at the subtree that was formerly rooted at z and is now rooted at the node we temporarily called b. (See Figure 4.6b.)

This trinode restructuring may reduce the height of the subtree rooted at b by 1, which may cause in turn an ancestor of b to become unbalanced. Thus, a single trinode restructuring may not restore the height-balance property globally after a removal. So, after rebalancing z, we continue walking up T looking for unbalanced nodes. If we find another unbalanced node, we perform a restructure operation to restore its balance, and continue marching up T looking for more, all the way to the root.

Since the height of T is $O(\log n)$, where n is the number of items, by Theorem 4.1, $O(\log n)$ trinode restructurings are sufficient to restore the height-balance property.

Pseudo-code for AVL Trees

Pseudo-code descriptions of the metods for performing the insertion and removal operations in an AVL tree are given in Algorithm 4.7.

We also include a common rebalancing method, rebalanceAVL, which restores the balance to an AVL tree after performing either an insertion or a removal.

This method, in turn, makes use of the trinode restructure operation to restore local balance to a node after an update. The rebalanceAVL method continues testing for unbalance up the tree, and restoring balance to any unbalanced nodes it finds, until it reaches the root.

Summarizing the Analysis of AVL Trees

We summarize the analysis of the performance of AVL trees as follows. (See Table 4.8.) Operations find, insert, and remove visit the nodes along a root-to-leaf path of T, plus, possibly their siblings, and spend $O(1)$ time per node. The insertion and removal methods perform this path traversal twice, actually, once down this path to locate the node containing the update key and once up this path after the update has occurred, to update height values (ranks) and do any necessary rotations to restore balance. Thus, since the height of T is $O(\log n)$ by Theorem 4.1, each of the above operations takes $O(\log n)$ time. That is, we have the following theorem.

Theorem 4.2: *An AVL tree for n key-element items uses $O(n)$ space and executes the operations* find, insert *and* remove *to each take $O(\log n)$ time.*

Operation	Time	Structural Changes
find	$O(\log n)$	none
insert	$O(\log n)$	$O(1)$
remove	$O(\log n)$	$O(\log n)$

Table 4.8: Performance of an n-element AVL tree. The space usage is $O(n)$.

Algorithm insertAVL(k, e, T):

> **Input:** A key-element pair, (k, e), and an AVL tree, T
>
> **Output:** An update of T to now contain the item (k, e)
>
> $v \leftarrow$ IterativeTreeSearch(k, T)
> **if** v is not an external node **then**
> > **return** "An item with key k is already in T"
>
> Expand v into an internal node with two external-node children
> v.key $\leftarrow k$
> v.element $\leftarrow e$
> v.height $\leftarrow 1$
> rebalanceAVL(v, T)

Algorithm removeAVL(k, T):

> **Input:** A key, k, and an AVL tree, T
>
> **Output:** An update of T to now have an item (k, e) removed
>
> $v \leftarrow$ IterativeTreeSearch(k, T)
> **if** v is an external node **then**
> > **return** "There is no item with key k in T"
>
> **if** v has no external-node child **then**
> > Let u be the node in T with key nearest to k
> > Move u's key-value pair to v
> > $v \leftarrow u$
>
> Let w be v's smallest-height child
> Remove w and v from T, replacing v with w's sibling, z
> rebalanceAVL(z, T)

Algorithm rebalanceAVL(v, T):

> **Input:** A node, v, where an imbalance may have occurred in an AVL tree, T
>
> **Output:** An update of T to now be balanced
>
> v.height $\leftarrow 1 + \max\{v$.leftChild().height, v.rightChild().height$\}$
> **while** v is not the root of T **do**
> > $v \leftarrow v$.parent()
> > **if** $|v$.leftChild().height $- v$.rightChild().height$| > 1$ **then**
> > > Let y be the tallest child of v and let x be the tallest child of y
> > > $v \leftarrow$ restructure(x) // trinode restructure operation
> >
> > v.height $\leftarrow 1 + \max\{v$.leftChild().height, v.rightChild().height$\}$

Algorithm 4.7: Methods for item insertion and removal in an AVL tree, as well as the method for rebalancing an AVL tree. This version of the rebalance method does not include the heuristic of stopping as soon as balance is restored, and instead always performs any needed rebalancing operations all the way to the root.

4.3 Red-Black Trees

The data structure we discuss in this section, the red-black tree, is a binary search tree that uses a kind of "pseudo-depth" to achieve balance using the approach of a depth-bounded search tree. In particular, a ***red-black tree*** is a binary search tree with nodes colored red and black in a way that satisfies the following properties:

External-Node Property: Every external node is black.

Internal-node Property: The children of a red node are black.

Black-depth Property: All the external nodes have the same ***black depth***, that is, the same number of black nodes as proper ancestors.

Some definitions of red-black trees also require that the root of a red-black tree be black. An example of a red-black tree is shown in Figure 4.9.

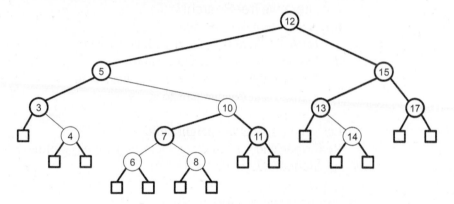

Figure 4.9: An example binary search tree that is a red-black tree. We used thin lines to denote red nodes and the edges from red nodes to their parents. Each external node of this red-black tree has three black proper ancestors; hence, each such node has black depth 3.

As is our convention in this book, we assume that items are stored in the internal nodes of a red-black tree, with the external nodes being empty placeholders. That is, we assume that red-black trees are proper binary search trees, so that every internal node has exactly two children. This allows us to describe search and update algorithms assuming external nodes are real, but we note in passing that at the expense of slightly more complicated search and update methods, external nodes could be **null** or references to a NULL_NODE object, as long as we can still imagine them as existing.

The reason behind all these properties that define red-black trees is that they lead to the following.

Theorem 4.3: *The height of a red-black tree storing n items is $O(\log n)$.*

Proof: Let n_d denote the minimum number of internal nodes in a red-black tree where all its external nodes have black depth d. Then

- $n_1 = 1$, since we could have a single internal node with two black external-node children.
- $n_d = 1 + 2n_{d-1}$, since we get the fewest number of internal nodes when we have a black root with two black children.

This implies that $n_d = 2^d - 1$, that is, $d = \log(n_d + 1)$. Now, let T be a red-black tree storing n items (in its internal nodes), and let d be the common black depth of each external node in T and let h be the height of T. By the definition of n_d, $d \leq \log(n + 1)$. Notice that the internal-node property of red-black trees implies that it is impossible to have two consecutive red nodes on any root-to-external-node path. Thus, if an external node, v, has black depth d, then the actual depth of v can be at most $2d + 1$ (since the root is allowed to be red). Therefore,

$$h \leq 2d + 1 \leq 2\log(n + 1) + 1.$$

■

We assume that a red-black tree is realized with a linked structure for binary trees, in which we store an item and a color indicator at each node. Moreover, this color indicator only needs to be a single bit, since there are only two possible colors—red or black.

The algorithm for searching in a red-black tree T is the same as that for a standard binary search tree. That is, we traverse down T to either an internal node holding an item with key equal to the search key or to an external node (without finding an item with the desired key). Thus, searching in a red-black tree takes $O(\log n)$ time.

Performing the update operations in a red-black tree is similar to that of a binary search tree, except that we must additionally restore the color properties. Unfortunately, the methods for doing this restoration are a bit complicated when dealing directly with node colors; hence, as a first step toward simpler algorithms for performing updates in a red-black tree, we provide an alternative definition of red-black trees, which is equivalent to the standard definition given above.

A Rank-Based Definition of Red-Black Trees

One of the biggest challenges in designing algorithms for red-black trees is that any change to a red-black tree has to maintain the black-depth property, which is somewhat difficult to work with. Thus, it is useful to have an alternative definition of red-black trees that avoids an explicit black-depth property.

So, instead of assigning colors to the nodes of a binary search tree, T, let us instead assign an integer, $r(v)$, to each node, v, in T, which we refer to as the **rank** of v. In order for an assignment of ranks to be valid, the rank of any node can never be greater than the rank of its parent. For each node v in T other than the root, we define the *rank difference* of v as the difference between the rank of v and the rank of v's parent.

We say that an assignment of ranks to the nodes of a binary search tree is *red-black-equivalent* if it satisfies the following properties.

External-Node Property: Every external node has rank 0 and its parent, if it exists, has rank 1.

Parent Property: The rank difference of every node, other than the root, is 0 or 1.

Grandparent Property: Any node with rank difference 0 is either a child of the root or its parent has rank difference 1.

We can show that this set of properties is equivalent to the standard properties for red-black trees. (See Figure 4.10.)

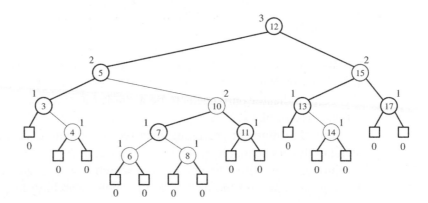

Figure 4.10: An example binary search tree that is a red-black tree, both by the color-based definition and the rank-based definition. We show the rank next to each node. Note that red nodes have rank difference equal to zero.

Theorem 4.4: *Every red-black tree has a red-black-equivalent rank assignment.*

Proof: Suppose T is a red-black tree. Without loss of generality, we can assume the root of T is black. Define the ***black height*** of each node v in T as the number of black descendants of v (not counting v) on a path from v to an external node. Note that the black-depth property implies that this notion is well-defined. Now, assign ranks to the nodes of T according to the following.

Rank-Assignment Rule: Give each black node, v, in T a rank, $r(v)$, equal to its black height, and give each red node, v, a rank, $r(v)$, equal to the rank of its (black) parent.

Then this assignment of ranks satisfies all the properties for being red-black-equivalent. In particular, every external node will have rank 0 and a parent of rank 1, the rank differences of every node will be 0 or 1, and any node with rank difference 0 will have a parent with rank difference 1. ∎

We also have the following result.

Theorem 4.5: *Every tree with a red-black-equivalent rank assignment can be colored as a red-black tree.*

Proof: Suppose T is a binary tree with a red-black-equivalent rank assignment. To come up with a coloring of T, use the following.

Color-Assignment Rule: If a node has rank difference 0, then color it red; otherwise, color it black.

Thus, by the rules for a red-black-equivalent ranking, every external node will be colored black and every red node will have a black parent. To see that every external node has the same black depth, note that we can easily prove by induction that the black depth of every external node in a subtree of T rooted at v is equal to the black height of v, since every node has rank difference 0 or 1. Therefore, all the external nodes are at the same black depth from the root. ∎

This rank-based definition of red-black trees is still not quite what we need to design simple update algorithms, but it is a good first step. In the next section, we provide an alternative rank-based balancing scheme, which results in balanced search trees that are structurally red-black trees but have improved performance and simpler update algorithms. Thus, we omit from this book a description of the complicated update algorithms for red-black trees. Let us, instead, take as a given that red-black trees can achieve $O(\log n)$-time performance for insertions and deletions.

Table 4.11 summarizes the running times of the main operations of a red-black tree. The main take-away message from this table is that a red-black tree achieves logarithmic worst-case running times for both searching and updating.

Operation	Time
find	$O(\log n)$
insert	$O(\log n)$
remove	$O(\log n)$

Table 4.11: Performance of an n-element red-black tree. The space usage is $O(n)$.

4.4 Weak AVL Trees

In this section, we discuss a type of rank-balanced trees, known as *weak AVL trees* or *wavl trees*, that have features of both AVL trees and red-black trees. That is, as we will show, every AVL tree is a weak AVL tree, and every weak AVL tree can be colored as a red-black tree. Weak AVL trees achieve balance by enforcing rules about integer ranks assigned to nodes, which are a kind of "stand in" for height rather than having nodes have ranks exactly equal to their heights, as in AVL trees. Also, by using such ranks, wavl trees are able to achieve efficiency and have simple update methods.

In a *weak AVL* tree, T, we assign an integer rank, $r(v)$, to each node, v in T, such that the rank of any node is less than the rank of its parent. For each node v in T, the *rank difference* for v is the difference between the rank of v and the rank of v's parent. An internal node is a $1, 1$-*node* if its children each have rank difference 1. It is a $2, 2$-*node* if its children each have rank difference 2. And it is a $1, 2$-*node* if it has one child with rank difference 1 and one child with rank difference 2. The ranks assigned to the nodes in a wavl tree must satisfy the following properties.

Rank-Difference Property: The rank difference of any non-root node is 1 or 2.

External-Node Property: Every external node has rank 0.

Internal-Node Property: An internal node with two external-node children cannot be a $2, 2$-node.

Note that just by the rank-difference and external-node properties, the height of a wavl tree, T, is less than or equal to the rank of the root of T. (See Figure 4.12.)

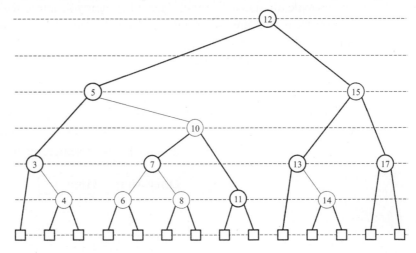

Figure 4.12: Example of a wavl tree. The nodes are placed at y-coordinates equal to their ranks.

Theorem 4.6: *The height of a wavl tree storing n items is at most $2\log(n+1)$.*

Proof: Let n_r denote the minimum number of internal nodes in a wavl tree whose root has rank r. Then, by the rules for ranks in a wavl tree,

$$n_0 = 0$$
$$n_1 = 1$$
$$n_2 = 2$$
$$n_r = 1 + 2n_{r-2}, \text{ for } r \geq 3.$$

This implies that $n_r \geq 2^{r/2} - 1$, that is, $r \leq 2\log(n_r+1)$. Thus, by the definition of n_r, $r \leq 2\log(n+1)$. That is, the rank of the root is at most $2\log(n+1)$, which implies that the height of the tree is bounded by $2\log(n+1)$, since the height of a wavl tree is never more than the rank of its root. ∎

Thus, wavl trees are balanced binary search trees. We also have the following.

Theorem 4.7: *Every AVL tree is a weak AVL tree.*

Proof: Suppose we are given an AVL tree, T, with a rank assignment, $r(v)$, for the nodes of T, as described in Section 4.2, so that $r(v)$ is equal to the height of v in T. Then, every external node in T has rank 0. In addition, by the height-balance property for AVL trees, every internal node is either a $1,1$-node or $1,2$-node; that is, there are no $2,2$-nodes. Thus, the standard rank assignment, $r(v)$, for an AVL tree implies T is a weak AVL tree. ∎

Put another way, an AVL tree is just a weak AVL tree with no $2,2$-nodes, which motivates the name, "weak AVL tree." We also get a relationship that goes from wavl trees to red-black trees.

Theorem 4.8: *Every wavl tree can be colored as a red-black tree.*

Proof: Suppose we are given a wavl tree, T, with a rank assignment, $r(v)$. For each node v in T, assign a new rank, $r'(v)$, to each node v as follows:

$$r'(v) = \lfloor r(v)/2 \rfloor.$$

Then each external node still has rank 0 and the rank difference for any node is 0 or 1. In addition, note that the rank difference, in the $r(v)$ rank assignment, between a node and its grandparent must be at least 2; hence, in the $r'(v)$ rank assignment, the parent of any node with rank difference 0 must have rank difference 1. Thus, the $r'(v)$ rank assignment is red-black-equivalent; hence, by Theorem 4.5, T can be colored as a red-black tree. ∎

Nevertheless, the relationship does not go the other way, as there are some red-black trees that cannot be given rank assignments to make them be wavl trees (e.g., see Exercise R-4.16). In particular, the internal-node property distinguishes wavl trees from red-black trees. Without this property, the two types of trees are equivalent, as Theorem 4.8 and the following theorem show.

Theorem 4.9: *Every red-black tree can be given a rank assignment that satisfies the rank-difference and external-node properties.*

Proof: Let T be a red-black tree. For each black node in v, let $r(v)$ be 2 times the black height of v. If v is red, on the other hand, let $r(v)$ be 1 more than the (same) rank of its black children. Then the rank of every external node is 0 and the rank difference for any node is 1 or 2. ∎

Insertion

The insertion algorithm for weak AVL trees is essentially the same as for AVL trees, except that we use node ranks for wavl trees instead of node ranks that are exactly equal to node heights. Let q denote the node in a wavl tree where we just performed an insertion, and note that q previously was an external node. Now q has two external-node children; hence, we increase the rank of q by 1, which in an action called a ***promotion*** at q. We then proceed according to the following rebalancing operation:

- If q has rank difference 1 after promotion, or if q is the root, then we are done with the rebalancing operation. Otherwise, if q now has rank-difference 0, with its parent, p, then we proceed according to the following two cases.

  1. q's sibling has rank-difference 1. In this case, we promote q's parent, p. See Figure 4.13. This fixes the rank-difference property for q, but it may cause a violation for p. So, we replace q by p and we repeat the rebalancing operation for this new version of q.
  2. q's sibling has rank-difference 2. Let t denote a child of q that has rank-difference 1. By induction, such a child always exists. We perform a trinode restructuring operation at t by calling the method, restructure(t), described in Algorithm 4.2. See Figure 4.14. We then set the rank of the node replacing p (i.e., the one temporarily labeled b) with the old rank p and we set the ranks of its children so that they both have rank-difference 1. This terminates the rebalancing operation, since it repairs all rule violations without creating any new ones.

As mentioned above, this insertion algorithm is essentially the same as that for AVL trees. Moreover, it doesn't create any $2, 2$-nodes. Thus, if we construct a weak AVL tree, T, via a sequence of n insertions and don't perform any deletions, then the height of T is the same as that for a similarly constructed AVL tree, namely, at most $1.441 \log{(n + 1)}$. (See Exercise C-4.4.)

In addition, note that we perform at most $O(1)$ restructuring operations for any insertion in a weak AVL tree. Interestingly, unlike AVL trees, this same efficiency also holds for deletion in a wavl tree.

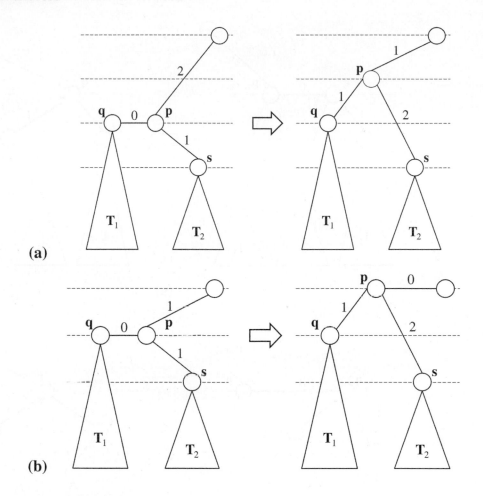

Figure 4.13: Case 1 of rebalancing in a wavl tree after an insertion: node q has rank-difference 0 (a violation) and its sibling, s, has rank-difference 1. To resolve the rank-difference violation for node q, we promote p, the parent of q. (a) If p had rank difference 2, we are done. (b) Else (p had rank-difference 1), we now have a violation at p.

Deletion

Let us next consider how to perform a deletion in a wavl tree T. Recall that a deletion in a binary search tree operates on a node v with an external-node child u and another child q (which may also be an external node). Note that if q is an internal node, q has rank 1 and v has rank 2. Else (q is an external node), q has rank 0 and v has rank 1.

To perform the deletion, nodes u and v are removed. If v was the root, then q becomes the new root. Otherwise, let p be the former parent of v. Node q now becomes a child of p. Note that p is either null or has rank 2, 3, or 4. Still, it

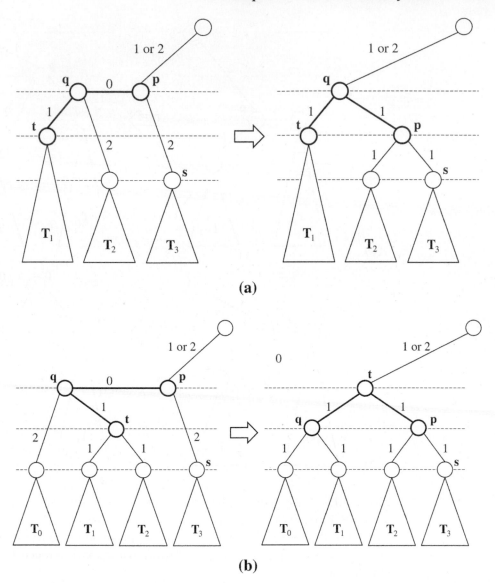

(a)

(b)

Figure 4.14: Case 2 of rebalancing in a wavl tree after an insertion: node q has rank-difference 0 (a violation) and its sibling, s, has rank-difference 2. To resolve the violation for node q, we perform a trinode restructuring operation at t.

cannot be the case that q has rank 0 and p has rank 4, since that would mean v had rank 2 with two rank-0 children, which is a violation of the internal-node property. Thus, after deletion, q has rank-difference 2 or 3 unless it is the root. If q has rank-difference 3, the deletion has caused a violation of the rank-difference property. To remedy this violation we perform a rebalancing operation. Let s be the sibling of q. We consider two cases:

1. If s has rank difference 2 with p, then we reduce the rank of p by 1, which is called a ***demotion***, as shown in Figure 4.15. The demotion of p repairs the violation of the rank-difference property at q. But it may case a violation of the rank-difference property at p. So, in this case, we relabel p as q, and we repeat the rebalancing operation.

2. Else (s has rank difference 1 with p), we consider two subcases:

   (a) Both children of s have rank-difference 2. In this case, we demote both p and s, as shown in Figure 4.16. These demotions repair the rank-difference violation at q (and avoid a violation at s). But they may create a rank-difference violation at p. So, in this case, we relabel p as q, and we repeat the rebalancing operation.

   (b) Node s has at least one child, t, with rank-difference 1. When both children of s have rank-difference 1, we pick t as follows: if s is a left child, then t is the left child of s, else t is the right child of s. In this case, we perform a trinode restructuring operation at t, by calling method, restructure(t), described in Algorithm 4.2. See Figure 4.17, which also shows how to set the ranks of p, s and t. These actions repair the rank-difference violation at q and do not create any new violations.

Thus, we can restore the balance after a deletion in a wavl tree after a sequence of at most $O(\log n)$ demotions followed by a single trinode restructuring operation.

Table 4.18 summarizes the performance of wavl trees, as compared to AVL trees and red-black trees (with black roots).

	AVL trees	**red-black trees**	**wavl trees**
$H(n)$	$1.441 \log{(n+1)}$	$2 \log{(n+1)}$	$2 \log{(n+1)}$
$IH(n)$	$1.441 \log{(n+1)}$	$2 \log{(n+1)}$	$1.441 \log{(n+1)}$
$IR(n)$	1	1	1
$DR(n)$	$O(\log n)$	2	1
search time	$O(\log n)$	$O(\log n)$	$O(\log n)$
insertion time	$O(\log n)$	$O(\log n)$	$O(\log n)$
deletion time	$O(\log n)$	$O(\log n)$	$O(\log n)$

Table 4.18: Comparing the performance of an n-element AVL tree, red-black tree, and wavl tree, respectively. Here, $H(n)$ denotes the worst-case height of the tree, $IH(n)$ denotes the worst-case height of the tree if it is built by doing n insertions (starting from an empty tree) and no deletions, $IR(n)$ denotes the worst-case number of trinode restructuring operations that are needed after an insertion, and $DR(n)$ denotes the worst-case number of trinode restructuring operations that are needed after performing a deletion in order to restore balance. The space usage is $O(n)$ for all of these balanced binary search trees.

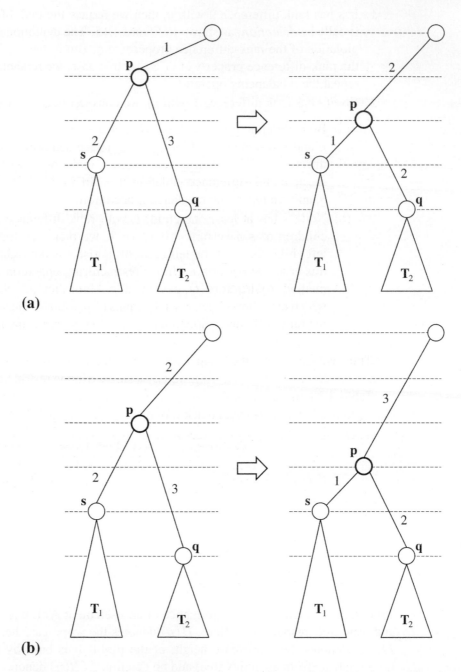

Figure 4.15: Case 1 of rebalancing in a wavl tree after a deletion: node q has rank-difference 3 (a violation) and its sibling, s, has rank-difference 2. To resolve the rank-difference violation for node q, we demote p, the parent of q. (a) If p had rank difference 1, we are done. (b) Else (p had rank-difference 2), we now have a violation at p.

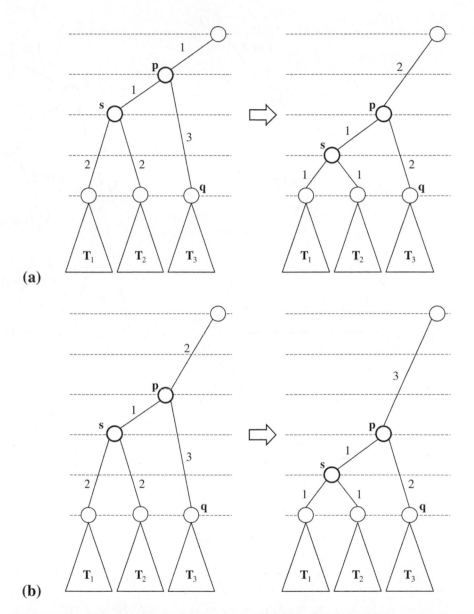

Figure 4.16: Case 2.a of rebalancing in a wavl tree after a deletion: node q has rank-difference 3 (a violation), its sibling, s, has rank-difference 1, and both children of s have rank-difference 2. To resolve the rank-difference violation for node q, we demote both s and p, the parent of q. (a) If p had rank difference 1, we are done. (b) Else (p had rank-difference 2), we now have a violation at p.

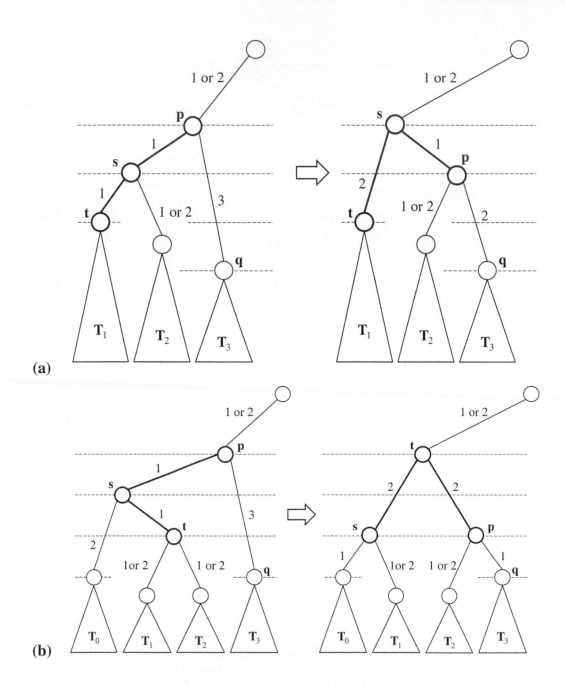

(a)

(b)

Figure 4.17: Case 2.b of rebalancing in a wavl tree after a deletion: node q has rank-difference 3 (a violation), its sibling, s, has rank-difference 1, and a child, t, of s has rank-difference 1. To resolve the violation for node q, we perform a trinode restructuring operation at t.

4.5 Splay Trees

The final balanced binary search tree data structure we discuss in this chapter is the *splay tree*. This structure is conceptually quite different from the previously discussed balanced search trees (AVL, red-black, and wavl trees), for a splay tree does not use any explicit ranks or rules to enforce its balance. Instead, it applies a certain move-to-root operation, called *splaying* after every access, in order to keep the search tree balanced in an amortized sense. The splaying operation is performed at the bottommost node x reached during an insertion, deletion, or even a search. The surprising thing about splaying is that it allows us to guarantee amortized running times for insertions, deletions, and searches that are logarithmic. The structure of a *splay tree* is simply a binary search tree T. In fact, there are no additional height, balance, or color labels that we associate with the nodes of this tree.

Splaying

Given an internal node x of a binary search tree T, we *splay* x by moving x to the root of T through a sequence of restructurings. The particular restructurings we perform are important, for it is not sufficient to move x to the root of T by just any sequence of restructurings. The specific operation we perform to move x up depends upon the relative positions of x, its parent y, and (if it exists) x's grandparent z. There are three cases that we consider.

zig-zig: The node x and its parent y are both left or right children. (See Figure 4.19.) We replace z by x, making y a child of x and z a child of y, while maintaining the inorder relationships of the nodes in T.

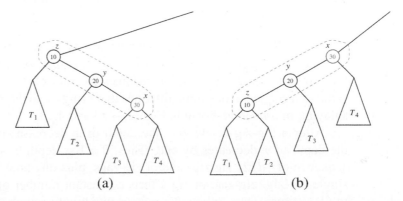

(a)   (b)

Figure 4.19: Zig-zig: (a) before; (b) after. There is another symmetric configuration where x and y are left children.

zig-zag: One of x and y is a left child and the other is a right child. (See Figure 4.20.) In this case, we replace z by x and make x have as its children the nodes y and z, while maintaining the inorder relationships of the nodes in T.

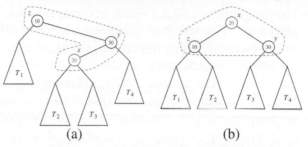

(a)   (b)

Figure 4.20: Zig-zag: (a) before; (b) after. There is another symmetric configuration where x is a right child and y is a left child.

zig: x does not have a grandparent (or we are not considering x's grandparent for some reason). (See Figure 4.21.) In this case, we rotate x over y, making x's children be the node y and one of x's former children w, so as to maintain the relative inorder relationships of the nodes in T.

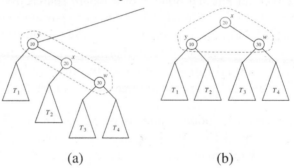

(a)   (b)

Figure 4.21: Zig: (a) before; (b) after. There is another symmetric configuration where x and w are left children.

We perform a zig-zig or a zig-zag when x has a grandparent, and we perform a zig when x has a parent but not a grandparent. A ***splaying*** step consists of repeating these restructurings at x until x becomes the root of T. Note that this is not the same as a sequence of simple rotations that brings x to the root. An example of the splaying of a node is shown in Figures 4.22 and 4.23.

After a zig-zig or zig-zag, the depth of x decreases by two, and after a zig the depth of x decreases by one. Thus, if x has depth d, splaying x consists of a sequence of $\lfloor d/2 \rfloor$ zig-zigs and/or zig-zags, plus one final zig if d is odd. Since a single zig-zig, zig-zag, or zig affects a constant number of nodes, it can be done in $O(1)$ time. Thus, splaying a node x in a binary search tree T takes time $O(d)$, where d is the depth of x in T. In other words, the time for performing a splaying step for a node x is asymptotically the same as the time needed just to reach that node in a top-down search from the root of T.

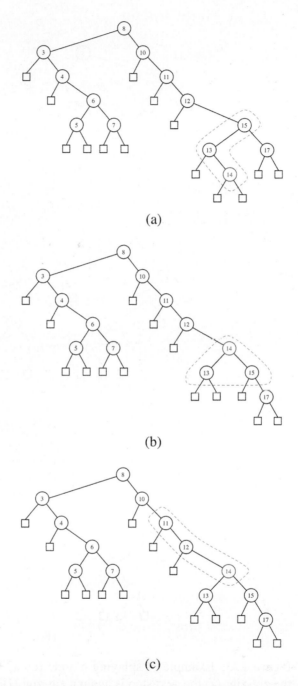

Figure 4.22: Example of splaying a node: (a) splaying the node storing 14 starts with a zig-zag; (b) after the zig-zag; (c) the next step is a zig-zig.

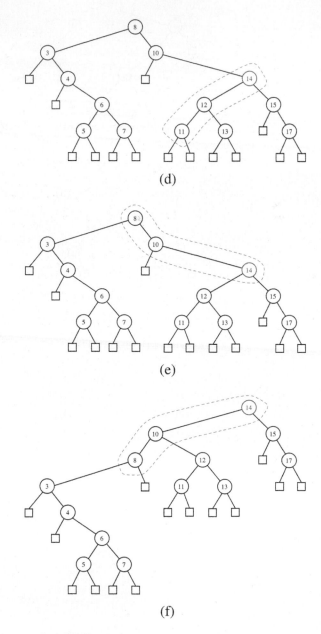

(d)

(e)

(f)

Figure 4.23: Example of splaying a node (continued from Figure 4.22): (d) after the zig-zig; (e) the next step is again a zig-zig; (f) after the zig-zig.

When to Splay

The rules that dictate when splaying is performed are as follows:

- When searching for key k, if k is found at a node x, we splay x, else we splay the parent of the external node at which the search terminates unsuccessfully. For example, the splaying in Figures 4.22 and 4.23 would be performed after searching successfully for key 14 or unsuccessfully for key 14.5.
- When inserting key k, we splay the newly created internal node where k gets inserted. For example, the splaying in Figures 4.22 and 4.23 would be performed if 14 were the newly inserted key. We show a sequence of insertions in a splay tree in Figure 4.24.

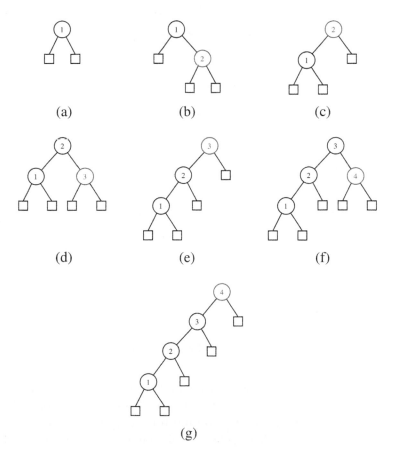

Figure 4.24: A sequence of insertions in a splay tree: (a) initial tree; (b) after inserting 2; (c) after splaying; (d) after inserting 3; (e) after splaying; (f) after inserting 4; (g) after splaying.

Thus, a payment of $O(\log n)$ cyber-dollars is sufficient to maintain the invariant when a new node is inserted.

When deleting a node v from a splay tree with n keys, the ranks of all the ancestors of v are decreased. Thus, the total variation of $r(T)$ caused by the deletion is negative, and we do not need to make any payment to maintain the invariant. Therefore, we may summarize our amortized analysis in the following theorem.

Theorem 4.12: *Consider a sequence of m operations on a splay tree, each a search, insertion, or deletion, starting from an empty splay tree with zero keys. Also, let n_i be the number of keys in the tree after operation i, and n be the total number of insertions. The total running time for performing the sequence of operations is*

$$O\left(m + \sum_{i=1}^{m} \log n_i\right),$$

which is $O(m \log n)$.

In other words, the amortized running time of performing a search, insertion, or deletion in a splay tree is $O(\log n)$, where n is the size of the splay tree at the time. Thus, a splay tree can achieve logarithmic time amortized performance for searching and updating. This amortized performance matches the worst-case performance of AVL trees, red-black trees, and wavl trees, but it does so using a simple binary tree that does not need any extra balance information stored at each of its nodes. In addition, splay trees have a number of other interesting properties that are not shared by these other balanced search trees. We explore one such additional property in the following theorem (which is sometimes called the "Static Optimality" theorem for splay trees).

Theorem 4.13: *Consider a sequence of m operations on a splay tree, each a search, insertion, or deletion, starting from a tree T with no keys. Also, let $f(i)$ denote the number of times the item i is accessed in the splay tree, that is, its **frequency**, and let n be total number of items. Assuming that each item is accessed at least once, then the total running time for performing the sequence of operations is*

$$O\left(m + \sum_{i=1}^{n} f(i) \log\left(m/f(i)\right)\right).$$

We leave the proof of this theorem as an exercise. The remarkable thing about this theorem is that it states that the amortized running time of accessing an item i is $O(\log\left(m/f(i)\right))$. For example, if a sequence of operations accesses some item i as many as $m/4$ times, then the amortized running time of each of these accesses is $O(1)$ when we use a splay tree. Contrast this to the $\Omega(\log n)$ time needed to access this item in an AVL tree, red-black tree, or wavl tree. Thus, an additional nice property of splay trees is that they can "adapt" to the ways in which items are being accessed so as to achieve faster running times for the frequently accessed items.

4.6 Exercises

Reinforcement

R-4.1 Consider the insertion of items with the following keys (in the given order) into an initially empty AVL tree: 30, 40, 24, 58, 48, 26, 11, 13. Draw the final tree that results.

R-4.2 Consider the insertion of items with the following keys (in the given order) into an initially empty wavl tree: 12, 44, 52, 58, 38, 27, 41, 11. Draw the final tree that results.

R-4.3 Consider the insertion of items with the following keys (in the given order) into an initially empty splay tree: 0, 2, 4, 6, 8, 10, 12, 14, 16, 18. Draw the final tree that results.

R-4.4 A certain Professor Amongus claims that the order in which a fixed set of elements is inserted into an AVL tree does not matter—the same tree results every time. Give a small example that proves Professor Amongus wrong.

R-4.5 Professor Amongus claims he has a "patch" to his claim from the previous exercise, namely, that the order in which a fixed set of elements is inserted into a wavl tree does not matter—the same tree results every time. Give a small example that proves that Professor Amongus is still wrong.

R-4.6 What is the minimum number of nodes in an AVL tree of height 7?

R-4.7 What is the minimum number of nodes in a red-black tree of height 8?

R-4.8 What is the minimum number of nodes in a wavl tree of height 7?

R-4.9 What is the minimum number of nodes in a splay tree of height 9?

R-4.10 Is the rotation done in Figure 4.5 a single or a double rotation? What about the rotation in Figure 4.6?

R-4.11 Draw the AVL tree resulting from the insertion of an item with key 52 into the AVL tree of Figure 4.6b.

R-4.12 Draw the AVL tree resulting from the removal of the item with key 62 from the AVL tree of Figure 4.6b.

R-4.13 Draw the wavl tree resulting from the insertion of an item with key 52 into the tree of Figure 4.6b.

R-4.14 Draw the wavl tree resulting from the removal of the item with key 62 from the tree of Figure 4.6b.

R-4.15 Draw an example red-black tree that is not an AVL tree. Your tree should have at least 6 nodes, but no more than 16.

R-4.16 Draw an example of a red-black tree that is not structurally equivalent to a wavl tree.

R-4.17 For each of the following statements about wavl trees, determine whether it is true or false. If you think it is true, provide a justification. If you think it is false, give a counterexample.

      a. A subtree of a wavl tree is itself a wavl tree.

      b. The sibling of an external node is either external or it has rank 1.

R-4.18 What does a splay tree look like if its items are accessed in increasing order by their keys?

R-4.19 How many trinode restructuring operations are needed to perform the zig-zig, zig-zag, and zig updates in splay trees? Use figures to explain your counting.

R-4.20 Describe how to implement the methods, insert(k, v) and remove(k), as well methods, and min() and max(), which return the key-value pair with smallest and largest key, respectively, in $O(\log n)$ time each using a balanced binary search tree.

Creativity

C-4.1 Show that any n-node binary tree can be converted to any other n-node binary tree using $O(n)$ rotations.

    Hint: Show that $O(n)$ rotations suffice to convert any binary tree into a *left chain*, where each internal node has an external right child.

C-4.2 The *Fibonacci sequence* is the sequence of numbers,

$$0, 1, 1, 2, 3, 5, 8, 13, 21, 34, 55, 89, \ldots,$$

defined by the base cases, $F_0 = 0$ and $F_1 = 1$, and the general-case recursive definition, $F_k = F_{k-1} + F_{k-2}$, for $k \geq 2$. Show, by induction, that, for $k \geq 3$,

$$F_k \geq \varphi^{k-2},$$

where $\varphi = (1 + \sqrt{5})/2 \approx 1.618$, which is the well-known *golden ratio* that traces its history to the ancient Greeks.

    Hint: Note that $\varphi^2 = \varphi + 1$; hence, $\varphi^k = \varphi^{k-1} + \varphi^{k-2}$, for $k \geq 3$.

C-4.3 Show, by induction, that the minimum number, n_h, of internal nodes in an AVL tree of height h, as defined in the proof of Theorem 4.1, satisfies the following identity, for $h \geq 1$:

$$n_h = F_{h+2} - 1,$$

where F_k denotes the *Fibonacci number* of order k, as defined in the previous exercise.

C-4.4 Use the facts given in the previous two exercises (and a scientific calculator) to show that an AVL tree storing n items has height at most $1.441 \log (n+1)$, where, as is the custom in this book, we take the base of the "log" function to be 2.

C-4.5 Describe how to perform the operation findAllElements(k), which returns all the items with keys equal to k in a balanced search tree, and show that it runs in time $O(\log n + s)$, where n is the number of elements stored in the tree and s is the number of items returned.

C-4.6 Describe how to perform the operation removeAllElements(k), which removes all elements with keys equal to k, in a balanced search tree T, and show that this method runs in time $O(s \log n)$, where n is the number of elements stored in the tree and s is the number of elements with key k.

C-4.7 Draw an example of an AVL tree such that a single remove operation could require $\Theta(\log n)$ trinode restructurings (or rotations) from a leaf to the root in order to restore the height-balance property. (Use triangles to represent subtrees that are not affected by this operation.)

C-4.8 Show that at most one node in an AVL tree becomes unbalanced after operation removeAboveExternal is performed within the execution of a remove operation.

C-4.9 Show that at most one trinode restructure operation (which corresponds to one single or double rotation) is needed to restore balance after any insertion in an AVL tree.

C-4.10 Let T and U be wavl trees storing n and m items, respectively, such that all the items in T have keys less than the keys of all the items in U. Describe an $O(\log n + \log m)$ time method for *joining* T and U into a single tree that stores all the items in T and U (destroying the old versions of T and U).

C-4.11 Justify Theorem 20.1.

C-4.12 The Boolean used to mark nodes in a red-black tree as being "red" or "black" is not strictly needed when storing a set of distinct keys. Describe a scheme for implementing a red-black tree without adding any extra space to binary search tree nodes in this case.

C-4.13 Let T be a wavl tree storing n items, and let k be the key of an item in T. Show how to construct from T, in $O(\log n)$ time, two wavl trees T' and T'', such that T' contains all the keys of T less than k, and T'' contains all the keys of T greater than k. This operation destroys T.

C-4.14 Show that the nodes of any AVL tree T can be colored "red" and "black" so that T becomes a red-black tree.

C-4.15 A *mergeable heap* supports operations insert(k, x), remove(k), unionWith(h), and min(), where the unionWith(h) operation performs a union of the mergeable heap h with the present one, destroying the old versions of both, and min() returns the element with minimum key. Describe a implementation of a mergeable heap that achieves $O(\log n)$ performance for all its operations. For simplicity, you may assume that all keys in existing mergeable heaps are distinct, although this is not strictly necessary.

C-4.16 Consider a variation of splay trees, called *half-splay trees*, where splaying a node at depth d stops as soon as the node reaches depth $\lfloor d/2 \rfloor$. Perform an amortized analysis of half-splay trees.

C-4.17 The standard splaying step requires two passes, one downward pass to find the node x to splay, followed by an upward pass to splay the node x. Describe a method for splaying and searching for x in one downward pass. Each substep now requires that you consider the next two nodes in the path down to x, with a possible zig substep performed at the end. Describe the details for performing each of the zig-zig, zig-zag, and zig substeps.

C-4.18 Describe a sequence of accesses to an n-node splay tree T, where n is odd, that results in T consisting of a single chain of internal nodes with external node children, such that the internal-node path down T alternates between left children and right children.

C-4.19 Justify Theorem 4.13. A way to establish this justification is to note that we can redefine the "size" of a node as the sum of the access frequencies of its children and show that the entire justification of Theorem 4.11 still goes through.

C-4.20 Suppose we are given a sorted sequence S of items $(x_0, x_1, \ldots, x_{n-1})$ such that each item x_i in S is given a positive integer weight a_i. Let A denote the total weight of all elements in S. Construct an $O(n \log n)$-time algorithm that builds a search tree T for S such that the depth of each item a_i is $O(\log A/a_i)$.

Hint: Find the item x_j with largest j such that $\sum_{i=0}^{j-1} a_i < A/2$. Consider putting this item at the root and recursing on the two subsequences that this induces.

C-4.21 Design a linear-time algorithm for the previous problem.

Applications

A-4.1 Suppose you are working for a large dog adoption organization and are asked to build a website showing all the dogs that your organization currently knows of that are waiting to be placed in loving homes. You are being asked to create a separate web page for each such dog, with these pages ordered by age, so that the web page for a waiting dog, d, has a link to the dog just younger than d and a link to the dog just older than d (with ties broken arbitrarily). Describe an efficient scheme for designing an automated way to add and remove dogs from this website (as they are respectively put up for adoption and placed in loving homes). Sketch your methods for adding and removing dogs, and characterize the running times of these methods in terms of n, the number of dogs currently displayed on the website.

A-4.2 Suppose you are working for a fast-growing startup company, which we will call "FastCo," and it is your job to write a software package that can maintain the set, E, of all the employees working for FastCo. In particular, your software has to maintain, for each employee, x in E, the vital information about x, such as his or her name and address, as well as the number of shares of stock in FastCo that the CEO has promised to x. When an employee first joins FastCo they start out with 0 shares of stock. Every Friday afternoon, the CEO hosts a party for all the FastCo employees and kicks things off by promising every employee that they are getting y more shares of stock, where the value of y tends to be different every Friday. Describe how to implement this software so that it can simultaneously achieve the following goals:

- The time to insert or remove an employee in E should be $O(\log n)$, where n is the number of employees in E.
- Your system must be able to list all the employees in E in alphabetical order in $O(n)$ time, showing, for each x in E, the number of shares of FastCo the CEO has promised to x.
- Your software must be able to process each Friday promise from the CEO in $O(1)$ time, to reflect the fact that everyone working for FastCo on that day is being promised y more shares of stock. (Your system needs to be this fast so that processing this update doesn't make you miss too much of the party.)

A-4.3 Suppose a used car dealer, Jalopy Joe, has asked you to build a website for his car dealership. He wants this website to allow users to be able to search for a set of cars on his lot that are in their price range. That is, viewed abstractly, he would like you to build a system that can maintain an ordered collection, D, of key-value pairs, such that, in addition to the standard insert and removal methods, the implementation for D can support the following operation:

findAllInRange(k_1, k_2): Return all the elements in D with key k such that $k_1 \leq k \leq k_2$.

In this case, of course, the keys are car prices. Describe an algorithm to implement this method in $O(\log n + s)$ time, where n is the number of cars in D and s is the number of cars returned by an instance of this range query.

A-4.4 Suppose you are working for a victim-support group to build a website for maintaining a set, S, containing the names of all the registered sex offenders in a given area. The system should be able to list out the names of the people in S ordered by their Zip codes, and, within each Zip code, ordered alphabetically. It should also be able to list out the names of the people in S just for a given Zip code. The running time for a full listing should be $O(n)$, where n is the number of people in S, and the running time for a listing for a given Zip code should be $O(\log n + s)$, where s is the number of names returned. Insertions and removals from S should run in $O(\log n)$ time. Describe a scheme for achieving these bounds.

A-4.5 Suppose you are hired as a consultant to a professor, Dr. Bob Loblaw, from the Sociology department. He is asking that you build him a software system that can maintain a set, P, of people from a country, Phishnonia, that he is studying. People in Phishnonia are free to come and go as they please, so Dr. Bob Loblaw is asking that your system support fast insertions and deletions. In addition, he is also interested in doing queries that respectively return the mean and median ages of the people in P. His thesis is that if the median age is much smaller than the mean, then the Phishnonia is ripe for revolution, for it implies that there are a disproportionate number of young people. Describe a scheme for maintaining P that can support median and mean age queries, subject to insertions and removals, with each of these operations running in at most $O(\log n)$ time, where n is the number of people in P.

A-4.6 Suppose your neighbor, sweet Mrs. McGregor, has invited you to her house to help her with a computer problem. She has a huge collection of JPEG images of bunny rabbits stored on her computer and a shoebox full of 1 gigabyte USB drives. She is asking that you help her copy her images onto the drives in a way that minimizes the number of drives used. It is easy to determine the size of each image, but finding the optimal way of storing images on the fewest number of drives is an instance of the *bin packing* problem, which is a difficult problem to solve in general. Nevertheless, Mrs. McGregor has suggested that you use the *first fit* heuristic to solve this problem, which she recalls from her days as a young computer scientist. In applying this heuristic here, you would consider the images one at a time and, for each image, I, you would store it on the first USB drive where it would fit, considering the drives in order by their remaining storage capacity. Unfortunately, Mrs. McGregor's way of doing this results in an algorithm with a running time of $O(mn)$, where m is the number of images and $n < m$ is the number of USB drives. Describe how to implement the first fit algorithm here in $O(m \log n)$ time instead.

A-4.7 Suppose there is a computer game, Land-of-Candy (LoC), where a player moves through a three-dimensional world defined by the cells in an $n \times n \times n$ array, C. Each cell, $C[i, j, k]$, specifies the number of points that a player in LoC gets when they are at position (i, j, k). At the start of a game in LoC, there are only $O(n)$ nonzero cells in C; all the other $O(n^3)$ cells in C are equal to 0. During the course of the game, if a player moves to a position (i, j, k) such that $C[i, j, k]$ is nonzero, then all the points in $C[i, j, k]$ are awarded to the player and the value of $C[i, j, k]$ is reduced to 0. Then the game picks another position, (i', j', k'), at random and adds 100 points to $C[i', j', k']$. The problem is that this game was designed for playing on a large computer and now must be adapted to run on a smartphone, which has much less memory. So you cannot afford to use $O(n^3)$ space to represent C, as in the original version. Describe an efficient way to represent C, which uses only $O(n)$ space. Also describe how to lookup the value of any cell, $C[i, j, k]$, and how to add 100 points to any cell, $C[i, j, k]$, efficiently so that looking up the value of any cell, $C[i, j, k]$, can be done in $O(\log n)$ worst-case time or better.

Chapter Notes

AVL trees are due to Adel'son-Vel'skii and Landis [2]. Average-height analyses for binary search trees can be found in the books by Aho, Hopcroft, and Ullman [9]. The handbook by Gonnet and Baeza-Yates [85] contains a number of theoretical and experimental comparisons among search-tree implementations. Red-black trees were defined by Bayer [22], and are discussed further by Guibas and Sedgewick [94]. Weak AVL trees were introduced by Haeupler, Sen, and Tarjan [96]. Splay trees were invented by Sleator and Tarjan [197] (see also [207]). Additional reading can be found in the books by Mehlhorn [157] and Tarjan [207], and the chapter by Mehlhorn and Tsakalidis [160]. Knuth [131] provides excellent additional reading that includes early approaches to balancing trees. Exercise C-4.21 is inspired by a paper by Mehlhorn [156]. We are thankful to Siddhartha Sen and Bob Tarjan for several helpful discussions regarding the topics of this chapter.

Chapter

5

Priority Queues and Heaps

Wall Street during the Bankers Panic of 1907. From the New York Public Library's Digital Gallery, in the Irma and Paul Milstein Division of United States History, Local History and Genealogy. 1907. Public domain image.

Contents

5.1	Priority Queues	157
5.2	PQ-Sort, Selection-Sort, and Insertion-Sort	158
5.3	Heaps	163
5.4	Heap-Sort	174
5.5	Extending Priority Queues	179
5.6	Exercises	182

Instead of having people perform stock transactions by yelling at each other on a trading floor, the NASDAQ uses a massive network of computers to process the buying and selling of stocks of listed companies. At the heart of this network are highly reliable systems known as **matching engines**, which match the trades of buyers and sellers. A simplification of how such a system works is in terms of a **continuous limit order book**, where buyers post bids to buy a number of shares in a given stock at or below a specified price and sellers post offers to sell a number of shares of a given stock at or above a specified price. For example, suppose a company, Example.com, has a continuous limit order book that has the following bids and offers currently open:

STOCK: EXAMPLE.COM

Buy Orders			Sell Orders		
Shares	**Price**	**Time**	**Shares**	**Price**	**Time**
1000	4.05	20 s	500	4.06	13 s
100	4.05	6 s	2000	4.07	46 s
2100	4.03	20 s	400	4.07	22 s
1000	4.02	3 s	3000	4.10	54 s
2500	4.01	81 s	500	4.12	2 s
			3000	4.20	58 s
			800	4.25	33 s
			100	4.50	92 s

Buy and sell orders are organized according to a **price-time priority**, meaning that price has highest priority and if there are multiple orders for the same price, then ones that have been in the order book the longest have higher priority. When a new order is entered into the order book, the matching engine determines if a trade can be immediately executed and if so, then it performs the appropriate matches according to price-time priority. For example, if a new buy order for Example.com came in for 1000 shares at a price of at most 4.10, then it would be matched with the sell order for 500 shares at 4.06 and 500 shares of the sell order for 2000 shares at 4.07. This transaction would reduce the latter sell order to 1500 shares at 4.07. Similarly, if a new sell order came in for 100 shares at 4.00, it would be matched with 100 shares of the buy order for 1000 shares at 4.05. Note in this case that the new sell order would not be matched with the buy order for 100 shares at 4.05, because the one for 1000 shares is older.

Such systems amount to two instances of the data structure we discuss in this chapter—the **priority queue**—one for buy orders and one for sell orders. This data structure performs element removals based on priorities assigned to elements when they are inserted. Dealing with such priorities efficiently requires more effort than is needed for simple stacks and queues, however, and we give an efficient priority queue implementation in this chapter known as the **heap**. In addition, we show how priority queues can be used for sorting purposes, giving rise to sorting algorithms known as **selection-sort**, **insertion-sort**, and **heap-sort**.

5.1 Priority Queues

Applications, such as in a matching engine for performing stock trades, often require ranking objects according to parameters or properties, called "keys," that are assigned for each object in a collection. Formally, we define a *key* to be an object that is assigned to an element as a specific attribute for that element, which can be used to identify, rank, or weight that element. Note that the key is assigned to an element, typically by a user or application.

Total Orders

The concept of a key as an arbitrary object type is therefore quite general. But, in order to deal consistently with such a general definition for keys and still be able to discuss when one key has priority over another, we need a way of robustly defining a rule for comparing keys. That is, a priority queue needs a comparison rule that will never contradict itself. In order for a comparison rule, denoted by $\leq$, to be robust in this way, it must define a *total order* relation, which is to say that the comparison rule is defined for every pair of keys and it must satisfy the following properties:

- **Reflexive property**: $k \leq k$.
- **Antisymmetric property**: if $k_1 \leq k_2$ and $k_2 \leq k_1$, then $k_1 = k_2$.
- **Transitive property**: if $k_1 \leq k_2$ and $k_2 \leq k_3$, then $k_1 \leq k_3$.

Any comparison rule, $\leq$, that satisfies these three properties will never lead to a comparison contradiction. In fact, such a rule defines a linear ordering relationship among a set of keys. Thus, if a (finite) collection of elements has a total order defined for it, then the notion of a *smallest* key, $k_{\min}$, is well-defined. Namely, it is a key in which $k_{\min} \leq k$, for any other key k in our collection.

Methods for Priority Queues

A *priority queue* is a container of elements, each having an associated key that is provided at the time the element is inserted. The name "priority queue" is motivated from the fact that keys determine the "priority" used to pick elements to be removed. The two fundamental methods of a priority queue P are as follows:

insert(k, e): Insert an element e with key k into P.

removeMin(): Return and remove from P an element with the smallest key, that is, an element whose key is less than or equal to that of every other element in P.

5.2   PQ-Sort, Selection-Sort, and Insertion-Sort

In this section, we discuss how to use a priority queue to sort a set of elements.

PQ-Sort: Using a Priority Queue to Sort

In the *sorting* problem, we are given a collection C of n elements that can be compared according to a total order relation, and we want to rearrange them in increasing order (or at least in nondecreasing order if there are ties). The algorithm for sorting C with a priority queue Q is quite simple and consists of the following two phases:

1. In the first phase, we put the elements of C into an initially empty priority queue P by means of a series of n insert operations, one for each element.

2. In the second phase, we extract the elements from P in nondecreasing order by means of a series of n removeMin operations, putting them back into C in order.

We give pseudocode for this algorithm in Algorithm 5.1, assuming that C is an array of n elements. The algorithm works correctly for any priority queue P, no matter how P is implemented. However, the running time of the algorithm is determined by the running times of operations insert and removeMin, which do depend on how P is implemented. Indeed, **PQ-Sort** should be considered more a sorting "scheme" than a sorting "algorithm," because it does not specify how the priority queue P is implemented. The **PQ-Sort** scheme is the paradigm of several popular sorting algorithms, including selection-sort, insertion-sort, and heap-sort.

Algorithm PQ-Sort(C, P):

    Input: An n-element array, C, index from 1 to n, and a priority queue P that
        compares keys, which are elements of C, using a total order relation
    Output: The array C sorted by the total order relation

    for $i \leftarrow 1$ **to** n **do**
        $e \leftarrow C[i]$
        P.insert(e, e)   // the key is the element itself
    for $i \leftarrow 1$ **to** n **do**
        $e \leftarrow P$.removeMin()   // remove a smallest element from P
        $C[i] \leftarrow e$

Algorithm 5.1: Algorithm **PQ-Sort**. Note that the elements of the input array C serve both as keys and elements of the priority queue P.

5.2.1   Selection-Sort

As our first implementation of a priority queue P, consider storing the elements of P and their keys in an unordered list, S. Let us say that S is a general list implemented with either an array or a doubly linked list (the choice of specific implementation will not affect performance, as we will see). Thus, the elements of S are pairs (k, e), where e is an element of P and k is its key. A simple way of implementing method insert(k, e) of P is to add the new pair object $p = (k, e)$ at the end of the list S. This implementation of method insert takes $O(1)$ time, independent of whether the list is implemented using an array or a linked list (see Section 2.2.2). This choice also means that S will be unsorted, for always inserting items at the end of S does not take into account the ordering of the keys. As a consequence, to perform the operation removeMin on P, we must inspect all the elements of list S to find an element $p = (k, e)$ of S with minimum k. Thus, no matter how the list S is implemented, these search methods on P each take $O(n)$ time, where n is the number of elements in P at the time the method is executed. Moreover, each search method runs in $\Omega(n)$ time even in the best case, since each requires searching the entire list to find a minimum element. That is, each such method runs in $\Theta(n)$ time. Thus, by using an unsorted list to implement a priority queue, we achieve constant-time insertion, but the removeMin operation takes linear time.

Analysis of PQ-Sort with an Unsorted List

If we implement the priority queue P with an unsorted list, as described above, then the first phase of PQ-Sort takes $O(n)$ time, for we can insert each element in constant time. In the second phase, assuming we can compare two keys in constant time, the running time of each removeMin operation is proportional to the number of elements currently in P. Thus, the bottleneck computation in this implementation is the repeated "selection" of the minimum element from an unsorted list in phase 2. For this reason, this sorting algorithm is better known as *selection-sort*. (See Figure 5.2 for an illustration of this algorithm and Algorithm 5.3 for a pseudocode description.)

The size of P starts at n and incrementally decreases with each removeMin until it becomes 0. Thus, the first removeMin operation takes time $O(n)$, the second one takes time $O(n - 1)$, and so on, until the last (nth) operation takes time $O(1)$. Therefore, the total time needed for the second phase is proportional to the sum

$$n + (n - 1) + \cdots + 2 + 1 = \sum_{i=1}^{n} i$$

By Theorem 1.13, we have $\sum_{i=1}^{n} i = \frac{n(n+1)}{2}$. Thus, the second phase takes time $O(n^2)$, as does the entire selection-sort algorithm.

		List S	*Priority Queue P*
Input		$(7, 4, 8, 2, 5, 3, 9)$	$()$
Phase 1	(a)	$(4, 8, 2, 5, 3, 9)$	(7)
	(b)	$(8, 2, 5, 3, 9)$	$(7, 4)$
	⋮	⋮	⋮
	(g)	$()$	$(7, 4, 8, 2, 5, 3, 9)$
Phase 2	(a)	(2)	$(7, 4, 8, 5, 3, 9)$
	(b)	$(2, 3)$	$(7, 4, 8, 5, 9)$
	(c)	$(2, 3, 4)$	$(7, 8, 5, 9)$
	(d)	$(2, 3, 4, 5)$	$(7, 8, 9)$
	(e)	$(2, 3, 4, 5, 7)$	$(8, 9)$
	(f)	$(2, 3, 4, 5, 7, 8)$	(9)
	(g)	$(2, 3, 4, 5, 7, 8, 9)$	$()$

Figure 5.2: An illustration of selection-sort run on list $S = (7, 4, 8, 2, 5, 3, 9)$. This algorithm follows the two-phase **PQ-Sort** scheme and uses a priority queue P implemented with an unsorted list. In the first phase, we repeatedly remove the first element from S and insert it into P, as the last element of the list implementing P. Note that at the end of the first phase, P is a copy of what was initially S. In the second phase, we repeatedly perform removeMin operations on P, each of which requires that we scan the entire list implementing P, and we add the elements returned at the end of S.

Algorithm SelectionSort(A):

　　Input: An array A of n comparable elements, indexed from 1 to n
　　Output: An ordering of A so that its elements are in nondecreasing order

　　for $i \leftarrow 1$ **to** $n - 1$ **do**
　　　　// Find the index, s, of the smallest element in $A[i..n]$.
　　　　$s \leftarrow i$
　　　　for $j \leftarrow i + 1$ **to** n **do**
　　　　　　if $A[j] < A[s]$ **then**
　　　　　　　　$s \leftarrow j$
　　　　if $i \neq s$ **then**
　　　　　　// Swap $A[i]$ and $A[s]$
　　　　　　$t \leftarrow A[s]$; $A[s] \leftarrow A[i]$; $A[i] \leftarrow t$
　　return A

Algorithm 5.3: The selection-sort algorithm, described as an ***in-place*** algorithm, where the input list, S, is given as an array, A, and only a constant amount of memory is used in addition to that used by A. In each iteration, $A[1..i - 1]$ is the sorted portion and $A[i..n]$ is the unsorted priority queue.

5.2.2 Insertion-Sort

An alternative implementation of a priority queue P also uses a list S, except this time let us store items ordered by key values. Thus, the first element in S is always an element with smallest key in P. Therefore, we can implement the removeMin method of P simply by removing the first element in S. Assuming that S is implemented with a linked list or an array that supports constant-time front-element removal (see Section 2.2.2), finding and removing the minimum in P in this case takes $O(1)$ time. Thus, using a sorted list allows for simple and fast implementations of priority queue access and removal methods.

This benefit comes at a cost, however, for now the insert method of P requires that we scan through the list S to find the appropriate place to insert the new element and key. Thus, implementing the insert method of P now requires $O(n)$ time, where n is the number of elements in P at the time the method is executed. In summary, when using a sorted list to implement a priority queue, insertion runs in linear time whereas finding and removing the minimum can be done in $O(1)$ time.

Analysis of PQ-Sort with a Sorted List

If we implement the priority queue P using a sorted list, as described above, then we improve the running time of the second phase of the PQ-Sort method to $O(n)$, for each operation removeMin on P now takes $O(1)$ time. Unfortunately, the first phase now becomes the bottleneck for the running time. Indeed, in the worst case, the running time of each insert operation is proportional to the number of elements that are currently in the priority queue, which starts out having size zero and increases in size until it has size n. The first insert operation takes time $O(1)$, the second one takes time $O(2)$, and so on, until the last (nth) operation takes time $O(n)$, in the worst case. Thus, if we use a sorted list to implement P, then the first phase becomes the bottleneck phase. This sorting algorithm is therefore better known as ***insertion-sort***, for the bottleneck in this sorting algorithm involves the repeated "insertion" of a new element at the appropriate position in a sorted list. (See Figure 5.4 for an illustration of this algorithm and Algorithm 5.5 for a pseudocode description.)

Analyzing the running time of insertion-sort, we note that the first phase takes $O(\sum_{i=1}^{n} i)$ time in the worst case. Again, by recalling Theorem 1.13, the first phase runs in $O(n^2)$ time, and hence so does the entire algorithm. Therefore, both selection-sort and insertion-sort both have a running time that is $O(n^2)$.

Still, although selection-sort and insertion-sort are similar, they actually have some interesting differences. For instance, note that selection-sort always takes $\Omega(n^2)$ time, for selecting the minimum in each step of the second phase requires scanning the entire priority-queue sequence. The running time of insertion-sort, on the other hand, varies depending on the input sequence. For example, if the input sequence S is in reverse order, then insertion-sort runs in $O(n)$ time.

		list S	*priority queue P*
Input		$(7, 4, 8, 2, 5, 3, 9)$	$()$
Phase 1	(a)	$(4, 8, 2, 5, 3, 9)$	(7)
	(b)	$(8, 2, 5, 3, 9)$	$(4, 7)$
	(c)	$(2, 5, 3, 9)$	$(4, 7, 8)$
	(d)	$(5, 3, 9)$	$(2, 4, 7, 8)$
	(e)	$(3, 9)$	$(2, 4, 5, 7, 8)$
	(f)	(9)	$(2, 3, 4, 5, 7, 8)$
	(g)	$()$	$(2, 3, 4, 5, 7, 8, 9)$
Phase 2	(a)	(2)	$(3, 4, 5, 7, 8, 9)$
	(b)	$(2, 3)$	$(4, 5, 7, 8, 9)$
	⋮	⋮	⋮
	(g)	$(2, 3, 4, 5, 7, 8, 9)$	$()$

Figure 5.4: Schematic visualization of the execution of insertion-sort on list $S = (7, 4, 8, 2, 5, 3, 9)$. This algorithm follows the two-phase PQ-Sort scheme and uses a priority queue P, implemented by means of a sorted list. In the first phase, we repeatedly remove the first element of S and insert it into P, by scanning the list implementing P, until we find the correct position for the element. In the second phase, we repeatedly perform removeMin operations on P, each of which returns the first element of the list implementing P, and we add the element at the end of S.

Algorithm InsertionSort(A):

    Input: An array, A, of n comparable elements, indexed from 1 to n

    Output: An ordering of A so that its elements are in nondecreasing order.

    for $i \leftarrow 2$ **to** n **do**

        $x \leftarrow A[i]$

        // Put x in the right place in $A[1..i]$, moving larger elements up as needed.

        $j \leftarrow i$

        while $j > 1$ **and** $x < A[j-1]$ **do**

            $A[j] \leftarrow A[j-1]$ // move $A[j-1]$ up one cell

            $j \leftarrow j - 1$

        $A[j] \leftarrow x$

    return A

Algorithm 5.5: The insertion-sort algorithm, described as an ***in-place*** algorithm, where the input list, S, is given as an array, A, and only a constant amount of memory is used in addition to that used by A. In each iteration, $A[1..i-1]$ is the sorted priority queue and $A[i..n]$ is the unsorted input list.

5.3 Heaps

An implementation of a priority queue that is efficient for both the insert(k, e) and removeMin() operations is to use a ***heap***. This data structure allows us to perform both insertions and removals in logarithmic time. The fundamental way the heap achieves this improvement is to abandon the idea of storing elements and keys in a list and store elements and keys in a binary tree instead.

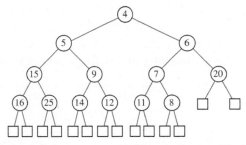

Figure 5.6: Example of a heap storing 13 integer keys. The last node is the one storing key 8, and external nodes are empty.

A heap (see Figure 5.6) is a binary tree T that stores a collection of keys at its internal nodes and that satisfies two additional properties: a relational property defined in terms of the way keys are stored in T and a structural property defined in terms of T itself. Also, in our definition of a heap, we assume the external nodes of T do not store keys or elements and serve only as "place-holders." The relational property for T is the following:

Heap-Order Property: In a heap T, for every node v other than the root, the key stored at v is greater than or equal to the key stored at v's parent.

As a consequence of this property, the keys encountered on a path from the root to an external node of T are in nondecreasing order. Also, a minimum key is always stored at the root of T. For the sake of efficiency, we want the heap T to have as small a height as possible. We enforce this desire by insisting that the heap T satisfy an additional structural property:

Complete Binary Tree: A binary tree T with height h is ***complete*** if the levels $0, 1, 2, \ldots, h - 1$ have the maximum number of nodes possible (that is, level i has 2^i nodes, for $0 \le i \le h - 1$) and in level $h - 1$ all the internal nodes are to the left of the external nodes.

By saying that all the internal nodes on level $h - 1$ are "to the left" of the external nodes, we mean that all the internal nodes on this level will be visited before any external nodes on this level in an inorder traversal. (See Figure 5.6.) By insisting that a heap T be complete, we identify another important node in a heap T, other than the root—namely, the ***last node*** of T, which we define to be the right-most, deepest internal node of T. (See Figure 5.6.)

Implementing a Priority Queue with a Heap

Our heap-based priority queue consists of the following (see Figure 5.7):

- *heap*: A complete binary tree T whose elements are stored at internal nodes and have keys satisfying the heap-order property. For each internal node v of T, we denote the key of the element stored at v as $k(v)$.
- *last*: A reference to the last node of T.
- *comp*: A comparison rule that defines the total order relation among the keys. Without loss of generality, we assume that *comp* maintains the minimum element at the root. If instead we wish the maximum element to be at the root, then we can redefine our comparison rule accordingly.

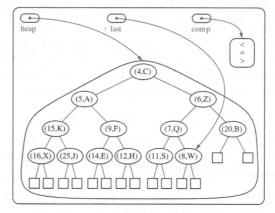

Figure 5.7: A heap-based priority queue storing integer keys and text elements.

The efficiency of this implementation is based on the following fact.

Theorem 5.1: *A heap T storing n keys has height $h = \lceil \log(n+1) \rceil$.*

Proof: Since T is complete, the number of internal nodes of T is at least

$$1 + 2 + 4 + \cdots + 2^{h-2} + 1 = 2^{h-1} - 1 + 1 = 2^{h-1}.$$

This lower bound is achieved when there is only one internal node on level $h - 1$. Alternately, we observe that the number of internal nodes of T is at most

$$1 + 2 + 4 + \cdots + 2^{h-1} = 2^h - 1.$$

This upper bound is achieved when all the 2^{h-1} nodes on level $h - 1$ are internal. Since the number of internal nodes is equal to the number n of keys, $2^{h-1} \leq n$ and $n \leq 2^h - 1$. Thus, by taking logarithms of both sides of these two inequalities, we see that $h \leq \log n + 1$ and $\log(n+1) \leq h$, which implies that $h = \lceil \log(n+1) \rceil$. ■

Thus, if we can perform update operations on a heap in time proportional to its height, then those operations will run in logarithmic time.

5.3.1   An Array-Based Structure for Binary Trees

A simple structure for representing a binary tree T, especially when it is complete, is based on a straightforward way of numbering the nodes of T.

Level Numbering the Nodes of a Binary Tree

For every node v of T, let $p(v)$ be the integer defined as follows:

- If v is the root of T, then $p(v) = 1$.
- If v is the left child of node u, then $p(v) = 2p(u)$.
- If v is the right child of node u, then $p(v) = 2p(u) + 1$.

The numbering function p is known as a **_level numbering_** of the nodes in a binary tree T, because it numbers the nodes on each level of T in increasing order from left to right, although it may skip some numbers. (See Figure 5.8.)

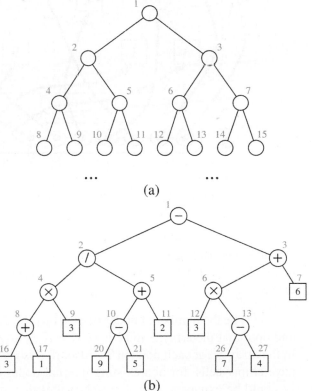

Figure 5.8: Example binary tree level numberings. (a) a complete binary tree; (b) a binary expression tree that is not complete.

Using Level Numbers as Array Indices

The level numbering function p suggests a representation of a binary tree T using an array, S, such that node v of T is associated with the element of S at index $p(v)$. (See Figure 5.9.) Alternatively, we could realize the S using an extendable array. (See Section 1.4.2.)

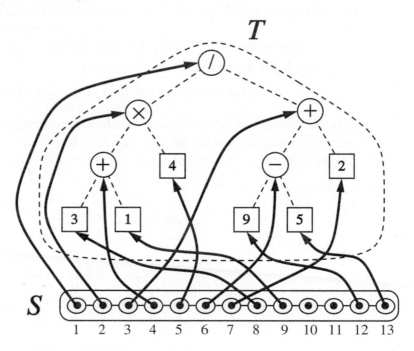

Figure 5.9: Representing a binary tree T using an array S.

Such an implementation is simple and fast, for we can use it to easily perform the methods root, parent, leftChild, rightChild, sibling, isInternal, isExternal, and isRoot by using simple arithmetic operations on the numbers $p(v)$. (See Exercise R-5.3.)

Let n be the number of nodes of T, let p_M be the maximum value of $p(v)$ for T, and note that the array S must have size $N \geq p_M$, since we need to store a value in the array S for each node in T. Also, if T is not complete, then the array S may have empty cells, for non-existing internal nodes of T. In fact, in the worst case, N could be exponential in n, which makes this implementation a poor choice for general binary trees. Nevertheless, if T is a heap, and, hence, T is complete and all its external nodes are empty, then we can save additional space by restricting S to exclude external nodes whose index is past that of the last internal node in the tree. Thus, if T is a heap, then we can set N to be $O(n)$.

An Array-Based Representation of a Heap

When a heap, T, is implemented with an array, as described above, the index of the last node w is always equal to n, and the first empty external node z has index equal to $n + 1$. (See Figure 5.10.) Note that this index for z is valid even for the following cases:

- If the current last node w is the right-most node on its level, then z is the left-most node of the bottommost level (see Figure 5.10b).

- If T has no internal nodes (that is, the priority queue is empty and the last node in T is not defined), then z is the root of T.

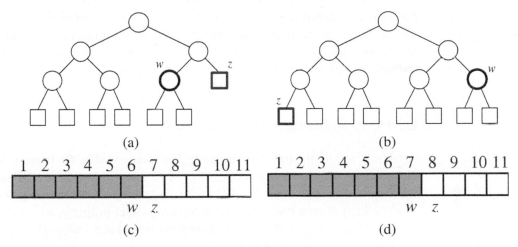

(a)

(b)

(c)

(d)

Figure 5.10: Last node w and first external node z in a heap: (a) regular case where z is right of w; (b) case where z is left-most on bottom level. The array representation of (a) is shown in (c); the representation of (b) is shown in (d).

The simplifications that come from representing the heap T with an array aid in our methods for implementing a priority queue. For example, adding a new node in a heap implemented with an array can be done in $O(1)$ time (assuming no array expansion is necessary), for it simply involves assigning an element to a single cell in the array. Likewise, removing a node in a heap implemented with an array just involves clearing out a cell in the array, which also can be done in $O(1)$ time. In addition, finding the element with smallest key can easily be performed in $O(1)$, just by accessing the item stored at the root of the heap (which is at index 1 in the array). Moreover, because T is a complete binary tree, the array associated with heap T in an array-based implementation of a binary tree has $2n + 1$ elements, $n + 1$ of which are place-holder external nodes by our convention. Indeed, since all the external nodes have indices higher than any internal node, we don't even have to explicitly store all the external nodes. (See Figure 5.10.)

5.3.2   Insertion in a Heap

Let us consider how to perform the insert method for a priority queue implemented with a heap, T. In order to store a new key-element pair (k, e) into T, we need to add a new internal node to T. In order to keep T as a complete binary tree, we must add this new node so that it becomes the new last node of T. That is, we must identify the correct external node z where we can perform an expandExternal(z) operation, which replaces z with an internal node (with empty external-node children), and then insert the new element at z. (See Figure 5.11a–b.) Node z is called the ***insertion position***.

Usually, node z is the external node immediately to the right of the last node w. (See Figure 5.10a.) In any case, by our array implementation of T, the insertion position z is stored at index $n + 1$, where n is the current size of the heap. Thus, we can identify the node z in constant time in the array implementing T. After then performing expandExternal(z), node z becomes the last node, and we store the new key-element pair (k, e) in it, so that $k(z) = k$.

Up-Heap Bubbling after an Insertion

After this action, the tree T is complete, but it may violate the heap-order property. Hence, unless node z is the root of T (that is, the priority queue was empty before the insertion), we compare key $k(z)$ with the key $k(u)$ stored at the parent u of z. If $k(u) > k(z)$, then we need to restore the heap-order property, which can be locally achieved by swapping the key-element pairs stored at z and u. (See Figure 5.11c–d.) This swap causes the new key-element pair (k, e) to move up one level. Again, the heap-order property may be violated, and we continue swapping going up in T until no violation of heap-order property occurs. (See Figure 5.11e–h.)

The upward movement by means of swaps is conventionally called ***up-heap bubbling***. A swap either resolves the violation of the heap-order property or propagates it one level up in the heap. In the worst case, up-heap bubbling causes the new key-element pair to move all the way up to the root of heap T. (See Figure 5.11.) Thus, in the worst case, the running time of method insert is proportional to the height of T, that is, it is $O(\log n)$ because T is complete.

If T is implemented with an array, then we can find the new last node z immediately in $O(1)$ time. For example, we could extend an array-based implementation of a binary tree, so as to add a method that returns the node with index $n + 1$, that is, with level number $n + 1$, as defined in Section 5.3.1. Alternately, we could even define an add method, which adds a new element at the first external node z, at rank $n + 1$ in the array. If, on the other hand, the heap T is implemented with a linked structure, then finding the insertion position z is a little more involved. (See Exercise C-5.4.)

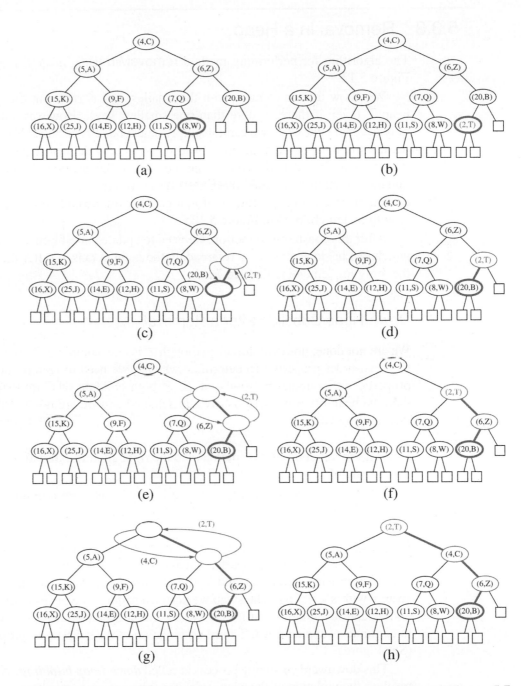

Figure 5.11: Insertion of a new element with key 2 into the heap of Figure 5.7: (a) initial heap; (b) adding a new last node to the right of the old last node; (c)–(d) swap to locally restore the partial order property; (e)–(f) another swap; (g)–(h) final swap.

5.3.3   Removal in a Heap

The algorithm for performing method removeMin using heap T is illustrated in Figure 5.12.

We know that an element with the smallest key is stored at the root r of the heap T (even if there is more than one smallest key). However, unless r is the only internal node of T, we cannot simply delete node r, because this action would disrupt the binary tree structure. Instead, we access the last node w of T, copy its key-element pair to the root r, and then delete the last node by performing the update operation removeAboveExternal(u), where $u = T$.rightChild(w). This operation removes the parent, w, of u, together with the node u itself, and replaces w with its left child. (See Figure 5.12a–b.)

After this constant-time action, we need to update our reference to the last node, which can be done simply by referencing the node at rank n (after the removal) in the array implementing the tree T.

Down-Heap Bubbling after a Removal

We are not done, however, for, even though T is now complete, T may now violate the heap-order property. To determine whether we need to restore the heap-order property, we examine the root r of T. If both children of r are external nodes, then the heap-order property is trivially satisfied and we are done. Otherwise, we distinguish two cases:

- If the left child of r is internal and the right child is external, let s be the left child of r.
- Otherwise (both children of r are internal), let s be a child of r with the smallest key.

If the key $k(r)$ stored at r is greater than the key $k(s)$ stored at s, then we need to restore the heap-order property, which can be locally achieved by swapping the key-element pairs stored at r and s. (See Figure 5.12c–d.) Note that we shouldn't swap r with s's sibling. The swap we perform restores the heap-order property for node r and its children, but it may violate this property at s; hence, we may have to continue swapping down T until no violation of the heap-order property occurs. (See Figure 5.12e–h.)

This downward swapping process is called ***down-heap bubbling***. A swap either resolves the violation of the heap-order property or propagates it one level down in the heap. In the worst case, a key-element pair moves all the way down to the level immediately above the bottom level. (See Figure 5.12.) Thus, the running time of method removeMin is, in the worst case, proportional to the height of heap T, that is, it is $O(\log n)$.

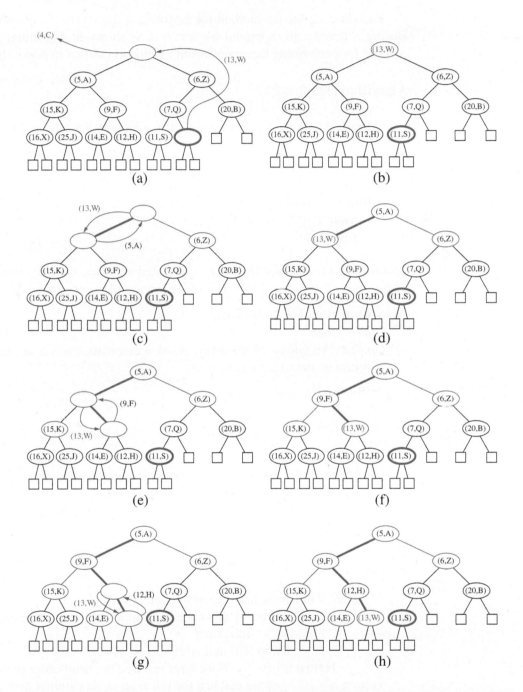

Figure 5.12: Removal of the element with the smallest key from a heap: (a)–(b) deletion of the last node, whose key-element pair gets stored into the root; (c)–(d) swap to locally restore the heap-order property; (e)–(f) another swap; (g)–(h) final swap.

Pseudo-code for the method for performing the insert(k, e) method in a heap storing n items with an extendable array, A, is shown in Algorithm 5.13, and the method for performing the removeMin() method is shown in Algorithm 5.13.

Algorithm HeapInsert(k, e):

> *Input:* A key-element pair
>
> *Output:* An update of the array, A, of n elements, for a heap, to add (k, e)
>
> $n \leftarrow n + 1$
> $A[n] \leftarrow (k, e)$
> $i \leftarrow n$
> **while** $i > 1$ **and** $A[\lfloor i/2 \rfloor] > A[i]$ **do**
>> Swap $A[\lfloor i/2 \rfloor]$ and $A[i]$
>> $i \leftarrow \lfloor i/2 \rfloor$

Algorithm 5.13: Insertion in a heap represented with an array. We identify the parent of i as the cell at index $\lfloor i/2 \rfloor$. The while-loop implements up-heap bubbling.

Algorithm HeapRemoveMin():

> *Input:* None
>
> *Output:* An update of the array, A, of n elements, for a heap, to remove and
>>   return an item with smallest key
>
> $temp \leftarrow A[1]$
> $A[1] \leftarrow A[n]$
> $n \leftarrow n - 1$
> $i \leftarrow 1$
> **while** $i < n$ **do**
>> **if** $2i + 1 \leq n$ **then**   // this node has two internal children
>>> **if** $A[i] \leq A[2i]$ **and** $A[i] \leq A[2i + 1]$ **then**
>>>> **return** $temp$ // we have restored the heap-order property
>>>
>>> **else**
>>>> Let j be the index of the smaller of $A[2i]$ and $A[2i + 1]$
>>>> Swap $A[i]$ and $A[j]$
>>>> $i \leftarrow j$
>>
>> **else**   // this node has zero or one internal child
>>> **if** $2i \leq n$ **then**   // this node has one internal child (the last node)
>>>> **if** $A[i] > A[2i]$ **then**
>>>>> Swap $A[i]$ and $A[2i]$
>>>
>>> **return** $temp$ // we have restored the heap-order property
>
> **return** $temp$ // we reached the last node or an external node

Algorithm 5.13: Removing the minimum item in a heap represented with an array. We identify the two children of i as the cells at indices $2i$ and $2i+1$. The while-loop implements down-heap bubbling.

Performance

Table 5.14 shows the running time of the priority queue methods for the heap implementation of a priority queue, assuming that the heap T is itself implemented with an array.

Operation	Time
insert	$O(\log n)$
removeMin	$O(\log n)$

Table 5.14: Performance of a priority queue that is implemented with a heap, which is in turn implemented with an array-based structure for a binary tree. We denote with n the number of elements in the priority queue at the time a method is executed. The space requirement is $O(N)$, where $N \geq n$ is the size of the array used to implement the heap.

In short, each of the fundamental priority queue methods can be performed in $O(\log n)$ time, where n is the number of elements at the time the method is executed. We can also implement a method for simply returning, but not removing, the minimum item, in $O(1)$ time (just by returning the item stored at the root of the heap).

The above analysis of the running time of the methods of a priority queue implemented with a heap is based on the following facts:

- The height of heap T is $O(\log n)$, since T is complete.

- In the worst case, up-heap and down-heap bubbling take time proportional to the height of T.

- Finding the insertion position in the execution of insert and updating the last node position in the execution of removeMin takes constant time.

- The heap T has n internal nodes, each storing a reference to a key and a reference to an element.

We conclude that the heap data structure is an efficient implementation of a priority queue. The heap implementation achieves fast running times for both insertion and removal, unlike the list-based priority queue implementations. Indeed, an important consequence of the efficiency of the heap-based implementation is that it can speed up priority-queue sorting to be much faster than the list-based insertion-sort and selection-sort algorithms.

5.4　Heap-Sort

Let us consider again the PQ-Sort sorting scheme from Section 5.2, which uses a priority queue P to sort a list S. If we implement the priority queue P with a heap, then, during the first phase, each of the n insert operations takes time $O(\log k)$, where k is the number of elements in the heap at the time. Likewise, during the second phase, each of the n removeMin operations also runs in time $O(\log k)$, where k is the number of elements in the heap at the time. Since we always have $k \leq n$, each such operation runs in $O(\log n)$ time in the worst case. Thus, each phase takes $O(n \log n)$ time, so the entire priority-queue sorting algorithm runs in $O(n \log n)$ time when we use a heap to implement the priority queue. This sorting algorithm is better known as **heap-sort**, and its performance is summarized in the following theorem.

Theorem 5.2: *The heap-sort algorithm sorts a list S of n comparable elements in $O(n \log n)$ time.*

Recalling Table 1.7, we stress that the $O(n \log n)$ running time of heap-sort is much better than the $O(n^2)$ running time for selection-sort and insertion-sort. In addition, there are several modifications we can make to the heap-sort algorithm to improve its performance in practice.

If the list S to be sorted is implemented with an array, we can speed up heap-sort and reduce its space requirement by a constant factor using a portion of the list S itself to store the heap, thus avoiding the use of an external heap data structure. This is accomplished by modifying the algorithm as follows:

1. We use a maximum-based comparison rule, which corresponds to a heap where the largest element is at the top. At any time during the execution of the algorithm, we use the left portion of S, up to a certain rank $i - 1$, to store the elements in the heap, and the right portion of S, from rank i to $n - 1$ to store the elements in the list. Thus, the first i elements of S (at ranks $0, \ldots, i-1$) provide the array representation of the heap (with modified level numbers starting at 0 instead of 1), that is, the element at rank k is greater than or equal to its "children" at ranks $2k + 1$ and $2k + 2$.

2. In the first phase of the algorithm, we start with an empty heap and move the boundary between the heap and the list from left to right, one step at a time. In step i ($i = 1, \ldots, n$), we expand the heap by adding the element at rank $i - 1$.

3. In the second phase of the algorithm, we start with an empty list and move the boundary between the heap and the list from right to left, one step at a time. At step i ($i = 1, \ldots, n$), we remove a maximum element from the heap and store it at rank $n - i$.

The above variation of heap-sort is ***in-place***, since we use only a constant amount of space in addition to the list itself. Instead of transferring elements out of the list and then back in, we simply rearrange them. We illustrate in-place heap-sort in Figure 5.15. In general, we say that a sorting algorithm is in-place if it uses only a constant amount of memory in addition to the memory needed for the objects being sorted themselves. The advantage of an in-place sorting algorithm in practice is that such an algorithm can make the most efficient use of the main memory of the computer it is running on.

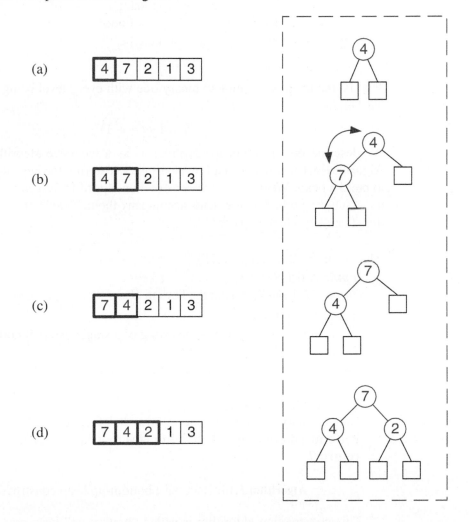

Figure 5.15: First three steps of Phase 1 of in-place heap-sort. The heap portion of the array is highlighted with thick lines. Next to the array, we draw a binary tree view of the heap, even though this tree is not actually constructed by the in-place algorithm.

Bottom-Up Heap Construction

The analysis of the heap-sort algorithm shows that we can construct a heap storing n key-element pairs in $O(n \log n)$ time, by means of n successive insert operations, and then use that heap to extract the elements in order. However, if all the keys to be stored in the heap are given in advance, there is an alternative ***bottom-up*** construction method that runs in $O(n)$ time.

We describe this method here, observing that it could be used in the heap-sort algorithm instead of filling up the heap using a series of n insert operations. For simplicity of exposition, we describe this bottom-up heap construction assuming the number n of keys is an integer of the type

$$n = 2^h - 1.$$

That is, the heap is a complete binary tree with every level being full, so the heap has height

$$h = \log(n + 1).$$

We describe bottom-up heap construction as a recursive algorithm, as shown in Algorithm 5.16, which we call by passing a list storing the keys for which we wish to build a heap. We describe the construction algorithm as acting on keys, with the understanding that their elements accompany them. That is, the items stored in the tree T are key-element pairs.

Algorithm BottomUpHeap(S):

    Input: A list S storing $n = 2^h - 1$ keys

    Output: A heap T storing the keys in S.

    if S is empty **then**

        return an empty heap (consisting of a single external node).

    Remove the first key, k, from S.

    Split S into two lists, S_1 and S_2, each of size $(n - 1)/2$.

    $T_1 \leftarrow$ BottomUpHeap(S_1)

    $T_2 \leftarrow$ BottomUpHeap(S_2)

    Create binary tree T with root r storing k, left subtree T_1, and right subtree T_2.

    Perform a down-heap bubbling from the root r of T, if necessary.

    return T

Algorithm 5.16: Recursive bottom-up heap construction.

This construction algorithm is called "bottom-up" heap construction because of the way each recursive call returns a subtree that is a heap for the elements it stores. That is, the "heapification" of T begins at its external nodes and proceeds up the tree as each recursive call returns. For this reason, some authors refer to the bottom-up heap construction as the "heapify" operation.

We illustrate bottom-up heap construction in Figure 5.17 for $h = 4$.

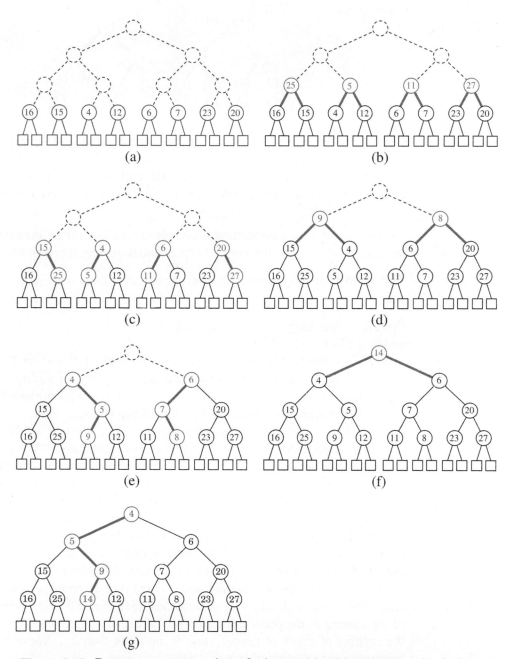

Figure 5.17: Bottom-up construction of a heap with 15 keys: (a) we begin by constructing 1-key heaps on the bottom level; (b)–(c) we combine these heaps into 3-key heaps and then (d)–(e) 7-key heaps, until (f)–(g) we create the final heap. The paths of the down-heap bubblings are highlighted with thick lines.

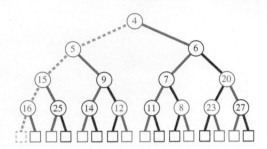

Figure 5.18: Visual justification of the linear running time of bottom-up heap construction, where the paths associated with the internal nodes have been highlighted alternating gray and black. For example, the path associated with the root consists of the internal nodes storing keys 4, 6, 7, and 11, plus an external node.

Bottom-up heap construction is asymptotically faster than incrementally inserting n keys into an initially empty heap, as the following theorem shows.

Theorem 5.3: *The bottom-up construction of a heap with n items takes $O(n)$ time.*

Proof: We analyze bottom-up heap construction using a "visual" approach, which is illustrated in Figure 5.18.

Let T be the final heap, let v be an internal node of T, and let $T(v)$ denote the subtree of T rooted at v. In the worst case, the time for forming $T(v)$ from the two recursively formed subtrees rooted at v's children is proportional to the height of $T(v)$. The worst case occurs when down-heap bubbling from v traverses a path from v all the way to a bottommost external node of $T(v)$. Consider now the path $p(v)$ of T from node v to its inorder successor external node, that is, the path that starts at v, goes to the right child of v, and then goes down leftward until it reaches an external node. We say that path $p(v)$ is **associated with** node v. Note that $p(v)$ is not necessarily the path followed by down-heap bubbling when forming $T(v)$. Clearly, the length (number of edges) of $p(v)$ is equal to the height of $T(v)$. Hence, forming $T(v)$ takes time proportional to the length of $p(v)$, in the worst case. Thus, the total running time of bottom-up heap construction is proportional to the sum of the lengths of the paths associated with the internal nodes of T.

Note that for any two internal nodes u and v of T, paths $p(u)$ and $p(v)$ do not share edges, although they may share nodes. (See Figure 5.18.) Therefore, the sum of the lengths of the paths associated with the internal nodes of T is no more than the number of edges of heap T, that is, no more than $2n$. We conclude that the bottom-up construction of heap T takes $O(n)$ time.   ∎

To summarize, Theorem 5.3 says that the first phase of heap-sort can be implemented to run in $O(n)$ time. Unfortunately, the running time of the second phase of heap-sort is $\Omega(n \log n)$ in the worst case. We will not justify this lower bound until Chapter 8, however.

5.5 Extending Priority Queues

We can additionally augment the two fundamental methods for a priority queue with supporting methods, such as size(), isEmpty(), and the following:

minElement(): Return (but do not remove) an element of P with the smallest key.

minKey(): Return (but do not remove) the smallest key in P.

Both of these methods return error conditions if the priority queue is empty. If we implement a priority queue using an ordered list or a heap, then we can perform these operations in $O(1)$ time each.

Comparators

In addition, we can augment a priority queue to support parameterizing the data structure in the way it does comparisons, by using a concept known a ***comparator***. This pattern specifies the way in which we compare keys, and is designed to support the most general and reusable form of a priority queue. For such a design, we should not rely on the keys to provide their comparison rules, for such rules might not be what a user desires (particularly for multidimensional data). Instead, we use special ***comparator*** objects that are external to the keys to supply the comparison rules. A comparator is an object that compares two keys. We assume that a priority queue P is given a comparator when P is constructed, and we might also imagine the ability of a priority queue to be given a new comparator if its old one ever becomes "out of date." When P needs to compare two keys, it uses the comparator it was given to perform the comparison. Thus, a programmer can write a general priority queue implementation that can work correctly in a wide variety of contexts. Formally, a comparator object provides the following methods, each of which takes two keys and compares them (or reports an error if the keys are incomparable). The methods of a comparator include the following:

isLess(a, b): True if and only if a is less than b.

isLessOrEqualTo(a, b): True if and only if a is less than or equal to b.

isEqualTo(a, b): True if and only if a and b are equal.

isGreater(a, b): True if and only if a is greater than b.

isGreaterOrEqualTo(a, b): True if and only if a is greater than or equal to b.

isComparable(a): True if and only if a can be compared.

Locators

We conclude this section by discussing a concept that allows us to extend a priority queue to have additional functionality, which will be useful, for example, in some of the graph algorithms discussed later in this book. As we saw with lists and binary trees, abstracting positional information in a container is a very powerful tool.

There are applications where we need to keep track of elements as they are being moved around inside a container, however. A concept that fulfills this need is the ***locator***. A locator is a mechanism for maintaining the association between an element and its current position in a container. A locator "sticks" with a specific element, even if the element changes its position in the container.

A locator is like a coat check; we can give our coat to a coat-room attendant, and we receive back a coat check, which is a "locator" for our coat. The position of our coat relative to the other coats can change, as other coats are added and removed, but our coat check can always be used to retrieve our coat. The important thing to remember about a locator is that it follows its item, even if it changes position.

Like a coat check, we can now imagine getting something back when we insert an element in a container—we can get back a locator for that element. This locator in turn can be used later to refer to the element within the container, for example, to specify that this element should be removed from the container. Viewed abstractly, a locator ℓ supports the following methods:

element(): Return the element of the item associated with ℓ.

key(): Return the key of the item associated with ℓ.

For the sake of concreteness, we next discuss how we can use locators to extend the repertoire of operations of a priority queue to include methods that return locators and take locators as arguments.

Using Locators with a Priority Queue

We can use locators in a natural way in the context of a priority queue. A locator in such a scenario stays attached to an item inserted in the priority queue, and allows us to access the item in a generic manner, independent of the specific implementation of the priority queue. This ability is important for a priority queue implementation, for there are no positions, *per se*, in a priority queue, since we do not refer to items by any notions of "index" or "node," and instead are based on the use of keys.

Locator-Based Priority Queue Methods

By using locators, we can extend a priority queue with the following methods that access and modify a priority queue P:

min(): Return the locator to an item of P with smallest key.

insert(k, e): Insert a new item with element e and key k into P and return a locator to the item.

remove(ℓ): Remove from P the item with locator ℓ.

replaceElement(ℓ, e): Replace with e and return the element of the item of P with locator ℓ.

replaceKey(ℓ, k): Replace with k and return the key of the item of P with locator ℓ.

Locator-based access runs in $O(1)$ time, while a key-based access, which must look for the element via a search in an entire list or heap, runs in $O(n)$ time in the worst case. In addition, some applications call for us to restrict the operation replaceKey so that it only increases or decreases the key. This restriction can be done by defining new methods increaseKey or decreaseKey, for example, which would take a locator as an argument, which can be implemented to run in amortized $O(1)$ time using more sophisticated heap structures, such as Fibonacci heaps, which we don't discuss here. Further applications of such priority queue methods are given in Chapter 14.

Comparison of Different Priority Queue Implementations

In Table 5.19, we compare running times of the priority queue methods defined in this section for the unsorted-list, sorted-list, and heap implementations.

Method	Unsorted List	Sorted List	Heap
key, replaceElement	$O(1)$	$O(1)$	$O(1)$
minElement, min, minKey	$O(n)$	$O(1)$	$O(1)$
insert	$O(1)$	$O(n)$	$O(\log n)$
removeMin	$O(n)$	$O(1)$	$O(\log n)$
remove	$O(1)$	$O(1)$	$O(\log n)$
replaceKey	$O(1)$	$O(n)$	$O(\log n)$

Table 5.19: Comparison of the running times of the priority queue methods for the unsorted-list, sorted-list, and heap implementations. We denote with n the number of elements in the priority queue at the time a method is executed.

incrementally in order to $N + n - 1$. The packets are usually not received in this order, however. Thus, to reconstruct the file at the receiving computer, your method must re-order the packets so that they are sorted by their sequence numbers. In studying example inputs, you notice that the input sequence of packets is usually not that far from being sorted. That is, you notice in the examples you studied that each input packet is *proximate* to its output position, which means that if a packet is at position i in the input sequence, then its position in the sorted output sequence is somewhere in the range $[i-50, i+50]$. Describe a method for sorting a sequence of n such packets by their sequence numbers in $O(n)$ time, assuming that every input packet is proximate to its output position.

Chapter Notes

Knuth's book on sorting and searching [131] describes the motivation and history for the selection-sort, insertion-sort, and heap-sort algorithms. The heap-sort algorithm is due to Williams [216], and the linear-time heap construction algorithm is due to Floyd [73]. Additional algorithms and analyses for heaps and heap-sort variations can be found in papers by Bentley [29], Carlsson [41], Gonnet and Munro [86], McDiarmid and Reed [150], and Schaffer and Sedgewick [185]. The locator pattern (also described in [89]) appears to be new. Higham [97] studies the numerical stability of several floating-point summation algorithms, including the one discussed in Exercise A-5.5.

Chapter

6

Hash Tables

Operating a card sorter, 1920. U.S. Census Bureau.

Contents

6.1   Maps 189
6.2   Hash Functions 192
6.3   Handling Collisions and Rehashing 198
6.4   Cuckoo Hashing 206
6.5   Universal Hashing 212
6.6   Exercises 215

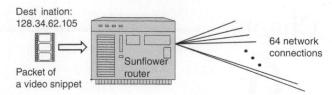

Suppose you are working on a development team that is designing the next generation of a network router for a major technology company. Such devices processes information packets, allowing them to move through networks having lots of interconnections. In this case, your team's job is to design a router, code named "Sunflower," that can process 64 streams of high-definition video at a time.

When a packet is received from one of the 64 cables that connect to the Sunflower router, it must examine destination information stored in the beginning of that packet and quickly decide along which of the 63 remaining cables to send it. Indeed, to avoid introducing annoying pauses in a video stream, the Sunflower router needs to process each such packet in at most 25 microseconds. Your job is to write the software that processes the destination information for deciding where to send each packet.

Viewed abstractly, each packet can be modeled as a pair, (k, x), where k is a key indicating the destination for this packet and x is the data contained in this packet, which would, in this case, be a snippet of some video stream. To process such a packet, your software needs to maintain a collection of pairs, (k, c), each of which indicates the cable, c, where the Sunflower router should send a packet with the destination k. Your system must support an operation, put(k, c), which adds a key-cable pair to the collection, and an operation, get(k), which returns the cable number in the collection for a given destination key, k.

One possibility, of course, is to use a linked list to store (k, c) pairs. This implementation choice would allow you to perform the put(k, c) operation in $O(1)$ time, since you could simply put each new pair at the beginning of the list. But you have correctly realized that such a solution would take $O(n)$ time to process a single get(k) operation on a collection of n pairs, since you would, in general, have to search through the entire list of n pairs to find a pair with the key k. Therefore, such a solution would put your team significantly over the 25 microsecond time limit if n is relatively large. Fortunately, there is a better choice, which is to use an instance of the **hash table** data structure we discuss in this chapter.

This data structure is able to achieve $O(1)$ expected time for both get and put operations. Indeed, we describe variations of this data structure that can achieve worst-case $O(1)$ time performance for either get or put operations, with the other operation still running in $O(1)$ expected time. Because of such performance bounds, hash tables are used in a host of different applications besides network routers, including operating systems, computer games, and bioinformatics.

6.1 Maps

The main idea at the heart of the hash table data structure is that it allows users to assign keys to elements and then use those keys later to look up or remove elements. (See Figure 6.1.) This functionality defines a data structure known as a ***dictionary*** or ***map***. That is, this structure supports methods for the insertion, removal, and searching of values in terms of keys associated with those values.

Figure 6.1: A conceptual illustration of a map data structure. Keys are like labels assigned to file folders, which serve as the values. The resulting item (labeled file folders) is then inserted into the map (file cabinet) by a file clerk. The keys can be used later to retrieve or remove the items. (Included image: LC-DIG-ppmsca-03084, 1945. U.S. government image, U.S. Office of War Information.)

6.1.1 The Map Definition

A map stores a collection of key-value pairs, (k, v), which we call ***items***, where k is a key and v is a value that is associated with that key. For example, in a map storing student records (such as the student's name, address, and course grades), the key might be the student's ID number. That is, a ***key*** is an identifier that is assigned by an application or user to an associated value, which we allow to be any data element.

For the sake of generality, some definitions allow a map to associated multiple values with the same key. Nevertheless, in most applications we would probably want to disallow items with the same key (for example, in a map storing student records, we would probably want to disallow two students having the same ID). In such cases when keys are unique, then the key associated with an object can be viewed as an "address" for that object in memory. Indeed, such maps are sometimes referred to as "associative stores," because the key associated with an object determines its "location" in the map. Thus, we assume here that keys are unique and we refer to a map that allows for multiple values for the same key as a ***multimap***.

As ***map*** data structure, M, supports the following fundamental methods:

get(k): If M contains an item with key equal to k, then return the value of such an item; else return a special element NULL.

put(k, v): Insert an item with key k and value v; if there is already an item with key k, then replace its value with v.

remove(k): Remove from M an item with key equal to k, and return this item. If M has no such item, then return the special element NULL.

Note that when operations get(k) and remove(k) are unsuccessful (that is, the map M has no item with key equal to k), we use the convention of returning a special element NULL. Such a special element is known as a ***sentinel***. Alternatively, we could have had these methods indicate an error or exception in such cases, but it would not normally be considered an error to search for a key that happens not to be present in a map.

In addition, a map can implement other supporting methods, such as size() and isEmpty() methods for containers. Moreover, we could include methods for listing out the items, values, or keys in M. Still, the above three methods are the essential ones for a Map structure.

As mentioned above, the keys associated with values in a map are often meant to be "addresses" for those values. In addition to their applications in Internet routers, as in the Sunflower router mentioned above, another application of a map is in a compiler's symbol table, where each name in a program is a key associated with a variable, function, or class. In this case, we would store name-value associations, where each name serves as the "address" for properties about a variable's type and value.

6.1.2 Lookup Tables

In some cases, the universe of keys that will be used for a map is the set of integers in the range $[0, N - 1]$, for a reasonably small value of N. In such a scenario, there is an almost trivial way of implementing a map—namely, we can allocate an array, A, of size N, where each cell of A is thought of as a "bucket" that can hold a single key-element pairs (or a pointer to such a pair). Since we assume that keys are distinct, we can use A to store any key-value pair (k, v) by placing that pair in the cell $A[k]$. In this case, we refer to this implementation as a ***lookup table***, since the key k allows us to simply "look up" the item for k by a single array-indexing operation.

Performing the essential operations for a map in this case is quite simple. We begin by allocating the array A so that every cell is initially associated with the special NULL object. Then, we perform the map operations as follows:

- To perform a put(k, v) operation, we assign (k, v) to $A[k]$.
- To perform a get(k) operation, we return $A[k]$.
- To perform a remove(k) operation, we return $A[k]$ and then we assign the NULL item to $A[k]$.

(See Figure 6.2.)

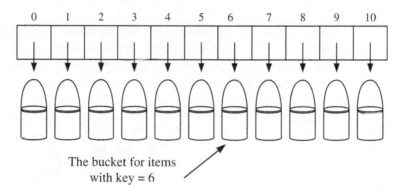

The bucket for items
with key = 6

Figure 6.2: How a lookup table works.

Analysis of a Lookup Table

The analysis of the performance of a lookup table is also simple. Each of the essential map methods runs in $O(1)$ time in worst case. Thus, in terms for time performance, the lookup table is optimal.

There are some drawbacks with this implementation, however. In terms of space usage, we note that the total amount of memory used for a lookup table is $\Theta(N)$. In this case, we refer to the size, N, of the array A as being the ***capacity*** of this map implementation. Such an amount of space is certainly reasonable if the number of items, n, being stored in the map is close to N. But if N is large relative to n, then one drawback of this implementation is that it is wasteful of space. Another drawback with this implementation is that it requires keys be unique integers in the range $[0, N-1]$, which is often not the case. Thus, it would be nice to have a mechanism to overcome these drawbacks while still achieving simple and fast methods for implementing the essential operations for a map.

6.2   Hash Functions

If we cannot assume that keys are unique integers in the range $[0, N - 1]$, but we
nevertheless still want to use something akin to a lookup table for storing key-value
pairs, then we need a good way of assigning keys to integers in this range. That is,
we need a function, h, called a ***hash function***, that maps each key k in our map to
an integer in the range $[0, N - 1]$, where N is the capacity of the underlying array
for this table. The use of such a function allows us to treat objects, such as strings,
as numbers.

Using a Hash Function with a Lookup Table

Equipped with such a function, h, we can apply the lookup table approach to arbitrary keys. The main idea of this approach is to use the hash value, $h(k)$, as an
index into our array, A, instead of the key k itself. That is, the idea is to try to store
the item (k, v) in the bucket $A[h(k)]$. (See Figure 6.3.)

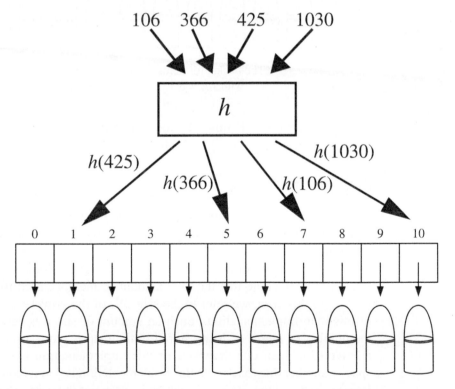

Figure 6.3: How a hash function, h, works with a lookup table. For simplicity, we
only show keys, not values.

Collisions

One complication that we have to deal with when using this approach, however, is that it is entirely possible that the hash function, h, could map two distinct keys to the same location in A. That is, we could have $h(k) = h(l)$, for $k \neq l$, for two keys k and l in our map. We refer to such a pair of keys with the same hash value, j, as causing a **collision** at j. Likewise, we say that a hash function is "good" if it maps the keys in our map so as to minimize collisions as much as possible. In other words, we would like the hash function h to look as random as possible, since a truly random function would automatically minimize the expected number of collisions for any given hash value, j. For practical reasons, we also would like the evaluation of a given hash function to be fast and easy to compute.

Viewing Keys as Bit Strings, Tuples, or Integers

Any kind of key that is of interest in a computing application must be representable as a binary string. Thus, without loss of generality, we can assume that any key used with a map data structure is a binary string. Of course, any such binary string can be interpreted as belonging to any one of a large number of different data types. Nevertheless, the standard convention for hash functions is to view keys in one of two ways:

- Each key, k, is a tuple of integers, $(x_1, x_2, \ldots, x_d)$, with each x_i being an integer in the range $[0, M - 1]$, for some M and d.
- Each key, k, is a nonnegative integer, which could possibly be very large.

For example, if our keys are character strings, such as in the case of the variable names in a programming language or words taken from web pages, then it is probably most natural to view such keys as tuples. Alternatively, if our keys are fixed-length IP addresses of destination domains on the Internet, then it is probably most natural to view them as single integers.

Depending on which of these two viewpoints we take, there are a number of different kinds of hash functions that we can consider. In fact, there are a large number of different hash functions that have been published over the years, each of which is based on the goal of minimizing collisions. Rather than survey all the different existing hash functions, however, we restrict our discussion in this section to some important representative hash functions. This collection is representative of existing hash functions in that most of the existing functions contain elements from the ones we discuss and assume that keys come in one of the above two forms. In some cases, a hashing scheme might use both forms of keys, for instance, first viewing an input key as a tuple and mapping that to some integer based on one hash function, and then further mapping that single integer to some other value based on yet another hash function.

6.2.1   Summing Components

In the case when each of our keys, k, is a d-tuple, of the form

$$(x_1, x_2, \ldots, x_d),$$

where each x_i is an integer, one possible hash function we could use is to sum up the different components in each key. That is, we could compute $h(k)$ as

$$h(k) = \sum_{i=1}^{d} x_i,$$

where this sum is taken over either the integers or is done so that every addition is modulo some integer, p, so that the result is in the range $[0, p-1]$.

A slight variation on this theme is to compute an exclusive-or of all the components of a key, which could be written mathematically as

$$h(k) = \oplus_{i=1}^{d} x_i,$$

where $\oplus$ denotes the bitwise exclusive-or (XOR) operation. Using an XOR is sometimes preferred over addition in that there are no extra complications regarding carry bits when one is doing XORs and the XOR operation itself is often a fast built-in operation for most CPUs. But there are some caveats, as the XOR of a number and itself is always 0, so care should be taken if there are duplicate components in a tuple.

How Symmetry Can Cause Collisions

Unfortunately, such hash functions, which consist of either summing or XORing the components of each key, are actually not that good in most applications. In particular, such a function is fairly poor at avoiding collisions for the case when keys are character strings or other multiple-length objects that can be viewed as tuples of the form $(x_1, x_2, \ldots, x_k)$, as used above, where the order of the x_i's is significant.

For example, consider such a hash function for a character string s that sums the ASCII (or Unicode) values of the characters in s. This hash function produces lots of unwanted collisions for common groups of strings. For instance, `"temp01"` and `"temp10"` collide using this function, as do the four words,

`"stop"`, `"tops"`, `"pots"`, and `"spot"`.

A better hash code in such cases should somehow take into consideration the positions of the x_i's. That is, each index, i, should play a role in the hash function in some way.

6.2.2 Polynomial-Evaluation Functions

An alternative hash code, which does a better job at factoring in the positional information of the components in a key $k = (x_1, x_2, \ldots, x_d)$, is to choose a nonzero constant, $a \neq 1$, and use as a hash function the following:

$$h(k) = x_1 a^{d-1} + x_2 a^{d-2} + \cdots + x_{d-1} a + x_d,$$

which, by Horner's rule (see Exercise C-1.14), can be rewritten as

$$h(k) = x_d + a(x_{d-1} + a(x_{d-2} + \cdots + a(x_3 + a(x_2 + ax_1))\cdots)).$$

Note that we can evaluate such a hash function in a simple for-loop, which has $d - 1$ iterations; hence, this function can be evaluated using $d - 1$ additions and $d - 1$ multiplications. Mathematically speaking, the hash function, h, in this case is a $(d - 1)$-degree polynomial, which is being evaluated for the argument a, and has the components $(x_1, x_2, \ldots, x_d)$ as its coefficients. We therefore refer to this hash function as a ***polynomial-evaluation*** hash function.

Intuitively, a polynomial-evaluation hash function uses multiplication by the constant a as a way of "making room" for each component in a tuple of values while also preserving a characterization of the previous components. Of course, on a typical computer, evaluating a polynomial will be done using the finite bit representation for a hash code; hence, the value will periodically overflow the bits used for an integer. Since we are more interested in a good spread of the object x with respect to other keys, we simply ignore such overflows or we assume that all the arithmetic is being done modulo some prime number, p. In any case, one of the critical design decisions in using this hash function is choosing the constant, a. Intuitively, a should have some higher-order bits to "shift" over the running partial sum to make room for the new term while also having some lower-order bits to allow each new term to be factored in.

Special Values for English Words

We have done some experimental studies that suggest that 33, 37, 39, and 41 are good choices for a when working with character strings that are English words. In fact, in a list of over 50,000 English words formed as the union of the word lists provided in two variants of Unix, we found that taking a to be 33, 37, 39, or 41 produced less than 7 collisions in each case. It should come as no surprise, then, to learn that actual character string hash functions often choose the polynomial hash function using one of these constants for a. For the sake of speed, however, some implementations only apply the polynomial hash function to a fraction of the characters in long strings, say, every eight characters.

6.2.3   Tabulation-Based Hashing

For the case when each key can be viewed as a tuple, $k = (x_1, x_2, \ldots, x_d)$, for a fixed d, there is another class of hash functions we can use, which involve simple table lookups. These are known as ***tabulation-based hash functions***, and they can be applied even for hashing on small devices, since they make no use of addition or multiplication.

So, let us assume that all our keys are of the form $k = (x_1, x_2, \ldots, x_d)$, for a fixed d, and each x_i is in the range $[0, M - 1]$. Then we can initialize d tables, $T_1, T_2, \ldots, T_d$, of size M each, so that each $T_i[j]$ is a uniformly chosen independent random number in the range $[0, N - 1]$. We then can compute the hash function, $h(k)$, as

$$h(k) = T_1[x_1] \oplus T_2[x_2] \oplus \cdots \oplus T_d[x_d].$$

Note, in addition, that we might as well assume that $N \le M^d$, for otherwise we could simply use each key, k, as an integer index for hashing, as in the standard lookup table implementation. Also, recall that the number of keys, n, may be different than the capacity, N, of our hash table.

Because the values in the tables are themselves chosen at random, such a function is itself fairly random. For instance, it can be shown that such a function will cause two distinct keys to collide at the same hash value with probability $1/N$, which is what we would get from a perfectly random function. In addition, this function only uses the XOR operation; hence, it can be evaluated without doing any additions and multiplications, which may take more time than XOR operations on some machines.

6.2.4   Modular Division

In the case that we can view the key k as a single integer, perhaps the simplest hash function is to use modular division to compress k into the range $[0, N - 1]$ as follows:

$$h(k) = k \bmod N.$$

If we take N to be a prime number, then the division compression map helps "spread out" the distribution of hashed values. Indeed, if N is not prime, there is a higher likelihood that patterns in the distribution of keys will be repeated in the distribution of hash codes, thereby causing collisions. For example, if we hash the keys $\{200, 205, 210, 215, 220, \ldots, 600\}$ to a bucket array of size 100, then each hash code will collide with three others. But if this same set of keys is hashed to a bucket array of size 101, then there will be no collisions. If we can assume that the set of keys is uniformly randomly distributed among an integer range much larger than N, then the modular-division hash function should guarantee that the probability of two different keys being hashed to the same value is at most $1/N$.

Choosing N to be a prime number and having uniformly distributed keys is not always enough to avoid such collisions, however, if the keys are not also random. For example, if there is a repeated pattern of key values of the form $iN + j$ for several different i's, then such a set of keys would be uniformly distributed but they will all collide at the hash value j.

6.2.5 Random Linear and Polynomial Functions

A more sophisticated compression function, which helps mitigate repeated patterns in a set of integer keys is to use a ***random linear hash function***. In this case, we define a ***random linear hash function***, h, for an integer key, k, as

$$h(k) = (ak + b) \bmod N,$$

where N is a prime number, and $0 < a < N$ and $0 \le b < N$ are independent uniform random integers. This hash function is chosen in order to reduce the number of collisions caused by repeated patterns in a set of hash values and thereby get us closer to having a "good" hash function, that is, one where the probability any two different keys collide is $1/N$. In fact, we prove below, in Section 6.5, that a random linear hash function can be used to guarantee such a probability bound on pairwise collisions.

Random Polynomial Functions

In some cases, we may need a hash function that guarantees that the probabilities that larger numbers of hash values collide is the same as what one would get with a random function. One way to achieve such a result for an integer key, k, is to use a ***random polynomial hash function***, h, which is defined as

$$h(k) = a_d + k(a_{d-1} + k(a_{d-2} + \cdots + k(a_3 + k(a_2 + ka_1))\cdots)) \bmod N,$$

where N is prime and the a_i's are independent uniformly random integers in the range $[0, N - 1]$, such that at least one of the coefficients in $\{a_1, a_2, \ldots, a_{d-1}\}$ is nonzero. For such a hash function, although we don't include a proof here, one can show that the probability that any $2 \le c \le d$ distinct keys collide at the same hash value is $1/N^{c-1}$.

Thus, adding this hash function to the bunch we have already discussed, we clearly have a rich collection of hash functions, each of which is designed to minimize the number of collisions. Even so, it is not likely that we can completely avoid collisions with any of these schemes. Therefore, in addition to choosing a good hash function, we also need to come up with a graceful way of handling collisions when they occur.

6.3   Handling Collisions and Rehashing

Recall that the main idea of a hash table is to take a lookup table, A, and a hash function, h, and use them to implement a map by storing each item (k, v) in the "bucket" $A[h(k)]$. This simple idea is challenged, however, when we have two distinct keys, k_1 and k_2, such that $h(k_1) = h(k_2)$. The existence of such *collisions* prevents us from simply inserting a new item (k, v) directly in the bucket $A[h(k)]$. They also complicate our procedure for performing the get(k) operation. Thus, we need consistent strategies for resolving collisions.

6.3.1   Separate Chaining

A simple and efficient way for dealing with collisions is to have each bucket $A[i]$ store a reference to a set, S_i, that stores all the items that our hash function has mapped to the bucket $A[i]$ in a linked list. The set S_i can be viewed as a miniature map, implemented using the underlying linked list, but restricted to only hold items (k, v) such that $h(k) = i$. This *collision resolution* rule is known as *separate chaining*. Assuming that we implement each nonempty bucket in this way, we can perform the fundamental map operations as follows:

- get(k):
    $B \leftarrow A[h(k)]$
    if $B =$ NULL **then**
        return NULL
    else
        return B.get(k)   // do a lookup in the list B

- put(k, v):
    if $A[h(k)] =$ NULL **then**
        Create a new initially empty linked-list-based map, B
        $A[h(k)] \leftarrow B$
    else
        $B \leftarrow A[h(k)]$
    B.put(k, v)   // put (k, v) at the end of the list B

- remove(k):
    $B \leftarrow A[h(k)]$
    if $B =$ NULL **then**
        return NULL
    else
        return B.remove(k)   // remove the item with key k from the list B

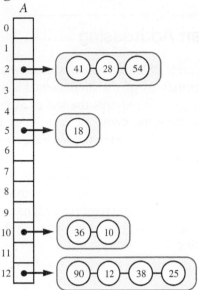

Figure 6.4: Example of a hash table of size 13, storing 10 integer keys, with collisions resolved by the chaining method. The hash function in this case is $h(k) = k \bmod 13$.

Thus, for each map operation involving a key k, we delegate the handling of this operation to the miniature linked-list-based map stored at $A[h(k)]$. So, an insertion will put the new item at the beginning of this list in $O(1)$ time, a find will search through this sequence until it reaches the end or finds an item with the desired key, and a remove will additionally remove an item after it is found. We can "get away" with using the simple linked-list implementation in these cases, because the spreading properties of the hash function help keep each such list small. Indeed, a good hash function will try to minimize collisions as much as possible, which will imply that most of our buckets are either empty or store just a single item.

In Figure 6.4, we give an illustration of a simple hash table that uses the modular division hash function and separate chaining to resolve collisions.

For the sake of analyzing separate chaining, let us assume that our hash function, h, maps keys to independent uniform random values in the range $[0, N - 1]$. Thus, if we let X be a random variable representing the number of items that map to a bucket, i, in the array A, then the expected value of X,

$$E(X) = \frac{n}{N},$$

where n is the number of items in the map, since each of the N locations in A is equally likely for each item to be placed. This parameter, n/N, which is the ratio of the number of items in a hash table, n, and the capacity of the table, N, is called the ***load factor*** of the hash table. If it is $O(1)$, then the above analysis says that the expected time for hash table operations is $O(1)$ when collisions are handled with separate chaining.

6.3.2   Open Addressing

The separate chaining rule has many nice properties, such as allowing for simple implementations of the fundamental map operations, but it nevertheless has one disadvantage: it requires the use of auxiliary data structures—namely, the linked lists that store the items for each index in the array. We can handle collisions in other ways besides using the separate chaining rule, however. In particular, if space is of a premium, then we can use the alternative approach of always storing each item directly in a bucket, at most one item per bucket. This approach saves space because no auxiliary structures are employed—it only uses the space in the bucket array, A, itself—but it requires a bit more complexity to deal with collisions. There are several methods for implementing this approach, which is referred to as ***open addressing***.

6.3.3   Linear Probing

One of the simplest open addressing collision-handling strategy is ***linear probing***. In this strategy, if we try to insert an item (k, v) into a bucket $A[i]$ that is already occupied, where $i = h(k)$, then we try next at $A[(i + 1) \bmod N]$. If $A[(i + 1) \bmod N]$ is occupied, then we try $A[(i + 2) \bmod N]$, and so on, until we find an empty bucket in A that can accept the new item. Once this bucket is located, we simply insert the item (k, v) here. Of course, using this collision resolution strategy requires that we change the implementation of the get(k) operation. In particular, to perform such a search we must examine consecutive buckets, starting from $A[h(k)]$, until we either find an item with key equal to k or we find an empty bucket (in which case the search is unsuccessful). (See Figure 6.5.)

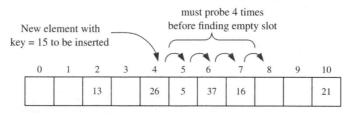

Figure 6.5: An insertion into a hash table using linear probing to resolve collisions. Here we use the compression map $h(k) = k \bmod 11$.

The operation remove(k) is more complicated, however. In particular, to fully implement this method, we should restore the contents of the bucket array to look as though the item with key k was never inserted in its bucket $A[i]$ in the first place. The algorithms for the three fundamental map methods are as follows, where, for the sake of simplicity, we assume that the table, A, is not completely full.

- get(k):

    $i \leftarrow h(k)$
    while $A[i] \neq$ NULL **do**
        if $A[i]$.key $= k$ **then**
            return $A[i]$
        $i \leftarrow (i + 1) \bmod N$
    return NULL

- put(k, v):

    $i \leftarrow h(k)$
    while $A[i] \neq$ NULL **do**
        if $A[i]$.key $= k$ **then**
            $A[i] \leftarrow (k, v)$ // replace the old (k, v')
        $i \leftarrow (i + 1) \bmod N$
    $A[i] \leftarrow (k, v)$

- remove(k):

    $i \leftarrow h(k)$
    while $A[i] \neq$ NULL **do**
        if $A[i]$.key $= k$ **then**
            $temp \leftarrow A[i]$
            $A[i] \leftarrow$ NULL
            Call Shift(i) to restore A to a stable state without k
            return $temp$
        $i \leftarrow (i + 1) \bmod N$
    return NULL

- Shift(i):

    $s \leftarrow 1$ // the current shift amount
    while $A[(i + s) \bmod N] \neq$ NULL **do**
        $j \leftarrow h(A[(i + s) \bmod N]$.key$)$ // preferred index for this item
        if $j \notin (i, i + s] \bmod N$ **then**
            $A[i] \leftarrow A[(i + s) \bmod N]$ // fill in the "hole"
            $A[(i + s) \bmod N] \leftarrow$ NULL   // move the "hole"
            $i \leftarrow (i + s) \bmod N$
            $s \leftarrow 1$
        else
            $s \leftarrow s + 1$

One alternative to the shifting done above for remove(k) is to replace the deleted item by a special "deactivated item" object. With this special marker possibly occupying buckets in our hash table, we would then need to modify our search algorithm for remove(k) or get(k), so that the search for a key k should skip over deactivated items and continue probing until reaching the desired item or an empty bucket. Likewise, the put(k, v) algorithm should stop at a deactivated item and replace it with the new item to be inserted. (See Exercise C-6.1.)

Analyzing Linear Probing

Recall that, in the linear-probing scheme for handling collisions, whenever an insertion at a cell i would cause a collision, then we instead insert the new item in the first cell of $i+1$, $i+2$, and so on, until we find an empty cell, wrapping our indices to the beginning of the table if necessary. In order to analyze how long this takes on average, we are going to use one of the Chernoff bounds, which we also discuss in Sections 1.2.4 and 19.5.

Let $X_1, X_2, \ldots, X_n$ be a set of mutually independent indicator random variables, such that each X_i is 1 with some probability $p_i > 0$ and 0 otherwise. Let $X = \sum_{i=1}^{n} X_i$ be the sum of these random variables, and let μ denote the mean of X, that is, $\mu = E(X) = \sum_{i=1}^{n} p_i$. The following bound, which is due to Chernoff (and which we derive in Section 19.5), establishes that, for $\delta > 0$,

$$\Pr(X > (1+\delta)\mu) < \left[\frac{e^\delta}{(1+\delta)^{(1+\delta)}}\right]^\mu.$$

Having presented this Chernoff bound, we can now analyze the expected running time for doing a search or update in a hash table that is implemented using the linear-probing collision-handling scheme. For this analysis, let us assume that we are storing n items in a hash table of size $N = 2n$, that is, our hash table has a load factor of $1/2$. If our actual load factor is less than this, then this analysis still applies, of course. If the load factor is much more than this, however, then the performance of linear probing can degrade significantly.

Let X denote a random variable equal to the number of probes that we would perform in doing a search or update operation in our hash table for some key, k. Furthermore, let X_i be a 0/1 indicator random variable that is 1 if and only if $i = h(k)$, and let Y_i be a random variable that is equal to the length of a run of contiguous nonempty cells that begins at position i, wrapping around the end of the table if necessary. By the way that linear probing works, and because we assume that our hash function $h(k)$ is random,

$$X = \sum_{i=0}^{N-1} X_i(Y_i + 1),$$

which implies that

$$
\begin{aligned}
E(X) &= \sum_{i=0}^{N-1} \frac{1}{2n} E(Y_i + 1) \\
&= 1 + (1/2n)E\left(\sum_{i=0}^{N-1} Y_i\right).
\end{aligned}
$$

Thus, if we can bound the expected value of the sum of Y_i's, then we can bound the expected time for a search or update operation in a linear-probing hashing scheme.

Consider, then, a maximal contiguous sequence, S, of k nonempty table cells, that is, a contiguous group of occupied cells that has empty cells next to its opposite ends. Any search or update operation that lands in S will, in the worst case, march all the way to the end of S. That is, if a search lands in the first cell of S, it would make k wasted probes, if it lands in the second cell of S, it would make $k - 1$ wasted probes, and so on. So the total cost of all the searches that land in S can be at most k^2. Thus, if we let $Z_{i,k}$ be a 0/1 indicator random variable for the existence of a maximal sequence of nonempty cells of length k, then

$$\sum_{i=0}^{N-1} Y_i \leq \sum_{i=0}^{N-1} \sum_{k=1}^{2n} k^2 Z_{i,k}.$$

Put another way, it is as if we are "charging" each maximal sequence of nonempty cells for all the searches that land in that sequence.

So, to bound the expected value of the sum of the Y_i's, we need to bound the probability that $Z_{i,k}$ is 1, which is something we can do using the Chernoff bound given above. Let Z_k denote the number of items that are mapped to a given sequence of k cells in our table. Then,

$$\Pr(Z_{i,k} = 1) \leq \Pr(Z_k \geq k).$$

Because the load factor of our table is $1/2$, $E(Z_k) = k/2$. Thus, by the above Chernoff bound,

$$\begin{aligned}
\Pr(Z_k \geq k) &= \Pr(Z_k > 2(k/2)) \\
&\leq (e/4)^{k/2} \\
&< 2^{-k/4}.
\end{aligned}$$

Therefore, putting all the above pieces together,

$$\begin{aligned}
E(X) &= 1 + (1/2n)E\left(\sum_{i=0}^{N-1} Y_i\right) \\
&\leq 1 + (1/2n)\sum_{i=0}^{N-1} \sum_{k=1}^{2n} k^2 2^{-k/4} \\
&\leq 1 + \sum_{k=1}^{\infty} k^2 2^{-k/4} \\
&= O(1).
\end{aligned}$$

That is, the expected running time for doing a search or update operation with linear probing is $O(1)$, so long as the load factor in our hash table is at most $1/2$.

Linear probing saves space, but it admittedly complicates removals. In addition, if the load factor of the hash table goes too high, then the linear-probing collision-handling strategy tends to cluster the items of the map into contiguous runs, which causes searches to slow down.

6.3.4   Quadratic Probing

Another open addressing strategy, known as **quadratic probing**, involves iteratively trying the buckets $A[(i + f(j)) \bmod N]$, for $j = 0, 1, 2, \ldots$, where $f(j) = j^2$, until finding an empty bucket. As with linear probing, the quadratic probing strategy complicates the removal operation, but it does avoid the kinds of clustering patterns that occur with linear probing.

Secondary Clustering

Nevertheless, when the load factor approaches 1, it creates its own kind of clustering, called **secondary clustering**, where the set of filled array cells "bounces" around the array in a fixed pattern. If N is not chosen as a prime, then the quadratic probing strategy may not find an empty bucket in A even if one exists. In fact, even if N is prime, this strategy may not find an empty slot, if the bucket array is at least half full.

6.3.5   Double Hashing

Another open addressing strategy that does not cause clustering of the kind produced by linear probing or the kind produced by quadratic probing is the **double hashing** strategy. In this approach, we choose a secondary hash function, h', and if h maps some key k to a bucket $A[i]$, with $i = h(k)$, that is already occupied, then we iteratively try the buckets $A[(i + f(j)) \bmod N]$ next, for $j = 1, 2, 3, \ldots$, where $f(j) = j \cdot h'(k)$. In this scheme, the secondary hash function is not allowed to evaluate to zero; a common choice is $h'(k) = q - (k \bmod q)$, for some prime number $q < N$. Also, N should be a prime.

Moreover, in using the double hashing technique, we should choose a secondary hash function that will attempt to minimize clustering as much as possible. If the functions h and f are assumed to be random functions, then it is fairly straightforward to prove that the expected running time for a search is $O(1)$, for example, see Exercise C-6.3.

Trade-offs for Open Addressing

These **open addressing** schemes save some space over the separate chaining method, but they are not necessarily faster. In experimental and theoretical analyses, the chaining method is either competitive or faster than the other methods, if the load factor is relatively close to 1, and open addressing tends to be faster than separate chaining if the load factor is less than $1/2$ (because it avoids an extra pointer hop).

6.3.6   Rehashing

As shown above, the ***load factor***, n/N, which is the ratio of the number of items in a hash table, n, and the capacity of the table, N, has a big impact on the performance of a hash table. The load factor of a hash table correlates to the probability that a newly inserted item will collide with an existing item, and, as discussed above, the load factor impacts the running times for hash table operations for both separate chaining and open addressing methods for handling collisions. For instance, given a constant load factor, the above analysis for separate chaining implies that the expected running time of the operations get, put, and remove in a map implemented with a hash table with separate chaining is $O(\lceil n/N \rceil) = O(1)$. Thus, we can implement the standard map operations to run in constant expected time, assuming we can maintain our hash table to have a bounded load factor. Therefore, we should always keep the load factor of our hash table below a small constant sufficiently smaller than 1.

Keeping a hash table's load factor below a constant (like $1/2$ or $3/4$) requires additional work whenever we add an item that would cause us to exceed this bound. In such cases, in order to keep the load factor below the specified constant, we need to increase the size of our bucket array, A, and change our hash function to match this new size. Moreover, we must then insert all the existing hash-table elements into the new bucket array using the new hash function. Such a size increase and hash table rebuild is called ***rehashing***. Following the approach of the extendable array (Section 1.4.2), a good choice is to rehash into an array roughly double the size of the original array. Such a choice implies that the additional amortized cost required for rehashing is $O(1)$ per insertion operation. (See Figure 6.6.)

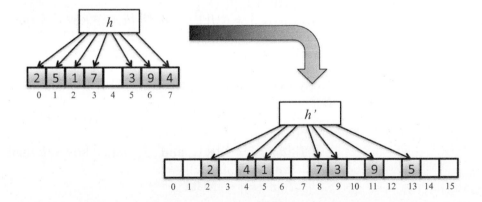

Figure 6.6: Rehashing a hash table with capacity 8 and load factor $7/8$ into a hash table with capacity 16 and load factor $7/16$. Note that all the items are placed into their new locations according to a new hash function, h'. So, for example, the item with key 7 was placed in bucket 3 in the old table, since $h(7) = 3$, but is placed in bucket 8 in the new table, since $h'(7) = 8$. (We only show keys, not values.)

6.4 Cuckoo Hashing

In the separate chaining and open addressing hashing schemes, the running time for doing a search is expected to be $O(1)$, but it can be as bad as $O(n)$ in the worst case (albeit with very low probability). In the case of separate chaining, the running time of the $\text{put}(k, v)$ method runs in $O(1)$ time in the worst case, however. In most applications, we would expect to perform more searches than insertions, so it would be nice to have a collision-handling scheme that can guarantee that searches run in $O(1)$ time in the worst case, while allowing for insertions to run in $O(1)$ time as an expected bound. Interestingly, the ***cuckoo hashing*** scheme we describe in this section achieves this performance goal while still being an open addressing scheme, like linear probing.

The Power of Two Choices

In the cuckoo hashing scheme, we use two lookup tables, T_0 and T_1, each of size N, where N is greater than n, the number of items in the map, by at least a constant factor, say, $N \geq 2n$. In addition, we use a hash function, h_0, for T_0, and a different hash function, h_1, for T_1. For any key, k, there are only two possible places where we are allowed to store an item with key k, namely, either in $T_0[h_0(k)]$ or $T_1[h_1(k)]$. (See Figure 6.7.)

The way we perform the $\text{get}(k)$ method in this scheme is quite simple:

- $\text{get}(k)$:
   if $T_0[h_0(k)] \neq$ NULL **and** $T_0[h_0(k)]$.key $= k$ **then**
      return $T_0[h_0(k)]$
   if $T_1[h_1(k)] \neq$ NULL **and** $T_1[h_1(k)]$.key $= k$ **then**
      return $T_1[h_1(k)]$
   return NULL

This is clearly a constant-time operation, and performing the $\text{remove}(k)$ operation is similar:

- $\text{remove}(k)$:
   if $T_0[h_0(k)] \neq$ NULL **and** $T_0[h_0(k)]$.key $= k$ **then**
      $temp \leftarrow T_0[h_0(k)]$
      $T_0[h_0(k)] \leftarrow$ NULL
      return $temp$
   if $T_1[h_1(k)] \neq$ NULL **and** $T_1[h_1(k)]$.key $= k$ **then**
      $temp \leftarrow T_1[h_1(k)]$
      $T_1[h_1(k)] \leftarrow$ NULL
      return $temp$
   return NULL

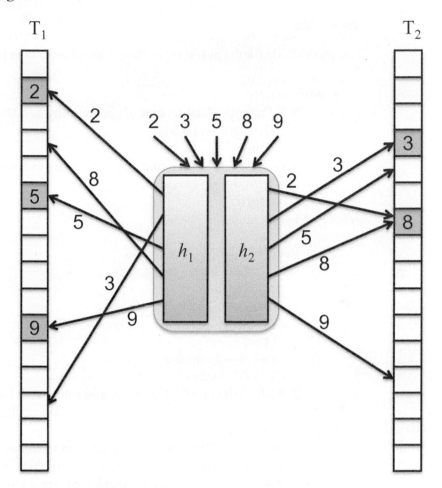

Figure 6.7: Cuckoo hashing. Each of the keys in the set $S = \{2, 3, 5, 8, 9\}$ has two possible locations it can go, one in the table T_1 and one in the table T_2. Note that there is a collision of 2 and 8 in T_2, but that is okay, since there is no collision for 2 in its alternative location, in T_1.

The name "cuckoo hashing" comes from the way the $\text{put}(k, v)$ operation is performed in this scheme, because it mimics the breeding habits of the Common Cuckoo bird. The Common Cuckoo is a brood parasite—it lays its egg in the nest of another bird after first evicting an egg out of that nest. Similarly, if a collision occurs in the insertion operation in the cuckoo hashing scheme, then we evict the previous item in that cell and insert the new one in its place. This forces the evicted item to go to its alternate location in the other table and be inserted there, which may repeat the eviction process with another item, and so on. Eventually, we either find an empty cell and stop or we repeat a previous eviction, which indicates an eviction cycle. If we discover an eviction cycle, then we stop the insertion process and rehash all the items in the two tables using new, hopefully better, hash functions.

Insertions

The pseudocode for the $\text{put}(k, v)$ method is as follows. (See Figure 6.8.)

- $\text{put}(k, v)$:
    if $T_0[h_0(k)] \neq \text{NULL}$ **and** $T_0[h_0(k)].\text{key} = k$ **then**
        $T_0[h_0(k)] \leftarrow (k, v)$
        return
    if $T_1[h_1(k)] \neq \text{NULL}$ **and** $T_1[h_1(k)].\text{key} = k$ **then**
        $T_1[h_1(k)] \leftarrow (k, v)$
        return
    $i \leftarrow 0$
    repeat
        if $T_i[h_i(k)] = \text{NULL}$ **then**
            $T_i[h_i(k)] \leftarrow (k, v)$
            return
        $temp \leftarrow T_i[h_i(k)]$
        $T_i[h_i(k)] \leftarrow (k, v)$ // cuckoo eviction
        $(k, v) \leftarrow temp$
        $i \leftarrow (i + 1) \bmod 2$
    until a cycle occurs
    Rehash all the items, plus (k, v), using new hash functions, h_0 and h_1.

Note that the above pseudocode has a condition for detecting a cycle in the sequence of insertions. There are several ways to formulate this condition. For example, we could count the number of iterations for this loop and consider there to be a cycle if we go over a certain threshold, like n or $\log n$.

Analysis of Cuckoo Hashing

Let us analyze the expected running time for doing an insertion in the cuckoo hashing scheme. Throughout this analysis, we assume $N \geq 2n$, where N is the size of each table and n is the number of items in our map. Central to this analysis is an analysis of the possibility that a sequence of evictions could start at a cell, x_1, and evict an item that goes to a cell, x_2, and evicts an item that goes to a cell, x_3, and so on. Ignoring the direction that such a sequence of evictions goes in, say that there is a potential sequence of evictions of *length* 1 between x and y if there is an item that maps to both x and y as its two possible locations. Likewise, say that there is a potential sequence of evictions of *length* L between x and y if there is a possible sequence of evictions of length $L - 1$ between x and some cell, z, and there is also an item that maps to both z and y as its two possible locations. We begin our analysis with a useful fact about the probability that there will be a possible sequence of evictions of length L between a cell, x, and a cell, y, in $T_0 \cup T_1$.

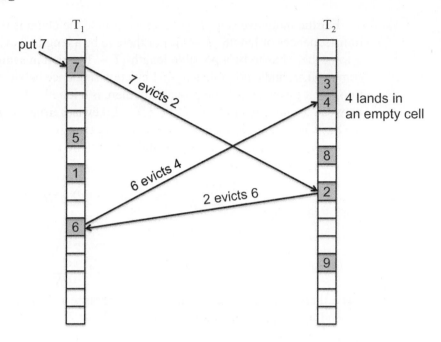

Figure 6.8: An eviction sequence of length 3.

Bounding the Probability of Long Eviction Sequences

The following lemma gives us a way of bounding the probability that we might have long eviction sequences for any put operation.

Lemma 6.1: *The probability that there is a possible sequence of evictions of length L between a cell, x, and a cell, y, in $T_0 \cup T_1$, is at most $1/(2^L N)$.*

Proof: The proof is by induction. For the base case, $L = 1$, note that there is a possible length-1 eviction sequence between x and y if and only if we choose x and y as the two possible locations for some item. The hash functions h_0 and h_1 effectively choose 1 cell each out of N possible cells in T_0 and T_1, respectively. Thus, the probability that a particular item chooses both x and y as its two locations is at most $1/N^2$, and the probability that *any* of the n items in our set, S, chooses both x and y is at most

$$\sum_{(k,v) \in S} \frac{1}{N^2} \;=\; \frac{n}{N^2}$$

$$\leq\; \frac{1}{2} \cdot \frac{1}{N},$$

because of our assumption that $N \geq 2n$. Note that the probability that there is a possible eviction sequence of length 1 between x and y is 0 if both x and y are in the same table, T_i, but this probability is clearly bounded by $1/(2N)$. So this completes the proof for the base case, $L = 1$.

For the inductive step, $L \geq 2$, let us assume the claim is true for possible eviction sequences of length $(L-1)$. For there to be a length-L eviction sequence from x to y, there has to be a possible length-$(L-1)$ eviction sequence between x and some cell, z, and a possible length-1 eviction sequence between z and y. By induction, for a given cell, z, the probability there is a length-$(L-1)$ eviction sequence between x and z is at most $1/(2^{L-1}N)$. Likewise, from the above discussion for the base case, there is a length-1 eviction sequence between z and y with probability at most $1/(2N)$. Thus, the probability that there is a length-L eviction sequence between x and y is at most

$$
\sum_z \frac{1}{2^{L-1}N} \cdot \frac{1}{2N} = \sum_z \frac{1}{2^L N^2}
$$
$$
\leq \frac{N}{2^L N^2}
$$
$$
= \frac{1}{2^L N},
$$

since there are only N candidates for z, because it has to be in either T_0 or T_1, depending, respectively, on whether y is in T_1 or T_0.   ∎

Counting the Expected Number of Possible Evictions

Say that two keys k and l are in the same "bucket" if there is a sequence of evictions (of any length) between a possible cell for k and a possible cell for l. Thus, for k and l to be in the same bucket, there has to be an eviction sequence between one of the cells $T_0[h_0(k)]$ or $T_1[h_1(k)]$ and one of the cells $T_0[h_0(l)]$ or $T_1[h_1(l)]$. Note that there are 4 such possible sequences, depending on where we stop and end, since we are ignoring the direction that a sequence of evictions can take. Then, by Lemma 6.1, and summing across all possible lengths, the probability that k and l are in the same bucket is bounded by

$$
4 \sum_{L=1}^{\infty} \frac{1}{2^L N} = \frac{4}{N} \sum_{L=1}^{\infty} \frac{1}{2^L}
$$
$$
= \frac{4}{N}.
$$

Note that, by this notion of a "bucket," the running time for performing an insertion in a cuckoo table is certainly bounded by the number of items that map to the same bucket as the item being inserted, so long as we don't cause a rehash. Thus, the expected time to insert an item with key k in this case is bounded by

$$
\sum_{\text{keys in } S} \frac{4}{N} = 4n/N \leq 2.
$$

In other words, the expected running time for performing a $\mathsf{put}(k, v)$ operation for a cuckoo table is $O(1)$, assuming this insertion does not cause a rehash.

Allowing for Rehash Operations

So, let us consider the expected number of rehashes we may have to do. By the description of the insertion algorithm, a rehash occurs if there is a cycle of evictions, that is, a length-L sequence of evictions that starts and ends at the same cell. Then, by Lemma 6.1, and the fact that we need only consider even-length sequences of evictions (to form a cycle), the probability that there is a cycle of evictions that starts and ends at some cell, x, is bounded by

$$\sum_{L=1}^{\infty} \frac{1}{2^{2L}N} = \sum_{L=1}^{\infty} \frac{1}{4^L N}$$

$$= \frac{1}{N} \sum_{L=1}^{\infty} \frac{1}{4^L}$$

$$= \frac{1}{N} \cdot \frac{1/4}{1 - 1/4}$$

$$= \frac{1}{3N}.$$

Therefore, the probability that there is a cycle anywhere can be bounded by summing this value over all $2N$ cells in the cuckoo tables. That is, the probability that any of the n items in our cuckoo hash table forms a cycle of evictions is at most $2/3$. In other words, with probability at most $2/3$ we will have to do a rehash during the insertion of these n items, and, with probability at most $(2/3)^2$ we would have to do 2 rehashes, and, with probability at most $(2/3)^3$ we would have to do 3 rehashes, and so on. If the time to do a rehash is $O(n)$, then the expected time to perform n insertions and the rehashes they may cause is bounded by

$$O(n) + O(n) \cdot \sum_{i=1}^{\infty} (2/3)^i,$$

which is $O(n)$. Thus, the expected amortized time to perform any single insertion in a cuckoo table is $O(1)$.

Summary

So, to sum up, a cuckoo hash table achieves worst-case constant time for lookups and removals, and expected constant time for insertions. This is primarily because there are exactly two possible places for any item to be in a cuckoo hash table, which shows the power of two choices.

6.5 Universal Hashing

In this section, we show how a random linear hash function can be probabilistically shown to be good. Recall that in this case we assume that our set of keys are integers in some range. Let $[0, M-1]$ be this range. Thus, we can view a hash function h as a mapping from integers in the range $[0, M-1]$ to integers in the range $[0, N-1]$, and we can view the set of candidate hash functions we are considering as a ***family*** H of hash functions. Such a family is ***universal*** if for any two integers j and k in the range $[0, M-1]$ and for a hash function chosen uniformly at random from H,

$$\Pr(h(j) = h(k)) \leq \frac{1}{N}.$$

Such a family is also known as a ***2-universal*** family of hash functions. The goal of choosing a good hash function can therefore be viewed as the problem of selecting a small universal family H of hash functions that are easy to compute. The reason universal families of hash functions are useful is that they result in a low expected number of collisions.

Theorem 6.2: *Let j be an integer in the range $[0, M-1]$, let S be a set of n integers in this same range, and let h be a hash function chosen uniformly, at random, from a universal family of hash functions from integers in the range $[0, M-1]$ to integers in the range $[0, N-1]$. Then the expected number of collisions between j and the integers in S is at most n/N.*

Proof: Let $c_h(j, S)$ denote the number of collisions between j and integers in S (that is, $c_h(j, S) = |\{k \in S : h(j) = h(k)\}|$). The quantity we are interested in is the expected value $E(c_h(j, S))$. We can write $c_h(j, S)$ as

$$c_h(j, S) = \sum_{k \in S} X_{j,k},$$

where $X_{j,k}$ is a random variable that is 1 if $h(j) = h(k)$ and is 0 otherwise (that is, $X_{j,k}$ is an ***indicator*** random variable for a collision between j and k). By the linearity of expectation,

$$E(c_h(j, S)) = \sum_{s \in S} E(X_{j,k}).$$

Also, by the definition of a universal family, $E(X_{j,k}) \leq 1/N$. Thus,

$$E(c_h(j, S)) \leq \sum_{s \in S} \frac{1}{N} = \frac{n}{N}.$$

■

Put another way, this theorem states that the expected number of collisions between a hash code j and the keys already in a hash table (using a hash function chosen at random from a universal family H) is at most the current load factor of the hash table. Since the time to perform a search, insertion, or deletion for a key j in a hash table that uses the chaining collision-resolution rule is proportional to the number of collisions between j and the other keys in the table, this implies that the expected running time of any such operation is proportional to the hash table's load factor. This is exactly what we want.

Let us turn our attention, then, to the problem of constructing a small universal family of hash functions that are easy to compute. The set of hash functions we construct is actually similar to the final family we considered at the end of the previous section. Let p be a prime number greater than or equal to the number of hash codes M but less than $2M$ (and there must always be such a prime number, according to a mathematical fact known as **Bertrand's Postulate**).

Define H as the set of hash functions of the form

$$h_{a,b}(k) = (ak + b \bmod p) \bmod N.$$

The following theorem establishes that this family of hash functions is universal.

Theorem 6.3: *The family $H = \{h_{a,b} : 0 < a < p \text{ and } 0 \le b < p\}$ is universal.*

Proof: Let Z denote the set of integers in the range $[0, p-1]$. Let us separate each hash function $h_{a,b}$ into the functions

$$f_{a,b}(k) = (ak + b) \bmod p$$

and

$$g(k) = k \bmod N,$$

so that $h_{a,b}(k) = g(f_{a,b}(k))$. The set of functions $f_{a,b}$ defines a family of hash functions F that map integers in Z to integers in Z. We claim that each function in F causes no collisions at all. To justify this claim, consider $f_{a,b}(j)$ and $f_{a,b}(k)$ for some pair of different integers j and k in Z. If $f_{a,b}(j) = f_{a,b}(k)$, then we would have a collision. But, recalling the definition of the modulo operation, this would imply that

$$aj + b - \left\lfloor \frac{aj+b}{p} \right\rfloor p = ak + b - \left\lfloor \frac{ak+b}{p} \right\rfloor p.$$

Without loss of generality, we can assume that $k < j$, which implies that

$$a(j - k) = \left(\left\lfloor \frac{aj+b}{p} \right\rfloor - \left\lfloor \frac{ak+b}{p} \right\rfloor \right) p.$$

Since $a \ne 0$ and $k < j$, this in turn implies that $a(j - k)$ is a multiple of p. But $a < p$ and $j - k < p$, so there is no way that $a(j - k)$ can be a positive multiple of p, because p is prime (remember that every positive integer can be factored into a product of primes). So it is impossible for $f_{a,b}(j) = f_{a,b}(k)$ if $j \ne k$. To put this another way, each $f_{a,b}$ maps the integers in Z to the integers in Z in a way that defines a one-to-one correspondence. Since the functions in F cause no collisions, the only way that a function $h_{a,b}$ can cause a collision is for the function g to cause a collision.

Let j and k be two different integers in Z. Also, let $c(j,k)$ denote the number of functions in H that map j and k to the same integer (that is, that cause j and k to collide). We can derive an upper bound for $c(j,k)$ by using a simple counting argument. If we consider any integer x in Z, there are p different functions $f_{a,b}$ such that $f_{a,b}(j) = x$ (since we can choose a b for each choice of a to make this so). Let us now fix x and note that each such function $f_{a,b}$ maps k to a unique integer

$$y = f_{a,b}(k)$$

in Z with $x \neq y$. Moreover, of the p different integers of the form $y = f_{a,b}(k)$, there are at most

$$\lceil p/N \rceil - 1$$

such that $g(y) = g(x)$ and $x \neq y$ (by the definition of g). Thus, for any x in Z, there are at most $\lceil p/N \rceil - 1$ functions $h_{a,b}$ in H such that

$$x = f_{a,b}(j) \quad \text{and} \quad h_{a,b}(j) = h_{a,b}(k).$$

Since there are p choices for the integer x in Z, the above counting arguments imply that

$$c(j,k) \;\leq\; p\left(\left\lceil \frac{p}{N} \right\rceil - 1\right)$$
$$\leq\; \frac{p(p-1)}{N}.$$

There are $p(p-1)$ functions in H, since each function $h_{a,b}$ is determined by a pair (a,b) such that $0 < a < p$ and $0 \leq b < p$. Thus, picking a function uniformly at random from H involves picking one of $p(p-1)$ functions. Therefore, for any two different integers j and k in Z,

$$\Pr(h_{a,b}(j) = h_{a,b}(k)) \;\leq\; \frac{p(p-1)/N}{p(p-1)}$$
$$=\; \frac{1}{N}.$$

That is, the family H is universal. ■

In addition to being universal, the functions in H have a number of other nice properties. Each function in H is easy to select, since doing so simply requires that we select a pair of random integers a and b such that $0 < a < p$ and $0 \leq b < p$. In addition, each function in H is easy to compute in $O(1)$ time, requiring just one multiplication, one addition, and two applications of the modulus function. Thus, any hash function chosen uniformly at random in H will result in an implementation of a map so that the fundamental operations all have expected running times that are $O(\lceil n/N \rceil)$, since we are using the chaining rule for collision resolution.

6.6 Exercises

Reinforcement

R-6.1 Alice says that a hash table with collisions handled using separate chaining can have a load factor greater than 1. Bob says that this is impossible. Who is right, and why?

R-6.2 Bob says that a hash table with collisions handled using open addressing can have a load factor greater than 1. Alice says that this is impossible. Who is right, and why?

R-6.3 Describe the limitations of using a linked list to store a collection of key-value pairs subject to $put(k, v)$ and $get(k)$.

R-6.4 Draw the 11-item hash table resulting from hashing the keys 12, 44, 13, 88, 23, 94, 11, 39, 20, 16, and 5, using the hash function $h(i) = (2i + 5) \bmod 11$ and assuming collisions are handled by chaining.

R-6.5 What is the result of the previous exercise, assuming collisions are handled by linear probing?

R-6.6 Show the result of Exercise R-6.4, assuming collisions are handled by quadratic probing, up to the point where the method fails because no empty slot is found.

R-6.7 What is the result of Exercise R-6.4 assuming collisions are handled by double hashing using a secondary hash function $h'(k) = 7 - (k \bmod 7)$?

R-6.8 Give a pseudocode description of an insertion into a hash table that uses quadratic probing to resolve collisions, assuming we also use the trick of replacing deleted items with a special "deactivated item" object.

R-6.9 Show the result of rehashing the hash table shown in Figure 6.4 into a table of size 19 using the new hash function $h(k) = 2k \bmod 19$.

Creativity

C-6.1 Give the pseudocode description for performing insertion, searching, and removal from a hash table that uses linear probing to resolve collisions where we use a special marker to represent deleted elements.

C-6.2 In our description of hashing with the separate chaining rule, we assumed each cell in the array, A, was a pointer to a linked list, which wastes space in the case where the list holds only one item. Show how to modify our implementation so that we don't waste space on additional pointers to linked-list nodes for the cells in A that hold only one item.

C-6.3 Suppose that both the hash function, h, and the hash function, f, used in the double hashing open addressing scheme are random functions. Show that the expected time to perform the $get(k)$ operation is $O(1)$.

C-6.4 Dr. Wayne has a new way to do open addressing, where, for a key k, if the cell $h(k)$ is occupied, then he suggests trying $(h(k) + i \cdot f(k)) \bmod N$, for $i = 1, 2, 3, \ldots$, until finding an empty cell, where $f(k)$ is a random hash function returning values from 1 to $N - 1$. Explain what can go wrong with Dr. Wayne's scheme if N is not prime.

C-6.5 Describe a different way of detecting an eviction cycle in the cuckoo hashing scheme than in counting iterations.

Hint: You are allowed to use additional memory or to mark the cells of the two tables.

C-6.6 A *multimap* is data structure that allows for multiple values to be associated with the same key. It has a put(k, v) method, which inserts an item with key k and value v even if there is already an item with key k (but not the same key-value pair), and a FindAll(k) method, which returns all the values that have the key k. Describe a scheme that implements a multimap so that the put(k, v) method runs in $O(1)$ expected time and the FindAll(k) method runs in $O(1 + s)$ time, where s is the number of values with key k.

C-6.7 Suppose you would like to build a hash table for images, where the key for each image is a "thumbnail" image of 75×75 pixels, with each pixel being one of 256 possible colors. Describe a hash function for a set of such images. Your hash function should be fast to compute and it should strive to map different images to different hash values. In particular, reflections and $90°$ rotations of the same image should, in general, map to different hash values.

Applications

A-6.1 Suppose you are working in the information technology department for a large hospital. The people working at the front office are complaining that the software to discharge patients is taking too long to run. Indeed, on most days around noon there are long lines of people waiting to leave the hospital because of this slow software. After you ask if there are similar long lines of people waiting to be admitted to the hospital, you learn that the admissions process is quite fast in comparison. After studying the software for admissions and discharges, you notice that the set of patients currently admitted in the hospital is being maintained as a linked list, with new patients simply being added to the end of this list when they are admitted to the hospital. Describe a modification to this software that can allow both admissions and discharges to go fast. Characterize the running times of your solution for both admissions and discharges.

A-6.2 Perform a comparative analysis that studies the collision rates for various hash functions for character strings, such as various polynomial hash codes for different values of the parameter a. Use a hash table to determine collisions, but only count collisions where different strings map to the same hash code (not if they map to the same location in this hash table). Test these hash codes on text files found on the Internet.

A-6.3 In a *double-entry accounting* system, every business transaction has to be entered as two separate transactions, in different two accounts, once as a *debit* and once as a *credit*. For example, if a business borrows $10,000 from a bank, the business should enter a debit of $10,000 to its Cash account a credit of $10,000 to its Notes Payable account. In order to be in balance, every debit in such a system must have a matching credit. Describe an efficient algorithm to test if a double-entry accounting system is in balance. What is the running time of your method in terms of n, the number of business transactions?

A-6.4 Sports announcers are expected to keep talking during a broadcast of a sporting event even when there is nothing actually happening, such as during half-time. One common way to fill empty time is with sports trivia. Suppose, then, that you are going to be a sports announcer for the big game between the Bears and the Anteaters. To fill the empty time during half-time, you would like to say that this is the nth time that a game between the Bears and Anteaters has had a score of i-versus-j at half-time. The problem is that you don't know the values of i and j yet, of course, because the game hasn't happened yet, and, once half-time arrives you won't have time to look through the entire list of Bear-Anteater half-time scores to count the number of times the pair (i, j) appears. Describe an efficient scheme for processing the list of Bear-Anteater half-time scores before the game so that you can quickly say, right at the start of half-time, how many times the pair (i, j) has occurred at similar moments in the past. Ideally, you would like the processing task to take time proportional to the number of previous games and the querying task to take constant time.

A-6.5 Imagine that you are building an online plagiarism checker, which allows teachers in the land of Edutopia to submit papers written by their students and check if any of those students have copied whole sections from a set, D, of documents written in the Edutopian language that you have collected from the Internet. You have at your disposal a parser, P, that can take any document, d, and separate it into a sequence of its n words in their given order (with duplicates included) in $O(n)$ time. You also have a perfect hash function, h, that maps any Edutopian word to an integer in the range from 1 to 1,000,000, with no collisions, in constant time. It is considered an act of plagiarism if any student uses a sequence of m words (in their given order) from a document in D, where m is a parameter set by parliament. Describe a system whereby you can read in an Edutopian document, d, of n words, and test if it contains an act of plagiarism. Your system should process the set of documents in D in expected time proportional to their total length, which is done just once. Then, your system should be able to process any given document, d, of n words, in expected $O(n+m)$ time (not $O(nm)$ time!) to detect a possible act of plagiarism.

A-6.6 It is well known that in a room of n people, the probability that at least two of them have the same birthday is over $1/2$ if $n > 23$, which is a phenomenon known as the **birthday paradox**. Suppose, then, that you have a list of n people and their birthdays. Describe a way, in $O(n)$ expected time, to test whether two of the people on this list have the same birthday.

A-6.7 One way to measure the reading difficulty of a book is to count the number of unique words it contains. For example, *Green Eggs and Ham*, by Dr. Seuss, contains 50 unique words, whereas the book of Isaiah, from the Bible, contains almost 2,000 unique (Hebrew) words. Suppose you have a book, B, containing n total words (including duplicates). Describe an efficient scheme to count the number of unique words in B. You may assume that you have a parser that returns the n words in B as a sequence of character strings in $O(n)$ time. What is the running time of your method?

A-6.8 Imagine that you work for an insurance company that is insuring people against identity theft. You have just learned about a major security breach at a prominent bank used by many of your customers. Through back channels, you have obtained the list of Social Security numbers of the bank customers whose banking records were stolen, and, of course, you know the Social Security numbers for your own customers. Describe an efficient scheme for identifying which of your customers were victims in this security breach. What is the running time of your method in terms of n, the number of customers of your insurance company, and m, the number of bank customers who were victims in this security breach?

A-6.9 A popular tool for visualizing the themes in a speech is to draw a word cluster diagram, where the unique words from the speech are drawn in a group, with each word's size being in proportion to the number of times it is used in the speech. Given a speech containing n total words, describe an efficient method for counting the number of times each word is used in that speech. You may assume that you have a parser that returns the n words in a given speech as a sequence of character strings in $O(n)$ time. What is the running time of your method?

A-6.10 Most modern text processing systems have a built-in spelling checker, which checks to make sure words are spelled correctly and offers suggested corrections when words are misspelled. Suppose you have a dictionary, D, of n English words and would like to build such a spelling checker for two common spelling mistakes: transpositions, where two consecutive letters are swapped, and substitutions, where a single letter is replaced with a different letter. Describe a scheme to process the dictionary D in expected $O(n)$ time and then process any m-letter word, w, to see if w is spelled correctly, and, if not, to collect all the suggested correct English words that differ from w in a single transposition or substitution. The processing of any such w should take $O(m + s)$ time, where s is the total length of all the suggested alternatives to w.

Chapter Notes

Classic discussions of hashing can be found in well-known books by Knuth [131] and Gonnet and Baeza-Yates [85], including descriptions of separate chaining and open addressing schemes for handling collisions. Vitter and Chen [212] discuss coalesced hashing, which is a hybrid of these two collision-handling strategies. Discussions concerning rehashing can be found in works by Fagin *et al.* [69] and Litwin [145]. Eppstein [67] has a simplified analysis of linear probing that avoids Chernoff bounds, which we have adapted to an analysis based on Chernoff bounds in this chapter. A nice discussion of tabulation hashing can be found in a paper by Patrascu and Thorup [171]. Cuckoo hashing is due to Pagh and Rodler [167]. The analysis of cuckoo hashing given in this chapter is based on an unpublished manuscript, "Cuckoo Hashing for Undergraduates," by Pasmus Pagh. Universal hashing is due to Carter and Wegman [42].

Chapter

7

Union-Find Structures

Merging galaxies, NGC 2207 and IC 2163. Combined image from NASA's
Spitzer Space Telescope and Hubble Space Telescope. 2006. U.S. government
image. NASA/JPL-Caltech/STSci/Vassar.

Contents

7.1   Union-Find and Its Applications 221
7.2   A List-Based Implementation 225
7.3   A Tree-Based Implementation 228
7.4   Exercises 236

Social networking research studies how relationships between various people can influence behavior. Thus, a critical part of this research involves understanding how such relationships define groups or communities within a social network. Formally, given a set, S, of people, we can define a ***social network*** for S by creating an element, x, for each person and then create a set, E, of ***edges*** or ***ties*** between pairs of people that have a certain kind of relationship. For example, in a friendship network, ties would be defined by pairs of friends, in a sexual-relations network, ties would be defined by pairs of people who were physically intimate, and in an enemies network, ties would be defined by pairs of enemies. For the sake of being concrete, let us consider a friendship network.

Social networking researchers are often interested in identifying ***connected components*** in a friendship network. A connected component is a subset, T, of people from S that satisfies the following properties:

- Every person in T is related through friendship, that is, for any x and y in T, either x and y are friends or there is a chain of friendship, such as through a friend of a friend of a friend, that connects x and y.
- No one in T is friends with anyone outside of T.

Such community identifications are useful, since they allow researchers to study the degree to which being connected through friendship can influence behavior, such as how people vote or shop or whether they are more likely to gain weight or lose weight. Thus, from an algorithmic perspective, it is useful to have an efficient data structure that can be used to identify the connected components in a social network. The types of data structures we discuss in this chapter, ***union-find structures***, fit this bill perfectly.

In the context of a social network, a union-find structure gives us a way of maintaining a collection of disjoint sets of people, so as to support the following three operations:

- Make a set, which initially contains just a single person, x, and has that person's name, "X," as the name of the set
- Union two sets, A and B, together, naming the result as being one of "A" or "B," so that everyone that was in A or B is now identified as belonging to this union
- Find the name of the set containing a particular person, x.

Given such a data structure, we can determine all the connected components in a social network simply by making a set for each person in the network and doing a union operation for every pair of friends, x and y, that belong to different sets at the point we consider their edge, (x, y). As we study in this chapter, this algorithm has a surprising "almost" linear-time behavior.

7.1 Union-Find and Its Applications

A *partition* or *union-find* structure is a data structure supporting a collection of disjoint sets. We define the methods for this structure assuming we have a constant-time way to access a node associated with an item, e. For instance, items could themselves be nodes or we could maintain some kind of lookup table or map for finding the node associated with an item, e, in constant time. Given such an ability, the methods include the following:

makeSet(e): Create a singleton set containing the element e and name this set "e".

union(A, B): Update A and B to create $A \cup B$, naming the result as "A" or "B".

find(e): Return the name of the set containing the element e.

We refer to an implementation supporting these methods as a ***union-find structure***.

7.1.1 Connected Components

Consider again the connected components problem mentioned above. That is, suppose we are given a social network, N, defined by a set, S, of people, and a set, E, of edges defining relationships between pairs of people, in no particular order, and we are asked to find all the connected components for N. (See Figure 7.1.)

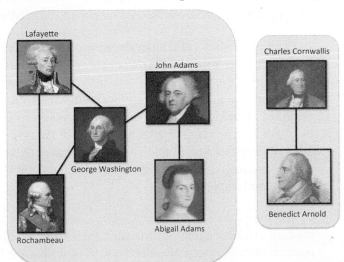

Figure 7.1: Connected components in a friendship network of some of the key figures in the American Revolutionary War. All images are in the public domain.

A Connected Components Algorithm

We give a pseudocode description of an algorithm for solving the connected components problem using a union-find structure in Algorithm 7.2. The output from this algorithm is an identification, for each person x in S, of the connected component to which x belongs. For instance, for the social network shown in Figure 7.1, the output would identify Lafayette, Rochambeau, George Washington, John Adams, and Abigail Adams as belonging to the "Washington" connected component, and Charles Cornwallis and Benedict Arnold as belonging to the "Cornwallis" connected component.

Algorithm UFConnectedComponents(S, E):

> *Input:* A set, S, of n people and a set, E, of m pairs of people from S defining pairwise relationships
>
> *Output:* An identification, for each x in S, of the connected component containing x

> **for** each x in S **do**
>> makeSet(x)
>
> **for** each (x, y) in E **do**
>> **if** find(x) $\neq$ find(y) **then**
>>> union(find(x), find(y))
>
> **for** each x in S **do**
>> Output "Person x belongs to connected component" find(x)

Algorithm 7.2: A connected components algorithm using union and find.

This algorithm's efficiency depends on how we implement the union-find structure, of course. If performing a sequence of m union and find operations, starting with n singleton sets created with the makeSet method, takes $O(t(n, m))$ time, then the running time of the UFConnectedComponents algorithm can be characterized as being $O(t(n, n + m))$, since we do two find operations for each edge in E and then one find operation for each of the n members of S. Using the implementations described in this chapter, we can achieve a running time that is either $O((n+m) \log n)$, using a list-based implementation, or "almost" $O(n+m)$, using a tree-based implementation.

As we explore in Chapter 13, if we are given the set E in sorted order (say, according to a lexicographic ordering), then we can actually design a connected components algorithm that runs in $O(n+m)$ time. But the UFConnectedComponents algorithm is the fastest way we know of for solving the connected components problem if we cannot make any assumptions about the ordering of E and we only get to scan through it once.

7.1.2 Maze Construction and Percolation Theory

Another application of union-find structures, which might at first seem to be purely for entertainment purposes, is for constructing mazes. In this application, we consider a **maze** to be a two-dimensional visual puzzle, defined by cells, which can be traversed, and walls, which are barriers. The goal is to find a path from a start location to a finish location that traverses connected cells in the maze without crossing any walls. (See Figure 7.3.)

Figure 7.3: A maze defined from a 30×30 square grid.

One challenge for people who like mazes is to find interesting mazes to solve. Thus, it is useful to have an automated way to construct mazes that have exactly one solution such that finding that solution is nontrivial. There are several possibilities for constructing such mazes, of course, but one that has turned out to be able to consistently construct interesting, solvable mazes is the method given in Algorithm 7.4.

Algorithm MazeGenerator(G, E):

Input: A grid, G, consisting of n cells and a set, E, of m "walls," each of
which divides two cells, x and y, such that the walls in E initially separate
and isolate all the cells in G

Output: A subset, R of E, such that removing the edges in R from E creates a
maze defined on G by the remaining walls

while R has fewer than $n - 1$ edges **do**

    Choose an edge, (x, y), in E uniformly at random from among those pre-
viously unchosen

    if find(x) $\neq$ find(y) **then**

        union(find(x), find(y))

        Add the edge (x, y) to R

return R

    Algorithm 7.4: A randomized algorithm for constructing mazes.

Given a grid, G, of n cells, and a set, E, of m walls separating pairs of cells
in G, this maze construction algorithm considers the walls in E in random order.
For each wall in this ordering that joins two previously separated connected components of cells, we add that wall to the set we are going to remove and we union
the two connected components it separated. Since we repeat this step until the set
of removed walls is equal to $n - 1$, we guarantee that the final maze has a single
connected component. Thus, it has a solution and it is likely to have lots of pas-
sages where a puzzle solver will reach a dead end. Indeed, the maze in Figure 7.3
was constructed using this algorithm.

Given a random ordering of the edges in E, the running time of this algorithm
is $O(t(n, m))$, where $O(t(n, m))$ is the running time for performing m union and
find operations on an initial set of n singleton sets.

Although this problem is motivated by a recreation, it is related to the science
of ***percolation theory***, which is the study of how liquids permeate porous materials.
For instance, a porous material might be modeled as a three-dimensional $n \times n \times n$
grid of cells. The barriers separating adjacent pairs of cells might then be removed
virtually with some probability p and remain with probability $1 - p$. The scientific
question to answer for this virtual material would then be whether a liquid poured
on top of the grid will make it to the bottom—that is, whether any top cell is connected to some bottom cell. Such a question can be answered by connecting every
top cell to a special "super-top" cell and connecting every bottom cell to a special "super-bottom" cell, performing a union operation for every pair of connected
cells, and then asking if the super-top and super-bottom cell are in the same set.
Repeating this experiment for several instances of the three-dimensional grid and
for different values of p can then provide insights into how liquids permeate porous
materials. Thus, the same thinking behind maze construction can be used to answer
scientific questions, and both can be performed using union-find structures.

7.2 A List-Based Implementation

A simple implementation of a union-find structure is to use a collection of linked lists, one for each set, where the list for a set A contains a **head** node, which stores

- the size of A
- the name of A
- a pointer to the first and last nodes of a linked list containing pointers to all the elements of A.

Each node of the linked list for A stores a pointer to an element belonging to that set and a pointer to the **head** node for A. (See Figure 7.5.)

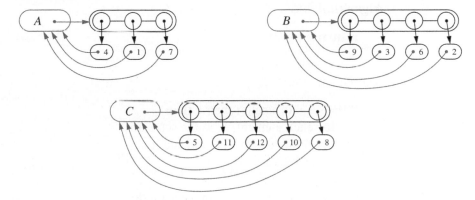

Figure 7.5: A list-based implementation of a union-find structure consisting of three sets: $A = \{1, 4, 7\}$, $B = \{2, 3, 6, 9\}$, and $C = \{5, 8, 10, 11, 12\}$.

Thus, we can perform operation $\mathsf{find}(e)$ in $O(1)$ time simply by following the pointer from the node for e to the **head** node and returning the name of the set identified by that node. Likewise, $\mathsf{makeSet}$ also takes $O(1)$ time, since it involves the creation of a new **head** node and a linked list containing a single element. The operation $\mathsf{union}(A, B)$ is not a simple constant-time procedure, however, since it requires that we join the two linked lists for A and B into one list and update the **head** pointers for all the nodes in one of these two lists (to now point to the **head** node of the other list). In order to save some time, let us choose to implement this operation by always changing the **head** pointers for whichever list, for A or B, has the smaller size (breaking ties arbitrarily). Hence, this implementation of the operation $\mathsf{union}(A, B)$ takes time $O(\min(|A|, |B|))$, which is $O(n)$ in the worst-case, because, in the worst case, $|A| = |B| = n/2$, where n is the number of singleton sets we start with. Nevertheless, as we show below, an amortized analysis reveals that this implementation is much better than first appears from this worst-case analysis.

Details for a List-Based Implementation for Disjoint Sets

We give pseudocode descriptions for implementing the fundamental methods of the disjoint sets data structures using linked lists in Algorithm 7.6.

Algorithm makeSet():

    for each singleton element, x **do**
        create a linked-list header node, u,
        u.name ← "x"
        add x to the list u
        x.head ← u

Algorithm find(x):

    return x.head

Algorithm union(u, v):

    if the set u is smaller than v **then**
        for each element, x, in the set u **do**
            remove x from u and add it v
            x.head ← v
    else
        for each element, x, in the set v **do**
            remove x from v and add it u
            x.head ← u

Algorithm 7.6: The fundamental disjoint-set methods for an implementation based on linked lists.

Analysis of the List-Based Implementation

The above linked list implementation is simple, and it might at first appear to be inefficient, but, as the following theorem shows, this implementation is actually not that slow.

Theorem 7.1: *Performing a sequence, σ, of m union and find operations, starting from n singleton sets, using the above list-based implementation of a union-find structure, takes $O(n \log n + m)$ time.*

Proof: We use the accounting method to analyze the time for us to perform all the operations in σ. We assume that 1 cyber-dollar can pay for the constant amount of time it takes to perform a find operation, or to update a head pointer during a union operation.

In the case of a find operation, we charge the operation itself 1 cyber-dollar, and, in the case of a union operation, we charge 1 cyber-dollar to each node for which we change its head pointer. Note that we charge nothing to the union operations themselves. Also, observe that there can be at most $n - 1$ union operations before all the singleton sets have been merged into one. Finally, note that the total charges to find operations can be at most $O(m)$, since m is the number of operations in σ.

Consider, then, the number of charges made to nodes on behalf of union operations. The important observation is that each time we update the head pointer for some node, the size of the new set at least doubles. This property is due to the fact that we always link the smaller set into the larger one, with ties broken arbitrarily. Thus, any node can have its head pointer changed at most $\log n$ times; hence, each such node can be charged at most $O(\log n)$ cyber-dollars, since we assume that the partition starts with n singleton sets. Thus, the total amount of cyber-dollars charged to all the nodes in this implementation of a union-find structure is $O(n \log n)$. ∎

The amortized running time of an operation in a series of makeSet, union, and find operations, is the total time taken for the series divided by the number of operations. Note, in addition, that, for the sake of analysis of a sequence of union, find, and makeSet operations, we can assume without loss of generality that all the makeSet operations come first. We conclude from the above theorem that, for a list-based implementation of a union-find structure, as described above, the amortized running time of each union operation is $O(\log n)$ and the amortized running time for each makeSet and find operation is $O(1)$. Thus, we can summarize the performance of our simple list-based implementation as follows.

Theorem 7.2: *Using a list-based implementation of a union-find structure, in a series of* makeSet, union, *and* find *operations, involving a total of n initially singleton sets, the amortized running of each* union *operation is $O(\log n)$ and the amortized running time for each* makeSet *and* find *operation is $O(1)$.*

We would like to stress that in this list-based implementation of a union-find structure, the running time of the union operations is the computational bottleneck, since the running time of this method is proportional to the size of the smaller set involved in the union. In the next section, we describe a tree-based implementation of a union-find structure where find operations are the bottleneck, but the amortized time performance for each operation is much better than $O(\log n)$.

7.3   A Tree-Based Implementation

An alternative data structure for implementing a union-find structure, starting from n singleton sets, is to use a collection of trees to store the elements in sets, where each tree is associated with a different set. In particular, we implement a tree T with a linked data structure, where each node u of T stores an element of the set associated with T, and a **parent** pointer to the parent node of u. If u is the root, then its **parent** pointer points to itself. As in the list-based implementation, we assume that either we have a constant-time way of accessing the node associated with an element from the element itself or that the nodes of in our data structure serve as the elements in our partition. Also, in this implementation, we identify each set with the root of its associated tree. (See Figure 7.7.)

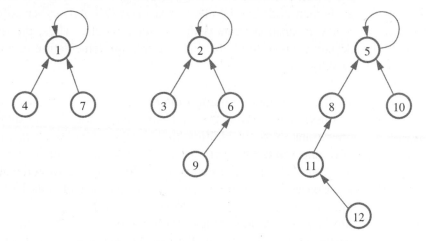

Figure 7.7: A tree-based implementation of a union-find structure for three disjoint sets: $A = \{1, 4, 7\}$, $B = \{2, 3, 6, 9\}$, and $C = \{5, 8, 10, 11, 12\}$.

With this data structure, the operation **union** is performed by making one of the two trees a subtree of the other (Figure 7.8a), which can be done in $O(1)$ time by setting the **parent** pointer of the root of one tree to point to the root of the other tree. Operation **find** for an element e is performed by walking up to the root of the tree containing e (Figure 7.8b), which takes $O(n)$ time in the worst case.

Note that this representation of a tree is a specialized data structure used to implement a union-find structure, and it is not meant to be a realization of a general tree data structure. Indeed, this representation has only **parent** links, and does not provide a way to access the children of a given node.

At first, this implementation may seem to be no better than the list-based implementation of a union-find structure, but we add the following simple heuristics to make it run faster.

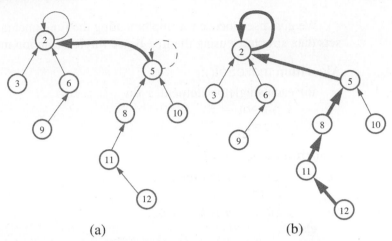

Figure 7.8: Tree-based implementation of a partition: (a) operation union(A, B); (b) operation find(ℓ), where ℓ denotes the node for element 12.

Union-by-Size: Store with each node v the size of the subtree rooted at v, denoted by $n(v)$. In a union, we now make the tree of the smaller set a subtree of the other tree, and update the size field of the root of the resulting tree.

Path Compression: In a find operation, for each node v that the find visits, reset the parent pointer from v to point to the root. (See Figure 7.9.)

These heuristics increase the running time of an operation by a constant factor, but as we show in the section that follows, they significantly improve the amortized running time for performing a sequence of union and find operations.

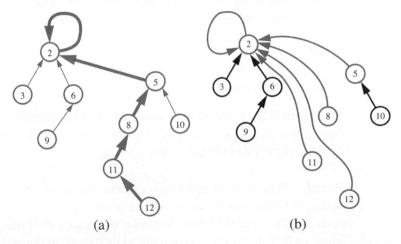

Figure 7.9: Path-compression heuristic: (a) path traversed by operation find on element 12; (b) restructured tree.

We give pseudocode for implementing the fundamental methods of the disjoint sets data structures using the tree-based implementation in Algorithm 7.10.

Algorithm makeSet():

> **for** each singleton element, x **do**
>> x.parent $\leftarrow x$
>> x.size $\leftarrow 1$

Algorithm union(x, y):

> **if** x.size $< y$.size **then**
>> x.parent $\leftarrow y$
>> y.size $\leftarrow y$.size $+ x$.size
>
> **else**
>> y.parent $\leftarrow x$
>> x.size $\leftarrow x$.size $+ y$.size

Algorithm find(x):

> $r \leftarrow x$
> **while** r.parent $\neq r$ **do**   // find the root
>> $r \leftarrow r$.parent
>
> $z \leftarrow x$
> **while** z.parent $\neq z$ **do**   // path compression
>> $w \leftarrow z$
>> $z \leftarrow z$.parent
>> w.parent $\leftarrow r$

Algorithm 7.10: The fundamental disjoint-set methods for an implementation based on trees defined by "parent" pointers for every element. Note: the x and y parameters for the union method must both be roots of their respective trees.

The above tree-based implementation has a very interesting analysis, which we give in the next section. Before giving that analysis, however, let us first give a simple analysis for the above implementation.

Theorem 7.3: *Performing a sequence, σ, of m union and find operations, starting from n singleton sets, using the above tree-based implementation of a union-find structure, takes $O(n + m \log n)$ time.*

Proof: There are at most $O(n)$ union operations, and each runs in $O(1)$ time; hence, the total time for doing all the union operations is $O(n)$. We only change a node's parent pointer when we union its set into a set that is at least as large as it. Thus, each time we go from a node to its parent, in doing a find operation, the size of the set rooted at that node must at least double. Therefore, the longest sequence of parent pointers that we can march through in doing a find is $O(\log n)$.   ∎

7.3.1 Analyzing the Tree-Based Implementation

Our analysis of the tree-based implementation of the union-find operations is based on the use of a very slow-growing function, $\alpha(n)$, which is the inverse of a very fast-growing function, known as the *Ackermann function*.

The Ackermann Function

The Ackermann function is named after Wilhelm Ackermann, a German mathematician who was a student of the well-known mathematician David Hilbert. There are actually several versions of the Ackermann function, including one originally proposed by Wilhelm Ackermann, each of which is more or less equivalent with the others. Each version of the Ackermann function defines a very fast-growing function, which has the interesting property that it cannot be computed using only Pascal-style for-loops (as it also requires the use of while-loops). We are not primarily interested in this structural property of the Ackermann function, however, which was Ackermann's original motivation for proposing it. Instead, we are interested in the Ackermann function because it is useful for analyzing the tree-based implementation of union-find operations.

The version of the Ackermann function we use is based on an indexed function, A_i, which is defined as follows, for integers $x \geq 0$ and $i > 0$:

$$\begin{aligned} A_0(x) &= x + 1 \\ A_{i+1}(x) &= A_i^{(x)}(x), \end{aligned}$$

where $f^{(k)}$ denotes the k-fold composition of the function f with itself. That is,

$$\begin{aligned} f^{(0)}(x) &= x \\ f^{(k)}(x) &= f(f^{(k-1)}(x)). \end{aligned}$$

So, in other words, $A_{i+1}(x)$ involves making x applications of the A_i function on itself, starting with x. This indexed function actually defines a progression of functions, with each function growing much faster than the previous one:

- $A_0(x) = x + 1$, which is the increment-by-one function
- $A_1(x) = 2x$, which is the multiply-by-two function
- $A_2(x) = x2^x \geq 2^x$, which is the power-of-two function
- $A_3(x) \geq 2^{2^{\cdot^{\cdot^{\cdot^2}}}}$ (with x number of 2's), which is the tower-of-twos function
- $A_4(x)$ is greater than or equal to the tower-of-tower-of-twos function
- and so on.

We then define the ***Ackermann function*** as

$$\mathcal{A}(x) = A_x(2),$$

which is an incredibly fast-growing function. To get some perspective, note that $\mathcal{A}(3) = 2048$ and $\mathcal{A}(4)$ is greater than or equal to a tower of 2048 twos, which is much larger than the number of subatomic particles in the universe. Likewise, its inverse,

$$\alpha(n) = \min\{x\colon \mathcal{A}(x) \geq n\},$$

is an incredibly slow-growing function. Still, even though $\alpha(n)$ is indeed growing as n goes to infinity, for all practical purposes, $\alpha(n) \leq 4$.

An Amortized Analysis

Let us use an amortization argument to analyze the running time of a sequence, σ, of m union and find operations on a partition that initially consists of n single-element sets.

Let U be the tree defined by all the union operations in σ ***without*** our having performed any path compressions. For each node v, let $n(v)$ denote the number of nodes in the subtree of U rooted at v, and define the ***rank*** of v, which we denote as $r(v)$, as follows:

$$r(v) = \lfloor \log n(v) \rfloor + 2.$$

Thus, we immediately get that $n(v) \geq 2^{r(v)-2}$. Also, since there are at most n nodes in U, $r(v) \leq \lfloor \log n \rfloor + 2$, for each node v.

Lemma 7.4: *If node w is the parent of node v, then*

$$r(v) < r(w).$$

Proof: We make v point to w only if the size of w before the union is at least as large as the size of v. Let $n(w)$ denote the size of w before the union and let $n'(w)$ denote the size of w after the union. Thus, after the union we get

$$
\begin{aligned}
r(v) \;&=\; \lfloor \log n(v) \rfloor + 2 \\
&<\; \lfloor \log n(v) + 1 \rfloor + 2 \\
&=\; \lfloor \log 2n(v) \rfloor + 2 \\
&\leq\; \lfloor \log(n(v) + n(w)) \rfloor + 2 \\
&=\; \lfloor \log n'(w) \rfloor + 2 \\
&\leq\; r(w).
\end{aligned}
$$

∎

Put another way, this theorem states that ranks are ***strictly*** increasing as we follow parent pointers up the union tree. It also implies the following.

Lemma 7.5: *The number of nodes of rank s, $0 \leq s \leq \lfloor \log n \rfloor + 2$, is at most*

$$\frac{n}{2^{s-2}}.$$

Proof: By the previous theorem, $r(v) < r(w)$, for any node v with parent w, and ranks are strictly increasing as we follow parent pointers up any tree. Thus, if $r(v) = r(w)$ for two nodes v and w, then the nodes counted in $n(v)$ must be separate and distinct from the nodes counted in $n(w)$. By the definition of rank, if a node v is of rank s, then $n(v) \geq 2^{s-2}$. Therefore, since there are at most n nodes total, there can be at most $n/2^{s-2}$ that are of rank s. ∎

Let us now consider the time it takes to perform the m union and find operations in the sequence σ. In particular, let us develop an amortized analysis, assuming that it takes 1 cyber-dollar to perform $O(1)$ amount of work during our performance of σ. We have already observed that performing a union takes $O(1)$ time. We therefore charge each union operation 1 cyber-dollar to pay for this. This implies that the total charges to all union operations is $O(n)$, since there can be at most $n - 1$ union operations in all.

Analyzing Path Compression

To characterize the performance of the other operations in σ, let us therefore consider how path compression affects the performance of find operations. As we perform path compressions, for each node v, we may be changing the parent, $p(v)$, of v. Note that, by Lemma 7.4, every time we change $p(v)$ during the execution of σ, we increase the value of $r(p(v))$, the rank of v's parent.

For the sake of our amortized analysis, let us define a ***labeling function***, $L(v)$, for each node v, which changes over the course of the execution of the operations in σ. In particular, at each step t in the sequence σ, define $L(v)$ as follows:

$$L(v) = \text{the largest } i \text{ for which } r(p(v)) \geq A_i(r(v)).$$

Note that if v has a parent, then $L(v)$ is well-defined and is at least 0, since

$$r(p(v)) \geq r(v) + 1 = A_0(r(v)),$$

because ranks are strictly increasing as we go up the tree U. Also, for $n \geq 5$, the maximum value for $L(v)$ is $\alpha(n) - 1$, since, if $L(v) = i$, then

$$
\begin{aligned}
n &> \lfloor \log n \rfloor + 2 \\
&\geq r(p(v)) \\
&\geq A_i(r(v)) \\
&\geq A_i(2).
\end{aligned}
$$

Or, put another way,

$$L(v) < \alpha(n),$$

for all v and t.

The main computational task in performing a find operation is in following parent pointers along a path, P, from a some node u up to the root, z, of the tree containing u at time t. We can account for all of this work by paying 1 cyber-dollar for each parent pointer we traverse. Let v be some node along P. We use two rules for charging a cyber-dollar for following the parent pointer for v:

- If v has an ancestor w in P such that $L(v) = L(w)$, at this point in time, then we charge 1 cyber-dollar to v itself.
- If v has no such ancestor, then we charge 1 cyber-dollar to this find operation.

Thus, the maximum number of cyber-dollars any find can get charged is bounded by the number of distinct $L(v)$ values for nodes on the path P, which is less than $\alpha(n)$, as we observed above. The total amount of cyber-dollars charged to all the find operations is therefore $O(m\,\alpha(n))$.

Let us next consider all the charges that are made to a vertex v over the course of performing the find operations in σ. For such a charge to occur at time t, then v must have an ancestor w such that $L(v) = L(w) = i$, for some i. So, at time t,

$$r(p(v)) \geq A_i(r(v))$$

and

$$r(p(w)) \geq A_i(r(w)).$$

Suppose, in particular, that

$$r(p(v)) \geq A_i^{(k)}(r(v)),$$

where $k \geq 1$. Recall that z denotes the last vertex on the path P. Then at time t,

$$
\begin{aligned}
r(z) &\geq r(p(w)) \\
&\geq A_i(r(w)) \\
&\geq A_i(r(p(v))) \\
&\geq A_i(A_i^{(k)}(r(v))) \\
&\geq A_i^{(k+1)}(r(v)).
\end{aligned}
$$

Therefore, since z becomes the new parent of v at time $t + 1$, because of path compression, we have at time $t + 1$,

$$r(p(v)) \geq A_i^{(k+1)}(r(v)).$$

This implies that at most $r(v)$ charges can be made to v before

$$
\begin{aligned}
r(p(v)) &\geq A_i^{(r(v))}(r(v)) \\
&= A_{i+1}(r(v)),
\end{aligned}
$$

at which point $L(v) = i + 1$. Thus, after at most $r(v)$ cyber-dollars are charged against v, $L(v)$ increases by at least 1. Since $L(v)$ can increase at most $\alpha(n) - 1$ times, this means that there can be at most $r(v)$ times $\alpha(n)$ cyber-dollars charged to v in total. Combining this fact with Lemma 7.5, there are at most

$$s \, \alpha(n) \frac{n}{2^{s-2}} = n \, \alpha(n) \frac{s}{2^{s-2}}$$

cyber-dollars charged to all the vertices of rank s. Summing over all possible ranks, the total number of cyber-dollars charged to all nodes is at most

$$\sum_{s=0}^{\lfloor \log n \rfloor + 2} n \, \alpha(n) \frac{s}{2^{s-2}} \;\leq\; \sum_{s=0}^{\infty} n \, \alpha(n) \frac{s}{2^{s-2}}$$

$$=\; n \, \alpha(n) \sum_{s=0}^{\infty} \frac{s}{2^{s-2}}$$

$$\leq\; 8n \, \alpha(n),$$

by a well-known summation bound (see Theorem A.15 in the appendix). That is, the total charges made to all nodes is $O(n \, \alpha(n))$, which gives us the following:

Theorem 7.6: *In a sequence σ of m* union *and* find *operations performed using union-by-size and path compression, starting with a collection of n single-element sets, the total time to perform the operations in σ is $O((n + m)\alpha(n))$.*

7.4 Exercises

Reinforcement

R-7.1 Suppose we have a social network with members A, B, C, D, E, F, and G, and the set of friendship ties,

$$\{(A, B), (B, C), (C, A), (D, E), (F, G)\}.$$

What are the connected components?

R-7.2 Suppose a social network, N, contains n people, m edges, and c connected components. What is the exact number of times that each of the methods, makeSet, union, and find, are called in computing the connected components for N using Algorithm 7.2?

R-7.3 How many walls were erased to construct the maze in Figure 7.3, not counting the start and finish walls?

R-7.4 For the sake of analysis, if we have a sequence of union, find, and makeSet operations, why can we can assume without loss of generality that all the makeSet operations come first?

R-7.5 One additional feature of the list-based implementation of a union-find structure is that it allows for the contents of any set in a partition to be listed in time proportional to the size of the set. Describe how this can be done.

R-7.6 Suppose we have 20 singleton sets, numbered 0 through 19, and we call the operation union(find(i),find($i + 5$)), for $i = 0, 1, 2, \ldots, 14$. Draw a picture of a list-based representation of the sets that result.

R-7.7 Suppose we have 20 singleton sets, numbered 0 through 19, and we call the operation union(find(i),find($i + 5$)), for $i = 0, 1, 2, \ldots, 14$. Draw a picture of a tree-based representation of the sets that result, assuming we don't implement the union-by-size and path compression heuristics.

R-7.8 Answer the previous exercise assuming that we implement both the union-by-size and path compression heuristics.

Creativity

C-7.1 Describe how to implement a union-find structure using extendable arrays, which each contains the elements in a single set, instead of linked lists. Show how this solution can be used to process a sequence of m union-find operations on an initial collection of n singleton sets in $O(n \log n + m)$ time.

C-7.2 Consider a method, remove(e), which removes e from whichever list it belongs to, in a list-based implementation of a union-find structure. Describe how to modify the list-based implementation so that this method runs in time $O(1)$.

C-7.3 Suppose that we implement a union-find structure by representing each set using a balanced search tree. Describe and analyze algorithms for each of the methods for a union-find structure so that every operation runs in at most $O(\log n)$ time in the *worst case*.

C-7.4 Let A be a collection of objects. Describe an efficient method for converting A into a set. That is, remove all duplicates from A. What is the running time of this method?

C-7.5 Suppose we implement the tree-based union-find data structure using the union-by-size heuristic and a *partial* path-compression heuristic. The partial path compression in this case means that, after performing a sequence of pointer hops for a find operation, we update the parent pointer for each node u along this path to point to its grandparent. Show that the total running time for performing m union and find operations, starting with n singleton sets, is still $O((n+m)\alpha(n))$ in this case.

C-7.6 Suppose we implement the tree-based union-find data structure using the union-by-size and path-compression heuristics. Show that the total running time for performing a sequence of m union and find operations, starting with n singleton sets, is $O(n + m)$ if all the unions come before all the finds.

C-7.7 Suppose we implement the tree-based union-find data structure using the union-by-size heuristic and path-compression heuristics. Show that the total running time for performing a sequence of m union and find operations, starting with n singleton sets, is $O(m)$, if $m \geq n \log n$.

C-7.8 Suppose we implement the tree-based union-find data structure, but we don't use the union-by-size heuristic nor the path-compression heuristic. Show that the total running time for performing a sequence of n union and find operations, starting with n singleton sets, is $\Theta(n^2)$ in this case. That is, provide a proof that it is $O(n^2)$ and an example that requires $\Omega(n^2)$ time.

Applications

A-7.1 Another problem of interest in percolation theory is to determine the threshold probability where a liquid will permeate a porous material. One way to model this is to consider the barriers between pairs of adjacent cells in some random order and remove them in this order. At the point when the top and bottom are connected, we would then take the ratio of r/s as an approximation to this threshold probability, where r is the number of barriers considered up to this point and s is the total number of barriers. Describe an algorithm for efficiently computing this threshold value right at the moment it occurs, given a random listing of the pairwise barriers in the porous material as input.

A-7.2 One of the tasks for an operating system is the job of scheduling computations to be performed by the processor(s) that are part of that system. A subtask that comes up in some processor scheduling problems is to solve a sequence σ of $O(n)$ priority queue operations, where each operation in σ is either an insert(i) or removeMin(), such that i is a distinct integer in the range from 1 to n. This problem is known as the *offline-min problem*, since the entire sequence, σ, is given in advance. Interestingly, the offline nature of this problem gives us a faster way of answering the operations in σ than using a heap. Namely, if k is the smallest integer inserted somewhere in σ, then we know the very next removeMin() in σ will return k. Likewise, after we have matched up k and this removeMin(), and deleted both from σ, then we can repeat this argument on the operations that remain. Use this observation to design an algorithm for answering all the operations in σ in $O(n\alpha(n))$ time, and thereby solve the offline-min problem.

A-7.3 In image-processing applications, such as for optical character recognition, it is often useful to group together contiguous sets of similarly colored pixels in an image. (See Figure 7.11.) For instance, in a black-and-white image, we might say that a black pixel, p, is adjacent with another black pixel, q, if q shares a boundary with p's North, East, South, or West boundary. Typically, the way an image is represented imposes constraints on an algorithm for finding the contiguous parts of similarly colored pixels, and, as an image-processing algorithm designer, we often don't get to dictate the order in which pixels are presented. Design an efficient algorithm that can take a sequence of black or white pixels, given in an arbitrary order, taken from some image, and output all the contiguous shapes in that image. You may assume that each time a pixel is given, you are told its (x, y)-coordinates and the colors of its North, East, South, and West neighbors.

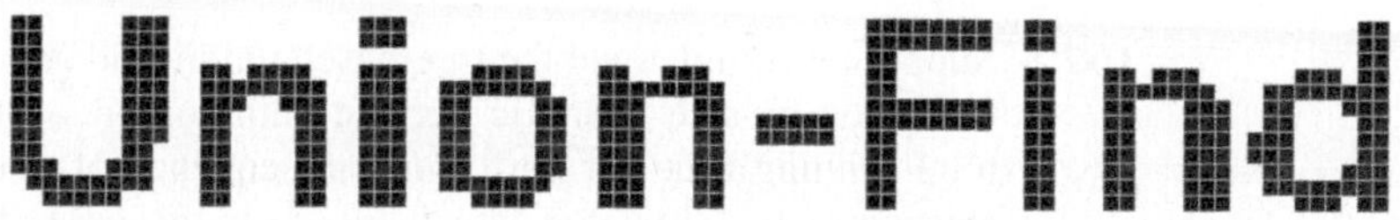

Figure 7.11: Contiguous regions of similarly colored pixels in an image. This image has 12 such regions.

A-7.4 The game of *Hex* is said to have, as one of its inventors, the mathematician John Nash, who is the subject of the book and movie *A Beautiful Mind*. In this game, two players, one playing black and the other playing white, take turns placing stones of their respective colors on an $n \times n$ hexagonal grid. Once a stone is placed, it cannot be moved. The black player's goal is to connect the top and bottom sides of the grid, and the white player's goal is to connect the left and right sides of the grid, using stones of their respective colors. Two cells are considered connected if they share an edge and both have the same color stone. (See Figure 7.12.) Describe an efficient scheme where you can determine after each move whether black or white has just won a game of Hex.

A-7.5 Consider the game of Hex, as in the previous exercise, but now with a twist. Suppose some number, k, of the cells in the game board are colored gold and if the set of stones that connect the two sides of a winning player's board are also connected to $k' \le k$ of the gold cells, then that player gets k' bonus points.

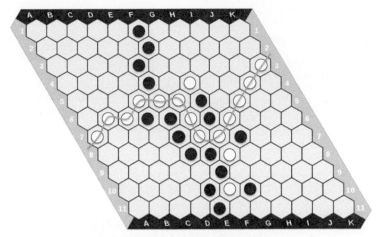

Figure 7.12: An 11×11 instance of the game of Hex. In this case, the white player has just placed a stone to create a winning configuration. (Background Hex board image is in the public domain; credit: Tiltec.)

Describe an efficient way to detect when a player wins and also, at that same moment, determine how many bonus points they get. What is the running time of your method over the course of a game consisting of n moves?

Chapter Notes

Tarjan [206] was the first to show that a sequence of n union and find operations, implemented as described in this chapter, can be performed in $O(n\,\alpha(n))$ time, and this bound is tight in the worst case (see also [207, 209]). The analysis we give for the tree-based implementation of the union-find operations is based on related discussions by Hopcroft and Ullman [103] and Kozen [135]. Cormen *et al.* [51] provide an alternative analysis based on a potential argument and another analysis can be found in a more recent paper by Seidel and Sharir [192].

Kaplan *et al.* [116] and Alstrup *et al.* [11] study an efficient way to support deletions as well as union-find operations. Agarwal *et al.* [5] study the union-find problem in the external-memory model and explore several applications in terrain analysis. Gabow and Tarjan [77] show that certain special cases of the union-find problem can be solved in linear time, including instances that arise in the offline-min problem, and Frederickson [75] shows a connection between processor scheduling and the offline-min problem. Dillencourt *et al.* [57] study the problem of finding contiguous sets of similarly colored pixels in an image and show that if an image is given in raster order, this problem can be solved in linear time by exploiting special properties in the union-find problems that arise in this application. For more algorithms for social networks, see the book by Easley and Kleinberg [60].

Chapter 8

Merge-Sort and Quick-Sort

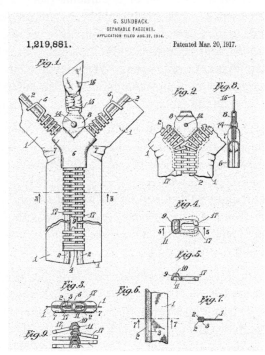

G. SUNDBACK.
SEPARABLE FASTENER.
APPLICATION FILED AUG. 27, 1914.

1,219,881.   Patented Mar. 20, 1917.

Fig.1.

Fig.2.

Fig.8.

Fig.4.

Fig.5.

Fig.3.

Fig.6.

Fig.7.

Fig.9.

Separable Fastener, U.S. Patent 1,219,881, 1917.
Public domain image.

Contents

8.1 Merge-Sort 243
8.2 Quick-Sort 250
8.3 A Lower Bound on Comparison-Based Sorting 257
8.4 Exercises 259

Recall that in the sorting problem, we are given a collection of n comparable items and we are asked to place them in order.

Efficient sorting algorithms have a wide range of applications, including uses in the underlying technologies behind Internet search engines Sorting arises, for example, in the steps needed to build a data structure that allows a search engine to quickly return a list of the documents that contain a given keyword. This data structure is known as the *inverted file*.

Given a collection of documents (such as the web pages found by a search engine when it was crawling the web), an inverted file is a lookup table that matches words to the documents containing those words. It is indexed by keywords found in the document collection and it includes, for each keyword, a list of the documents where that keyword appears. This lookup table allows the search engine to quickly return the documents containing a given keyword just by doing a lookup for that keyword in the table.

The data is not given in this format, however. In fact, it starts out as just a collection of documents. To construct an inverted file, we must first create a set of keyword-document pairs, (k, d), where k is a keyword and d is the identifier for a document where k appears. Fortunately, constructing such a set of keyword-document pairs is fairly easy—we can simply scan the contents of each document, d, and output a pair, (k, d), for each keyword, k, found in d. Thus, we can assume that we can start with a set of keyword-document pairs, from which we then want to build an inverted file.

Building an inverted file data structure from a set of keyword-document pairs requires that we bring together, for each keyword, k, all the documents that contain k. Bringing all such documents together can be done simply by sorting the set of keyword-document pairs by keywords. This places all the (k, d) pairs with the same keyword, k, right next to one another in the output list. From this sorted list, it is then a simple computation to scan the list and build a lookup table of documents for each keyword that appears in this sorted list.

In practice, most search engines go one step further, and not only sort the set of keyword-document pairs by keywords, but break ties between (k, d) pairs with the same keyword, k, by using a relevance (or ranking) score for the document, d, as a secondary key (following a *lexicographic* ordering rule). Taking this approach implies that the (k, d) pairs with the same keyword, k, will be ordered in the sorted list according to the score of their document, d. Thus, having a fast algorithm for sorting can be very helpful for a search engine, particularly if that algorithm is designed to work quickly for large sets of input data. We study two sorting algorithms in this chapter. The first algorithm, called merge-sort, is ideally suited for very large data sets, which must be accessed on a hard drive or network storage system. The second algorithm, called quick-sort, is very efficient for moderately large data sets that fit in the computer's main memory (RAM).

8.1 Merge-Sort

In this section, we present a sorting technique, called *merge-sort*, that can be described in a simple and compact way using recursion.

8.1.1 Divide-and-Conquer

Merge-sort is based on an algorithmic paradigm called *divide-and-conquer*. The divide-and-conquer paradigm can be described in general terms as consisting of the following three steps (see Figure 8.1):

1. *Divide:* If the input size is smaller than a certain threshold (say, 10 elements), solve the problem directly using a straightforward method and return the solution so obtained. Otherwise, divide the input data into two or more disjoint subsets.

2. *Recur:* Recursively solve the subproblems associated with the subsets.

3. *Conquer:* Take the solutions to the subproblems and "merge" them into a solution to the original problem.

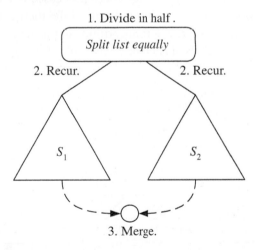

Figure 8.1: A visual schematic of the divide-and-conquer paradigm, applied to a problem involving a list that is divided equally in two in the divide step.

Merge-sort applies the divide-and-conquer technique to the sorting problem, where, for the sake of generality, let us consider the sorting problem to take a sequence, S, of objects as input, which could be represented with either a list or an array, and returns S in sorted order.

For the problem of sorting a sequence S with n elements, the three divide-and-conquer steps are as follows:

1. ***Divide:*** If S has zero or one element, return S immediately; it is already sorted. Otherwise (S has at least two elements), put the elements of S into two sequences, S_1 and S_2, each containing about half of the elements of S; that is, S_1 contains the first $\lceil n/2 \rceil$ elements of S, and S_2 contains the remaining $\lfloor n/2 \rfloor$ elements.

2. ***Recur:*** Recursively sort the sequences S_1 and S_2.

3. ***Conquer:*** Put back the elements into S by merging the sorted sequences S_1 and S_2 into a sorted sequence.

We can visualize an execution of the merge-sort algorithm using a binary tree T, called the ***merge-sort tree***. (See Figure 8.2.) Each node of the merge-sort tree, T, represents a recursive call of the merge-sort algorithm. We associate with each node v of T the sequence S that is processed by the call associated with v. The children of node v are associated with the recursive calls that process the subsequences S_1 and S_2 of S. The external nodes of T are associated with individual elements of S, corresponding to instances of the algorithm that make no recursive calls.

Figure 8.2 summarizes an execution of the merge-sort algorithm by showing the input and output sequences processed at each node of the merge-sort tree. This algorithm visualization in terms of the merge-sort tree helps us analyze the running time of the merge-sort algorithm. In particular, since the size of the input sequence roughly halves at each recursive call of merge-sort, the height of the merge-sort tree is about $\log n$ (recall that the base of log is 2 if omitted).

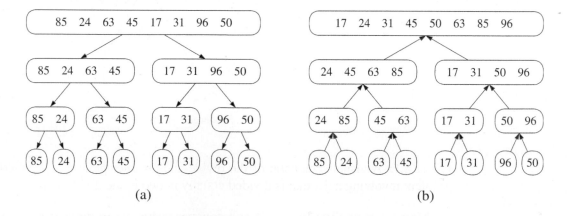

(a)   (b)

Figure 8.2: Merge-sort tree T for an execution of the merge-sort algorithm on a sequence with eight elements: (a) input sequences processed at each node of T; (b) output sequences generated at each node of T.

Having given an overview of merge-sort and an illustration of how it works, let us consider each of the steps of this divide-and-conquer algorithm in more detail. The divide and recur steps of the merge-sort algorithm are simple; dividing a sequence of size n involves separating it at the element with rank $\lceil n/2 \rceil$, and the recursive calls simply involve passing these smaller sequences as parameters. The difficult step is the conquer step, which merges two sorted sequences into a single sorted sequence. We provide a pseudocode description of the method for merging two sorted arrays in Algorithm 8.3. It merges two sorted arrays, S_1 and S_2, by iteratively removing a smallest element from one of these two and adding it to the end of an output array, S, until one of these two arrays is empty, at which point we copy the remainder of the other array to the output array.

Algorithm merge(S_1, S_2, S):
> **Input:** Two arrays, S_1 and S_2, of size n_1 and n_2, respectively, sorted in non-decreasing order, and an empty array, S, of size at least $n_1 + n_2$
> **Output:** S, containing the elements from S_1 and S_2 in sorted order
>
> $i \leftarrow 1$
> $j \leftarrow 1$
> **while** $i \leq n$ **and** $j \leq n$ **do**
>> **if** $S_1[i] \leq S_2[j]$ **then**
>>> $S[i + j - 1] \leftarrow S_1[i]$
>>> $i \leftarrow i + 1$
>>
>> **else**
>>> $S[i + j - 1] \leftarrow S_2[j]$
>>> $j \leftarrow j + 1$
>
> **while** $i \leq n$ **do**
>> $S[i + j - 1] \leftarrow S_1[i]$
>> $i \leftarrow i + 1$
>
> **while** $j \leq n$ **do**
>> $S[i + j - 1] \leftarrow S_2[j]$
>> $j \leftarrow j + 1$

Algorithm 8.3: Merging two sorted arrays, with indexing beginning at 1.

One of the nice properties of this merge algorithm is that the while loops involve simple scans of the input arrays, S_1 and S_2. For large data sets, this kind of data access is efficient, because of the sequential way that data is typically accessed in external storage devices, like disk drives. The trade-off for this benefit, however, is that we have to use an output array, S, rather than reusing the space in the input arrays themselves.

If we want to merge two sorted sequences given as linked lists, instead of arrays, then we would use a similar method to the array-based merge algorithm, which would involve our comparing the front elements in the two lists, removing the smaller one from its list, and adding that element to the end of an output linked list. Once one of the lists is empty, we would then copy the remainder of the other list to the output list.

We show an example execution of a list-based merge algorithm in Figure 8.4.

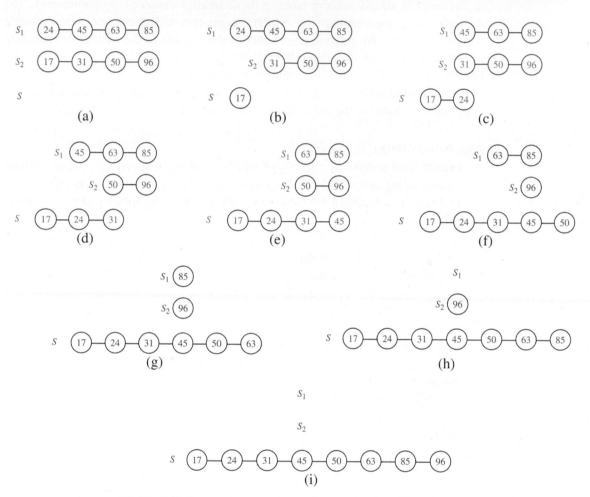

Figure 8.4: Example execution of a merge algorithm for sorted linked lists.

Analysis of the Merge-Sort Algorithm

Our analysis for the merge-sort algorithm begins with the **merge** algorithm. Let n_1 and n_2 be the number of elements of S_1 and S_2, respectively. Algorithm **merge** has three **while** loops. The operations performed inside each loop take $O(1)$ time each. The key observation is that during each iteration of any one of the loops, one element is added to the output array S and is never considered again. This observation implies that the overall number of iterations of the three loops is $n_1 +$

n_2. Thus, the running time of algorithm merge is $O(n_1 + n_2)$, as we summarize:

Theorem 8.1: *Merging two sorted arrays S_1 and S_2 takes $O(n_1 + n_2)$ time, where n_1 is the size of S_1 and n_2 is the size of S_2.*

Having given the details of the merge algorithm, let us analyze the running time of the entire merge-sort algorithm, assuming it is given an input sequence of n elements. For simplicity, let us also assume n is a power of 2. We analyze the merge-sort algorithm by referring to the merge-sort tree, T.

First, we analyze the height of the merge-sort tree, T, referring to Figure 8.5.

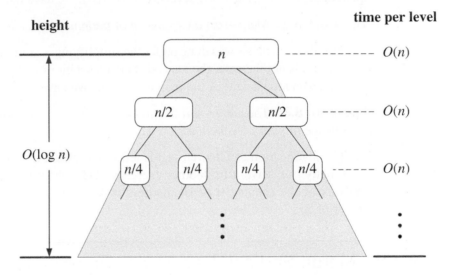

Total time: $O(n \log n)$

Figure 8.5: A visual analysis of the running time of merge-sort. Each node of the merge-sort tree is labeled with the size of its subproblem.

We observe that the length of the subsequence stored at a node of T with depth (distance from the root) i is $n/2^i$ since we halve the length of the sequence each time we go down one level. Thus, a node at depth $i = \log n$ stores a single-element subsequence and therefore is a leaf of the tree. We conclude that the height of the merge-sort tree is $\log n$.

We call the *time spent at a node* v of T the running time of the recursive call associated with v, excluding the time taken waiting for the recursive calls associated with the children of v to terminate. In other words, the time spent at node v includes the running times of the divide and conquer steps, but excludes the running time of the recur step. We have already observed that the details of the divide step are straightforward; this step runs in time proportional to the size of the sequence for v. Also, as shown in Theorem 8.1, the conquer step, which consists of merging two sorted subsequences, also takes linear time. That is, letting i denote the depth of node v, the time spent at node v is $O(n/2^i)$, since the size of the sequence handled by the recursive call associated with v is equal to $n/2^i$.

Looking at the tree T more globally, as shown in Figure 8.5, we see that, given our definition of "time spent at a node," the running time of merge-sort is equal to the sum of the times spent at the nodes of T. Observe that T has exactly 2^i nodes at depth i. This simple observation has an important consequence, for it implies that the overall time spent at all the nodes of T at depth i is $O(2^i \cdot n/2^i)$, which is $O(n)$. We have previously seen that the height of T is $\log n$. Thus, since the time spent at each of the $\log n + 1$ levels of T is $O(n)$, we have the following result:

Theorem 8.2: *Merge-sort on sequence of n elements runs in $O(n \log n)$ time.*

The above analysis was done under the simplifying assumption that n is a power of 2. If this is not the case, the analysis becomes a bit more complicated.

Regarding the height of the merge-sort tree, we have:

Theorem 8.3: *The merge-sort tree associated with an execution of merge-sort on a sequence of size n has height $\lceil \log n \rceil$.*

The justification of Theorem 8.3 is left to a simple exercise (R-8.1).

Finally, we leave it to another exercise (R-8.3) how to extend the rest of the analysis of the running time of merge-sort to the general case when n is not a power of 2.

8.1.2 Merge-Sort and Recurrence Equations

There is another way to justify that the running time of the merge-sort algorithm is $O(n \log n)$. Let the function $t(n)$ denote the worst-case running time of merge-sort on an input sequence of size n. Since merge-sort is recursive, we can characterize function $t(n)$ by means of the following equalities, where function $t(n)$ is recursively expressed in terms of itself, as follows:

$$t(n) = \begin{cases} b & \text{if } n = 1 \text{ or } n = 0 \\ t(\lceil n/2 \rceil) + t(\lfloor n/2 \rfloor) + cn & \text{otherwise} \end{cases}$$

where $b > 0$ and $c > 0$ are constants. A characterization of a function such as the one above is called a **recurrence equation** (Sections 1.1.4 and 11.1), since the function appears on both the left- and right-hand sides of the equal sign. Although such a characterization is correct and accurate, what we really desire is a big-Oh type of characterization of $t(n)$ that does not involve the function $t(n)$ itself (that is, we want a **closed-form** characterization of $t(n)$).

In order to provide a closed-form characterization of $t(n)$, let us restrict our attention to the case when n is a power of 2. We leave the problem of showing that our asymptotic characterization still holds in the general case as an exercise (R-8.3). In this case, we can simplify the definition of $t(n)$ as follows:

$$t(n) = \begin{cases} b & \text{if } n = 1 \\ 2t(n/2) + cn & \text{otherwise.} \end{cases}$$

But, even so, we must still try to characterize this recurrence equation in a closed-form way. One way to do this is to iteratively apply this equation, assuming n is relatively large. For example, after one more application of this equation, we can write a new recurrence for $t(n)$ as follows:

$$\begin{aligned} t(n) &= 2\left(2t\left(n/2^2\right) + (cn/2)\right) + cn \\ &= 2^2 t\left(n/2^2\right) + 2cn. \end{aligned}$$

If we apply the equation again, we get

$$t(n) = 2^3 l\left(n/2^3\right) + 3cn.$$

Applying the equation once again, we obtain

$$t(n) = 2^4 t\left(n/2^4\right) + 4cn.$$

Now, a clear pattern emerges, and we infer that after applying this equation i times, we get

$$t(n) = 2^i t\left(n/2^i\right) + icn.$$

The issue that remains, then, is to determine when to stop this process. To see when to stop, recall that we switch to the closed form $t(n) = b$ when $n = 1$, which occurs when $2^i = n$. In other words, this will occur when $i = \log n$. Making this substitution yields

$$\begin{aligned} t(n) &= 2^{\log n} t\left(n/2^{\log n}\right) + (\log n)cn \\ &= nt(1) + cn \log n \\ &= nb + cn \log n. \end{aligned}$$

That is, we get an alternative justification of the fact that $t(n)$ is $O(n \log n)$.

8.2 Quick-Sort

The quick-sort algorithm sorts a sequence S using a simple divide-and-conquer approach, whereby we divide S into subsequences, recur to sort each subsequence, and then combine the sorted subsequences by a simple concatenation. In particular, the quick-sort algorithm consists of the following three steps (see Figure 8.6):

1. ***Divide:*** If S has at least two elements (nothing needs to be done if S has zero or one element), select a specific element x from S, which is called the ***pivot***. As is common practice, choose the pivot x to be the last element in S. Remove all the elements from S and put them into three sequences:

   - L, storing the elements in S less than x
   - E, storing the elements in S equal to x
   - G, storing the elements in S greater than x.

   (If the elements of S are all distinct, E holds just one element—the pivot.)

2. ***Recur:*** Recursively sort sequences L and G.

3. ***Conquer:*** Put the elements back into S in order by first inserting the elements of L, then those of E, and finally those of G.

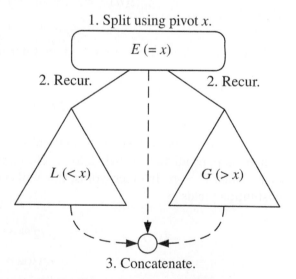

Figure 8.6: A visual schematic of the quick-sort algorithm.

Like merge-sort, we can visualize quick-sort using a binary recursion tree, called the *quick-sort tree*. Figure 8.7 visualizes the quick-sort algorithm, showing example input and output sequences for each node of the quick-sort tree.

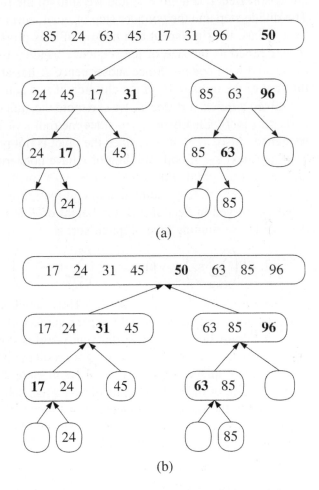

Figure 8.7: Quick-sort tree T for an execution of the quick-sort algorithm on a sequence with eight elements: (a) input sequences processed at each node of T; (b) output sequences generated at each node of T. The pivot used at each level of the recursion is shown in bold.

Unlike merge-sort, however, the height of the quick-sort tree associated with an execution of quick-sort is linear in the worst case. This happens, for example, if the sequence consists of n distinct elements and is already sorted. Indeed, in this case, the standard choice of the pivot as the largest element yields a subsequence L of size $n - 1$, while subsequence E has size 1 and subsequence G has size 0. Hence, the height of the quick-sort tree is $n - 1$ in the worst case.

Running Time of Quick-Sort

We can analyze the running time of quick-sort with the same technique used for merge-sort in Section 8.1.1. Namely, we identify the time spent at each node of the quick-sort tree T (Figure 8.7) and we sum up the running times for all the nodes. The divide step and the conquer step of quick-sort are easy to implement in linear time. Thus, the time spent at a node v of T is proportional to the *input size* $s(v)$ of v, defined as the size of the sequence handled by the invocation of quick-sort associated with node v. Since subsequence E has at least one element (the pivot), the sum of the input sizes of the children of v is at most $s(v) - 1$.

Given a quick-sort tree T, let s_i denote the sum of the input sizes of the nodes at depth i in T. Clearly, $s_0 = n$, since the root r of T is associated with the entire sequence. Also, $s_1 \leq n - 1$, since the pivot is not propagated to the children of r. Consider next s_2. If both children of r have nonzero input size, then $s_2 = n - 3$. Otherwise (one child of the root has zero size, the other has size $n-1$), $s_2 = n-2$. Thus, $s_2 \leq n - 2$. Continuing this line of reasoning, we obtain that $s_i \leq n - i$.

As observed in Section 8.2, the height of T is $n - 1$ in the worst case. Thus, the worst-case running time of quick-sort is

$$O\left(\sum_{i=0}^{n-1} s_i\right), \quad \text{which is} \quad O\left(\sum_{i=0}^{n-1} (n-i)\right) \quad \text{that is,} \quad O\left(\sum_{i=1}^{n} i\right).$$

By Theorem 1.13, $\sum_{i=1}^{n} i$ is $O(n^2)$. Thus, quick-sort runs in $O(n^2)$ worst-case time. Given its name, we would expect quick-sort to run quickly. However, the above quadratic bound indicates that quick-sort is slow in the worst case. Paradoxically, this worst-case behavior occurs for problem instances when sorting should be easy—if the sequence is already sorted. Still, note that the best case for quick-sort on a sequence of distinct elements occurs when subsequences L and G happen to have roughly the same size. Indeed, in this case we save one pivot at each internal node and make two equal-sized calls for its children. Thus, we save 1 pivot at the root, 2 at level 1, 2^2 at level 2, and so on. That is, in the best case, we have

$$
\begin{aligned}
s_0 &= n \\
s_1 &= n - 1 \\
s_2 &= n - (1 + 2) = n - 3 \\
&\;\vdots \\
s_i &= n - (1 + 2 + 2^2 + \cdots + 2^{i-1}) = n - (2^i - 1),
\end{aligned}
$$

and so on. Thus, in the best case, T has height $O(\log n)$ and quick-sort runs in $O(n \log n)$ time. We leave the justification of this fact as an exercise (R-8.6).

The informal intuition behind the expected behavior of quick-sort is that at each invocation the pivot will probably divide the input sequence about equally. Thus, we expect the average running time of quick-sort to be similar to the best-case running time, that is, $O(n \log n)$. We will see in the next section that introducing randomization makes quick-sort behave exactly as described above.

8.2.1 Randomized Quick-Sort

One common method for analyzing quick-sort is to assume that the pivot will always divide the sequence almost equally. We feel such an assumption would presuppose knowledge about the input distribution that is typically not available, however. For example, we would have to assume that we will rarely be given "almost" sorted sequences to sort, which are actually common in many applications. Fortunately, this assumption is not needed in order for us to match our intuition to quick-sort's behavior.

Since the goal of the partition step of the quick-sort method is to divide the sequence S almost equally, let us use a new rule to pick the pivot—choose a ***random element*** of the input sequence. As we show next, the resulting algorithm, called ***randomized quick-sort***, has an expected running time of $O(n \log n)$ given a sequence with n elements.

Theorem 8.4: *The expected running time of randomized quick-sort on a sequence of size n is $O(n \log n)$.*

Proof: We make use of a simple fact from probability theory:

> *The expected number of times that a fair coin must be flipped until it shows "heads" k times is $2k$.*

Consider now a particular recursive invocation of randomized quick-sort, and let m denote the size of the input sequence for this invocation. Say that this invocation is "good" if the pivot chosen creates subsequences L and G that have size at least $m/4$ and at most $3m/4$ each. Since the pivot is chosen uniformly at random and there are $m/2$ pivots for which this invocation is good, the probability that an invocation is good is $1/2$ (the same as the probability a coin comes up heads).

If a node v of the quick-sort tree T, as shown in Figure 8.8, is associated with a "good" recursive call, then the input sizes of the children of v are each at most $3s(v)/4$ (which is the same as $s(v)/(4/3)$). If we take any path in T from the root to an external node, then the length of this path is at most the number of invocations that have to be made (at each node on this path) until achieving $\log_{4/3} n$ good invocations. Applying the probabilistic fact reviewed above, the expected number of invocations we must make until this occurs is $2 \log_{4/3} n$ (if a path terminates before this level, that is all the better). Thus, the expected length of any path from the root to an external node in T is $O(\log n)$. Recalling that the time spent at each level of T is $O(n)$, the expected running time of randomized quick-sort is $O(n \log n)$. ∎

We note that the expectation in the running time is taken over all the possible choices the algorithm makes, and is independent of any assumptions about the distribution of input sequences the algorithm is likely to encounter. Actually, by using powerful facts from probability, we can show that the running time of randomized quick-sort is $O(n \log n)$ with high probability. (See Exercise C-8.4.)

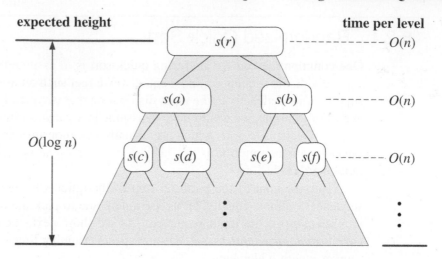

total expected time: $O(n \log n)$

Figure 8.8: A visual time analysis of the quick-sort tree T.

8.2.2   In-Place Quick-Sort

Recall from Section 5.4 that a sorting algorithm is ***in-place*** if it uses only a small amount of memory in addition to that needed for the objects being sorted themselves. The merge-sort algorithm, as we have described it above, is not in-place, and making it be in-place seems quite difficult. In-place sorting is not inherently difficult, however. For, as with heap-sort, quick-sort can be adapted to be in-place.

Performing the quick-sort algorithm in-place requires a bit of ingenuity, however, for we must use an input array itself to store the subarrays for all the recursive calls. We show algorithm inPlaceQuickSort, which performs in-place quick-sort, in Algorithm 8.9. Algorithm inPlaceQuickSort assumes that the input array, S, has distinct elements. The reason for this restriction is explored in Exercise R-8.7. The extension to the general case is discussed in Exercise C-8.8.

In-place quick-sort modifies the input sequence using swapElements operations and does not explicitly create subsequences. Indeed, a subsequence of the input sequence is implicitly represented by a range of positions specified by a left-most rank l and a right-most rank r. The divide step is performed by scanning the sequence simultaneously from l forward and from r backward, swapping pairs of elements that are in reverse order, as shown in Figure 8.10. When these two indices "meet," subsequences L and G are on opposite sides of the meeting point. The algorithm completes by recursing on these two subsequences. In-place quick-sort reduces the running time, caused by the creation of new sequences and the movement of elements between them, by a constant factor.

Algorithm inPlacePartition(S, a, b):

    Input: An array, S, of distinct elements; integers a and b such that $a \leq b$

    Output: An integer, l, such that the subarray $S[a .. b]$ is partitioned into $S[a..l-1]$ and $S[l..b]$ so that every element in $S[a..l-1]$ is less than each element in $S[l..b]$

    Let r be a random integer in the range $[a, b]$

    Swap $S[r]$ and $S[b]$

    $p \leftarrow S[b]$ // the pivot

    $l \leftarrow a$ // l will scan rightward

    $r \leftarrow b - 1$ // r will scan leftward

    while $l \leq r$ **do** // find an element larger than the pivot

        while $l \leq r$ **and** $S[l] \leq p$ **do**

            $l \leftarrow l + 1$

        while $r \geq l$ **and** $S[r] \geq p$ **do** // find an element smaller than the pivot

            $r \leftarrow r - 1$

        if $l < r$ **then**

            Swap $S[l]$ and $S[r]$

    Swap $S[l]$ and $S[b]$ // put the pivot into its final place

    return l

Algorithm inPlaceQuickSort(S, a, b):

    Input: An array, S, of distinct elements; integers a and b

    Output: The subarray $S[a .. b]$ arranged in nondecreasing order

    if $a \geq b$ **then return**   // subrange with 0 or 1 elements

    $l \leftarrow$ inPlacePartition(S, a, b)

    inPlaceQuickSort($S, a, l - 1$)

    inPlaceQuickSort($S, l + 1, b$)

Algorithm 8.9: In-place randomized quick-sort for an array, S.

Dealing with the Recursion Stack

Actually, the above description of quick-sort is not quite in-place, as it could, in the worst case, require a linear amount of additional space besides the input array. Of course, we are using no additional space for the subsequences, and we are using only a constant amount of additional space for local variables (such as l and r).

So, where does this additional space come from?

It comes from the recursion, since we need space for a stack proportional to the depth of the recursion tree in order to keep track of the recursive calls for quick-sort. This stack can become as deep as $\Theta(n)$, in fact, if we have a series of bad pivots, since we need to have a method frame for every active call when we make the call for the deepest node in the quick-sort tree.

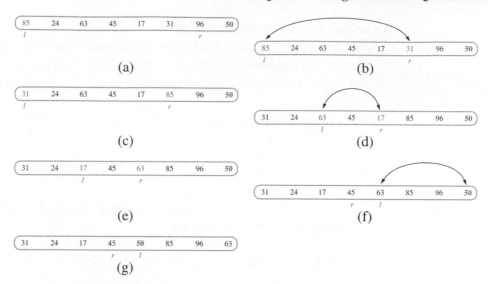

Figure 8.10: An example execution of the inPlacePartition algorithm.

Fortunately, we can fix our quick-sort algorithm to actually be in-place, and use only $O(\log n)$ additional space, by changing the way we do the recursive calls. The key detail for such an implementation is that if we always do the recursive call for the smaller subproblem first, then we can replace the second recursive call with a loop, since it comes last. This ability to change a recursive call into an iteration if it is the last operation in a recursive procedure is known as ***tail recursion***. The details are shown in Algorithm 8.11.

The depth of recursion and, hence, the amount of additional space used for the method stack in Algorithm 8.11 is $O(\log n)$. To see this, note that by doing a recursive call only for the smaller subproblem each time, we guarantee that the size of any recursive subproblem is at most half the size of the subproblem that is making that call. Thus, the depth of the recursion stack is never more than $O(\log n)$.

Algorithm CorrectInPlaceQuickSort(S, a, b):

    Input: An array, S, of distinct elements; integers a and b

    Output: The subarray $S[a .. b]$ arranged in nondecreasing order

    while $a < b$ **do**

        $l \leftarrow$ inPlacePartition(S, a, b)   // from Algorithm 8.9

        if $l - a < b - l$ **then**   // first subarray is smaller

            CorrectInPlaceQuickSort($S, a, l - 1$)

            $a \leftarrow l + 1$

        else

            CorrectInPlaceQuickSort($S, l + 1, b$)

            $b \leftarrow l - 1$

Algorithm 8.11: Correct version of in-place randomized quick-sort for an array, S.

8.3 A Lower Bound on Comparison-Based Sorting

Recapping our discussions on sorting to this point, we have described several methods with either a worst-case or expected running time of $O(n \log n)$ on an input sequence of size n. These methods include merge-sort and quick-sort, described in this chapter, as well as heap-sort, described in Section 5.4. A natural question to ask, then, is whether it is possible to sort any faster than in $O(n \log n)$ time.

In this section, we show that if the computational primitive used by a sorting algorithm is the comparison of two elements, then this is the best we can do—comparison-based sorting has an $\Omega(n \log n)$ worst-case lower bound on its running time. (Recall the notation $\Omega(\cdot)$ from Section 1.1.5.) To focus on the main cost of comparison-based sorting, let us only count the comparisons that a sorting algorithm performs. Since we want to derive a lower bound, this will be sufficient.

Suppose we are given a sequence $S = (x_1, x_2, \ldots, x_n)$ that we wish to sort, and let us assume that all the elements of S are distinct (this is not a restriction since we are deriving a lower bound). Each time a sorting algorithm compares two elements x_i and x_j (that is, it asks, "is $x_i < x_j$?"), there are two outcomes: "yes" or "no." Based on the result of this comparison, the sorting algorithm may perform some internal calculations (which we are not counting here) and will eventually perform another comparison between two other elements of S, which again will have two outcomes. Therefore, we can represent a comparison-based sorting algorithm with a decision tree T. That is, each internal node v in T corresponds to a comparison and the edges from node v' to its children correspond to the computations resulting from either a "yes" or "no" answer (see Figure 8.12).

It is important to note that the hypothetical sorting algorithm in question probably has no explicit knowledge of the tree T. We simply use T to represent all the possible sequences of comparisons that a sorting algorithm might make, starting from the first comparison (associated with the root) and ending with the last comparison (associated with the parent of an external node) just before the algorithm terminates its execution.

Each possible initial ordering, or ***permutation***, of the elements in S will cause our hypothetical sorting algorithm to execute a series of comparisons, traversing a path in T from the root to some external node. Let us associate with each external node v in T, then, the set of permutations of S that cause our sorting algorithm to end up in v. The most important observation in our lower-bound argument is that each external node v in T can represent the sequence of comparisons for at most one permutation of S. The justification for this claim is simple: if two different permutations P_1 and P_2 of S are associated with the same external node, then there are at least two objects x_i and x_j, such that x_i is before x_j in P_1 but x_i is after x_j in P_2. At the same time, the output associated with v must be a specific reordering of S, with either x_i or x_j appearing before the other. But if P_1 and P_2 both cause the sorting algorithm to output the elements of S in this order, then that implies there is a way to trick the algorithm into outputting x_i and x_j in the wrong order. Since this cannot be allowed by a correct sorting algorithm, each external node of T must be associated with exactly one permutation of S. We use this property of the decision tree associated with a sorting algorithm to prove the following result:

Theorem 8.5: *The running time of any comparison-based algorithm for sorting an n-element sequence is $\Omega(n \log n)$ in the worst case.*

Proof: The running time of a comparison-based sorting algorithm must be greater than or equal to the height of the decision tree T associated with this algorithm, as described above. (See Figure 8.12.) By the above argument, each external node in T must be associated with one permutation of S. Moreover, each permutation of S must result in a different external node of T. The number of permutations of n objects is

$$n! = n(n-1)(n-2)\cdots 2 \cdot 1.$$

Thus, T must have at least $n!$ external nodes. By Theorem 2.7, the height of T is at least $\log(n!)$. This immediately justifies the theorem, because there are at least $n/2$ terms that are greater than or equal to $n/2$ in the product $n!$; hence

$$\log(n!) \geq \log\left(\frac{n}{2}\right)^{\frac{n}{2}} = \frac{n}{2} \log \frac{n}{2},$$

which is $\Omega(n \log n)$.   ∎

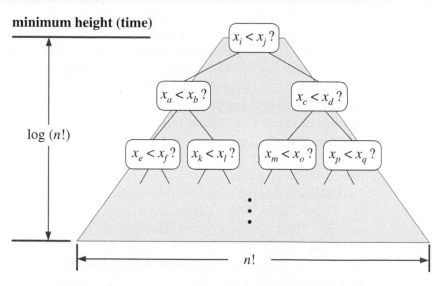

Figure 8.12: Visualizing the lower bound for comparison-based sorting.

8.4 Exercises

Reinforcement

R-8.1 Give a complete justification of Theorem 8.3.

R-8.2 Give a pseudocode description of the merge-sort algorithm assuming the input is given as a linked list.

R-8.3 Show that the running time of the merge-sort algorithm on an n-element sequence is $O(n \log n)$, even when n is not a power of 2.

R-8.4 Suppose we modify the deterministic version of the quick-sort algorithm so that, instead of selecting the last element in an n-element sequence as the pivot, we choose the element at index $\lfloor n/2 \rfloor$, that is, an element in the middle of the sequence. What is the running time of this version of quick-sort on a sequence that is already sorted?

R-8.5 Consider again the modification of the deterministic version of the quick-sort algorithm so that, instead of selecting the last element in an n-element sequence as the pivot, we choose the element at index $\lfloor n/2 \rfloor$. Describe the kind of sequence that would cause this version of quick-sort to run in $\Theta(n^2)$ time.

R-8.6 Show that the best-case running time of quick-sort on a sequence of size n with distinct elements is $O(n \log n)$.

R-8.7 Suppose that algorithm inPlaceQuickSort (Algorithm 8.9) is executed on a sequence with duplicate elements. Show that, in this case, the algorithm correctly sorts the input sequence, but the result of the divide step may differ from the high-level description given in Section 8.2 and may result in inefficiencies. In particular, what happens in the partition step when there are elements equal to the pivot? What is the running time of the algorithm if all the elements of the input sequence are equal?

Creativity

C-8.1 Describe a variation of the merge-sort algorithm that is given a single array, S, as input, and uses only an additional array, T, as a workspace. No other memory should be used other than a constant number of variables.

C-8.2 Let A be a collection of objects. Describe an efficient method for converting A into a set. That is, remove all duplicates from A. What is the running time of this method?

C-8.3 Suppose we are given two n-element sorted sequences A and B that should not be viewed as sets (that is, A and B may contain duplicate entries). Describe an $O(n)$-time method for computing a sequence representing the set $A \cup B$ (with no duplicates).

C-8.4 Show that randomized quick-sort runs in $O(n \log n)$ time with probability $1 - 1/n^2$.

Hint: Use the **Chernoff bound** that states that if we flip a coin k times, then the probability that we get fewer than $k/16$ heads is less than $2^{-k/8}$.

C-8.5 Suppose we are given a sequence S of n elements, each of which is colored red or blue. Assuming S is represented as an array, give an in-place method for ordering S so that all the blue elements are listed before all the red elements. Can you extend your approach to three colors?

C-8.6 Suppose we are given two sequences A and B of n elements, possibly containing duplicates, on which a total order relation is defined. Describe an efficient algorithm for determining if A and B contain the same set of elements (possibly in different orders). What is the running time of this method?

C-8.7 Suppose we are given a sequence S of n elements, on which a total order relation is defined. Describe an efficient method for determining whether there are two equal elements in S. What is the running time of your method?

C-8.8 Modify Algorithm inPlaceQuickSort (Algorithm 8.9) to handle the general case efficiently when the input array, S, may have duplicate keys.

C-8.9 Let S be an array of n elements on which a total order relation is defined. An *inversion* in S is a pair of indices i and j such that $i < j$ but $S[i] > S[j]$. Describe an algorithm running in $O(n \log n)$ time for determining the **number** of inversions in S (which can be as large as $O(n^2)$).

Hint: Try to modify the merge-sort algorithm to solve this problem.

C-8.10 Give an example of a sequence of n integers with $\Omega(n^2)$ inversions. (Recall the definition of inversion from Exercise C-8.9.)

C-8.11 Let A and B be two sequences of n integers each. Given an integer x, describe an $O(n \log n)$-time algorithm for determining if there is an integer a in A and an integer b in B such that $x = a + b$.

C-8.12 Given a sequence of numbers, $(x_1, x_2, \ldots, x_n)$, the **mode** is the value that appears the most number of times in this sequence. Give an efficient algorithm to compute the mode for a sequence of n numbers. What is the running time of your method?

C-8.13 Suppose you would like to sort n music files, but you only have an old, unreliable computer, which you have nicknamed "Rustbucket." Every time Rustbucket compares two music files, x and y, there is an independent 50-50 chance that it has an internal disk fault and returns the value 0, instead of the correct result, 1, for "**true**" or -1, for "**false**," to the question, "$x \le y$?" That is, for each comparison of music files that Rustbucket is asked to perform, it is as if it flips a fair coin and answers the comparison correctly if the coin turns up "heads" and answers with 0 if the coin turns up "tails." Moreover, this behavior occurs independent of previous comparison requests, even for the same pair of music files. Otherwise, Rustbucket correctly performs every other kind of operation (not involving the comparison of two music files), including if-statements, for-loops, and while-loops based on comparisons of integers. Describe an efficient algorithm that can use Rustbucket to sort n music files correctly and show that your algorithm has an expected running time that is $O(n \log n)$.

Applications

A-8.1 Suppose you are given a new hardware device that can merge $k > 2$ different sorted lists of total size n into a single sorted list in $O(n)$ time, independent of the value of k. Such a device could, for example, be based on a hardware streaming system or could be based on a network protocol. Show that you can use this device to sort n elements in $O(n \log n / \log k)$ time. That is, if k is $\Theta(\sqrt{n})$, then you can use this device to sort in linear time.

A-8.2 Suppose we are given an n-element sequence S such that each element in S represents a different vote in an election, where each vote is given as an integer representing the ID of the chosen candidate. Without making any assumptions about who is running or even how many candidates there are, design an $O(n \log n)$-time algorithm to see who wins the election S represents, assuming the candidate with the most votes wins.

A-8.3 Consider the voting problem from the previous exercise, but now suppose that we know the number $k < n$ of candidates running. Describe an $O(n \log k)$-time algorithm for determining who wins the election.

A-8.4 Bob has a set, A, of n nuts and a set, B, of n bolts, such that each nut has a unique matching bolt. Unfortunately, the nuts in A all look the same, and the bolts in B all look the same as well. The only comparison that Bob can make is to take a nut-bolt pair (a, b), such that $a \in A$ and $b \in B$, and test if the threads of a are larger, smaller, or a perfect match with the threads of b. Describe an efficient algorithm for Bob to match up all of his nuts and bolts. What is the running time of this algorithm?

A-8.5 As mentioned above, for each word, w, in a collection of documents, an inverted file stores a list of documents that contain the word, w. In addition, search engines typically order the list for each word by a ranking score. Modern search engines must be able to answer more than just single-word queries, however. Describe an efficient method for computing a list of the documents that contain two words, w and u, ordered by the ranking scores assigned to the documents. What is the running time of your method in terms of n_w and n_u, the respective sizes of the lists for w and u?

A-8.6 In cloud computing, it is common for a client, "Alice," to store her data on an external server owned by a cloud storage provider, "Bob." Because Bob is likely to be honest, but curious, Alice wants to keep the contents of her data private from Bob. Of course, she can encrypt her data using a secret key that only she knows, but that is not enough, since she may reveal information about her data simply based on the pattern in which she accesses her data. Since Bob can see the access pattern for Alice's data, even if she encrypts it, Alice should consider using an algorithm that has a data access pattern that does not depend on any of its input values. Such an algorithm is said to be *data-oblivious*. Suppose, then, that Alice wants to sort an array, A, of elements stored on Bob's computer, but do so in a data-oblivious fashion, so that she sorts privately, even though each time she accesses some item, $A[i]$, in the array, A, Bob learns that she is accessing the item at index i. She can use a constant amount of local private memory, e.g., to store indices, pointers, or to perform a comparison and swap, if the elements

Algorithm OddEvenMerge(A, B, C):

    Input: Two sorted arrays, $A = [a_1, a_2, \ldots, a_n]$ and $B = [b_1, b_2, \ldots, b_n]$, and an empty array, C, of size $2n$

    Output: C, containing the elements from A and B in sorted order

    Let $O_1 \leftarrow [a_1, a_3, a_5, \ldots, a_{n-1}]$

    Let $O_2 \leftarrow [b_1, b_3, b_5, \ldots, b_{n-1}]$

    Let $E_1 \leftarrow [a_2, a_4, a_6, \ldots, a_n]$

    Let $E_2 \leftarrow [b_2, b_4, b_6, \ldots, b_n]$

    Call OddEvenMerge(O_1, O_2, O), where $O = [o_1, o_2, \ldots, o_n]$

    Call OddEvenMerge(E_1, E_2, E), where $E = [e_1, e_2, \ldots, e_n]$

    Let $C \leftarrow [o_1, e_1, o_2, e_2, \ldots, o_n, e_n]$

    for $i \leftarrow 1$ **to** n **do**

        Do a compare-exchange of $C[2i - 1]$ and $C[2i]$

    return C

Algorithm 8.13: Odd-even merge.

are out of order, as an atomic action called a ***compare-exchange***. For example, she could use bubble-sort (Algorithm 5.20) to sort A, since this algorithms is data-oblivious when implemented using the compare-exchange primitive. But this would require $O(n^2)$ time, which is quite inefficient for solving the sorting problem. An alternative is to use the ***odd-even merge-sort*** algorithm, which is the same as the merge-sort algorithm given above, except that the merge step is replaced with the merge method shown in Algorithm 8.13. Argue why the odd-even merge-sort algorithm is data-oblivious, and analyze the running time of the resulting sorting algorithm.

A-8.7 In computer games and also in simulations of card-playing scenarios, we sometimes need to use a computer to simulate the way that person would shuffle a deck of cards. Given two decks of n cards each, the ***riffle shuffle*** algorithm involves repeatedly choosing one of the two decks at random and then removing the bottom card from that deck and placing that card on the top of an output deck. This card-choosing step is repeated until all the original cards are placed in the output deck. Define a ***recursive-riffle*** algorithm, which cuts a deck of n cards into two decks of $n/2$ each, where n is a power of 2, and then calls the recursive-riffle algorithm on each half. When these recursive calls return, the recursive-riffle algorithm then performs a riffle shuffle of the two decks to produce the shuffled result. Show that every card in the original deck has an equal probability of being the top card after a recursive-riffle is performed on the deck, and analyze the running time of the recursive-riffle algorithm using a recurrence equation.

A-8.8 Many states require that candidate names appear on a ballot in random order, so as to minimize biases that can arise from the order in which candidate names appear on a ballot for a given election. For instance, in the 2012 general election, the Secretary of State of California performed a random drawing that determined that candidate names for that election must appear in alphabetical order based on the following ordering of letters:

    (I,X,C,A,P,U,Z,S,W,H,K,T,D,F,Q,V,G,M,R,J,L,Y,E,B,P,N).

For example, if three candidates in that election had the last names, "BROWN," "BLACK," and "WHITE," then they would appear on the ballot in the order, (WHITE, BROWN, BLACK). Describe an efficient algorithm that takes, as input, an array, A, specifying an ordering of letters such as this, and a collection of names, and sorts the collection of names using a lexicographic order based on the alternative ordering of letters given in A. What is the running time of your method in terms of m, the size of the array, A, and n, the number of names to be sorted? (You may assume the length of each name is bounded by some constant, but you may not assume that m or n is a constant.)

A-8.9 A *floating-point number* is a pair, (m, d), of integers, which represents the number $m \times b^d$, where b is either 2 or 10. In any real-world programming environment, the sizes of m and d are limited; hence, each arithmetic operation involving two floating-point numbers may have some *roundoff error*. The traditional way to account for this error is to introduce a *machine precision* parameter, $\epsilon < 1$, for the given programming environment, and bound roundoff errors in terms of this parameter. For instance, in the case of floating-point addition, $fl(x + y)$, for summing two floating-point numbers, x and y, we can write

$$fl(x + y) = (x + y) \cdot (1 + \delta_{x,y}),$$

where $|\delta_{x,y}| \leq \epsilon$. Consider, then, using an accumulation algorithm for summing a sequence, $(x_1, x_2, \ldots, x_n)$, of positive floating-point numbers, as shown in Algorithm 8.14. Assuming that ϵ is small enough so that ϵ^2 times any floating-point number is negligibly small, then we can use a term, e_n, to estimate an upper bound for the roundoff error for summing these numbers in this way as

$$e_n = \epsilon \sum_{i=1}^{n} (n - i + 1) x_i.$$

Prove that the optimal order for summing any set of n positive floating-point number according to the standard accumulation algorithm, so as to minimize the error term, e_n, is to sum them in nondecreasing order. Also, give an $O(n \log n)$-time method for arranging the numbers in the sequence $(x_1, x_2, \ldots, x_n)$ so that the standard accumulation summation algorithm minimizes the error term, e_n.

Algorithm FloatSum$(x_1, x_2, \ldots, x_n)$:
   Input: A sequence, $(x_1, x_2 \ldots, x_n)$, of n positive floating-point numbers
   Output: A floating-point representation of the sum of the n numbers
   $s \leftarrow 0.0$
   for $i \leftarrow 1$ **to** n **do**
      $s \leftarrow fl(s + x_i)$
   return s

Algorithm 8.14: An accumulation algorithm for summing n floating-point numbers.

Chapter Notes

Knuth's classic text on *Sorting and Searching* [131] contains an extensive history of the sorting problem and algorithms for solving it, starting with the census card sorting machines of the late 19th century. Huang and Langston [107] describe how to merge two sorted lists in-place in linear time. The standard quick-sort algorithm is due to Hoare [100]. A tighter analysis of randomized quick-sort can be found in the book by Motwani and Raghavan [162]. Gonnet and Baeza-Yates [85] provide experimental comparisons and theoretical analyses of a number of different sorting algorithms. Kao and Wang [115] study the problem of minimizing the numerical error in summing n floating-point numbers.

Chapter

9

Fast Sorting and Selection

Antarctica Gentoo Penguins. U.S. government image, 2010.
Credit: Lt. Elizabeth Crapo/NOAA.

Contents

9.1 Bucket-Sort and Radix-Sort 267

9.2 Selection 270

9.3 Weighted Medians 276

9.4 Exercises 279

Most teachers keep grades recorded on computers these days. The analysis and record-keeping functions that computers provide are simply no match for paper and pencil. For instance, teachers can easily compute averages, minimums, maximums, and other statistics using functions that involve fast computations. One common computation in such applications, for instance, is bucketing or histogramming. In this computation, n students are assigned integer scores in some range, such as 0 to 100, and are then sorted based on these scores. From this sorting step, the teacher can then display a histogram that shows how many students have received each possible score, which can then be used to determine cutoffs for various letter grades. (See Figure 9.1.)

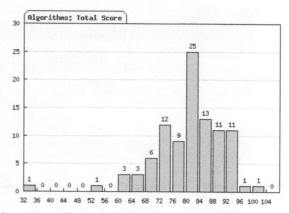

Figure 9.1: A histogram of scores from a recent Algorithms course taught by one of the authors.

When we think about the algorithmic issues in performing such a computation, it is easy to see that this is a type of sorting problem. But it is not the most general kind of sorting problem, since the keys the teacher is using to sort is simply integers in a given range. So a natural question to ask is whether we can sort n elements faster than in $O(n \log n)$ time for such specialized sorting problems; hence, beating the lower-bound on the time to sort n elements using a comparison-based algorithm, as was established in Section 8.3. Interestingly, as we explore in this chapter, it is possible to sort n elements as fast as $O(n)$ time, provided the keys being used to sort these elements are integers in a reasonably small range.

Another common computation for teachers to perform is to compute a median score, that is, a score from among n scores such that there are at most $n/2$ elements larger than this score and at most $n/2$ elements smaller than this score. Of course, such a number can be found easily if we were to sort the scores, but it would be ideal if we could find medians in $O(n)$ time without having to perform a sorting operation. As we show in this chapter, even if elements simply have a pairwise comparison rule that defines a total order, then we can find the kth smallest element in $O(n)$ time, for any value of k, including $k = n/2$. Thus, we can find medians in $O(n)$ time.

9.1 Bucket-Sort and Radix-Sort

In the previous chapter, we showed that $\Omega(n \log n)$ time is necessary, in the worst case, to sort an n-element sequence with a comparison-based sorting algorithm. A natural question to ask, then, is whether there are other kinds of sorting algorithms that can be designed to run asymptotically faster than $O(n \log n)$ time. Interestingly, such algorithms exist, but they require special assumptions about the input sequence to be sorted. Even so, such scenarios often arise in practice, so discussing them is worthwhile. In this section, we consider the problem of sorting a sequence of items, each a key-element pair.

9.1.1 Bucket-Sort

Consider a sequence, S, of n items whose keys are integers in the range $[0, N-1]$, for some integer $N \geq 2$, and suppose that S should be sorted according to the keys of the items. In this case, it is possible to sort S in $O(n + N)$ time. It might seem surprising, but this implies, for example, that if N is $O(n)$, then we can sort S in $O(n)$ time. Of course, the crucial point is that, because of the restrictive assumption about the format of the elements, we can avoid using comparisons.

The main idea is to use an algorithm called *bucket-sort*, which is not based on comparisons, but on using keys as indices into a bucket array, B, that has entries from 0 to $N-1$. An item with key k is placed in the "bucket" $B[k]$, which itself is a list (of items with key k). After inserting each item of the input sequence S into its bucket, we can put the items back into S in sorted order by enumerating the contents of the buckets $B[0], B[1], \ldots, B[N-1]$ in order. We give a pseudocode description of bucket-sort in Algorithm 9.2.

Algorithm bucketSort(S):

    Input: Sequence S of items with integer keys in the range $[0, N-1]$
    Output: Sequence S sorted in nondecreasing order of the keys

    let B be an array of N lists, each of which is initially empty
    for each item x in S **do**
        let k be the key of x
        remove x from S and insert it at the end of bucket (list) $B[k]$
    for $i \leftarrow 0$ to $N-1$ **do**
        for each item x in list $B[i]$ **do**
            remove x from $B[i]$ and insert it at the end of S

Algorithm 9.2: Bucket-sort.

Analysis and the Property of Being a Stable Sorting Algorithm

It is easy to see that bucket-sort runs in $O(n + N)$ time and uses $O(n + N)$ space, just by examining the two **for** loops. Namely, the first loop runs in time $O(n)$ and the second loop runs in time $O(n + N)$. Also, sequence S uses $O(n)$ space and array B has size N. Thus, bucket-sort is efficient when the range N of values for the keys is small compared to the sequence size n, say $N = O(n)$ or $N = O(n \log n)$. Still, the performance of bucket-sort deteriorates as N grows compared to n.

In addition, an important property of the bucket-sort algorithm is that it works correctly even if there are many different elements with the same key. Indeed, we described it in a way that anticipates such occurrences.

When sorting key-element items, an important issue is how equal keys are handled. Let $S = ((k_0, e_0), \ldots, (k_{n-1}, e_{n-1}))$ be a sequence of items. We say that a sorting algorithm is **stable** if, for any two items (k_i, e_i) and (k_j, e_j) of S such that $k_i = k_j$ and (k_i, e_i) precedes (k_j, e_j) in S before sorting (that is, $i < j$), we have that item (k_i, e_i) also precedes item (k_j, e_j) after sorting. Stability is important for a sorting algorithm because applications may want to preserve the initial ordering of elements with the same key.

Our informal description of bucket-sort in Algorithm 9.2 does not guarantee stability. This is not inherent in the bucket-sort method itself, however, for we can easily modify our description to make bucket-sort stable, while still preserving its $O(n + N)$ running time. Indeed, we can obtain a stable bucket-sort algorithm by always removing the *first* element from sequence S and from each list $B[i]$ during the execution of the algorithm.

9.1.2 Radix-Sort

One of the reasons that stable sorting is so important is that it allows the bucket-sort approach to be applied to more general contexts than to sort integers. Suppose, for example, that we want to sort items with keys that are pairs (k, l), where k and l are integers in the range $[0, N - 1]$, for some integer $N \geq 2$. In a context such as this, it is natural to define an ordering on these items using the *lexicographical* (dictionary) convention, where $(k_1, l_1) < (k_2, l_2)$ if

- $k_1 < k_2$ or
- $k_1 = k_2$ and $l_1 < l_2$.

This is a pair-wise version of the lexicographic comparison function, usually applied to equal-length character strings (and it easily generalizes to tuples of d numbers for $d > 2$).

The *radix-sort* algorithm sorts a sequence of pairs such as S, by applying a stable bucket-sort on the sequence twice; first using one component of the pair as the ordering key and then using the second component. But which order is correct? Should we first sort on the k's (the first component) and then on the l's (the second component), or should it be the other way around?

Before we answer this question, we consider the following example.

Example 9.1: *Consider the following sequence S:*

$$S = ((3,3),(1,5),(2,5),(1,2),(2,3),(1,7),(3,2),(2,2)).$$

If we stably sort S on the first component, then we get the sequence

$$S_1 = ((1,5),(1,2),(1,7),(2,5),(2,3),(2,2),(3,3),(3,2)).$$

If we then stably sort this sequence S_1 using the second component, then we get the sequence

$$S_{1,2} = ((1,2),(2,2),(3,2),(2,3),(3,3),(1,5),(2,5),(1,7)),$$

which is not exactly a sorted sequence. On the other hand, if we first stably sort S using the second component, then we get the sequence

$$S_2 = ((1,2),(3,2),(2,2),(3,3),(2,3),(1,5),(2,5),(1,7)).$$

If we then stably sort sequence S_2 using the first component, then we get the sequence

$$S_{2,1} = ((1,2),(1,5),(1,7),(2,2),(2,3),(2,5),(3,2),(3,3)),$$

which is indeed sequence S lexicographically ordered.

So, from this example, we are led to believe that we should first sort using the second component and then again using the first component. This intuition is exactly right. By first stably sorting by the second component and then again by the first component, we guarantee that if two elements are equal in the second sort (by the first component), then their relative order in the starting sequence (which is sorted by the second component) is preserved. Thus, the resulting sequence is guaranteed to be sorted lexicographically every time. We leave the determination of how this approach can be extended to triples and other d-tuples of numbers to a simple exercise (R-9.2). We can generalize the results of this section as follows:

Theorem 9.2: *Let S be a sequence of n key-element items, each of which has a key $(k_1, k_2, \ldots, k_d)$, where k_i is an integer in the range $[0, N-1]$ for some integer $N \geq 2$. We can sort S lexicographically in time $O(d(n+N))$ using radix-sort.*

As important as it is, sorting is not the only interesting problem dealing with a total order relation on a set of elements. There are some applications, for example, that do not require an ordered listing of an entire set, but nevertheless call for some amount of ordering information about the set.

9.2 Selection

There are a number of applications in which we are interested in identifying a single element in terms of its rank relative to an ordering of the entire set. Examples include identifying the minimum and maximum elements, but we may also be interested in, say, identifying the *median* element, that is, the element such that half of the other elements are smaller and the remaining half are larger. In general, queries that ask for an element with a given rank are called *order statistics*.

In this section, we discuss the general order-statistic problem of selecting the kth smallest element from an unsorted collection of n comparable elements. This is known as the *selection* problem. Of course, we can solve this problem by sorting the collection and then indexing into the sorted sequence at rank index $k-1$. Using the best comparison-based sorting algorithms, this approach would take $O(n \log n)$ time. Thus, a natural question to ask is whether we can achieve an $O(n)$ running time for all values of k, including the interesting case of finding the median, where $k = \lceil n/2 \rceil$.

Prune-and-Search

This may come as a small surprise, but we can indeed solve the selection problem in $O(n)$ time for any value of k. Moreover, the technique we use to achieve this result involves an interesting algorithmic technique, which is known as *prune-and-search*. In applying this technique, we solve a given problem that is defined on a collection of n objects by pruning away a fraction of the n objects and recursively solving the smaller problem. When we have finally reduced the problem to one defined on a constant-sized collection of objects, then we solve the problem using some brute-force method. Returning back from all the recursive calls completes the construction. In some cases, we can avoid using recursion, in which case we simply iterate the prune-and-search reduction step until we can apply a brute-force method and stop.

9.2.1 Randomized Quick-Select

In applying the prune-and-search technique to the selection problem, we can design a simple and practical method, called *randomized quick-select*, for finding the kth smallest element in an unordered sequence of n elements on which a total order relation is defined. Randomized quick-select runs in $O(n)$ *expected* time, taken over all possible random choices made by the algorithm, and this expectation does not depend whatsoever on any randomness assumptions about the input distribution. We note though that randomized quick-select runs in $O(n^2)$ time in the *worst case*, the justification of which is left as an exercise (R-9.5).

Suppose we are given an unsorted sequence S of n comparable elements together with an integer $k \in [1, n]$. At a high level, the quick-select algorithm for finding the kth smallest element in S is similar in structure to the randomized quicksort algorithm described in Section 8.2.1. We pick an element x from S at random and use this as a "pivot" to subdivide S into three subsequences L, E, and G, storing the elements of S less than x, equal to x, and greater than x, respectively. This is the prune step. Then, based on the value of k, we determine which of these sets should then be solved recursively. We describe randomized quick-select in Algorithm 9.3, and we illustrate it in Figure 9.4.

Algorithm quickSelect(S, k):

    Input: Sequence S of n comparable elements, and an integer $k \in [1, n]$

    Output: The kth smallest element of S

    if $n = 1$ **then**

        return the (first) element of S

    pick a random element x of S

    remove all the elements from S and put them into three sequences:

- L, storing the elements in S less than x
- E, storing the elements in S equal to x
- G, storing the elements in S greater than x.

    if $k \le |L|$ **then**

        quickSelect(L, k)

    else if $k \le |L| + |E|$ **then**

        return x // each element in E is equal to x

    else

        quickSelect$(G, k - |L| - |E|)$

Algorithm 9.3: Randomized quick-select algorithm.

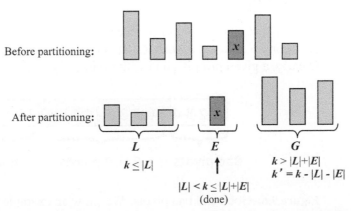

Figure 9.4: A schematic illustration of the quick-select algorithm.

Analyzing Randomized Quick-Select

We mentioned above that the randomized quick-select algorithm runs in expected $O(n)$ time. Fortunately, justifying this claim requires only the simplest of probabilistic arguments. The main probabilistic fact that we use is the ***linearity of expectation***. Recall that this fact states that if X and Y are random variables and c is a number, then $E(X + Y) = E(X) + E(Y)$ and $E(cX) = cE(X)$, where we use $E(\mathcal{Z})$ to denote the expected value of the expression $\mathcal{Z}$.

Let $t(n)$ denote the running time of randomized quick-select on a sequence of size n. Since the randomized quick-select algorithm depends on the outcome of random events, its running time, $t(n)$, is a random variable. We are interested in bounding $E(t(n))$, the expected value of $t(n)$. Moreover, since quick-select is a recursive algorithm that makes at most one additional recursive call with each invocation, the recursion tree for quick-select is simply a path. (See Figure 9.5.)

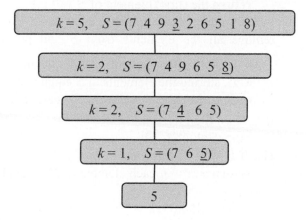

Figure 9.5: An example recursion tree for the quick-select algorithm. For each invocation, we show the integer, k, the list, S, and we underline the random pivot that is chosen.

Say that a pivot used in an invocation of randomized quick-select is "good" if it partitions S so that the size of L and G is at most $3n/4$, and it is "bad" otherwise. Clearly, a given pivot is good with probability $1/2$. (See Figure 9.6.)

Figure 9.6: Good and bad pivots. We show an example list of 16 elements in sorted order, even though the list, S, will usually be unsorted.

Let $g(n)$ denote the number of consecutive recursive invocations (including the present one) before getting a good invocation. Then

$$t(n) \le bn \cdot g(n) + t(3n/4),$$

where $b > 0$ is a constant (to account for the overhead of each call). We are, of course, focusing on the case where n is larger than 1, for we can easily characterize in a closed form that $t(1) = b$. Applying the linearity of expectation property to the general case, then, we get

$$E\left(t(n)\right) \le E\left(bn \cdot g(n) + t(3n/4)\right) = bn \cdot E\left(g(n)\right) + E\left(t(3n/4)\right).$$

Since a recursive call is good with probability $1/2$, and whether a recursive call is good or not is independent of its parent call being good, the expected value of $g(n)$ is the same as the expected number of times we must flip a fair coin before it comes up "heads." This implies that $E(g(n)) = 2$. Thus, if we let $T(n)$ be a shorthand notation for $E(t(n))$ (the expected running time of the randomized quick-select algorithm), then we can write the case for $n > 1$ as

$$T(n) \le T(3n/4) + 2bn.$$

As with the merge-sort recurrence equation, we would like to convert this equation into a closed form. To do this, let us again iteratively apply this equation assuming n is large. So, for example, after two iterative applications, we get

$$T(n) \le T((3/4)^2 n) + 2b(3/4)n + 2bn.$$

At this point, we see that the general case is

$$T(n) \le 2bn \cdot \sum_{i=0}^{\lceil \log_{4/3} n \rceil} (3/4)^i.$$

In other words, the expected running time of randomized quick-select is $2bn$ times the sum of a geometric progression whose base is a positive number less than 1. Thus, by Theorem 1.12 on geometric summations, we obtain the result that $T(n)$ is $O(n)$.

To summarize, we have the following:

Theorem 9.3: *The expected running time of randomized quick-select on a sequence of size n is $O(n)$.*

As we mentioned earlier, there is a variation of quick-select that does not use randomization and runs in $O(n)$ worst-case time, which we discuss next.

9.2.2   Deterministic Selection

In this section, we discuss how to modify the quick-select algorithm to make it deterministic, yet still run in $O(n)$ time on an n-element sequence. The main idea is to modify the way we choose the pivot so that it is chosen deterministically, not randomly, based on the following approach:

1. Partition the set S into $\lceil n/5 \rceil$ groups of size 5 each (except, possibly, for one group).
2. Sort each group and identify its median element.
3. Apply the algorithm recursively on these $\lceil n/5 \rceil$ "baby medians" to find their median.
4. Use this element (the median of the baby medians) as the pivot and proceed as in the quick-select algorithm.

We give the details for this method in Algorithm 9.7.

Algorithm DeterministicSelect(S, k):

    Input: Sequence S of n comparable elements, and an integer $k \in [1, n]$

    Output: The kth smallest element of S

    if $n = 1$ **then**

        return the (first) element of S

    Divide S into $g = \lceil n/5 \rceil$ groups, $S_1, \ldots, S_g$, such that each of groups $S_1, \ldots, S_{g-1}$ has 5 elements and group S_g has at most 5 elements.

    for $i \leftarrow 1$ to g **do**

        Find the baby median, x_i, in S_i (using any method)

    $x \leftarrow$ DeterministicSelect($\{x_1, \ldots, x_g\}, \lceil g/2 \rceil$)

    remove all the elements from S and put them into three sequences:

        • L, storing the elements in S less than x

        • E, storing the elements in S equal to x

        • G, storing the elements in S greater than x.

    if $k \leq |L|$ **then**

        DeterministicSelect(L, k)

    else if $k \leq |L| + |E|$ **then**

        return x // each element in E is equal to x

    else

        DeterministicSelect($G, k - |L| - |E|$)

Algorithm 9.7: The deterministic selection algorithm.

Analysis of Deterministic Selection

We now show that the above deterministic selection algorithm runs in linear time.

The algorithm has two recursive calls. The first one is performed on the set of baby medians, which has size

$$g = \lceil n/5 \rceil.$$

The second recursive call is made on either set L (elements smaller than the pivot, x) or set G (elements larger than the pivot, x). Recall that each group but one contains 5 elements and our pivot, x, is the median of the baby medians from all of these groups. Thus, we have that for $\lceil g/2 \rceil$ groups, at least half of the group elements are less than or equal to x. Since group S_g could be part of this half, we have that number of elements in S that are less than or equal to x is at least

$$3 \left(\left\lceil \frac{g}{2} \right\rceil - 1 \right) + 1 = 3 \left\lceil \frac{1}{2} \cdot \left\lceil \frac{n}{5} \right\rceil \right\rceil - 2 \geq \frac{3n}{10} - 2.$$

With a similar argument, we obtain that the above value is also a lower bound on the number of elements of S less than or equal to x.

We conclude that the second recursive call is performed on a set of size at most

$$n - \left(\frac{3n}{10} - 2 \right) = \frac{7n}{10} + 2.$$

Overall, for a sufficiently large value of n, the running time for the deterministic selection algorithm, $T(n)$, can be characterized by the following recurrence relation:

$$T(n) \leq T(n/5 + 1) + T(7n/10 + 2) + bn.$$

where $b > 0$ is a constant.

To solve the recurrence, we guess that $T(n) \leq cn$, for some constant $c > 0$. Expanding the recurrence, we have the following:

$$
\begin{aligned}
T(n) &\leq T(n/5 + 1) + T(7n/10 + 2) + bn \\
&\leq cn/5 + c + 7cn/10 + 2c + bn \\
&= 9cn/10 + bn + 3c.
\end{aligned}
$$

Pick $c = 11b$. We obtain

$$T(n) \leq 9cn/10 + bn + 3c \leq 9cn/10 + cn/11 + 3c.$$

Thus, we have $T(n) \leq cn$ for n large enough such that

$$cn/11 + 3c \leq cn/10,$$

that is, for $n \geq 330$. Therefore, the running time of the deterministic selection algorithm is $O(n)$.

We summarize the above analysis with the following theorem.

Theorem 9.4: *Given an input sequence with n elements, the deterministic selection algorithm runs in $O(n)$ time.*

Admittedly, the constant in the $O(n)$ running time for deterministic selection, as estimated by the analysis, is fairly high. Thus, in practice, it is probably more efficient to use the randomized quick-select algorithm than this deterministic selection algorithm. Still, it is useful to know that we can match the expected $O(n)$ running time for randomized quick-select with a deterministic algorithm.

9.3 Weighted Medians

In some applications, elements have weights and we wish to find a median of the elements that respects these weights. For example, suppose we have a set of people with distinct ages and weights, who want to cross a river, and we have a ship that has capacity to support roughly half the total weight, W, of all the people. Suppose further that these people are willing to admit to their ages, but not their weights. Thus, we would like to announce to them that everyone who is younger than some amount, x, can go on the first sailing and everyone else can go on the sailing after that. That is, we are interested in finding the age, x, such that the total weight of everyone younger than x is at most $W/2$, and the total weight of everyone older than x is at most $W/2$.

Formal Definition of a Weighted Median

Formally, let us assume we are given a set,

$$X = \{x_1, x_2, \ldots, x_n\},$$

of n distinct elements taken from some total order, such that each element x_i has a positive weight w_i. Suppose further that these weights sum up to

$$W = \sum_{i=1}^{n} w_i.$$

We are interested in finding an element, x_m in X, such that

$$\sum_{x_i < x_m} w_i \leq \frac{W}{2}$$

and

$$\sum_{x_i > x_m} w_i \leq \frac{W}{2}.$$

Note that these sums do not include the weight of the element, w_m, itself. Note that the above conditions imply that the smallest x_m such that

$$\sum_{x_i \leq x_m} w_i > \frac{W}{2},$$

is a weighted median element.

A Solution Based on Sorting

For a first cut at a solution, let us consider an algorithm based on sorting. Specifically, imagine that we sort the elements in X by their values (and not their weights). Then we can scan this sorted sequence, from the beginning, while keeping a running total of the weights of the elements we have encountered so far. As soon as this running total goes over $W/2$, then we will have found a weighted median, w_m. (See Algorithm 9.8.)

Algorithm SortedMedian(X):

    Input: A set, X, of distinct elements, with each x_i in X having a positive weight, w_i

    Output: The weighted median for X

    Let W be the sum of all the weights of the elements in X

    Let the sequence $(x_1, x_2, \ldots, x_n)$ be the result of sorting X

    $w \leftarrow 0$

    for $i \leftarrow 1$ to n **do**

        $w \leftarrow w + w_i$

        if $w > W/2$ **then**

            return x_i

Algorithm 9.8: A sorting-based algorithm for the weighted median problem.

This algorithm is clearly correct, since it incrementally builds the set of elements less than the weighted median until it is found, based on the formal characterization given above. The total running time of this method is dominated by the running time for the sorting step, which takes $O(n \log n)$ time, since we are assuming only that the elements in X come from some total order.

A Solution Based on Prune-and-Search

We can design a more efficient algorithm for the weighted median problem, however, by using the prune-and-search technique. The main idea is reminiscent of binary search. Use the linear-time selection algorithm from the previous section to find the median, y, in X, without taking weights into consideration. Then compute the weight of every element less than y and the weight of every element less than or equal to y. If the first of these is greater than $W/2$, then y is too large; hence, we should recursively solve the problem on elements less than y. If the second of these sums is less than $W/2$, then y is too small; hence, we should recursively solve the problem on elements greater than y. Otherwise, y is the weighted median. The method, PruneMedian, which is shown in Algorithm 9.9, performs this computation, where we initially pass in the set X and half its total weight, $W/2$, of the elements in X.

Algorithm PruneMedian(X, W):

> ***Input:*** A set, X, of distinct elements, $\{x_1, \ldots, x_n\}$, with each x_i in X having
> a positive weight, w_i; and a weight, W
>
> ***Output:*** The element, y, in X, such that the total weight of the elements in X
> less than y is at most W and the total weight of the elements in X less than
> or equal to y is greater than or equal to W

> **if** $n = 1$ **then**
>> **return** x_1
>
> Let $y \leftarrow$ DeterministicSelect$(X, \lceil n/2 \rceil)$
> Let $w_1 \leftarrow \sum_{x_i < y} w_i$
> Let $w_2 \leftarrow \sum_{x_i \leq y} w_i$
> **if** $w_1 > W$ **then**   // y is too large
>> Let X' be the set of elements in X that are less than y
>> Call PruneMedian(X', W)
>
> **else if** $w_2 < W$ **then**   // y is too small
>> Let X' be the set of elements in X greater than y
>> Let W' be the sum of the weights of the elements in $X - X'$
>> Call PruneMedian$(X', W - W')$
>
> **else**
>> **return** y

Algorithm 9.9: A prune-and-search algorithm for the weighted median problem.

Analysis of the Prune-and-Search Weighted Median Algorithm

The running time, $T(n)$, for this algorithm can be characterized by $T(n)$ being at
most a constant if $n = 1$, and the following recurrence equation otherwise:

$$T(n) \leq T(\lceil n/2 \rceil) + bn,$$

where $b > 0$ is a constant. This gives us the following:

Theorem 9.5: *The weighted median problem can be solved in $O(n)$ time.*

Proof: To see that the prune-and-search weighted median algorithm runs in
$O(n)$ time, we will prove the claim that $T(n) \leq cn$, for some constant $c > 0$ by
induction. For the case when $n < 4$, we take c larger than the constant time needed
for the algorithm when this is the input size. Otherwise, for $n \geq 4$,

$$
\begin{aligned}
T(n) & \leq & T(\lceil n/2 \rceil) + bn \\
& \leq & T(n/2 + 1) + bn \\
& \leq & cn/2 + c + bn \\
& \leq & cn,
\end{aligned}
$$

for $c \geq 4b$, since, in this case, $cn/4 \geq bn$ and $cn/4 \geq c$.   ∎

Therefore, we can solve the weighted median problem in linear time using the
prune-and-search technique.

9.4 Exercises

Reinforcement

R-9.1 Which, if any, of the algorithms bubble-sort, heap-sort, merge-sort, and quick-sort are stable?

R-9.2 Describe a radix-sort method for lexicographically sorting a sequence S of triplets (k, l, m), where k, l, and m are integers in the range $[0, N-1]$, for some $N \geq 2$. How could this scheme be extended to sequences of d-tuples $(k_1, k_2, \ldots, k_d)$, where each k_i is an integer in the range $[0, N-1]$?

R-9.3 Is the bucket-sort algorithm in-place? Why or why not?

R-9.4 Give a pseudocode description of an in-place quick-select algorithm.

R-9.5 Show that the worst-case running time of quick-select on an n-element sequence is $\Omega(n^2)$.

R-9.6 Explain where the induction proof for showing that deterministic selection runs in $O(n)$ time would fail if we formed groups of size 3 instead of groups of size 5.

R-9.7 What does the weighted median algorithm return if the weights of all the elements are equal?

Creativity

C-9.1 Show that any comparison-based sorting algorithm can be made to be stable, without affecting the asymptotic running time of this algorithm.

Hint: Change the way elements are compared with each other.

C-9.2 Suppose we are given two sequences A and B of n integers, possibly containing duplicates, in the range from 1 to $2n$. Describe a linear-time algorithm for determining if A and B contain the same set of elements (possibly in different orders).

C-9.3 Suppose we are given a sequence S of n elements, each of which is an integer in the range $[0, n^2 - 1]$. Describe a simple method for sorting S in $O(n)$ time.

Hint: Think of alternate ways of viewing the elements.

C-9.4 Let $S_1, S_2, \ldots, S_k$ be k different sequences whose elements have integer keys in the range $[0, N-1]$, for some parameter $N \geq 2$. Describe an algorithm running in $O(n + N)$ time for sorting all the sequences (not as a union), where n denotes the total size of all the sequences.

C-9.5 Suppose we are given a sequence, S, of n integers in the range from 1 to n^3. Give an $O(n)$-time method for determining whether there are two equal numbers in S.

C-9.6 Let A and B be two sequences of n integers each, in the range $[1, n^4]$. Given an integer x, describe an $O(n)$-time algorithm for determining if there is an integer a in A and an integer b in B such that $x = a + b$.

C-9.7 Given an unordered sequence S of n comparable elements, describe a linear-time method for finding the $\lceil \sqrt{n} \rceil$ items whose rank in an ordered version of S is closest to that of the median.

C-9.8 Show how a deterministic $O(n)$-time selection algorithm can be used to design a quick-sort-like sorting algorithm that runs in $O(n \log n)$ ***worst-case*** time on an n-element sequence.

C-9.9 Given an unsorted sequence S of n comparable elements, and an integer k, give an $O(n \log k)$ expected-time algorithm for finding the $O(k)$ elements that have rank $\lceil n/k \rceil$, $2\lceil n/k \rceil$, $3\lceil n/k \rceil$, and so on.

C-9.10 Suppose you are given two sorted lists, A and B, of n elements each, all of which are distinct. Describe a method that runs in $O(\log n)$ time for finding the median in the set defined by the union of A and B.

C-9.11 Given a set of n elements that come from a total order, show that you can find the second smallest element in this set using $n + \lceil \log n \rceil - 2$ comparisons.

C-9.12 Given an array, A, of n numbers in the range from 1 to n, describe an $O(n)$-time method for finding the ***mode***, that is, the number that occurs most frequently in A.

C-9.13 Suppose instead of choosing a single pivot in the quick-select algorithm, we chose $\log n$ pivots. Show that the probability that at least one of them is good is at least $1 - 1/n$.

Applications

A-9.1 Suppose you would like to find the most average kitten in your collection of n kitten photographs, based on cuteness. So as to avoid your own personal biases, any time you would need to compare two kitten photos, x and y, rather than doing this yourself, you use an online crowdsourcing application, Decider, to decide which kitten is cuter. You may assume that there is a total ordering of your kitten photographs, based on cuteness, but, for any given time that you make a call to Decider to compare two kittens, x and y, there is an independent 50-50 chance that the people Decider picks to perform this comparison cannot agree on which kitten is cuter. That is, for each comparison of two kittens that Decider is asked to perform, it is as if it flips a fair coin and answers the comparison accurately if the coin turns up "heads" and answers "cannot decide" if the coin turns up "tails." Moreover, this behavior occurs independent of previous comparison requests, even for the same pair of kitten photographs. Describe an efficient algorithm that can correctly use Decider to find the median kitten photograph, based on cuteness, and show that your algorithm makes an expected number of calls to Decider that is $O(n)$.

A-9.2 Search engines often index their collections of documents so that they can easily return an ordered set of documents that contain a given query word, w. Such a data structure is known as an ***inverted file***. In order to construct an inverted file, we might start with a set of n triples of the form, (w, d, r), where w is a word, d is an identifier for a document that contains the word w, and r is a rank score for the popularity of the document d. Often, the next step is to sort these triples, ordered first by w, then by r, and then by d. Assuming each of the values, w, d, and r, are represented as integers in the range from 1 to $4n$, describe a linear-time algorithm for sorting a given set of n such triples.

A-9.3 Suppose you are the postmaster in charge of putting a new post office in a small town, where all the houses are along one street, where the new post office should go as well. Let us view this street as a line and the houses on it as a set of real numbers, $\{x_1, x_2, \ldots, x_n\}$, corresponding to points on this line. To make everyone in town as happy as possible, the location, p, for the new post office should minimize the sum,

$$\sum_{i=1}^{n} |p - x_i|.$$

Describe an efficient algorithm for finding the optimal location for the new post office, show that your algorithm is correct, and analyze its running time.

A-9.4 Suppose University High School (UHS) is electing its student-body president. Suppose further that everyone at UHS is a candidate and voters write down the student number of the person they are voting for, rather than checking a box. Let A be an array containing n such votes, that is, student numbers for candidates receiving votes, listed in no particular order. Your job is to determine if one of the candidates got a majority of the votes, that is, more than $n/2$ votes. Describe an $O(n)$-time algorithm for determining if there is a student number that appears more than $n/2$ times in A.

A-9.5 Consider the election problem from the previous exercise, but now describe an algorithm running in $O(n)$ time to determine the student numbers of every candidate that received more than $n/3$ votes.

A-9.6 Computational *metrology* deals with algorithms for the science of measurement. For instance, suppose we are given a set, S, of n points in 3-dimensional spaces, which is defined by sampling the surface of a manufactured part with a laser range-finding device. A possible problem in computational metrology is to precisely determine how flat the points in S are, based on some mathematical definition of "flatness." But in order to determine how flat a set of points is in 3-dimensional space, we must have some reference plane. Therefore, let us define the reference plane for S to be the plane, $z = c$, that minimizes the sum of distances from points in S to this plane, that is, the plane that minimizes the sum

$$F(S) = \sum_{p \in S} |z(p) - c|,$$

where $z(p)$ denotes the z-coordinate of the point p. The *flatness* of S is then defined as $F(S)$. Describe an efficient algorithm for computing the flatness of S defined in this way. What is the running time of your method?

A-9.7 Suppose you are the owner of a chain of premium coffee shops that sell high-priced coffee with fancy Italian names to college students. You have learned that there is a street in a large college town that is lined with n dormitories and there currently is no coffee shop on this street. Your goal is to place a new coffee shop on this street so as to optimize the distance from this shop to the various dormitories. To simplify things, let us model the street as a line and each dormitory as a point, d_i, which is a real number on this line. In addition, we know the number of people, p_i, who live in each dormitory, d_i. You are interested in finding the location, x, that minimizes the cost function,

$$\sum_{i=1}^{n} p_i|d_i - x|.$$

Describe an efficient algorithm for finding the point, x, where to place your coffee shop, that minimizes this cost. What is the running time of your algorithm?

Chapter Notes

Knuth's classic text on *Sorting and Searching* [131] contains an extensive history of the sorting problem and algorithms for solving it, starting with the census card sorting machines of the late 19th century. Gonnet and Baeza-Yates [85] provide experimental comparisons and theoretical analyses of a number of different sorting algorithms. The term "prune-and-search" originally comes from the computational geometry literature (such as in the work of Clarkson [45] and Megiddo [154, 155]).

Chapter

10

The Greedy Method

Civil War Knapsack. U.S. government image. Vicksburg National Military Park. Public domain.

Contents

10.1 The Fractional Knapsack Problem 286

10.2 Task Scheduling 289

10.3 Text Compression and Huffman Coding 292

10.4 Exercises 298

Suppose you are designing a new online auction website that is intended to process bids for **multi-lot** auctions. That is, this website should be able to handle a single auction for 100 units of the same digital camera or 500 units of the same smartphone, where bids could be of the form, "x units for $\$y$," meaning that the bidder wants a quantity of x of the items being sold and is willing to pay $\$y$ for all x of them. The challenge for your website is that it must allow for a large number of bidders to place such multi-lot bids and it must decide which bidders to choose as the winners.

Naturally, in order to maximize sales commissions, the website managers are interested in you designing the website so that it always chooses a set of winning bids that maximizes the total amount of money paid for the items being auctioned. So how do you decide which bidders to choose as the winners?

One way is to use the technique we discuss in this chapter—the **greedy method**. This algorithm design paradigm involves repeatedly making choices that optimize some objective function, like repeatedly accepting the bid that maximizes the price-per-unit. The trick in applying this technique is guaranteeing that such a local "greedy" choice can always lead to an optimal solution.

Proving that the greedy method can indeed lead to an optimal solution can often require deeper understanding of the problem being solved, though, so we may need to make additional assumptions in order for it to work. For instance, for the problem of deciding which bidders to accept, this greedy strategy can work only if you are allowed to partially satisfy bids. That is, the greedy strategy works if you can satisfy a bid to buy x units for $\$y$ by selling $k < x$ units for $\$yk/x$. In fact, this problem is equivalent to a problem we study in more detail in this chapter—the fractional knapsack problem.

In the **knapsack** problem, we are given a set of n items, each having a weight and a benefit, and we are interested in choosing the set of items that maximize our total benefit while not going over the weight capacity of the knapsack. So, in this case, each bid is an item, with its "weight" being the number of units being requested and its benefit being the amount of money being offered. In this particular instance, where bids can be satisfied with a partial fulfillment, then it is an instance of the **fractional knapsack** problem, for which the greedy method works to find an optimal solution. Interestingly, for the "0-1" version of the problem, where fractional choices are not allowed, then the greedy method may not work. In fact, solving this problem for all possible inputs is quite difficult—it is discussed in Section 17.5 in the context of **NP**-completeness.

Still, there are several other problems, which we discuss in this chapter, for which the greedy methods works to find an optimal solution. These include problems for task scheduling and text compression. Incidentally, this technique is also used in Chapter 14, to derive efficient algorithms for finding shortest paths in weighted graphs, Chapter 15, to construct minimum spanning trees, and Section 18.2.2, to find approximate solutions to the SET-COVER problem.

The Greedy Method

The **greedy method** is applied to optimization problems—that is, problems that involve searching through a set of **configurations** to find one that minimizes or maximizes an **objective function** defined on these configurations. The general formula of the greedy method could not be simpler—in order to solve a given optimization problem, we proceed by a sequence of choices. The sequence of choices starts from some well-understood starting configuration, and then iteratively makes the decision that is best from all of those that are currently possible, in terms of improving the objective function. (See Figure 10.1.)

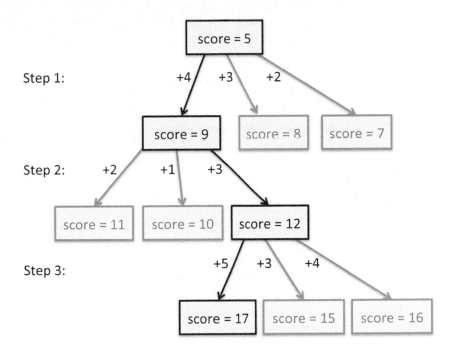

Figure 10.1: An example of the greedy method. Each rectangle represents a configuration whose score is the objective function. A configuration has three choices, each of which provides a different incremental improvement to the score. The bold choices are the ones that are picked in each step according to the greedy strategy.

This greedy approach does not always lead to an optimal solution, but there are several problems that it does work optimally for, and such problems are said to possess the **greedy-choice** property. This is the property that a global optimal configuration can be reached by a series of locally optimal choices (that is, choices that are the best from among the possibilities available at the time), starting from a well-defined configuration.

10.1   The Fractional Knapsack Problem

Consider the *fractional knapsack* problem, where we are given a set S of n items, such that each item i has a positive benefit b_i and a positive weight w_i, and we wish to find the maximum-benefit subset that does not exceed a given weight W. If we are restricted to entirely accepting or rejecting each item, then we would have the 0-1 version of this problem (for which we give a dynamic programming solution in Section 12.6). Let us now allow ourselves to take arbitrary fractions of some elements, however. The motivation for this fractional knapsack problem is that we are going on a trip and we have a single knapsack that can carry items that together have weight at most W. In addition, we are allowed to break items into fractions arbitrarily. That is, we can take an amount x_i of each item i such that

$$0 \leq x_i \leq w_i \text{ for each } i \in S \quad \text{and} \quad \sum_{i \in S} x_i \leq W.$$

The total benefit of the items taken is determined by the objective function

$$\sum_{i \in S} b_i(x_i/w_i).$$

(See Figure 10.2.)

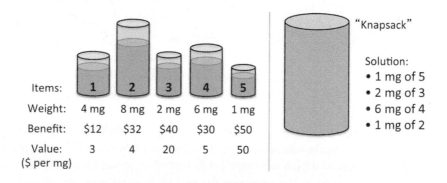

Figure 10.2: The fractional knapsack problem.

Consider, for example, a student who is going to an outdoor sporting event and must fill a knapsack full of foodstuffs to take along. As long as each candidate foodstuff is something that can be easily divided into fractions, such as drinks, potato chips, popcorn, and pizza, then this would be an instance of the fractional knapsack problem.

Using the Greedy Method to Solve the Fractional Knapsack Problem

When considering the fractional knapsack problem, this is one place where the greedy method can be applied successfully, for we can solve the fractional knapsack problem using the greedy approach.

In applying the greedy method, the most important decision is to determine the objective function that we wish to optimize. For example, we could choose to include items into our knapsack based on their weights, say, taking items in order by increasing weights. The intuition behind this approach is that the lower-weight items consume the least amount of the weight resource of the knapsack. Unfortunately, this first idea doesn't work. It is easy to construct examples where choosing items in order by their weights leads to suboptimal solutions. For example, even with just two items, with weight-benefit pairs of $(1, 10)$ and $(10, 200)$, this weight-based greedy approach, with a knapsack of weight 10, chooses 1 unit of item 1 and 9 units of item 2, for a total benefit of $10 + 180 = 190$, whereas just taking item 2 would get a benefit of 200.

Another possibility is to choose items in order based on their benefits, but again it is easy to construct examples where this results in a suboptimal strategy (see Exercise C-10.1). A much better approach is to rank the items by their *value*, which we define to be the ratio of their benefits and weights. The intuition behind this is that benefit-per-weight-unit is a natural measurement of the inherent value that each item possesses. Indeed, this approach leads to an efficient algorithm that finds an optimal solution to the fractional knapsack problem. We describe the details of this approach in Algorithm 10.3.

Algorithm FractionalKnapsack(S, W):

 Input: Set S of items, such that each item $i \in S$ has a positive benefit b_i and a positive weight w_i; positive maximum total weight W

 Output: Amount x_i of each item $i \in S$ that maximizes the total benefit while not exceeding the maximum total weight W

for each item $i \in S$ **do**
 $x_i \leftarrow 0$
 $v_i \leftarrow b_i/w_i$ // *value index* of item i
$w \leftarrow 0$ // total weight
while $w < W$ and $S \neq \emptyset$ **do**
 remove from S an item i with highest value index // greedy choice
 $a \leftarrow \min\{w_i, W - w\}$ // more than $W - w$ causes a weight overflow
 $x_i \leftarrow a$
 $w \leftarrow w + a$

Algorithm 10.3: A greedy algorithm for the fractional knapsack problem.

Analyzing the Greedy Algorithm for the Fractional Knapsack Problem

The above FractionalKnapsack algorithm can be implemented in $O(n \log n)$ time, where n is the number of items in S. Specifically, we can use a heap-based priority queue (Section 5.3) to store the items of S, where the key of each item is its value index. With this data structure, each greedy choice, which removes the item with greatest value index, takes $O(\log n)$ time.

Alternatively, we could even sort the items by their benefit-to-weight values, and then process them in this order. This would require $O(n \log n)$ time to sort the items and then $O(n)$ time to process them in the while-loop of Algorithm 10.3. Either way, we have that the greedy algorithm for solving the fractional knapsack problem can be implemented in $O(n \log n)$ time. The following theorem summarizes this fact and also shows that this algorithm is correct.

Theorem 10.1: *Given a collection S of n items, such that each item i has a benefit b_i and weight w_i, we can construct a maximum-benefit subset of S, allowing for fractional amounts, that has a total weight W in $O(n \log n)$ time.*

Proof: To see that our algorithm (10.3) for solving the fractional knapsack problem is correct, suppose, for the sake of contradiction, that there is an optimal solution better than the one chosen by this greedy algorithm. Then there must be two items i and j such that

$$x_i < w_i, \quad x_j > 0, \quad \text{and} \quad v_i > v_j.$$

Let

$$y = \min\{w_i - x_i, x_j\}.$$

But then we could then replace an amount y of item j with an equal amount of item i, thus increasing the total benefit without changing the total weight, which contradicts the assumption that this non-greedy solution is optimal. Therefore, we can correctly compute optimal amounts for the items by greedily choosing items by increasing benefit-to-weight values. ∎

The proof of this theorem uses an ***exchange argument*** to show that the greedy method works to solve this problem optimally. The general structure of such an argument is a proof by contradiction, where we assume, for the sake of reaching a contradiction, that there is a better solution than one found by the greedy algorithm. We then argue that there is an exchange that we could make among the components of this solution that would lead to a better solution. In this case, this approach shows that the greedy method can effectively be used to solve the fractional knapsack problem. Incidentally, the all-or-nothing, or "0-1" version of the knapsack problem does not have an efficient greedy solution, however, and solving this version of the problem is much harder, as we explore in Sections 12.6 and 17.5.

10.2 Task Scheduling

Suppose we are given a set T of n **tasks** such that each task i has a **start time**, s_i, and a **finish time**, f_i (where $s_i < f_i$). Task i must start at time s_i and must finish by time f_i. Each task has to be performed on a **machine** and each machine can execute only one task at a time. Two tasks i and j are said to be **nonconflicting** if they do not overlap in time, i.e., $f_i \le s_j$ or $f_j \le s_i$. Clearly, two tasks can be scheduled to be executed on the same machine only if they are nonconflicting.

The **task scheduling** problem we consider here is to schedule all the tasks in T on the fewest machines possible in a nonconflicting way. Alternatively, we can think of the tasks as meetings that we must schedule in as few conference rooms as possible. (See Figure 10.4.)

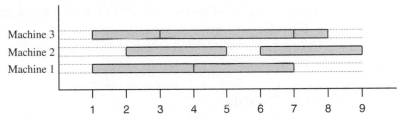

Figure 10.4: An illustration of a solution to the task scheduling problem, for tasks whose collection of pairs of start times and finish times is $\{(1,3), (1,4), (2,5), (3,7), (4,7), (6,9), (7,8)\}$.

There are several ways we might wish to solve this problem using the greedy method. As with any greedy strategy, the challenge is to find the right objective function. For example, we might consider the tasks from longest to shortest, assigning them to machines based on the first one available, since the longest tasks seem like they would be the hardest to schedule. Unfortunately, this approach does not necessarily result in an optimal solution, as is shown in Figure 10.5.

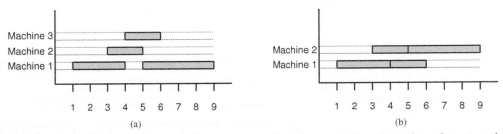

(a)   (b)

Figure 10.5: Why the longest-first strategy doesn't work, for the pairs of start and finish times in the set $\{(1,4), (5,9), (3,5), (4,6)\}$; (a) the solution chosen by the longest-first strategy; (b) the optimal solution. Note that the longest-first strategy uses three machines, whereas the optimal strategy uses only two.

A Better Greedy Approach to Task Scheduling

Another greedy approach is to consider the tasks ordered by increasing start times. In this case, we would consider each task by the order of its start time, and assign it to the first machine that is available at that time. If there are no available machines, however, then we would need to allocate a new machine and schedule this task on that machine. The intuition behind this approach is that, by processing tasks by their start times, when we process a task for a given start time we will have already processed all the other tasks that would conflict with this starting time. We give the details of this greedy algorithm in Algorithm 10.6.

Algorithm TaskSchedule(T):

    Input: A set T of tasks, such that each task has a start time s_i and a finish time f_i

    Output: A nonconflicting schedule of the tasks in T using a minimum number of machines

    $m \leftarrow 0$ // optimal number of machines
    while $T \neq \emptyset$ **do**
        remove from T the task i with smallest start time s_i
        if there is a machine j with no task conflicting with task i **then**
            schedule task i on machine j
        else
            $m \leftarrow m + 1$ // add a new machine
            schedule task i on machine m

Algorithm 10.6: A greedy algorithm for the task scheduling problem.

We show an example solution produced by this algorithm in Figure 10.7, using the same set of tasks used in Figure 10.4. Note that even though this is an optimal solution, it is not the same as the optimal solution shown in Figure 10.4.

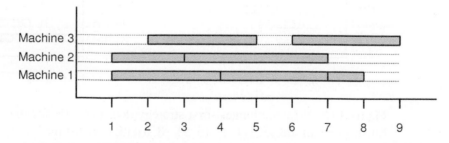

Figure 10.7: An example solution produced by the greedy algorithm based on considering tasks by increasing start times.

Analysis of the Greedy Task Scheduling Algorithm

So, in words, in the above algorithm, TaskSchedule, we begin with no machines and we consider the tasks in a greedy fashion, ordered by their start times. For each task i, if we have a machine that can handle task i, then we schedule i on that machine, say, choosing the first such available machine. Otherwise, we allocate a new machine, schedule i on it, and repeat this greedy selection process until we have considered all the tasks in T.

The following theorem states that greedy method TaskSchedule (Algorithm 10.6) produces an optimal solution, because we are always considering a task starting at a given time after we have already processed all the tasks that might conflict with this start time.

Theorem 10.2: *Given a set of n tasks specified by their start and finish times, the Algorithm* TaskSchedule *produces, in $O(n \log n)$ time, a schedule for the tasks using a minimum number of machines.*

Proof: Let k be the last machine allocated by algorithm TaskSchedule, and let i be the first task scheduled on k. When we scheduled i, each of the machines 1 through $k - 1$ contained tasks that conflict with i. Since they conflict with i and because we consider tasks ordered by their start times, all the tasks currently conflicting with task i must have start times less than or equal to s_i, the start time of i, and have finish times after s_i. In other words, these tasks not only conflict with task i, they all conflict with each other. But this means we have k tasks in our set T that conflict with each other, which implies it is impossible for us to schedule all the tasks in T using only $k - 1$ machines. Therefore, k is the minimum number of machines needed to schedule all the tasks in T.

We leave as a simple exercise (R-10.2) the job of showing how to implement the Algorithm TaskSchedule in $O(n \log n)$ time. ∎

Note that the proof of this theorem does not use an exchange argument to prove the correctness of the greedy algorithm we used in this case. Instead, the above proof uses a *lower-bound* argument, which is another technique for proving greedy algorithms are correct. In using this technique, we argue that any solution to our problem will require a cost of at least some given parameter and we then show that the greedy algorithm achieves this lower bound as an upper bound. In the above proof, we used the parameter k for this purpose.

10.3   Text Compression and Huffman Coding

In this section, we consider another application of the greedy method—to *text compression*. In this problem, we are given a string X defined over some alphabet, such as the ASCII or Unicode character sets, and we want to efficiently encode X into a small binary string Y (using only the characters 0 and 1). Text compression is useful in any situation where we are communicating over a low-bandwidth channel, such as a slow wireless or satellite connection, and we wish to minimize the time needed to transmit our text. Likewise, text compression is also useful for storing collections of large documents more efficiently, to allow a computational device with a small amount of storage to contain as many documents as possible.

Standard encoding schemes, such as the ASCII and Unicode systems, use fixed-length binary strings to encode characters, with 7 bits in the ASCII system and 16 in the Unicode system. So, for example, an English document whose length is 100 million characters would require at least 7 megabits to represent in ASCII and 16 megabits to represent in Unicode. This is a waste of bits, however, since there are some characters that are hardly ever used and others, like the letters "e" and "t," that are used so often that is shame to be using the same number of bits for them as the seldomly used characters.

An alternative to such fixed-length encoding schemes, then, is a *variable-length encoding scheme*, where the codes for various characters are allowed to have different lengths. Ideally, we would like the most-frequently used characters to use the fewest number of bits, and the least-frequently used characters to use the most. To encode a string X, we would then represent each character in X with its associated variable-length code word, and we concatenate all these code words in order to produce a binary representation, Y, for X.

In order to avoid ambiguities in this approach, we insist that our encoding scheme be a *prefix code*, that is, we insist that no code word in our scheme is a prefix of any other code word in our scheme. The advantage of using such a prefix code is that decoding can be accomplished by using the greedy strategy of processing the bits of Y in order, repeatedly matching bits to the first code word they represent. Moreover, the savings produced by a variable-length prefix code can be significant, particularly if there is a wide variance in character frequencies (as is the case for natural language text in almost every spoken language).

The challenge, of course, is that to get the maximum compression possible with this approach we want to guarantee that high-frequency characters are assigned to short code words and low-frequency characters are assigned to longer code words. In other words, to get the maximum compression for X based on this approach, our code words must be chosen based on the frequencies of how characters appear in X. So, let us assume that we have, for each character, c, in X, a count, $f(c)$, of the number of times c appears in the string X.

Huffman Coding

An interesting greedy approach to solving the text compression problem using this approach is ***Huffman coding***. This method produces a variable-length prefix code for X based on the construction of a proper binary tree T that represents the code. Each edge in T represents a bit in a code word, with each edge to a left child representing a "0" and each edge to a right child representing a "1." Each external node v is associated with a specific character, and the code word for that character is defined by the sequence of bits associated with the edges in the path from the root of T to v.

Since characters are associated only with external nodes, and no internal node is associated with any code word, such a scheme produces a prefix code. Put another way, if we start matching bits in X based on the path that they trace out in T, then the external node that we reach will correspond to the character represented by the code word this string of bits is equal to. (See Figure 10.8.)

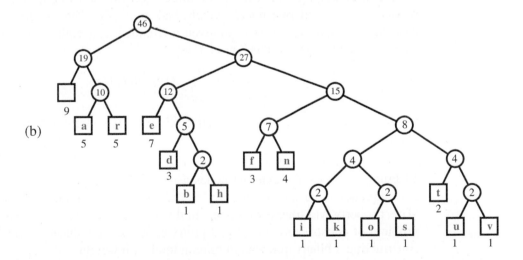

Figure 10.8: An illustration of an example Huffman code for the input string $X = $ "a fast runner need never be afraid of the dark": (a) frequency of each character of X; (b) Huffman tree T for string X. The code for a character c is obtained by tracing the path from the root of T to the external node where c is stored, and associating a left child with 0 and a right child with 1. For example, the code for "a" is 010, and the code for "f" is 1100.

The Huffman Coding Algorithm

The critical part of the Huffman coding algorithm is to construct the tree, T, so that it represents a good prefix code. We begin with a collection, C, of characters, with each character c in C having a numeric weight, $f(c)$, which we think of as its frequency.

Each external node v in T is associated with a character and has a *frequency*, $f(v)$, which is the frequency in X of the character associated with v. For each internal node, v, in T, we associate a total frequency, $f(v)$, which is the sum of the frequencies of all the external nodes in the subtree rooted at v. The remaining optimization problem involves choosing how T is structured so as to determine an optimal prefix code.

Let T be a binary tree, defined as above, with a numeric weight, $f(v)$, assigned to each external node, v in T, and a weight, $f(v)$, assigned to each internal node, v, that is the sum of the weights of its external-node descendants. Define the *total path weight*, $p(T)$, of T to be the sum of all the weights in T. That is, define $p(T)$ as follows:

$$p(T) = \sum_{v \in T} f(v).$$

Note that this is equivalent to us summing, over all the external nodes of T, the product of each external node's weight and its depth. That is, given a set C of characters, where each c in C is given a (frequency) weight, $f(c)$, we can also characterize the total path weight of T as

$$p(T) = \sum_{c \in C} f(c) \cdot d(v_c),$$

where v_c is the external node associated with the character c in C and $d(v_c)$ is the depth of v_c in T.

The goal is for us to construct T so that it has minimum total path weight over all binary trees having external nodes associated with the characters in C, using the frequency of each character in C as the weight of its associated external node. (This property was true, for instance, in the tree shown in Figure 10.8b.) Thus, the problem of constructing an optimal prefix code can be reduced to the problem of constructing a binary tree with minimum total path weight.

The Huffman coding algorithm begins with a set, C, of characters that are the d distinct characters from the string X, such that each such character is associated with the root node of a single-node binary tree. The algorithm proceeds in a series of rounds. In each round, the algorithm takes the two binary trees with the smallest weight at their respective roots and merges them into a single binary tree, giving the root of the new tree the sum of the roots of the two merged trees. The algorithm then repeats this process until only one tree is left. (See Algorithm 10.9.)

Algorithm Huffman(C):

> *Input:* A set, C, of d characters, each with a given weight, $f(c)$
> *Output:* A coding tree, T, for C, with minimum total path weight

> Initialize a priority queue Q.
> **for each** character c in C **do**
> > Create a single-node binary tree T storing c.
> > Insert T into Q with key $f(c)$.
> **while** Q.size() > 1 **do**
> > $f_1 \leftarrow Q$.minKey()
> > $T_1 \leftarrow Q$.removeMin()
> > $f_2 \leftarrow Q$.minKey()
> > $T_2 \leftarrow Q$.removeMin()
> > Create a new binary tree T with left subtree T_1 and right subtree T_2.
> > Insert T into Q with key $f_1 + f_2$.
> **return** tree Q.removeMin()

Algorithm 10.9: Huffman coding algorithm.

Analysis of the Huffman Coding Algorithm

Each iteration of the while-loop in the Huffman coding algorithm can be implemented in $O(\log d)$ time using a priority queue represented with a heap. In addition, each iteration takes two binary trees out of Q and adds one in, all of which can be done in $O(\log d)$ time. This process is repeated $d - 1$ times before exactly one node is left in Q. Thus, this algorithm runs in $O(d \log d)$ time, assuming we are given the set, C, of d distinct characters in the string X as input. In addition, we can construct C from X in $O(n)$ time, including the calculation, for each c in C, of the frequency, $f(c)$, of how many times the character c appears in X, where n is the length of X; see Exercise C-10.3.

The correctness argument for the Huffman coding algorithm begins with the following lemma.

Lemma 10.3: *If T is a binary tree, T, with minimum total path weight for a set, C, of characters, with each c in C having a positive weight, $f(c)$, then T is proper, that is, each internal node in T has two children.*

Proof: Suppose, for the sake of contradiction, that T has an internal node, v, with only one child, w. Then we can replace v with w and T will have the same set of external nodes as before, but each node in the subtree rooted at T will have its depth reduced by 1. Since the weights for the characters in C are positive, this implies that the total path weight for the new tree is less than T, which is impossible, since T is a binary tree with minimum total path weight. ∎

In addition, the following lemma is also important.

Lemma 10.4: *Given a set, C, of characters, with a positive weight, $f(c)$, defined for each c in C, two characters, b and c, with the smallest two weights, are associated with nodes that have the maximum depth and are siblings in a binary tree, T, with minimum total path weight for C.*

Proof: Let T be a binary tree with minimum total path weight for C. Suppose that the node for one of b or c does not have maximum depth in T, and let v be this node and, without loss of generality, let c be the associated character. Then there must be another external node, w, associated with a character, e, such that $f(e) \geq f(c)$ and $d(w) > d(v)$. We can swap the characters for v and w, which will cause a change in the total path weight of T by the amount

$$f(c)(d(w) - d(v)) \ - \ f(e)(d(w) - d(v)),$$

which cannot be positive. Thus, c can be associated with a maximum-depth node without increasing the total weight of T; hence, there is an optimal tree having a maximum-depth node associated with c.

   To see that b and c can be siblings, note that, since we have already shown that b and c are at maximum depth in an optimal tree, T, and an optimal tree is proper, by Lemma 10.3, we can swap a sibling of either b or c to make these two be siblings without changing the total path weight of T.   ∎

   We use this lemma to prove the following.

Theorem 10.5: *The Huffman coding algorithm constructs an optimal prefix code for a string of length n with d distinct characters in $O(n + d \log d)$ time.*

Proof: We have already established the time bound for the Huffman coding algorithm, as well as the fact that an optimal prefix code can be derived from a binary tree, T, with minimum total path weight, $p(T)$, for a set of characters and weights associated with its external nodes.

   We can prove the correctness of the Huffman coding algorithm by induction on d, the number of characters in C. For the basis, note that for $d = 1$, the optimal tree is a single (root) node, and that this is the tree constructed by the Huffman coding algorithm.

   Let T be a tree constructed by the Huffman coding algorithm for a set, C, of $d > 1$ characters. After merging two lowest-frequency characters, b and c, in C into a single tree having a root, r, which has the two associated nodes as its children, note that the iterative structure of the algorithm is the same as if we had started with $d - 1$ characters, including a character for r with frequency $f(r)$. Thus, we can assume inductively that the tree, T', constructed for this set of characters is optimal. In addition, since b and c are associated with the children of r,

$$p(T) = p(T') + f(b) + f(c).$$

   Now, let U be an optimal tree for the set C, where, by Lemma 10.4, the nodes for b and c are siblings. Let U' be the tree derived from U by removing the nodes for b and c, but keeping their parent node, which has weight $f(b) + f(c)$. That is, U' is defined on the same set of characters and frequencies as T', and

$$p(U) = p(U') + f(b) + f(c).$$

In addition, since T' is optimal,

$$p(T') \leq p(U').$$

Therefore,

$$
\begin{aligned}
p(T) &= p(T') + f(b) + f(c) \\
&\leq p(U') + f(b) + f(c) \\
&= p(U).
\end{aligned}
$$

In other words, T has weight less than or equal to U. But, since U is an optimal tree, this means that T must be an optimal tree. ■

How the Huffman Coding Algorithm Uses the Greedy Method

The Huffman coding algorithm for building an optimal prefix code is another application of the **greedy method**. As mentioned above, this technique is applied to optimization problems, where we are trying to construct some structure while minimizing or maximizing some property of that structure.

Indeed, the Huffman coding algorithm closely follows the general formula for the greedy method. Namely, in order to solve the given optimization code problem using the greedy method, we proceed by a sequence of choices. The sequence starts from a well-understood starting condition, and computes the cost for that initial condition. Finally, we iteratively make additional choices by identifying the decision that achieves the best cost improvement from all of the choices that are currently possible. This approach does not always lead to an optimal solution, but it does indeed find the optimal prefix code when used according to the approach of the Huffman coding algorithm.

This global optimality for the Huffman coding algorithm is due to the fact that the optimal prefix coding problem possesses the **greedy-choice** property. This is the property that a global optimal condition can be reached by a series of locally optimal choices (that is, choices that are each the current best from among the possibilities available at the time), starting from a well-defined starting condition. In this case, the general condition is defined by a set of disjoint binary trees, each with a given weight for its root, and the greedy choice is to combine two lowest-weight trees into a single tree.

10.4 Exercises

Reinforcement

R-10.1 Let $S = \{a, b, c, d, e, f, g\}$ be a collection of objects with benefit-weight values, $a: (12, 4)$, $b: (10, 6)$, $c: (8, 5)$, $d: (11, 7)$, $e: (14, 3)$, $f: (7, 1)$, $g: (9, 6)$. What is an optimal solution to the fractional knapsack problem for S assuming we have a sack that can hold objects with total weight 18? Show your work.

R-10.2 Describe how to implement the TaskSchedule method to run in $O(n \log n)$ time.

R-10.3 Suppose we are given a set of tasks specified by pairs of the start times and finish times as $T = \{(1, 2), (1, 3), (1, 4), (2, 5), (3, 7), (4, 9), (5, 6), (6, 8), (7, 9)\}$. Solve the task scheduling problem for this set of tasks.

R-10.4 Draw the frequency table and Huffman tree for the following string:

"dogs do not spot hot pots or cats".

R-10.5 Give an example set of 10 characters and their associated frequencies so that, in the Huffman tree for this set, every internal node has an external-node child.

R-10.6 Give an example set of 8 characters and their associated frequencies so that the Huffman tree for this set is a complete binary tree.

R-10.7 Fred says that he ran the Huffman coding algorithm for the four characters, A, C, G, and T, and it gave him the code words, 0, 10, 111, 110, respectively. Give examples of four frequencies for these characters that could have resulted in these code words or argue why these code words could not possibly have been output by the Huffman coding algorithm.

R-10.8 Repeat the previous exercise for the code words, 0, 10, 101, 111.

R-10.9 Repeat the previous exercise for the code words, 00, 100, 101, 11.

R-10.10 Indicate for each of the lemmas used in the proof of correctness for the Huffman coding algorithm whether the proof of that lemma uses an exchange argument or a lower-bound argument?

Creativity

C-10.1 Provide an example instance of the fractional knapsack problem where a greedy strategy based on repeatedly choosing as much of the highest-benefit item as possible results in a suboptimal solution.

C-10.2 Suppose you are given an instance of the fractional knapsack problem in which all the items have the same weight. Show that you can solve the fractional knapsack problem in this case in $O(n)$ time.

C-10.3 Given a character string X of length n, describe an $O(n)$-time algorithm to construct the set, C, of distinct characters that appear in C, along with a count, $f(c)$, for each c in C, of how many times the character c appears in X. You may assume that the characters in X are encoded using a standard character indexing scheme, like the ASCII system.

C-10.4 A native Australian named Anatjari wishes to cross a desert carrying only a single water bottle. He has a map that marks all the watering holes along the way. Assuming he can walk k miles on one bottle of water, design an efficient algorithm for determining where Anatjari should refill his bottle in order to make as few stops as possible. Argue why your algorithm is correct.

C-10.5 Describe an efficient greedy algorithm for making change for a specified value using a minimum number of coins, assuming there are four denominations of coins (called quarters, dimes, nickels, and pennies), with values 25, 10, 5, and 1, respectively. Argue why your algorithm is correct.

C-10.6 Give an example set of denominations of coins so that a greedy change making algorithm will not use the minimum number of coins.

C-10.7 Suppose T is a Huffman tree for a set of characters having frequencies equal to the first n nonzero Fibonacci numbers, $\{1, 1, 2, 3, 5, 8, 13, 21, 34, \ldots\}$, where $f_0 = 1$, $f_1 = 1$, and $f_i = f_{i-1} + f_{i-2}$. Prove that every internal node in T has an external-node child.

C-10.8 Suppose you've been sent back in time and have arrived at the scene of an ancient Roman battle. Moreover, suppose you have just learned that it is your job to assign n spears to n Roman soldiers, so that each man has a spear. You observe that the men and spears are of various heights, and you have been told (in Latin) that the army is at its best if you can minimize the total difference in heights between each man and his spear. That is, if the ith man has height m_i and his spear has height s_i, then you want to minimize the sum,

$$\sum_{i=1}^{n} |m_i - s_i|.$$

Consider a greedy strategy of repeatedly matching the man and spear that minimizes the difference in heights between these two. Prove or disprove that this greedy strategy results in the optimal assignment of spears to men.

C-10.9 Consider again the time-travel problem of the previous exercise, but now consider a greedy algorithm that sorts the men by increasing heights and sorts the spears by increasing heights, and then assigns the ith spear in the ordered list of spears to the ith man in the ordered list of Roman soldiers. Prove or disprove that this greedy strategy results in the optimal assignment of spears to men.

C-10.10 Suppose you are organizing a party for a large group of your friends. Your friends are pretty opinionated, though, and you don't want to invite two friends if they don't like each other. So you have asked each of your friends to give you an "enemies" list, which identifies all the other people among your friends that they dislike and for whom they know the feeling is mutual. Your goal is to invite the largest set of friends possible such that no pair of invited friends dislike each other. To solve this problem quickly, one of your relatives (who is not one of your friends) has offered a simple greedy strategy, where you would repeatedly invite the person with the fewest number of enemies from among your friends who is not an enemy of someone you have already invited, until there is no one left who can be invited. Show that your relative's greedy algorithm may not always result in the maximum number of friends being invited to your party.

Applications

A-10.1 In the ***art gallery guarding*** problem we are given a line L that represents a long hallway in an art gallery. We are also given a set $X = \{x_0, x_1, \ldots, x_{n-1}\}$ of real numbers that specify the positions of paintings in this hallway. Suppose that a single guard can protect all the paintings within distance at most 1 of his or her position (on both sides). Design an algorithm for finding a placement of guards that uses the minimum number of guards to guard all the paintings with positions in X.

A-10.2 Consider a single ***machine scheduling*** problem, where we are given a set, T, of tasks specified by their start times and finish times, as in the task scheduling problem, except now we have only one machine and we wish to maximize the number of tasks that this single machine performs. Design a greedy algorithm for this single machine scheduling problem and show that it is correct. What is the running time of this algorithm?

A-10.3 A *floating-point number* is a pair, (m, d), of integers, which represents the number $m \times b^d$, where b is either 2 or 10. In any real-world programming environment, the sizes of m and d are limited; hence, each arithmetic operation involving two floating-point numbers may have some ***roundoff error***. The traditional way to account for this error is to introduce a ***machine precision*** parameter, $\epsilon < 1$, for the given programming environment, and bound roundoff errors in terms of this parameter. For instance, in the case of floating-point addition, $fl(x + y)$, for summing two floating-point numbers, x and y, we can write

$$fl(x + y) = (x + y) \cdot (1 + \delta_{x,y}),$$

where

$$|\delta_{x,y}| \leq \epsilon.$$

Suppose we are given a set of positive floating-point numbers, $\{x_1, x_2, \ldots, x_n\}$, and we wish to sum up all these numbers. Any such summation algorithm can be modeled with a binary expression tree, T, that has each x_i associated with one of its external nodes, with each internal node, v, representing the floating-point sum of the floating point numbers computed by v's children. Given the machine-precision approach to bounding floating-point errors, and assuming that ϵ is small enough so that ϵ^2 times any floating-point number is negligibly small, then we can use a term, e_n, to estimate an upper bound for the roundoff error for summing these numbers using the tree T as

$$e_n = \epsilon \sum_{i=1}^{n} x_i d(v_{x_i}),$$

where v_{x_i} is the external node associated with x_i and $d(v_{x_i})$ is the depth of this node in T. Design an efficient algorithm for constructing the binary expression tree, T, that minimizes e_n. What is the running time of your method?

A-10.4 Whenever a word processor or web browser displays a long passage of text, it must be broken up into lines of text that are displayed one on top of the other. Determining where to make these breaks is known as the ***line breaking*** problem. The most natural place to make such breaks are between words. So, suppose you are given a sequence, W, of n words, $W = (w_1, w_2, \ldots, w_n)$, where each word, w_i in W, has a given length, l_i. Also, for the sake of simplicity, let us ignore any spaces or punctuation that might come before or after any of these words. Suppose further that you are given a line length, L, that is an upper bound on the sum of the lengths of words that can fit on a single line. We specify how to break W into lines, by a sequence of indices, $(i_1, i_2, \ldots, i_k)$, where $i_1 = 1$, $i_k = n$, to indicate that we should break W into the lines, $w_{i_j} \ldots w_{i_{j+1}-1})$, for $j = 1, 2, \ldots, k-1$, subject to the constraints that $i_j < i_{j+1}$ and

$$\sum_{r=i_j}^{i_{j+1}-1} l_r \le L.$$

In addition, define the ***penalty*** for such a set of line breaks to be

$$\sum_{j=1}^{k} \left| L - \sum_{r=i_j}^{i_{j+1}-1} l_r \right|.$$

Describe an efficient greedy algorithm for breaking a sequence of words, W, into lines and prove that your method minimizes this penalty. What is the running time of your method?

A-10.5 Consider the line breaking problem from the previous exercise, but now consider changing the penalty for line breaks, so that it is now

$$\sum_{j=1}^{k} \left(L - \sum_{r=i_j}^{i_{j+1}-1} l_r \right)^2.$$

Show that a greedy strategy of scanning W from beginning to end and making the choice that minimizes the term,

$$\left(L - \sum_{r=i_j}^{i_{j+1}-1} l_r \right)^2,$$

based on previous choices, while maintaining each line to be of length at most L, does not necessarily result in an optimal set of line breaks.

A-10.6 In the 2003 California gubernatorial recall election, the ballot contained 135 candidates, including people with various listings for their current job, including "actor," "comedian," and even "adult film actress." The winner was the actor-businessman Arnold Schwarzenegger, who got over 48% of the vote. Suppose we have the election results from such an election, with a large number, n, of candidates, and the only tool we can use to determine the winner is to encode the names of all the candidates using the Huffman coding algorithm, based on the number of votes each candidate got in this election. Suppose further that a friend of yours is guessing that if the winning candidate gets more than 40% of the votes, then his or her name will be encoded with a single bit. Prove that this conjecture is true and analyze the running time of this election-counting algorithm.

A-10.7 When data is transmitted across a noisy channel, information can be lost during the transmission. For example, a message that is sent through a noisy channel as

> "WHO PARKED ON HARRY POTTER'S SPOT?"

could be received as the message,

> "HOP ON POP"

That is, some characters could be lost during the transmission, so that only a selected portion of the original message is received. We can model this phenomenon using character strings, where, given a string $X = x_1 x_2 \ldots x_n$, we say that a string $Y = y_1 y_2 \ldots y_m$ is a **subsequence** of X if there are a set of indices $\{i_1, i_2, \ldots, i_k\}$, such that $y_1 = x_{i_1}$, $y_2 = x_{i_2}$, ..., $y_k = x_{i_k}$, and $i_j < i_{j+1}$, for $j = 1, 2, \ldots, k - 1$. In a case of transmission along a noisy channel, it could be useful to know if our transcription of a received message is indeed a subsequence of the message sent. Therefore, describe an $O(n + m)$-time method for determining if a given string, Y, of length m is a subsequence of a given string, X, of length n.

Chapter Notes

The term "greedy algorithm" was coined by Edmonds [63] in 1971, although the concept existed before then. For more information about the greedy method and the theory that supports it, which is known as matroid theory, please see the book by Papadimitriou and Steiglitz [169]. The application of the greedy method we gave to the coding problem comes from Huffman [108].

Chapter

11

Divide-and-Conquer

Grand Canyon from South Rim, 1941. Ansel Adams. U.S. government image. U.S. National Archives and Records Administration.

Contents

11.1 Recurrences and the Master Theorem 305
11.2 Integer Multiplication 313
11.3 Matrix Multiplication 315
11.4 The Maxima-Set Problem 317
11.5 Exercises 319

Imagine that you are getting ready to go on a vacation and are looking for a hotel. Suppose that for you, the only criteria that matter when you judge a hotel are the size of its pool and the quality of its restaurant, as measured by a well-known restaurant guide. You have gone to the restaurant guide website and several hotel websites and have discovered, for each of n hotels, the size of its pool and the quality of its restaurant.

With so many hotels to choose from, it would be useful if you could rule out some possibilities. For instance, if there is a hotel whose pool is smaller and restaurant is of lower quality than another hotel, then it can be eliminated as a possible choice, as both of your criteria for the first hotel are dominated by the second hotel. We can visualize the various trade-offs by plotting each hotel as a two-dimensional point, (x, y), where x is the pool size and y is the restaurant quality score. We say that such a point is a ***maximum*** point in a set if there is no other point, (x', y'), in that set such that $x \le x'$ and $y \le y'$. (See Figure 11.1.)

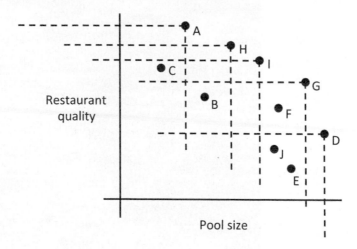

Figure 11.1: A set of hotels visualized as two-dimensional points, in terms of their pool size and restaurant quality scores. The points that are maxima are shown with dashed lines indicating the set of other points they dominate. For example, Hotel B is dominated by Hotels G, H, and I. The maxima set is $\{A, D, G, H, I\}$.

Given such a set of points, then, we are interested in designing an efficient algorithm that can identify the ***maxima set***. The other points can be pruned from consideration, since each of them is dominated by some other point. As we show in Section 11.4, the algorithmic technique we discuss in this chapter, ***divide-and-conquer***, is well suited for solving this problem. In addition, in this chapter, we discuss how to apply this technique to integer and matrix multiplication, and we give a general way, called the master theorem, for analyzing divide-and-conquer algorithms. Incidentally, we also discuss divide-and-conquer algorithms, merge-sort and quick-sort, in Chapter 8, and the fast Fourier transform, in Chapter 25.

11.1 Recurrences and the Master Theorem

The ***divide-and-conquer*** technique involves solving a particular computational problem by dividing it into one or more subproblems of smaller size, recursively solving each subproblem, and then "merging" or "marrying" the solutions to the subproblem(s) to produce a solution to the original problem.

We can model the divide-and-conquer approach by using a parameter n to denote the size of the original problem, and let $S(n)$ denote this problem. We solve the problem $S(n)$ by solving a collection of k subproblems $S(n_1)$, $S(n_2)$, ..., $S(n_k)$, where $n_i < n$ for $i = 1, \ldots, k$, and then merging the solutions to these subproblems.

For example, in the classic merge-sort algorithm (Section 8.1), $S(n)$ denotes the problem of sorting a sequence of n numbers. Merge-sort solves problem $S(n)$ by dividing it into two subproblems $S(\lfloor n/2 \rfloor)$ and $S(\lceil n/2 \rceil)$, recursively solving these two subproblems, and then merging the resulting sorted sequences into a single sorted sequence that yields a solution to $S(n)$. The merging step takes $O(n)$ time. Thus, the total running time of the merge-sort algorithm is $O(n \log n)$.

As with the merge-sort algorithm, the general divide-and-conquer technique can be used to build algorithms that have fast running times.

To analyze the running time of a divide-and-conquer algorithm, we often use a ***recurrence equation*** (Section 1.1.4). That is, we let a function $T(n)$ denote the running time of the algorithm on an input of size n, and we characterize $T(n)$ using an equation that relates $T(n)$ to values of the function T for problem sizes smaller than n. In the case of the merge-sort algorithm, we get the recurrence equation

$$
T(n) = \begin{cases} b & \text{if } n < 2 \\ 2T(n/2) + bn & \text{if } n \geq 2, \end{cases}
$$

for some constant $b \geq 1$, taking the simplifying assumption that n is a power of 2. In fact, throughout this section, we take the simplifying assumption that n is an appropriate power, so that we can avoid using floor and ceiling functions. Every asymptotic statement we make about recurrence equations will still be true, even if we relax this assumption (see Exercise C-11.5). As we observed in Chapter 8, we can show that $T(n)$ is $O(n \log n)$ in this case. In general, however, we may get a recurrence equation that is more challenging to solve than this one. Thus, it is useful to develop some general ways of solving the kinds of recurrence equations that arise in the analysis of divide-and-conquer algorithms.

The Iterative Substitution Method

One way to solve a divide-and-conquer recurrence equation is to use the *iterative substitution* method, which is more colloquially known as the "plug-and-chug" method. In using this method, we assume that the problem size n is fairly large and we then substitute the general form of the recurrence for each occurrence of the function T on the right-hand side. For example, performing such a substitution with the merge-sort recurrence equation yields the equation

$$
\begin{aligned}
T(n) &= 2(2T(n/2^2) + b(n/2)) + bn \\
&= 2^2 T(n/2^2) + 2bn.
\end{aligned}
$$

Plugging the general equation for T in again yields the equation

$$
\begin{aligned}
T(n) &= 2^2(2T(n/2^3) + b(n/2^2)) + 2bn \\
&= 2^3 T(n/2^3) + 3bn.
\end{aligned}
$$

The hope in applying the iterative substitution method is that at some point we will see a pattern that can be converted into a general closed-form equation (with T only appearing on the left-hand side). In the case of the merge-sort recurrence equation, the general form is

$$
T(n) = 2^i T(n/2^i) + ibn.
$$

Note that the general form of this equation shifts to the base case, $T(n) = b$, when $n = 2^i$, that is, when $i = \log n$, which implies

$$
T(n) = bn + bn \log n.
$$

In other words, $T(n)$ is $O(n \log n)$. In a general application of the iterative substitution technique, we hope that we can determine a general pattern for $T(n)$ and that we can also figure out when the general form of $T(n)$ shifts to the base case.

From a mathematical point of view, there is one point in the use of the iterative substitution technique that involves a bit of a logical "jump." This jump occurs at the point where we try to characterize the general pattern emerging from a sequence of substitutions. Often, as was the case with the merge-sort recurrence equation, this jump is quite reasonable. Other times, however, it may not be so obvious what a general form for the equation should look like. In these cases, the jump may be more dangerous. To be completely safe in making such a jump, we must fully justify the general form of the equation, possibly using induction. Combined with such a justification, the iterative substitution method is completely correct and an often useful way of characterizing recurrence equations. By the way, the colloquialism "plug-and-chug," used to describe the iterative substitution method, comes from the way this method involves "plugging" in the recursive part of an equation for $T(n)$ and then often "chugging" through a considerable amount of algebra in order to get this equation into a form where we can infer a general pattern.

The Recursion Tree

Another way of characterizing recurrence equations is to use the *recursion tree* method. Like the iterative substitution method, this technique uses repeated substitution to solve a recurrence equation, but it differs from the iterative substitution method in that, rather than being an algebraic approach, it is a visual approach. In using the recursion tree method, we draw a tree R where each node represents a different substitution of the recurrence equation. Thus, each node in R has a value of the argument n of the function $T(n)$ associated with it. In addition, we associate an *overhead* with each node v in R, defined as the value of the nonrecursive part of the recurrence equation for v. For divide-and-conquer recurrences, the overhead corresponds to the running time needed to merge the subproblem solutions coming from the children of v. The recurrence equation is then solved by summing the overheads associated with all the nodes of R. This is commonly done by first summing values across the levels of R and then summing up these partial sums for all the levels of R.

Example 11.1: *Consider the following recurrence equation:*

$$T(n) = \begin{cases} b & \text{if } n < 3 \\ 3T(n/3) + bn & \text{if } n \geq 3. \end{cases}$$

This is the recurrence equation that we get, for example, by modifying the merge-sort algorithm so that we divide an unsorted sequence into three equal-sized sequences, recursively sort each one, and then do a three-way merge of three sorted sequences to produce a sorted version of the original sequence. In the recursion tree R for this recurrence, each internal node v has three children and has a size and an overhead associated with it, which corresponds to the time needed to merge the subproblem solutions produced by v's children. We illustrate the tree R in Figure 11.2. Note that the overheads of the nodes of each level sum to bn. Thus, observing that the depth of R is $\log_3 n$, we have that $T(n)$ is $O(n \log n)$.

Overhead

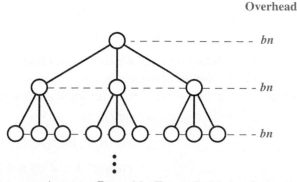

Figure 11.2: The recursion tree R used in Example 11.1, where we show the cumulative overhead of each level.

The Guess-and-Test Method

Another method for solving recurrence equations is the ***guess-and-test*** technique. This technique involves first making an educated guess as to what a closed-form solution of the recurrence equation might look like and then justifying that guess, usually by induction. For example, we can use the guess-and-test method as a kind of "binary search" for finding good upper bounds on a given recurrence equation. If the justification of our current guess fails, then it is possible that we need to use a faster-growing function, and if our current guess is justified "too easily," then it is possible that we need to use a slower-growing function. However, using this technique requires our being careful, in each mathematical step we take, in trying to justify that a certain hypothesis holds with respect to our current "guess." We explore an application of the guess-and-test method in the examples that follow.

Example 11.2: *Consider the following recurrence equation (assuming the base case $T(n) = b$ for $n < 2$):*

$$T(n) = 2T(n/2) + bn \log n.$$

This looks very similar to the recurrence equation for the merge-sort routine, so we might make the following as our first guess:

$$\text{First guess: } T(n) \leq cn \log n,$$

for some constant $c > 0$. We can certainly choose c large enough to make this true for the base case, so consider the case when $n \geq 2$. If we assume our first guess is an inductive hypothesis that is true for input sizes smaller than n, then we have

$$
\begin{aligned}
T(n) &= 2T(n/2) + bn \log n \\
&\leq 2(c(n/2) \log(n/2)) + bn \log n \\
&= cn(\log n - \log 2) + bn \log n \\
&= cn \log n - cn + bn \log n.
\end{aligned}
$$

But there is no way that we can make this last line less than or equal to $cn \log n$ for $n \geq 2$. Thus, this first guess was not sufficient. Let us therefore try

$$\text{Better guess: } T(n) \leq cn \log^2 n,$$

for some constant $c > 0$. We can again choose c large enough to make this true for the base case, so consider the case when $n \geq 2$. If we assume this guess as an inductive hypothesis that is true for input sizes smaller than n, then we have

$$
\begin{aligned}
T(n) &= 2T(n/2) + bn \log n \\
&\leq 2(c(n/2) \log^2(n/2)) + bn \log n \\
&= cn(\log^2 n - 2 \log n + 1) + bn \log n \\
&= cn \log^2 n - 2cn \log n + cn + bn \log n \\
&\leq cn \log^2 n,
\end{aligned}
$$

provided $c \geq b$. Thus, we have shown that $T(n)$ is indeed $O(n \log^2 n)$ in this case.

We must take care in using this method. Just because one inductive hypothesis for $T(n)$ does not work, that does not necessarily imply that another one proportional to this one will not work.

Example 11.3: *Consider the following recurrence equation (assuming the base case $T(n) = b$ for $n < 2$):*

$$T(n) = 2T(n/2) + \log n.$$

This recurrence is the running time for the bottom-up heap construction discussed in Section 5.4, which we have shown is $O(n)$. Nevertheless, if we try to prove this fact with the most straightforward inductive hypothesis, we will run into some difficulties. In particular, consider the following:

First guess: $T(n) \leq cn$,

for some constant $c > 0$. We can choose c large enough to make this true for the base case, certainly, so consider the case when $n \geq 2$. If we assume this guess as an inductive hypothesis that is true for input sizes smaller than n, then we have

$$
\begin{aligned}
T(n) &= 2T(n/2) + \log n \\
&\leq 2(c(n/2)) + \log n \\
&= cn + \log n.
\end{aligned}
$$

But there is no way that we can make this last line less than or equal to cn for $n \geq 2$. Thus, this first guess was not sufficient, even though $T(n)$ is indeed $O(n)$. Still, we can show this fact is true by using

Better guess: $T(n) \leq c(n - \log n)$,

for some constant $c > 0$. We can again choose c large enough to make this true for the base case; in fact, we can show that it is true any time $n < 8$. So consider the case when $n \geq 8$. If we assume this guess as an inductive hypothesis that is true for input sizes smaller than n, then we have

$$
\begin{aligned}
T(n) &= 2T(n/2) + \log n \\
&\leq 2c((n/2) - \log(n/2)) + \log n \\
&= cn - 2c\log n + 2c + \log n \\
&= c(n - \log n) - c\log n + 2c + \log n \\
&\leq c(n - \log n),
\end{aligned}
$$

provided $c \geq 3$ and $n \geq 8$. Thus, we have shown that $T(n)$ is indeed $O(n)$ in this case.

The guess-and-test method can be used to establish either an upper or lower bound for the asymptotic complexity of a recurrence equation. Even so, as the above example demonstrates, it requires that we have developed some skill with mathematical induction.

11.1.1   The Master Theorem

Each of the methods described above for solving recurrence equations is ad hoc and requires mathematical sophistication in order to be used effectively. There is, nevertheless, one method for solving divide-and-conquer recurrence equations that is quite general and does not require explicit use of induction to apply correctly. It is the *master theorem*. The master theorem is a "cookbook" method for determining the asymptotic characterization of a wide variety of recurrence equations. Namely, it is used for recurrence equations of the form

$$T(n) = \begin{cases} c & \text{if } n < d \\ aT(n/b) + f(n) & \text{if } n \geq d, \end{cases}$$

where $d \geq 1$ is an integer constant, $a \geq 1$, $c > 0$, and $b > 1$ are real constants, and $f(n)$ is a function that is positive for $n \geq d$. Such a recurrence equation would arise in the analysis of a divide-and-conquer algorithm that divides a given problem into a subproblems of size at most n/b each, solves each subproblem recursively, and then "merges" the subproblem solutions into a solution to the entire problem. The function $f(n)$, in this equation, denotes the total additional time needed to divide the problem into subproblems and merge the subproblem solutions into a solution to the entire problem. Each of the recurrence equations given above uses this form, as do each of the recurrence equations used to analyze divide-and-conquer algorithms given earlier in this book. Thus, it is indeed a general form for divide-and-conquer recurrence equations.

The master theorem for solving such recurrence equations involves simply writing down the answer based on whether one of the three cases applies. Each case is distinguished by comparing $f(n)$ to the special function $n^{\log_b a}$ (we will show later why this special function is so important).

Theorem 11.4 [The Master Theorem]: *Let $f(n)$ and $T(n)$ be defined as above.*

1. *If there is a small constant $\epsilon > 0$, such that $f(n)$ is $O(n^{\log_b a - \epsilon})$, then $T(n)$ is $\Theta(n^{\log_b a})$.*

2. *If there is a constant $k \geq 0$, such that $f(n)$ is $\Theta(n^{\log_b a} \log^k n)$, then $T(n)$ is $\Theta(n^{\log_b a} \log^{k+1} n)$.*

3. *If there are small constants $\epsilon > 0$ and $\delta < 1$, such that $f(n)$ is $\Omega(n^{\log_b a + \epsilon})$ and $af(n/b) \leq \delta f(n)$, for $n \geq d$, then $T(n)$ is $\Theta(f(n))$.*

Case 1 characterizes the situation where $f(n)$ is polynomially smaller than the special function, $n^{\log_b a}$. Case 2 characterizes the situation when $f(n)$ is asymptotically close to the special function, and Case 3 characterizes the situation when $f(n)$ is polynomially larger than the special function.

Some Example Applications of the Master Theorem

We illustrate the usage of the master theorem with a few examples (with each taking the assumption that $T(n) = c$ for $n < d$, for constants $c \geq 1$ and $d \geq 1$).

Example 11.5: *Consider the recurrence*

$$T(n) = 4T(n/2) + n.$$

In this case, $n^{\log_b a} = n^{\log_2 4} = n^2$. Thus, we are in Case 1, for $f(n)$ is $O(n^{2-\epsilon})$ for $\epsilon = 1$. This means that $T(n)$ is $\Theta(n^2)$ by the master theorem.

Example 11.6: *Consider the recurrence*

$$T(n) = 2T(n/2) + n \log n,$$

which is one of the recurrences given above. In this case, $n^{\log_b a} = n^{\log_2 2} = n$. Thus, we are in Case 2, with $k = 1$, for $f(n)$ is $\Theta(n \log n)$. This means that $T(n)$ is $\Theta(n \log^2 n)$ by the master theorem.

Example 11.7: *Consider the recurrence*

$$T(n) = T(n/3) + n,$$

which is the recurrence for a geometrically decreasing summation that starts with n. In this case, $n^{\log_b a} = n^{\log_3 1} = n^0 = 1$. Thus, we are in Case 3, for $f(n)$ is $\Omega(n^{0+\epsilon})$, for $\epsilon = 1$, and $af(n/b) = n/3 = (1/3)f(n)$. This means that $T(n)$ is $\Theta(n)$ by the master theorem.

Example 11.8: *Consider the recurrence*

$$T(n) = 9T(n/3) + n^{2.5}.$$

In this case, $n^{\log_b a} = n^{\log_3 9} = n^2$. Thus, we are in Case 3, since $f(n)$ is $\Omega(n^{2+\epsilon})$ (for $\epsilon = 1/2$) and $af(n/b) = 9(n/3)^{2.5} = (1/3)^{1/2}f(n)$. This means that $T(n)$ is $\Theta(n^{2.5})$ by the master theorem.

Example 11.9: *Finally, consider the recurrence*

$$T(n) = 2T(n^{1/2}) + \log n.$$

Unfortunately, this equation is not in a form that allows us to use the master theorem. We can put it into such a form, however, by introducing the variable $k = \log n$, which lets us write

$$T(n) = T(2^k) = 2T(2^{k/2}) + k.$$

Substituting into this the equation $S(k) = T(2^k)$, we get that

$$S(k) = 2S(k/2) + k.$$

Now, this recurrence equation allows us to use master theorem, which specifies that $S(k)$ is $O(k \log k)$. Substituting back for $T(n)$ implies $T(n)$ is $O(\log n \log \log n)$.

High-Level Justification of the Master Theorem

Rather than rigorously prove Theorem 11.4, we instead discuss the justification behind the master theorem at a high level.

If we apply the iterative substitution method to the general divide-and-conquer recurrence equation, we get

$$
\begin{aligned}
T(n) &= aT(n/b) + f(n) \\
&= a(aT(n/b^2) + f(n/b)) + f(n) = a^2 T(n/b^2) + af(n/b) + f(n) \\
&= a^3 T(n/b^3) + a^2 f(n/b^2) + af(n/b) + f(n) \\
&\;\;\vdots \\
&= a^{\log_b n} T(1) + \sum_{i=0}^{\log_b n - 1} a^i f(n/b^i) \\
&= n^{\log_b a} T(1) + \sum_{i=0}^{\log_b n - 1} a^i f(n/b^i),
\end{aligned}
$$

where the last substitution is based on the identity,

$$
a^{\log_b n} = n^{\log_b a}.
$$

Indeed, this equation is where the special function comes from.

Given this closed-form characterization of $T(n)$, we can intuitively see how each of the three cases is derived:

- Case 1 comes from the situation when $f(n)$ is small and the first term above dominates.

- Case 2 denotes the situation when each of the terms in the above summation is proportional to the others, so the characterization of $T(n)$ is $f(n)$ times a logarithmic factor.

- Finally, Case 3 denotes the situation when the first term is smaller than the second and the summation above is a sum of geometrically-decreasing terms that start with $f(n)$; hence, $T(n)$ is itself proportional to $f(n)$.

The proof of Theorem 11.4 formalizes this intuition, but instead of giving the details of this proof, we present more applications of the master theorem in the remainder of the chapter, for the analysis of various divide-and-conquer algorithms, including integer and matrix multiplication and the maxima-set problem.

11.2 Integer Multiplication

We consider, in this subsection, the problem of multiplying *big integers*, that is, integers represented by a large number of bits that cannot be handled directly by the arithmetic unit of a single processor. Multiplying big integers has applications to data security, where big integers are used in encryption schemes.

Given two big integers I and J represented with n bits each, we can easily compute $I + J$ and $I - J$ in $O(n)$ time. Efficiently computing the product $I \cdot J$ using the common grade-school algorithm requires, however, $O(n^2)$ time. In the rest of this section, we show that by using the divide-and-conquer technique, we can design a subquadratic-time algorithm for multiplying two n-bit integers.

Let us assume that n is a power of two (if this is not the case, we can pad I and J with 0's). We can therefore divide the bit representations of I and J in half, with one half representing the *higher-order* bits and the other representing the *lower-order* bits. In particular, if we split I into I_h and I_l and J into J_h and J_l, then

$$
\begin{aligned}
I &= I_h 2^{n/2} + I_l, \\
J &= J_h 2^{n/2} + J_l.
\end{aligned}
$$

Also, observe that multiplying a binary number I by a power of two, 2^k, is trivial—it simply involves shifting left (that is, in the higher-order direction) the number I by k bit positions. Thus, provided a left-shift operation takes constant time, multiplying an integer by 2^k takes $O(k)$ time.

Let us focus on the problem of computing the product $I \cdot J$. Given the expansion of I and J above, we can rewrite $I \cdot J$ as

$$
I \cdot J = (I_h 2^{n/2} + I_l) \cdot (J_h 2^{n/2} + J_l) = I_h J_h 2^n + I_l J_h 2^{n/2} + I_h J_l 2^{n/2} + I_l J_l.
$$

Thus, we can compute $I \cdot J$ by applying a divide-and-conquer algorithm that divides the bit representations of I and J in half, recursively computes the product as four products of $n/2$ bits each (as described above), and then merges the solutions to these subproducts in $O(n)$ time using addition and multiplication by powers of two. We can terminate the recursion when we get down to the multiplication of two 1-bit numbers, which is trivial. This divide-and-conquer algorithm has a running time that can be characterized by the following recurrence:

$$
T(n) = \begin{cases} c & \text{if } n < 2 \\ 4T(n/2) + cn, & \text{if } n \geq 2, \end{cases}
$$

for some constant $c > 0$. We can then apply the master theorem to note that the special function $n^{\log_b a} = n^{\log_2 4} = n^2$ in this case; hence, we are in Case 1 and $T(n)$ is $\Theta(n^2)$. Unfortunately, this is no better than the grade-school algorithm.

A Better Algorithm

The master theorem gives us some insight into how we might improve this algorithm. If we can reduce the number of recursive calls, then we will reduce the complexity of the special function used in the master theorem, which is currently the dominating factor in our running time. Fortunately, if we are a little more clever in how we define subproblems to solve recursively, we can in fact reduce the number of recursive calls by one. In particular, consider the product

$$(I_h - I_l) \cdot (J_l - J_h) = I_h J_l - I_l J_l - I_h J_h + I_l J_h.$$

This is admittedly a strange product to consider, but it has an interesting property. When expanded out, it contains two of the products we want to compute (namely, $I_h J_l$ and $I_l J_h$) and two products that can be computed recursively (namely, $I_h J_h$ and $I_l J_l$). Thus, we can compute $I \cdot J$ as follows:

$$I \cdot J = I_h J_h 2^n + [(I_h - I_l) \cdot (J_l - J_h) + I_h J_h + I_l J_l] 2^{n/2} + I_l J_l.$$

This computation requires the recursive computation of three products of $n/2$ bits each, plus $O(n)$ additional work. Thus, it results in a divide-and-conquer algorithm with a running time characterized by the following recurrence equation (for $n \geq 2$):

$$T(n) = \begin{cases} c & \text{if } n < 2 \\ 3T(n/2) + cn, & \text{if } n \geq 2, \end{cases}$$

for some constant $c > 0$.

Theorem 11.10: *We can multiply two n-bit integers in $O(n^{\log_2 3})$ time, which is $O(n^{1.585})$.*

Proof: We apply the master theorem with the special function,

$$n^{\log_b a} = n^{\log_2 3}.$$

Thus, we are in Case 1, which implies that $T(n)$ is $\Theta(n^{\log_2 3})$, which is itself $O(n^{1.585})$.   ∎

Using divide-and-conquer, we have designed an algorithm for integer multiplication that is asymptotically faster than the straightforward quadratic-time method. We can actually do even better than this, achieving a running time that is "almost" $O(n \log n)$, by using a more complex divide-and-conquer algorithm called the *fast Fourier transform*, which we discuss in Chapter 25.

11.3 Matrix Multiplication

Suppose we are given two $n \times n$ matrices X and Y, and we wish to compute their product $Z = XY$, which is defined so that

$$Z[i,j] = \sum_{k=0}^{e-1} X[i,k] \cdot Y[k,j],$$

which is an equation that immediately gives rise to a simple $O(n^3)$-time algorithm.

Another way of viewing this product is in terms of submatrices. That is, let us assume that n is a power of two and let us partition X, Y, and Z each into four $(n/2) \times (n/2)$ matrices, so that we can rewrite $Z = XY$ as

$$\begin{pmatrix} I & J \\ K & L \end{pmatrix} = \begin{pmatrix} A & B \\ C & D \end{pmatrix} \begin{pmatrix} E & F \\ G & H \end{pmatrix}.$$

Thus,

$$
\begin{aligned}
I &= AE + BG \\
J &= AF + BH \\
K &= CE + DG \\
L &= CF + DH.
\end{aligned}
$$

We can use this set of equations in a divide-and-conquer algorithm that computes $Z = XY$ by computing I, J, K, and L from the subarrays A through G. By the above equations, we can compute I, J, K, and L from the eight recursively computed matrix products on $(n/2) \times (n/2)$ subarrays, plus four additions that can be done in $O(n^2)$ time. Thus, the above set of equations give rise to a divide-and-conquer algorithm whose running time $T(n)$ is characterized by the recurrence

$$T(n) = 8T(n/2) + bn^2,$$

for some constant $b > 0$. Unfortunately, this equation implies that $T(n)$ is $O(n^3)$ by the master theorem; hence, it is no better than the straightforward matrix multiplication algorithm.

Interestingly, there is an algorithm known as ***Strassen's Algorithm***, which organizes arithmetic involving the subarrays A through G so that we can compute I, J, K, and L using just seven recursive matrix multiplications. We begin Strassen's algorithm with seven submatrix products:

$$
\begin{aligned}
S_1 &= A(F - H) \\
S_2 &= (A + B)H \\
S_3 &= (C + D)E \\
S_4 &= D(G - E) \\
S_5 &= (A + D)(E + H) \\
S_6 &= (B - D)(G + H) \\
S_7 &= (A - C)(E + F).
\end{aligned}
$$

Given these seven submatrix products, we can compute I as

$$
\begin{aligned}
I &= S_5 + S_6 + S_4 - S_2 \\
&= (A+D)(E+H) + (B-D)(G+H) + D(G-E) - (A+B)H \\
&= AE + BG.
\end{aligned}
$$

We can compute J as

$$
\begin{aligned}
J &= S_1 + S_2 \\
&= A(F-H) + (A+B)H \\
&= AF - AH + AH + BH \\
&= AF + BH.
\end{aligned}
$$

We can compute K as

$$
\begin{aligned}
K &= S_3 + S_4 \\
&= (C+D)E + D(G-E) \\
&= CE + DE + DG - DE \\
&= CE + DG.
\end{aligned}
$$

Finally, we can compute L as

$$
\begin{aligned}
L &= S_1 - S_7 - S_3 + S_5 \\
&= A(F-H) - (A-C)(E+F) - (C+D)E + (A+D)(E+H) \\
&= CF + DH.
\end{aligned}
$$

Thus, we can compute $Z = XY$ using seven recursive multiplications of matrices of size $(n/2) \times (n/2)$. Thus, we can characterize the running time $T(n)$ as

$$
T(n) = 7T(n/2) + bn^2,
$$

for some constant $b > 0$. Thus, by the master theorem, we have the following:

Theorem 11.11: *We can multiply two $n \times n$ matrices in $O(n^{\log 7})$ time.*

Thus, with a fair bit of additional complication, we can perform the multiplication for $n \times n$ matrices in time $O(n^{2.808})$, which is $o(n^3)$ time. As admittedly complicated as Strassen's matrix multiplication is, there are actually much more complicated matrix multiplication algorithms, with running times as low as $O(n^{2.376})$.

11.4 The Maxima-Set Problem

Let us now return to the problem of finding a *maxima set* for a set, S, of n points in the plane. This problem is motivated from *multi-objective optimization*, where we are interested in optimizing choices that depend on multiple variables. For instance, in the introduction we used the example of someone wishing to optimize hotels based on the two variables of pool size and restaurant quality. A point is a *maximum* point in S if there is no other point, (x', y'), in S such that $x \le x'$ and $y \le y'$. Points that are not members of the maxima set can be eliminated from consideration, since they are dominated by another point in S. Thus, finding the maxima set of points can act as a kind of filter that selects out only those points that should be candidates for optimal choices. Moreover, such a filter can be quite effective, as we explore in Exercise A-11.4.

Given a set, S, of n points in the plane, there is a simple divide-and-conquer algorithm for constructing the maxima set of points in S. If $n \le 1$, the maxima set is just S itself. Otherwise, let p be the median point in S according to a lexicographic ordering of the points in S, that is, where we order based primarily on x-coordinates and then by y-coordinates if there are ties. If the points have distinct x-coordinates, then we can imagine that we are dividing S using a vertical line through p. Next, we recursively solve the maxima-set problem for the set of points on the left of this line and also for the points on the right. Given these solutions, the maxima set of points on the right are also maxima points for S. But some of the maxima points for the left set might be dominated by a point from the right, namely the point, q, that is leftmost. So then we do a scan of the left set of maxima, removing any points that are dominated by q, until reaching the point where q's dominance extends. (See Figure 11.3.) The union of remaining set of maxima from the left and the maxima set from the right is the set of maxima for S. We give the details in Algorithm 11.4.

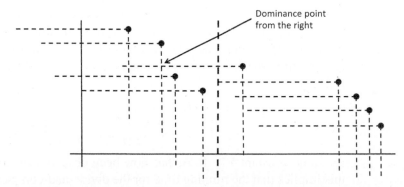

Figure 11.3: The combine step for the divide-and-conquer maxima-set algorithm.

Algorithm MaximaSet(S):

> *Input:* A set, S, of n points in the plane
> *Output:* The set, M, of maxima points in S
>
> **if** $n \leq 1$ **then**
> >   **return** S
>
> Let p be the median point in S, by lexicographic (x, y)-coordinates
> Let L be the set of points lexicographically less than p in S
> Let G be the set of points lexicographically greater than or equal to p in S
> $M_1 \leftarrow$ MaximaSet(L)
> $M_2 \leftarrow$ MaximaSet(G)
> Let q be the lexicographically smallest point in M_2
> **for** each point, r, in M_1 **do**
> >   **if** $x(r) \leq x(q)$ **and** $y(r) \leq y(q)$ **then**
> > >   Remove r from M_1
>
> **return** $M_1 \cup M_2$

Algorithm 11.4: A divide-and-conquer algorithm for the maxima-set problem.

Analysis of the Divide-and-Conquer Maxima-Set Algorithm

To analyze the divide-and-conquer maxima-set algorithm, there is a minor implementation detail in Algorithm 11.4 that we need to work out. Namely, there is the issue of how to efficiently find the point, p, that is the median point in a lexicographical ordering of the points in S according to their (x, y)-coordinates. There are two immediate possibilities. One choice is to use a linear-time median-finding algorithm, such as that given in Section 9.2. This achieves a good asymptotic running time, but adds some implementation complexity. Another choice is to sort the points in S lexicographically by their (x, y)-coordinates as a preprocessing step, prior to calling the MaxmaSet algorithm on S. Given this preprocessing step, the median point is simply the point in the middle of the list. Moreover, each time we perform a recursive call, we can be passing a sorted subset of S, which maintains the ability to easily find the median point each time. In either case, the rest of the nonrecursive steps can be performed in $O(n)$ time, so this implies that, ignoring floor and ceiling functions (as allowed by the analysis of Exercise C-11.5), the running time for the divide-and-conquer maxima-set algorithm can be specified as follows:

$$T(n) = \begin{cases} b & \text{if } n < 2 \\ 2T(n/2) + bn & \text{if } n \geq 2, \end{cases}$$

for some constant $b \geq 1$. As has now been observed several times in this chapter, this implies that the running time for the divide-and-conquer maxima-set algorithm is $O(n \log n)$.

11.5 Exercises

Reinforcement

R-11.1 Characterize each of the following recurrence equations using the master theorem (assuming that $T(n) = c$ for $n < d$, for constants $c > 0$ and $d \geq 1$).

   a. $T(n) = 2T(n/2) + \log n$
   b. $T(n) = 8T(n/2) + n^2$
   c. $T(n) = 16T(n/2) + (n \log n)^4$
   d. $T(n) = 7T(n/3) + n$
   e. $T(n) = 9T(n/3) + n^3 \log n$

R-11.2 Use the divide-and-conquer algorithm, from Section 11.2, to compute $10110011 \cdot 10111010$ in binary. Show your work.

R-11.3 Use Strassen's matrix multiplication algorithm to multiply the matrices

$$X = \begin{pmatrix} 3 & 2 \\ 4 & 8 \end{pmatrix} \quad \text{and} \quad Y = \begin{pmatrix} 1 & 5 \\ 9 & 6 \end{pmatrix}.$$

R-11.4 A complex number $a + b\mathbf{i}$, where $\mathbf{i} = \sqrt{-1}$, can be represented by the pair (a, b). Describe a method performing only three real-number multiplications to compute the pair (e, f) representing the product of $a + b\mathbf{i}$ and $c + d\mathbf{i}$.

R-11.5 What is the maxima set from the following set of points:

$$\{(7, 2), (3, 1), (9, 3), (4, 5), (1, 4), (6, 9), (2, 6), (5, 7), (8, 6)\}?$$

R-11.6 Give an example of a set of n points in the plane such that every point is a maximum point, that is, no point in this set is dominated by any other point in this set.

Creativity

C-11.1 Consider the recurrence equation,

$$T(n) = 2T(n-1) + 1,$$

for $n > 1$, where $T(n) = 1$ for $n = 1$. Prove that $T(n)$ is $O(2^n)$.

C-11.2 There are several cases of divide-and-conquer recurrence relations that are not covered in the master theorem. Nevertheless, the intuition for the master theorem can still give us some guidance. Derive and prove a general solution, like that given in the master theorem, to the following recurrence equation (assuming $T(n)$ is a constant for n less than or equal to a given constant, $a \geq 2$):

$$T(n) = a\,T(n/a) + n \log \log n.$$

C-11.3 There is a sorting algorithm, "Stooge-sort," which is named after the comedy team, "The Three Stooges." if the input size, n, is 1 or 2, then the algorithm sorts the input immediately. Otherwise, it recursively sorts the first $2n/3$ elements, then the last $2n/3$ elements, and then the first $2n/3$ elements again. The details are shown in Algorithm 11.5. Show that Stooge-sort is correct and characterize the running time, $T(n)$, for Stooge-sort, using a recurrence equation, and use the master theorem to determine an asymptotic bound for $T(n)$.

Algorithm StoogeSort(A, i, j):
    Input: An array, A, and two indices, i and j, such that $1 \leq i \leq j \leq n$
    Output: Subarray, $A[i..j]$, sorted in nondecreasing order
    $n \leftarrow j - i + 1$ // The size of the subarray we are sorting
    if $n = 2$ **then**
        if $A[i] > A[j]$ **then**
            Swap $A[i]$ and $A[j]$
    else if $n > 2$ **then**
        $m \leftarrow \lfloor n/3 \rfloor$
        StoogeSort($A, i, j - m$)   // Sort the first part
        StoogeSort($A, i + m, j$)   // Sort the last part
        StoogeSort($A, i, j - m$)   // Sort the first part again
    return A

Algorithm 11.5: Stooge-sort.

C-11.4 Consider the Stooge-sort algorithm, shown in Algorithm 11.5, and suppose we change the assignment statement for m (on line 6) to the following:

$$m \leftarrow \max\{1, \lfloor n/4 \rfloor\}$$

Characterize the running time, $T(n)$, in this case, using a recurrence equation, and use the master theorem to determine an asymptotic bound for $T(n)$.

C-11.5 Consider a version of the divide-and-conquer recurrence equation based on use of the ceiling function, as follows:

$$T(n) = a\,T(\lceil n/b \rceil) + f(n),$$

where $a \geq 1$ and $b > 1$ are constants, and $f(n)$ is $\Theta(n^{\log_b a} \log^k n)$, for some integer constant, $k \geq 0$. Show that, by using the inequality,

$$T(n) \leq a\,T(n/b + 1) + f(n),$$

for sufficiently large n, $T(n)$ is $O(n^{\log_b a} \log^{k+1} n)$.

Applications

A-11.1 A very common problem in computer graphics is to approximate a complex shape with a ***bounding box***. For a set, S, of n points in 2-dimensional space, the idea is to find the smallest rectangle, R, with sides parallel to the coordinate axes that contains all the points in S. Once S is approximated by such a bounding box, we can often speed up lots of computations that involve S. For example, if R is completely obscured some object in the foreground, then we don't need to render any of S. Likewise, if we shoot a virtual ray and it completely misses R, then it is guarantee to completely miss S. So doing comparisons with R instead of S can often save time. But this savings is wasted if we spend a lot of time constructing R; hence, it would be ideal to have a fast way of computing a bounding box, R, for a set, S, of n points in the plane. Note that the construction of R can be reduced to two instances of the problem of simultaneously finding the minimum and the maximum in a set of n numbers; namely, we need only do this for the x-coordinates in S and then for the y-coordinates in S. Therefore, design a divide-and-conquer algorithm for finding both the minimum and the maximum element of n numbers using no more than $3n/2$ comparisons.

A-11.2 Given a set, P, of n teams in some sport, a ***round-robin tournament*** is a collection of games in which each team plays each other team exactly once. Such round-robin tournaments are often used as the first round for establishing the order of teams (and their seedings) for later single- or double-elimination tournaments. Design an efficient algorithm for constructing a round-robin tournament for a set, P, of n teams assuming n is a power of 2.

A-11.3 In some multi-objective optimization problems (such as that exemplified by the choosing of hotels based on the sizes of their pools and quality scores of their restaurants), we may have different kinds of constraints involving the variables instead of the desire to avoid points dominated by others. Suppose, for example, that we have a two-variable optimization problem where we have a set, C, of constraints of the form,

$$y \geq m_i x + b_i,$$

for real numbers, m_i and b_i, for $i = 1, 2, \ldots, n$. In such a case, we would like to restrict our attention to points that satisfy all the linear inequality constraints in C. One way to address this desire is to construct the ***upper envelope*** for C, which is a representation of the function, $f(x)$, defined as

$$f(x) = \max_{1 \leq i \leq n} \{m_i x + b_i\},$$

where the (m_i, b_i) pairs are from the inequalities in C. Equivalently, the upper envelope is a representation of the part of the plane determined by the intersection of all the halfplanes determined by the inequalities in C. If we consider how this function behaves as x goes from $-\infty$ to $+\infty$, we note that each inequality in C can appear at most once during this process. Thus, we can represent f in terms of a set, $S = \{(a_1, b_1, i_1), (a_2, b_2, i_2), \ldots, (a_k, b_k, i_k)\}$, such that each triple, (a_j, b_j, i_j) in S, represents the fact that interval $[a_j, b_j]$ is a maximal interval such that $f(x) = m_{i_j} x + b_{i_j}$. Describe an $O(n \log n)$-time algorithm for computing such a representation, S, of the upper envelope of the linear inequalities in C.

A-11.4 Selecting out a maxima set of points from among a set of points in the plane seems is intended to filter away a lot of points from consideration in a multi-objective optimization problem. For example, if we grade hotels by the sizes of their pools and the quality of their restaurants, then we would hope to have a small set of hotels to choose from that are not dominated by any other hotel along these axes. So let us analyze the expected size of a maxima set of randomly chosen points in the plane with distinct x- and y-coordinates. We can model such as set by defining a random set of n points in the plane by first randomly permuting the sequence of numbers, $(1, 2, \ldots, n)$, giving $(y_1, y_2, \ldots, y_n)$. Let us then define a set of two dimensional points as the set,

$$R = \{(1, y_1), (2, y_2), \ldots, (n, y_n)\}.$$

Since it is the relative order of points that determines whether a point is a maximum point or not, this set of points with integer coordinates fully captures all the possibilities, with respect to the maxima-set problem, for any random set of points in the plane with distinct x- and y-coordinates. So as to show just how effective it is to select out the maxima set of points from such a set as a filtering step (hence, it should be a good filter in practice), show that the expected size of the maxima set for R is $O(\log n)$.

A-11.5 Suppose you have a high-performance computer, which has a CPU containing a dedicated bank of $k > 2$ *optimization* registers. This bank of registers supports the insertion of key-value pair, (x, y), into the bank of registers in $O(1)$ time, assuming that there are fewer than k numbers already stored in the bank. In addition, this bank of registers allows you to remove and return a key-value pair, (x, y), with smallest key, x, from the bank of registers in $O(1)$ time. Show that you can use this high-performance computer to sort n numbers in $O(n \log n / \log k)$ time.

A-11.6 Suppose you have a geometric description of the buildings of Manhattan and you would like to build a representation of the New York skyline. That is, suppose you are given a description of a set of rectangles, all of which have one of their sides on the x-axis, and you would like to build a representation of the union of all these rectangles. Formally, since each rectangle has a side on the x-axis, you can assume that you are given a set, $S = \{[a_1, b_1], [a_2, b_2], \ldots, [a_n, b_n]\}$ of subintervals in the interval $[0, 1]$, with $0 \le a_i < b_i \le 1$, for $i = 1, 2, \ldots, n$, such that there is an associated height, h_i, for each interval $[a_i, b_i]$ in S. The *skyline* of S is defined to be a list of pairs $[(x_0, c_0), (x_1, c_1), (x_2, c_2), \ldots, (x_m, c_m), (x_{m+1}, 0)]$, with $x_0 = 0$ and $x_{m+1} = 1$, and ordered by x_i values, such that, each subinterval, $[x_i, x_{i+1}]$, is the maximal subinterval that has a single highest interval, which is at height c_i, in S, containing $[x_i, x_{i+1}]$, for $i = 0, 1, \ldots, m$. Design an $O(n \log n)$-time algorithm for computing the skyline of S.

Chapter Notes

The master theorem for solving divide-and-conquer recurrences traces its origins to a paper by Bentley, Haken, and Saxe [30]. The divide-and-conquer algorithm for multiplying two large integers in $O(n^{1.585})$ time is generally attributed to the Russians Karatsuba and Ofman [117]. The matrix multiplication algorithm we present is due to Strassen [202]. Kung, Luccio, and Preparata [138] present a divide-and-conquer algorithm for finding maxima sets. The Stooge-sort algorithm was first given by Cormen *et al.* (e.g., see [51]).

Chapter

12

Dynamic Programming

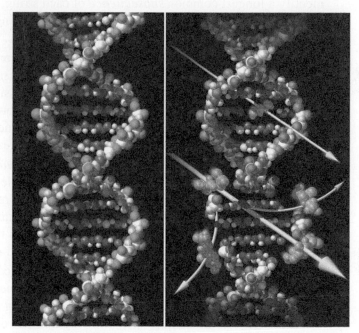

Effects of radiation on DNA's double helix, 2003. U.S. government image. NASA-MSFC.

Contents

12.1 Matrix Chain-Products	325
12.2 The General Technique	329
12.3 Telescope Scheduling	331
12.4 Game Strategies	334
12.5 The Longest Common Subsequence Problem	339
12.6 The 0-1 Knapsack Problem	343
12.7 Exercises	346

DNA sequences can be viewed as strings of A, C, G, and T characters, which represent nucleotides, and finding the similarities between two DNA sequences is an important computation performed in bioinformatics. For instance, when comparing the DNA of different organisms, such alignments can highlight the locations where those organisms have identical DNA patterns. Similarly, places that don't match can show possible mutations between these organisms and a common ancestor, including mutations causing substitutions, insertions, and deletions of nucleotides. Computing a best way to align to DNA strings, therefore, is useful for identifying regions of similarity and difference. For instance, one simple way is to identify a longest common ***subsequence*** of each string, that is, a longest string that can be defined by selecting characters from each string in order in the respective strings, but not necessarily in a way that is contiguous. (See Figure 12.1.)

From an algorithmic perspective, such similarity computations can appear quite challenging at first. For instance, the most obvious solution for finding the best match between two strings of length n is to try all possible ways of defining subsequences of each string, test if they are the same, and output the one that is longest. Unfortunately, however, there are 2^n possible subsequences of each string; hence, this algorithm would run in $O(n2^{2n})$ time, which makes this algorithm impractical.

In this chapter, we discuss the ***dynamic programming*** technique, which is one of the few algorithmic techniques that can take problems, such as this, that seem to require exponential time and produce polynomial-time algorithms to solve them. For example, we show how to solve this problem of finding a longest common subsequence between two strings in time proportional to the product of their lengths, rather than the exponential time of the straightforward method mentioned above.

Moreover, the algorithms that result from applications of the dynamic programming technique are usually quite simple—often needing little more than a few lines of code to describe some nested loops for filling in a table. We demonstrate this effectiveness and simplicity by showing how the dynamic programming technique can be applied to several different types of problems, including matrix chain-products, telescope scheduling, game strategies, the above-mentioned longest common subsequence problem, and the 0-1 knapsack problem. In addition to the topics we discuss in this chapter, dynamic programming is also used for other problems mentioned elsewhere, including maximum subarray-sum (Section 1.3), transitive closure (Section 13.4.2), and all-pairs shortest paths (Section 14.5).

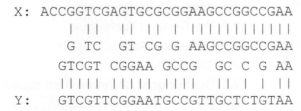

Figure 12.1: Two DNA sequences, X and Y, and their alignment in terms of a longest subsequence, GTCGTCGGAAGCCGGCCGAA, that is common to these two strings.

12.1 Matrix Chain-Products

Rather than starting out with an explanation of the general components of the dynamic programming technique, we start out instead by giving a classic, concrete example. Suppose we are given a collection of n two-dimensional matrices for which we wish to compute the product

$$A_0 \cdot A_1 \cdot A_2 \cdots A_{n-1},$$

where A_i is a $d_i \times d_{i+1}$ matrix, for $i = 0, 1, 2, \ldots, n - 1$. In the standard matrix multiplication algorithm (which is the one we will use), to multiply a $d \times e$ matrix A times an $e \times f$ matrix B, we compute the (i, j) entry of the $d \times f$ matrix product, C, as follows (see Figure 12.2):

$$C[i, j] = \sum_{k=0}^{e-1} A[i, k] \cdot B[k, j].$$

Thus, the computation of a single entry of the product matrix $B \cdot C$ takes e (scalar) multiplications. Overall, the computation of all the entries takes def (scalar) multiplications.

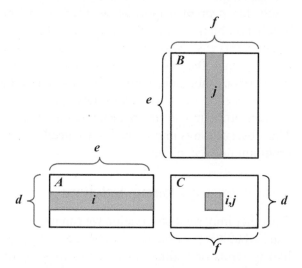

Figure 12.2: Multiplication of a $d \times e$ matrix, A, and an $e \times f$ matrix, B, which produces a $d \times f$ matrix, C.

This definition implies that matrix multiplication is associative, that is, it implies that $B \cdot (C \cdot D) = (B \cdot C) \cdot D$. Thus, we can parenthesize the expression for A any way we wish and we will end up with the same answer. We will not necessarily perform the same number of scalar multiplications in each parenthesization, however, as is illustrated in the following example.

Example 12.1: *Let B be a 2×10 matrix, let C be a 10×50 matrix, and let D be a 50×20 matrix. Computing $B \cdot (C \cdot D)$ requires $2 \cdot 10 \cdot 20 + 10 \cdot 50 \cdot 20 = 10400$ multiplications, whereas computing $(B \cdot C) \cdot D$ requires $2 \cdot 10 \cdot 50 + 2 \cdot 50 \cdot 20 = 3000$ multiplications.*

The *matrix chain-product* problem is to determine the parenthesization of the expression defining the product A that minimizes the total number of scalar multiplications performed. Of course, one way to solve this problem is to simply enumerate all the possible ways of parenthesizing the expression for A and determine the number of multiplications performed by each one. Unfortunately, the set of all different parenthesizations of the expression for A is equal in number to the set of all different binary trees that have n external nodes. This number is exponential in n. Thus, this straightforward ("brute-force") algorithm runs in exponential time, for there are an exponential number of ways to parenthesize an associative arithmetic expression (the number is equal to the nth *Catalan number*, which is $\Omega(4^n/n^{3/2})$).

Defining Subproblems

We can improve the performance achieved by the brute-force algorithm significantly, however, by making a few observations about the nature of the matrix chain-product problem. The first observation is that the problem can be split into *subproblems*. In this case, we can define a number of different subproblems, each of which is to compute the best parenthesization for some subexpression $A_i \cdot A_{i+1} \cdots A_j$. As a concise notation, we use $N_{i,j}$ to denote the minimum number of multiplications needed to compute this subexpression. Thus, the original matrix chain-product problem can be characterized as that of computing the value of $N_{0,n-1}$. This observation is important, but we need one more in order to apply the dynamic programming technique.

Characterizing Optimal Solutions

The other important observation we can make about the matrix chain-product problem is that it is possible to characterize an optimal solution to a particular subproblem in terms of optimal solutions to its subproblems. We call this property the *subproblem optimality* condition.

In the case of the matrix chain-product problem, we observe that, no matter how we parenthesize a subexpression, there has to be some final matrix multiplication that we perform. That is, a full parenthesization of a subexpression $A_i \cdot A_{i+1} \cdots A_j$ has to be of the form $(A_i \cdots A_k) \cdot (A_{k+1} \cdots A_j)$, for some $k \in \{i, i+1, \ldots, j-1\}$. Moreover, for whichever k is the right one, the products $(A_i \cdots A_k)$ and $(A_{k+1} \cdots A_j)$ must also be solved optimally. If this were not so, then there would be a global optimal that had one of these subproblems solved suboptimally. But this is impossible, since we could then reduce the total number of multiplications by replacing the current subproblem solution by an optimal solution for the subproblem. This observation implies a way of explicitly defining the optimization problem for $N_{i,j}$ in terms of other optimal subproblem solutions. Namely, we can compute $N_{i,j}$ by considering each place k where we could put the final multiplication and taking the minimum over all such choices.

Designing a Dynamic Programming Algorithm

The above discussion implies that we can characterize the optimal subproblem solution $N_{i,j}$ as

$$N_{i,j} = \min_{i \le k < j} \{N_{i,k} + N_{k+1,j} + d_i d_{k+1} d_{j+1}\},$$

where we recall that each A_i is a $d_i \times d_{i+1}$ matrix. Also, note that $N_{i,i} = 0$, since no work is needed for a subexpression comprising a single matrix. That is, $N_{i,j}$ is the minimum, taken over all possible places to perform the final multiplication, of the number of multiplications needed to compute each subexpression plus the number of multiplications needed to perform the final matrix multiplication.

The equation for $N_{i,j}$ looks similar to the recurrence equations we derive for divide-and-conquer algorithms, but this is only a superficial resemblance, for there is an aspect of the equation for $N_{i,j}$ that makes it difficult to use divide-and-conquer to compute $N_{i,j}$. In particular, there is a ***sharing of subproblems*** going on that prevents us from dividing the problem into completely independent subproblems (as we would need to do to apply the divide-and-conquer technique). We can, nevertheless, use the equation for $N_{i,j}$ to derive an efficient algorithm by computing $N_{i,j}$ values in a bottom-up fashion, and storing intermediate values in a table of $N_{i,j}$ values. We can begin simply enough by assigning $N_{i,i} = 0$ for $i = 0, 1, \ldots, n - 1$. We can then apply the general equation for $N_{i,j}$ to compute $N_{i,i+1}$ values, since they depend only on $N_{i,i}$ and $N_{i+1,i+1}$ values, which are available. Given the $N_{i,i+1}$ values, we can then compute the $N_{i,i+2}$ values, and so on. Therefore, we can build $N_{i,j}$ values up from previously computed values until we can finally compute the value of $N_{0,n-1}$, which is the number that we are searching for. The details of this ***dynamic programming*** solution are given in Algorithm 12.3.

Analyzing the Matrix Chain-Product Algorithm

Thus, we can compute $N_{0,n-1}$ with an algorithm that consists primarily of three nested for-loops. The outside loop is executed n times. The loop inside is executed at most n times. And the inner-most loop is also executed at most n times. Therefore, the total running time of this algorithm is $O(n^3)$.

Theorem 12.2: *Given a chain-product of n two-dimensional matrices, we can compute a parenthesization of this chain that achieves the minimum number of scalar multiplications in $O(n^3)$ time.*

Algorithm MatrixChain($d_0, \ldots, d_n$):

    Input: Sequence $d_0, \ldots, d_n$ of integers

    Output: For $i, j = 0, \ldots, n - 1$, the minimum number of multiplications $N_{i,j}$
        needed to compute the product $A_i \cdot A_{i+1} \cdots A_j$, where A_k is a $d_k \times d_{k+1}$
        matrix

    for $i \leftarrow 0$ **to** $n - 1$ **do**
        $N_{i,i} \leftarrow 0$
    for $b \leftarrow 1$ **to** $n - 1$ **do**
        for $i \leftarrow 0$ **to** $n - b - 1$ **do**
            $j \leftarrow i + b$
            $N_{i,j} \leftarrow +\infty$
            for $k \leftarrow i$ **to** $j - 1$ **do**
                $N_{i,j} \leftarrow \min\{N_{i,j},\ N_{i,k} + N_{k+1,j} + d_i d_{k+1} d_{j+1}\}.$

Algorithm 12.3: Dynamic programming algorithm for the matrix chain-product problem.

Proof: We have shown above how we can compute the optimal ***number*** of scalar multiplications. But how do we recover the actual parenthesization?

The method for computing the parenthesization itself is actually quite straightforward. We modify the algorithm for computing $N_{i,j}$ values so that any time we find a new minimum value for $N_{i,j}$, we store, with $N_{i,j}$, the index k that allowed us to achieve this minimum. ∎

In Figure 12.4, we illustrate the way the dynamic programming solution to the matrix chain-product problem fills in the array N.

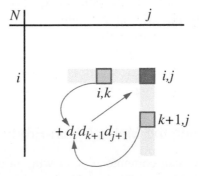

Figure 12.4: Illustration of the way the matrix chain-product dynamic-programming algorithm fills in the array N.

Now that we have worked through a complete example of the use of the dynamic programming method, we discuss in the next section the general aspects of the dynamic programming technique as it can be applied to other problems.

12.2 The General Technique

The dynamic programming technique is used primarily for *optimization* problems, where we wish to find a "best" way of doing something. Often the number of different ways of doing that "something" is exponential, so a brute-force search for the best is computationally infeasible for all but the smallest problem sizes. We can apply the dynamic programming technique in such situations, however, if the problem has a certain amount of structure that we can exploit. This structure involves the following three components:

Simple Subproblems: There has to be some way of breaking the global optimization problem into subproblems, each having a similar structure to the original problem. Moreover, there should be a simple way of defining subproblems with just a few indices, like i, j, k, and so on.

Subproblem Optimality: An optimal solution to the global problem must be a composition of optimal subproblem solutions, using a relatively simple combining operation. We should not be able to find a globally optimal solution that contains suboptimal subproblems.

Subproblem Overlap: Optimal solutions to unrelated subproblems can contain subproblems in common. Indeed, such overlap allows us to improve the efficiency of a dynamic programming algorithm by storing solutions to subproblems.

This last property is particularly important for dynamic programming algorithms, because it allows them to take advantage of *memoization*, which is an optimization that allows us to avoid repeated recursive calls by storing intermediate values. Typically, these intermediate values are indexed by a small set of parameters, and we can store them in an array and look them up as needed.

As an illustration of the power of memoization, consider the Fibonacci series, $f(n)$, defined as

$$
\begin{aligned}
f(0) &= 0 \\
f(1) &= 1 \\
f(n) &= f(n-1) + f(n-2).
\end{aligned}
$$

If we implement this equation literally, as a recursive program, then the running time of our algorithm, $T(n)$, as a function of n, has the following behavior:

$$
\begin{aligned}
T(0) &= 1 \\
T(1) &= 1 \\
T(n) &= T(n-1) + T(n-2).
\end{aligned}
$$

But this implies that, for $n \geq 2$,

$$
T(n) \geq 2T(n-2) = 2^{n/2}.
$$

In other words, if we implement this equation recursively as written, then our running time is exponential in n. But if we store Fibonacci numbers in an array, F, then we can instead calculate the Fibonacci number, $F[n]$, iteratively, as follows:

$$F[0] \leftarrow 0$$
$$F[1] \leftarrow 1$$
for $i = 2$ to n **do**
$$\qquad F[i] \leftarrow F[i-1] + F[i-2]$$

This algorithm clearly runs in $O(n)$ time, and it illustrates the way memoization can lead to improved performance when subproblems overlap and we use table lookups to avoid repeating recursive calls. (See Figure 12.5.)

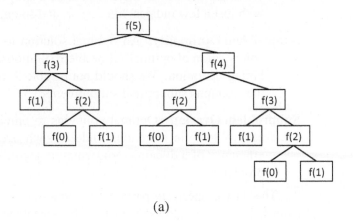

(a)

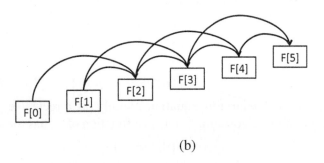

(b)

Figure 12.5: The power of memoization. (a) all the function calls needed for a fully recursive definition of the Fibonacci function; (b) the data dependencies in an iterative definition.

12.3 Telescope Scheduling

Large, powerful telescopes are precious resources that are typically oversubscribed by the astronomers who request times to use them. This high demand for observation times is especially true, for instance, for the Hubble Space Telescope, which receives thousands of observation requests per month. In this section, we consider a simplified version of the problem of scheduling observations on a telescope, which factors out some details, such as the orientation of the telescope for an observation and who is requesting that observation, but which nevertheless keeps some of the more important aspects of this problem.

The input to this ***telescope scheduling*** problem is a list, L, of observation requests, where each request, i, consists of the following elements:

- a requested start time, s_i, which is the moment when a requested observation should begin
- a finish time, f_i, which is the moment when the observation should finish (assuming it begins at its start time)
- a positive numerical benefit, b_i, which is an indicator of the scientific gain to be had by performing this observation.

The start and finish times for an observation request are specified by the astronomer requesting the observation; the benefit of a request is determined by an administrator or a review committee for the telescope. To get the benefit, b_i, for an observation request, i, that observation must be performed by the telescope for the entire time period from the start time, s_i, to the finish time, f_i. Thus, two requests, i and j, ***conflict*** if the time interval $[s_i, f_i]$, intersects the time interval, $[s_j, f_j]$. Given the list, L, of observation requests, the optimization problem is to schedule observation requests in a nonconflicting way so as to maximize the total benefit of the observations that are included in the schedule.

There is an obvious exponential-time algorithm for solving this problem, of course, which is to consider all possible subsets of L and choose the one that has the highest total benefit without causing any scheduling conflicts. We can do much better than this, however, by using the dynamic programming technique.

As a first step towards a solution, we need to define subproblems. A natural way to do this is to consider the observation requests according to some ordering, such as ordered by start times, finish times, or benefits. Start times and finish times are essentially symmetric, so we can immediately reduce the choice to that of picking between ordering by finish times and ordering by benefits.

The greedy strategy would be to consider the observation requests ordered by nonincreasing benefits, and include each request that doesn't conflict with any chosen before it. This strategy doesn't lead to an optimal solution, however, which we can see after considering a simple example. For instance, suppose we had a list containing just 3 requests—one with benefit 100 that conflicts with two nonconflicting

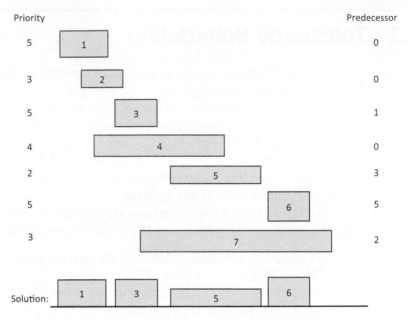

Figure 12.6: The telescope scheduling problem. The left and right boundary of each rectangle represent the start and finish times for an observation request. The height of each rectangle represents its benefit. We list each request's benefit on the left and its predecessor on the right. The requests are listed by increasing finish times. The optimal solution has total benefit 17.

requests with benefit 75 each. The greedy algorithm would choose the observation with benefit 100, in this case, whereas we could achieve a total benefit of 150 by taking the two requests with benefit 75 each. So a greedy strategy based on repeatedly choosing a nonconflicting request with maximum benefit won't work.

Let us assume, therefore, that the observation requests in L are sorted by nondecreasing finish times, as shown in Figure 12.6. The idea in this case would be to consider each request according to this ordering. So let us define our set of subproblems in terms of a parameter, B_i, which is defined as follows:

$B_i =$ the maximum benefit that can be achieved with the first i requests in L.

So, as a boundary condition, we get that $B_0 = 0$.

One nice observation that we can make for this ordering of L by nondecreasing finish times is that, for any request i, the set of other requests that conflict with i form a contiguous interval of requests in L. Define the **_predecessor_**, $\mathrm{pred}(i)$, for each request, i, then, to be the largest index, $j < i$, such that requests i and j don't conflict. If there is no such index, then define the predecessor of i to be 0. (See Figure 12.6.)

The definition of the predecessor of each request lets us easily reason about the effect that including or not including an observation request, i, in a schedule that includes the first i requests in L. That is, in a schedule that achieves the optimal value, B_i, for $i \geq 1$, either it includes the observation i or it doesn't; hence, we can reason as follows:

- If the optimal schedule achieving the benefit B_i includes observation i, then $B_i = B_{\text{pred}(i)} + b_i$. If this were not the case, then we could get a better benefit by substituting the schedule achieving $B_{\text{pred}(i)}$ for the one we used from among those with indices at most $\text{pred}(i)$.
- On the other hand, if the optimal schedule achieving the benefit B_i does not include observation i, then $B_i = B_{i-1}$. If this were not the case, then we could get a better benefit by using the schedule that achieves B_{i-1}.

Therefore, we can make the following recursive definition:

$$B_i = \max\{B_{i-1}, B_{\text{pred}(i)} + b_i\}.$$

Notice that this definition exhibits subproblem overlap. Thus, it is most efficient for us to use memoization when computing B_i values, by storing them in an array, B, which is indexed from 0 to n. Given the ordering of requests by finish times and an array, P, so that $P[i] = \text{pred}(i)$, then we can fill in the array, B, using the following simple algorithm:

$B[0] \leftarrow 0$
for $i = 1$ to n **do**
$\quad B[i] \leftarrow \max\{B[i-1], B[P[i]] + b_i\}$

After this algorithm completes, the benefit of the optimal solution will be $B[n]$, and, to recover an optimal schedule, we simply need to trace backward in B from this point. During this trace, if $B[i] = B[i-1]$, then we can assume observation i is not included and move next to consider observation $i-1$. Otherwise, if $B[i] = B[P[i]] + b_i$, then we can assume observation i is included and move next to consider observation $P[i]$.

It is easy to see that the running time of this algorithm is $O(n)$, but it assumes that we are given the list L ordered by finish times and that we are also given the predecessor index for each request i. Of course, we can easily sort L by finish times if it is not given to us already sorted according to this ordering. To compute the predecessor of each request, note that it is sufficient that we also have the requests in L sorted by start times. In particular, given a listing of L ordered by finish times and another listing, L', ordered by start times, then a merging of these two lists, as in the merge-sort algorithm (Section 8.1), gives us what we want. The predecessor of request i is literally the index of the predecessor in L of the value, s_i, in L'. Therefore, we have the following:

Theorem 12.3: *Given a list, L, of n observation requests, provided in two sorted orders, one by nondecreasing finish times and one by nondecreasing start times, we can solve the telescope scheduling problem for L in $O(n)$ time.*

12.4   Game Strategies

There are many types of games, some that are completely random and others where players benefit by employing various kinds of strategies. In this section, we consider two simple games in which dynamic programming can be employed to come up with optimal strategies for playing these games. These are not the only game scenarios where dynamic programming applies, however, as it has been used to analyze strategies for many other games as well, including baseball, American football, and cricket.

12.4.1   Coins in a Line

The first game we consider is reported to arise in a problem that is sometimes asked during job interviews at major software and Internet companies (probably because it is so tempting to apply a greedy strategy to this game, whereas the optimal strategy uses dynamic programming).

In this game, which we will call the ***coins-in-a-line game***, an even number, n, of coins, of various denominations from various countries, are placed in a line. Two players, who we will call Alice and Bob, take turns removing one of the coins from either end of the remaining line of coins. That is, when it is a player's turn, he or she removes the coin at the left or right end of the line of coins and adds that coin to his or her collection. The player who removes a set of coins with larger total value than the other player wins, where we assume that both Alice and Bob know the value of each coin in some common currency, such as dollars. (See Figure 12.7.)

Alice: (1, $6), (6, $5), (4, $7)   Total value = $18

Bob: (2, $5), (5, $3), (3, $2)   Total value = $10

Figure 12.7: The coins-in-a-line game. In this instance, Alice goes first and ultimately ends up with $18 worth of coins. U.S. government images. Credit: U.S. Mint.

A Dynamic Programming Solution

It is tempting to start thinking of various greedy strategies, such as always choosing the largest-valued coin, minimizing the two remaining choices for the opponent, or even deciding in advance whether it is better to choose all the odd-numbered coins or even-numbered coins. Unfortunately, none of these strategies will consistently lead to an optimal strategy for Alice to play the coins-in-a-line game, assuming that Bob follows an optimal strategy for him.

To design an optimal strategy, we apply the dynamic programming technique. In this case, since Alice and Bob can remove coins from either end of the line, the appropriate way to define subproblems is in terms of a range of indices for the coins, assuming they are initially numbered from 1 to n, as in Figure 12.7. Thus, let us define the following indexed parameter:

$$M_{i,j} = \begin{cases} \text{the maximum value of coins taken by Alice, for coins} \\ \text{numbered } i \text{ to } j, \text{ assuming Bob plays optimally.} \end{cases}$$

Therefore, the optimal value for Alice is determined by $M_{1,n}$.

Let us assume that the values of the coins are stored in an array, V, so that coin 1 is of Value $V[1]$, coin 2 is of Value $V[2]$, and so on. To determine a recursive definition for $M_{i,j}$, we note that, given the line of coins from coin i to coin j, the choice for Alice at this point is either to take coin i or coin j and thereby gain a coin of value $V[i]$ or $V[j]$. Once that choice is made, play turns to Bob, who we are assuming is playing optimally. Thus, he will make the choice among his possibilities that minimizes the total amount that Alice can get from the coins that remain. In other words, Alice must choose based on the following reasoning:

- If $j = i + 1$, then she should pick the larger of $V[i]$ and $V[j]$, and the game is over.
- Otherwise, if Alice chooses coin i, then she gets a total value of
$$\min\{M_{i+1,j-1}, M_{i+2,j}\} + V[i].$$
- Otherwise, if Alice chooses coin j, then she gets a total value of
$$\min\{M_{i,j-2}, M_{i+1,j-1}\} + V[j].$$

Since these are all the choices that Alice has, and she is trying to maximize her returns, then we get the following recurrence equation, for $j > i+1$, where $j-i+1$ is even:

$$M_{i,j} = \max\left\{\min\{M_{i+1,j-1}, M_{i+2,j}\} + V[i], \min\{M_{i,j-2}, M_{i+1,j-1}\} + V[j]\right\}.$$

In addition, for $i = 1, 2, \ldots, n-1$, we have the initial conditions

$$M_{i,i+1} = \max\{V[i], V[i+1]\}.$$

We can compute the $M_{i,j}$ values, then, using memoization, by starting with the definitions for the above initial conditions and then computing all the $M_{i,j}$'s where $j - i + 1$ is 4, then for all such values where $j - i + 1$ is 6, and so on. Since there are $O(n)$ iterations in this algorithm and each iteration runs in $O(n)$ time, the total time for this algorithm is $O(n^2)$. Of course, this algorithm simply computes all the relevant $M_{i,j}$ values, including the final value, $M_{1,n}$. To recover the actual game strategy for Alice (and Bob), we simply need to note for each $M_{i,j}$ whether Alice should choose coin i or coin j, which we can determine from the definition of $M_{i,j}$. And given this choice, we then know the optimal choice for Bob, and that determines if the next choice for Alice is based on $M_{i+2,j}$, $M_{i+1,j-1}$, or $M_{i,j-2}$. Therefore, we have the following.

Theorem 12.4: *Given an even number, n, of coins in a line, all of known values, we can determine in $O(n^2)$ time the optimal strategy for the first player, Alice, to maximize her returns in the coins-in-a-line game, assuming Bob plays optimally.*

12.4.2 Probabilistic Game Strategies and Backward Induction

In addition to games, like chess and the coins-in-a-line game, which are purely strategic, there are lots of games that involve some combination of strategy and randomness (or events that can be modeled probabilistically), like backgammon and sports. Another application of dynamic programming in the context of games arises in these games, in a way that involves combining probability and optimization. To illustrate this point, we consider in this section a strategic decision that arises in the game of American football, which hereafter we refer to simply as "football."

Extra Points in Football

After a team scores a touchdown in football, they have a choice between kicking an extra point, which involves kicking the ball through the goal posts to add 1 point to their score if this is successful, or attempting a two-point conversion, which involves lining up again and advancing the ball into the end zone to add 2 points to their score if this is successful. In professional football teams, extra-point attempts are successful with a probability of at least .98 and two-point conversion have a success probability between .40 and .55, depending on the team.

In addition to these probabilistic considerations, the choice of whether it is better to attempt a two-point conversion also depends on the difference in the scores between the two teams and how many possessions are left in the game (a possession is a sequence of plays where one team has control of the ball).

Developing a Recurrence Equation

Let us characterize the state of a football game in terms of a triple, (k, d, n), where these parameters have the following meanings:

- k is the number of points scored at the end of a possession (0 for no score, 3 for a field goal, and 6 for a touchdown, as we are ignoring safeties and we are counting the effects of extra points after a touchdown separately). Possessions alternate between team A and team B.
- d is the difference in points between team A and team B (which is positive when A is in the lead and negative when B is in the lead).
- n is the number of possessions remaining in the game.

For the sake of this analysis, let us assume that n is a potentially unbounded parameter that is known to the two teams, whereas k is always a constant and d can be considered a constant as well, since no professional football team has come back from a point deficit of -30 to win.

We can then define $V_A(k, d, n)$ to be the probability that team A wins the game given that its possession ended with team A scoring k points to now have a score deficit of d and n more possessions remaining in the game. Similarly, define $V_B(k, d, n)$ to be the probability that team A wins the game given that team B's possession ended with team B scoring k points to now cause team A to have a score deficit of d with n more possessions remaining in the game. Thus, team A is trying to maximize V_A and team B is trying to minimize V_B.

To derive recursive definitions for V_A and V_B, note that at the end of the game, when $n = 0$, the outcome is determined. Thus, $V_A(k, d, 0) = 1$ if and only if $d > 0$, and similarly for $V_B(k, d, 0)$. We assume, based on past performance, that we know the probability that team A or B will score a touchdown or field goal in a possession, and that these probabilities are independent of k, d, or n. Thus, we can determine $V(k, d, n)$, the probability that A wins after completing a possession with no score ($k = 0$) or a field goal ($k = 3$) as follows:

$$
\begin{aligned}
V_A(0, d, n) \;=\; V_A(3, d, n) \;=\; & \Pr(\text{TD by B})V_B(6, d - 6, n - 1) \\
& + \Pr(\text{FG by B})V_B(3, d - 3, n - 1) \\
& + \Pr(\text{NS by B})V_B(0, d, n - 1).
\end{aligned}
$$

The first term quantifies the impact of team B scoring a touchdown (TD) on the next possession, the second term quantifies the impact of team B scoring a field goal (FG) on the next possession, and the third term quantifies the impact of team B having no score (NS) at the end of the next possession. Similar equations hold for V_B, with the roles of A and B reversed. For professional football teams, the average probability of a possession ending in a touchdown is .20, the average probability of a possession ending in a field goal is .12; hence, for such an average team, we would take the probability of a possession ending with no score for team B to be .68. The main point of this exercise, however, is to characterize the case when $k = 6$, that is, when a possession ends with a touchdown.

Let p_1 denote the probability of success for an extra-point attempt and p_2 denote the probability of success for a two-point conversion. Then we have

1. Pr(Team A wins if it makes an extra-point attempt in state $(6, d, n)$)

$$
\begin{aligned}
= \; & p_1 \left[\text{Pr(TD by B)} V_B(6, d-5, n-1) \right. \\
& + \text{Pr(FG by B)} V_B(3, d-2, n-1) \\
& \left. + \text{Pr(NS by B)} V_B(0, d+1, n-1) \right] \\
& + (1 - p_1) \left[\text{Pr(TD by B)} V_B(6, d-6, n-1) \right. \\
& \quad + \text{Pr(FG by B)} V_B(3, d-3, n-1) \\
& \quad \left. + \text{Pr(NS by B)} V_B(0, d, n-1) \right].
\end{aligned}
$$

2. Pr(Team A wins if it tries a two-point conversion in state $(6, d, n)$)

$$
\begin{aligned}
= \; & p_2 \left[\text{Pr(TD by B)} V_B(6, d-4, n-1) \right. \\
& + \text{Pr(FG by B)} V_B(3, d-1, n-1) \\
& \left. + \text{Pr(NS by B)} V_B(0, d+2, n-1) \right] \\
& + (1 - p_2) \left[\text{Pr(TD by B)} V_B(6, d-6, n-1) \right. \\
& \quad + \text{Pr(FG by B)} V_B(3, d-3, n-1) \\
& \quad \left. + \text{Pr(NS by B)} V_B(0, d, n-1) \right].
\end{aligned}
$$

The value of $V_A(6, d, n)$ is the maximum of the above two probabilities. Similar bounds hold for V_B, except that $V_B(6, d, n)$ is the minimum of the two similarly defined probabilities. Given our assumptions about k and d, these equations imply that we can compute $V(k, d, n)$ in $O(n)$ time, by incrementally increasing the value of n in the above equations and applying memoization. Note that this amounts to reasoning about the game backward, in that we start with an ending state and use a recurrence equation to reason backward in time. For this reason, this analysis technique is called ***backward induction***.

In the case of the decision we are considering, given known statistics for an average professional football team, the values of n for when it is better to attempt a two-point conversion are shown in Table 12.8.

behind by $(-d)$	1	2	3	4	5	6	7	8	9	10
n **range**	$\emptyset$	$[0, 15]$	$\emptyset$	$\emptyset$	$[2, 14]$	$\emptyset$	$\emptyset$	$[2, 8]$	$[4, 9]$	$[2, 5]$

ahead by (d)	0	1	2	3	4	5	6	7	8	9	10
n **range**	$\emptyset$	$[1, 7]$	$[4, 10]$	$\emptyset$	$\emptyset$	$[1, 15]$	$\emptyset$	$\emptyset$	$\emptyset$	$\emptyset$	$\emptyset$

Table 12.8: When it is preferential to attempt a two-point conversion after a touchdown, based on n, the number of possessions remaining in a game. Each interval indicates the range of values of n for which it is better to make such an attempt.

12.5 The Longest Common Subsequence Problem

A common text processing problem, which, as we mentioned in the introduction, arises in genetics, is to test the similarity between two text strings. Recall that, in the genetics application, the two strings correspond to two strands of DNA, which could, for example, come from two individuals, who we will consider genetically related if they have a long subsequence common to their respective DNA sequences. There are other applications, as well, such as in software engineering, where the two strings could come from two versions of source code for the same program, and we may wish to determine which changes were made from one version to the next. In addition, the data gathering systems of search engines, which are called *web crawlers*, must be able to distinguish between similar web pages to avoid needless web page requests. Indeed, determining the similarity between two strings is considered such a common operation that Unix-like operating systems come with a program, called "diff," for comparing text files.

12.5.1 Problem Definition

There are several different ways we can define the similarity between two strings. Even so, we can abstract a simple, yet common, version of this problem using character strings and their subsequences. Given a string X of size n, a *subsequence* of X is any string that is of the form

$$X[i_1]X[i_2]\cdots X[i_k], \quad i_j < i_{j+1} \text{ for } j = 1,\ldots,k-1;$$

that is, it is a sequence of characters that are not necessarily contiguous but are nevertheless taken in order from X. For example, the string $AAAG$ is a subsequence of the string $CGATAATTGAGA$. Note that the concept of *subsequence* of a string is different from the one of *substring* of a string.

The specific text similarity problem we address here is the *longest common subsequence* (LCS) problem. In this problem, we are given two character strings, X of size n and Y of size m, over some alphabet and are asked to find a longest string S that is a subsequence of both X and Y.

One way to solve the longest common subsequence problem is to enumerate all subsequences of X and take the largest one that is also a subsequence of Y. Since each character of X is either in or not in a subsequence, there are potentially 2^n different subsequences of X, each of which requires $O(m)$ time to determine whether it is a subsequence of Y. Thus, the brute-force approach yields an exponential algorithm that runs in $O(2^n m)$ time, which is very inefficient. In this section, we discuss how to use *dynamic programming* to solve the longest common subsequence problem much more quickly than this.

12.5.2   Applying Dynamic Programming to the LCS Problem

We can solve the LCS problem much more quickly than exponential time using dynamic programming. As mentioned above, one of the key components of the dynamic programming technique is the definition of simple subproblems that satisfy the subproblem optimization and subproblem overlap properties.

Recall that in the LCS problem, we are given two character strings, X and Y, of length n and m, respectively, and are asked to find a longest string S that is a subsequence of both X and Y. Since X and Y are character strings, we have a natural set of indices with which to define subproblems—indices into the strings X and Y. Let us define a subproblem, therefore, as that of computing the length of the longest common subsequence of $X[0..i]$ and $Y[0..j]$, denoted $L[i, j]$.

This definition allows us to rewrite $L[i, j]$ in terms of optimal subproblem solutions. We consider the following two cases. (See Figure 12.9.)

Case 1: $X[i] = Y[j]$. Let $c = X[i] = Y[j]$. We claim that a longest common subsequence of $X[0..i]$ and $Y[0..j]$ ends with c. To prove this claim, let us suppose it is not true. There has to be some longest common subsequence $X[i_1]X[i_2]\ldots X[i_k] = Y[j_1]Y[j_2]\ldots Y[j_k]$. If $X[i_k] = c$ or $Y[j_k] = c$, then we get the same sequence by setting $i_k = i$ and $j_k = j$. Alternately, if $X[j_k] \neq c$, then we can get an even longer common subsequence by adding c to the end. Thus, a longest common subsequence of $X[0..i]$ and $Y[0..j]$ ends with $c = X[i] = Y[j]$. Therefore, we set

$$L[i, j] = L[i-1, j-1] + 1 \quad \text{if } X[i] = Y[j]. \tag{12.1}$$

Case 2: $X[i] \neq Y[j]$. In this case, we cannot have a common subsequence that includes both $X[i]$ and $Y[j]$. That is, a common subsequence can end with $X[i]$, $Y[j]$, or neither, but not both. Therefore, we set

$$L[i, j] = \max\{L[i-1, j], \, L[i, j-1]\} \quad \text{if } X[i] \neq Y[j]. \tag{12.2}$$

In order to make Equations 12.1 and 12.2 make sense in the boundary cases when $i = 0$ or $j = 0$, we define $L[i, -1] = 0$ for $i = -1, 0, 1, \ldots, n-1$ and $L[-1, j] = 0$ for $j = -1, 0, 1, \ldots, m-1$.

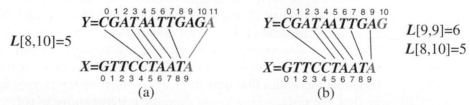

Figure 12.9: The two cases for $L[i, j]$: (a) $X[i] = Y[j]$; (b) $X[i] \neq Y[j]$.

The LCS Algorithm

The above definition of $L[i, j]$ satisfies subproblem optimization, for we cannot have a longest common subsequence without also having longest common subsequences for the subproblems. Also, it uses subproblem overlap, because a subproblem solution $L[i, j]$ can be used in several other problems (namely, the problems $L[i + 1, j]$, $L[i, j + 1]$, and $L[i + 1, j + 1]$).

Turning this definition of $L[i, j]$ into an algorithm is actually quite straightforward. We initialize an $(n + 1) \times (m + 1)$ array, L, for the boundary cases when $i = 0$ or $j = 0$. Namely, we initialize $L[i, -1] = 0$ for $i = -1, 0, 1, \ldots, n - 1$ and $L[-1, j] = 0$ for $j = -1, 0, 1, \ldots, m - 1$. (This is a slight abuse of notation, since in reality, we would have to index the rows and columns of L starting with 0.) Then, we iteratively build up values in L until we have $L[n - 1, m - 1]$, the length of a longest common subsequence of X and Y. We give a pseudocode description of how this approach results in a dynamic programming solution to the longest common subsequence (LCS) problem in Algorithm 12.10. Note that the algorithm stores only the $L[i, j]$ values, not the matches.

Algorithm LCS(X, Y):
  Input: Strings X and Y with n and m elements, respectively
  Output: For $i = 0, \ldots, n - 1, j = 0, \ldots, m - 1$, the length $L[i, j]$ of a longest
    common subsequence of $X[0..i]$ and $Y[0..j]$

  for $i \leftarrow -1$ to $n - 1$ **do**
    $L[i, -1] \leftarrow 0$
  for $j \leftarrow 0$ to $m - 1$ **do**
    $L[-1, j] \leftarrow 0$
  for $i \leftarrow 0$ to $n - 1$ **do**
    for $j \leftarrow 0$ to $m - 1$ **do**
      if $X[i] = Y[j]$ **then**
        $L[i, j] \leftarrow L[i - 1, j - 1] + 1$
      else
        $L[i, j] \leftarrow \max\{L[i - 1, j], \ L[i, j - 1]\}$
  return array L

Algorithm 12.10: Dynamic programming algorithm for the LCS problem.

Performance

The running time of Algorithm 12.10 is easy to analyze, for it is dominated by two nested for-loops, with the outer one iterating n times and the inner one iterating m times. Since the if-statement and assignment inside the loop each requires $O(1)$ primitive operations, this algorithm runs in $O(nm)$ time. Thus, the dynamic programming technique can be applied to the longest common subsequence problem to improve significantly over the exponential-time brute-force solution to the LCS problem.

Algorithm 12.10 (LCS) computes the length of the longest common subsequence (stored in $L[n-1, m-1]$), but not the subsequence itself. As shown in the following theorem, a simple postprocessing step can extract the longest common subsequence from the array L returned by the algorithm.

Theorem 12.5: *Given a string X of n characters and a string Y of m characters, we can find the longest common subsequence of X and Y in $O(nm)$ time.*

Proof: We have already observed that Algorithm LCS computes the **length** of a longest common subsequence of the input strings X and Y in $O(nm)$ time. Given the table of $L[i, j]$ values, constructing a longest common subsequence is straightforward. One method is to start from $L[n-1, m-1]$ and work back through the table, reconstructing a longest common subsequence from back to front. At any position $L[i, j]$, we determine whether $X[i] = Y[j]$. If this is true, then we take $X[i]$ as the next character of the subsequence (noting that $X[i]$ is **before** the previous character we found, if any), moving next to $L[i-1, j-1]$. If $X[i] \neq Y[j]$, then we move to the larger of $L[i, j-1]$ and $L[i-1, j]$. (See Figure 12.11.) We stop when we reach a boundary entry (with $i = -1$ or $j = -1$). This method constructs a longest common subsequence in $O(n + m)$ additional time. ∎

L	-1	0	1	2	3	4	5	6	7	8	9	10	11
-1	0	0	0	0	0	0	0	0	0	0	0	0	0
0	0	0	1	1	1	1	1	1	1	1	1	1	1
1	0	0	1	1	2	2	2	2	2	2	2	2	2
2	0	0	1	1	2	2	2	3	3	3	3	3	3
3	0	1	1	1	2	2	2	3	3	3	3	3	3
4	0	1	1	1	2	2	2	3	3	3	3	3	3
5	0	1	1	1	2	2	2	3	4	4	4	4	4
6	0	1	1	2	2	3	3	3	4	4	5	5	5
7	0	1	1	2	2	3	4	4	4	4	5	5	6
8	0	1	1	2	3	3	4	5	5	5	5	5	6
9	0	1	1	2	3	4	4	5	5	5	6	6	6

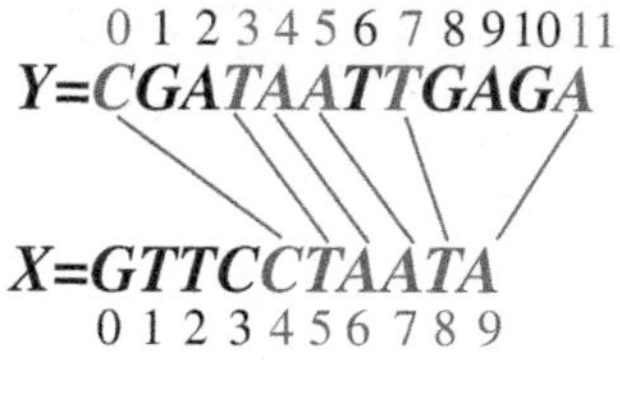

```
              0 1 2 3 4 5 6 7 8 9 10 11
          Y=C G A T A A T T G A G A

          X=G T T C C T A A T A
            0 1 2 3 4 5 6 7 8 9
```

Figure 12.11: Illustration of the algorithm for constructing a longest common subsequence from the array L.

12.6 The 0-1 Knapsack Problem

Suppose a hiker is about to go on a trek through a rainforest carrying a single knapsack. Suppose further that she knows the maximum total weight W that she can carry, and she has a set S of n different useful items that she can potentially take with her, such as a folding chair, a tent, and a copy of this book. Let us assume that each item i has an integer weight w_i and a benefit value b_i, which is the utility value that our hiker assigns to item i. Her problem, of course, is to optimize the total value of the set T of items that she takes with her, without going over the weight limit W. That is, she has the following objective:

$$\text{maximize} \sum_{i \in T} b_i \quad \text{subject to} \quad \sum_{i \in T} w_i \leq W.$$

Her problem is an instance of the *0-1 knapsack problem*. This problem is called a "0-1" problem, because each item must be entirely accepted or rejected. We consider the fractional version of this problem in Section 10.1, and we study how knapsack problems arise in the context of Internet auctions in Exercise R-12.9.

A Pseudo-Polynomial Time Dynamic Programming Algorithm

We can easily solve the 0-1 knapsack problem in $\Theta(2^n)$ time, of course, by enumerating all subsets of S and selecting the one that has highest total benefit from among all those with total weight not exceeding W. This would be an inefficient algorithm, however. Fortunately, we can derive a dynamic programming algorithm for the 0-1 knapsack problem that runs much faster than this in most cases.

As with many dynamic programming problems, one of the hardest parts of designing such an algorithm for the 0-1 knapsack problem is to find a nice characterization for subproblems (so that we satisfy the three properties of a dynamic programming algorithm). To simplify the discussion, number the items in S as $1, 2, \ldots, n$ and define, for each $k \in \{1, 2, \ldots, n\}$, the subset

$$S_k = \{\text{items in } S \text{ labeled } 1, 2, \ldots, k\}.$$

One possibility is for us to define subproblems by using a parameter k so that subproblem k is the best way to fill the knapsack using only items from the set S_k. This is a valid subproblem definition, but it is not at all clear how to define an optimal solution for index k in terms of optimal subproblem solutions. Our hope would be that we would be able to derive an equation that takes the best solution using items from S_{k-1} and considers how to add the item k to that. Unfortunately, if we stick with this definition for subproblems, then this approach is fatally flawed. For, as we show in Figure 12.12, if we use this characterization for subproblems, then an optimal solution to the global problem may actually contain a suboptimal subproblem.

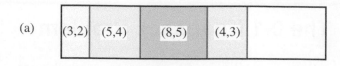

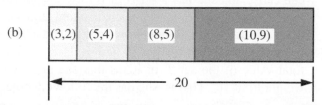

Figure 12.12: An example showing that our first approach to defining a knapsack subproblem does not work. The set S consists of five items denoted by the (***weight, benefit***) pairs $(3, 2)$, $(5, 4)$, $(8, 5)$, $(4, 3)$, and $(10, 9)$. The maximum total weight is $W = 20$: (a) best solution with the first four items; (b) best solution with the first five items. We shade each item in proportion to its benefit.

One of the reasons that defining subproblems only in terms of an index k is fatally flawed is that there is not enough information represented in a subproblem to provide much help for solving the global optimization problem. We can correct this difficulty, however, by adding a second parameter w. Let us therefore formulate each subproblem as that of computing $B[k, w]$, which is defined as the maximum total value of a subset of S_k from among all those subsets having total weight *at most* w. We have $B[0, w] = 0$ for each $w \leq W$, and we derive the following relationship for the general case

$$B[k, w] = \begin{cases} B[k - 1, w] & \text{if } w_k > w \\ \max\{B[k - 1, w], \ B[k - 1, w - w_k] + b_k\} & \text{else.} \end{cases}$$

That is, the best subset of S_k that has total weight at most w is either the best subset of S_{k-1} that has total weight at most w or the best subset of S_{k-1} that has total weight at most $w - w_k$ plus item k. Since the best subset of S_k that has total weight w must either contain item k or not, one of these two choices must be the right choice. Thus, we have a subproblem definition that is simple (it involves just two parameters, k and w) and satisfies the subproblem optimization condition. Moreover, it has subproblem overlap, for an optimal subset of total weight at most w may be used by many future subproblems.

In deriving an algorithm from this definition, we can make one additional observation, namely, that the definition of $B[k, w]$ is built from $B[k - 1, w]$ and possibly $B[k - 1, w - w_k]$. Thus, we can implement this algorithm using only a single array B, which we update in each of a series of iterations indexed by a parameter k so that, at the end of iteration k, $B[w] = B[k, w]$. This gives us Algorithm 12.13.

Algorithm 01Knapsack(S, W):

Input: Set S of n items, such that item i has positive benefit b_i and positive integer weight w_i; positive integer maximum total weight W

Output: For $w = 0, \ldots, W$, maximum benefit $B[w]$ of a subset of S with total weight at most w

for $w \leftarrow 0$ to W **do**
    $B[w] \leftarrow 0$
for $k \leftarrow 1$ to n **do**
    for $w \leftarrow W$ downto w_k **do**
        if $B[w - w_k] + b_k > B[w]$ **then**
            $B[w] \leftarrow B[w - w_k] + b_k$

Algorithm 12.13: Dynamic programming algorithm for the 0-1 knapsack problem.

The running time of the 01Knapsack algorithm is dominated by the two nested for-loops, where the outer one iterates n times and the inner one iterates at most W times. After it completes we can find the optimal value by locating the value $B[w]$ that is greatest among all $w \leq W$. Thus, we have the following:

Theorem 12.6: *Given an integer W and a set S of n items, each of which has a positive benefit and a positive integer weight, we can find the highest benefit subsct of S with total weight at most W in $O(nW)$ time.*

Proof: We have given Algorithm 12.13 (01Knapsack) for constructing the *value* of the maximum-benefit subset of S that has total weight at most W using an array B of benefit values. We can easily convert our algorithm into one that outputs the items in a best subset, however. We leave the details of this conversion as an exercise. ∎

In addition to being another useful application of the dynamic programming technique, Theorem 12.6 states something very interesting. Namely, it states that the running time of our algorithm depends on a parameter W that strictly speaking is not proportional to the size of the input (the n items, together with their weights and benefits, plus the *number* W). Assuming that W is encoded in some standard way (such as a binary number), then it takes only $O(\log W)$ bits to encode W. Moreover, if W is very large (say $W = 2^n$), then this dynamic programming algorithm would actually be asymptotically slower than the brute-force method. Thus, technically speaking, this algorithm is not a polynomial-time algorithm, for its running time is not actually a polynomial function of the *size* of the input. It is common to refer to an algorithm such as our knapsack dynamic programming algorithm as being a *pseudo-polynomial-time* algorithm, for its running time depends polynomially on the magnitude of a number given in the input, not its encoding size.

12.7 Exercises

Reinforcement

R-12.1 What is the best way to multiply a chain of matrices with dimensions that are 10×5, 5×2, 2×20, 20×12, 12×4, and 4×60? Show your work.

R-12.2 Design an efficient algorithm for the matrix chain multiplication problem that outputs a fully parenthesized expression for how to multiply the matrices in the chain using the minimum number of operations.

R-12.3 Suppose that during the playing of the coins-in-a-line game that Alice's opponent, Bob, makes a choice that is suboptimal for him. Does this require that Alice recompute her table of remaining $M_{i,j}$ values to plan her optimal strategy from this point on?

R-12.4 Suppose that in an instance of the coins-in-a-line game the coins have the following values in the line:

$$(9, 1, 7, 3, 2, 8, 9, 3).$$

What is the maximum that the first player, Alice, can win, assuming that the second player, Bob, plays optimally?

R-12.5 Let $S = \{a, b, c, d, e, f, g\}$ be a collection of objects with benefit-weight values, a: $(12, 4)$, b: $(10, 6)$, c: $(8, 5)$, d: $(11, 7)$, e: $(14, 3)$, f: $(7, 1)$, g: $(9, 6)$. What is an optimal solution to the 0-1 knapsack problem for S assuming we have a sack that can hold objects with total weight 18? Show your work.

R-12.6 Suppose we are given a set of telescope observation requests, specified by triples of (s_i, f_i, b_i), defining the start times, finish times, and benefits of each observation request as

$$L = \{(1, 2, 5), (1, 3, 4), (2, 4, 7), (3, 5, 2), (1, 6, 3), (4, 7, 5), (6, 8, 7), (7, 9, 4)\}.$$

Solve the telescope scheduling problem for this set of observation requests.

R-12.7 Suppose we define a probabilistic event so that $V(i, 0) = 1$ and $V(0, j) = 0$, for all i and j, and $V(i, j)$, for $i, j \geq 1$, is defined as

$$V(i, j) = 0.5V(i - 1, j) + 0.5V(i, j - 1).$$

What is the probability of the event, $V(2, 2)$?

R-12.8 Show the longest common subsequence table, L, for the following two strings:

$$X = \texttt{"skullandbones"}$$

$$Y = \texttt{"lullabybabies"}.$$

What is a longest common subsequence between these strings?

R-12.9 Sally is hosting an Internet auction to sell n widgets. She receives m bids, each of the form "I want k_i widgets for d_i dollars," for $i = 1, 2, \ldots, m$. Characterize her optimization problem as a knapsack problem. Under what conditions is this a 0-1 versus fractional problem?

Creativity

C-12.1 *Binomial coefficients* are a family of positive integers that have a number of useful properties and they can be defined in several ways. One way to define them is as an indexed recursive function, $C(n, k)$, where the "C" stands for "choice" or "combinations." In this case, the definition is as follows:

$$C(n, 0) = 1,$$

$$C(n, n) = 1,$$

and, for $0 < k < n$,

$$C(n, k) = C(n - 1, \, k - 1) + C(n - 1, \, k).$$

(a) Show that, if we don't use memoization, and n is even, then the running time for computing $C(n, \, n/2)$ is at least $2^{n/2}$.

(b) Describe a scheme for computing $C(n, k)$ using memoization. Give a big-oh characterization of the number of arithmetic operations needed for computing $C(n, \lceil n/2 \rceil)$ in this case.

C-12.2 Show that, in the coins-in-a-line game, a greedy strategy of having the first player, Alice, always choose the available coin with highest value will not necessarily result in an optimal solution (or even a winning solution) for her.

C-12.3 Show that, in the coins-in-a-line game, a greedy-denial strategy of having the first player, Alice, always choose the available coin that minimizes the maximum value of the coin available to Bob will not necessarily result in an optimal solution for her.

C-12.4 Design an $O(n)$-time non-losing strategy for the first player, Alice, in the coins-in-a-line game. Your strategy does not have to be optimal, but it should be guaranteed to end in a tie or better for Alice.

C-12.5 Show that we can solve the telescope scheduling problem in $O(n)$ time even if the list of n observation requests is not given to us in sorted order, provided that start and finish times are given as integer indices in the range from 1 to n^2.

C-12.6 Given a sequence $S = (x_0, x_1, x_2, \ldots, x_{n-1})$ of numbers, describe an $O(n^2)$-time algorithm for finding a longest subsequence $T = (x_{i_0}, x_{i_1}, x_{i_2}, \ldots, x_{i_{k-1}})$ of numbers, such that $i_j < i_{j+1}$ and $x_{i_j} > x_{i_{j+1}}$. That is, T is a longest decreasing subsequence of S.

C-12.7 Describe an $O(n \log n)$-time algorithm for the previous problem.

C-12.8 Show that a sequence of n distinct numbers contains a decreasing or increasing subsequence of size at least $\lfloor \sqrt{n} \rfloor$.

C-12.9 Define the *edit distance* between two strings X and Y of length n and m, respectively, to be the number of edits that it takes to change X into Y. An edit consists of a character insertion, a character deletion, or a character replacement. For example, the strings `"algorithm"` and `"rhythm"` have edit distance 6. Design an $O(nm)$-time algorithm for computing the edit distance between X and Y.

C-12.10 A *substring* of some character string is a contiguous sequence of characters in that string (which is different than a subsequence, of course). Suppose you are given two character strings, X and Y, with respective lengths n and m. Describe an efficient algorithm for finding a *longest common substring* of X and Y.

C-12.11 Let A, B, and C be three length-n character strings taken over the same constant-sized alphabet Σ. Design an $O(n^3)$-time algorithm for finding a longest substring that is common to all three of A, B, and C.

C-12.12 How can we modify the dynamic programming algorithm from simply computing the best benefit value for the 0-1 knapsack problem to computing the assignment that gives this benefit?

C-12.13 Suppose we are given a collection $A = \{a_1, a_2, \ldots, a_n\}$ of n positive integers that add up to N. Design an $O(nN)$-time algorithm for determining whether there is a subset $B \subset A$ such that $\sum_{a_i \in B} a_i = \sum_{a_i \in A-B} a_i$.

C-12.14 Let P be a convex polygon (Section 22.1). A *triangulation* of P is an addition of diagonals connecting the vertices of P so that each interior face is a triangle. The *weight* of a triangulation is the sum of the lengths of the diagonals. Assuming that we can compute lengths and add and compare them in constant time, give an efficient algorithm for computing a minimum-weight triangulation of P.

C-12.15 A *grammar* G is a way of generating strings of "terminal" characters from a nonterminal symbol S, by applying simple substitution rules, called *productions*. If $B \to \beta$ is a production, then we can convert a string of the form $\alpha B \gamma$ into the string $\alpha \beta \gamma$. A grammar is in *Chomsky normal form* if every production is of the form "$A \to BC$" or "$A \to a$," where A, B, and C are nonterminal characters and a is a terminal character. Design an $O(n^3)$-time dynamic programming algorithm for determining if string $x = x_0 x_1 \cdots x_{n-1}$ can be generated from the start symbol S.

C-12.16 Suppose we are given an n-node rooted tree T, such that each node v in T is given a weight $w(v)$. An *independent set* of T is a subset S of the nodes of T such that no node in S is a child or parent of any other node in S. Design an efficient dynamic programming algorithm to find the maximum-weight independent set of the nodes in T, where the weight of a set of nodes is simply the sum of the weights of the nodes in that set. What is the running time of your algorithm?

C-12.17 Suppose you are given an ordered set, K, of n keys, $k_1 < k_2 < \cdots < k_n$. In addition, for each key, k_i, suppose you know the probability, p_i, that any given query will be for the key k_i. The cost of a binary search tree, T, for K, is defined as

$$C(T) = \sum_{i=1}^{n} (d_T(k_i) + 1) p_i,$$

where $d_T(k_i)$ denotes the depth of k_i in T. Describe an algorithm to find an *optimal binary search tree*, for K, that is, a binary search tree, T, that minimizes $C(T)$. What is the running time of your algorithm?

Hint: First, define $P(i,j) = \sum_{k=i}^{j} p_k$, for $1 \le i \le j \le n$. Then, consider how to compute $C(i,j)$, the cost of an optimal binary search tree for the keys that range from k_i to k_j.

Applications

A-12.1 Suppose that the coins of the fictional country of Combinatoria come in the denominations, $d_1, d_2, \ldots, d_k$, where $d_1 = 1$ and the other d_i values form a set of distinct integers greater than 1. Given an integer, $n > 0$, the problem of **making change** is to find the fewest number of Combinatorian coins whose values sum to n.

(a) Give an instance of the making-change problem for which it is suboptimal to use the standard greedy algorithm, which repeatedly chooses a highest-valued coin whose value is at most n until the sum of chosen coins equals n.

(b) Describe an efficient algorithm for solving the problem of making change. What is the running time of your algorithm?

A-12.2 Every web browser and word processor needs a way of breaking English paragraphs into lines at word boundaries that is both fast and looks good. Some systems even have ways of hyphenating words to make good line breaks, but let us ignore that complication here. Say that the width of each line on a computer screen or browser window is M characters, and we are given a list,

$$\mathcal{W} = (W_1, W_2, \ldots, W_n),$$

of n words forming a paragraph that we wish to display, where the word, W_i, has length, L_i. The **word wrapping** problem is to break $\mathcal{W}$ into lines of length at most M in a way that minimizes a total cost penalizing the wasted space. The cost of breaking a single line to hold the words $W_i, W_{i+1}, \ldots, W_j$, has the following cost:

$$C(i,j) = \left(M - (j - i) - \sum_{k=i}^{j} L_k \right)^3,$$

assuming this cost is nonnegative. If this cost is negative, then we instead set $C(i,j) = +\infty$, to show that the set of words from W_i to W_j doesn't fit on a single line. In addition, if this cost is positive, but $j = n$, then we set $C(i,j) = 0$, to show that there is no wasted space in the last line of the paragraph. Describe an efficient algorithm for solving the word wrapping problem, so as to minimize the total cost of all the lines used to display the paragraph formed by the words $W_1, \ldots, W_n$. What is the running time of your algorithm?

A-12.3 An American spy is deep undercover in the hostile country of Phonemia. In order not to waste scarce resources, any time he wants to send a message back home, he removes all the punctuation from his message and converts all the letters to uppercase. So, for example, to send the message,

"Abort the plan! Meet at the Dark Cabin."

he would transmit

ABORTTHEPLANMEETATTHEDARKCABIN

Given such a string, S, of n uppercase letters, describe an efficient way of breaking it into a sequence of valid English words. You may assume that you have a function, valid(s), which can take a character string, s, and return **true** if and only if s is a valid English word. What is the running time of your algorithm, assuming each call to the function, valid, runs in $O(1)$ time?

A-12.4 The comedian, Demetri Martin, is the author of a 224-word palindrome poem. That is, like any **palindrome**, the letters of this poem are the same whether they are read forward or backward. At some level, this is no great achievement, because there is a palindrome inside every poem, which we explore in this exercise. Describe an efficient algorithm for taking any character string, S, of length n, and finding the longest subsequence of S that is a palindrome. For instance, the string, "I EAT GUITAR MAGAZINES" has "EATITAE" and "IAGAGAI" as palindrome subsequences. Your algorithm should run in time $O(n^2)$.

A-12.5 Scientists performing DNA sequence alignment often desire a more parametrized way of aligning two strings than simply computing a longest common subsequence between these two strings. One way to achieve such flexibility is to use the **Smith-Waterman algorithm**, which is generalization of the dynamic programming algorithm for computing a longest common subsequence so that it can handle weighted scoring functions. In particular, for two strings, X and Y, suppose we are given functions, defined on characters, a, from X, and b from Y, as follows:

$$M(a, b) = \text{the positive benefit for a match, if } a = b$$

$$M(a, b) = \text{the negative cost for a mismatch, if } a \neq b$$

$$I(a) = \text{the negative cost for inserting } a \text{ at a position in } X$$

$$D(b) = \text{the negative cost of deleting } b \text{ from some position in } Y.$$

Given a string, X, of length n and a string, Y, of length m, describe an algorithm running in $O(nm)$ time for finding the maximum-weight way of transforming X into Y, according to the above weight functions, using the operations of matching, substitution, insertion in X, and deletion from Y.

A-12.6 The pointy-haired boss (PHB) of an office in a major technology company would like to throw a party. Based on the performance reviews he has done, the PHB has assigned an integer "fun factor" score, $F(x)$, for each employee, x, in his office. In order for the party to be as crazy as possible, the PHB has one rule: an employee, x, may be invited to the party only if x's immediate supervisor is not invited. Suppose you are the PHB's administrative assistant, and it is your job to figure out who to invite, subject to this rule, given the list of $F(x)$ values and the office organizational chart, which is a tree, T, rooted at the PHB, containing the n employees as nodes, so that each employee's parent in T is the immediate supervisor of that employee. Describe an algorithm for solving this **office party problem**, by choosing a group of employees to invite to the party such that this group has the largest total fun factor while satisfying the PHB's rule and also guaranteeing that you are invited, which, of course, means that the PHB is not. What is the running time of your algorithm?

A-12.7 Consider a variant of the telescope scheduling problem, where we are given a list, L, of n observational requests for a large telescope, but now these requests are specified differently. Instead of having a start time, finish time, and benefit, each request i is now specified by a deadline, d_i, by when the observation must be completed, an exposure time, t_i, which is the length of uninterrupted telescope time this observation needs once it begins, and a benefit, b_i, which, as before, is a positive integer indicating the benefit to science for performing this observation. Assume that time is broken up into discrete units, such as seconds, so that all d_i's are integers, and observation times have an upper limit, so that all t_i's are integers in the range from 1 to n. Describe an algorithm for solving this version of the telescope scheduling problem, to maximize the total benefit of the included observations so that all the included observations are completed by their deadlines. Characterize the running time of your algorithm in terms of n.

A-12.8 Speech recognition systems need to match audio streams that represent the same words spoken at different speeds. Suppose, therefore, that you are given two sequences of numbers, $X = (x_1, x_2, \ldots, x_n)$, and $Y = (y_1, y_2, \ldots, y_m)$, representing two different audio streams that need to be matched. A *mapping* between X and Y is a list, M, of distinct pairs, (i, j), that is ordered lexicographically, such that, for each $i \in [1, n]$, there is at least one pair, (i, j), in M, and for each $j \in [1, m]$, there is at least one pair, (i, j), in M. Such a mapping is *monotonic* if, for any (i, j) and (k, l) in M, with (i, j) coming before (k, l) in M, we have $i \leq k$ and $j \leq l$. For example, given

$$X = (3, 9, 9, 5) \text{ and } Y = (3, 3, 9, 5, 5),$$

one possible monotonic mapping between X and Y would be

$$M = [(1, 1), (1, 2), (2, 3), (3, 3), (4, 4), (4, 5)].$$

The *dynamic time warping* problem is to find a monotonic mapping, M, between X and Y, that minimizes the distance, $D(X, Y)$, between X and Y, subject to M, which is defined as

$$D(X, Y) = \sum_{(i,j) \in M} |x_i - y_j|,$$

where this minimization is taken over all possible monotonic mappings between X and Y. For instance, in the example X, Y, and M, given above, we have $D(X, Y) = 0$. Describe an efficient algorithm for solving the dynamic time warping problem. What is the running time of your algorithm?

A-12.9 Consider a variant of the coins-in-a-line game, which we are calling *houses-in-a-row*. In this game, two real estate moguls, Alice and Bob, take turns divvying up n houses that are lined up in a row, with Alice going first. When it is a player's turn, he or she must choose one or more of the remaining houses, starting from either the left end of the row or the right, with the set of houses he or she picks in this turn being consecutive. For example, in a row of houses numbered 1 to 100, Alice could choose houses numbered 1, 2, and 3 in her first turn, and, following that, Bob could choose houses numbered 100 and 99 in his first turn, which could be then followed by Alice choosing house number 98, and so on, until all the houses are chosen. There is no limit on the number of houses that Alice or Bob can choose during a turn, but the values of the houses can be either positive or negative. For instance, a house could have a negative value if it is contains a hazardous waste site that costs more to clean up than the house is worth. Describe an efficient algorithm for determining how Alice can maximize the total net value of all the houses she chooses, assuming Bob plays optimally as well. What is the running time of your algorithm?

A-12.10 Suppose, at some distance point in the future, the World Series in major league baseball becomes a best-of-n series, where n is an arbitrary odd number set by the Commissioner of Baseball in that year, based on advertising revenue. Suppose the Anteaters and the Bears are meeting in the World Series in that year, and, based on past experience, we know that in each game they play, the Anteaters have a probability p of winning; hence, the Bears have a probability of $1 - p$ of winning, with all games being independent. Consider a parameter, $V(i, j)$, which is the probability that the Anteaters will have won i games and the Bears will have won j games after the two teams have played $i + j$ against each other. Give an equation for defining $V(i, j)$, including the special cases, $V(i, 0)$, $V(0, j)$, $V(\lceil n/2 \rceil, j)$ and $V(i, \lceil n/2 \rceil)$, and describe an algorithm for determining the overall probability that the Anteaters will win the World Series.

A-12.11 Suppose n computers in a wired local-area network are arranged in a tree, T, which is rooted at one of these computers (say, one that is connected to the Internet). That is, the computers in this network form the nodes of T, and the edges of T are determined by the pairs of computers that have cables connecting them to each other. The administrator of this network is concerned about reliability and wants to buy some network monitoring devices to continuously check the quality of the connections in T. If such a monitoring device is installed on a computer, x, then x is able to continuously monitor all the direct connections that x has with other computers. To save money, he is asking that you determine the fewest number of monitoring devices needed in order to have at least one device monitoring every connection in T. For example, if every computer in T other than the root were a child of the root, then the administrator would need only one monitoring device (placed at the root). Describe an efficient algorithm for solving this problem, which is known as the ***vertex-cover*** problem, for T. What is the running time of your algorithm?

Chapter Notes

Dynamic programming was developed in the operations research community and formalized by Bellman [25]. The matrix chain-product solution we described is due to Godbole [82]. The asymptotically fastest method is due to Hu and Shing [105, 106]. Our presentation of the analysis of when it is better to attempt a two-point conversion after a touchdown in American football is based on an analysis by Sackrowitz [180] (see also [198, 201]). The dynamic programming algorithm for the knapsack problem is found in the book by Hu [104]. Hirschberg [99] shows how to solve the longest common substring problem with the same running time as given above but with linear space (see also [52]). More information about dynamic time warping and sequence comparison algorithms can be found in an edited book by Sankoff and Kruskal [183]. Additional information about telescope scheduling can be found in a paper by Johnston [113].

Chapter

13

Graphs and Traversals

The metropolitan area of Milan, Italy at night. Astronaut photograph ISS026-E-28829, 2011. U.S. government image. NASA-JSC.

Contents

13.1 Graph Terminology and Representations 355

13.2 Depth-First Search 365

13.3 Breadth-First Search 370

13.4 Directed Graphs 373

13.5 Biconnected Components 386

13.6 Exercises 392

Connectivity information is present in a multitude of different applications, including social networks, road networks, computer games and puzzles, and computer networks. In computer networks, for instance, computers are connected together using routers, switches, and (wired or radio) communication links. Information flows in the form of individual packets, from one computer to another, by tracing out paths that hop through intermediate connections. Alternatively, in computer puzzle and game applications, game positions are connected by the transitions that are allowed between them. In either case, however, we might be interested in paths that can be mapped out in the connectivity structures that are represented in these applications. For instance, a path in a puzzle application could be a solution that starts from an initial game position and leads to a goal position.

In some applications, we might not really care whether we find a shortest path from a source to a destination, whereas in others we might be interested in finding the shortest paths possible. For example, in interactive applications, such as in online games or video chat sessions, we would naturally want packets to flow in our computer network along shortest paths, since we want to minimize any delays that occur between one person's action and the reaction of communicating partner. In other applications, such as in solving a maze puzzle, there may be only a single path between a source and destination, with several dead ends that need to be ruled out in order find this path. Thus, we would like to design algorithms that can efficiently identify paths in connectivity structures.

In addition to these motivating applications, connectivity information can be defined by all kinds of relationships that exist between pairs of objects. Additional examples include mapping (in geographic information systems), transportation (in road and flight networks), and electrical engineering (in circuits). The topic we study in this chapter—*graphs*—is therefore focused on representations and algorithms for dealing efficiently with such relationships. That is, a graph is a set of objects, called "vertices," together with a collection of pairwise connections between them, which define "edges."

Because applications for graphs are so widespread and diverse, people have developed a great deal of terminology to describe different components and properties of graphs, which we also explore in this chapter. Fortunately, since most graph applications are relatively recent developments, this terminology is fairly intuitive.

We begin this chapter by discussing much of this terminology and some elementary properties of graphs. We also present ways of representing graphs. As highlighted above, traversals are important computations for graphs, both for shortest paths and for arbitrary paths, and we discuss in Section 13.2. We discuss directed graphs in Section 13.4, where pairwise relationships have a given direction, and connectivity problems become more complicated.

13.1 Graph Terminology and Representations

A **graph** G is a set, V, of **vertices** and a collection, E, of pairs of vertices from V, which are called **edges**. Thus, a graph is a way of representing connections or relationships between pairs of objects from some set V. Incidentally, some people use different terminology for graphs and refer to what we call vertices as "nodes" and what we call edges as "arcs" or "ties."

Edges in a graph are either **directed** or **undirected**. An edge (u, v) is said to be **directed** from u to v if the pair (u, v) is ordered, with u preceding v. An edge (u, v) is said to be **undirected** if the pair (u, v) is not ordered. Undirected edges are sometimes denoted with set notation, as $\{u, v\}$, but for simplicity we use the pair notation (u, v), noting that in the undirected case (u, v) is the same as (v, u). Graphs are typically visualized by drawing the vertices as circles or rectangles and the edges as segments or curves connecting pairs of these circles or rectangles.

Example 13.1: *We can visualize collaborations among the researchers of a certain discipline by constructing a graph whose vertices are associated with the researchers themselves, and whose edges connect pairs of vertices associated with researchers who have coauthored a paper or book. (See Figure 13.1.) Such edges are undirected because coauthorship is a* **symmetric relation***; that is, if A has coauthored something with B, then B necessarily has coauthored something with A.*

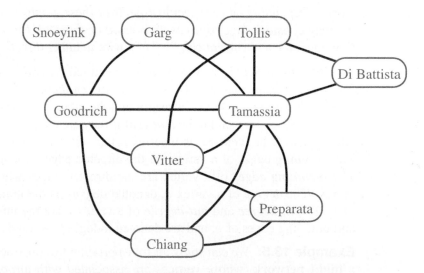

Figure 13.1: Graph of coauthorships among some authors.

13.1.1   Some Graph Terminology

If all the edges in a graph are undirected, then we say the graph is an ***undirected graph***. Likewise, a ***directed graph***, also called a ***digraph***, is a graph whose edges are all directed. A graph that has both directed and undirected edges is often called a ***mixed graph***. Note that an undirected or mixed graph can be converted into a directed graph by replacing every undirected edge (u, v) by the pair of directed edges (u, v) and (v, u). It is often useful, however, to keep undirected and mixed graphs represented as they are, for such graphs have several applications.

Example 13.2: *We can associate with an object-oriented program a graph whose vertices represent the classes defined in the program, and whose edges indicate inheritance between classes. There is an edge from a vertex v to a vertex u if the class for v extends the class for u. Such edges are directed because the inheritance relation only goes in one direction (that is, it is* **asymmetric***).*

Example 13.3: *A city map can be modeled by a graph whose vertices are intersections or dead ends, and whose edges are stretches of streets without intersections. This graph has both undirected edges, which correspond to stretches of two-way streets, and directed edges, which correspond to stretches of one-way streets. Thus, a graph modeling a city map is a mixed graph.*

Example 13.4: *Physical examples of graphs are present in the electrical wiring and plumbing networks of a building. Such networks can be modeled as graphs, where each connector, fixture, or outlet is viewed as a vertex, and each uninterrupted stretch of wire or pipe is viewed as an edge. Such graphs are actually components of much larger graphs, namely the local power and water distribution networks. Depending on the specific aspects of these graphs that we are interested in, we may consider their edges as undirected or directed, for, in principle, water can flow in a pipe and current can flow in a wire in either direction.*

The two vertices joined by an edge are called the ***end vertices*** of the edge. The end vertices of an edge are also known as the ***endpoints*** of that edge. If an edge is directed, its first endpoint is its ***origin*** and the other is the ***destination*** of the edge.

Two vertices are said to be ***adjacent*** if they are endpoints of the same edge. An edge is said to be ***incident*** on a vertex if the vertex is one of the edge's endpoints. The ***outgoing edges*** of a vertex are the directed edges whose origin is that vertex. The ***incoming edges*** of a vertex are the directed edges whose destination is that vertex. The ***degree*** of a vertex v, denoted $\deg(v)$, is the number of incident edges of v. The ***in-degree*** and ***out-degree*** of a vertex v are the number of the incoming and outgoing edges of v, and are denoted $\text{indeg}(v)$ and $\text{outdeg}(v)$, respectively.

Example 13.5: *We can study air transportation by constructing a graph G, called a* **flight network***, whose vertices are associated with airports, and whose edges are associated with flights. (See Figure 13.2.) In graph G, the edges are directed because a given flight has a specific travel direction (from the origin airport to the* *destination airport). The endpoints of an edge e in G correspond respectively to the origin and destination for the flight corresponding to e. Two airports are adjacent in G if there is a flight that flies between them, and an edge e is incident upon a vertex v in G if the flight for e flies to or from the airport for v. The outgoing edges of a vertex v correspond to the out-bound flights from v's airport, and the incoming edges correspond to the in-bound flights to v's airport. Finally, the in-degree of a vertex v of G corresponds to the number of in-bound flights to v's airport, and the out-degree of a vertex v in G corresponds to the number of out-bound flights.*

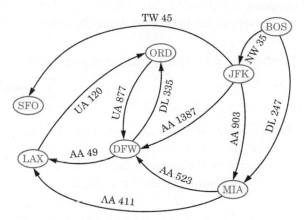

Figure 13.2: Example of a directed graph representing a flight network. The endpoints of edge UA 120 are LAX and ORD; hence, LAX and ORD are adjacent. The in-degree of DFW is 3, and the out-degree of DFW is 2.

The definition of a graph groups edges in a ***collection***, not a ***set***, thus allowing for two undirected edges to have the same end vertices, and for two directed edges to have the same origin and destination. Such edges are called ***parallel edges*** or ***multiple edges***. Parallel edges may exist in a flight network (Example 13.5), in which case multiple edges between the same pair of vertices could indicate different flights operating on the same route at different times of the day. Another special type of edge is one that connects a vertex to itself. In this case, we say that an edge (undirected or directed) is a ***self-loop*** if its two endpoints coincide. A self-loop may occur in a graph associated with a city map (Example 13.3), where it would correspond to a "circle" (a curving street that returns to its starting point).

With few exceptions, like those mentioned above, graphs do not have parallel edges or self-loops. Such graphs are said to be ***simple***. Thus, we can usually say that the edges of a simple graph are a ***set*** of vertex pairs (and not just a collection). Throughout this chapter, we shall assume that a graph is simple unless otherwise specified. This assumption simplifies the presentation of data structures and algorithms for graphs. Extending the results of this chapter to general graphs, with self-loops and/or parallel edges, is straightforward but tedious.

In the theorems that follow, we explore a few important properties of degrees and the number of edges in a graph. These properties relate the number of vertices and edges to each other and to the degrees of the vertices in a graph.

Theorem 13.6: *If G is a graph with m edges, then*

$$\sum_{v \in G} deg(v) = 2m.$$

Proof: An edge (u, v) is counted twice in the above summation: once by its endpoint u and once by its endpoint v. Thus, the total contribution of the edges to the degrees of the vertices is twice the number of edges.   ■

Theorem 13.7: *If G is a directed graph with m edges, then*

$$\sum_{v \in G} indeg(v) = \sum_{v \in G} outdeg(v) = m.$$

Proof: In a directed graph, an edge (u, v) contributes one unit to the out-degree of its origin u and one unit to the in-degree of its destination v. Thus, the total contribution of the edges to the out-degrees of the vertices is equal to the number of edges, and similarly for the in-degrees.   ■

Theorem 13.8: *Let G be a simple graph with n vertices and m edges. If G is undirected, then $m \leq n(n-1)/2$, and if G is directed, then $m \leq n(n-1)$.*

Proof: Suppose that G is undirected. Since no two edges can have the same endpoints and there are no self-loops, the maximum degree of a vertex in G is $n-1$ in this case. Thus, by Theorem 13.6, $2m \leq n(n-1)$. Now suppose that G is directed. Since no two edges can have the same origin and destination, and there are no self-loops, the maximum in-degree of a vertex in G is $n-1$ in this case. Thus, by Theorem 13.7, $m \leq n(n-1)$.   ■

Put another way, Theorem 13.8 states that a simple graph with n vertices has $O(n^2)$ edges.

A **path** in a graph is a sequence of alternating vertices and edges that starts at a vertex and ends at a vertex, such that each edge is incident to its predecessor and successor vertex. A **cycle** is a path with the same start and end vertices. We say that a path is **simple** if each vertex in the path is distinct, and we say that a cycle is **simple** if each vertex in the cycle is distinct, except for the first and last one. A **directed path** is a path such that all the edges are directed and are traversed along their direction. A **directed cycle** is defined similarly.

Example 13.9: *Given a graph G representing a city map (see Example 13.3), we can model a couple driving from their home to dinner at a recommended restaurant as traversing a path though G. If they know the way, and don't accidentally go* *through the same intersection twice, then they traverse a simple path in G. Likewise, we can model the entire trip the couple takes, from their home to the restaurant and back, as a cycle. If they go home from the restaurant in a completely different way than how they went, not even going through the same intersection twice, then their entire round trip is a simple cycle. Finally, if they travel along one-way streets for their entire trip, then we can model their night out as a directed cycle.*

A *subgraph* of a graph G is a graph H whose vertices and edges are subsets of the vertices and edges of G, respectively. A *spanning subgraph* of G is a subgraph of G that contains all the vertices of the graph G. A graph is **connected** if, for any two vertices, there is a path between them. If a graph G is not connected, its maximal connected subgraphs are called the **connected components** of G. A *forest* is a graph without cycles. A *tree* is a connected forest, that is, a connected graph without cycles.

Note that this definition of a tree is somewhat different from the one given in Section 2.3. Namely, in the context of graphs, a tree has no root. Whenever there is ambiguity, the trees of Section 2.3 should be called *rooted trees*, while the trees of this chapter should be called *free trees*. The connected components of a forest are (free) trees. A *spanning tree* of a graph is a spanning subgraph that is a (free) tree.

Example 13.10: *Perhaps the most talked about graph today is the Internet, which can be viewed as a graph whose vertices are computers and whose (undirected) edges are communication connections between pairs of computers on the Internet. The computers and the connections between them in a single domain, like* wiley.com, *form a subgraph of the Internet. If this subgraph is connected, then two users on computers in this domain can send e-mail to one another without having their information packets ever leave their domain. Suppose the edges of this subgraph form a spanning tree. This implies that, even if a single connection goes down (for example, because someone pulls a communication cable out of the back of a computer in this domain), then this subgraph will no longer be connected.*

There are a number of simple properties of trees, forests, and connected graphs.

Theorem 13.11: *Let G be an undirected graph with n vertices and m edges. Then we have the following:*

- *If G is connected, then $m \geq n - 1$.*
- *If G is a tree, then $m = n - 1$.*
- *If G is a forest, then $m \leq n - 1$.*

We leave the justification of this theorem as an exercise (C-13.1).

13.1.2   Operations on Graphs

In spite of their simplicity, graphs are a rich abstraction. This richness derives partly from the fact that graphs contain two kinds of objects—vertices and edges—and also because edges can be directed or undirected. There are, therefore, a number of operations that we can consider performing for a graph, G, including the following:

- Return the number, n, of vertices in G.
- Return the number, m, of edges in G.
- Return a set or list containing all n vertices in G.
- Return a set or list containing all m edges in G.
- Return some vertex, v, in G.
- Return the degree, $\deg(v)$, of a given vertex, v, in G.
- Return a set or list containing all the edges incident upon a given vertex, v, in G.
- Return a set or list containing all the vertices adjacent to a given vertex, v, in G.
- Return the two end vertices of an edge, e, in G; if e is directed, indicate which vertex is the origin of e and which is the destination of e.
- Return whether two given vertices, v and w, are adjacent in G.

When we allow for some or all the edges in a graph to be directed, then there are several additional methods we should consider including in the set of operations that could be supported by a graph, such as the following:

- Indicate whether a given edge, e, is directed in G.
- Return the in-degree of v, inDegree(v).
- Return a set or list containing all the incoming (or outgoing) edges incident upon a given vertex, v, in G.
- Return a set or list containing all the vertices adjacent to a given vertex, v, along incoming (or outgoing) edges in G.

We can also allow for update methods that add or delete edges and vertices, such as the following:

- Insert a new directed (or undirected) edge, e, between two given vertices, v and w, in G.
- Insert a new (isolated) vertex, v, in G.
- Remove a given edge, e, from G.
- Remove a given vertex, v, and all its incident edges from G.

In addition, we can allow any edge or vertex to store additional information, including numeric weights, Boolean values, or even pointers to general objects.

There are admittedly a lot of operations than one can perform with a graph, and the above list is not even exhaustive. The number of operations is to a certain extent unavoidable, however, since graphs are such rich structures.

13.1.3   Data Structures for Representing Graphs

There are two data structures that people often use to represent graphs, the ***adjacency list*** and the ***adjacency matrix***. In both of these representations, if vertices or edges are used to store data, then we assume there is some way of mapping vertices and edges to data that is associated with them. For example, we may use a lookup structure to store objects using vertex or edge names as keys, or we may represent edges or vertices as multiple-field objects and store the data associated with the edges or vertices in these fields. As we explain below, the main difference between these two graph representations are that we may get different time performances for various graph operations depending on how our graph is represented. Also, for a graph G with n vertices and m edges, an adjacency list representation uses $O(n + m)$ space, whereas an adjacency matrix representation uses $O(n^2)$ space.

The Adjacency List Structure

The ***adjacency list*** structure for a graph, G, includes the following components:

- A collection, V, of n vertices. This collection could be a set, list, or array, or it could even be defined implicitly as simply the integers from 1 to n. If vertices can "store" data, there also needs to be some way to map each vertex, v, to the data associated with v.

- A collection, E, of m edges, that is, pairs of vertices. This collection could be a set, list, or array, or it could even be defined implicitly by the pairs of vertices that are determined by adjacency lists. If edges can "store" data, there also needs to be some way to map each edge, e, to the data associated with e.

- For each vertex, v, in V, we store a list, called the ***adjacency list for*** v, that represents all the edges incident on v. This is implemented either as a list of references to each vertex, w, such that (v, w) is an edge in E, or it is implemented as a list of references to each edge, e, that is incident on v. If G is a directed graph, then the adjacency list for v is typically divided into two parts—one representing the incoming edges for v and one representing the outgoing edges for v.

We illustrate the adjacency list structure of a directed graph in Figure 13.3. For a vertex v, the space used by the adjacency list for v is proportional to the degree of v, that is, it is $O(\deg(v))$. Thus, by Theorem 13.6, the space requirement of the adjacency list structure for a graph, G, of n vertices and m edges is $O(n + m)$.

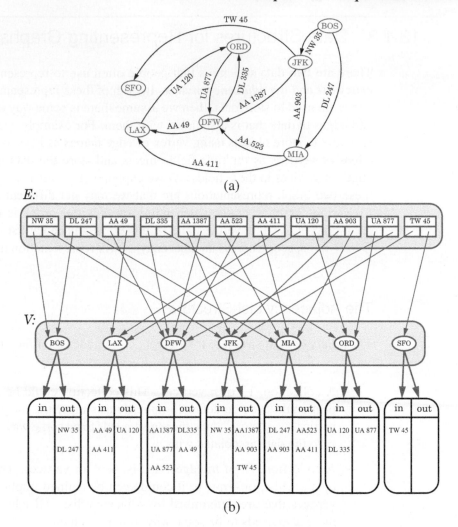

(a)

(b)

Figure 13.3: (a) A directed graph G; (b) a schematic representation of the adjacency list structure of G. In this example, we have a set of vertex objects and set of edge objects. Each edge object has pointers to its two end vertices and each vertex object has pointers to the two parts of its adjacency list, which store references to incident edges, one part for incoming edges and one for outgoing edges.

In addition, the adjacency list structure has the following performance properties:

- Returning the incident edges or adjacent vertices for a vertex, v, run in $O(\deg(v))$ time.
- Determining whether two vertices, u and v, are adjacent can be performed by inspecting either the adjacency list for u or that of v. By choosing the smaller of the two, we get $O(\min\{\deg(u), \deg(v)\})$ running time for this operation.

The Adjacency Matrix Structure

In the *adjacency matrix* representation of a graph, G, we represent the edges in G using (a two-dimensional array) matrix, A. This representation allows us to determine adjacencies between pairs of vertices in constant time. As we shall see, the trade-off in achieving this speedup is that the space usage for representing a graph of n vertices is $O(n^2)$, even if the graph has few edges.

In the adjacency matrix representation, we number the vertices, $1, 2, \ldots, n$, and we view the edges as being pairs of such integers. Historically, the adjacency matrix was the first representation used for graphs, with the adjacency matrix being a Boolean $n \times n$ matrix, A, defined as follows:

$$A[i,j] = \begin{cases} 1 & \text{if } (i,j) \text{ is an edge in } G \\ 0 & \text{otherwise.} \end{cases}$$

Thus, the adjacency matrix has a natural appeal as a mathematical structure (for example, an undirected graph has a symmetric adjacency matrix).

Modern instances of an adjacency matrix representation often update this historical perspective slightly to follow an object-oriented framework. In this case, we represent a graph, G, with an $n \times n$ array, A, such that $A[i,j]$ stores a reference to an edge object, e, if there is an edge $e = (i,j)$ in G. If there is no edge, (i,j) in G, then $A[i,j]$ is null.

In addition, if vertices or edges have some kind of data that is associated with them, then we would also need some way of mapping vertex numbers to vertex data and vertex pairs, (i,j), to associated edge data.

Using an adjacency matrix A, we can determine whether two vertices, v and w, are adjacent in $O(1)$ time. We can achieve this performance by accessing the vertices v and w to determine their respective indices i and j, and then testing whether the cell $A[i,j]$ is null or not. This performance achievement is traded off by an increase in the space usage, however, which is now $O(n^2)$, and in the running time of some other graph operations as well. For example, listing out the incident edges or adjacent vertices for a vertex v now requires that we examine an entire row or column of the array, A, representing the graph, which takes $O(n)$ time.

Deciding which representation to use for a particular graph, G, typically boils down to determining how *dense* G is. For instance, if G has close to a quadratic number of edges, then the adjacency matrix is often a good choice for representing G, but if G has close to a linear number of edges, then the adjacency list representation is probably superior. The graph algorithms we examine in this chapter tend to run most efficiently when acting upon a graph stored using an adjacency list representation.

We illustrate an example adjacency matrix in Figure 13.4.

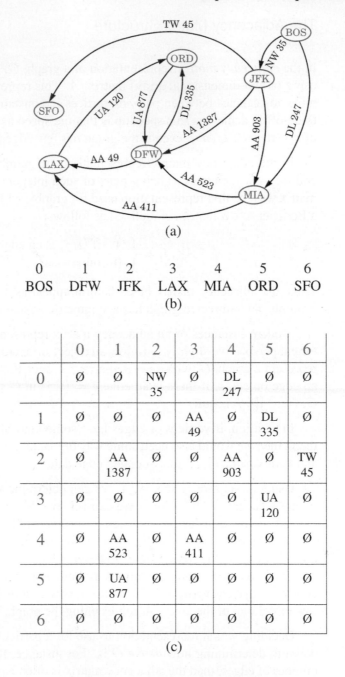

(a)

0	1	2	3	4	5	6
BOS	DFW	JFK	LAX	MIA	ORD	SFO

(b)

	0	1	2	3	4	5	6
0	Ø	Ø	NW 35	Ø	DL 247	Ø	Ø
1	Ø	Ø	Ø	AA 49	Ø	DL 335	Ø
2	Ø	AA 1387	Ø	Ø	AA 903	Ø	TW 45
3	Ø	Ø	Ø	Ø	Ø	UA 120	Ø
4	Ø	AA 523	Ø	AA 411	Ø	Ø	Ø
5	Ø	UA 877	Ø	Ø	Ø	Ø	Ø
6	Ø	Ø	Ø	Ø	Ø	Ø	Ø

(c)

Figure 13.4: Schematic representation of an adjacency matrix structure. (a) A directed graph G; (b) a numbering of its vertices; (c) the adjacency matrix A for G, using a modern object-oriented viewpoint, where each cell, $A[i, j]$, holds a pointer to the edge object, $e = (i, j)$, or is null if there is no such edge in G.

13.2 Depth-First Search

In this section, we explore a fundamental kind of algorithmic operation that we might wish to perform on a graph—traversing the edges and the vertices of that graph. Specifically, a ***traversal*** is a systematic procedure for exploring a graph by examining all of its vertices and edges. For example, a web ***spider***, or ***crawler***, which is the data collecting part of a search engine, must explore a graph of hypertext documents by examining its vertices, which are the documents, and its edges, which are the hyperlinks between documents. A traversal is efficient if it visits all the vertices and edges in time proportional to their number, that is, in linear time.

The first traversal algorithm we consider is ***depth-first search*** (DFS) in an undirected graph. Depth-first search is useful for performing a number of computations on graphs, including finding a path from one vertex to another, determining whether a graph is connected, and computing a spanning tree of a connected graph.

Traversing a Graph Using the Backtracking Technique

Depth-first search in an undirected graph G applies the ***backtracking*** technique and is analogous to wandering in a labyrinth with a string and a can of paint without getting lost. We begin at a specific starting vertex s in G, which we initialize by fixing one end of our string to s and painting s as "explored." The vertex s is now our "current" vertex—call our current vertex v. We then traverse G by considering an (arbitrary) edge (v, w) incident to the current vertex, v. If the edge (v, w) leads us to an already explored (that is, painted) vertex w, then we immediately backtrack to vertex v. If, on the other hand, (v, w) leads to an unexplored vertex, w, then we unroll our string, and go to w. We then paint w as "explored" and make it the current vertex, repeating the above computation. Eventually, we will get to a "dead end," that is, a current vertex, v, such that all the edges incident on v lead to vertices already explored. To get out of this impasse, we roll our string back up, backtracking along the edge that brought us to v, going back to a previously visited vertex, u. We then make u our current vertex and repeat the above computation for any edges incident upon u that we have not looked at before. If all of u's incident edges lead to visited vertices, then we again roll up our string and backtrack to the vertex we came from to get to u, and repeat the procedure at that vertex. Thus, we continue to backtrack along the path that we have traced so far until we find a vertex that has yet unexplored edges, at which point we take one such edge and continue the traversal. The process terminates when our backtracking leads us back to the start vertex, s, and there are no more unexplored edges incident on s. This simple process traverses the edges of G in an elegant, systematic way. (See Figure 13.5.)

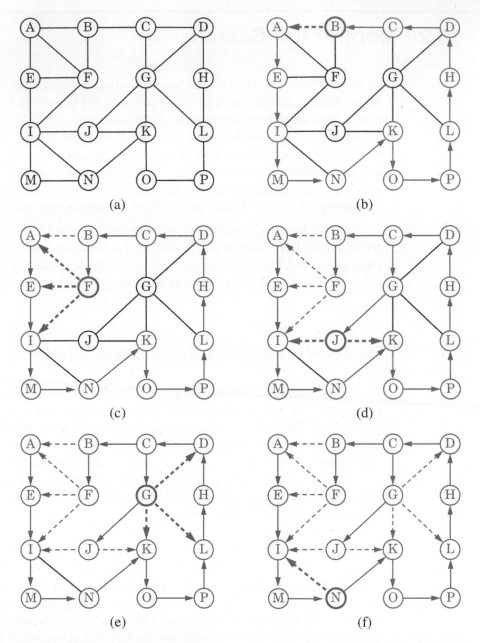

Figure 13.5: Example of depth-first search traversal on a graph starting at vertex A. Discovery edges are drawn with solid lines and back edges are drawn with dashed lines. The current vertex is drawn with a thick line: (a) input graph; (b) path of discovery edges traced from A until back edge (B,A) is hit; (c) reaching F, which is a dead end; (d) after backtracking to C, resuming with edge (C,G), and hitting another dead end, J; (e) after backtracking to G; (f) after backtracking to N.

Visualizing Depth-First Search

We can visualize a DFS traversal by orienting the edges along the direction in which they are explored during the traversal, distinguishing the edges used to discover new vertices, called *discovery edges*, or *tree edges*, from those that lead to already explored vertices, called *back edges*. (See Figure 13.5f.) In the analogy above, discovery edges are the edges where we unroll our string when we traverse them, and back edges are the edges where we immediately return without unrolling any string. The discovery edges form a spanning tree of the connected component of the starting vertex s, called *DFS tree*. We call the edges not in the DFS tree "back edges," because, assuming that the DFS tree is rooted at the start vertex, each such edge leads back from a vertex in this tree to one of its ancestors in the tree.

Recursive Depth-First Search

The pseudocode for a DFS traversal starting at a vertex v follows our analogy with string and paint based on the backtracking technique. We use recursion to implement this approach. We assume that we have a mechanism (similar to the painting analogy) to determine if a vertex or edge has been explored or not, and to label the edges as discovery edges or back edges.

A pseudocode description of recursive DFS is given in Algorithm 13.6.

Algorithm DFS(G, v):

    Input: A graph G and a vertex v in G

    Output: A labeling of the edges in the connected component of v as discovery edges and back edges, and the vertices in the connected component of v as explored

    Label v as explored
    for each edge, e, that is incident to v in G **do**
        if e is unexplored **then**
            Let w be the end vertex of e opposite from v
            if w is unexplored **then**
                Label e as a discovery edge
                DFS(G, w)
            else
                Label e as a back edge

Algorithm 13.6: A recursive description of the DFS algorithm for searching from a vertex, v.

13.3   Breadth-First Search

In this section, we consider the ***breadth-first search*** (BFS) traversal algorithm. Like DFS, BFS traverses a connected component of a graph, and in so doing, defines a useful spanning tree. Instead of searching recursively, however, BFS proceeds in rounds and subdivides the vertices into *levels*, which represent the minimum number of edges from the start vertex to each vertex.

BFS starts at a given start vertex, s, which is at level 0 and defines the "anchor" for our string. In the first round, we explore all the vertices we can reach in one edge, marking each as explored. These vertices are placed into level 1. In the second round, we explore all the vertices that can be reached in two edges from the start vertex. These new vertices, which are adjacent to level 1 vertices and not previously assigned to a level, are placed into level 2, and so on. The BFS traversal terminates when every vertex has been visited. Pseudo-code for a BFS traversal starting at a vertex s is shown in Algorithm 13.8. We use auxiliary space to label edges, mark visited vertices, and store lists associated with levels. That is, the lists L_0, L_1, L_2, and so on, store the nodes that are in level 0, level 1, level 2, and so on.

Algorithm BFS(G, s):

    Input: A graph G and a vertex s of G

    Output: A labeling of the edges in the connected component of s as discovery
        edges and cross edges

    Create an empty list, L_0

    Mark s as explored and insert s into L_0

    $i \leftarrow 0$

    while L_i is not empty **do**

        create an empty list, L_{i+1}

        for each vertex, v, in L_i **do**

            for each edge, $e = (v, w)$, incident on v in G **do**

                if edge e is unexplored **then**

                    if vertex w is unexplored **then**

                        Label e as a discovery edge

                        Mark w as explored and insert w into L_{i+1}

                  else

                    Label e as a cross edge

        $i \leftarrow i + 1$

Algorithm 13.8: BFS traversal of a graph.

We illustrate a BFS traversal in Figure 13.9.

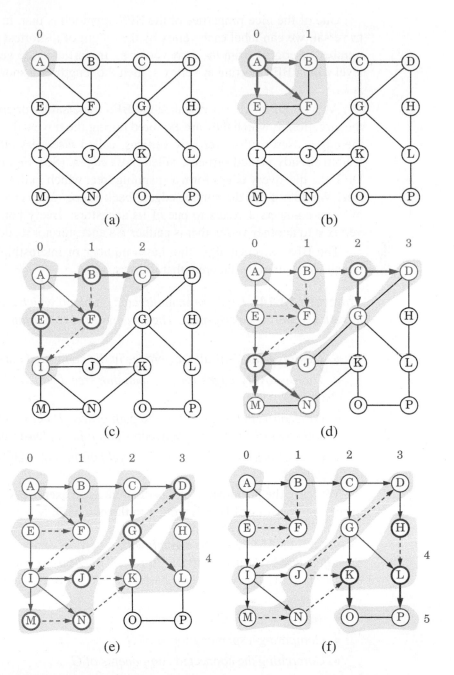

Figure 13.9: Example of breadth-first search traversal. The discovery edges are shown with solid lines and the cross edges are shown with dashed lines: (a) graph before the traversal; (b) discovery of level 1; (c) discovery of level 2; (d) discovery of level 3; (e) discovery of level 4; (f) discovery of level 5.

One of the nice properties of the BFS approach is that, in performing the BFS traversal, we can label each vertex by the length of a shortest path (in terms of the number of edges) from the start vertex s. In particular, if vertex v is placed into level i by a BFS starting at vertex s, then the length of a shortest path from s to v is i.

As with DFS, we can visualize the BFS traversal by orienting the edges along the direction in which they are explored during the traversal, and by distinguishing the edges used to discover new vertices, called ***discovery edges***, from those that lead to already visited vertices, called ***cross edges***. (See Figure 13.9f.) As with the DFS, the discovery edges form a spanning tree, which in this case we call the ***BFS tree***. We do not call the nontree edges "back edges" in this case, however, for none of them connects a vertex to one of its ancestors. Every nontree edge connects a vertex v to another vertex that is neither v's ancestor nor its descendant.

The BFS traversal algorithm has a number of interesting properties, some of which we state in the theorem that follows.

Theorem 13.14: *Let G be an undirected graph on which a BFS traversal starting at vertex s has been performed. Then we have the following:*

- *The traversal visits all the vertices in the connected component of s.*
- *The discovery edges form a spanning tree T of the connected component of s.*
- *For each vertex v at level i, the path of tree T between s and v has i edges, and any other path of G between s and v has at least i edges.*
- *If (u, v) is a cross edge, then the level numbers of u and v differ by at most 1.*

We leave the justification of this theorem as an exercise (C-13.17). The analysis of the running time of BFS is similar to the one of DFS.

Theorem 13.15: *Let G be a graph with n vertices and m edges represented with the adjacency list structure. A BFS traversal of G takes $O(n+m)$ time. Also, there exist $O(n+m)$-time algorithms based on BFS for the following problems:*

- *Testing whether G is connected*
- *Computing a spanning forest of G*
- *Computing the connected components of G*
- *Given a start vertex s of G, computing, for every vertex v of G, a path with the minimum number of edges between s and v, or reporting that no such path exists*
- *Computing a cycle in G, or reporting that G has no cycles.*

13.4 Directed Graphs

In this section, we consider issues that are specific to directed graphs. Recall that a directed graph, or *digraph*, is a graph that has only directed edges.

A fundamental issue with directed graphs is the notion of *reachability*, which deals with determining where we can get to in a directed graph. For example, in a graph whose vertices represent college courses and whose directed edges represent prerequisites, it is important to know which courses depend on a given other course as an explicit or implicit prerequisite. A traversal in a directed graph always goes along directed paths, that is, paths where all the edges are traversed according to their respective directions. Given vertices u and v of a digraph $\vec{G}$, we say that u *reaches* v (and v is *reachable* from u) if $\vec{G}$ has a directed path from u to v.

A digraph $\vec{G}$ is *strongly connected* if, for any two vertices u and v of $\vec{G}$, u reaches v and v reaches u. A *directed cycle* of $\vec{G}$ is a cycle where all the edges are traversed according to their respective directions. (Note that $\vec{G}$ may have a cycle consisting of two edges with opposite direction between the same pair of vertices.) A digraph $\vec{G}$ is *acyclic* if it has no directed cycles. (See Figure 13.10 for examples.)

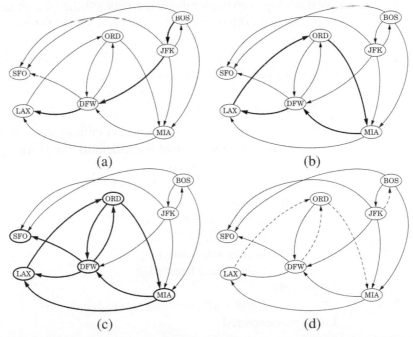

Figure 13.10: Examples of reachability in a digraph: (a) a directed path from BOS to LAX is drawn with thick lines; (b) a directed cycle (ORD, MIA, DFW, LAX, ORD) is drawn with thick lines; its vertices induce a strongly connected subgraph; (c) the subgraph of the vertices and edges reachable from ORD is shown with thick lines; (d) removing the dashed edges gives an acyclic digraph.

The ***transitive closure*** of a digraph, $\vec{G}$, is the digraph $\vec{G}^*$ such that the vertices of $\vec{G}^*$ are the same as the vertices of $\vec{G}$, and $\vec{G}^*$ has an edge (u, v), whenever $\vec{G}$ has a directed path from u to v. That is, we define $\vec{G}^*$ by starting with the digraph, $\vec{G}$, and adding in an extra edge (u, v), for each u and v such that v is reachable from u (and there isn't already an edge (u, v) in $\vec{G}$).

Interesting problems that deal with reachability in a digraph, $\vec{G}$, include finding all the vertices of $\vec{G}$ that are reachable from a given vertex s, determining whether $\vec{G}$ is strongly connected, determining whether $\vec{G}$ is acyclic, and computing the transitive closure $\vec{G}^*$ of $\vec{G}$.

13.4.1 Traversing a Digraph

As with undirected graphs, we can explore a digraph in a systematic way with slight modifications to the depth-first search (DFS) and breadth-first search (BFS) algorithms defined previously for undirected graphs (Sections 13.2 and 13.3). Such explorations can be used, for example, to answer reachability questions. The directed depth-first search and breadth-first search methods we develop in this section for performing such explorations are very similar to their undirected counterparts. In fact, the main difference is that the directed depth-first search and breadth-first search methods only traverse edges according to their respective directions. For instance, see Algorithm 13.11 for a possible extension of DFS to directed graphs (and see Exercise C-13.13 for another).

Algorithm DirectedDFS(G, v):

    Label v as active   // Every vertex is initially unexplored

    for each outgoing edge, e, that is incident to v in G **do**

        if e is unexplored **then**

            Let w be the destination vertex for e

            if w is unexplored and not active **then**

                Label e as a discovery edge

                DirectedDFS(G, w)

            else if w is active **then**

                Label e as a back edge

            else

                Label e as a forward/cross edge

    Label v as explored

Algorithm 13.11: A recursive description of the DirectedDFS algorithm for searching from a vertex, v.

We illustrate a directed version of DFS starting at a vertex, BOS, in Figure 13.12.

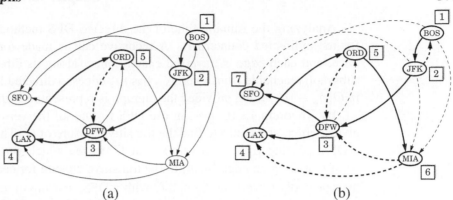

Figure 13.12: An example of a DFS in a digraph: (a) intermediate step, where, for the first time, an already visited vertex (DFW) is reached; (b) the completed DFS. The order in which the vertices are visited is indicated by a label next to each vertex. Discovery edges are shown with thick solid lines, back edges are shown with thick dashed lines, and forward edges are shown with thin dashed lines. For instance, (ORD,DFW) is a back edge and (DFW,ORD) is a forward edge. If there were an edge (SFO,LAX), it would be a cross edge.

A directed DFS on a digraph, $\vec{G}$, partitions the edges of $\vec{G}$ reachable from the starting vertex into *discovery edges* or *tree edges*, which lead us to discover a new vertex, and *nontree edges*, which take us to a previously visited vertex. The discovery edges form a tree rooted at the starting vertex, called the *directed DFS tree*. Also, we can distinguish three kinds of nontree edges (see Figure 13.12b):

- *back edges*, which connect a vertex to an ancestor in the DFS tree
- *forward edges*, which connect a vertex to a descendant in the DFS tree
- *cross edges*, which connect a vertex to a vertex that is neither its ancestor nor its descendant.

Theorem 13.16: *Let $\vec{G}$ be a digraph. Depth-first search on $\vec{G}$, starting at a vertex s, visits all the vertices of $\vec{G}$ that are reachable from s. Also, the DFS tree contains directed paths from s to every vertex reachable from s.*

Proof: Let V_s be the subset of vertices of $\vec{G}$ visited by DFS starting at vertex s. We want to show that V_s contains s and every vertex reachable from s belongs to V_s. Suppose, for the sake of a contradiction, that there is a vertex w reachable from s that is not in V_s. Consider a directed path from s to w, and let (u, v) be the first edge on such a path taking us out of V_s, that is, u is in V_s but v is not in V_s. When DFS reaches u, it explores all the outgoing edges of u, and thus must also reach vertex v via edge (u, v). Hence, v should be in V_s, and we have obtained a contradiction. Therefore, V_s must contain every vertex reachable from s. ∎

Analyzing the running time of the directed DFS method is analogous to that for its undirected counterpart. A recursive call is made for each vertex exactly once, and each edge is traversed exactly once (along its direction). Hence, if the subgraph reachable from a vertex s has m_s edges, a directed DFS starting at s runs in $O(n_s + m_s)$ time, provided the digraph is represented with an adjacency list.

By Theorem 13.16, we can use DFS to find all the vertices reachable from a given vertex, and hence to find the transitive closure of $\vec{G}$. That is, we can perform a DFS, starting from each vertex v of $\vec{G}$, to see which vertices w are reachable from v, adding an edge (v, w) to the transitive closure for each such w. Likewise, by repeatedly traversing digraph $\vec{G}$ with a DFS, starting in turn at each vertex, we can easily test whether $\vec{G}$ is strongly connected. Therefore, $\vec{G}$ is strongly connected if each DFS visits all the vertices of $\vec{G}$.

Theorem 13.17: *Let $\vec{G}$ be a digraph with n vertices and m edges. The following problems can be solved by an algorithm that runs in $O(n(n + m))$ time:*

- *Computing, for each vertex v of $\vec{G}$, the subgraph reachable from v*
- *Testing whether $\vec{G}$ is strongly connected*
- *Computing the transitive closure $\vec{G}^*$ of $\vec{G}$.*

Testing for Strong Connectivity

Actually, we can determine if a directed graph $\vec{G}$ is strongly connected much faster than $O(n(n + m))$ time, just using two depth-first searches. We begin by performing a DFS of our directed graph $\vec{G}$ starting at an arbitrary vertex s. If there is any vertex of $\vec{G}$ that is not visited by this DFS, and is not reachable from s, then the graph is not strongly connected. So, if this first DFS visits each vertex of $\vec{G}$, then we reverse all the edges of $\vec{G}$ (using the reverseDirection method) and perform another DFS starting at s in this "reverse" graph. If every vertex of $\vec{G}$ is visited by this second DFS, then the graph is strongly connected, for each of the vertices visited in this DFS can reach s. Since this algorithm makes just two DFS traversals of $\vec{G}$, it runs in $O(n + m)$ time.

Directed Breadth-First Search

As with DFS, we can extend breadth-first search (BFS) to work for directed graphs. A pseudocode description is essentially the same as that shown in Algorithm 13.8. The algorithm still visits vertices level by level and partitions the set of edges into *tree edges* (or *discovery edges*), which together form a directed *breadth-first search tree* rooted at the start vertex, and *nontree edges*. Unlike the directed DFS method, however, the directed BFS method only leaves two kinds of nontree edges:

- *back edges*, which connect a vertex to one of its ancestors
- *cross edges*, which connect a vertex to another vertex that is neither its ancestor nor its descendant.

Modifying BFS for Directed Graphs

Thus, the only change needed in order to modify the pseudocode description of BFS shown in Algorithm 13.8 to work for directed graphs is to label each nontree edge as a back/cross edge. We explore how to distinguish between back and cross nontree edges with respect to a directed BFS tree in Exercise C-13.11. There are no forward edges, which is a fact we explore in an exercise (C-13.12).

13.4.2 Transitive Closure

In this section, we explore an alternative technique for computing the transitive closure of a digraph. That is, we describe a direct method for determining all pairs of vertices (v, w) in a directed graph such that w is reachable from v. Such information is useful, for example, in computer networks, for it allows us to immediately know if we can route a message from a node v to a node w, or whether it is appropriate to say "you can't get there from here" with respect to this message.

The Floyd-Warshall Algorithm

Let $\vec{G}$ be a digraph with n vertices and m edges. We compute the transitive closure of $\vec{G}$ in a series of rounds. We initialize $\vec{G}_0 = \vec{G}$. We also arbitrarily number the vertices of $\vec{G}$ as

$$v_1, v_2, \ldots, v_n.$$

We then begin the computation of the rounds, beginning with round 1. In a generic round k, we construct digraph $\vec{G}_k$ starting with $\vec{G}_k = \vec{G}_{k-1}$ and adding to $\vec{G}_k$ the directed edge (v_i, v_j) if digraph $\vec{G}_{k-1}$ contains both the edges (v_i, v_k) and (v_k, v_j). In this way, we will enforce a simple rule embodied in the lemma that follows.

Lemma 13.18: *For $i = 1, \ldots, n$, digraph $\vec{G}_k$ has an edge (v_i, v_j) if and only if digraph $\vec{G}$ has a directed path from v_i to v_j, whose intermediate vertices (if any) are in the set $\{v_1, \ldots, v_k\}$. In particular, $\vec{G}_n$ is equal to $\vec{G}^*$, the transitive closure of $\vec{G}$.*

This lemma suggests a simple ***dynamic programming*** algorithm (Chapter 12) for computing the transitive closure of $\vec{G}$, which is known as the ***Floyd-Warshall algorithm***. Pseudo-code for this method is given in Algorithm 13.13.

Algorithm FloydWarshall($\vec{G}$):

   Input: A digraph $\vec{G}$ with n vertices

   Output: The transitive closure $\vec{G}^*$ of $\vec{G}$

   Let $v_1, v_2, \ldots, v_n$ be an arbitrary numbering of the vertices of $\vec{G}$

   $\vec{G}_0 \leftarrow \vec{G}$

   for $k \leftarrow 1$ **to** n **do**

      $\vec{G}_k \leftarrow \vec{G}_{k-1}$

      for $i \leftarrow 1$ **to** $n, i \neq k$ **do**

         for $j \leftarrow 1$ **to** $n, j \neq i, k$ **do**

            if both edges (v_i, v_k) and (v_k, v_j) are in $\vec{G}_{k-1}$ **then**

               if $\vec{G}_k$ does not contain directed edge (v_i, v_j) **then**

                  add directed edge (v_i, v_j) to $\vec{G}_k$

  return $\vec{G}_n$

Algorithm 13.13: The Floyd-Warshall algorithm. This dynamic programming algorithm computes the transitive closure $\vec{G}^*$ of G by incrementally computing a series of digraphs $\vec{G}_0, \vec{G}_1, \ldots, \vec{G}_n$, for $k = 1, \ldots, n$.

Analysis of the Floyd-Warshall Algorithm

The running time of the Floyd-Warshall algorithm is easy to analyze. The main loop is executed n times and the inner loop considers each of $O(n^2)$ pairs of vertices, performing a constant-time computation for each pair. If we use a data structure, such as the adjacency matrix structure, that supports methods areAdjacent and insertDirectedEdge in $O(1)$ time, we have that the total running time is $O(n^3)$. Thus, we have the following.

Theorem 13.19: *Let $\vec{G}$ be a digraph with n vertices represented by the adjacency matrix structure. The Floyd-Warshall algorithm computes the transitive closure $\vec{G}^*$ of $\vec{G}$ in $O(n^3)$ time.*

Let us now compare the running time of the Floyd-Warshall algorithm with that of the more complicated algorithm of Theorem 13.17, which repeatedly performs a DFS n times, starting at each vertex. If the digraph is represented by an adjacency matrix structure, then a DFS traversal takes $O(n^2)$ time (we explore the reason for this in an exercise). Thus, running DFS n times takes $O(n^3)$ time, which is no better than a single execution of the Floyd-Warshall algorithm.

If the digraph is represented by an adjacency list structure, then running the DFS algorithm n times would take $O(n(n + m))$ time. Even so, if the graph is *dense*, that is, if it has $\Theta(n^2)$ edges, then this approach still runs in $O(n^3)$ time.

Thus, the only case where the algorithm of Theorem 13.17 is better than the Floyd-Warshall algorithm is when the graph is not dense and is represented using an adjacency list structure.

We illustrate an example run of the Floyd-Warshall algorithm in Figure 13.14.

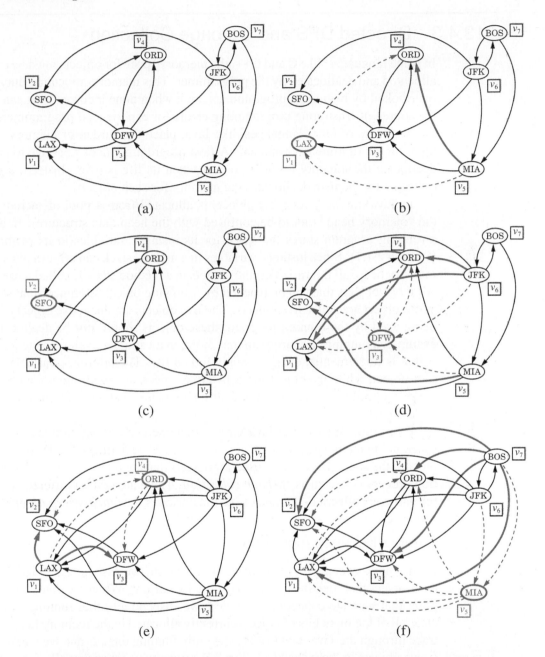

Figure 13.14: Sequence of digraphs computed by the Floyd-Warshall algorithm: (a) initial digraph $\vec{G} = \vec{G}_0$ and numbering of the vertices; (b) digraph $\vec{G}_1$; (c) $\vec{G}_2$; (d) $\vec{G}_3$; (e) $\vec{G}_4$; (f) $\vec{G}_5$. Note that $\vec{G}_5 = \vec{G}_6 = \vec{G}_7$. If digraph $\vec{G}_{k-1}$ has the edges (v_i, v_k) and (v_k, v_j), but not the edge (v_i, v_j), in the drawing of digraph $\vec{G}_k$, we show edges (v_i, v_k) and (v_k, v_j) with dashed thin lines, and edge (v_i, v_j) with a solid thick line.

13.4.3 Directed DFS and Garbage Collection

In some languages, like C and C++, the memory space for objects must be explicitly allocated and deallocated by the programmer. This memory-allocation duty is often overlooked by beginning programmers, and, when done incorrectly, it can even be the source of frustrating programming errors for experienced programmers. Thus, the designers of other languages, like Java, place the burden of memory management on the runtime environment. A Java programmer does not have to explicitly deallocate the memory for some object when its life is over. Instead, a *garbage collector* mechanism deallocates the memory for such objects.

In Java, memory for most objects is allocated from a pool of memory called the "memory heap" (not to be confused with the heap data structure). In addition, a running program stores the space for its instance variables in its method stack (Section 2.1.1). Since instance variables in a method stack can refer to objects in the memory heap, all the variables and objects in a method stack is called a *root object*. All those objects that can be reached by following object references that start from a root object are called *live objects*. The live objects are the active objects currently being used by the running program; these objects should *not* be deallocated. For example, a running Java program may store, in a variable, a reference to a sequence S that is implemented using a doubly linked list. The reference variable to S is a root object, while the object for S is a live object, as are all the node objects that are referenced from this object and all the elements that are referenced from these node objects.

From time to time, the Java virtual machine (JVM) may notice that available space in the memory heap is becoming scarce. At such times, the JVM can elect to reclaim the space that is being used for objects that are no longer live. This reclamation process is known as *garbage collection*. There are several different algorithms for garbage collection, but one of the most used is the *mark-sweep algorithm*.

The Mark-Sweep Algorithm

In the mark-sweep garbage collection algorithm, we associate a "mark" bit with each object that identifies if that object is live or not. When we determine at some point that garbage collection is needed, we suspend all other running threads and clear all of the mark bits of objects currently allocated in the memory heap. We then trace through the Java stacks of the currently running threads and we mark all of the (root) objects in these stacks as "live." We must then determine all of the other live objects—the ones that are reachable from the root objects. To do this efficiently, we should use the directed-graph version of the depth-first search traversal. In this case, each object in the memory heap is viewed as a vertex in a directed graph, and the reference from one object to another is viewed as an edge. By performing a directed DFS from each root object, we can correctly identify and mark each live object. This process is known as the "mark" phase. Once this process has completed, we then scan through the memory heap and reclaim any space that is being used for an object that has not been marked. This scanning process is known as the "sweep" phase, and when it completes, we resume running the suspended threads. Thus, the mark-sweep garbage collection algorithm will reclaim unused space in time proportional to the number of live objects and their references plus the size of the memory heap.

Performing DFS In-place

The mark-sweep algorithm correctly reclaims unused space in the memory heap, but there is an important issue we must face during the mark phase. Since we are reclaiming memory space at a time when available memory is scarce, we must take care not to use extra space during the garbage collection itself. The trouble is that the DFS algorithm, in the recursive way we have described it, can use space proportional to the number of vertices in the graph. In the case of garbage collection, the vertices in our graph are the objects in the memory heap; hence, we don't have this much memory to use. So our only alternative is to find a way to perform DFS in-place rather than recursively, that is, we must perform DFS using only a constant amount of additional storage.

The main idea for performing DFS in-place is to simulate the recursion stack using the edges of the graph (which in the case of garbage collection correspond to object references). Whenever we traverse an edge from a visited vertex v to a new vertex w, we change the edge (v, w) stored in v's adjacency list to point back to v's parent in the DFS tree. When we return back to v (simulating the return from the "recursive" call at w), we can now switch the edge we modified to point back to w. Of course, we need to have some way of identifying which edge we need to change back. One possibility is to number the references going out of v as 1, 2, and so on, and store, in addition to the mark bit (which we are using for the "visited" tag in our DFS), a count identifier that tells us which edges we have modified.

Using a count identifier of course requires an extra word of storage per object. This extra word can be avoided in some implementations, however. For example, many implementations of the Java virtual machine represent an object as a composition of a reference with a type identifier (which indicates if this object is an Integer or some other type) and as a reference to the other objects or data fields for this object. Since the type reference is always supposed to be the first element of the composition in such implementations, we can use this reference to "mark" the edge we changed when leaving an object v and going to some object w. We simply swap the reference at v that refers to the type of v with the reference at v that refers to w. When we return to v, we can quickly identify the edge (v, w) we changed, because it will be the first reference in the composition for v, and the position of the reference to v's type will tell us the place where this edge belongs in v's adjacency list. Thus, whether we use this edge-swapping trick or a count identifier, we can implement DFS in-place without affecting its asymptotic running time.

13.4.4   Directed Acyclic Graphs

A directed graph without cycles is referred to as a ***directed acyclic graph***, or ***dag***, for short. Applications of such graphs include the following:

- Inheritance between C++ classes or Java interfaces
- Prerequisites between courses of a degree program
- Scheduling constraints between the tasks of a project.

Example 13.20: *In order to manage a large project, it is convenient to break it up into a collection of smaller tasks. The tasks, however, are rarely independent, because scheduling constraints exist between them. (For example, in a house building project, the task of ordering nails obviously precedes the task of nailing shingles to the roof deck.) Clearly, scheduling constraints cannot have circularities, because a circularity would make the project impossible. (For example, in order to get a job you need to have work experience, but in order to get work experience you need to have a job.) The scheduling constraints impose restrictions on the order in which the tasks can be executed. Namely, if a constraint says that task a must be completed before task b is started, then a must precede b in the order of execution of the tasks. Thus, if we model a feasible set of tasks as vertices of a directed graph, and we place a directed edge from v to w whenever the task for v must be executed before the task for w, then we define a directed acyclic graph.*

The above example motivates the following definition. Let $\vec{G}$ be a digraph with n vertices. A ***topological ordering*** of $\vec{G}$ is an ordering $(v_1, v_2, \ldots, v_n)$ of the vertices of $\vec{G}$ such that for every edge (v_i, v_j) of $\vec{G}$, $i < j$. That is, a topological ordering is an ordering such that any directed path in $\vec{G}$ traverses vertices in increasing order. (See Figure 13.15.) Note that a digraph may have more than one topological ordering.

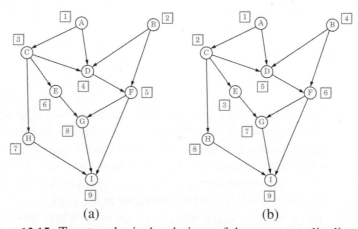

(a)   (b)

Figure 13.15: Two topological orderings of the same acyclic digraph.

Theorem 13.21: *A digraph has a topological ordering if and only if it is acyclic.*

Proof: The necessity (the "only if" part of the statement) is easy to demonstrate. Suppose $\vec{G}$ is topologically ordered. Assume, for the sake of a contradiction, that $\vec{G}$ has a cycle consisting of edges $(v_{i_0}, v_{i_1}), (v_{i_1}, v_{i_2}), \ldots, (v_{i_{k-1}}, v_{i_0})$. Because of the topological ordering, we must have $i_0 < i_1 < \cdots < i_{k-1} < i_0$, which is clearly impossible. Thus, $\vec{G}$ must be acyclic.

We now argue sufficiency (the "if" part). Suppose $\vec{G}$ is acyclic. We describe an algorithm to build a topological ordering for $\vec{G}$. Since $\vec{G}$ is acyclic, $\vec{G}$ must have a vertex with no incoming edges (that is, with in-degree 0). Let v_1 be such a vertex. Indeed, if v_1 did not exist, then in tracing a directed path from an arbitrary start vertex we would eventually encounter a previously visited vertex, thus contradicting the acyclicity of $\vec{G}$. If we remove v_1 from $\vec{G}$, together with its outgoing edges, the resulting digraph is still acyclic. Hence, the resulting digraph also has a vertex with no incoming edges, and we let v_2 be such a vertex. By repeating this process until $\vec{G}$ becomes empty, we obtain an ordering $v_1, \ldots, v_n$ of the vertices of $\vec{G}$. Because of the above construction, if (v_i, v_j) is an edge of $\vec{G}$, then v_i must be deleted before v_j can be deleted, and thus $i < j$. Thus, $v_1, \ldots, v_n$ is a topological ordering. ∎

The above proof suggests Algorithm 13.16, called *topological sorting*.

Algorithm TopologicalSort($\vec{G}$):
> *Input:* A digraph $\vec{G}$ with n vertices.
> *Output:* A topological ordering $v_1, \ldots, v_n$ of $\vec{G}$ or $\vec{G}$ has a cycle.
>
> Let S be an initially empty stack
> **for** each vertex u of $\vec{G}$ **do**
> > incounter(u) ← indeg(u)
> > **if** incounter(u) = 0 **then**
> > > S.push(u)
>
> $i \leftarrow 1$
> **while** S is not empty **do**
> > $u \leftarrow S$.pop()
> > number u as the i-th vertex v_i
> > $i \leftarrow i + 1$
> > **for** each edge $e \in \vec{G}$.outIncidentEdges(u) **do**
> > > $w \leftarrow \vec{G}$.opposite(u, e)
> > > incounter(w) ← incounter(w) − 1
> > > **if** incounter(w) = 0 **then**
> > > > S.push(w)
>
> **if** $i > n$ **then**
> > **return** $v_1, \cdots, v_n$
> **return** "digraph $\vec{G}$ has a directed cycle"

Algorithm 13.16: Topological sorting algorithm.

13.5 Biconnected Components

Let G be a connected undirected graph. A *separation edge* of G is an edge whose removal disconnects G. A *separation vertex* is a vertex whose removal disconnects G. Separation edges and vertices correspond to single points of failure in a network; hence, we often wish to identify them. A connected graph G is *biconnected* if, for any two vertices u and v of G, there are two disjoint paths between u and v, that is, two paths sharing no common edges or vertices, except u and v. A *biconnected component* of G is a subgraph satisfying one of the following (see Figure 13.19):

- A subgraph of G that is biconnected and for which adding any additional vertices or edges of G would force it to stop being biconnected
- A single edge of G consisting of a separation edge and its endpoints.

If G is biconnected, it has one biconnected component: G itself. If G has no cycles, on the other hand, then each edge of G is a biconnected component. Biconnected components are important in computer networks, where vertices represent routers and edges represent connections, for even if a router in a biconnected component fails, messages can still be routed in that component using the remaining routers.

As stated in the following lemma, whose proof is left as an exercise (C-13.5), biconnectivity is equivalent to the absence of separation vertices and edges.

Lemma 13.23: *Let G be a connected graph. The following are equivalent:*

1. *G is biconnected.*
2. *For any two vertices of G, there is a simple cycle containing them.*
3. *G does not have separation vertices or separation edges.*

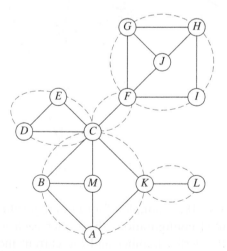

Figure 13.19: Biconnected components, shown circled with dashed lines. C, F, and K are separation vertices; (C, F) and (K, L) are separation edges.

Equivalence Classes and the Linked Relation

Any time we have a collection C of objects, we can define a Boolean relation, $R(x, y)$, for each pair x and y in C. That is, $R(x, y)$ is defined for each x and y in C as being either true or false. The relation R is an *equivalence relation* if it has the following properties:

- *Reflexive Property*: $R(x, x)$ is true for each x in C.
- *Symmetric Property*: $R(x, y) = R(y, x)$, for each pair x and y in C.
- *Transitive Property*: If $R(x, y)$ is true and $R(y, z)$ is true, then $R(x, z)$ is true, for every x, y, and z in C.

For example, the usual "equals" operator ($=$) is an equivalence relation for any set of numbers. The *equivalence class* for any object x in C is the set of all objects y, such that $R(x, y)$ is true. Note that any equivalence relation R for a set C partitions the set C into disjoint subsets that consist of the equivalence classes of the objects in C.

We can define an interesting *link relation* on the edges of a graph G. We say two edges e and f of G are *linked* if $e = f$ or G has a simple cycle containing both e and f. The following lemma gives fundamental properties of the link relation.

Lemma 13.24: *Let G be a connected graph. Then,*

1. *The link relation forms an equivalence relation on the edges of G.*
2. *A biconnected component of G is the subgraph induced by an equivalence class of linked edges.*
3. *An edge e of G is a separation edge if and only if e forms a single-element equivalence class of linked edges.*
4. *A vertex v of G is a separation vertex if and only if v has incident edges in at least two distinct equivalence classes of linked edges.*

Proof: It is readily seen that the link relation is reflexive and symmetric. To show that it is transitive, suppose that edges f and g are linked, and edges g and h are linked. If $f = g$ or $g = h$, then $f = h$ or there is a simple cycle containing f and h; hence, f and h are linked. Suppose, then, that f, g, and h are distinct. That is, there is a simple cycle C_{fg} through f and g, and there is a simple cycle C_{gh} through g and h. Consider the graph obtained by the union of cycles C_{fg} and C_{gh}. While this graph may not be a simple cycle itself (although we could have $C_{fg} = C_{gh}$), it contains a simple cycle C_{fh} through f and h. Thus, f and h are linked. Therefore, the link relation is an equivalence relation.

The correspondence between equivalence classes of the link relation and biconnected components of G is a consequence of Lemma 13.23.   ∎

A Linked Approach to Computing Biconnected Components via DFS

Since the equivalence classes of the link relation on the edges of G are the same as the biconnected components, by Lemma 13.24, to construct the biconnected components of G we need only compute the equivalence classes of the link relation among G's edges. To perform this computation, let us begin with a DFS traversal of G, and construct an ***auxiliary graph*** B as follows (see Figure 13.20):

- The vertices of B are the edges of G.
- For every back edge e of G, let $f_1, \ldots, f_k$ be the discovery edges of G that form a cycle with e. Graph B contains the edges $(e, f_1), \ldots, (e, f_k)$.

Since there are $m - n + 1$ back edges and each cycle induced by a back edge has at most $O(n)$ edges, the graph B has at most $O(nm)$ edges.

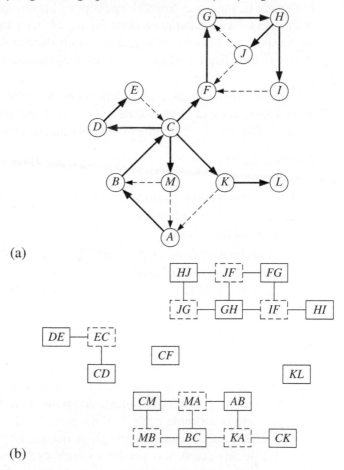

Figure 13.20: Auxiliary graph used to compute link components: (a) graph G on which a DFS traversal has been performed (the back edges are drawn with dashed lines); (b) auxiliary graph associated with G and its DFS traversal.

An $O(nm)$-Time Algorithm

From Figure 13.20, it appears that each connected component in B corresponds to an equivalence class in the link relation for the graph G. After all, we included an edge (e, f) in B for each back edge e found on the cycle containing f that was induced by e and the DFS spanning tree.

The following lemma, whose proof is left as an exercise (C-13.7), establishes a strong relationship between the graph B and the equivalence classes in the link relation on G's components of G, where, for brevity, we call the equivalence classes in the link relation the ***link components*** of G.

Lemma 13.25: *The connected components of the auxiliary graph B correspond to the link components of the graph G that induced B.*

Lemma 13.25 yields the following $O(nm)$-time algorithm for computing all the link components of a graph G with n vertices and m edges:

1. Perform a DFS traversal T on G.
2. Compute the auxiliary graph B by identifying the cycles of G induced by each back edge with respect to T.
3. Compute the connected components of B, for example, by performing a DFS traversal of the auxiliary graph B.
4. For each connected component of B, output the vertices of B (which are edges of G) as a link component of G.

From the identification of the link components in G, we can then determine the biconnected components, separation vertices, and separation edges of the graph G in linear time. Namely, after the edges of G have been partitioned into equivalence classes with respect to the link relation, the biconnected components, separation vertices, and separation edges of G can be identified in $O(n + m)$ time, using the simple rules listed in Lemma 13.24. Unfortunately, constructing the auxiliary graph B can take as much as $O(nm)$ time; hence, the bottleneck computation in this algorithm is the construction of B.

But note that we don't actually need all of the auxiliary graph B in order to find the biconnected components of G. We only need to identify the connected components in B. Thus, it would actually be sufficient if we were to simply compute a spanning tree for each connected component in B, that is, a spanning forest for B. Since the connected components in a spanning forest for B are the same as in the graph B itself, we don't actually need all the edges of B—just enough of them to construct a spanning forest of B.

Therefore, let us concentrate on how we can apply this more efficient spanning-forest approach to compute the equivalence classes of the edges of G with respect to the link relation.

A Linear-Time Algorithm

As outlined above, we can reduce the time required to compute the link components of G to $O(m)$ time by using an auxiliary graph of smaller size, which is a spanning forest of B. The algorithm is described in Algorithm 13.21.

Algorithm LinkComponents(G):

    Input: A connected graph G

    Output: The link components of G

Let F be an initially empty auxiliary graph.

Perform a DFS traversal of G starting at an arbitrary vertex s.

Add each DFS discovery edge f as a vertex in F and mark f "unlinked."

For each vertex v of G, let $p(v)$ be the parent of v in the DFS spanning tree.

for each vertex v, in increasing rank order as visited in the DFS traversal **do**

    for each back edge $e = (u, v)$ with destination v **do**

        Add e as a vertex of the graph F.

        // March up from u to s adding edges to F only as necessary.

        while $u \neq v$ **do**

            Let f be the vertex in F corresponding to the discovery edge $(u, p(u))$.

            Add the edge (e, f) to F.

            if f is marked "unlinked" **then**

                Mark f as "linked."

                $u \leftarrow p(u)$

            else

                $u \leftarrow v$ // shortcut to the end of the while loop

Compute the connected components of the graph F.

Algorithm 13.21: A linear-time algorithm for computing the link components. Note that a connected component in F consisting of an individual "unlinked" vertex corresponds to a separation edge (related only to itself in the link relation).

Let us analyze the running time of LinkComponents, from Algorithm 13.21. The initial DFS traversal of G takes $O(m)$ time. The main computation, however, is the construction of the auxiliary graph F, which takes time proportional to the number of vertices and edges of F. Note that at some point in the execution of the algorithm, each edge of G is added as a vertex of F. We use an accounting charge method to account for the edges of F. Namely, each time we add to F an edge (e, f), from a newly encountered back edge e to a discover edge f, let us charge this operation to f if f is marked "unlinked" and to e otherwise. From the construction of the inner while-loop, we see that we charge each vertex of F at most once during the algorithm using this scheme. We conclude that the construction of F takes $O(m)$ time. Finally, the computation of the connected components of F, which correspond to the link components of G, takes $O(m)$ time.

The correctness of the above algorithm follows from the fact that the graph F in LinkComponents is a spanning forest of the graph B mentioned in Lemma 13.25. For details, see Exercise C-13.8. Therefore, we summarize with the following theorem and give an example of LinkComponents in Figure 13.22.

Theorem 13.26: *Given a connected graph G with m edges, we can compute G's biconnected components, separation vertices, and separation edges in $O(m)$ time.*

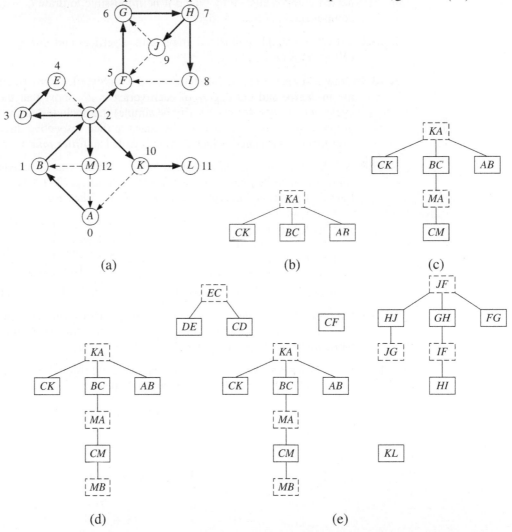

Figure 13.22: Sample execution of algorithm LinkComponents (Algorithm 13.21): (a) input graph G after a DFS traversal (the vertices are labeled by their rank in the visit order, and the back edges are drawn with dashed lines); auxiliary graph F after processing (b) back edge (K, A), (c) back edge (M, A), and (d) back edge $(M.B)$; (e) graph F at the end of the algorithm.

13.6 Exercises

Reinforcement

R-13.1 Draw a simple undirected graph G that has 12 vertices, 18 edges, and 3 connected components. Why would it be impossible to draw G with 3 connected components if G had 66 edges?

R-13.2 Let G be a simple connected graph with n vertices and m edges. Explain why $O(\log m)$ is $O(\log n)$.

R-13.3 Draw a simple connected directed graph with 8 vertices and 16 edges, such that the in-degree and out-degree of each vertex is 2. Show that there is a single cycle (which may not necessarily be simple) that includes all the edges of your graph, that is, you can trace all the edges in their respective directions without ever lifting your pencil. (Such a cycle is called an **Euler tour**.)

R-13.4 Bob loves foreign languages and wants to plan his course schedule to take the following nine language courses: LA15, LA16, LA22, LA31, LA32, LA126, LA127, LA141, and LA169. The course prerequisites are:

- LA15: (none)
- LA16: LA15
- LA22: (none)
- LA31: LA15
- LA32: LA16, LA31

- LA126: LA22, LA32
- LA127: LA16
- LA141: LA22, LA16
- LA169: LA32.

Find a sequence of courses that allows Bob to satisfy all the prerequisites.

R-13.5 Suppose we represent a graph G having n vertices with an adjacency matrix. Why, in this case, would inserting an undirected edge in G run in $O(1)$ time while inserting a new vertex would take $O(n^2)$ time?

R-13.6 Let G be a graph whose vertices are the integers 1 through 8, and let the adjacent vertices of each vertex be given by the table below:

vertex	adjacent vertices
1	(2, 3, 4)
2	(1, 3, 4)
3	(1, 2, 4)
4	(1, 2, 3, 6)
5	(6, 7, 8)
6	(4, 5, 7)
7	(5, 6, 8)
8	(5, 7)

Assume that, in a traversal of G, the adjacent vertices of a given vertex are returned in the same order as they are listed in the above table.

a. Draw G.

b. Order the vertices as they are visited in a DFS traversal starting at vertex 1.

c. Order the vertices as they are visited in a BFS traversal starting at vertex 1.

R-13.7 Would you use the adjacency list structure or the adjacency matrix structure in each of the following cases? Justify your choice.

    a. The graph has 10,000 vertices and 20,000 edges, and it is important to use as little space as possible.

    b. The graph has 10,000 vertices and 20,000,000 edges, and it is important to use as little space as possible.

    c. You need to answer the query areAdjacent as fast as possible, no matter how much space you use.

R-13.8 Explain why the DFS traversal runs in $\Theta(n^2)$ time on an n-vertex simple graph that is represented with the adjacency matrix structure.

R-13.9 Draw the transitive closure of the directed graph shown in Figure 13.2.

R-13.10 Compute a topological ordering for the vertices in the directed graph drawn with solid edges in Figure 13.10d.

R-13.11 Can we use a queue instead of a stack as an auxiliary data structure in the topological sorting algorithm shown in Algorithm 13.16?

R-13.12 Give the order in which the edges are labeled by the DFS traversal shown in Figure 13.5.

R-13.13 Give the order in which the edges are labeled by the BFS traversal shown in Figure 13.9.

R-13.14 Give the order in which the edges are labeled by the DFS traversal shown in Figure 13.12.

R-13.15 How many biconnected components would be in the graph shown in Figure 13.5a if we were to remove the edge (B,C) and the edge (N,K)?

Creativity

C-13.1 Justify Theorem 13.11.

C-13.2 Describe the details of an $O(n + m)$-time algorithm for computing all the connected components of an undirected graph G with n vertices and m edges.

C-13.3 Let T be the spanning tree rooted at the start vertex produced by the depth-first search of a connected, undirected graph, G. Argue why every edge of G, not in T, goes from a vertex in T to one of its ancestors, that is, it is a ***back edge***.

Hint: Suppose that such a nontree edge is a cross edge, and argue based upon the order the DFS visits the end vertices of this edge how this leads to a contradiction.

C-13.4 Suppose G is a graph with n vertices and m edges. Describe a way to represent G using $O(n + m)$ space so as to support in $O(\log n)$ time an operation that can test, for any two vertices v and w, whether v and w are adjacent.

C-13.5 Give a proof of Lemma 13.23.

C-13.6 Show that if a graph G has at least three vertices, then it has a separation edge only if it has a separation vertex.

C-13.7 Give a proof of Lemma 13.25.

C-13.8 Supply the details of the proof of correctness of the LinkComponents algorithm (Algorithm 13.21).

C-13.9 Show how to perform a BFS traversal using, as an auxiliary data structure, a single queue instead of the level containers $L_0, L_1, \ldots$.

C-13.10 Show that, if T is a BFS tree produced for a connected graph G, then, for each vertex v at level i, the path of T between s and v has i edges, and any other path of G between s and v has at least i edges.

C-13.11 The directed version of the BFS algorithm classifies nontree edges as being either back edges or cross edges, but it does not distinguish between these two types. Given a BFS spanning tree, T, for a directed graph, $\vec{G}$, and a set of nontree edges, E', describe an algorithm that can correctly label each edge in E' as being either a back edge or cross edge. Your algorithm should run in $O(n + m)$ time, where n is the number of vertices and m is the number of edges.

Hint: Consider first constructing an Euler tour traversal of the tree T.

C-13.12 Explain why there are no forward nontree edges with respect to a BFS tree constructed for a directed graph.

C-13.13 In the pseudocode description of the directed DFS traversal algorithm we did not distinguish the labeling of cross edges and forward edges. Describe how to modify the directed DFS algorithm so that it correctly labels each nontree edge as a back edge, forward edge, or cross edge.

C-13.14 Explain why the strong connectivity testing algorithm given in Section 13.4.1 is correct.

C-13.15 Let G be an undirected graph with n vertices and m edges. Describe an $O(n + m)$-time algorithm to determine whether G contains at least two cycles.

C-13.16 Let G be an undirected graph with n vertices and m edges. Describe an algorithm running in $O(n + m)$ time that can determine whether G contains exactly two cycles that have no edges in common.

C-13.17 Justify Theorem 13.14.

C-13.18 Show that it is possible to count the total number of paths in a directed acyclic graph, $\vec{G}$, with n vertices and m edges using $O(n + m)$ additions. Also, show that there is a graph, $\vec{G}$, where this number is at least $2^{n/2}$.

Applications

A-13.1 A *road network* is a mixed graph defined by the roads in a geographic region. Vertices in this graph are defined by road intersections and dead ends, and edges are defined by the portions of roads that connect such vertices. An edge is directed if its associated road is a one-way street; otherwise, an edge is undirected. Imagine that you are the manager of a post office delivery system, and that you need to map out the route that a postal worker should drive to deliver mail to all the houses on the roads in a given geographic region. Furthermore, suppose that all the streets in this region are one-way, so the road network for this region is a directed graph, $\vec{G}$. An ***Euler tour*** of such a directed graph, $\vec{G}$, is a cycle that traverses each edge of $\vec{G}$ exactly once according to its direction. Note that an Euler tour is necessarily the shortest route that starts at the post office (assuming it is one of the vertices in $\vec{G}$) and visits every street in the road network represented by $\vec{G}$ in the appropriate direction (where u-turns are allowed at a vertex with an outgoing edge going back to the origin of an incoming edge). Such a tour always exists if $\vec{G}$ is connected and the in-degree equals the out-degree of each vertex in $\vec{G}$. Describe an $O(n + m)$-time algorithm for finding an Euler tour of such a digraph, $\vec{G}$, if such a tour exists, starting from some vertex, v, where n is the number of vertices in $\vec{G}$ and m is the number of edges in $\vec{G}$.

A-13.2 Suppose you are given a connected road network, G, as described in the previous exercise, except that none of the edges in G are directed. Describe an efficient method for designing a tour of G that starts at some vertex, v, and traverses each edge of G exactly once in each direction (with u-turns allowed). What is the running time of your algorithm?

A-13.3 Suppose you work for a company that is giving a smartphone to each of its employees. Unfortunately, the companies that make apps for these smartphones are constantly suing each other over their respective intellectual property. Say that two apps, A and B, are ***litigation-conflicting*** if A contains some disputed technology that is also contained in B. Your job is to pre-install a set of apps on the company smartphones, but you have been asked by the company lawyers to avoid installing any litigation-conflicting apps. To make your job a little easier, these lawyers have given you a graph, G, whose vertices consist of all the possible apps you might want to install and whose edges consist of all the pairs of litigation-conflicting apps. An independent set of such an undirected graph, $G = (V, E)$, is a subset, I, of V, such that no two vertices in I are adjacent. That is, if $u, v \in I$, then $(u, v) \notin E$. A ***maximal independent set*** M is an independent set such that, if we were to add any additional vertex to M, then it would not be independent any longer. In the case of the graph, G, of litigation-conflicting apps, a maximal independent set in G corresponds to a set of nonconflicting apps such that if we were to add any other app to this set, it would conflict with at least one of the apps in the set. Give an efficient algorithm that computes a maximal independent set for a such a graph, G. What is the running time of your algorithm?

A-13.4 Tamarindo University and many other schools worldwide are doing a joint project on multimedia. A computer network is built to connect these schools using communication links that form a free tree. The schools decide to install a file server at one of the schools to share data among all the schools. Since the transmission time on a link is dominated by the link setup and synchronization, the cost of a data transfer is proportional to the number of links used. Hence, it is desirable to choose a "central" location for the file server. Given a free tree T and a node v of T, the *eccentricity* of v is the length of a longest path from v to any other node of T. A node of T with minimum eccentricity is called a *center* of T.

    a. Design an efficient algorithm that, given an n-node free tree T, computes a center of T.

    b. Is the center unique? If not, how many distinct centers can a free tree have?

A-13.5 The time delay of a long-distance call can be determined by multiplying a small fixed constant by the number of communication links on the telephone network between the caller and callee. Suppose the telephone network of a company named RT&T is a free tree. The engineers of RT&T want to compute the maximum possible time delay that may be experienced in a long-distance call. Given a free tree T, the *diameter* of T is the length of a longest path between two nodes of T. Give an efficient algorithm for computing the diameter of T.

A-13.6 A company named RT&T has a network of n stations connected by m high-speed communication links. Each customer's phone is connected to one station in his or her area. The engineers of RT&T have developed a prototype video-phone system that allows two customers to see each other during a phone call. In order to have acceptable image quality, however, the number of links used to transmit video signals between the two parties cannot exceed 4. Suppose that RT&T's network is represented by a graph. Design an efficient algorithm that computes, for each station, the set of stations it can reach using no more than 4 links.

A-13.7 Imagine that you are a medical practitioner for a developing country, Strategia, and it is your job to inoculate people in each village in Strategia so as to limit the ability of the Kissoba virus to spread in Strategia. The Kissoba virus can only be spread between two people if they kiss. For each village, you are given a *kissing* graph, G, whose vertices are the people in that village and whose edges are pairs of people who regularly kiss. Unfortunately, you don't have an unlimited supply of the Kissoba vaccine, and each shot is expensive. So the president of Strategia has asked that you limit the people you vaccinate to those who are *central* kissers, where a central kisser is a person, p, such that there are no two people, r and q, who are kissed by p such that there is a sequence of kissing pairs of people that starts with r and leads to q while avoiding p. Given a graph, G, representing the kissing graph for a village in Strategia, describe an efficient algorithm for identifying all the central kissers in G, and analyze its running time.

Chapter Notes

DFS is a part of the "folklore" of computer science, but Hopcroft and Tarjan [102, 205] showed how useful this algorithm is for solving several different graph problems. Knuth [129] discusses the topological sorting problem. The simple linear-time algorithm in Section 13.4.1 for determining if a directed graph is strongly connected is due to Kosaraju. The Floyd-Warshall algorithm appears in a paper by Floyd [72] and is based upon a theorem of Warshall [214]. The mark-sweep garbage collection method we describe is one of many different algorithms for performing garbage collection. We encourage the reader interested in further study of garbage collection to examine the book by Jones [114]. To learn about algorithms for drawing graphs, see the book by Di Battista *et al.* [55] and the handbook edited by Tamassia [203]. The reader interested in further study of graph algorithms is referred to the books by Ahuja, Magnanti, and Orlin [10], Cormen, Leiserson, and Rivest [50], Even [68], Gibbons [81], Mehlhorn [158], and Tarjan [207], and the book chapter by van Leeuwen [210]. For more applications of graph algorithms to social networks, see the book by Easley and Kleinberg [60].

Chapter

14

Shortest Paths

Lightning strike, 2009. U.S. government image. NOAA.

Contents

14.1 Single-Source Shortest Paths 399

14.2 Dijkstra's Algorithm 400

14.3 The Bellman-Ford Algorithm 407

14.4 Shortest Paths in Directed Acyclic Graphs 410

14.5 All-Pairs Shortest Paths 412

14.6 Exercises 418

In a *road network*, the interconnection structure of a set of roads is modeled as a graph whose vertices are intersections and dead ends in the set of roads, and edges are defined by segments of road that exists between pairs of such vertices. In such contexts, we often would like to find the shortest path that exists between two vertices in the road network. For example, such problems arise in GPS mapping contexts where we are interested in minimizing the driving distance between two points. Here, it typically would be inappropriate to consider one path shorter than another simply because it uses a fewer number of edges. Edges in a road network usually have varying lengths, and it can take longer to traverse some edges than it does others. Thus, edges in road networks have lengths, which represent some notion of distance for the edges, such as driving distance or driving time. Therefore, the length of a path in a road network is the sum of the lengths of the edges in that path, not the number of edges in the path.

In general, a *weighted graph* is a graph that has a numeric label, $w(e)$, associated with each edge, e, called the *weight* of edge e. Edge weights can be integers, rational numbers, or real numbers, which represent a concept such as distance, connection costs, or affinity. We explore in this chapter how to solve shortest path problems for weighted graphs, so as to solve such problems as finding optimal driving directions in road networks. We show an example of a weighted graph in Figure 14.1.

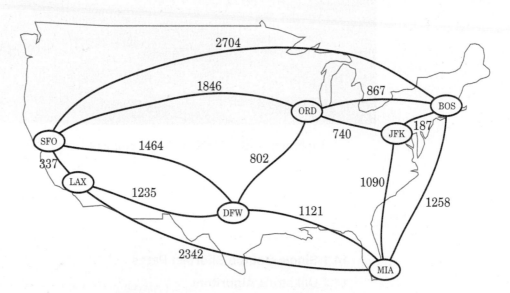

Figure 14.1: A weighted graph whose vertices represent major U.S. airports and whose edge weights represent distances in miles. This graph has a path from JFK to LAX of total weight 2,777 (going through ORD and DFW). This is the shortest path in the graph from JFK to LAX.

14.1 Single-Source Shortest Paths

Let G be a weighted graph. The *length* (or *weight*) of a path, P, in G, is the sum of the weights of the edges of P. That is, if P consists of edges, $e_0, e_1, \ldots, e_{k-1}$, then the length of P, denoted $w(P)$, is defined as

$$w(P) = \sum_{i=0}^{k-1} w(e_i).$$

The *distance* from a vertex v to a vertex u in G, denoted $d(v, u)$, is the length of a minimum length path (also called *shortest path*) from v to u, if such a path exists.

People often use the convention that $d(v, u) = +\infty$ if there is no path at all from v to u in G. Even if there is a path from v to u in G, the distance from v to u may not be defined, however, if there is a cycle in G whose total weight is negative. For example, suppose vertices in G represent cities, and the weights of edges in G represent how much money it costs to go from one city to another. If someone were willing to actually pay us to go from, say, JFK to ORD, then the "cost" of the edge (JFK,ORD) would be negative. If someone else were willing to pay us to go from ORD to JFK, then there would be a negative-weight cycle in G and distances would no longer be defined. That is, anyone can now build a path (with cycles) in G from any city A to another city B that first goes to JFK and then cycles as many times as he or she likes from JFK to ORD and back, before going on to B. The existence of such paths allows us to build arbitrarily low negative-cost paths (and in this case make a fortune in the process). But distances cannot be arbitrarily low negative numbers. Thus, any time we use edge weights to represent distances, we must be careful not to introduce any negative-weight cycles.

Suppose we are given a weighted graph G, and we are asked to find a shortest path from some vertex v to each other vertex in G, viewing the weights on the edges as distances. In the next few sections, we explore efficient ways of finding all such *single-source shortest paths*, if they exist.

The first algorithm we discuss is for the simple, yet common, case when all the edge weights in G are nonnegative (that is, $w(e) \geq 0$ for each edge e of G); hence, we know in advance that there are no negative-weight cycles in G. Recall that the special case of computing a shortest path when all weights are 1 was solved with the BFS traversal algorithm presented in Section 13.3. There is an interesting approach for solving this single-source shortest problem based on the *greedy method* (Chapter 10), which is known as Dijkstra's algorithm.

The second single-source algorithm we discuss, the Bellman-Ford algorithm, is for the case where edges can have negative weights, and it does not use a greedy strategy. The next single-source algorithm we consider also allows for negative-weight edges, but it is specialized for directed acyclic graphs and it is instead based on a greedy strategy.

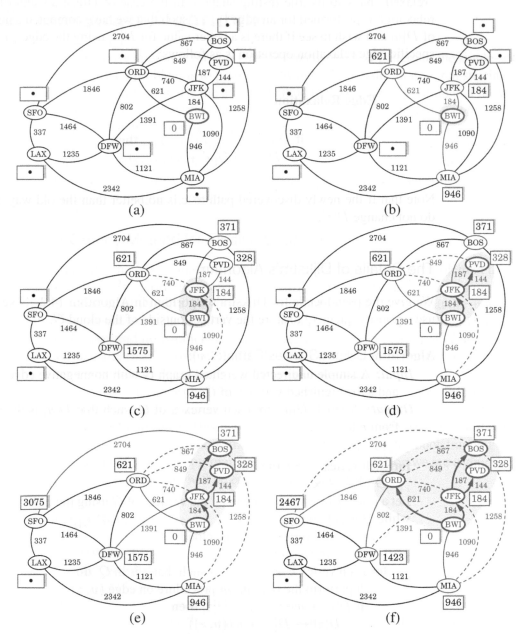

Figure 14.3: An execution of Dijkstra's algorithm on a weighted graph. The start vertex is BWI. A box next to each vertex u stores the label $D[u]$. The symbol • is used instead of $+\infty$. The edges of the shortest-path tree are drawn as thick arrows, and for each vertex u outside the "cloud" we show the current best edge for pulling in u with a solid line. (Continued in Figure 14.4.)

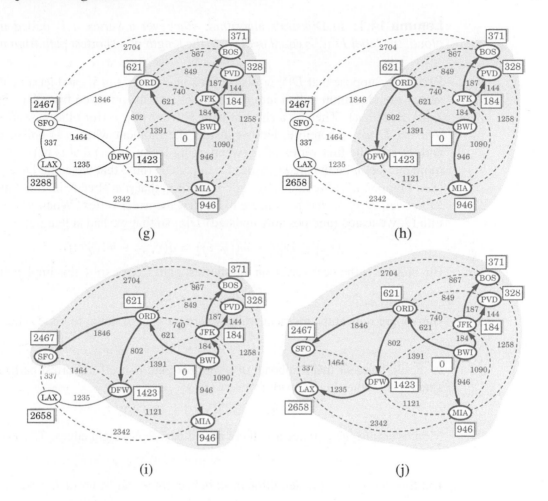

Figure 14.4: Visualization of Dijkstra's algorithm. (Continued from Figure 14.3.)

Why It Works

The interesting, and possibly even a little surprising, aspect of the Dijkstra algorithm is that, at the moment a vertex u is pulled into C, its label $D[u]$ stores the correct length of a shortest path from v to u. Thus, when the algorithm terminates, it will have computed the shortest-path distance from v to every vertex of G. That is, it will have solved the single-source shortest path problem.

It is probably not immediately clear why Dijkstra's algorithm correctly finds the shortest path from the start vertex v to each other vertex u in the graph. Why is it that the distance from v to u is equal to the value of the label $D[u]$ at the time vertex u is pulled into the cloud C (which is also the time u is removed from the priority queue Q)? The answer to this question depends on there being no negative-weight edges in the graph, for it allows the greedy method to work correctly, as we show in the lemma that follows.

Lemma 14.1: *In Dijkstra's algorithm, whenever a vertex u is pulled into the cloud, the label $D[u]$ is equal to $d(v, u)$, the length of a shortest path from v to u.*

Proof: Suppose that $D[t] > d(v, t)$ for some vertex t in V, and let u be the *first* vertex the algorithm pulled into the cloud C (that is, removed from Q), such that $D[u] > d(v, u)$. There is a shortest path P from v to u (for otherwise $d(v, u) = +\infty = D[u]$). Therefore, let us consider the moment when u is pulled into C, and let z be the first vertex of P (when going from v to u) that is not in C at this moment. Let y be the predecessor of z in path P (note that we could have $y = v$). (See Figure 14.5.) We know, by our choice of z, that y is already in C at this point. Moreover, $D[y] = d(v, y)$, since u is the *first* incorrect vertex. When y was pulled into C, we tested (and possibly updated) $D[z]$ so that we had at that point

$$D[z] \leq D[y] + w((y, z)) = d(v, y) + w((y, z)).$$

But since z is the next vertex on the shortest path from v to u, this implies that

$$D[z] = d(v, z).$$

But we are now at the moment when we are picking u, not z, to join C; hence,

$$D[u] \leq D[z].$$

It should be clear that a subpath of a shortest path is itself a shortest path. Hence, since z is on the shortest path from v to u,

$$d(v, z) + d(z, u) = d(v, u).$$

Moreover, $d(z, u) \geq 0$ because there are no negative-weight edges. Therefore,

$$D[u] \leq D[z] = d(v, z) \leq d(v, z) + d(z, u) = d(v, u).$$

But this contradicts the definition of u; hence, there can be no such vertex u.   ∎

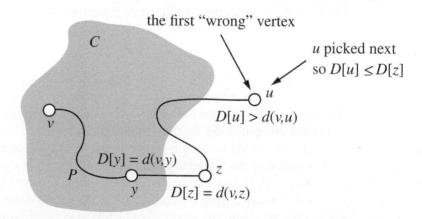

Figure 14.5: A schematic illustration for the justification of Lemma 14.1.

The Running Time of Dijkstra's Algorithm

Let us analyze the time complexity of Dijkstra's algorithm, where we use n and m to denote the number of vertices and edges of the input graph G, respectively. We assume that the edge weights can be added and compared in constant time. Because of the high level of the description we gave for Dijkstra's algorithm in Algorithm 14.2, analyzing its running time requires that we give more details on its implementation. Specifically, we should indicate the data structures used and how they are implemented.

Let us first assume that we are representing the graph G using an adjacency list structure. This data structure allows us to step through the vertices adjacent to u during the relaxation step in time proportional to their number. It still does not settle all the details for the algorithm, however, for we must say more about how to implement the other main data structure in the algorithm—the priority queue Q.

An efficient implementation of the priority queue Q uses a heap (see Section 5.3). This allows us to extract the vertex u with smallest D label, by calling the removeMin method, in $O(\log n)$ time. As noted in the pseudocode, each time we update a $D[z]$ label we need to update the key of z in the priority queue. If Q is implemented as a heap, then this key update can, for example, be done by first removing and then inserting z with its new key. The standard heap data structure doesn't normally support a removal method for arbitrary elements, however. Instead, it supports insertion of items given as key-value pairs and the repeated removal of an item with smallest key. We can extend our priority queue implementation to support a removal operation, however, by using the locator concept described in Section 5.5. In Dijkstra's algorithm, this approach is roughly equivalent to our maintaining a pointer with each vertex, v, that supports constant-time access to the node in our heap that is holding v. Given a pointer to this node, we can remove v or update its key and perform the associated up-heap or down-heap bubbling as needed in $O(\log n)$ time.

Assuming this implementation of Q, implies that Dijkstra's algorithm runs in $O((n + m) \log n)$ time. Referring back to Algorithm 14.2, the details of this analysis are as follows:

- Inserting all the vertices in Q with their initial key value can be done in $O(n \log n)$ time by repeated insertions, or in $O(n)$ time using bottom-up heap construction (see Section 5.4).
- At each iteration of the **while** loop, we spend $O(\log n)$ time to remove vertex u from Q, and $O(\deg(v) \log n)$ time to perform the relaxation procedure on the edges incident on u.
- The overall running time of the **while** loop is

$$\sum_{v \in G} (1 + \deg(v)) \log n,$$

which is $O((n + m) \log n)$ by Theorem 13.6.

Thus, we can implement Dijkstra's algorithm in $O(m \log n)$ time, but this is not the only way to implement this algorithm. There is an alternative implementation of Dijkstra's algorithm based on implementing the priority queue, Q, using an unsorted doubly linked list. This, of course, requires that we spend $O(n)$ time to remove the item with minimum key, but it allows for very fast key updates, provided Q supports use of the locator pattern or something like it. That is, we would need to support constant-time access from any vertex, v, to the node in the linked list for Q that is holding v. For example, maintaining a pointer for each vertex, v, to the node in Q that is holding v would suffice for this purpose.

This approach would allow us to implement each key update done in a relaxation step in $O(1)$ time, since we could simply change the key value once we locate the item in Q to update. Hence, this implementation results in a running time that is $O(n^2 + m)$, which can be simplified to $O(n^2)$, since G is simple.

Thus, we have at least two choices for implementing the priority queue in Dijkstra's algorithm. The two implementations we explored above are a locator-based heap implementation, which yields an algorithm with an $O(m \log n)$ running time, and a locator-based unsorted sequence implementation, which yields an $O(n^2)$-time algorithm. (In addition, we explore yet another way of implementing Dijkstra's algorithm in Exercise C-14.3, which avoids the use of locators.) Thus, we have the following.

Theorem 14.2: *Given a simple weighted graph G with n vertices and m edges, such that the weight of each edge is nonnegative, and a vertex v of G, Dijkstra's algorithm computes the distance from v to all other vertices of G in $O(m \log n)$ time, or, alternatively, in $O(n^2)$ time.*

In Exercise R-14.3, we explore how to modify Dijkstra's algorithm to output a tree T rooted at v, such that the path in T from v to a vertex u is a shortest path in G from v to u. In addition, extending Dijkstra's algorithm for directed graphs is fairly straightforward. We cannot extend Dijkstra's algorithm to work on graphs with negative-weight edges, however, as Figure 14.6 illustrates.

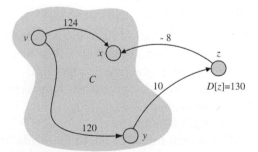

Figure 14.6: An illustration of why Dijkstra's algorithm fails for graphs with negative-weight edges. Bringing z into C and performing edge relaxations will invalidate the previously computed shortest-path distance (124) to x.

14.3 The Bellman-Ford Algorithm

There is another algorithm, which is due to Bellman and Ford, that can find shortest paths in graphs that have negative-weight edges. We must, in this case, insist that the graph be directed, for otherwise any negative-weight undirected edge would immediately imply a negative-weight cycle, where we traverse this edge back and forth in each direction. We cannot allow such edges, since a negative cycle invalidates the notion of distance based on edge weights.

Let $\vec{G}$ be a weighted directed graph, possibly with some negative-weight edges. The Bellman-Ford algorithm for computing the shortest-path distance from some vertex v in $\vec{G}$ to every other vertex in $\vec{G}$ is very simple. It shares the notion of edge relaxation from Dijkstra's algorithm, but does not use it in conjunction with the greedy method (which would not work in this context; see Exercise C-14.2). That is, as in Dijkstra's algorithm, the Bellman-Ford algorithm uses a label $D[u]$ that is always an upper bound on the distance $d(v, u)$ from v to u, and is iteratively "relaxed" until it exactly equals this distance.

The Bellman-Ford method is shown in Algorithm 14.7. It performs $n - 1$ times a relaxation of every edge in the digraph. We illustrate an execution of the Bellman-Ford algorithm in Figure 14.8.

Algorithm BellmanFordShortestPaths($\vec{G}, v$):

> ***Input:*** A weighted directed graph $\vec{G}$ with n vertices, and a vertex v of $\vec{G}$
>
> ***Output:*** A label $D[u]$, for each vertex u of $\vec{G}$, such that $D[u]$ is the distance from v to u in $\vec{G}$, or an indication that $\vec{G}$ has a negative-weight cycle
>
> $D[v] \leftarrow 0$
> **for** each vertex $u \neq v$ of $\vec{G}$ **do**
> > $D[u] \leftarrow +\infty$
>
> **for** $i \leftarrow 1$ to $n - 1$ **do**
> > **for** each (directed) edge (u, z) outgoing from u **do**
> > > // Perform the ***relaxation*** operation on (u, z)
> > > **if** $D[u] + w((u, z)) < D[z]$ **then**
> > > > $D[z] \leftarrow D[u] + w((u, z))$
>
> **if** there are no edges left with potential relaxation operations **then**
> > **return** the label $D[u]$ of each vertex u
>
> **else**
> > **return** "$\vec{G}$ contains a negative-weight cycle"

Algorithm 14.7: The Bellman-Ford single-source shortest-path algorithm.

Lemma 14.3: *If, at the end of the execution of Algorithm 14.7, there is an edge (u, z) such that $D[u] + w((u, z)) < D[z]$, then the input digraph, $\vec{G}$, contains a negative-weight cycle. Otherwise, $D[u] = d(v, u)$ for each vertex u in $\vec{G}$.*

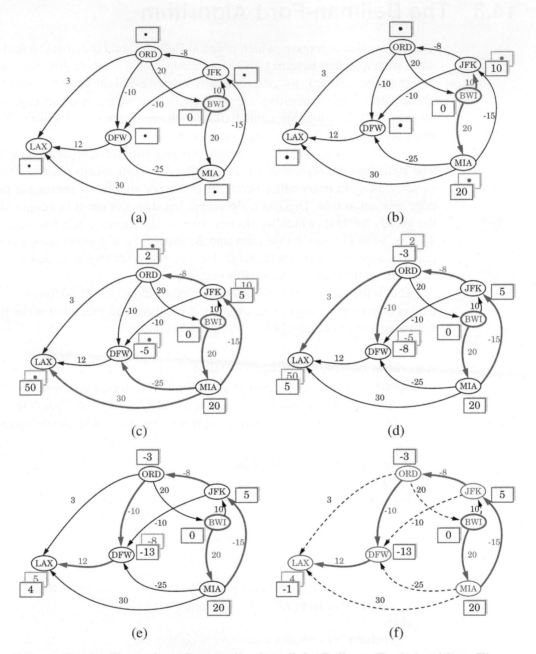

Figure 14.8: An illustration of an application of the Bellman-Ford algorithm. The start vertex is BWI. A box next to each vertex u stores the label $D[u]$, with "shadows" showing values revised during relaxations; the thick edges are causing such relaxations.

Proof: For the sake of this proof, let us introduce a new notion of distance in a digraph. Specifically, let $d_i(v, u)$ denote the length of a path from v to u that is shortest among all paths from v to u that contain at most i edges. We call $d_i(v, u)$ the *i-edge distance* from v to u. We claim that after iteration i of the main for-loop in the Bellman-Ford algorithm $D[u] = d_i(v, u)$ for each vertex in $\vec{G}$. This is certainly true before we even begin the first iteration, for $D[v] = 0 = d_0(v, v)$ and, for $u \neq v$, $D[u] = +\infty = d_0(v, u)$. Suppose this claim is true before iteration i (we will now show that if this is the case, then this claim will be true after iteration i as well). In iteration i, we perform a relaxation step for every edge in the digraph. The i-edge distance $d_i(v, u)$, from v to a vertex u, is determined in one of two ways. Either $d_i(v, u) = d_{i-1}(v, u)$ or $d_i(v, u) = d_{i-1}(v, z) + w((z, u))$ for some vertex z in $\vec{G}$. Because we do a relaxation for *every* edge of $\vec{G}$ in iteration i, if it is the former case, then after iteration i we have $D[u] = d_{i-1}(v, u) = d_i(v, u)$, and if it is the latter case, then after iteration i we have $D[u] = D[z] + w((z, u)) = d_{i-1}(v, z) + w((z, u)) = d_i(v, u)$. Thus, if $D[u] = d_{i-1}(v, u)$ for each vertex u before iteration i, then $D[u] = d_i(v, u)$ for each vertex u after iteration i.

Therefore, after $n - 1$ iterations, $D[u] = d_{n-1}(v, u)$ for each vertex u in $\vec{G}$. Now observe that if there is still an edge in $\vec{G}$ that can be relaxed, then there is some vertex u in $\vec{G}$, such that the n-edge distance from v to u is less than the $(n - 1)$-edge distance from v to u, that is, $d_n(v, u) < d_{n-1}(v, u)$. But there are only n vertices in $\vec{G}$; hence, if there is a shortest n-edge path from v to u, it must repeat some vertex z in $\vec{G}$ twice. That is, it must contain a cycle. Moreover, since the distance from a vertex to itself using zero edges is 0 (that is, $d_0(z, z) = 0$), this cycle must be a negative-weight cycle. Thus, if there is an edge in $\vec{G}$ that can still be relaxed after running the Bellman-Ford algorithm, then $\vec{G}$ contains a negative-weight cycle. If, on the other hand, there is no edge in $\vec{G}$ that can still be relaxed after running the Bellman-Ford algorithm, then $\vec{G}$ does not contain a negative-weight cycle. Moreover, in this case, every shortest path between two vertices will have at most $n - 1$ edges; hence, for each vertex u in $\vec{G}$, $D[u] = d_{n-1}(v, u) = d(v, u)$. ■

Thus, the Bellman-Ford algorithm is correct and even gives us a way of telling when a digraph contains a negative-weight cycle. The running time of the Bellman-Ford algorithm is easy to analyze. We perform the main for-loop $n - 1$ times, and each such loop involves spending $O(1)$ time for each edge in $\vec{G}$. Therefore, the running time for this algorithm is $O(nm)$. We summarize as follows:

Theorem 14.4: *Given a weighted directed graph $\vec{G}$ with n vertices and m edges, and a vertex v of $\vec{G}$, the Bellman-Ford algorithm computes the distance from v to all other vertices of G or determines that $\vec{G}$ contains a negative-weight cycle in $O(nm)$ time.*

14.4   Shortest Paths in Directed Acyclic Graphs

As mentioned above, both Dijkstra's algorithm and the Bellman-Ford algorithm work for directed graphs. We can solve the single-source shortest paths problem faster than these algorithms can, however, if the digraph has no directed cycles, that is, it is a weighted directed acyclic graph (DAG).

Recall from Section 13.4.4 that a topological ordering of a DAG $\vec{G}$ is a listing of its vertices $(v_1, v_2, \ldots, v_n)$, such that if (v_i, v_j) is an edge in $\vec{G}$, then $i < j$. Also, recall that we can use the depth-first search algorithm to compute a topological ordering of the n vertices in an m-edge DAG $\vec{G}$ in $O(n+m)$ time. Interestingly, given a topological ordering of such a weighted DAG $\vec{G}$, we can compute all shortest paths from a given vertex v in $O(n + m)$ time.

The method, which is given in Algorithm 14.9, involves visiting the vertices of $\vec{G}$ according to the topological ordering, relaxing the outgoing edges with each visit.

Algorithm DAGShortestPaths($\vec{G}, s$):
  Input: A weighted directed acyclic graph (DAG) $\vec{G}$ with n vertices and m
       edges, and a distinguished vertex s in $\vec{G}$
  Output: A label $D[u]$, for each vertex u of $\vec{G}$, such that $D[u]$ is the distance
       from v to u in $\vec{G}$

  Compute a topological ordering $(v_1, v_2, \ldots, v_n)$ for $\vec{G}$
  $D[s] \leftarrow 0$
  for each vertex $u \neq s$ of $\vec{G}$ **do**
      $D[u] \leftarrow +\infty$
  for $i \leftarrow 1$ to $n - 1$ **do**
      // Relax each outgoing edge from v_i
      for each edge (v_i, u) outgoing from v_i **do**
          if $D[v_i] + w((v_i, u)) < D[u]$ **then**
              $D[u] \leftarrow D[v_i] + w((v_i, u))$
  Output the distance labels D as the distances from s.

Algorithm 14.9: Shortest-path algorithm for a directed acyclic graph.

The running time of the shortest-path algorithm for a DAG is easy to analyze. Assuming the digraph is represented using an adjacency list, we can process each vertex in constant time plus an additional time proportional to the number of its outgoing edges. In addition, we have already observed that computing the topological ordering of the vertices in $\vec{G}$ can be done in $O(n + m)$ time. Thus, the entire algorithm runs in $O(n + m)$ time. We illustrate this algorithm in Figure 14.10.

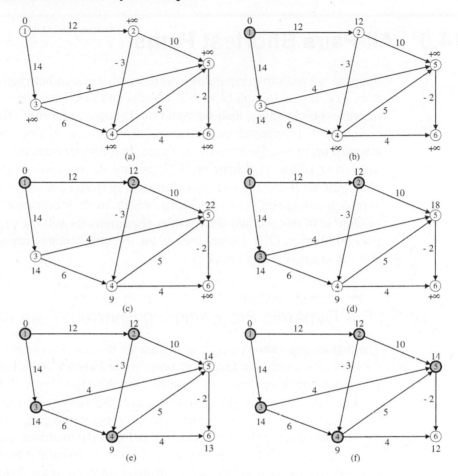

Figure 14.10: An illustration of the shortest-path algorithm for a DAG.

Theorem 14.5: DAGShortestPaths *computes the distance from a start vertex s to each other vertex in a directed n-vertex graph $\vec{G}$ with m edges in $O(n+m)$ time.*

Proof: Suppose, for the sake of a contradiction, that v_i is the first vertex in the topological ordering such that $D[v_i]$ is not the distance from s to v_i. First, note that $D[v_i] < +\infty$, for the initial D value for each vertex other than s is $+\infty$ and the value of a D label is only ever lowered if a path from s is discovered. Thus, if $D[v_j] = +\infty$, then v_j is unreachable from s. Therefore, v_i is reachable from s, so there is a shortest path from s to v_i. Let v_k be the penultimate vertex on a shortest path from s to v_i. Since the vertices are numbered according to a topological ordering, we have that $k < i$. Thus, $D[v_k]$ is correct (we may possibly have $v_k = s$). But when v_k is processed, we relax each outgoing edge from v_k, including the edge on the shortest path from v_k to v_i. Thus, $D[v_i]$ is assigned the distance from s to v_i. But this contradicts the definition of v_i; hence, no such vertex v_i can exist. ∎

14.5   All-Pairs Shortest Paths

Suppose we wish to compute the shortest-path distance between every pair of vertices in a directed graph $\vec{G}$ with n vertices and m edges. Of course, if $\vec{G}$ has no negative-weight edges, then we could run Dijkstra's algorithm from each vertex in $\vec{G}$ in turn. This approach would take $O(n(n + m) \log n)$ time, assuming $\vec{G}$ is represented using an adjacency list structure. In the worst case, this bound could be as large as $O(n^3 \log n)$. Likewise, if $\vec{G}$ contains no negative-weight cycles, then we could run the Bellman-Ford algorithm starting from each vertex in $\vec{G}$ in turn. This approach would run in $O(n^2 m)$ time, which, in the worst case, could be as large as $O(n^4)$. In this section, we consider algorithms for solving the all-pairs shortest path problem in $O(n^3)$ time, even if the digraph contains negative-weight edges (but not negative-weight cycles).

14.5.1   A Dynamic Programming Shortest-Path Algorithm

The first all-pairs shortest-path algorithm we discuss is a variation on an algorithm we have given earlier in this book, namely, the Floyd-Warshall algorithm for computing the transitive closure of a directed graph (Algorithm 13.13).

Let $\vec{G}$ be a given weighted directed graph. We number the vertices of $\vec{G}$ arbitrarily as $(v_1, v_2, \ldots, v_n)$. As in any dynamic programming algorithm (Chapter 12), the key construct in the algorithm is to define a parametrized cost function that is easy to compute and also allows us to ultimately compute a final solution. In this case, we use the cost function, $D_{i,j}^k$, which is defined as the distance from v_i to v_j using only intermediate vertices in the set $\{v_1, v_2, \ldots, v_k\}$. Initially,

$$D_{i,j}^0 = \begin{cases} 0 & \text{if } i = j \\ w((v_i, v_j)) & \text{if } (v_i, v_j) \text{ is an edge in } \vec{G} \\ +\infty & \text{otherwise.} \end{cases}$$

Given this parametrized cost function $D_{i,j}^k$, and its initial value $D_{i,j}^0$, we can then easily define the value for an arbitrary $k > 0$ as

$$D_{i,j}^k = \min\{D_{i,j}^{k-1}, D_{i,k}^{k-1} + D_{k,j}^{k-1}\}.$$

In other words, the cost for going from v_i to v_j using vertices numbered 1 through k is equal to the shorter of two possible paths. The first path is simply the shortest path from v_i to v_j using vertices numbered 1 through $k - 1$. The second path is the sum of the costs of the shortest path from v_i to v_k using vertices numbered 1 through $k - 1$ and the shortest path from v_k to v_j using vertices numbered 1 through $k - 1$. Moreover, there is no other shorter path from v_i to v_j using vertices of $\{v_1, v_2, \ldots, v_k\}$ than these two. If there was such a shorter path and it excluded v_k, then it would violate the definition of $D_{i,j}^{k-1}$, and if there was such a shorter

Algorithm AllPairsShortestPaths($\vec{G}$):

    Input: A simple weighted directed graph $\vec{G}$ without negative-weight cycles

    Output: A numbering $v_1, v_2, \ldots, v_n$ of the vertices of $\vec{G}$ and a matrix D, such that $D[i, j]$ is the distance from v_i to v_j in $\vec{G}$

    let $v_1, v_2, \ldots, v_n$ be an arbitrary numbering of the vertices of $\vec{G}$

    for $i \leftarrow 1$ **to** n **do**

        for $j \leftarrow 1$ **to** n **do**

            if $i = j$ **then**

                $D^0[i, i] \leftarrow 0$

            if (v_i, v_j) is an edge in $\vec{G}$ **then**

                $D^0[i, j] \leftarrow w((v_i, v_j))$

            else

                $D^0[i, j] \leftarrow +\infty$

    for $k \leftarrow 1$ **to** n **do**

        for $i \leftarrow 1$ **to** n **do**

            for $j \leftarrow 1$ **to** n **do**

                $D^k[i, j] \leftarrow \min\{D^{k-1}[i, j], D^{k-1}[i, k] + D^{k-1}[k, j]\}$

    return matrix D^n

Algorithm 14.11: A dynamic programming algorithm to compute all-pairs shortest-path distances in a digraph without negative cycles.

path and it included v_k, then it would violate the definition of $D_{i,k}^{k-1}$ or $D_{k,j}^{k-1}$. In fact, note that this argument still holds even if there are negative cost edges in $\vec{G}$, just so long as there are no negative cost cycles. In Algorithm 14.11, we show how this cost-function definition allows us to build an efficient solution to the all-pairs shortest path problem. The running time for this dynamic programming algorithm is clearly $O(n^3)$, which implies the following.

Theorem 14.6: *Given a simple weighted directed graph $\vec{G}$ with n vertices and no negative-weight cycles, Algorithm 14.11 (*AllPairsShortestPaths*) computes the shortest-path distances between each pair of vertices of $\vec{G}$ in $O(n^3)$ time.*

14.5.2 Computing Shortest Paths via Matrix Multiplication

We can view the problem of computing the shortest-path distances for all pairs of vertices in a directed graph $\vec{G}$ as a matrix problem. In this subsection, we describe how to solve the all-pairs shortest-path problem in $O(n^3)$ time using this approach. We first describe how to use this approach to solve the all-pairs problem in $O(n^4)$ time, and then we show how this can be improved to $O(n^3)$ time by studying the problem in more depth. This matrix-multiplication approach to shortest paths is especially useful in contexts where we represent graphs using the adjacency matrix data structure.

The Weighted Adjacency Matrix Representation

Let us number the vertices of $\vec{G}$ as $(v_0, v_1, \ldots, v_{n-1})$, returning to the convention of numbering the vertices starting at index 0. Given this numbering of the vertices of $\vec{G}$, there is a natural weighted view of the adjacency matrix representation for a graph, where we define $A[i, j]$ as follows:

$$A[i,j] = \begin{cases} 0 & \text{if } i = j \\ w((v_i, v_j)) & \text{if } (v_i, v_j) \text{ is an edge in } \vec{G} \\ +\infty & \text{otherwise.} \end{cases}$$

(Note that this is the same definition used for the cost function $D_{i,j}^0$ from the previous subsection.)

Shortest Paths and Matrix Multiplication

In other words, $A[i, j]$ stores the shortest-path distance from v_i to v_j using one or fewer edges in the path. Let us therefore use the matrix A to define another matrix A^2, such that $A^2[i, j]$ stores the shortest-path distance from v_i to v_j using at most two edges. A path with at most two edges is either empty (a zero-edge path) or it adds an extra edge to a zero-edge or one-edge path. Therefore, we can define $A^2[i, j]$ as

$$A^2[i,j] = \min_{l=0,1,\ldots,n-1} \{A[i,l] + A[l,j]\}.$$

Thus, given A, we can compute the matrix A^2 in $O(n^3)$ time, by using an algorithm very similar to the standard matrix multiplication algorithm.

In fact, we can view this computation as a matrix multiplication in which we have simply redefined what the operators "plus" and "times" mean in the matrix multiplication algorithm (the programming language C++ specifically allows for such operator overloading). If we let "plus" be redefined to mean "min" and we let "times" be redefined to mean "+," then we can write $A^2[i, j]$ as a true matrix multiplication:

$$A^2[i,j] = \sum_{l=0,1,\ldots,n-1} A[i,l] \cdot A[l,j].$$

Indeed, this matrix-multiplication viewpoint is the reason why we have written this matrix as "A^2," for it is the square of the matrix A.

Let us continue this approach to define a matrix A^k, so that $A^k[i, j]$ is the shortest-path distance from v_i to v_j using at most k edges. Since a path with at most k edges is equivalent to a path with at most $k - 1$ edges plus possibly one additional edge, we can define A^k so that

$$A^k[i,j] = \sum_{l=0,1,\ldots,n-1} A^{k-1}[i,l] \cdot A[l,j],$$

with the operators redefined so that "+" stands for "min" and "·" stands for "+."

The crucial observation is that if $\vec{G}$ contains no negative-weight cycles, then A^{n-1} stores the shortest-path distance between each pair of vertices in $\vec{G}$. This observation follows from the fact that any well-defined shortest path contains at most $n-1$ edges. If a path has more than $n-1$ edges, it must repeat some vertex; hence, it must contain a cycle. But a shortest path will never contain a cycle (unless there is a negative-weight cycle in $\vec{G}$). Thus, to solve the all-pairs shortest-path problem, all we need to do is to multiply A times itself $n-1$ times. Since each such multiplication can be done in $O(n^3)$ time, this approach immediately gives us the following.

Theorem 14.7: *Given a weighted directed n-vertex graph $\vec{G}$ containing no negative-weight cycles, and the weighted adjacency matrix A for $\vec{G}$, the all-pairs shortest path problem for $\vec{G}$ can be solved by computing A^{n-1}, which can be performed in $O(n^4)$ time.*

In Section 24.2.1, we discuss an exponentiation algorithm for numbers, which can be applied in the present context of matrix multiplication to compute A^{n-1} in $O(n^3 \log n)$ time. We can actually compute A^{n-1} in $O(n^3)$ time, however, by taking advantage of additional structure present in the all-pairs shortest-path problem.

Matrix Closure

As observed above, if $\vec{G}$ contains no negative-weight cycles, then A^{n-1} encodes all the shortest-path distances between pairs of vertices in $\vec{G}$. A well-defined shortest path can contain no cycles; hence, a shortest path restricted to contain at most $n-1$ edges must be a true shortest path. Likewise, a shortest path containing at most n edges is a true shortest path, as is a shortest path containing at most $n+1$ edges, $n+2$ edges, and so on. Therefore, if $\vec{G}$ contains no negative-weight cycles, then

$$A^{n-1} = A^n = A^{n+1} = A^{n+2} = \cdots.$$

The **closure** of a matrix A is defined as

$$A^* = \sum_{l=0}^{\infty} A^l,$$

if such a matrix exists. If A is a weighted adjacency matrix, then $A^*[i,j]$ is the sum of all possible paths from v_i to v_j. In our case, A is the weighted adjacency matrix for a directed graph $\vec{G}$ and we have redefined "+" as "min." Thus, we can write

$$A^* = \min_{i=0,\ldots,\infty} \{A^i\}.$$

Moreover, since we are computing shortest-path distances, the entries in A^{i+1} are never larger than the entries in A^i. Therefore, for the weighted adjacency matrix of an n-vertex digraph $\vec{G}$ with no negative-weight cycles,

$$A^* = A^{n-1} = A^n = A^{n+1} = A^{n+2} = \cdots.$$

That is, $A^*[i,j]$ stores the length of the shortest path from v_i to v_j.

14.6   Exercises

Reinforcement

R-14.1 Draw a simple, connected, weighted, undirected graph with 8 vertices and 16 edges, and with distinct edge weights. Identify one vertex as a "start" vertex and illustrate a running of Dijkstra's algorithm on this graph.

R-14.2 Show how to modify Dijkstra's algorithm for the case when the graph is directed and we want to compute shortest *directed paths* from the source vertex to all the other vertices.

R-14.3 Show how to modify Dijkstra's algorithm to not only output the distance from v to each vertex in G, but also to output a tree T rooted at v, such that the path in T from v to a vertex u is actually a shortest path in G from v to u.

R-14.4 Draw a (simple) directed weighted graph G with 10 vertices and 18 edges, such that G contains a minimum-weight cycle with at least 4 edges. Show that the Bellman-Ford algorithm will find this cycle.

R-14.5 The dynamic programming algorithm of Algorithm 14.11 uses $O(n^3)$ space. Describe a version of this algorithm that uses $O(n^2)$ space.

R-14.6 The dynamic programming algorithm of Algorithm 14.11 computes only shortest-path distances, not actual paths. Describe a version of this algorithm that outputs the set of all shortest paths between each pair of vertices in a directed graph. Your algorithm should still run in $O(n^3)$ time.

R-14.7 Consider the unsorted sequence implementation of the priority queue Q used in Dijkstra's algorithm. In this case, why is the best-case running time of Dijkstra's algorithm $\Omega(n^2)$ on an n-vertex graph?

Hint: Consider the size of Q each time the minimum element is extracted.

R-14.8 Describe the meaning of the graphical conventions used in Figures 14.3 and 14.4 illustrating Dijkstra's algorithm. What do the arrows signify? How about thick lines and dashed lines?

Creativity

C-14.1 Give an example of an n-vertex simple graph, G, that causes Dijkstra's algorithm to run in $\Omega(n^2 \log n)$ time when its implemented with a heap for the priority queue.

C-14.2 Give an example of a weighted directed graph, $\vec{G}$, with negative-weight edges, but no negative-weight cycle, such that Dijkstra's algorithm incorrectly computes the shortest-path distances from some start vertex v.

C-14.3 There is an alternative way of implementing Dijkstra's algorithm that avoids use of the locator pattern but increases the space used for the priority queue, Q, from $O(n)$ to $O(m)$ for a weighted graph, G, with n vertices and m edges. The main idea of this approach is simply to insert a new key-value pair, $(D[v], v)$, each time the $D[v]$ value for a vertex, v, changes, without ever removing the old key-value pair for v. This approach still works, even with multiple copies of each vertex being stored in Q, since the first copy of a vertex that is removed from Q is the copy with the smallest key. Describe the other changes that would be needed to the description of Dijsktra's algorithm for this approach to work. Also, what is the running time of Dijkstra's algorithm in this approach if we implement the priority queue, Q, with a heap?

C-14.4 Consider the following greedy strategy for finding a shortest path from vertex *start* to vertex *goal* in a given connected graph.

    1: Initialize *path* to *start*.
    2: Initialize *VisitedVertices* to {*start*}.
    3: If *start=goal*, return *path* and exit. Otherwise, continue.
    4: Find the edge (*start,v*) of minimum weight such that v is adjacent to *start* and v is not in *VisitedVertices*.
    5: Add v to *path*.
    6: Add v to *VisitedVertices*.
    7: Set *start* equal to v and go to step 3.

Does this greedy strategy always find a shortest path from *start* to *goal*? Either explain intuitively why it works, or give a counterexample.

C-14.5 Design an efficient algorithm for finding a ***longest*** directed path from a vertex s to a vertex t of an acyclic weighted digraph $\vec{G}$. Specify the graph representation used and any auxiliary data structures used. Also, analyze the time complexity of your algorithm.

C-14.6 Suppose we are given a directed graph $\vec{G}$ with n vertices, and let M be the $n \times n$ adjacency matrix corresponding to $\vec{G}$.

    a. Let the product of M with itself (M^2) be defined, for $1 \le i, j \le n$, as follows:

$$M^2(i, j) = M(i, 1) \odot M(1, j) \oplus \cdots \oplus M(i, n) \odot M(n, j),$$

    where "$\oplus$" is the Boolean **or** operator and "$\odot$" is Boolean **and**. Given this definition, what does $M^2(i, j) = 1$ imply about the vertices i and j? What if $M^2(i, j) = 0$?

    b. Suppose M^4 is the product of M^2 with itself. What do the entries of M^4 signify? How about the entries of $M^5 = (M^4)(M)$? In general, what information is contained in the matrix M^p?

    c. Now suppose that $\vec{G}$ is weighted and assume the following:
        1: for $1 \le i \le n$, $M(i, i) = 0$.
        2: for $1 \le i, j \le n$, $M(i, j) = weight(i, j)$ if $(i, j) \in E$.
        3: for $1 \le i, j \le n$, $M(i, j) = \infty$ if $(i, j) \notin E$.
    Also, let M^2 be defined, for $1 \le i, j \le n$, as follows:

$$M^2(i, j) = \min\{M(i, 1) + M(1, j), \ldots, M(i, n) + M(n, j)\}.$$

    If $M^2(i, j) = k$, what may we conclude about the relationship between vertices i and j?

C-14.7 Suppose you are given a connected weighted undirected graph, G, with n vertices and m edges, such that the weight of each edge in G is an integer in the interval $[1, c]$, for a fixed constant $c > 0$. Show how to solve the single-source shortest-paths problem, for any given vertex v, in G, in time $O(n + m)$.

Hint: Think about how to exploit the fact that the distance from v to any other vertex in G can be at most $O(cn) = O(n)$.

C-14.8 Suppose that every shortest path from some vertex, v, in an n-vertex weighted graph, G, to any other vertex in G has at most $k < n - 1$ edges. Show that it is sufficient to run the Bellman-Ford algorithm for only k iterations, instead of $n - 1$, to solve the single-source shortest-paths problem for v in G.

Applications

A-14.1 In a *side-scrolling video game*, a character moves through an environment from, say, left-to-right, while encountering obstacles, attackers, and prizes. The goal is to avoid or destroy the obstacles, defeat or avoid the attackers, and collect as many prizes as possible while moving from a starting position to an ending position. We can model such a game with a graph, G, where each vertex is a game position, given as an (x, y) point in the plane, and two such vertices, v and w, are connected by an edge, given as a straight line segment, if there is a single movement that connects v and w. Furthermore, we can define the cost, $c(e)$, of an edge to be a combination of the time, health points, prizes, etc., that it costs our character to move along the edge e (where earning a prize on this edge would be modeled as a negative term in this cost). A path, P, in G is *monotone* if traversing P involves a continuous sequence of left-to-right movements, with no right-to-left moves. Thus, we can model an optimal solution to such a side-scrolling computer game in terms of finding a minimum-cost monotone path in the graph, G, that represents this game. Describe and analyze an efficient algorithm for finding a minimum-cost monotone path in such a graph, G.

A-14.2 Suppose that CONTROL, a secret U.S. government counterintelligence agency based in Washington, D.C., has build a communication network that links n stations spread across the world using m communication channels between pairs of stations. Suppose further that the evil spy agency, KAOS, is able to eavesdrop on some number, k, of these channels and that CONTROL knows the k channels that have been compromised. Now, CONTROL has a message, M, that it wants to send from its headquarters station, s, to one of its field stations, t. The problem is that the message is super secret and should traverse a path that minimizes the number of compromised edges that occur along this path. Explain how to model this problem as a shortest-path problem, and describe and analyze an efficient algorithm to solve it.

A-14.3 Suppose you live far from work and are trying to determine the best route to drive from your home to your workplace. In order to solve this problem, suppose further that you have downloaded, from a government website, a weighted graph, G, representing the entire road network for your state. Although the edges in G are labeled with their lengths, you are more interested in the amount of time that it takes to traverse each edge. So you have found another website that has a function, $f_{i,j}$, defined for each edge, $e = (i, j)$, in G, such that each $f_{i,j}$ maps a time of day, t, to the amount of time it takes to go from i to j along the edge, $e = (i, j)$, if you enter that edge at time t. Here, time is measured in minutes and times of day are measured in terms of minutes since midnight. In addition, we assume that you will be leaving for work in the morning and you live close enough to your workplace so that you can get there before midnight. Moreover, the $f_{i,j}$ functions are defined to satisfy the normal rules of traffic flow, so that it is never possible to get to the end of an edge, (i, j), sooner than someone who entered that edge before you. That is, if $t_1 < t_2$, then

$$f_{i,j}(t_2) + t_2 - t_1 > f_{i,j}(t_1).$$

Describe an efficient algorithm that, given G and the $f_{i,j}$ functions for its edges, can determine, for any given time, t_0, that you might leave your home in the morning, the amount of time required for you to drive to work. What is the running time of your algorithm?

A-14.4 Suppose you are given a *timetable*, which consists of the following:

- A set $\mathcal{A}$ of n airports, and for each airport $a \in \mathcal{A}$, a minimum connecting time $c(a)$
- A set $\mathcal{F}$ of m flights, and the following, for each flight $f \in \mathcal{F}$:
  - Origin airport $a_1(f) \in \mathcal{A}$
  - Destination airport $a_2(f) \in \mathcal{A}$
  - Departure time $t_1(f)$
  - Arrival time $t_2(f)$.

Describe an efficient algorithm for the flight scheduling problem. In this problem, we are given airports a and b, and a time t, and we wish to compute a sequence of flights that allows one to arrive at the earliest possible time in b when departing from a at or after time t. Minimum connecting times at intermediate airports should be observed. What is the running time of your algorithm as a function of n and m?

A-14.5 As your reward for saving the Kingdom of Bigfunnia from the evil monster "Exponential Asymptotic," the king has given you the opportunity to earn a big reward. Behind the castle there is a maze, and along each corridor of the maze there is a bag of gold coins. The amount of gold in each bag varies. You will be given the opportunity to walk through the maze, picking up bags of gold. You may enter only through the door marked "ENTER" and exit through the door marked "EXIT." (These are distinct doors.) While in the maze you may not retrace your steps. Each corridor of the maze has an arrow painted on the wall. You may only go down the corridor in the direction of the arrow. There is no way to traverse a "loop" in the maze. You will receive a map of the maze, including the amount of gold in and the direction of each corridor. Describe and analyze an efficient algorithm to help you pick up the most gold in this maze while traversing a path from the start to the finish.

A-14.6 A part of doing business internationally involves the trading of different currencies, and the markets that facilitate such trades can fluctuate during a trading day in ways that create profit opportunities. For example, at a given moment during a trading day, 1 U.S. dollar might be worth 0.98 Canadian dollar, 1 Canadian dollar might be worth 0.81 euros, and 1 euro might be worth 1.32 U.S. dollars. Sometimes, as in this example, it is possible for us to perform a cyclic sequence of currency exchanges, all at the same time, and end up with more money than we started with, which is an action known as ***currency arbitrage***. For instance, with the above exchange rates, we could perform a cyclic sequence of trades from U.S. dollars, to Canadian dollars, to euros, and back to U.S. dollars, which could turn $1,000,000 into $1,047,816, ignoring the commissions and other overhead costs for performing currency exchanges (which we will indeed be ignoring in this exercise). Suppose you are given a complete directed graph, $\vec{G}$, that represents the currency exchange rates that exist at a given moment in time on a trading day. Each vertex in $\vec{G}$ is a currency, and each directed edge, (v, w), in $\vec{G}$, is labeled with an exchange rate, $r(v, w)$, which is the amount of currency w that would be exchanged for 1 unit of currency v. In order to profit from this information, you need to find, as quickly as possible, a cycle, $(v_1, v_2, \ldots, v_k, v_1)$, that maximizes the product,

$$r(v_1, v_2) \cdot r(v_2, v_3) \cdot \cdots \cdot r(v_k, v_1),$$

such that this product is strictly greater than 1. Describe and analyze an efficient dynamic programming algorithm for finding such a cycle, if it exists.

Chapter Notes

Dijkstra [56] published his single-source shortest-path algorithm in 1959. The Bellman-Ford algorithm is derived from separate publications of Bellman [24] and Ford [74].

Incidentally, the running time for Dijkstra's algorithm can actually be improved to be $O(n \log n + m)$ by implementing the queue Q with either of two more sophisticated data structures, the "Fibonacci Heap" [76] or the "Relaxed Heap" [58].

The reader interested in further study of graph algorithms is referred to the books by Ahuja, Magnanti, and Orlin [10], Even [68], Gibbons [81], Mehlhorn [158], and Tarjan [207], and the book chapter by van Leeuwen [210]. For applications of shortest paths to social networks, see the book by Easley and Kleinberg [60].

Chapter
15
Minimum Spanning Trees

Saguaros, Saguaro National Monument, 1941.
Ansel Adams. U.S. government image. U.S. National Archives and Records Administration.

Contents

15.1 Properties of Minimum Spanning Trees 425
15.2 Kruskal's Algorithm 428
15.3 The Prim-Jarník Algorithm 433
15.4 Barůvka's Algorithm 436
15.5 Exercises 439

Suppose the remote mountain country of Vectoria has been given a major grant to install a large Wi-Fi the center of each of its mountain villages. The grant pays for the installation and maintenance of the towers, but it doesn't pay the cost for running the cables that would be connecting all the towers to the Internet. Communication cables can run from the main Internet access point to a village tower and cables can also run between pairs of towers. The challenge is to interconnect all the towers and the Internet access point as cheaply as possible.

We can model this problem using a graph, G, where each vertex in G is the location of a Wi-Fi the Internet access point, and an edge in G is a possible cable we could run between two such vertices. Each edge in G could then be given a weight that is equal to the cost of running the cable that that edge represents. Thus, we are interested in finding a connected acyclic subgraph of G that includes all the vertices of G and has minimum total cost. That is, using the language of graph theory, we are interested in finding a minimum spanning tree of G, which is the topic we explore in this chapter. (See Figure 15.1.)

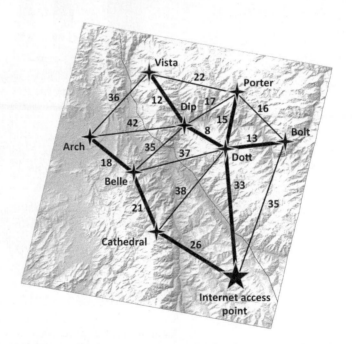

Figure 15.1: Connecting Wi-Fi Vectoria as cheaply as possible. Each edge is labeled with the cost, in millions of Vectoria dollars, of running a cable between its two endpoints. The edges that belong to the cheapest way to connect all the villages and the Internet access point are shown in bold. Note that this spanning tree is not the same as a shortest-path tree rooted at the Internet access point. For example, the shortest-path distance to Bolt is 35, but this edge is not included, since we can connect Bolt to Dott with an edge of cost 13. Background image is a Kashmir elevation map, 2005. U.S. government image. Credit: NASA.

15.1 Properties of Minimum Spanning Trees

As in the tower-connecting problem in Vectoria mentioned above, suppose we wish to connect all the computers in a new office building using the least amount of cable or suppose we have an undirected computer network in which each connection between two routers has a cost for usage and we want to connect all our routers at the minimum cost possible. As in the example of connecting villages in Vectoria, we can model these problems using a weighted graph, G, whose vertices represent the computers or routers, and whose edges represent all the possible pairs (u, v) of computers, where the weight $w((v, u))$ of edge (v, u) is equal to the amount of cable or network cost needed to connect computer v to computer u. Rather than computing a shortest-path tree from some particular vertex v, we are interested instead in finding a (free) tree T that contains all the vertices of G and has the minimum total weight over all such trees.

Given a weighted undirected graph G, we are interested in finding a tree T that contains all the vertices in G and minimizes the sum of the weights of the edges of T, that is,

$$w(T) = \sum_{e \in T} w(e).$$

Recall that a tree such as this, which contains every vertex of a connected graph G is a **spanning tree**. Computing a spanning tree T with smallest total weight is the problem of constructing a **minimum spanning tree** (or **MST**).

All the well-known efficient algorithms for finding minimum spanning trees are applications of the **greedy method**. As was discussed in Section 10, we apply the greedy method by iteratively choosing objects to join a growing collection, by incrementally picking an object that minimizes or maximizes the change in some objective function. Thus, algorithms for constructing minimum spanning trees based on this approach must define some kind of greedy ordering and some kind of objective function to optimize with each greedy step. The details for these definitions differ among the various well-known MST algorithms, however.

The first MST algorithm we discuss is Kruskal's algorithm, which "grows" the MST in clusters by considering edges in order of their weights. The second algorithm we discuss is the Prim-Jarník algorithm, which grows the MST from a single root vertex, much in the same way as Dijkstra's shortest-path algorithm. We conclude this chapter by discussing a third algorithm, due to Barůvka, which applies the greedy approach in a parallel way.

In order to simplify the description of the algorithms, we assume, in the following, that the input graph G is undirected (that is, all its edges are undirected) and simple (that is, it has no self-loops and no parallel edges). Hence, we denote the edges of G as unordered vertex pairs (u, z).

Crucial Facts about Minimum Spanning Trees

Before we discuss the details of efficient MST algorithms, however, let us give some crucial facts about minimum spanning trees that form the basis of these algorithms.

Lemma 15.1: *Let G be a weighted connected graph, and let T be a minimum spanning tree for T. If e is an edge of G that is not in T, then the weight of e is at least as great as any edge in the cycle created by adding e to T.*

Proof: Since T is a spanning tree (that is, a connected acyclic subgraph of G that contains all the vertices of G), adding e to T creates a cycle, C. Suppose, for the sake of contradiction, that there is an edge, f, whose weight is more than e's weight, that is, $w(e) < w(f)$. Then we can remove f from T and replace it with e, and this will result in a spanning tree, T', whose total weight is less than the total weight of T. But the existence of such a tree, T', would contradict the fact that T is a ***minimum*** spanning tree. So no such edge, f, can exist. (See Figure 15.2.)   ■

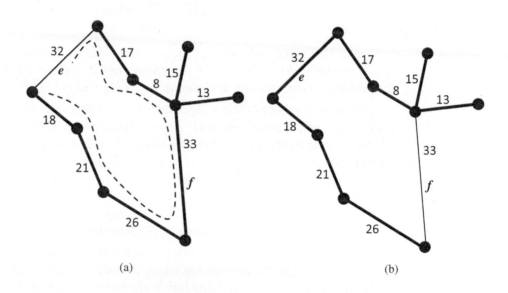

(a)   (b)

Figure 15.2: Any nontree edge must have weight that is at least as great as every edge in the cycle created by that edge and a minimum spanning tree. (a) Suppose a nontree edge, e, has lower weight than an edge, f, in the cycle created by e and a minimum spanning tree (shown with bold edges). (b) Then we could replace f by e and get a spanning tree with lower total weight, which would contradict the fact that we started with a ***minimum*** spanning tree.

In addition, all the MST algorithms we discuss in this chapter are based crucially on the following fact. (See Figure 15.3.)

e Belongs to a Minimum Spanning Tree

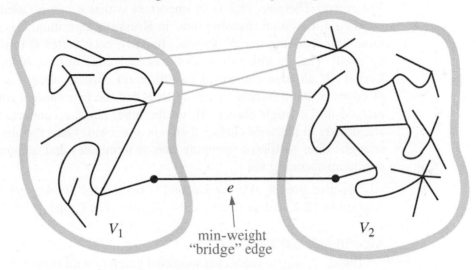

Figure 15.3: An illustration of a crucial fact about minimum spanning trees.

Theorem 15.2: *Let G be a weighted connected graph, and let V_1 and V_2 be a partition of the vertices of G into two disjoint nonempty sets. Furthermore, let e be an edge in G with minimum weight from among those with one endpoint in V_1 and the other in V_2. There is a minimum spanning tree T that has e as one of its edges.*

Proof: The proof is similar to that of Lemma 15.1. Let T be a minimum spanning tree of G. If T does not contain edge e, the addition of e to T must create a cycle. Therefore, there is some edge, f, of this cycle that has one endpoint in V_1 and the other in V_2. Moreover, by the choice of e, $w(e) \leq w(f)$. If we remove f from $T \cup \{e\}$, we obtain a spanning tree whose total weight is no more than before. Since T was a minimum spanning tree, this new tree must also be a minimum spanning tree. ∎

In fact, if the weights in G are distinct, then the minimum spanning tree is unique; we leave the justification of this less crucial fact as an exercise (C-15.3).

Also, note that Theorem 15.2 remains valid even if the graph G contains negative-weight edges or negative-weight cycles, unlike the algorithms we presented for shortest paths.

15.2   Kruskal's Algorithm

The reason Theorem 15.2 is so important is that it can be used as the basis for building a minimum spanning tree. In Kruskal's algorithm, it is used to build the minimum spanning tree in clusters. Initially, each vertex is in its own cluster all by itself. The algorithm then considers each edge in turn, ordered by increasing weight. If an edge e connects two different clusters, then e is added to the set of edges of the minimum spanning tree, and the two clusters connected by e are merged into a single cluster. If, on the other hand, e connects two vertices that are already in the same cluster, then e is discarded. Once the algorithm has added enough edges to form a spanning tree, it terminates and outputs this tree as the minimum spanning tree.

We give pseudocode for Kruskal's method for solving the MST problem in Algorithm 15.4, and we illustrate this algorithm in Figures 15.5, 15.6, and 15.7.

Algorithm KruskalMST(G):
   Input: A simple connected weighted graph G with n vertices and m edges
   Output: A minimum spanning tree T for G

   for each vertex v in G **do**
        Define an elementary cluster $C(v) \leftarrow \{v\}$.
   Let Q be a priority queue storing the edges in G, using edge weights as keys
   $T \leftarrow \emptyset$ // T will ultimately contain the edges of the MST
   while T has fewer than $n - 1$ edges **do**
        $(u, v) \leftarrow Q.\text{removeMin}()$
        Let $C(v)$ be the cluster containing v
        Let $C(u)$ be the cluster containing u
        if $C(v) \neq C(u)$ **then**
             Add edge (v, u) to T
             Merge $C(v)$ and $C(u)$ into one cluster, that is, union $C(v)$ and $C(u)$
   return tree T

Algorithm 15.4: Kruskal's algorithm for the MST problem.

As mentioned before, the correctness of Kruskal's algorithm follows from the crucial fact about minimum spanning trees from Theorem 15.2. Each time Kruskal's algorithm adds an edge (v, u) to the minimum spanning tree T, we can define a partitioning of the set of vertices V (as in the theorem) by letting V_1 be the cluster containing v and letting V_2 contain the rest of the vertices in V. This clearly defines a disjoint partitioning of the vertices of V and, more importantly, since we are extracting edges from Q in order by their weights, e must be a minimum-weight edge with one vertex in V_1 and the other in V_2. Thus, Kruskal's algorithm always adds a valid minimum spanning tree edge.

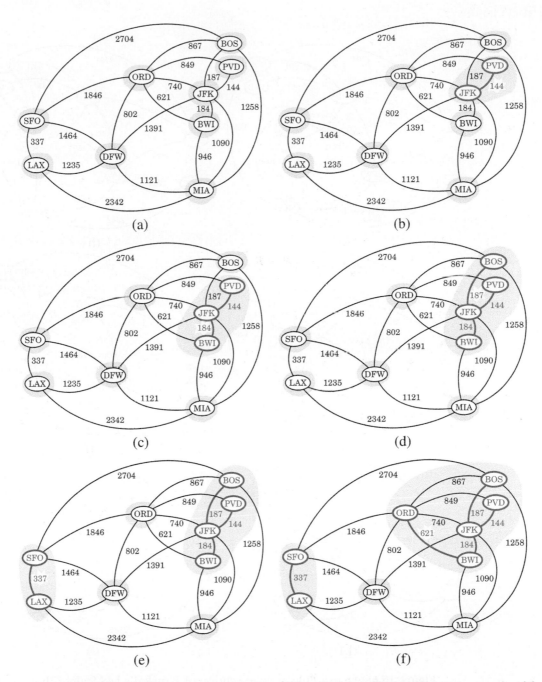

Figure 15.5: Example of an execution of Kruskal's MST algorithm on a graph with integer weights. We show the clusters as shaded regions, and we highlight the edge being considered in each iteration (continued in Figure 15.6).

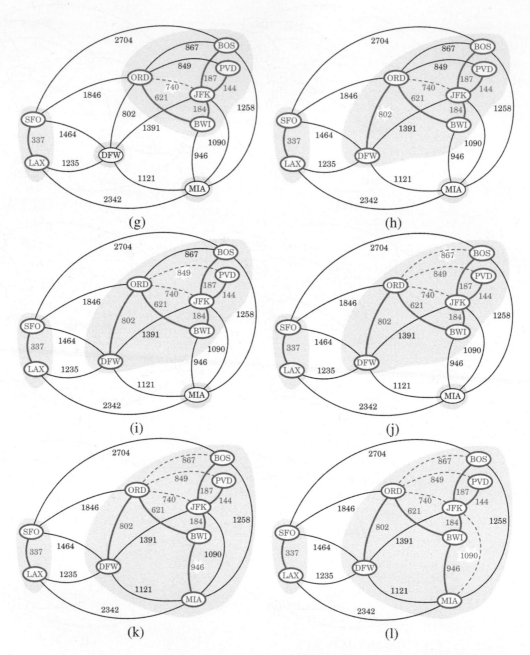

Figure 15.6: An example of an execution of Kruskal's MST algorithm (continued). Rejected edges are shown dashed (continued in Figure 15.7).

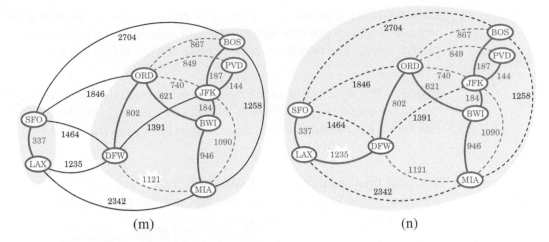

(m)   (n)

Figure 15.7: Example of an execution of Kruskal's MST algorithm (continued from Figures 15.5 and 15.6). The edge considered in (n) merges the last two clusters, which concludes this execution of Kruskal's algorithm.

Analyzing Kruskal's Algorithm

Suppose G is a connected, weighted, undirected graph with n vertices and m edges. We assume that the edge weights can be compared in constant time. Because of the high level of the description we gave for Kruskal's algorithm in Algorithm 15.4, analyzing its running time requires that we give more details on its implementation. Specifically, we should indicate the data structures used and how they are implemented.

We implement the priority queue Q using a heap. Thus, we can initialize Q in $O(m \log m)$ time by repeated insertions, or in $O(m)$ time using bottom-up heap construction (see Section 5.4). In addition, at each iteration of the **while** loop, we can remove a minimum-weight edge in $O(\log m)$ time, which actually is $O(\log n)$, since G is simple.

We can use a list-based implementation of a partition (Section 7.1) for the clusters. Namely, let us represent each cluster C with an unordered linked list of vertices, storing, with each vertex v, a reference to its cluster $C(v)$. With this representation, testing whether $C(u) \neq C(v)$ takes $O(1)$ time. When we need to merge two clusters, $C(u)$ and $C(v)$, we move the elements of the *smaller* cluster into the larger one and update the cluster references of the vertices in the smaller cluster. Since we can simply add the elements of the smaller cluster at the end of the list for the larger cluster, merging two clusters takes time proportional to the size of the smaller cluster. That is, merging clusters $C(u)$ and $C(v)$ takes $O(\min\{|C(u)|, |C(v)|\})$ time. There are other, more efficient, methods for merging clusters (see Section 7.1), but this simple approach will be sufficient.

Lemma 15.3: *Consider an execution of Kruskal's algorithm on a graph with n vertices, where clusters are represented with sequences and with cluster references at each vertex. The total time spent merging clusters is $O(n \log n)$.*

Proof: We observe that each time a vertex is moved to a new cluster, the size of the cluster containing the vertex at least doubles. Let $t(v)$ be the number of times that vertex v is moved to a new cluster. Since the maximum cluster size is n,

$$t(v) \leq \log n.$$

The total time spent merging clusters in Kruskal's algorithm can be obtained by summing up the work done on each vertex, which is proportional to

$$\sum_{v \in G} t(v) \leq n \log n.$$

■

Using Lemma 15.3 and arguments similar to those used in the analysis of Dijkstra's algorithm, we conclude that the total running time of Kruskal's algorithm is $O((n + m) \log n)$, which can be simplified as $O(m \log n)$ since G is simple and connected.

Theorem 15.4: *Given a simple connected weighted graph G with n vertices and m edges, Kruskal's algorithm constructs a minimum spanning tree for G in $O(m \log n)$ time.*

An Alternative Implementation

In some applications, we may be given the edges in sorted order by their weights. In such cases, we can implement Kruskal's algorithm faster than the analysis given above. Specifically, we can implement the priority queue, Q, in this case, simply as an ordered list. This approach allows us to perform all the removeMin operations in constant time.

Then, instead of using a simple list-based partition data structure, we can use the tree-based union-find structure given in Chapter 7. This implies that the sequence of $O(m)$ union-find operations runs in $O(m \, \alpha(n))$ time, where $\alpha(n)$ is the slow-growing inverse of the Ackermann function. Thus, we have the following.

Theorem 15.5: *Given a simple connected weighted graph G with n vertices and m edges, with the edges ordered by their weights, we can implement Kruskal's algorithm to construct a minimum spanning tree for G in $O(m \, \alpha(n))$ time.*

15.3 The Prim-Jarník Algorithm

In the Prim-Jarník algorithm, we grow a minimum spanning tree from a single cluster starting from some "root" vertex v. The main idea is similar to that of Dijkstra's algorithm. We begin with some vertex v, defining the initial "cloud" of vertices C. Then, in each iteration, we choose a minimum-weight edge $e = (v, u)$, connecting a vertex v in the cloud C to a vertex u outside of C. The vertex u is then brought into the cloud C and the process is repeated until a spanning tree is formed. Again, the crucial fact about minimum spanning trees from Theorem 15.2 is used here, for by always choosing the smallest-weight edge joining a vertex inside C to one outside C, we are assured of always adding a valid edge to the MST.

To efficiently implement this approach, we can take another cue from Dijkstra's algorithm. We maintain a label $D[u]$ for each vertex u outside the cloud C, so that $D[u]$ stores the weight of the best current edge for joining u to the cloud C. These labels allow us to reduce the number of edges that we must consider in deciding which vertex is next to join the cloud. We give the pseudocode in Algorithm 15.8.

Algorithm PrimJarníkMST(G):

    Input: A weighted connected graph G with n vertices and m edges

    Output: A minimum spanning tree T for G

    Pick any vertex v of G

    $D[v] \leftarrow 0$

    for each vertex $u \neq v$ **do**

        $D[u] \leftarrow +\infty$

    Initialize $T \leftarrow \emptyset$.

    Initialize a priority queue Q with an item $((u, \text{null}), D[u])$ for each vertex u, where (u, null) is the element and $D[u]$ is the key.

    while Q is not empty **do**

        $(u, e) \leftarrow Q.\text{removeMin}()$

        Add vertex u and edge e to T.

        for each vertex z adjacent to u such that z is in Q **do**

            // perform the relaxation procedure on edge (u, z)

            if $w((u, z)) < D[z]$ **then**

                $D[z] \leftarrow w((u, z))$

                Change to $(z, (u, z))$ the element of vertex z in Q.

                Change to $D[z]$ the key of vertex z in Q.

    return the tree T

Algorithm 15.8: The Prim-Jarník algorithm for the MST problem.

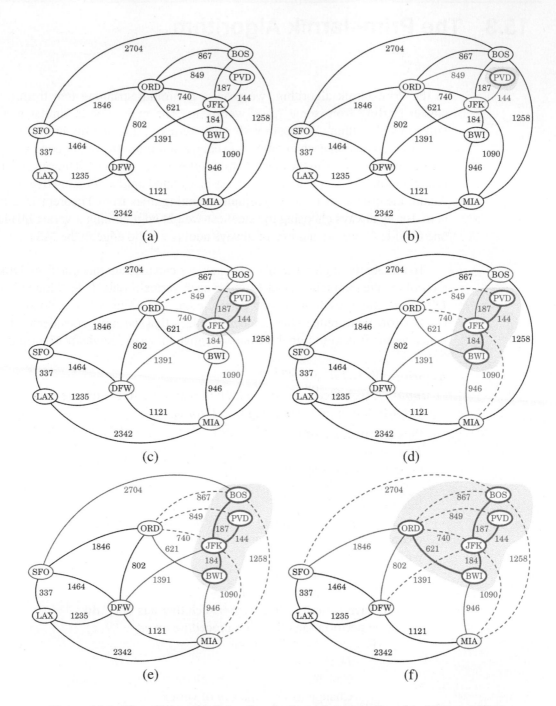

Figure 15.9: Visualizing the Prim-Jarník algorithm (continued in Figure 15.10).

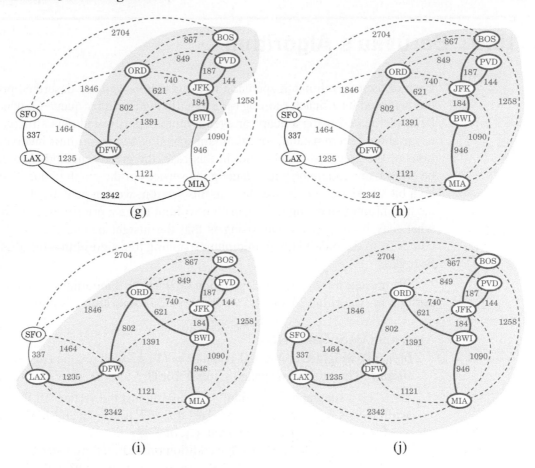

Figure 15.10: Visualizing the Prim-Jarník algorithm (continued from Figure 15.9).

Analyzing the Prim-Jarník Algorithm

Let n and m denote the number of vertices and edges of the input graph G, respectively. The implementation issues for the Prim-Jarník algorithm are similar to those for Dijkstra's algorithm. If we implement the priority queue Q as a heap that supports the locator-based priority queue methods (see Section 5.5), we can extract the vertex u in each iteration in $O(\log n)$ time.

In addition, we can update each $D[z]$ value in $O(\log n)$ time, as well, which is a computation considered at most once for each edge (u, z). The other steps in each iteration can be implemented in constant time. Thus, the total running time is $O((n + m) \log n)$, which is $O(m \log n)$. Hence, we can summarize as follows:

Theorem 15.6: *Given a simple connected weighted graph G with n vertices and m edges, the Prim-Jarník algorithm constructs a minimum spanning tree for G in $O(m \log n)$ time.*

We illustrate the Prim-Jarník algorithm in Figures 15.9 and 15.10.

15.4 Barůvka's Algorithm

Each of the two minimum spanning tree algorithms we have described previously has achieved its efficient running time by utilizing a priority queue Q, which could be implemented using a heap (or even a more sophisticated data structure). This usage should seem natural, for minimum spanning tree algorithms involve applications of the greedy method—and, in this case, the greedy method must explicitly be optimizing certain priorities among the vertices of the graph in question. It may be a bit surprising, but as we show in this section, we can actually design an efficient minimum spanning tree algorithm without using a priority queue. Moreover, what may be even more surprising is that the insight behind this simplification comes from the oldest known minimum spanning tree algorithm—the algorithm of Barůvka.

We present a pseudocode description of Barůvka's minimum spanning tree algorithm in Algorithm 15.11, and we illustrate this algorithm in Figure 15.12.

Algorithm BarůvkaMST(G):

  Input: A weighted connected graph $G = (V, E)$ with unique edge weights
  Output: The minimum spanning tree T for G.

  Let T be a subgraph of G initially containing just the vertices in V
  while T has fewer than $|V| - 1$ edges **do**   // T is not yet an MST
      for each connected component, C_i, of T **do**
          // Perform the MST edge addition procedure for cluster C_i
          Let $e = (v, u)$ be a smallest-weight edge in E with $v \in C_i$ and $u \notin C_i$
          Add e to T (unless e is already in T)
  return T

        Algorithm 15.11: Pseudo-code for Barůvka's algorithm.

Implementing Barůvka's algorithm to be efficient for a graph with n vertices and m edges is quite simple, requiring only that we be able to do the following:

- Maintain the forest T subject to edge insertion, which we can easily support in $O(1)$ time each using an adjacency list for T

- Traverse the forest T to identify connected components (clusters), which we can easily do in $O(n)$ time using a depth-first search of T

- Mark vertices with the name of the cluster they belong to, which we can do with an extra instance variable for each vertex

- Identify a smallest-weight edge in E incident upon a cluster C_i, which we can do by scanning the adjacency lists in G for the vertices in C_i.

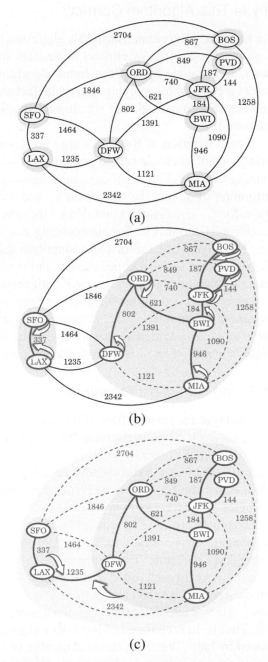

Figure 15.12: Example of an execution of Barůvka's algorithm. We show clusters as shaded regions. We highlight the edge chosen by each cluster with an arrow and we draw each such MST edge as a thick line. Edges determined not to be in the MST are shown dashed.

Why Is This Algorithm Correct?

Like Kruskal's algorithm, Barůvka's algorithm builds the minimum spanning tree by growing a number of clusters of vertices in a series of rounds, not just one cluster, as was done by the Prim-Jarník algorithm. But in Barůvka's algorithm, the clusters are grown by applying the crucial fact about minimum spanning trees from Theorem 15.2 to each cluster simultaneously. This approach adds many edges in each round.

In each iteration of Barůvka's algorithm, we choose the smallest-weight edge coming out of each connected component C_i of the current set T of minimum spanning tree edges. In each case, this edge is a valid choice, for if we consider a partitioning of V into the vertices in C_i and those outside of C_i, then the chosen edge e for C_i satisfies the condition of the crucial fact about minimum spanning trees from Theorem 15.2 for guaranteeing that e belongs to a minimum spanning tree. Moreover, because of our assumption that edge weights are unique, there will be just one such edge per cluster, and if two clusters are joined by the same minimum-weight edge, then they will both choose that edge.

Incidentally, if the edge weights in G are not initially unique, we can impose uniqueness by numbering the vertices 1 to n and taking the new weight of each edge $e = (u, v)$, written so that $u < v$, to be $(w(e), u, v)$, where $w(e)$ is the old weight of e and we use a lexicographic comparison rule for the new weights.

Analyzing Barůvka's Algorithm

Let us analyze the running time of Barůvka's algorithm (Algorithm 15.11). We can implement each round performing the searches to find the minimum-weight edge going out of each cluster by an exhaustive search through the adjacency lists of each vertex in each cluster. Thus, the total running time spent in searching for minimum-weight edges can be made to be $O(m)$, for it involves examining each edge (v, u) in G twice: once for v and once for u (since vertices are labeled with the number of the cluster they are in). The remaining computations in the main while-loop involve relabeling all the vertices, which takes $O(n)$ time, and traversing all the edges in T, which takes $O(n)$ time. Thus, each round in Barůvka's algorithm takes $O(m)$ time (since $n \le m$). In each round of the algorithm, we choose one edge coming out of each cluster, and we then merge each new connected component of T into a new cluster. Thus, each old cluster of T must merge with at least one other old cluster of T. That is, in each round of Barůvka's algorithm, the total number of clusters is reduced by half. Therefore, the total number of rounds is $O(\log n)$; hence, the total running time of Barůvka's algorithm is $O(m \log n)$. We summarize:

Theorem 15.7: *Barůvka's algorithm computes a minimum spanning tree for a connected weighted graph G with n vertices and m edges in $O(m \log n)$ time.*

15.5 Exercises

Reinforcement

R-15.1 Draw a simple, connected, undirected, weighted graph with 8 vertices and 16 edges, each with unique edge weights. Illustrate the execution of Kruskal's algorithm on this graph. (Note that there is only one minimum spanning tree for this graph.)

R-15.2 Repeat the previous problem for the Prim-Jarník algorithm.

R-15.3 Repeat the previous problem for Barůvka's algorithm.

R-15.4 Describe the meaning of the graphical conventions used in Figures 15.5 through 15.7, illustrating Kruskal's algorithm. What do thick lines and dashed lines signify?

R-15.5 Repeat Exercise R-15.4 for Figures 15.9 and 15.10, illustrating the Prim-Jarník algorithm.

R-15.6 Repeat Exercise R-15.4 for Figure 15.12, illustrating Barůvka's algorithm.

R-15.7 Give an alternative pseudocode description of Kruskal's algorithm that makes explicit use of the union and find operations.

R-15.8 Why do all the MST algorithms discussed in this chapter still work correctly even if the graph has negative-weight edges, and even negative-weight cycles?

R-15.9 Give an example of weighted, connected, undirected graph, G, such that the minimum spanning tree for G is different from every shortest-path tree rooted at a vertex of G.

R-15.10 Let G be a weighted, connected, undirected graph, and let V_1 and V_2 be a partition of the vertices of G into two disjoint nonempty sets. Furthermore, let e be an edge in the minimum spanning tree for G such that e has one endpoint in V_1 and the other in V_2. Give an example that shows that e is not necessarily the smallest-weight edge that has one endpoint in V_1 and the other in V_2.

Creativity

C-15.1 Suppose G is a weighted, connected, undirected graph and e is a smallest-weight edge in G. Show that there is a minimum spanning tree of G that contains e.

C-15.2 Suppose G is a weighted, connected, undirected, simple graph and e is a largest-weight edge in G. Prove or disprove the claim that there is no minimum spanning tree of G that contains e.

C-15.3 Suppose G is an undirected, connected, weighted graph such that the edges in G have distinct edge weights. Show that the minimum spanning tree for G is unique.

C-15.4 Suppose G is an undirected, connected, weighted graph such that the edges in G have distinct positive edge weights. Show that the minimum spanning tree for G is unchanged even if we square all the edge weights in G, that is, G has the same set of edges in its minimum spanning tree even if we replace the weight, $w(e)$, of each edge e in G, with $w(e)^2$.

C-15.5 Suppose G is an undirected, connected, weighted graph such that the edges in G have distinct edge weights, which may be positive or negative. Show that the minimum spanning tree for G may be changed if we square all the edge weights in G, that is, G may have a different set of edges in its minimum spanning tree if we replace the weight, $w(e)$, of each edge e in G, with $w(e)^2$.

C-15.6 Show how to modify the Prim-Jarník algorithm to run in $O(n^2)$ time.

C-15.7 Show how to modify Barůvka's algorithm so that it runs in $O(n^2)$ time.

Hint: Consider contracting the representation of the graph so that each connected component "cluster" is reduced to a single "super" vertex, with self-loops and parallel edges removed with each iteration. Then characterize the running time using a recurrence relation involving only n and show that this running time is $O(n^2)$.

C-15.8 Suppose you are given a weighted graph, G, with n vertices and m edges, such that the weight of each edge in G is a real number chosen independently at random from the interval $[0, 1]$. Show that the expected running time of the Prim-Jarník algorithm on G is $O(n \log^2 n + m)$, assuming the priority queue, Q, is implemented with a heap, as described in the chapter.

Hint: Think about first bounding the expected number of times the Prim-Jarník algorithm would change the value of $D[v]$ for any given vertex, v, in G.

C-15.9 Suppose G is a weighted, connected, undirected graph with each edge having a unique integer weight, which may be either positive or negative. Let G' be the same graph as G, but with each edge, e, in G' having weight that is 1 greater than e's weight in G. Show that G and G' have the same minimum spanning tree.

C-15.10 Suppose Joseph Kruskal had an evil twin, named Peter, who designed an algorithm that takes the exact opposite approach from his brother's algorithm for finding an MST in an undirected, weighted, connected graph, G. Also, for the sake of simplicity, suppose the edges of G have distinct weights. Peter's algorithm is as follows: consider the edges of G by decreasing weights. For each edge, e, in this order, if the removal of e from G would not disconnect G, then remove e from G. Peter claims that the graph that remains at the end of his algorithm is a minimum spanning tree. Prove or disprove Peter's claim.

C-15.11 Suppose Vojtěch Jarník had an evil twin, named Stanislaw, who designed a divide-and-conquer algorithm for finding minimum spanning trees. Suppose G is an undirected, connected, weighted graph, and, for the sake of simplicity, let us further suppose that the weights of the edges in G are distinct. Stanislaw's algorithm, MinTree(G), is as follows: If G is a single vertex, then it just returns, outputting nothing. Otherwise, it divides the set of vertices of G into two sets, V_1 and V_2, of equal size (plus or minus one vertex). Let e be the minimum-weight edge in G that connects V_1 and V_2. Output e as belonging to the minimum spanning tree. Let G_1 be the subgraph of G induced by V_1 (that is, G_1 consists of the vertices in V_1 plus all the edges of G that connect pairs of vertices in V_1). Similarly, let G_2 be the subgraph of G induced by V_2. The algorithm then recursively calls MinTree(G_1) and MinTree(G_2). Stanislaw claims that the edges output by his algorithm are exactly the edges of the minimum spanning tree of G. Prove or disprove Stanislaw's claim.

Applications

A-15.1 Suppose you are a manager in the IT department for the government of a corrupt dictator, who has a collection of computers that need to be connected together to create a communication network for his spies. You are given a weighted graph, G, such that each vertex in G is one of these computers and each edge in G is a pair of computers that could be connected with a communication line. It is your job to decide how to connect the computers. Suppose now that the CIA has approached you and is willing to pay you various amounts of money for you to choose some of these edges to belong to this network (presumably so that they can spy on the dictator). Thus, for you, the weight of each edge in G is the amount of money, in U.S. dollars, that the CIA will pay you for using that edge in the communication network. Describe an efficient algorithm, therefore, for finding a ***maximum spanning tree*** in G, which would maximize the money you can get from the CIA for connecting the dictator's computers in a spanning tree. What is the running time of your algorithm?

A-15.2 Suppose you are given a diagram of a telephone network, which is a graph G whose vertices represent switching centers, and whose edges represent communication lines between two centers. The edges are marked by their bandwidth, that is, the maximum speed, in bits per second, that information can be transmitted along that communication line. The bandwidth of a path in G is the bandwidth of its lowest-bandwidth edge. Give an algorithm that, given a diagram and two switching centers a and b, will output the maximum bandwidth of a path between a and b. What is the running time of your algorithm?

A-15.3 Suppose NASA wants to link n stations spread out over the solar system using ***free-space optical communication***, which is a technology that involves shooting lasers through space between pairs of stations to facilitate communication. Naturally, the energy needed to connect two stations in this way depends on the distance between them, with some connections requiring more energy than others. Therefore, each pair of stations has a different known energy that is needed to allow this pair of stations to communicate. NASA wants to connect all these stations together using the minimum amount of energy possible. Describe an algorithm for constructing such a communication network in $O(n^2)$ time.

A-15.4 Imagine that you just joined a company, GT&T, which set up its computer network a year ago for linking together its n offices spread across the globe. You have reviewed the work done at that time, and you note that they modeled their network as a connected, undirected graph, G, with n vertices, one for each office, and m edges, one for each possible connection. Furthermore, you note that they gave a weight, $w(e)$, for each edge in G that was equal to the annual rent that it costs to use that edge for communication purposes, and then they computed a minimum spanning tree, T, for G, to decide which of the m edges in G to lease. Suppose now that it is time renew the leases for connecting the vertices in G and you notice that the rent for one of the connections not used in T has gone down. That is, the weight, $w(e)$, of an edge in G that is not in T has been reduced. Describe an $O(n+m)$-time algorithm to update T to find a new minimum spanning, T', for G given the change in weight for the edge e.

A-15.5 Consider a scenario where you have a set of n players in a multiplayer game that we would like to connect to form a team. You are given a connected, weighted, undirected graph, G, with n vertices and m edges, which represents the n players and the m possible connections that can be made to link them together in a communicating team (that is, a connected subgraph of G). In this case, the weight on each edge, e, in G is an integer in the range $[1, n^2]$, which represents the amount of game points required to use the edge e for communication. Describe how to find a minimum spanning tree for G and thereby form this team with minimum cost, using an algorithm that runs in $O(m\,\alpha(n))$ time, where $\alpha(n)$ is the slow-growing inverse of the Ackermann function.

A-15.6 Suppose you have n rooms that you would like to connect in a communication network in one of the dormitories of Flash University. You have modeled the problem using a connected, undirected graph, G, where each of the n vertices in G is a room and each of the m edges in G is a possible connection that you can form by running a cable between the rooms represented by the end vertices of that edge. In this case, however, there are only two kinds of cables that you may possibly use, a 12-foot cable, which costs \$10 and is sufficient to connect some pairs of rooms, and a 50-foot cable, which costs \$30 and can be used to connect pairs of rooms that are farther apart. Describe an algorithm for finding a minimum-cost spanning tree for G in $O(n + m)$ time.

A-15.7 Suppose, for a data approximation application, you are given a set of n points in the plane and you would like to partition these points into two sets, A and B, such that each point in A is as close or closer to another point in A than it is to any point in B, and vice versa. Describe an efficient algorithm for doing this partitioning.

Chapter Notes

The first known minimum spanning tree algorithm is due to Barůvka [21], and was published in 1926. The Prim-Jarník algorithm was first published in Czech by Jarník [111] in 1930 and in English in 1957 by Prim [174]. Kruskal published his minimum spanning tree algorithm in 1956 [137]. The reader interested in further study of the history of the minimum spanning tree problem is referred to the paper by Graham and Hell [92]. The current asymptotically fastest minimum spanning tree algorithm is a randomized method of Karger, Klein, and Tarjan [119] that runs in $O(m)$ expected time.

Incidentally, the running time for the Prim-Jarník algorithm can be improved to be $O(n \log n + m)$ by implementing the queue Q with either of two more sophisticated data structures, the "Fibonacci Heap" [76] or the "Relaxed Heap" [58]. The reader interested in these implementations is referred to the papers that describe the implementation of these structures, and how they can be applied to minimum spanning tree problems.

Chapter

16

Network Flow and Matching

Yellowstone Falls, 1941. Ansel Adams. U.S. government image. U.S. National Archives and Records Administration.

Contents

16.1 Flows and Cuts 445
16.2 Maximum Flow Algorithms 452
16.3 Maximum Bipartite Matching 458
16.4 Baseball Elimination 460
16.5 Minimum-Cost Flow 462
16.6 Exercises 469

Consider a computer network modeled by a directed graph G in which each vertex represents a computer, each edge (u, v) represents a one-way communication channel from computer u to computer v, and the weight of each edge (u, v) represents the bandwidth of the channel, that is, the maximum number of bytes that can be sent from u to v in one second. Suppose that we would like to send a high-bandwidth streaming media connection from some computer s in G to some computer t in G, with as high a bandwidth as possible, possibly even higher than the maximum bandwidth of any single link in our network. This might seem impossible at first, but it might actually be possible if we can divide this media stream into lots of packets and route these packets through multiple paths in the network.

We can formulate this problem by imagining that each edge in G represents a "pipe" that can transport some commodity, with the weight of that edge representing the maximum amount it can transport per unit time interval. The optimization problem is then known as the **maximum flow** problem, where we are given a weighted directed graph and asked to find a way of transporting the maximum amount of the given commodity from some vertex s, called the **source**, to some vertex t, called the **sink**. (See Figure 16.1.)

Incidentally, the maximum flow problem is closely related to the problem of finding the maximum way of matching vertices of one type in a graph with vertices of another type. We therefore also study the maximum matching problem, showing how the maximum flow problem can be used to solve it efficiently.

Sometimes we have many different maximum flows. Although all are maximum in terms of how much flow they produce, these flows may in fact be different in how much they cost. Thus, in this chapter, we also study methods for computing maximum flows that are of minimum cost, when there are many different maximum flows and we have some way of measuring their relative costs.

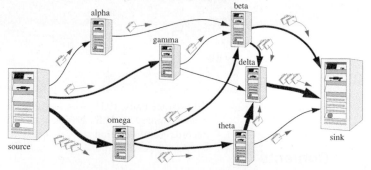

Figure 16.1: A flow in a graph representing a computer network, with the bandwidth of thick edges being 4 MB/s, medium edges being 2 MB/s, and thin edges being 1 MB/s. We indicate the flow using icons, where each folder corresponds to one MB/s going through the channel. Note that the total amount of flow sent from the source to the sink (6 MB/s) is not maximum. Indeed, one additional MB/s can be pushed from the source to gamma, from gamma to delta, and from delta to the sink. After this extra flow is added, the total flow will be maximum.

16.1 Flows and Cuts

The above example illustrates the rules that a legal flow must obey. In order to precisely say what these rules are, let us carefully define what we mean by a flow.

Flow Networks

A *flow network* N consists of the following:

- A connected directed graph G with nonnegative integer weights on the edges, where the weight of an edge e is called the ***capacity*** $c(e)$ of e
- Two distinguished vertices, s and t, of G, called the ***source*** and ***sink***, respectively, such that s has no incoming edges and t has no outgoing edges.

Given such a labeled graph, the challenge is to determine the maximum amount of some commodity that can be pushed from s to t under the constraint that the capacity of an edge determines the maximum flow that can go along that edge. (See Figure 16.2.)

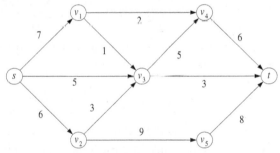

Figure 16.2: A flow network, N. Each edge e of N is labeled with its capacity, $c(e)$.

Of course, if we wish some commodity to flow from s to t, we need to be more precise about what we mean by a "flow." A *flow* for network N is an assignment of an integer value $f(e)$ to each edge e of G that satisfies the following properties:

- For each edge e of G,
$$0 \le f(e) \le c(e) \quad \textbf{\textit{(capacity rule)}}.$$

- For each vertex v of G distinct from the source s and the sink t
$$\sum_{e \in E^-(v)} f(e) = \sum_{e \in E^+(v)} f(e) \quad \textbf{\textit{(conservation rule)}},$$

where $E^-(v)$ and $E^+(v)$ denote the sets of incoming and outgoing edges of v, respectively.

In other words, a flow must satisfy the edge capacity constraints and must, for every vertex v other than s and t, have the total amount of flow going out of v equal to the total amount of flow coming into v. Each of the above rules is satisfied, for example, by the flow illustrated in Figure 16.3.

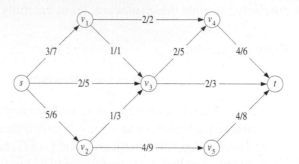

Figure 16.3: A flow, f (of value $|f| = 10$), for the flow network N of Figure 16.2.

The quantity $f(e)$ is called the *flow* of edge e. The *value* of a flow f, which we denote by $|f|$, is equal to the total amount of flow coming out from the source s:

$$|f| = \sum_{e \in E^+(s)} f(e).$$

It is easy to show that the flow value is also equal to the total amount of flow going into the sink t (see Exercise R-16.1):

$$|f| = \sum_{e \in E^-(t)} f(e).$$

That is, a flow specifies how some commodity is pushed out from s, through the network N, and finally into the sink t. A *maximum flow* for flow network N is a flow with maximum value over all flows for N (see Figure 16.4). Since a maximum flow is using a flow network most efficiently, we are most interested in methods for computing maximum flows.

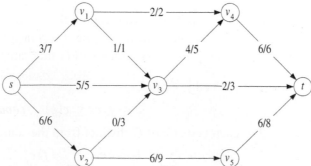

Figure 16.4: A maximum flow f^* (of value $|f^*| = 14$) for the flow network N of Figure 16.2.

16.1.1 Cuts

It turns out that flows are closely related to another concept, known as cuts. Intuitively, a cut is a division of the vertices of a flow network N into two sets, with s on one side and t on the other. Formally, a **cut** of N is a partition $\chi = (V_s, V_t)$ of the vertices of N such that $s \in V_s$ and $t \in V_t$. An edge e of N with origin $u \in V_s$ and destination $v \in V_t$ is said to be a **forward edge** of cut χ. An edge with origin in V_t and destination in V_s is said to be a **backward edge**. We envision a cut as a separation of s and t in N done by cutting across edges of N, with forward edges going from s's side to t's side and backward edges going in the opposite direction. (See Figure 16.5.)

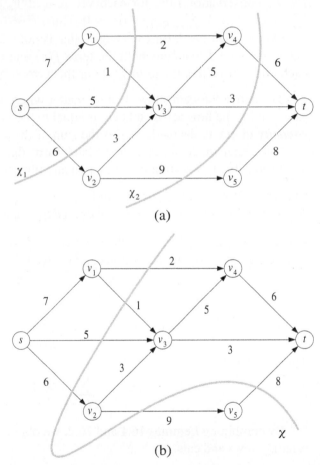

Figure 16.5: (a) Two cuts, χ_1 (on the left) and χ_2 (on the right), in the flow network N of Figure 16.2. These cuts have only forward edges and their capacities are $c(\chi_1) = 14$ and $c(\chi_2) = 18$. Cut χ_1 is a minimum cut for N. (b) A cut χ in N with both forward and backward edges. Its capacity is $c(\chi) = 22$.

Given a flow f for N, the ***flow across cut*** χ, denoted $f(\chi)$, is equal to the sum of the flows in the forward edges of χ minus the sum of the flows in the backward edges of χ. That is, $f(\chi)$ is the net amount of commodity that flows from s's side of χ to t's side of χ. The following lemma shows an interesting property of $f(\chi)$.

Lemma 16.1: *Let N be a flow network, and let f be a flow for N. For any cut χ of N, the value of f is equal to the flow across cut χ, that is, $|f| = f(\chi)$.*

Proof: Consider the sum

$$F = \sum_{v \in V_s} \left(\sum_{e \in E^+(v)} f(e) - \sum_{e \in E^-(v)} f(e) \right).$$

By the conservation rule, for each vertex v of V_s distinct from s, we have that $\sum_{e \in E^+(v)} f(e) - \sum_{e \in E^-(v)} f(e) = 0$. Thus, $F = |f|$.

On the other hand, for each edge e that is not a forward or a backward edge of cut χ, the sum F contains both the term $f(e)$ and the term $-f(e)$, which cancel each other, or neither the term $f(e)$ nor the term $-f(e)$. Thus, $F = f(\chi)$.   ■

The above theorem shows that no matter where we cut a flow network to separate s and t, the flow across that cut is equal to the flow for the entire network. The ***capacity*** of cut χ, denoted $c(\chi)$, is the sum of the capacities of the forward edges of χ (note that we do not include the backward edges). The next lemma shows that a cut capacity $c(\chi)$ is an upper bound on any flow across χ.

Lemma 16.2: *Let N be a flow network, and let χ be a cut of N. Given any flow f for N, the flow across cut χ does not exceed the capacity of χ, that is, $f(\chi) \leq c(\chi)$.*

Proof: Denote with $E^+(\chi)$ the forward edges of χ, and with $E^-(\chi)$ the backward edges of χ. By the definition of $f(\chi)$, we have

$$f(\chi) = \sum_{e \in E^+(\chi)} f(e) - \sum_{e \in E^-(\chi)} f(e).$$

Dropping nonpositive terms from the above sum, we obtain the simplified condition, $f(\chi) \leq \sum_{e \in E^+(\chi)} f(e)$. By the capacity rule, for each edge e, $f(e) \leq c(e)$. Thus, we have

$$f(\chi) \leq \sum_{e \in E^+(\chi)} c(e) = c(\chi).$$

■

By combining Lemmas 16.1 and 16.2, we obtain the following important result relating flows and cuts.

Theorem 16.3: *Let N be a flow network. Given any flow f for N and any cut χ of N, the value of f does not exceed the capacity of χ, that is, $|f| \leq c(\chi)$.*

In other words, given any cut χ for a flow network N, the capacity of χ is an upper bound on any flow for N. This upper bound holds even for a ***minimum cut*** of

N, which is a cut with minimum capacity, taken over all cuts of N. In the example of Figure 16.5, χ_1 is a minimum cut.

16.1.2 Residual Capacity and Augmenting Paths

Theorem 16.3 implies that the value of a maximum flow is no more than the capacity of a minimum cut. We will show in this section that these two quantities are actually equal. In the process, we will outline an approach for constructing a maximum flow.

Residual Capacity

In order to prove that a certain flow f is maximum, we need some way of showing that there is absolutely no more flow that can possibly be "squeezed" into f. Using the related concepts of residual capacity and augmenting paths, discussed next, we can provide just such a proof for when a flow f is maximum.

Let N be a flow network, which is specified by a graph G, capacity function c, source s, and sink t. Furthermore, let f be a flow for N. Given an edge e of G directed from vertex u to vertex v, the **residual capacity** from u to v with respect to the flow f, denoted $\Delta_f(u, v)$, is defined as

$$\Delta_f(u, v) = c(e) - f(e),$$

and the residual capacity from v to u is defined as

$$\Delta_f(v, u) = f(e).$$

Intuitively, the residual capacity defined by a flow f is any additional capacity that f has not fully taken advantage of in "pushing" its flow from s to t.

Let π be a path from s to t that is allowed to traverse edges in either the forward or backward direction, that is, we can traverse the edge $e = (u, v)$ from its origin u to its destination v or from its destination v to its origin u. Formally, a **forward edge** of π is an edge e of π such that, in going from s to t along path π, the origin of e is encountered before the destination of e. An edge of π that is not forward is said to be a **backward edge**. Let us extend our definition of **residual capacity** to an edge e in π traversed from u to v, so that $\Delta_f(e) = \Delta_f(u, v)$. In other words,

$$\Delta_f(e) = \begin{cases} c(e) - f(e) & \text{if } e \text{ is a forward edge} \\ f(e) & \text{if } e \text{ is a backward edge.} \end{cases}$$

That is, the residual capacity of an edge e going in the forward direction is the additional capacity of e that f has yet to consume, but the residual capacity in the opposite direction is the flow that f has consumed (and could potentially "give back" if that allows for another flow of higher value).

Augmenting Paths

The residual capacity, $\Delta_f(\pi)$, of a path π is the minimum residual capacity of its edges. That is,

$$\Delta_f(\pi) = \min_{e \in \pi} \Delta_f(e).$$

This value is the maximum amount of additional flow that we can possibly "push" down the path π without violating a capacity constraint. An ***augmenting path*** for flow f is a path π from the source s to the sink t with nonzero residual capacity, that is, for each edge e of π,

- $f(e) < c(e)$ if e is a forward edge
- $f(e) > 0$ if e is a backward edge.

We show in Figure 16.6 an example of an augmenting path.

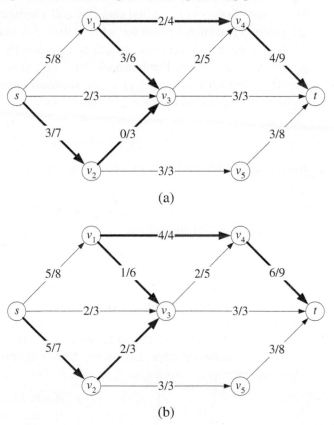

Figure 16.6: Example of an augmenting path: (a) network N, flow f, and an augmenting path π drawn with thick edges $((v_1, v_3)$ is a backward edge); (b) flow f' obtained from f by pushing $\Delta_f(\pi) = 2$ units of flow from s to t along path π.

As shown by the following lemma, we can always add the residual capacity of an augmenting path to an existing flow and get another valid flow.

Lemma 16.4: *Let π be an augmenting path for flow f in network N. There exists a flow f' for N of value $|f'| = |f| + \Delta_f(\pi)$.*

Proof: We compute the flow f' by modifying the flow of the edges of π:

$$f'(e) = \begin{cases} f(e) + \Delta_f(\pi) & \text{if } e \text{ is a forward edge} \\ f(e) - \Delta_f(\pi) & \text{if } e \text{ is a backward edge}. \end{cases}$$

Note that we subtract $\Delta_f(\pi)$ if e is a backward edge, for we are subtracting flow on e already taken by f in this case. In any case, because $\Delta_f(\pi) \geq 0$ is the minimum residual capacity of any edge in π, we will violate no capacity constraint on a forward edge by adding $\Delta_f(\pi)$ nor will we go below zero flow on any backward edge by subtracting $\Delta_f(\pi)$. Thus, f' is a valid flow for N, and the value of f' is $|f| + \Delta_f(\pi)$. ∎

By Lemma 16.4, the existence of an augmenting path π for a flow f implies that f is not maximum. Also, given an augmenting path π, we can modify f to increase its value by pushing $\Delta_f(\pi)$ units of flow from s to t along path π, as shown in the proof of Lemma 16.4.

What if there is no augmenting path for a flow f in network N? In this case, we have that f is a maximum flow, as stated by the following lemma.

Lemma 16.5: *If a network N does not have an augmenting path with respect to a flow f, then f is a maximum flow. Also, there is a cut χ of N such that $|f| = c(\chi)$.*

Proof: Let f be a flow for N, and suppose there is no augmenting path in N with respect to f. We construct from f a cut $\chi = (V_s, V_t)$ by placing in set V_s all the vertices v, such that there is a path from the source s to vertex v consisting of edges of nonzero residual capacity. Such a path is called an augmenting path from s to v. Set V_t contains the remaining vertices of N. Since there is no augmenting path for flow f, the sink t of N is in V_t. Thus, $\chi = (V_s, V_t)$ satisfies the definition of a cut.

By the definition of χ, each forward edge and backward edge of cut χ has zero residual capacity, that is,

$$f(e) = \begin{cases} c(e) & \text{if } e \text{ is a forward edge of } \chi \\ 0 & \text{if } e \text{ is a backward edge of } \chi. \end{cases}$$

Thus, the capacity of χ is equal to the value of f. That is,

$$|f| = c(\chi).$$

By Theorem 16.3, we have that f is a maximum flow. ∎

As a consequence of Theorem 16.3 and Lemma 16.5, we have the following:

Theorem 16.6 (The Max-Flow, Min-Cut Theorem): *The value of a maximum flow is equal to the capacity of a minimum cut.*

16.2 Maximum Flow Algorithms

In this section, we discuss two maximum flow algorithms in this section, starting with a classic algorithm, due to Ford and Fulkerson.

16.2.1 The Ford-Fulkerson Algorithm

The main idea of the *Ford-Fulkerson algorithm* is to incrementally increase the value of a flow in stages, where at each stage some amount of flow is pushed along an augmenting path from the source to the sink. Initially, the flow of each edge is equal to 0. At each stage, an augmenting path π is computed and an amount of flow equal to the residual capacity of π is pushed along π, as in the proof of Lemma 16.4. The algorithm terminates when the current flow f does not admit an augmenting path. Lemma 16.5 guarantees that f is a maximum flow in this case.

We provide a pseudocode description of the Ford-Fulkerson solution to the problem of finding a maximum flow in Algorithm 16.7.

Algorithm MaxFlowFordFulkerson(N):

    Input: Flow network $N = (G, c, s, t)$

    Output: A maximum flow f for N

    for each edge $e \in N$ **do**

        $f(e) \leftarrow 0$

    stop ← **false**

    repeat

        traverse G starting at s to find an augmenting path for f

        if an augmenting path π exists **then**

            // Compute the residual capacity $\Delta_f(\pi)$ of π

            $\Delta \leftarrow +\infty$

            for each edge $e \in \pi$ **do**

                if $\Delta_f(e) < \Delta$ **then**

                    $\Delta \leftarrow \Delta_f(e)$

            for each edge $e \in \pi$ **do**   // push $\Delta = \Delta_f(\pi)$ units along π

                if e is a forward edge **then**

                    $f(e) \leftarrow f(e) + \Delta$

                else

                    $f(e) \leftarrow f(e) - \Delta$ // e is a backward edge

        else

            stop ← **true**   // f is a maximum flow

    until *stop*

Algorithm 16.7: The Ford-Fulkerson algorithm.

We visualize the Ford-Fulkerson algorithm in Figure 16.8.

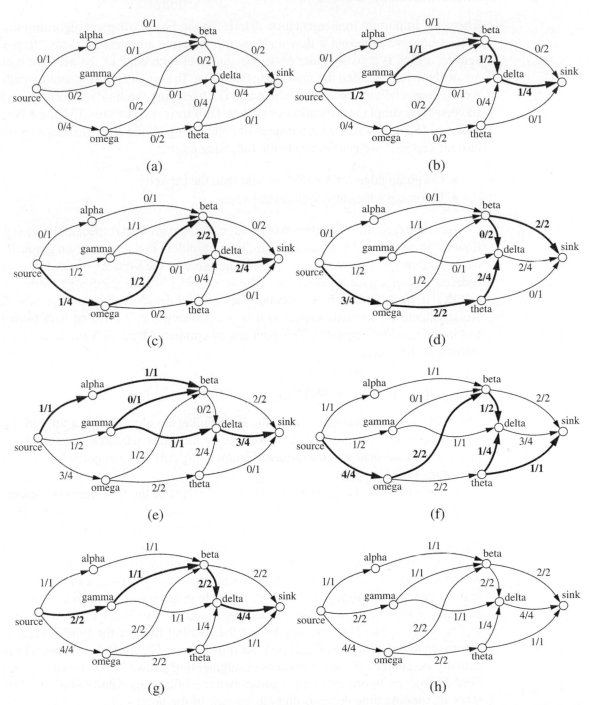

Figure 16.8: Example execution of the Ford-Fulkerson algorithm on the flow network of Figure 16.1. Augmenting paths are drawn with thick lines.

Implementation Details

There are important implementation details for the Ford-Fulkerson algorithm that impact how we represent a flow and how we compute augmenting paths. Representing a flow is actually quite easy. We can label each edge of the network with an attribute representing the flow along that edge. To compute an augmenting path, we use a specialized traversal of the graph G underlying the flow network. Such a traversal is a simple modification of either a DFS traversal (Section 13.2) or a BFS traversal (Section 13.3), where instead of considering all the edges incident on the current vertex v, we consider only the following edges:

- Outgoing edges of v with flow less than the capacity
- Incoming edges of v with nonzero flow.

Alternatively, the computation of an augmenting path with respect to the current flow f can be reduced to a simple path-finding problem in a new directed graph R_f derived from G. The vertices of R_f are the same as the vertices of G. For each ordered pair of adjacent vertices u and v of G, we add a directed edge from u to v if $\Delta_f(u, v) > 0$. Graph R_f is called the ***residual graph*** with respect to flow f. An augmenting path with respect to flow f corresponds to a directed path from s to t in the residual graph R_f. This path can be computed by a DFS traversal of R_f starting at the source.

Analyzing the Ford-Fulkerson Algorithm

The analysis of the running time of the Ford-Fulkerson algorithm is a little tricky. This is because the algorithm does not specify the exact way to find augmenting paths and, as we shall see, the choice of augmenting path has a major impact on the algorithm's running time.

Let n and m be the number of vertices and edges of the flow network, respectively, and let f^* be a maximum flow. Since the graph underlying the network is connected, we have that $n \leq m + 1$. Note that each time we find an augmenting path we increase the value of the flow by at least 1, since edge capacities and flows are integers. Thus, $|f^*|$, the value of a maximum flow, is an upper bound on the number of times the algorithm searches for an augmenting path. Also note that we can find an augmenting path by a simple graph traversal, such as a DFS or BFS traversal, which takes $O(m)$ time (see Theorems 13.13 and 13.15, and recall that $n \leq m + 1$). Thus, we can bound the running time of the Ford-Fulkerson algorithm as being at most $O(|f^*|m)$. As illustrated in Figure 16.9, this bound can actually be attained for some choices of augmenting paths. We conclude that the Ford-Fulkerson algorithm is a pseudo-polynomial-time algorithm (Section 12.6), since its running time depends on both the size of the input and also the value of a numeric parameter. Thus, the time bound of the Ford-Fulkerson algorithm can be quite slow if $|f^*|$ is large and augmenting paths are chosen poorly.

Finding an augmenting path   Augmenting the flow

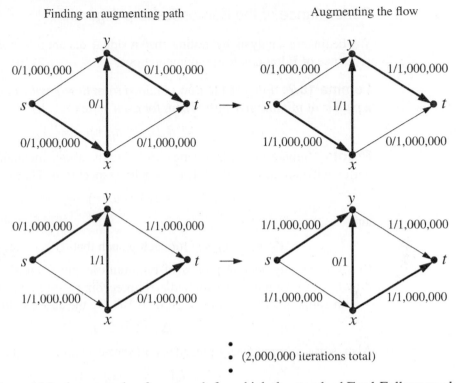

• • • (2,000,000 iterations total)

Figure 16.9: An example of a network for which the standard Ford-Fulkerson algorithm runs slowly. If the augmenting paths chosen by the algorithm alternate between (s, x, y, t) and (s, y, x, t), then the algorithm will make a total of $2,000,000$ iterations, even though two iterations would have sufficed.

16.2.2 The Edmonds-Karp Algorithm

The ***Edmonds-Karp algorithm*** is a variation of the Ford-Fulkerson algorithm. It uses a simple technique for finding good augmenting paths that results in a faster running time. This technique is based on the notion of being "more greedy" in our application of the greedy method to the maximum flow problem. Namely, at each iteration, we choose an augmenting path with the smallest number of edges, which can be easily done in $O(m)$ time by a modified BFS traversal. We will show that with these ***Edmonds-Karp augmentations***, the number of iterations is no more than nm, which implies an $O(nm^2)$ running time for the Edmonds-Karp algorithm.

We begin by introducing some notation. We call the ***length*** of a path π the number of edges in π. Let f be a flow for network N. Given a vertex v, we denote with $d_f(v)$ the minimum length of an augmenting path with respect to f from the source s to vertex v, and call this quantity the ***residual distance*** of v with respect to flow f. The following discussion shows how residual distance of each vertex impacts the running time of the Edmonds-Karp algorithm.

Performance of the Edmonds-Karp Algorithm

We begin our analysis by noting that residual distance is nondecreasing over a sequence of Edmonds-Karp augmentations.

Lemma 16.7: *Let g be the flow obtained from flow f with an augmentation along a path π of minimum length. Then, for each vertex v,*

$$d_f(v) \leq d_g(v).$$

Proof: Suppose there is a vertex violating the above inequality. Let v be such a vertex with smallest residual distance with respect to g. That is,

$$d_f(v) > d_g(v) \tag{16.1}$$

and

$$d_g(v) \leq d_g(u), \text{ for each } u \text{ such that } d_f(u) > d_g(u). \tag{16.2}$$

Consider an augmenting path γ of minimum length from s to v with respect to flow g. Let u be the vertex immediately preceding v on γ, and let e be the edge of γ with endpoints u and v (see Figure 16.10). By the above definition, we have

$$\Delta_g(u, v) > 0. \tag{16.3}$$

Also, since u immediately precedes v in shortest path, γ, we have

$$d_g(v) = d_g(u) + 1. \tag{16.4}$$

Finally, by (16.2) and (16.4), we have

$$d_f(u) \leq d_g(u). \tag{16.5}$$

We now show that $\Delta_f(u, v) = 0$. Indeed, if we had $\Delta_f(u, v) > 0$, we could go from u to v along an augmenting path with respect to flow f. This would imply

$$
\begin{aligned}
d_f(v) &\leq d_f(u) + 1 \\
&\leq d_g(u) + 1 \quad \text{by (16.5)} \\
&= d_g(v) \qquad\quad \text{by (16.4),}
\end{aligned}
$$

thus contradicting (16.1).

Since $\Delta_f(u, v) = 0$ and, by (16.3), $\Delta_g(u, v) > 0$, the augmenting path π, which produces g from f, must traverse the edge e from v to u (see Figure 16.10). Hence,

$$
\begin{aligned}
d_f(v) &= d_f(u) - 1 \quad \text{because } \pi \text{ is a shortest path} \\
&\leq d_g(u) - 1 \quad \text{by (16.5)} \\
&\leq d_g(v) - 2 \quad \text{by (16.4)} \\
&< d_g(v).
\end{aligned}
$$

Thus, we have obtained a contradiction with (16.1), which completes the proof. ■

Intuitively, Lemma 16.7 implies that each time we do an Edmonds-Karp augmentation, the residual distance from s to any vertex v can only increase or stay the same. This fact gives us the following.

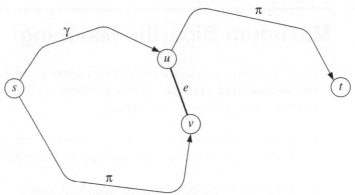

Figure 16.10: Illustration of the proof of Lemma 16.7.

Lemma 16.8: *When executing the Edmonds-Karp algorithm on a network with n vertices and m edges, the number of flow augmentations is no more than nm.*

Proof: Let f_i be the flow in the network before the ith augmentation, and let π_i be the path used in such augmentation. We say that an edge e of π_i is a ***bottleneck*** for π_i if the residual capacity of e is equal to the residual capacity of π_i. Clearly, every augmenting path used by the Edmonds-Karp algorithm has at least one bottleneck.

Consider a pair of vertices u and v joined by an edge e, and suppose that edge e is a bottleneck for two augmenting paths π_i and π_k, with $i < k$, that traverse e from u to v. The above assumptions imply each of the following:

- $\Delta_{f_i}(u, v) > 0$
- $\Delta_{f_{i+1}}(u, v) = 0$
- $\Delta_{f_k}(u, v) > 0$.

Thus, there must be an intermediate jth augmentation, with $i < j < k$ whose augmenting path π_j traverses edge e from v to u. We therefore obtain

$$
\begin{aligned}
d_{f_j}(u) \ &= \ d_{f_j}(v) + 1 \quad \text{(because } \pi_j \text{ is a shortest path)} \\
&\geq \ d_{f_i}(v) + 1 \quad \text{(by Lemma 16.7)} \\
&\geq \ d_{f_i}(u) + 2 \quad \text{(because } \pi_i \text{ is a shortest path).}
\end{aligned}
$$

Since the residual distance of a vertex is always less than the number of vertices n, each edge can be a bottleneck at most n times during the execution of the Edmonds-Karp algorithm ($n/2$ times for each of the two directions in which it can be traversed by an augmenting path). Hence, the overall number of augmentations is no more than nm. ∎

Since a single flow augmentation can be done in $O(m)$ time using a modified BFS strategy, we can summarize the above discussion as follows.

Theorem 16.9: *Given a flow network with n vertices and m edges, the Edmonds-Karp algorithm computes a maximum flow in $O(nm^2)$ time.*

16.3   Maximum Bipartite Matching

A problem that arises in a number of important applications is the ***maximum bipartite matching*** problem. In this problem, we are given a connected undirected graph with the following properties:

- The vertices of G are partitioned into two sets, X and Y.
- Every edge of G has one endpoint in X and the other endpoint in Y.

Such a graph is called a ***bipartite graph***. A ***matching*** in G is a set of edges that have no endpoints in common—such a set "pairs" up vertices in X with vertices in Y so that each vertex has at most one "partner" in the other set. The maximum bipartite matching problem is to find a matching with the greatest number of edges (over all matchings).

Example 16.10: *Let G be a bipartite graph where the set X represents a group of young men and the set Y represents a group of young women, who are all together at a community dance. Let there be an edge joining x in X and y in Y if x and y are willing to dance with one another. A maximum matching in G corresponds to a largest set of compatible pairs of men and women who can all be happily dancing at the same time.*

Example 16.11: *Let G be a bipartite graph where the set X represents a group of college courses and the set Y represents a group of classrooms. Let there be an edge joining x in X and y in Y if, based on its enrollment and audiovisual needs, the course x can be taught in classroom y. A maximum matching in G corresponds to a largest set of college courses that can be taught simultaneously without conflicting.*

These two examples provide a small sample of the kinds of applications that the maximum bipartite matching problem can be used to solve. Fortunately, there is a simple way of solving the maximum bipartite matching problem.

Reduction to the Maximum Flow Problem

Let G be a bipartite graph whose vertices are partitioned into sets X and Y. We create a flow network H such that a maximum flow in H can be immediately converted into a maximum matching in G:

- We begin by including all the vertices of G in H, plus a new source vertex s and a new sink vertex t.
- Next, we add every edge of G to H, but direct each such edge so that it is oriented from the endpoint in X to the endpoint in Y. In addition, we insert a directed edge from s to each vertex in X, and a directed edge from each vertex in Y to t. Finally, we assign to each edge of H a capacity of 1.

Given a flow f for H, we use f to define a set M of edges of G using the rule that an edge e is in M whenever $f(e) = 1$. (See Figure 16.11.) We now show that the set M is a matching. Since the capacities in H are all 1, the flow through each edge of H is either 0 or 1. Moreover, since each vertex x in X has exactly one incoming edge, the conservation rule implies that at most one outgoing edge of x has nonzero flow. Similarly, since each vertex y in Y has exactly one outgoing edge, at most one incoming edge of y has nonzero flow. Thus, each vertex in X will be paired by M with at most one vertex in Y, that is, set M is a matching. Also, we can easily see that the size of M is equal to $|f|$, the value of flow f.

A reverse transformation can also be defined. Namely, given a matching M in graph G, we can use M to define a flow f for H using the following rules:

- For each edge e of H that is also in G, $f(e) = 1$ if $e \in M$ and $f(e) = 0$ otherwise.
- For each edge e of H incident to s or t, $f(e) = 1$ if v is an endpoint of some edge of M and $f(e) = 0$ otherwise, where v denotes the other endpoint of e.

It is easy to verify that f is a flow for H and the value of f is equal to the size of M.

Therefore, any maximum flow algorithm can be used to solve the maximum bipartite matching problem on a graph G with n vertices and m edges. Namely,

1. We construct network H from the bipartite graph G. This step takes $O(n + m)$ time. Network H has $n + 2$ vertices and $n + m$ edges.
2. We compute a maximum flow for H using the standard Ford-Fulkerson algorithm. Since the value of the maximum flow is equal to $|M|$, the size of the maximum matching, and $|M| \leq n/2$, this step takes $O(n(n + m))$ time, which is $O(nm)$ because G is connected.

Theorem 16.12: *Let G be a bipartite graph with n vertices and m edges. A maximum matching in G can be computed in $O(nm)$ time.*

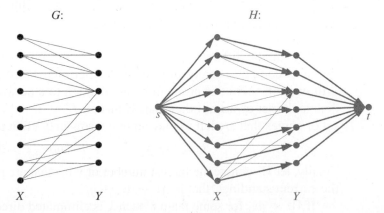

Figure 16.11: (a) A bipartite graph G. (b) Flow network H derived from G and a maximum flow in H; thick edges have unit flow and other edges have zero flow.

16.4　Baseball Elimination

Network flow has a lot of applications, with one of the more surprising being to a problem that arises in professional sports. Let T be a set of teams in a sports league, which, for historical reasons, let us assume is baseball. At any point during the season, each team, i, in T, will have some number, w_i, of wins, and will have some number, g_i, of games left to play. The **baseball elimination** problem is to determine whether it is possible for team i to finish the season in first place, given the games it has already won and the games it has left to play. Note that this depends on more than just the number of games left for team i, however; it also depends on the respective schedules of team i and the other teams. So let $g_{i,j}$ denote the number of games remaining between team i and team j, so that

$$g_i = \sum_{j \in T} g_{i,j}.$$

For example, see Table 16.12.

Team	Wins	Games Left	Schedule ($g_{i,j}$)			
i	w_i	g_i	LA	Oak	Sea	Tex
Los Angeles	81	8	-	1	6	1
Oakland	77	4	1	-	0	3
Seattle	76	7	6	0	-	1
Texas	74	5	1	3	1	-

Table 16.12: A set of teams, their standings, and their remaining schedule. Clearly, Texas is eliminated from finishing in first place, since it can win at most 79 games. In addition, even though it is currently in second place, Oakland is also eliminated, because it can win at most 81 games, but in the remaining games between LA and Seattle, either LA wins at least 1 game and finishes with at least 82 wins or Seattle wins 6 games and finishes with at least 82 wins.

With all the different ways for a team, k, to be eliminated, it might at first seem like it is computationally infeasible to determine whether team k is eliminated. Still, we can solve this problem by a reduction to a network flow problem. Let T' denote the set of teams other than k, that is, $T' = T - \{k\}$. Also, let L denote the set of games that are left to play among teams in T', that is,

$$L = \{\{i, j\}: \ i, j \in T' \text{ and } g_{i,j} > 0\}.$$

Finally, let W denote the largest number of wins that are possible for team k given the current standings, that is, $W = w_k + g_k$.

If $W < w_i$, for some team i, then k is eliminated directly by team i. So, let us assume that no single team eliminates team k. To consider how a combination of teams and game outcomes might eliminate team k, we create a graph, G, that has as its vertices a source, s, a sink, t, and the sets T' and L. Then, let us include the following edges in G (see Figure 16.13):

- For each game pair, $\{i, j\}$, in L, add an edge $(s, \{i, j\})$, and give it capacity $g_{i,j}$.
- For each game pair, $\{i, j\}$, in L, add edges $(\{i, j\}, i)$ and $(\{i, j\}, j)$, and give these edges capacity $+\infty$.
- For each team, i, add an edge (i, t) and give it capacity $W - w_i$, which cannot be negative in this case, since we ruled out the case when $W < w_i$.

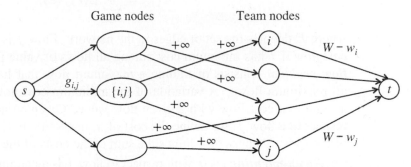

Figure 16.13: The network, G, to determine whether team k is eliminated.

The intuition behind the construction for G is that wins flow out from the source, s, are split at each game node, $\{i, j\}$, to allocate wins between each pair of teams, i and j, and then are absorbed by the sink, t. The flow on each edge, $(\{i, j\}, i)$, represents the number of games in which team i beats j, and the flow on each edge, (i, t), represents the number of remaining games that could be won by team i. Thus, maximizing the flow in G is equivalent to testing if it is possible to allocate wins among all the remaining games not involving team k so that no team goes above W wins. So we compute a maximum flow for G.

Suppose that the value of this maximum flow is

$$g(T') = \sum_{\{i,j\} \subseteq T'} g_{i,j},$$

which is the total number of games to be played by teams in T'. This implies that it is possible to allocate wins to all the remaining games so that no team has its win count go above W, that is, team k is not eliminated. If, on the other hand, the value of the maximum flow is strictly less than $g(T')$, then team k is eliminated, since it is not possible to allocate wins to all the remaining games with every team having a win count of at most W. Thus, we have the following:

Theorem 16.13: *We can solve the baseball elimination problem for any team in a set of n teams by solving a single maximum flow problem on a network with at most $O(n^2)$ vertices and edges.*

16.5 Minimum-Cost Flow

There is another variant of the maximum flow problem that applies in situations where there is a cost associated with sending a unit of flow through an edge. In this section, we extend the definition of a network by specifying a second nonnegative integer weight $w(e)$ for each edge e, representing the **cost** of edge e.

Given a flow f, we define the cost of f as

$$w(f) = \sum_{e \in E} w(e)f(e),$$

where E denotes the set of edges in the network. Flow f is said to be a **minimum-cost flow** if f has minimum cost among all flows of value $|f|$. The **minimum-cost flow problem** consists of finding a maximum flow that has the lowest cost over all maximum flows. A variation of the minimum-cost flow problem asks to find a minimum-cost flow with a given flow value. Given an augmenting path π with respect to a flow f, we define the cost of π, denoted $w(\pi)$, as the sum of the costs of the forward edges of π minus the sum of the costs of the backward edges of π.

An **augmenting cycle** with respect to flow f is an augmenting path whose first and last vertices are the same. In more mathematical terms, it is a directed cycle γ with vertices $v_0, v_1, \ldots, v(k-1), v_k = v_0$, such that $\Delta_f(v_i, v_{i+1}) > 0$ for $i = 0, \ldots, k-1$ (see Figure 16.14). The definitions of residual capacity (given in Section 16.1.2) and cost (given above) also apply to an augmenting cycle. In addition, note that since it is a cycle, we can add the flow of an augmenting cycle to an existing flow without changing its flow value.

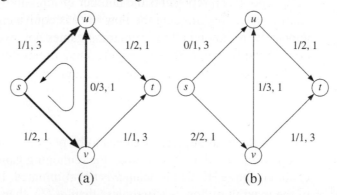

(a)   (b)

Figure 16.14: (a) Network with flow f, where each edge e is labeled with $f(e)/c(e), w(e)$. We have $|f| = 2$ and $w(f) = 8$. Augmenting cycle $\gamma = (s, v, u, s)$, drawn with thick edges. The residual capacity of γ is $\Delta_f(\gamma) = 1$. The cost of γ is $w(\gamma) = -1$. (b) Flow f' obtained from f by pushing one unit of flow along cycle γ. We have $|f'| = |f|$ and $w(f') = w(f) + w(\gamma)\Delta_f(\gamma) = 8 + (-1) \cdot 1 = 7$.

Adding the Flow from an Augmenting Cycle

The following lemma is analogous to Lemma 16.4, as it shows that a maximum flow can be changed into another maximum flow using an augmenting cycle.

Lemma 16.14: *Let γ be an augmenting cycle for flow f in network N. There exists a flow f' for N of value $|f'| = |f|$ and cost*

$$w(f') = w(f) + w(\gamma)\Delta_f(\gamma).$$

We leave the proof of Lemma 16.14 as an exercise (R-16.13).

A Condition for Minimum-Cost Flows

Note that Lemma 16.14 implies that if a flow f has an augmenting cycle of negative cost, then f does not have minimum cost. The following theorem shows that the converse is also true, giving us a condition for testing when a flow is in fact a minimum-cost flow.

Theorem 16.15: *A flow f has minimum cost among all flows of value $|f|$ if and only if there is no augmenting cycle of negative cost with respect to f.*

Proof: The "only-if" part follows immediately from Lemma 16.14. To prove the "if" part, suppose that flow f does not have minimum cost, and let g be a flow of value f with minimum cost. Flow g can be obtained from f by a series of augmentations along augmenting cycles. Since the cost of g is less than the cost of f, at least one of these cycles must have negative cost. ∎

An Algorithmic Approach for Finding Minimum-Cost Flows

Theorem 16.15 suggests an algorithm for the minimum-cost flow problem based on repeatedly augmenting flow along negative-cost cycles. We first find a maximum flow f^* using the Ford-Fulkerson algorithm or the Edmonds-Karp algorithm. Next, we determine whether flow f^* admits a negative-cost augmenting cycle. The Bellman-Ford algorithm (Section 14.3) can be used to find a negative cycle in time $O(nm)$. Let w^* denote the total cost of the initial maximum flow f^*. After each execution of the Bellman-Ford algorithm, the cost of the flow decreases by at least one unit. Hence, starting from maximum flow f^*, we can compute a maximum flow of minimum cost in time $O(w^*nm)$. Therefore, we have the following:

Theorem 16.16: *Given an n-vertex flow network N with costs associated with its m edges, together with a maximum flow f^*, we can compute a maximum flow of minimum cost in $O(w^*nm)$ time, where w^* is the total cost of f^*.*

We can do much better than this, however, by being more careful in how we compute augmenting cycles, as we show in the remainder of this section.

Successive Shortest Paths

In this section, we present an alternative method for computing a minimum-cost flow. The idea is to start from an empty flow and build up to a maximum flow by a series of augmentations along minimum-cost paths. The following theorem provides the foundation of this approach.

Theorem 16.17: *Let f be a minimum-cost flow, and let f' be a the flow obtained by augmenting f along an augmenting path π of minimum cost. Flow f' is a minimum-cost flow.*

Proof: The proof is illustrated in Figure 16.15.

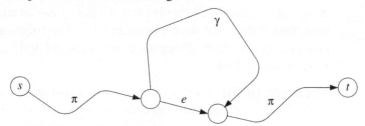

Figure 16.15: Illustrating the proof of Theorem 16.17.

Suppose, for the sake of a contradiction, that f' does not have minimum cost. By Theorem 16.15, f' has an augmenting cycle γ of negative cost. Cycle γ must have at least one edge e in common with path π and traverse e in the direction opposite to that of π, since otherwise γ would be an augmenting cycle of negative cost with respect to flow f, which is impossible, since f has minimum cost. Consider the path $\hat{\pi}$ obtained from π by replacing edge e with $\gamma - e$. The path $\hat{\pi}$ is an augmenting path with respect to flow f. Also path $\hat{\pi}$ has cost

$$w(\hat{\pi}) = w(\pi) + w(\gamma) < w(\pi).$$

This contradicts the assumption that π is an augmenting path of minimum cost with respect to flow f.   ∎

Starting from an initial null flow, we can compute a maximum flow of minimum cost by a repeated application of Theorem 16.17 (see Figure 16.16). Given the current flow f, we assign a weight to the edges of the residual graph R_f as follows (recall the definition of residual graph from Section 16.2). For each edge e, directed from u to v, of the original network, the edge of R_f from u to v, denoted (u, v), has weight $w(u, v) = w(e)$, while the edge (v, u) from v to u has weight $w(v, u) = -w(e)$. The computation of a shortest path in R_f can be done by using the Bellman-Ford algorithm (see Section 14.3) since, by Theorem 16.15, R_f does not have negative-cost cycles. Thus, we obtain a pseudo-polynomial-time algorithm (Section 12.6) that computes a maximum flow of minimum cost f^* in time $O(|f^*|nm)$.

An example execution of the above algorithm is shown in Figure 16.16.

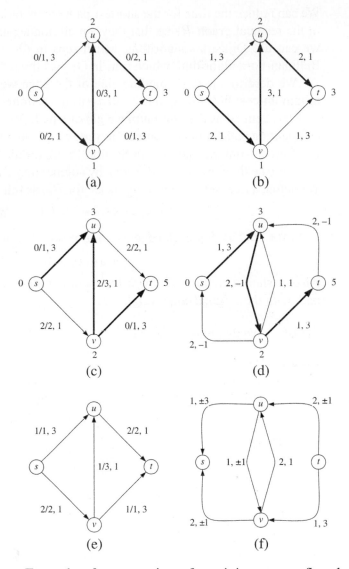

Figure 16.16: Example of computation of a minimum-cost flow by successive shortest-path augmentations. At each step, we show the network on the left and the residual network on the right. Vertices are labeled with their distance from the source. In the network, each edge e is labeled with $f(e)/c(e), w(e)$. In the residual network, each edge is labeled with its residual capacity and cost (edges with zero residual capacity are omitted). Augmenting paths are drawn with thick lines. A minimum-cost flow is computed with two augmentations. In the first augmentation, two units of flow are pushed along path (s, v, u, t). In the second augmentation, one unit of flow is pushed along path (s, u, v, t).

Modified Weights

We can reduce the time for the shortest-path computations by changing the weights in the residual graph R_f so that they are all nonnegative. After the modification, we can use Dijkstra's algorithm, which runs in $O(m \log n)$ time, instead of the Bellman-Ford algorithm, which runs in $O(nm)$ time.

We describe now the modification of the edge weights. Let f be the current minimum-cost flow. We denote with $d_f(v)$ the **distance** of vertex v from the source s in R_f, defined as the minimum weight of a path from s to v in R_f (the cost of an augmenting path from the source s to vertex v). Note that this definition of distance is different from the one used in Section 16.2.2 for the Edmonds-Karp algorithm.

Let g be the flow obtained from v by augmenting f along a minimum-cost path. We define a new set of edge weights w' for R_g, as follows (see Figure 16.17):

$$w'(u, v) = w(u, v) + d_f(u) - d_f(v).$$

Lemma 16.18: *For each edge (u, v) of residual network R_g, we have*

$$w'(u, v) \geq 0.$$

Also, a shortest path in R_g with the modified edge weights w' is also a shortest path with the original edge weights w.

Proof: We distinguish two cases.

Case 1: The edge (u, v) exists in R_f.
    In this case, the distance $d_f(v)$ of v from s is no more than the distance $d_f(u)$ of u from s plus the weight $w(u, v)$ of edge (u, v), that is,

$$d_f(v) \leq d_f(u) + w(u, v).$$

Thus, we have

$$w'(u, v) \geq 0.$$

Case 2: The edge (u, v) does not exist in R_f.
    In this case, (v, u) must be an edge of the augmenting path used to obtained flow g from flow f and we have

$$d_f(u) = d_f(v) + w(v, u).$$

Since $w(v, u) = -w(u, v)$, we have

$$w'(u, v) = 0.$$

Given a path π of R_g from s to t, the cost $w'(\pi)$ of π with respect to the modified edge weights differs from the cost $c(\pi)$ of π by a constant:

$$w'(\pi) = w(\pi) + d_f(s) - d_f(t) = w(\pi) - d_f(t).$$

Thus, a shortest path in R_g with respect to the original weights is also a shortest path with respect to the modified weights.   ■

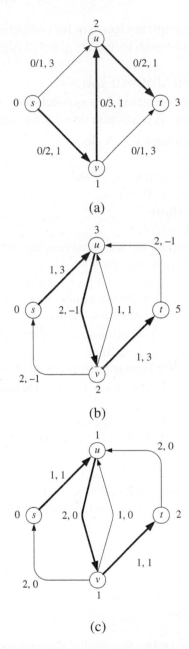

(a)

(b)

(c)

Figure 16.17: Modification of the edge costs in the computation of a minimum-cost flow by successive shortest-path augmentations. (a) Flow network N_f with initial null flow f and shortest augmenting path $\pi_1 = (s, v, u, t)$ with cost $w_1 = w(\pi_1) = 3$. Each vertex is labeled with its distance d_f from the source. (Same as Figure 16.16.b.) (b) Residual network R_g after augmenting flow f by two units along path π and shortest path $\pi_2 = (s, u, v, t)$ with cost $w(\pi_2) = 5$. (Same as Figure 16.16.d.) (c) Residual network R_g with modified edge weights. Path π_2 is still a shortest path. However, its cost is decreased by w_1.

The complete algorithm for computing a minimum-cost flow using the successive shortest-path method is given in Algorithm 16.18 (MinCostFlow).

Algorithm MinCostFlow(N):

    Input: Weighted flow network $N = (G, c, w, s, t)$

    Output: A maximum flow with minimum cost f for N

    for each edge $e \in N$ **do**

        $f(e) \leftarrow 0$

    for each vertex $v \in N$ **do**

        $d(v) \leftarrow 0$

    stop $\leftarrow$ **false**

    repeat

        compute the weighted residual network R_f

        for each edge $(u, v) \in R_f$ **do**

            $w'(u, v) \leftarrow w(u, v) + d(u) - d(v)$

        run Dijkstra's algorithm on R_f using the weights w'

        for each vertex $v \in N$ **do**

            $d(v) \leftarrow$ distance of v from s in R_f

        if $d(t) < +\infty$ **then**

            // π is an augmenting path with respect to f

            // Compute the residual capacity $\Delta_f(\pi)$ of π

            $\Delta \leftarrow +\infty$

            for each edge $e \in \pi$ **do**

                if $\Delta_f(e) < \Delta$ **then**

                    $\Delta \leftarrow \Delta_f(e)$

            // Push $\Delta = \Delta_f(\pi)$ units of flow along path π

            for each edge $e \in \pi$ **do**

                if e is a forward edge **then**

                    $f(e) \leftarrow f(e) + \Delta$

                else

                    $f(e) \leftarrow f(e) - \Delta$ // e is a backward edge

      else

            stop $\leftarrow$ **true**   // f is a maximum flow of minimum cost

    until *stop*

Algorithm 16.18: Successive shortest-path algorithm for computing a minimum-cost flow.

We summarize this section in the following theorem:

Theorem 16.19: *A minimum-cost maximum flow f for a network with n vertices and m edges can be computed in $O(|f| m \log n)$ time.*

16.6 Exercises

Reinforcement

R-16.1 Show that for a flow f, the total flow out of the source is equal to the total flow into the sink, that is,

$$\sum_{e \in E^+(s)} f(e) = \sum_{e \in E^-(t)} f(e).$$

R-16.2 Answer the following questions on the flow network N and flow f shown in Figure 16.6a:

- What are the forward and backward edges of augmenting path π?
- How many augmenting paths are there with respect to flow f? For each such path, list the sequence of vertices of the path and the residual capacity of the path.
- What is the value of a maximum flow in N?

R-16.3 Construct a minimum cut for the network shown in Figure 16.4 using the method in the proof of Lemma 16.5.

R-16.4 Illustrate the execution of the Ford-Fulkerson algorithm in the flow network of Figure 16.2.

R-16.5 Draw a flow network with 9 vertices and 12 edges. Illustrate an execution of the Ford-Fulkerson algorithm on it.

R-16.6 Find a minimum cut in the flow network of Figure 16.8a.

R-16.7 Show that, given a maximum flow in a network with m edges, a minimum cut of N can be computed in $O(m)$ time.

R-16.8 Find two maximum matchings for the bipartite graph of Figure 16.11a that are different from the maximum matching of Figure 16.11b.

R-16.9 Let G be a complete bipartite graph such that $|X| = |Y| = n$ and for each pair of vertices $x \in X$ and $y \in Y$, there is an edge joining x and y. Show that G has $n!$ distinct maximum matchings.

R-16.10 Illustrate the execution of the Ford-Fulkerson algorithm in the flow network of Figure 16.11b.

R-16.11 Illustrate the execution of the Edmonds-Karp algorithm in the flow network of Figure 16.8a.

R-16.12 Illustrate the execution of the Edmonds-Karp algorithm in the flow network of Figure 16.2.

R-16.13 Give a proof of Lemma 16.14.

R-16.14 Illustrate the execution of the minimum-cost flow algorithm based on successive augmentations along negative-cost cycles for the flow network of Figure 16.16a.

R-16.15 Illustrate the execution of the minimum-cost flow algorithm based on successive augmentations along minimum-cost paths for the flow network of Figure 16.2, where the cost of an edge (u, v) is given by $|\deg(u) - \deg(v)|$.

R-16.16 Is Algorithm 16.18 (MinCostFlow) a pseudo-polynomial-time algorithm?

Creativity

C-16.1 What is the worst-case running time of the Ford-Fulkerson algorithm if all edge capacities are bounded by a constant?

C-16.2 Improve the bound of Lemma 16.8 by showing that there are at most $nm/4$ augmentations in the Edmonds-Karp algorithm.

Hint: Use $d_f(u, t)$ in addition to $d_f(s, v)$.

C-16.3 Let N be a flow network with n vertices and m edges. Show how to compute an augmenting path with the largest residual capacity in $O((n + m) \log n)$ time.

C-16.4 Show that the Ford-Fulkerson algorithm runs in time $O(m^2 \log n \log |f^*|)$ when, at each iteration, the augmenting path with the largest residual capacity is chosen.

C-16.5 You want to increase the maximum flow of a network as much as possible, but you are only allowed to increase the capacity of one edge.

    a. How do you find such an edge? (Give pseudocode.) You may assume the existence of algorithms to compute max flow and min cut. What's the running time of your algorithm?

    b. Is it always possible to find such an edge? Justify your answer.

C-16.6 Given a flow network N and a maximum flow f for N, suppose that the capacity of an edge e of N is decreased by one, and let N' be the resulting network. Give an algorithm for computing a maximum flow in network N' by modifying f.

C-16.7 Give an algorithm that determines, in $O(n + m)$ time, whether a graph with n vertices and m edges is bipartite.

C-16.8 Give an algorithm for computing a flow of maximum value subject to the following two additional constraints:

    a. Each edge e has a lower bound $\ell(e)$ on the flow through it.

    b. There are multiple sources and sinks, and the value of the flow is computed as the total flow out of all the sources (equal to the total flow into all the sinks).

C-16.9 Show that in a flow network with noninteger capacities, the Ford-Fulkerson algorithm may not terminate.

C-16.10 In the context of the baseball elimination problem, one can show that if $w_i + g_i \leq w_k + g_k$ and team k is eliminated, then team i is also eliminated. Use this fact to show that among a set of n teams, one can determine all the eliminated teams by solving $O(\log n)$ maximum flow problems.

C-16.11 A *vertex cover* for a graph, G, is a set of vertices, C, such that every edge in G is incident to one of the vertices in C. The problem of finding a smallest vertex cover is useful in network monitoring and other applications, but it is a difficult problem for general graphs. Show that the problem of finding a smallest vertex cover in a bipartite graph can be solved in polynomial time.

Hint: Use the max-flow, min-cut theorem, and the reduction of Section 16.3, to prove that, for any bipartite graph, G, the number of vertices in a minimum vertex cover for G equals the number of edges in a maximum matching in G.

Applications

A-16.1 In 2006, the city of Beijing, China, instituted a policy that limits residents to own at most one dog per household. Imagine you are running an online pet adoption website for the city. Your website contains pictures of adorable puppies that are available for adoption, and it allows for dogless Beijing residents to click on as many puppies as they like, with the understanding that they can adopt at most one. Suppose now that you have collected the puppy preferences from among n Beijing residents for your m puppies. Describe an efficient algorithm for assigning puppies to residents that provides for the maximum number of puppy adoptions possible while satisfying the constraints that each resident will only adopt a puppy that he or she likes and that no resident can adopt more than one puppy.

A-16.2 The city of Irvine, California, allows for residents to own a maximum of three dogs per household without a breeder's license. Imagine you are running an online pet adoption website for the city, as in the previous exercise, but now for n Irvine residents and m puppies. Describe an efficient algorithm for assigning puppies to residents that provides for the maximum number of puppy adoptions possible while satisfying the constraints that each resident will only adopt puppies that he or she likes and that no resident can adopt more than three puppies.

A-16.3 Consider the previous exercise, but suppose the city of Irvine, California, changed its dog-owning ordinance so that it still allows for residents to own a maximum of three dogs per household, but now restricts each resident to own at most one dog of any given breed, such as poodle, terrier, or golden retriever. Describe an efficient algorithm for assigning puppies to residents that provides for the maximum number of puppy adoptions possible while satisfying the constraints that each resident will only adopt puppies that he or she likes, that no resident can adopt more than three puppies, and that no resident will adopt more than one dog of any given breed.

A-16.4 Imagine that you are working on creating a flow for a set of packets in a media stream, as described in the introduction to this chapter. So you are given a network, G, with a source, s, and sink, t, together with bandwidth constraints on each edge, which indicate the maximum speed that the communication link represented by that edge can support. As mentioned before, your goal is to produce a maximum flow from s to t, respecting the bandwidth constraints on the edges. Suppose now, however, that you also have a bandwidth constraint on each router in the network, which specifies the maximum amount of information, in bits per second, that can pass through that node. Describe an efficient algorithm for finding a maximum flow in the network, G, that satisfies the bandwidth capacity constraints on the edges as well as the vertices. What is the running time of your algorithm?

A-16.5 Suppose, as an interview question, you are told that you have a goat and a wolf that need to go from a node, s, to a node, t, in a directed acyclic graph, G. To avoid the wolf eating the goat, their paths must never share an edge. Describe a polynomial-time algorithm for finding two edge-disjoint paths in G, if such paths exist, to provide a way for the goat and the wolf to go from s to t without risk to the goat.

A-16.6 Suppose a friend of yours has created a simulation game based on J.R.R. Tolkien's epic *The Lord of the Rings*. The game environment is Middle Earth, which is populated by various noble creatures, including hobbits, humans, dwarves, and elves. Unfortunately, these noble creatures are under attack and need to get to safe havens, known as "strongholds." Some strongholds are larger than others, of course, and each stronghold, s, can only hold some number, N_s, of these creatures. Initially, let us assume each stronghold is empty, and the noble creatures are living in various regions, with each region, r, containing some number, N_r, of noble creatures. Moreover, we know, for each region, r, the set of strongholds, S_r, that can be reached from r in at most three days' travel. Your job is to figure out how to move the maximum number of noble creatures possible from the regions where they currently live to the various strongholds in three days' time while not overcrowding any stronghold. Describe and analyze an efficient algorithm to solve this game.

A-16.7 A limousine company must process pickup requests every day, for taking customers from their various homes to the local airport. Suppose this company receives pickup requests from n locations and there are n limos available, where the distance of limo i to location j is given by a number, d_{ij}. Describe an efficient algorithm for computing a dispatchment of the n limos to the n pickup locations that minimizes the total distance traveled by all the limos.

Chapter Notes

Ford and Fulkerson's network flow algorithm (16.2) is described in their book [74]. Edmonds and Karp [64] describe two methods for computing augmenting paths that cause the Ford-Fulkerson algorithm to run faster: shortest augmenting path (Section 16.2.2) and augmenting paths with maximum residual capacity (Exercise C-16.4). The minimum-cost flow algorithm based on successive augmentations along minimum-cost paths (Section 16.5) is also due to Edmonds and Karp [64].

The reader interested in further study of graph algorithms and flow networks is referred to the books by Ahuja, Magnanti, and Orlin [10], Even [68], Gibbons [81], Mehlhorn [158], and Tarjan [207], and the book chapter by van Leeuwen [210]. Schwartz [187] was the first to show that the baseball elimination problem could be reduced to a maximum flow problem. Our formulation of the baseball elimination problem follows that of Wayne [215]. For applications of network flow to social networks, see the book by Easley and Kleinberg [60].

Chapter

17

NP-Completeness

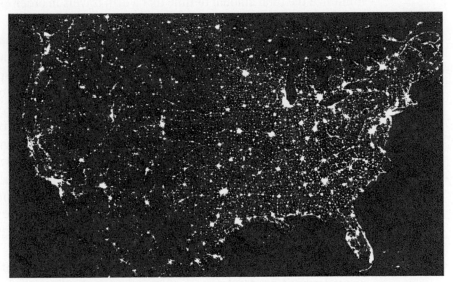

Composite satellite image of the United States at night, 1996. U.S. government image. NOAA/NGDC DMSP.

Contents

17.1 *P* and *NP* 476

17.2 *NP*-Completeness 483

17.3 CNF-SAT and 3SAT 489

17.4 VERTEX-COVER, CLIQUE, and SET-COVER 492

17.5 SUBSET-SUM and KNAPSACK 496

17.6 HAMILTONIAN-CYCLE and TSP 499

17.7 Exercises 502

Printed circuit boards connect electronic components, with the motherboard in a personal computer being a well-known example that connects memory chips, input/output ports, and a computer's CPU. The connections in a circuit board are made by an etching process that creates wires on its surface. Then holes are drilled into the board, allowing for the insertion of electronic components, which are subsequently soldered into the holes. Drilling all of the holes in such a board is a relatively slow step in this manufacturing process, and drilling time is wasted during the time the drill must move from one hole to the next. Thus, in order to manufacture a large number of identical printed circuit boards, it is worthwhile to minimize the total amount of time that a drill travels in order to drill all of the holes in a board.

Looking at this process as a computational problem, we can see that this manufacturing problem is actually an instance of a classic algorithmic problem—the *traveling salesperson problem* (*TSP*). In the traveling salesperson problem, we are given a set of "cities" that a traveling salesperson needs to visit. In addition, between every pair of cities, v and w, we are given "distance," $d(v, w)$, that is a number representing the cost (in time, miles, money, etc.) for traveling between city v and city w. The TSP objective is to find a tour that visits all of the cities and minimizes the total cost of all the traveling the salesperson needs to do. The problem of drilling all the holes in a printed circuit board is an instance of the traveling salesperson problem. Each of the holes represents a "city" and the distance between two of these cities is the time it would take to move a robotic drill from one hole to another, including the time it would take to change drill bits if the two holes are of different sizes. (See Figure 17.1.)

In addition to the example of optimizing the process of drilling holes in a printed circuit board, there are many other applications of the traveling salesperson problem. For instance, optimizing the delivery of packages in a UPS or FedEx truck, or the route that one should take to see all the points of interest on a vacation, are also traveling salesperson problems. Thus, it would be useful if we had a fast and simple algorithm for computing an optimal solution to any instance of the traveling salesperson problem. Unfortunately, this is a very difficult problem to always solve optimally.

Some computational problems, like the traveling salesperson problem, are hard. Moreover, even after lots of different researchers have worked on designing efficient algorithms for solving them, we may still not have a method that runs in polynomial time. Ideally, in such cases, we would like to prove that it is impossible to find a polynomial-time solution, so that we can clearly establish the difficulty of such a problem. Such a proof would be a great relief when an efficient algorithm evades us, for then we could take comfort from the fact that no efficient algorithm exists for this problem. Unfortunately, such proofs are typically also very difficult to discover.

Still, we can prove that certain problems are computationally as difficult as other problems, which is an indirect way of showing a problem is computationally difficult. In particular, the concept of *NP-completeness* allows us to rigorously show that finding an efficient algorithm for a certain problem is at least as hard as finding efficient algorithms for *all* the problems in a large class of problems called "*NP*." The formal notion of "efficient" we use here is that a problem has an algorithm running in time proportional to a polynomial function of its input size, n. (Recall that this notion of efficiency was already mentioned in Section 1.1.5.) That is, we consider an algorithm "efficient," for the discussion in this chapter, if it runs in time $O(n^k)$ on any input of size n, for some constant $k > 0$. The class *NP* contains some extremely difficult problems, for which polynomial-time solutions have eluded researchers for decades. Therefore, while showing that a problem is *NP*-complete is admittedly not the same as proving that an efficient algorithm for the problem is impossible, it is nevertheless a powerful statement. Basically, showing that a problem L is *NP*-complete says that, although we have been unable to find an efficient algorithm for L, neither has any computer scientist who has ever lived! Indeed, most computer scientists strongly believe it is impossible to solve any *NP*-complete problem in polynomial time.

In this chapter, we formally define the class *NP* and its related class *P*, and we show how to prove that some problems are *NP*-complete. We also discuss some of the best-known *NP*-complete problems, showing that each one is at least as hard as every other problem in *NP*. These problems include satisfiability, vertex cover, knapsack, and traveling salesperson.

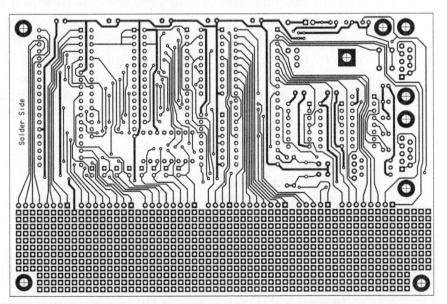

Figure 17.1: Artwork for a printed circuit board. Each circle in this diagram represents a hole that needs to be drilled. Optimizing the route that a drill should take to make these holes is an instance of the traveling salesperson problem (TSP). 8051 Development System Circuit Board, Paul Stoffregen, 2005, public domain image.

17.1 *P* and *NP*

In this section, we define ***P*** and ***NP***, which give us the basic tools for formally saying a problem is computationally difficult. But before we discuss the issue of intractability of computational problems, like the traveling salesperson problem, we need to revisit the definition of the running time of an algorithm.

In order to study ***NP***-completeness, we need to be more precise about running time. Namely, instead of the informal notion of input size as the number of "items" that form the input (see Chapter 1), we define the ***input size***, n, of a problem to be the number of bits used to encode an input instance. We also assume that characters and numbers in the input are encoded using a reasonable ***binary encoding*** scheme, so that each character uses a constant number of bits and each integer $M > 0$ is represented with at most $c \log M$ bits, for some constant $c > 0$. In particular, we disallow inputs that are specified using a ***unary encoding***, where an integer M is represented with M 1's.

Recall that we have, for most of the other chapters of this book, defined the input size, n, to be the number of "items" or "elements" in an input. In this chapter, however, we take n to be the number of bits used to represent an input, as mentioned above. Formally, we define the worst-case ***running time*** of an algorithm A to be the worst-case time taken by A as a function of n, taken over all inputs (with valid encodings) having n bits.

From the standpoint of polynomial-time algorithms, we don't actually lose much by focusing on bit-length as our definition of input size. For instance, if an algorithm has a running time that is polynomial in the number of input bits, n, then it also runs in polynomial time in the number of "items," N, in that same input, for $\sqrt{n} \leq N \leq n$. Likewise, any "reasonable" algorithm that runs in polynomial time in terms of the number of input items, N, will also run in polynomial time in terms of the number of input bits, n, where by "reasonable" we mean that numbers used by the algorithm can be represented using $O(\log N)$ bits or arrays of $O(\log N)$-bit numbers. Thus, under this restriction, n is $O(N \log N)$; hence, a reasonable algorithm with a running time that is polynomial in N will also have a running time that is polynomial in n. (See Figure 17.2 and also Exercise C-17.2.)

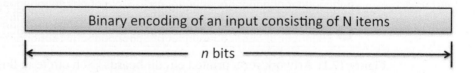

Figure 17.2: Viewing input size in terms of bits.

17.1.1   Defining the Complexity Classes *P* and *NP*

By the notion of a "reasonable" algorithm described above, we can easily show that, for the problems discussed elsewhere in this book, such as graph problems, text processing, or sorting, the polynomial-time algorithms given in those other chapters translate into polynomial-time algorithms using the notion of running time considered in this chapter.

Moreover, the class of polynomials is closed under addition, multiplication, and composition. That is, if $p(n)$ and $q(n)$ are polynomials, then so are $p(n) + q(n)$, $p(n) \cdot q(n)$, and $p(q(n))$. Thus, we can combine or compose polynomial-time algorithms to construct new polynomial-time algorithms. For example, if an algorithm, A, takes an input of size n and produces an output of size $q(n)$ in $O(q(n))$ time, and then an algorithm, B, takes the output of A as its input, where B runs in $O(p(m))$ time on inputs of size m, then this combined algorithm runs in time $O(q(n) + p(q(n)))$, which is polynomial if p and q are polynomials.

Decision Problems and Languages

To simplify our discussion, let us restrict our attention for the time being to *decision problems*, that is, to computational problems for which the intended output is either "yes" or "no." In other words, a decision problem's output is a single bit, which is either 0 or 1. For example, each of the following are decision problems:

- Given a string T and a string P, does P appear as a substring of T?
- Given two sets S and T, do S and T contain the same set of elements?
- Given a graph G with integer weights on its edges, and an integer k, does G have a minimum spanning tree of weight at most k?

As last problem illustrates, we can often turn an *optimization problem*, where we are trying to minimize or maximize some value, into a decision problem. We can introduce a parameter k and ask if the optimal value for the optimization problem is at most or at least k. Note that if we can show that a decision problem is hard, then its related optimization version must also be hard.

We say that an algorithm A *accepts* an input string x if A outputs "yes" on input x, and A *rejects* x if A outputs "no" on input x. Thus, we can view a *decision problem* as actually being just a set L of strings—the strings that should be accepted by an algorithm that correctly solves the problem. Indeed, we often use the letter "L" to denote such a decision problem, because a set of strings is often referred to as a *language*. We can extend this language-based viewpoint further to say that an algorithm A *decides* a language L if, for each string x, A outputs "yes" if x is in L and "no" otherwise. Throughout this chapter, we assume that if x is in an improper syntax, then an algorithm given x will output "no." In addition, we restrict our attention to algorithms, that is, computations that terminate on every input after a finite number of steps.

The Million-Dollar $P = NP$ Question

The *complexity class P* is the set of all decision problems (or languages) L that can be decided in worst-case polynomial time. That is, there is an algorithm A that, on input x, runs in $p(n)$ time, where n is the size of x and $p(n)$ is a polynomial, and, if $x \in L$, then A outputs "yes," and otherwise A outputs "no." The latter case refers to the *complement* of a language L, which consists of all binary strings that are not in L. Given an algorithm A that decides a language L in polynomial time, $p(n)$, we can easily construct a polynomial-time algorithm that decides the complement of L. In particular, given an input x, we can construct a complement algorithm B that simply runs A for $p(n)$ steps, where n is the size of x. If A outputs "yes," then B outputs "no," and if A outputs "no," then B outputs "yes." In either case, the complement algorithm, B, runs in polynomial time. Therefore, if a language L, representing some decision problem, is in *P*, then the complement of L is also in *P*.

The *complexity class NP* is defined to include the complexity class *P* but allow for the inclusion of languages that may not be in *P*. Specifically, with *NP* problems, we allow algorithms to perform an additional operation:

- **choose**(b): this operation chooses in a nondeterministic way a bit (that is, a value that is either 0 or 1) and assigns it to b.

When an algorithm A uses the **choose** primitive operation, then we say A is *nondeterministic*. We state that an algorithm A *nondeterministically accepts* a string x if there exists a set of outcomes to the **choose** calls that A could make on input x such that A would ultimately output "yes." In other words, it is as if we consider all possible outcomes to **choose** calls and only select those that lead to acceptance if there is such a set of outcomes.

The complexity class *NP* is the set of every decision problem (or language), L, that can be nondeterministically accepted in polynomial time, where we define the running time, $p(n)$, of a nondeterministic algorithm to be the maximum running time for A taken over all possible outcomes to its **choose** calls on an input of size n. That is, L is in *NP* if there is a nondeterministic algorithm A and polynomial $p(n)$ such that, on an input x of size n, if $x \in L$, then there is a set of outcomes to the **choose** calls in A so that it outputs "yes" and A runs in $p(n)$ time. If x is not in L, then every possible outcome to the **choose** calls in A results in A outputting "no."

Interestingly, unlike as was the case with *P*, just because a language L is in *NP* does not necessarily imply that the complement of L is also in *NP*. Indeed, there is a complexity class, called **co-NP**, that consists of all languages whose complement is in *NP*, and many researchers believe **co-NP** $\neq$ *NP*.

The Clay Mathematics Institute has offered \$1 million to the first person who proves whether $P = NP$. Although no one has, as of this writing, succeeded in claiming this prize, the majority of computer scientists believe that *P* is different than *NP*. That is, most computer scientists believe that the answer to the "$P = NP$?" question is "no."

An Alternative Definition of *NP*

There is actually another way to define the complexity class *NP*, which might be more intuitive for some readers. This alternative definition of *NP* is based on deterministic verification, instead of nondeterministic acceptance. We say that a language L can be ***verified*** by an algorithm A if, given any string x in L as input, there is another string y such that A outputs "yes" on input $z = x + y$, where we use the symbol "+" to denote concatenation. The string y is called a ***certificate*** for membership in L, for it helps us certify that x is indeed in L. Note that we make no claims about verifying when a string is not in L.

This notion of verification allows us to give an alternative definition of the complexity class *NP*. Namely, we can define *NP* to be the set of all languages L, defining decision problems, such that L can be verified in polynomial time. That is, there is a (deterministic) algorithm A that, for any x in L, verifies using some certificate y that x is indeed in L in polynomial time, $p(n)$, including the time A takes to read its input $z = x + y$, where n is the size of x. Note that this definition implies that the size of y is less than $p(n)$. As the following theorem shows, this verification-based definition of *NP* is equivalent to the nondeterminism-based definition given above.

Theorem 17.1: *A language L can be (deterministically) verified in polynomial time if and only if L can be nondeterministically accepted in polynomial time.*

Proof: Suppose there is a deterministic algorithm A that can verify in polynomial time, $p(n)$, that a string x is in L when given a polynomial-length certificate y. We can construct a nondeterministic algorithm B that takes the string x as input and calls the **choose** method to assign the value of each bit in y. After B has constructed a string $z = x + y$, it then calls A to verify that $x \in L$ given the certificate y. If there exists a certificate y such that A accepts z, then there is clearly a set of nondeterministic choices for B that result in B outputting "yes" itself. In addition, B will run in $O(p(n))$ steps.

Next, suppose that there is a nondeterministic algorithm A that, given a string x in L, performs $p(n)$ steps, which may include **choose** steps, such that, for some sequence of outcomes to these **choose** steps, A will output "yes." There is a deterministic verification algorithm B that, given x in L, uses as its certificate y the ordered concatenation of all the outcomes to **choose** calls that A makes on input x in order to ultimately output "yes." Since A runs in $p(n)$ steps, where n is the size of x, the algorithm B will also run in $O(p(n))$ steps given input $z = x + y$. ∎

The practical implication of this theorem is that, since both definitions of *NP* are equivalent, we can use either one for showing that a problem is in *NP*. That is, Theorem 17.1 implies that we can structure a nondeterministic algorithm so that all of its **choose** steps are performed first and the rest of the algorithm is just a verification. We illustrate this approach by showing some interesting decision problems to be in *NP* in the next subsection.

17.1.2   Some Interesting Problems in *NP*

Our first example problem in *NP* is the traveling salesperson problem, which we discussed above. Recall that in this problem we are given a set of N "cities" together with a distance function, $d(v, w)$, which assigns an integer cost to each pair of cities (so that $d(v, w) = d(w, v)$), and we are asked to find a tour of all the cities that has minimum total cost. Viewing this as a decision problem, or language TSP, we assume we are also given an integer k, and we are asked whether there is a cycle that visits each city exactly once, returning to the starting city, such that the total cost of the tour is at most k. (See Figure 17.3.)

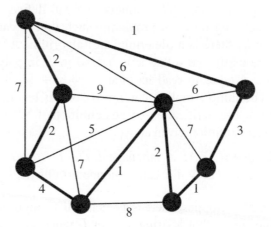

Figure 17.3: An example instance of the TSP decision problem, where $k = 18$ and the answer is "yes." City pairs with a finite cost between them are drawn as an edge along with its integer cost; missing edges are for city pairs with infinite cost between them. A tour with total cost at most k is drawn with bold edges.

Lemma 17.2: TSP *is in NP.*

Proof: Let us define a nondeterministic algorithm that accepts instances of TSP. Assume that the cities are numbered 1 to N. We iteratively call the choose method to determine a sequence S of $N + 1$ numbers from 1 to N. Then, we check that each number from 1 to N appears exactly once in S (for example, by sorting S), except for the first and last numbers in S, which should be the same. Then, we verify that the sequence S defines a cycle of cities and that the total cost of the tour defined by S is at most k. This algorithm clearly runs in polynomial time.

Observe that if there is a tour that visits each city exactly once, returning to the starting city, with total cost at most k, then our nondeterministic algorithm will output "yes." Likewise, if our algorithm outputs "yes," then it has found a tour visiting each city exactly once, returning to the starting city, with total cost at most k. Since this algorithm runs in polynomial time, this implies that TSP is in *NP*. ∎

Our next example is a problem related to circuit design testing. A **Boolean circuit** is a directed graph where each node, called a **logic gate**, corresponds to a simple Boolean function, AND, OR, or NOT. The incoming edges for a logic gate correspond to inputs for its Boolean function and the outgoing edges correspond to outputs, which will all be the same value, of course, for that gate. (See Figure 17.4.) Vertices with no incoming edges are **input** nodes, and a vertex with no outgoing edges is an **output** node.

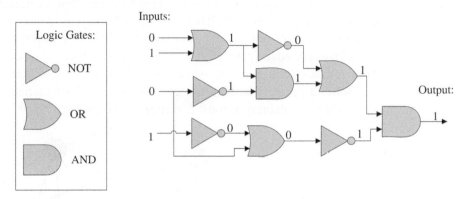

Figure 17.4: An example Boolean circuit.

CIRCUIT-SAT is the problem that takes as input a Boolean circuit with a single output node, and asks whether there is an assignment of values to the circuit's inputs so that its output value is "1." Such an assignment of values is called a **satisfying assignment**.

Lemma 17.3: CIRCUIT-SAT *is in NP*.

Proof: We construct a nondeterministic algorithm for accepting CIRCUIT-SAT in polynomial time. We first use the **choose** method to "guess" the values of the input nodes as well as the output value of each logic gate. Then, we simply visit each logic gate g in C, that is, each vertex with at least one incoming edge. We then check that the "guessed" value for the output of g is in fact the correct value for g's Boolean function, be it an AND, OR, or NOT, based on the given values for the inputs for g. This evaluation process can easily be performed in polynomial time. If any check for a gate fails, or if the "guessed" value for the output is 0, then we output "no." If, on the other hand, the check for every gate succeeds and the output is 1, the algorithm outputs "yes." Thus, if there is indeed a satisfying assignment of input values for C, then there is a possible collection of outcomes to the **choose** statements so that the algorithm will output "yes" in polynomial time. Likewise, if there is a collection of outcomes to the **choose** statements so that the algorithm outputs "yes" in polynomial-time algorithm, there must be a satisfying assignment of input values for C. Therefore, CIRCUIT-SAT is in **NP**. ∎

The next example problem is for a network monitoring problem. Suppose we are given a computer network, which is modeled using a graph G such that each vertex in G is a computer and each edge in G is a network connection between a pair of computers. We would like to monitor all of these connections by installing special monitoring devices on some of the computers, where a monitoring device placed on a computer can continuously check if all the network connections to that computer are working correctly. But these devices are relatively expensive, so we would like to minimize the number of such devices that we need to deploy. Viewed as a decision problem, which is known as VERTEX-COVER, we are given a graph G and an integer k, and we are asked whether there is a subset C of k vertices such that, for every edge (v, w) of G, $v \in C$ or $w \in C$ (possibly both). Such a subset is known as a ***vertex cover***. In other words, VERTEX-COVER is the decision problem that takes a graph G and an integer k as input, and asks whether there is a vertex cover for G containing at most k vertices. (See Figure 17.5.)

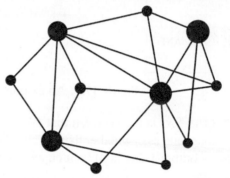

Figure 17.5: An instance of the VERTEX-COVER decision problem, where $k = 4$ and the answer is "yes." The vertices in the vertex cover are drawn as large disks.

Lemma 17.4: VERTEX-COVER *is in NP*.

Proof: Suppose we are given an integer k and a graph G, with its vertices numbered 1 to N. We use repeated calls to the **choose** method to form a collection C of k numbers that range from 1 to N. As a verification, we insert all the numbers of C into a dictionary, and then we examine each of the edges in G to make sure that, for each edge (v, w) in G, v is in C or w is in C. If we ever find an edge with neither of its end-vertices in G, then we output "no." If we run through all the edges of G so that each has an end-vertex in C, then we output "yes." Such a computation clearly runs in polynomial time. Note that if G has a vertex cover of size at most k, then there is an assignment of numbers to define the collection C so that each edge of G passes our test and our algorithm outputs "yes." Likewise, if our algorithm outputs "yes," then there must be a subset C of the vertices of size at most k, such that C is a vertex cover. Thus, VERTEX-COVER is in *NP*.   ∎

17.2 *NP*-Completeness

The notion of nondeterministic acceptance of a decision problem (or language) is admittedly strange. There is, after all, no conventional computer that can efficiently perform a nondeterministic algorithm with many calls to the choose method. Indeed, to date no one has shown how even an unconventional computer, such as a quantum computer or DNA computer, can efficiently simulate any nondeterministic polynomial-time algorithm using a polynomial amount of resources. Certainly, we can deterministically simulate a nondeterministic algorithm by trying out, one by one, all possible outcomes to the choose statements that the algorithm makes. But this simulation becomes an exponential-time computation for any nondeterministic algorithm that makes at least n^ϵ calls to the choose method, for any fixed constant $\epsilon > 0$. Indeed, there are hundreds of problems in the complexity class *NP* for which most computer scientists strongly believe there is no conventional deterministic method for solving them in polynomial time.

The usefulness of the complexity class *NP*, therefore, is that it formally captures a host of problems that many believe to be computationally difficult. In fact, there are some problems that are provably at least as hard as every other problem in *NP*, as far as polynomial-time solutions are concerned. This notion of hardness is based on the concept of polynomial-time reducibility, which we now discuss.

17.2.1 Polynomial-Time Reducibility and *NP*-Hardness

We say that a language L, defining some decision problem, is ***polynomial-time reducible*** to a language M, if there is a function f computable in polynomial time, that takes an input x to L, and transforms it to an input $f(x)$ of M, such that $x \in L$ if and only if $f(x) \in M$. In addition, we use a shorthand notation, saying $L \xrightarrow{\text{poly}} M$ to signify that language L is polynomial-time reducible to language M.

We say that a language M, defining some decision problem, is ***NP-hard*** if every other language L in *NP* is polynomial-time reducible to M. In more mathematical notation, M is *NP*-hard, if, for every $L \in NP$, $L \xrightarrow{\text{poly}} M$. If a language M is *NP*-hard and it is also in the class *NP* itself, then M is ***NP-complete***. Thus, an *NP*-complete problem is, in a very formal sense, one of the hardest problems in *NP*, as far as polynomial-time computability is concerned. For, if anyone ever shows that an *NP*-complete problem L is solvable in polynomial time, then that immediately implies that every other problem in the entire class *NP* is solvable in polynomial time. For, in this case, we could accept any other *NP* language M by reducing it to L and then running the algorithm for L. In other words, if anyone finds a deterministic polynomial-time algorithm for even one *NP*-complete problem, then ***P = NP***.

17.2.2   The Cook-Levin Theorem

At first, it might appear that the definition of *NP*-completeness is too strong. Still, as the following theorem shows, there is at least one *NP*-complete problem.

Theorem 17.5 (The Cook-Levin Theorem):   CIRCUIT-SAT *is NP-complete.*

Rather than give a formal proof of this theorem, which is somewhat cumbersome, let us instead provide a sketch of this proof, which highlights the main ideas. To begin, note that Lemma 17.3 shows that CIRCUIT-SAT is in *NP*. Thus, we have yet to show this problem is *NP*-hard. That is, we need to show that every problem in *NP* is polynomial-time reducible to CIRCUIT-SAT.

So, consider a language L, representing some decision problem that is in *NP*. Since L is in *NP*, there is a deterministic algorithm D that accepts any x in L in polynomial-time $p(n)$, given a polynomial-sized certificate y, where n is the size of x. The main idea of the proof is to build a large, but polynomial-sized, circuit C that simulates the algorithm D on an input x in such a way that C is satisfiable if and only if there is a certificate y such that D outputs "yes" on input $z = x + y$, where "+" denotes concatenation.

Configurations of a Computation

Recall (from Section 1.1.2) that any deterministic algorithm, such as D, can be implemented on a simple computational model (called the Random Access Machine, or RAM) that consists of a CPU and a bank M of addressable memory cells. In our case, the memory M contains the input, x, the certificate, y, the working storage, W, that D needs to perform its computations, and the code for the algorithm D itself. The working storage W for D includes all the registers used for temporary calculations and the stack frames for the procedures that D calls during its execution. The topmost such stack frame in W contains the program counter (PC) that identifies where D currently is in its program execution. Thus, there are no memory cells in the CPU itself. In performing each step of D, the CPU reads the next instruction i, which is pointed to by the PC, and performs the calculation indicated by i, be it a comparison, arithmetic operation, a conditional jump, a step in procedure call, etc., and then updates the PC to point to the next instruction to be performed. Thus, the current state of D is completely characterized by the contents of its memory cells. Moreover, since D accepts an x in L in a polynomial $p(n)$ number of steps, where n is the size of x, then the entire effective collection of its memory cells can be assumed to consist of just $p(n)$ bits. For in $p(n)$ steps, D can access at most $p(n)$ memory cells. Note also that the size of D's code is constant with respect to the sizes of x, y, and even W. We refer to the $p(n)$-sized collection M of memory cells for an execution of D as the ***configuration*** of the algorithm D.

Boolean Circuits Can Perform Computations

The heart of the reduction of L to CIRCUIT-SAT depends on our constructing a Boolean circuit that simulates the workings of the CPU in our computational model. We omit the details of such a construction in this proof sketch, but it is well known that a CPU can be designed as a Boolean circuit consisting of AND, OR, and NOT gates. For example, such constructions are studied in depth in courses on computer architecture. Moreover, let us further take for granted that this circuit, including its address unit for connecting to a memory of $p(n)$ bits, can be designed to take a configuration of D as input and provide as output the configuration resulting from processing the next computational step. In addition, let us assume that this simulation circuit, which we will call S, can be constructed to consist of at most $cp(n)^2$ AND, OR, and NOT gates, for some constant $c > 0$. We are admittedly making an important assumption here, which would be established formally in an actual proof of the Cook-Levin Theorem, but this assumption should at least be intuitive, for if it were not the case, then the CPUs that come inside modern computers and smartphones would not be as small as thcy are.

The Simulation

To then simulate the entire $p(n)$ steps of D, we make $p(n)$ copies of S, with the output from one copy serving as the input for the next. (See Figure 17.6.) Part of the input for the first copy of S consists of "hard-wired" values for the program for D, the value of x, the initial stack frame (complete with PC pointing to the first instruction of D), and the remaining working storage (initialized to all 0's). The only unspecified true inputs to the first copy of S are the cells of D's configuration for the certificate y. These are the true inputs to our circuit. Likewise, we ignore all the outputs from the final copy of S, except the single output that indicates the answer from D, with "1" for "yes" and "0" for "no." The total size of the circuit C is $O(p(n)^3)$, which of course is still polynomial in the size of x.

Completing the Proof Sketch

Consider an input x that D accepts for some certificate y after $p(n)$ steps. Then there is an assignment of values to the input to C corresponding to y, such that, by having C simulate D on this input and the hard-wired values for x, we will ultimately have C output a 1. Thus, C is satisfiable in this case. Conversely, consider a case when C is satisfiable. Then there is a set of inputs, which correspond to the certificate y, such that C outputs a 1. But, since C exactly simulates the algorithm D, this implies that there is an assignment of values to the certificate y, such that D outputs "yes." Thus, D will verify x in this case. Therefore, D accepts x with certificate y if and only if C is satisfiable.

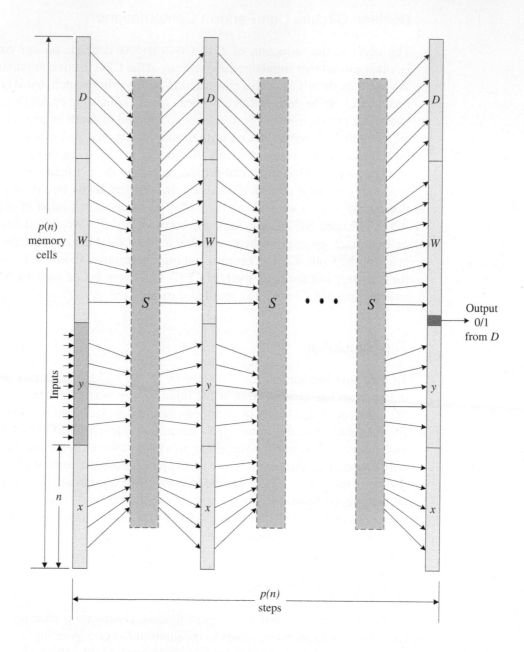

Figure 17.6: An illustration of the circuit used to prove that CIRCUIT-SAT is *NP*-hard. The only true inputs correspond to the certificate, y. The problem instance, x, the working storage, W, and the program code, D, are initially "hard-wired" values. The only output is the bit that determines whether the algorithm accepts x.

17.2.3   How to Prove Problems to be *NP*-Complete

Now that we are armed with one *NP*-complete problem, we can prove other problems are *NP*-complete using simple polynomial-time reductions. We explore a number of such reductions in the remainder of this chapter.

Given just a single *NP*-complete problem, we can now use polynomial-time reducibility to show other problems to be *NP*-complete. We will make repeated use of the following important lemma about polynomial-time reducibility.

Lemma 17.6: *If* $L_1 \xrightarrow{poly} L_2$ *and* $L_2 \xrightarrow{poly} L_3$, *then* $L_1 \xrightarrow{poly} L_3$.

Proof: Since $L_1 \xrightarrow{poly} L_2$, any instance, x, of size n, for L_1, can be converted in polynomial-time, $p(n)$, into an instance $f(x)$ for L_2, such that $x \in L_1$ if and only if $f(x) \in L_2$. Likewise, since $L_2 \xrightarrow{poly} L_3$, any instance, y, of size m, for L_2, can be converted in polynomial-time, $q(m)$, into an instance $g(y)$ for L_3, such that $y \in L_2$ if and only if $g(y) \in L_3$. Combining these two constructions, any instance, x, of size n, for L_1 can be converted in time, $p(n) + q(k)$, into an instance, $g(f(x))$, for L_3, such that $x \in L_1$ if and only if $g(f(x)) \in L_3$, where k is the size of $f(x)$. But, $k \le p(n)$, since $f(x)$ is constructed in $p(n)$ steps. Thus, $q(k) \le q(p(n))$. Since the composition of two polynomials always results in another polynomial, this inequality implies that $L_1 \xrightarrow{poly} L_3$.   ∎

In this section we establish several important problems to be *NP*-complete, using this lemma. All of the proofs have the same general structure. Given a new problem L, we first prove that L is in *NP*. Then, we reduce a known *NP*-complete problem to L in polynomial time, showing L to be *NP*-hard. Thus, we show L to be in *NP* and also *NP*-hard; hence, L has been shown to be *NP*-complete. (Why not do the reduction in the other direction?) These reductions generally take one of three forms:

- *Restriction*: This form shows a problem L is *NP*-hard by noting that a known *NP*-complete problem M is actually just a special case of L.
- *Local replacement*: This forms reduces a known *NP*-complete problem M to L by dividing instances of M and L into "basic units," and then showing how each basic unit of M can be locally converted into a basic unit of L.
- *Component design*: This form reduces a known *NP*-complete problem M to L by building components for an instance of L that will enforce important structural functions for instances of M. For example, some components might enforce a "choice" while others enforce an "evaluation" function.

The last of the three above forms tends to be the most difficult to construct; it is the form used, for example, by the proof of the Cook-Levin Theorem (17.5).

In Figure 17.7, we illustrate the problems we prove are *NP*-complete, together with the problems they are reduced from and the technique used in each polynomial-time reduction.

In the remainder of this chapter we study some important *NP*-complete problems. We treat most of them in pairs, with each pair addressing an important class of problems, including problems involving Boolean formulas, graphs, sets, and numbers. We begin with two problems involving Boolean formulas.

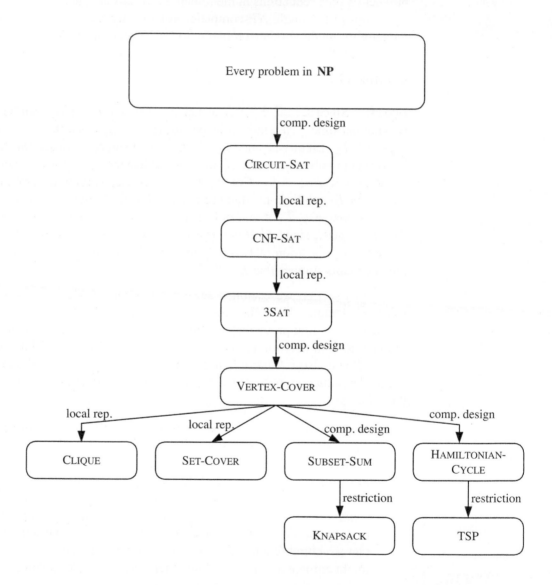

Figure 17.7: Illustration of the reductions used in some fundamental *NP*-completeness proofs. Each directed edge denotes a polynomial-time reduction, with the label on the edge indicating the primary form of that reduction. The topmost reduction is the Cook-Levin Theorem.

17.3 CNF-SAT and 3SAT

The first reductions we present are for problems involving Boolean formulas. A Boolean formula is a parenthesized expression that is formed from Boolean variables using Boolean operations, such as OR ($+$), AND ($\cdot$), NOT (drawn as a bar over the negated subexpression), IMPLIES ($\rightarrow$), and IF-AND-ONLY-IF ($\leftrightarrow$). A Boolean formula is in **conjunctive normal form** (CNF) if it is formed as a collection of subexpressions, called **clauses**, that are combined using AND, with each clause formed as the OR of Boolean variables or their negation, called **literals**. For example, the following Boolean formula is in CNF:

$$(\overline{x_1} + x_2 + x_4 + \overline{x_7})(x_3 + \overline{x_5})(\overline{x_2} + x_4 + \overline{x_6} + x_8)(x_1 + x_3 + x_5 + \overline{x_8}).$$

This formula evaluates to 1 if x_2, x_3, and x_4 are 1, where we use 0 for **false** and 1 for **true**. CNF is called a "normal" form, because any Boolean formula can be converted into this form.

CNF-SAT

Problem CNF-SAT takes a Boolean formula in CNF form as input and asks whether there is an assignment of Boolean values to its variables so that the formula evaluates to 1. It is easy to show that CNF-SAT is in *NP*, for, given a Boolean formula S, we can construct a simple nondeterministic algorithm that first "guesses" an assignment of Boolean values for the variables in S and then evaluates each clause of S in turn. If all the clauses of S evaluate to 1, then S is satisfied; otherwise, it is not.

To show that CNF-SAT is *NP*-hard, we will reduce the Circuit-SAT problem to it in polynomial time. So, suppose we are given a Boolean circuit, C. Without loss of generality, we assume that each AND and OR gate has two inputs and each NOT gate has one input. To begin the construction of a formula S equivalent to C, we create a variable x_i for each input for the entire circuit C. One might be tempted to limit the set of variables to just these x_i's and immediately start constructing a formula for C by combining subexpressions for inputs, but it is not clear that this approach would take polynomial time. (See Exercise C-17.5.) Instead, we create a variable y_i for each output of a gate in C. Then we create a short formula B_g that corresponds to each gate g in C as follows:

- If g is an AND gate with inputs a and b (which could be either x_i's or y_i's) and output c, then $B_g = (c \leftrightarrow (a \cdot b))$.
- If g is an OR gate with inputs a and b and output c, then $B_g = (c \leftrightarrow (a+b))$.
- If g is a NOT gate with input a and output b, then $B_g = (b \leftrightarrow \overline{a})$.

We wish to create our formula S by taking the AND of all of these B_g's, but such a formula would not be in CNF. So our method is to first convert each B_g to be in

a	b	c	$B = (c \leftrightarrow (a \cdot b))$
1	1	1	1
1	1	0	0
1	0	1	0
1	0	0	1
0	1	1	0
0	1	1	1
0	0	1	0
0	0	0	1

DNF formula for $\overline{B} = a \cdot b \cdot \overline{c} + a \cdot \overline{b} \cdot c + \overline{a} \cdot b \cdot c + \overline{a} \cdot \overline{b} \cdot c$

CNF formula for $B = (\overline{a} + \overline{b} + c) \cdot (\overline{a} + b + \overline{c}) \cdot (a + \overline{b} + \overline{c}) \cdot (a + b + \overline{c})$.

Figure 17.8: A truth table for a Boolean formula B over variables a, b, and c. The equivalent formula for $\overline{B}$ in DNF, and equivalent formula for B in CNF.

CNF, and then combine all of these transformed B_g's by AND operations to define the CNF formula S.

To convert a Boolean formula B into CNF, we construct a truth table for B, as shown in Figure 17.8. We then construct a short formula D_i for each table row that evaluates to 0. Each D_i consists of the AND of the variables for the table, with the variable negated if and only if its value in that row is 0. We create a formula D by taking the OR of all the D_i's. Such a formula, which is the OR of formulas that are the AND of variables or their negation, is said to be in *disjunctive normal form*, or *DNF*. In this case, we have a DNF formula D that is equivalent to $\overline{B}$, since it evaluates to 1 if and only if B evaluates to 0. To convert D into a CNF formula for B, we apply, to each D_i, De Morgan's laws, which establish that

$$\overline{(a + b)} = \overline{a} \cdot \overline{b} \quad \text{and} \quad \overline{(a \cdot b)} = \overline{a} + \overline{b}.$$

From Figure 17.8, we can replace each B_g that is of the form $(c \leftrightarrow (a \cdot b))$, by

$$(\overline{a} + \overline{b} + c)(\overline{a} + b + \overline{c})(a + \overline{b} + \overline{c})(a + b + \overline{c}),$$

which is in CNF. Likewise, for each B_g that is of the form $(b \leftrightarrow \overline{a})$, we can replace B_g by the equivalent CNF formula

$$(\overline{a} + \overline{b})(a + b).$$

We leave the CNF substitution for a B_g of the form $(c \leftrightarrow (a + b))$ as an exercise (R-17.2). Substituting each B_g in this way results in a CNF formula S' that corresponds exactly to each input and logic gate of the circuit, C. To construct the final Boolean formula S, then, we define $S = S' \cdot y$, where y is the variable that is associated with the output of the gate that defines the value of C itself. Thus, C is satisfiable if and only if S is satisfiable. Moreover, the construction from C to S builds a constant-sized subexpression for each input and gate of C; hence, this construction runs in polynomial time. Therefore, this local-replacement reduction gives us the following.

Theorem 17.7: CNF-SAT *is NP-complete.*

3Sat

Consider the 3Sat problem, which takes a Boolean formula S that is in conjunctive normal form (CNF) with each clause in S having exactly three literals, and asks whether S is satisfiable. Recall that a Boolean formula is in CNF if it is formed by the AND of a collection of clauses, each of which is the OR of a set of literals. For example, the following formula could be an instance of 3Sat:

$$(\overline{x_1} + x_2 + \overline{x_7})(x_3 + \overline{x_5} + x_6)(\overline{x_2} + x_4 + \overline{x_6})(x_1 + x_5 + \overline{x_8}).$$

Thus, the 3Sat problem is a restricted version of the CNF-Sat problem. (Note that we cannot use the restriction form of *NP*-hardness proof, however, for this proof form only works for reducing a restricted version to its more general form.) In this subsection, we show that 3Sat is *NP*-complete, using the local-replacement form of proof. Interestingly, the 2Sat problem, in which every clause has exactly two literals, can be solved in polynomial time. (See Exercises C-17.6 and C-17.7.)

Note that 3Sat is in *NP*, for we can construct a nondeterministic polynomial-time algorithm that takes a CNF formula S with 3-literals per clause, guesses an assignment of Boolean values for S, and then evaluates S to see if it is equal to 1.

To prove that 3Sat is *NP*-hard, we reduce the CNF-Sat problem to it in polynomial time. Let C be a given Boolean formula in CNF. We perform the following local replacement for each clause C_i in C:

- If $C_i = (a)$, that is, it has one term, which may be a negated variable, then we replace C_i with $S_i = (a + b + c) \cdot (a + \overline{b} + c) \cdot (a + b + \overline{c}) \cdot (a + \overline{b} + \overline{c})$, where b and c are new variables not used anywhere else.
- If $C_i = (a + b)$, that is, it has two terms, then we replace C_i with the subformula $S_i = (a + b + c) \cdot (a + b + \overline{c})$, where c is a new variable not used anywhere else.
- If $C_i = (a + b + c)$, that is, it has three terms, then we set $S_i = C_i$.
- If $C_i = (a_1 + a_2 + a_3 + \cdots + a_k)$, that is, it has $k > 3$ terms, then we replace C_i with $S_i = (a_1 + a_2 + b_1) \cdot (\overline{b_1} + a_3 + b_2) \cdot (\overline{b_2} + a_4 + b_3) \cdots (\overline{b_{k-3}} + a_{k-1} + a_k)$, where $b_1, b_2, \ldots, b_{k-1}$ are new variables not used anywhere else.

Notice that the value assigned to the newly introduced variables is completely irrelevant. No matter what we assign them, the clause C_i is 1 if and only if the small formula S_i is also 1. Thus, the original clause C is 1 if and only if S is 1. Moreover, note that each clause increases in size by at most a constant factor and that the computations involved are simple substitutions. Therefore, we have shown how to reduce an instance of the CNF-Sat problem to an equivalent instance of the 3Sat problem in polynomial time. This, together with the earlier observation about 3Sat belonging to *NP*, gives us the following theorem.

Theorem 17.8: *3Sat is NP-complete.*

17.4 VERTEX-COVER, CLIQUE, and SET-COVER

In the VERTEX-COVER problem, we are given a graph G and an integer k and asked whether there is a vertex cover for G containing at most k vertices. That is, VERTEX-COVER asks whether there is a subset C of vertices of size at most k, such that for each edge (v, w), we have $v \in C$ or $w \in C$. We showed, in Lemma 17.4, that VERTEX-COVER is in *NP*.

VERTEX-COVER is *NP*-Complete

Given that VERTEX-COVER is in *NP*, to show that VERTEX-COVER is *NP*-complete, we will show that VERTEX-COVER is *NP*-hard, by reducing the 3SAT problem to it in polynomial time. This reduction is interesting in two respects. First, it shows an example of reducing a logic problem to a graph problem. Second, it illustrates an application of the component-design proof technique.

Let S be a given instance of the 3SAT problem, that is, a CNF formula such that each clause has exactly three literals. We construct a graph G and an integer k such that G has a vertex cover of size at most k if and only if S is satisfiable. We begin our construction by adding the following:

- For each variable x_i used in the formula S, we add two vertices in G, one that we label with x_i and the other we label with $\overline{x_i}$. We also add the edge $(x_i, \overline{x_i})$ to G. (Note: These labels are for our own benefit; after we construct the graph G, we can always relabel vertices with integers if that is what an instance of the VERTEX-COVER problem should look like.)

Each edge $(x_i, \overline{x_i})$ is a "truth-setting" component, for, with this edge in G, a vertex cover must include at least one of x_i or $\overline{x_i}$. In addition, we add the following:

- For each clause $C_i = (a + b + c)$ in S, we form a triangle consisting of three vertices, $i1$, $i2$, and $i3$, and three edges, $(i1, i2)$, $(i2, i3)$, and $(i3, i1)$.

Note that any vertex cover will have to include at least two of the vertices in $\{i1, i2, i3\}$ for each such triangle. Each such triangle is a "satisfaction-enforcing" component. We then connect these two types of components, by adding, for each clause $C_i = (a + b + c)$, the edges $(i1, a)$, $(i2, b)$, and $(i3, c)$. (See Figure 17.9.) Finally, we set the integer parameter $k = n + 2m$, where n is the number of variables in S and m is the number of clauses. Thus, if there is a vertex cover of size at most k, it must have size exactly k. This completes the construction of an instance of the VERTEX-COVER problem. This construction clearly runs in polynomial time, so let us consider its correctness.

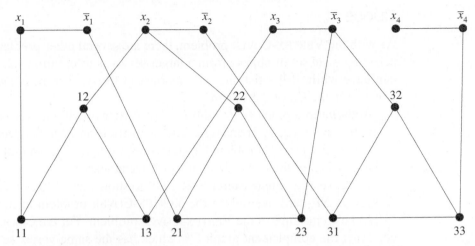

Figure 17.9: Example graph G as an instance of the VERTEX-COVER problem constructed from the formula $S = (x_1 + x_2 + x_3) \cdot (\overline{x_1} + x_2 + \overline{x_3}) \cdot (\overline{x_2} + \overline{x_3} + \overline{x_4})$.

Suppose there is an assignment of Boolean values to variables in S so that S is satisfied. From the graph G constructed from S, we can build a subset of vertices C that contains each literal a (in a truth-setting component) that is assigned 1 by the satisfying assignment. Likewise, for each clause $C_i = (a + b + c)$, the satisfying assignment sets at least one of a, b, or c to 1. Whichever one of a, b, or c is 1 (picking arbitrarily if there are ties), we include the other two in our subset C. This C is of size $n + 2m$. Moreover, notice that each edge in a truth-setting component and clause-satisfying component is covered, and two of every three edges incident on a clause-satisfying component are also covered. In addition, notice that an edge incident to a component associated clause C_i that is not covered by a vertex in the component must be covered by the node in C labeled with a literal, for the corresponding literal in C_i is 1.

Suppose then the converse, namely, that there is a vertex cover C of size at most $n+2m$. By construction, this set must have size exactly $n+2m$, for it must contain one vertex from each truth-setting component and two vertices from each clause-satisfying component. This leaves one edge incident to a clause-satisfying component that is not covered by a vertex in the clause-satisfying component; hence, this edge must be covered by the other endpoint, which is labeled with a literal. Thus, we can assign the literal in S associated with this node 1 and each clause in S is satisfied; hence, all of S is satisfied. Therefore, S is satisfiable if and only if G has a vertex cover of size at most k. This gives us the following.

Theorem 17.9: VERTEX-COVER *is NP-complete.*

As mentioned before, the above reduction illustrates the component-design technique. We constructed truth-setting and clause-satisfying components in our graph G to enforce important properties in the clause S.

CLIQUE

As with the VERTEX-COVER problem, there are several other problems that involve selecting a subset of objects from a larger set so as to optimize the size the subset can have while still satisfying an important property. The next such problem we consider is the CLIQUE problem.

A *clique* in a graph G is a subset C of vertices such that, for each v and w in C, with $v \neq w$, (v, w) is an edge. That is, there is an edge between every pair of distinct vertices in C. Problem CLIQUE takes a graph G and an integer k as input and asks whether there is a clique in G of size at least k.

We leave as a simple exercise (R-17.7) to show that CLIQUE is in *NP*. To show CLIQUE is *NP*-hard, we reduce the VERTEX-COVER problem to it. Therefore, let (G, k) be an instance of the VERTEX-COVER problem. For the CLIQUE problem, we construct the complement graph G^c, which has the same vertex set as G, but has the edge (v, w), with $v \neq w$, if and only if (v, w) is not in G. We define the integer parameter for CLIQUE as $n - k$, where k is the integer parameter for VERTEX-COVER. This construction runs in polynomial time and serves as a reduction, for G^c has a clique of size at least $n - k$ if and only if G has a vertex cover of size at most k. (See Figure 17.10.)

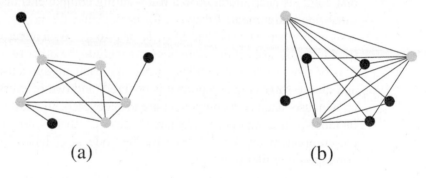

(a)   (b)

Figure 17.10: A graph G illustrating the proof that CLIQUE is *NP*-hard. (a) Shows the graph G with the nodes of a clique of size 5 shaded in gray. (b) Shows the graph G^c with the nodes of a vertex cover of size 3 shaded in gray.

Therefore, we have the following.

Theorem 17.10: CLIQUE *is NP-complete.*

Note how simple the above proof by local replacement is. Interestingly, the next reduction, which is also based on the local-replacement technique, is even simpler.

SET-COVER

Problem SET-COVER takes a collection of m sets S_1, S_2, ..., S_m and an integer parameter k as input and asks whether there is a subcollection of k sets S_{i_1}, S_{i_2},

..., S_{i_k}, such that

$$\bigcup_{i=1}^{m} S_i = \bigcup_{j=1}^{k} S_{i_j}.$$

That is, the union of the subcollection of k sets includes every element in the union of the original m sets.

We leave it to an exercise (R-17.14) to show SET-COVER is in *NP*. As to the reduction, we note that we can define an instance of SET-COVER from an instance G and k of VERTEX-COVER. Namely, for each vertex v of G, there is set S_v, which contains the edges of G incident on v. Clearly, there is a set cover among these sets S_v's of size k if and only if there is a vertex cover of size k in G. (See Figure 17.11.)

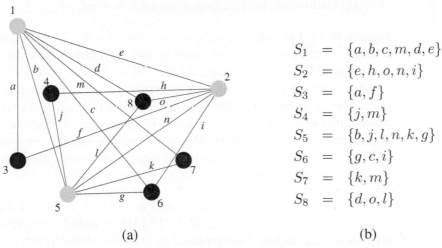

$$
\begin{aligned}
S_1 &= \{a, b, c, m, d, e\} \\
S_2 &= \{e, h, o, n, i\} \\
S_3 &= \{a, f\} \\
S_4 &= \{j, m\} \\
S_5 &= \{b, j, l, n, k, g\} \\
S_6 &= \{g, c, i\} \\
S_7 &= \{k, m\} \\
S_8 &= \{d, o, l\}
\end{aligned}
$$

(a)   (b)

Figure 17.11: A graph G illustrating the proof that SET-COVER is *NP*-hard. The vertices are numbered 1 through 8 and the edges are given letter labels a through o. (a) Shows the graph G with the nodes of a vertex cover of size 3 shaded in gray. (b) Shows the sets associated with each vertex in G, with the subscript of each set identifying the associated vertex. Note that $S_1 \cup S_2 \cup S_5$ contains all the edges of G.

Thus we have the following.

Theorem 17.11: SET-COVER *is NP-complete.*

This reduction illustrates how easily we can covert a graph problem into a set problem. In the next subsection, we show how we can actually reduce graph problems to number problems.

17.5　SUBSET-SUM and KNAPSACK

Some hard problems involve only numbers. In such cases, we must take extra care to use the size of the input in bits, for some numbers can be very large. To clarify the role that the size of numbers can make, researchers say that a problem L is ***strongly NP-hard*** if L remains ***NP***-hard even when we restrict the value of each number in the input to be bounded by a polynomial in the size (in bits) of the input. An input x of size n would satisfy this condition, for example, if each number i in x was represented using $O(\log n)$ bits. Interestingly, the number problems we study in this section are not strongly ***NP***-hard. (See Exercises C-17.14 and C-17.15.)

In the SUBSET-SUM problem, we are given a set S of n integers and an integer k, and we are asked whether there is a subset of integers in S that sum to k. This problem could arise, for example, as in the following.

Example 17.12: *Suppose we have an Internet web server, and we are presented with a collection of download requests. For each download request we can easily determine the size of the requested file. Thus, we can abstract each web request simply as an integer—the size of the requested file. Given this set of integers, we might be interested in determining a subset of them that exactly sums to the bandwidth our server can accommodate in one minute. Unfortunately, this problem is an instance of SUBSET-SUM. Moreover, because it is NP-complete, this problem will actually become harder to solve as our web server's bandwidth and request-handling ability improves.*

SUBSET-SUM might at first seem easy, and indeed showing that it belongs to ***NP*** is straightforward. (See Exercise R-17.15.) Unfortunately, it is ***NP***-complete, as we now show. Let G and k be given as an instance of the VERTEX-COVER problem. Number the vertices of G from 1 to n and the edges G from 1 to m, and construct the ***incidence matrix*** H for G, defined so that $H[i, j] = 1$ if and only if the edge numbered j is incident on the vertex numbered i; otherwise, $H[i, j] = 0$. (See Figure 17.12.)

We use H to define some admittedly large (but still polynomial-sized) numbers to use as inputs to the SUBSET-SUM problem. Namely, for each row i of H, which encodes all the edges incident on vertex i, we construct the number

$$a_i = 4^{m+1} + \sum_{j=1}^{m} H[i, j]4^j.$$

Note that this number adds in a different power of 4 for each 1-entry in the ith row of $H[i, j]$, plus a larger power of 4 for good measure. The collection of a_i's defines an "incidence component" to our reduction, for each power of 4 in an a_i, except for the largest, corresponds to a possible incidence between vertex i and some edge.

In addition to the above incidence component, we also define an "edge-covering

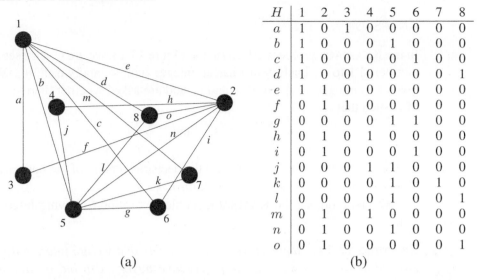

H	1	2	3	4	5	6	7	8
a	1	0	1	0	0	0	0	0
b	1	0	0	0	1	0	0	0
c	1	0	0	0	0	1	0	0
d	1	0	0	0	0	0	0	1
e	1	1	0	0	0	0	0	0
f	0	1	1	0	0	0	0	0
g	0	0	0	0	1	1	0	0
h	0	1	0	1	0	0	0	0
i	0	1	0	0	0	1	0	0
j	0	0	0	1	1	0	0	0
k	0	0	0	0	1	0	1	0
l	0	0	0	0	1	0	0	1
m	0	1	0	1	0	0	0	0
n	0	1	0	0	1	0	0	0
o	0	1	0	0	0	0	0	1

(a)   (b)

Figure 17.12: A graph G illustrating the proof that SUBSET-SUM is *NP*-hard. The vertices are numbered 1 through 8 and the edges are given letter labels a through o. (a) Shows the graph G; (b) shows the incidence matrix H for G. Note that there is a 1 for each edge in one or more of the columns for vertices 1, 2, and 5.

component," where, for each edge j, we define a number

$$b_j = 4^j.$$

We then set the sum we wish to attain with a subset of these numbers as

$$k' = k4^{m+1} + \sum_{j=1}^{m} 2 \cdot 4^j,$$

where k is the integer parameter for the VERTEX-COVER instance.

Let us consider how this reduction, which clearly runs in polynomial time, actually works. Suppose graph G has a vertex cover $C = \{i_1, i_2, \ldots, i_k\}$, of size k. Then we can construct a set of values adding to k' by taking every a_i with an index in C, that is, each a_{i_r} for $r = 1, 2, \ldots, k$. In addition, for each edge numbered j in G, if only one of j's endpoints is included in C, then we also include b_j in our subset. This set of numbers sums to k', for it includes k values of 4^{m+1} plus 2 values of each 4^j (either from two a_{i_r}'s such that this edge has both endpoints in C or from one a_{i_r} and one b_j if C contains just one endpoint of edge j).

Suppose there is a subset of numbers suming to k'. Since k' contains k values of 4^{m+1}, it must include exactly k a_i's. Let us include vertex i in our cover for each such a_i. Such a set is a cover, for each edge j, which corresponds to a power 4^j, must contribute two values to this sum. Since only one value can come from a b_j, one must have come from at least one of the chosen a_i's. Thus we have the following:

Theorem 17.13: SUBSET-SUM *is NP-complete.*

KNAPSACK

In the KNAPSACK problem, illustrated in Figure 17.13, we are given a set S of items, numbered 1 to n. Each item i has an integer size, s_i, and worth, w_i. We are also given two integer parameters, s, and w, and are asked whether there is a subset, T, of S such that

$$\sum_{i \in T} s_i \leq s, \quad \text{and} \quad \sum_{i \in T} w_i \geq w.$$

Problem KNAPSACK defined above is the decision version of the optimization problem "0-1 knapsack" discussed in Section 12.6.

We can motivate the KNAPSACK problem with the following Internet application.

Example 17.14: *Suppose we have s widgets that we are interested in selling at an Internet auction website. A prospective buyer i can bid on multiple lots by saying that he or she is interested in buying s_i widgets at a total price of w_i dollars. If multiple-lot requests, such as this, cannot be broken up (that is, buyer i wants exactly s_i widgets), then determining if we can earn w dollars from this auction gives rise to the KNAPSACK problem. (If lots can be broken up, then our auction optimization problem gives rise to the fractional knapsack problem, which can be solved efficiently using the greedy method of Section 10.1.)*

The KNAPSACK problem is in *NP*, for we can construct a nondeterministic polynomial-time algorithm that guesses the items to place in our subset T and then verifies that they do not violate the s and w constraints, respectively.

KNAPSACK is also *NP*-hard, as it actually contains the SUBSET-SUM problem as a special case. In particular, any instance of numbers given for the SUBSET-SUM problem can correspond to the items for an instance of KNAPSACK with each $w_i = s_i$ set to a value in the SUBSET-SUM instance and the targets for the size s and worth w both equal to k, where k is the integer we wish to sum to for the SUBSET-SUM problem. Thus, by the restriction proof technique, we have the following.

Theorem 17.15: KNAPSACK *is NP-complete.*

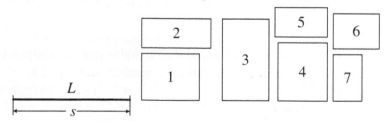

Figure 17.13: A geometric view of the KNAPSACK problem. Given a line L of length s, and a collection of n rectangles, can we translate a subset of the rectangles to have their bottom edge on L so that the total area of the rectangles touching L is at least w? Here, the width of rectangle i is s_i and its area is w_i.

17.6 HAMILTONIAN-CYCLE and TSP

The last two *NP*-complete problems we consider ask about the existence of certain kinds of cycles in a graph. Such problems are useful for optimizing the travel of robots and circuit-board drills, as discussed at the start of this chapter.

HAMILTONIAN-CYCLE

HAMILTONIAN-CYCLE is the problem that takes a graph G and asks whether there is a cycle in G that visits each vertex in G exactly once, returning to its starting vertex. (See Figure 17.14a.) It is relatively easy to show that HAMILTONIAN-CYCLE is in *NP*—guess a sequence of vertices and verify that each consecutive pair of vertices in this sequence is connected by an edge and that every vertex (other than the starting and ending vertex) is visited exactly once. To show that this problem is *NP*-complete, we will reduce VERTEX-COVER to it, using a component-design type of reduction.

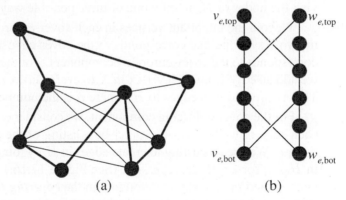

(a)   (b)

Figure 17.14: Illustrating the HAMILTONIAN-CYCLE problem and its *NP*-completeness proof. (a) Shows an example graph with a Hamiltonian cycle shown in bold. (b) Illustrates a cover-enforcer subgraph H_e used to show that HAMILTONIAN-CYCLE is *NP*-hard.

Let G and k be a given instance of the VERTEX-COVER problem. We will construct a graph H that has a Hamiltonian cycle if and only if G has a vertex cover of size k. We begin by including a set of k initially disconnected vertices $X = \{x_1, x_2, \ldots, x_k\}$ to H. This set of vertices will serve as a "cover-choosing" component, for they will serve to identify which nodes of G should be included in a vertex cover. In addition, for each edge $e = (v, w)$ in G we create a "cover-enforcer" subgraph H_e in H. This subgraph H_e has 12 vertices and 14 edges as shown in Figure 17.14b.

Six of the vertices in the cover-enforcer H_e for $e = (v, w)$ correspond to v and the other six correspond to w. Moreover, we label two vertices in cover-enforcer

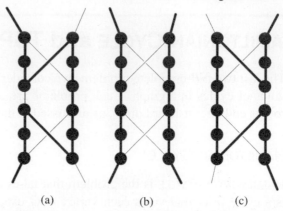

(a)   (b)   (c)

Figure 17.15: The three possible ways that a Hamiltonian cycle can visit the edges in a cover-enforcer H_e.

H_e that correspond to v as $v_{e,\text{top}}$ and $v_{e,\text{bot}}$, and we label two vertices in H_e that correspond to w as $w_{e,\text{top}}$ and $w_{e,\text{bot}}$. These are the only vertices in H_e that will be connected to any other vertices in H outside of H_e. Thus, a Hamiltonian cycle can visit the nodes of H_e in only one of three possible ways, as shown in Figure 17.15.

We join the important vertices in each cover-enforcer H_e to other vertices in H in two ways, one that corresponds to the cover-choosing component and one that corresponds to the cover-enforcing component. For the cover-choosing component, we add an edge from each vertex in X to every vertex $v_{e,\text{top}}$ and every vertex $v_{e,\text{bot}}$. That is, we add $2kn$ edges to H, where n is the number of vertices in G.

For the cover-enforcing component, we consider each vertex v in G in turn. For each such v, let $\{e_1, e_2, \ldots, e_{d(v)}\}$ be a listing of the edges of G that are incident upon v. We use this listing to create edges in H by joining $v_{e_i,\text{bot}}$ in H_{e_i} to $v_{e_{i+1},\text{top}}$ in $H_{e_{i+1}}$, for $i = 1, 2, \ldots, d - 1$. (See Figure 17.16.) We refer to the H_{e_i} components joined in this way as belonging to the **covering thread** for v. This completes the construction of the graph H. Note that this computation runs in polynomial time in the size of G.

We claim that G has a vertex cover of size k if and only if H has a Hamiltonian cycle. Suppose, first, that G has a vertex cover of size k. Let $C = \{v_{i_1}, v_{i_2}, \ldots, v_{i_k}\}$ be such a cover. We construct a Hamiltonian cycle in H, by connecting a series of paths P_j, where each P_j starts at x_j and ends at x_{j+1}, for $j = 1, 2, \ldots, k - 1$, except for the last path P_k, which starts at x_k and ends at x_1. We form such a path P_j as follows. Start with x_j, and then visit the entire covering thread for v_{i_j} in H, returning to x_{j+1} (or x_1 if $j = k$). For each cover-enforcer subgraph H_e in the covering thread for v_{i_j}, which is visited in this P_j, we write, without loss of generality, e as (v_{i_j}, w). If w is not also in C, then we visit this H_e as in Figure 17.15a or Figure 17.15c (with respect to v_{i_j}). Instead, if w is also in C, then we visit this H_e as in Figure 17.15b. In this way we will visit each vertex in H exactly once, since C is a vertex cover for G. Thus, this cycle is in fact a Hamiltonian cycle.

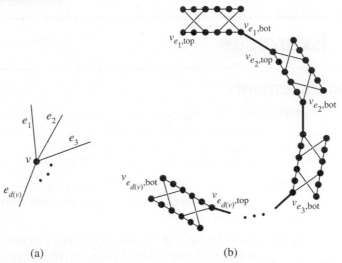

Figure 17.16: Connecting the cover-enforcers. (a) A vertex v in G and its set of incident edges $\{e_1, e_2, \ldots, e_{d(v)}\}$. (b) The connections made between the H_{e_i}'s in H for the edges incident upon v.

Suppose, conversely, that H has a Hamiltonian cycle. Since this cycle must visit all the vertices in X, we break this cycle up into k paths, $P_1, P_2, \ldots, P_k$, each of which starts and ends at a vertex in X. Moreover, by the structure of the cover-enforcer subgraphs H_e and the way that we connected them, each P_j must traverse a portion (possibly all) of a covering thread for a vertex v in G. Let C be the set of all such vertices in G. Since the Hamiltonian cycle must include the vertices from every cover-enforcer H_e and every such subgraph must be traversed in a way that corresponds to one (or both) of e's endpoints, C must be a vertex cover in G.

Therefore, G has a vertex cover of size k if and only if H has a Hamiltonian cycle. This gives us the following.

Theorem 17.16: *H* AMILTONIAN-CYCLE *is **NP**-complete.*

TSP

In the ***traveling salesperson problem***, or TSP, we are given an integer parameter k and a graph G, such that each edge e in G is assigned an integer cost $c(e)$, and we are asked whether there is a cycle in G that visits all the vertices in G (possibly more than once) and has total cost at most k. We have already established that TSP is in **NP**, in Lemma 17.2. Given this fact, showing that TSP is **NP**-complete is easy, as the TSP problem contains the HAMILTONIAN-CYCLE problem as a special case. Namely, given an instance G of the HAMILTONIAN-CYCLE problem, we can create an instance of TSP by assigning each edge in G the cost $c(e) = 1$ and setting the integer parameter $k = n$, where n is the number of vertices in G. Therefore, using the restriction form of reduction, we get the following.

Theorem 17.17: TSP *is **NP**-complete.*

17.7 Exercises

Reinforcement

R-17.1 Professor Amongus has shown that a decision problem L is polynomial-time reducible to an *NP*-complete problem M. Moreover, after 80 pages of dense mathematics, he has also just proven that L can be solved in polynomial time. Has he just proven that $P = NP$? Why, or why not?

R-17.2 Use a truth table to convert the Boolean formula $B = (a \leftrightarrow (b + c))$ into an equivalent formula in CNF. Show the truth table and the intermediate DNF formula for $\overline{B}$.

R-17.3 Show that the problem SAT, which takes an arbitrary Boolean formula S as input and asks whether S is satisfiable, is *NP*-complete.

R-17.4 Consider the problem DNF-SAT, which takes a Boolean formula S in disjunctive normal form (DNF) as input and asks whether S is satisfiable. Describe a deterministic polynomial-time algorithm for DNF-SAT.

R-17.5 Consider the problem DNF-DISSAT, which takes a Boolean formula S in disjunctive normal form (DNF) as input and asks whether S is dissatisfiable, that is, there is an assignment of Boolean values to the variables of S so that it evaluates to 0. Show that DNF-DISSAT is *NP*-complete.

R-17.6 Convert the Boolean formula $B = (x_1 \leftrightarrow x_2) \cdot (\overline{x_3} + x_4 x_5) \cdot (\overline{x_1 x_2} + x_3 \overline{x_4})$ into CNF.

R-17.7 Show that the CLIQUE problem is in *NP*.

R-17.8 Given the CNF formula $B = (x_1) \cdot (\overline{x_2} + x_3 + x_5 + \overline{x_6}) \cdot (x_1 + x_4) \cdot (x_3 + \overline{x_5})$, show the reduction of B into an equivalent input for the 3SAT problem.

R-17.9 Given $B = (x_1 + \overline{x_2} + x_3) \cdot (x_4 + x_5 + \overline{x_6}) \cdot (x_1 + \overline{x_4} + \overline{x_5}) \cdot (x_3 + x_4 + x_6)$, draw the instance of VERTEX-COVER that is constructed by the reduction from 3SAT of the Boolean formula B.

R-17.10 Draw an example of a graph with 10 vertices and 15 edges that has a vertex cover of size 2.

R-17.11 Draw an example of a graph with 10 vertices and 15 edges that has a clique of size 6.

R-17.12 Professor Amongus has just designed an algorithm that can take any graph G with n vertices and determine in $O(n^k)$ time whether G contains a clique of size k. Does Professor Amongus deserve the Turing Award for having just shown that $P = NP$? Why or why not?

R-17.13 Is there a subset of the numbers in $\{23, 59, 17, 47, 14, 40, 22, 8\}$ that sums to 100? What about 130? Show your work.

R-17.14 Show that the SET-COVER problem is in *NP*.

R-17.15 Show that the SUBSET-SUM problem is in *NP*.

R-17.16 Draw an example of a graph with 10 vertices and 20 edges that has a Hamiltonian cycle. Also, draw an example of a graph with 10 vertices and 20 edges that does not have a Hamiltonian cycle.

R-17.17 The *Manhattan distance* between two points (a, b) and (c, d) in the plane is $|a - c| + |b - d|$. Using Manhattan distance to define the cost between every pair of points, find an optimal traveling salesperson tour of the following set of points: $\{(1, 1), (2, 8), (1, 5), (3, -4), (5, 6), (-2, -6)\}$.

Creativity

C-17.1 Let n denote the size of an input in bits and N denote the size in a number of items. Define an algorithm to be *c-incremental* if any primitive operation involving one or two objects represented with b bits results in an object represented with at most $b + c$ bits, for $c \geq 0$. Show that an algorithm using multiplication as a primitive operation may not be c-incremental for any constant c.

C-17.2 Using the definition of a c-incremental algorithm from the previous exercise, show that, if a c-incremental algorithm A has a worst-case running time $t(N)$ in the RAM model, as a function of the number of input items, N, for some constant $c > 0$, then A has running time $O(n^2 t(n))$, in terms of the number, n, of bits in a standard binary encoding of the input.

C-17.3 Show that we can deterministically simulate in polynomial time any nondeterministic algorithm A that runs in polynomial time and makes at most $O(\log n)$ calls to the **choose** method, where n is the size of the input to A.

C-17.4 Show that every language L in $\boldsymbol{P}$ is polynomial-time reducible to the language $M = \{5\}$, that is, the language that simply asks whether the binary encoding of the input is equal to 5.

C-17.5 Show how to construct a Boolean circuit C such that, if we create variables only for the inputs of C and then try to build a Boolean formula that is equivalent to C, then we will create a formula exponentially larger than an encoding of C.

Hint: Use recursion to repeat subexpressions in a way that doubles their size each time they are used.

C-17.6 Show that the backtracking algorithm given in Section 18.4.1 for the CNF-SAT problem runs in polynomial time if every clause in the given Boolean formula has at most two literals. That is, it solves 2SAT in polynomial time.

C-17.7 Consider the 2SAT version of the CNF-SAT problem, in which every clause in the given formula S has exactly two literals. Note that any clause of the form $(a + b)$ can be thought of as two implications, $(\overline{a} \rightarrow b)$ and $(\overline{b} \rightarrow a)$. Consider a graph G from S, such that each vertex in G is associated with a variable, x, in S, or its negation, $\overline{x}$. Let there be a directed edge in G from $\overline{a}$ to b for each clause equivalent to $(\overline{a} \rightarrow b)$. Show that S is not satisfiable if and only if there is a variable x such that there is a path in G from x to $\overline{x}$ and a path from $\overline{x}$ to x. Derive from this rule a polynomial-time algorithm for solving this special case of the CNF-SAT problem. What is the running time of your algorithm?

C-17.8 Suppose an oracle has given you a magic computer, C, that when given any Boolean formula B in CNF will tell you in one step whether B is satisfiable. Show how to use C to construct an actual assignment of satisfying Boolean values to the variables in any satisfiable formula B. How many calls do you need to make to C in the worst case in order to do this?

C-17.9 Define SUBGRAPH-ISOMORPHISM as the problem that takes a graph, G, and another graph, H, and determines if H is isomorphic to a subgraph of G. That is, the problem is to determine whether there is a one-to-one mapping, f, of the vertices in H to a subset of the vertices in G such that, if (v, w) is an edge in H, then $(f(v), f(w))$ is an edge in G. Show that SUBGRAPH-ISOMORPHISM is *NP*-complete.

C-17.10 Define INDEPENDENT-SET as the problem that takes a graph G and an integer k and asks whether G contains an independent set of vertices of size k. That is, G contains a set I of vertices of size k such that, for any v and w in I, there is no edge (v, w) in G. Show that INDEPENDENT-SET is *NP*-complete.

C-17.11 Define HYPER-COMMUNITY to be the problem that takes a collection of n web pages and an integer k, and determines if there are k web pages that all contain hyperlinks to each other. Show that HYPER-COMMUNITY is *NP*-complete.

C-17.12 Define PARTITION as the problem that takes a set $S = \{s_1, s_2, \ldots, s_n\}$ of numbers and asks whether there is a subset T of S such that

$$\sum_{s_i \in T} s_i = \sum_{s_i \in S-T} s_i.$$

That is, it asks whether there is a partition of the numbers into two groups that sum to the same value. Show that PARTITION is *NP*-complete.

C-17.13 Show that the HAMILTONIAN-CYCLE problem on directed graphs is *NP*-complete.

C-17.14 Show that the SUBSET-SUM problem is solvable in polynomial time if the input is given in a unary encoding. That is, show that SUBSET-SUM is not strongly *NP*-hard. What is the running time of your algorithm?

C-17.15 Show that the KNAPSACK problem is solvable in polynomial time if the input is given in a unary encoding. That is, show that KNAPSACK is not strongly *NP*-hard. What is the running time of your algorithm?

C-17.16 Consider the special case of TSP where the vertices correspond to points in the plane, with the cost defined on an edge for every pair (p, q) being the usual Euclidean distance between p and q. Show that an optimal tour will not have any pair of crossing edges.

C-17.17 Given a graph G and two distinct vertices, v and w in G, define HAMILTONIAN-PATH to be the problem of determining whether there is a path that starts at v and ends at w and visits all the vertices of G exactly once. Show that the HAMILTONIAN-PATH problem is *NP*-complete.

Applications

A-17.1 Imagine that the annual university job fair is scheduled for next month and it is your job to book companies to host booths in the large Truman Auditorium during the fair. Unfortunately, at last year's job fair, a fight broke out between some people from competing companies, so the university president, Dr. Noah Drama, has issued a rule that prohibits any pair of competing companies from both being invited to this year's event. In addition, he has shown you a website that lists the competitors for every company that might be invited to this year's job fair and he has asked you to invite the maximum number of noncompeting companies as possible. Show that the decision version of the problem Dr. Drama has asked you to solve is *NP*-complete.

A-17.2 Suppose the football coach for the Anteaters has heard about your abilities to solve challenging problems and has hired you to write a computer program that can decide which of their many trophies to feature on their prized trophy shelf. He is asking that you do this as a computer program, rather than just coming up with a single decision, because the Anteaters are getting new trophies every year. The trophies come in all different shapes and sizes, and the ones on the prized trophy shelf have to be lined up next to one another. So the dimension that matters most is a trophy's width in centimeters, which is given as an integer. In addition, the coach has assigned an integer score to each trophy, so that a very prestigious trophy, like the one for winning the championship, would have a high score, whereas a less prestigious trophy, like the one for having the funniest uniforms, would have a low score. Moreover, given his eccentric nature, these scores can be arbitrarily large. He has asked that, given a listing of all the team's trophies along with their widths and prestige scores, your program should choose the set that maximizes the total prestige score and fits on the team's trophy shelf. Show that the decision version of the problem the coach has given you is *NP*-complete.

A-17.3 Consider the trophy-choosing problem from the previous exercise, but now suppose that each of the prestige scores is an integer in the range from 1 to 10. Describe how you can solve this version of the problem in polynomial time.

A-17.4 Suppose a friend of yours is rushing for one of the university fraternities, Tau Nu Tau (TNT). His job for this week is to arrange all the bottles in the TNT beer-bottle collection in a circle, subject to the constraint that each pair of consecutive bottles must be for beers that were both drunk in some TNT party. He has been given a listing of the beers in the TNT beer-bottle collection, and, for each beer on the list, he is told which other beers were drunk along with this one at some TNT party. Politely show that your friend has been asked to solve an *NP*-complete problem.

A-17.5 Suppose you are computer security expert working for a major company, Cable-Clock, any you have just discovered that many of the computers at CableClock are infected with malware that must have come from users visiting unsafe websites. For each infected computer, you are given a log file that lists all websites it has visited since the last time it was scanned for malware. Unfortunately, as you look over these log files, you notice that there isn't a single website that they all visited. You conclude, therefore, that there must be a number of websites that are able to inject this malware, and the most likely candidates would be in a smallest collection that is visited by all the infected computers. Show that the decision version of the problem of determining such a collection is *NP*-complete.

A-17.6 Imagine that you are a Hollywood movie producer who is trying to decide how your new movie should end. To help you make this decision, you would like to assemble a group of movie-goers together to do a focus group. To avoid biases, you have asked that the group be selected so that no two people in the group has previously seen the same movie. So, among the set of possible focus-group members, you have asked that each one fill out a list of all the movies they have seen, and you will be using these lists to make your decision about who to invite to the focus group. Show that the decision version of the problem of finding the largest set of movie-goers for this focus group such that no two people in the group has previously seen the same movie is *NP*-complete.

A-17.7 Suppose that you and a friend are both taking a Russian literature course and have agreed to buy all of your books together "fifty-fifty," so that for each book purchased, you paid half and your friend paid half. Suppose now that the course has ended and it is time to sell these books to the used-book buyer, who has posted the used-book values of all of your books on her website. Unfortunately, with your differing social calendars, there is no good time for you and your friend to go to the bookstore together to return your shared books. So you need to divide up the books between the two of you so that the total used-book value of the two sets is the same. Show that determining whether such a division of the books is possible, where there is an arbitrary number of books having arbitrary values, is *NP*-complete.

Chapter Notes

Computing models are discussed in the textbooks by Lewis and Papadimitriou [143], Savage [184] and Sipser [195].

The proof sketch of the Cook-Levin Theorem (17.5) given in this chapter is an adaptation of a proof sketch of Cormen, Leiserson, and Rivest [50]. Cook's original theorem [48] showed that CNF-SAT was *NP*-complete, and Levin's original theorem [141] was for a tiling problem. We refer to Theorem 17.5 as the "Cook-Levin" Theorem in honor of these two seminal papers, for their proofs were along the same lines as the proof sketch given for Theorem 17.5. Karp [122] demonstrated several more problems to be *NP*-complete, and subsequently hundreds of other problems have been shown to be *NP*-complete. Garey and Johnson [80] give a very nice discussion of *NP*-completeness as well as a catalog of many important *NP*-complete and *NP*-hard problems.

The reductions given in this chapter that use local replacement and restriction are well known in the computer science literature; for example, see Garey and Johnson [80] or Aho, Hopcroft, and Ullman [8]. The component-design proof that VERTEX-COVER is *NP*-complete is an adaptation of a proof of Garey and Johnson [80], as is the component-design proof that HAMILTONIAN-CYCLE is *NP*-complete, which itself is a combination of two reductions by Karp [122]. The component-design proof that SUBSET-SUM is *NP*-complete is an adaptation of a proof of Cormen, Leiserson, and Rivest [50].

Chapter

18

Approximation Algorithms

Lily pads, 2006. Michael T. Goodrich. Used with permission.

Contents

18.1 The Metric Traveling Salesperson Problem 511

18.2 Approximations for Covering Problems 515

18.3 Polynomial-Time Approximation Schemes 518

18.4 Backtracking and Branch-and-Bound 521

18.5 Exercises 525

Astronomers can determine the composition and distance of galaxies and stars by performing a spectrographic analysis of the light coming from these objects. Doing such an analysis involves collecting light from one of these objects over a relatively long period of time, and transmitting this light through a fiber-optic cable to a spectroscope. The spectrograph then splits this light into its various frequencies and measures the intensities of these light frequencies. By matching the patterns of high and low light frequencies coming from such an astronomical object to known patterns for the light emitted when various elements are burned, the astronomers can determine the elements that are present in the object. In addition, by observing the amount that these patterns are shifted to the red end of the spectrum, astronomers can also determine the distance of this object from earth. This distance can be determined using estimates for the speed at which the universe is expanding, because of the Doppler effect, where light wavelengths increase as an object is moving away from us.

As an optimization problem, one of the most time-consuming parts of this process is the first step—collecting the light from the galaxy or star over a given period of time. To do this with a telescope, a large aluminum disk the size of the diameter of the telescope is used. This disk is placed in the focal plane of the telescope, so that the light from each stellar objects in an observation falls in a specific spot on the disk. The astronomers know where these spots are located and, before the disk is placed in the focal plane, they use robotic drilling equipment to drill a hole in each spot of interest and they insert a fiber-optic cable into each such hole and connect it to a spectrograph. (See Figure 18.1.)

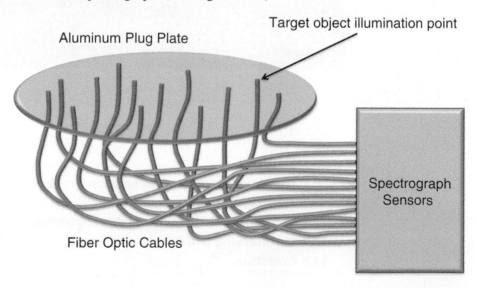

Figure 18.1: Aparatus for spectrographic analysis of stellar objects using an aluminum plug plate and fiber-optic cables. The aluminum plug plate is placed in the focal plane of a telescope.

As discussed at the beginning of Chapter 17, the problem of finding a fastest way to drill all these holes is an instance of the traveling salesperson problem (TSP). According to the abstract formulation of TSP, each of the hole locations is a "city" and the time it takes to move a robot drill from one hole to another corresponds to the distance between the cities corresponding to these two holes. Thus, a minimum-distance tour of the cities that starts and ends at the resting position for the robot drill is one that will drill the holes the fastest. Unfortunately, as we discuss in the previous chapter, the decision version of this optimization problem is NP-complete. Nevertheless, even though this is a difficult problem, it still needs to be solved in order to do the spectrographic analysis. The astronomers doing spectrographic analyses might not require the absolutely best solution, however. They might be happy with a solution that comes close to the optimum, especially if one can prove that it won't be too far from this optimum.

In addition to the problem of quickly drilling the holes in a plug plate for a spectrographic analysis, another optimization problem arises in this application as well. This problem is to minimize the number of observations needed in order to collect the spectra of all the stellar objects of interest. In this case, the astronomers have a map of all the stellar objects of interest and they want to cover it with the minimum number of disks having the same diameter as the telescope. (See Figure 18.2.) This optimization problem is an instance of the ***set cover*** problem. Each of the distinct sets of objects that can be included in a single observation is given as an input set and the optimization problem is to minimize the number of sets whose union includes all the objects of interest. As with TSP, the decision version of this problem is also NP-complete, but it is a problem for which an approximation to the optimum might be sufficient.

Approximation Ratios

In general, many optimization problems whose decision versions are NP-complete correspond to problems whose solution in the real world can oftentimes save money, time, or other resources. Thus, the main topic of this chapter is on approximate ways of dealing with ***NP***-completeness. One of the most effective methods is to construct polynomial-time algorithms that come close to solving difficult problems. Although such algorithms do not always produce optimal solutions, in some cases we can guarantee how close such an approximation algorithm will come to an optimal solution. Indeed, we explore several such approximations in this chapter, including algorithms for the knapsack, vertex cover, traveling salesperson, and set cover problems.

The general situation is that we have some problem instance x, which could be an encoding of a set of numbers, a graph, etc. In addition, for the problem we are interested in solving for x, there will often be a large set, $\mathcal{F}$, of ***feasible*** solutions for x. We also have a cost function, c, that determines a numeric cost $c(S)$ for any solution $S \in \mathcal{F}$. In the general optimization problem, we are interested in finding

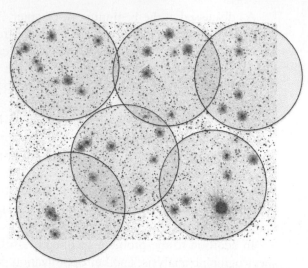

Figure 18.2: An example disk cover for a set of significant stellar objects (smaller objects are not included). Background image is from Omega Centauri, 2009. U.S. government image. Credit: NASA, ESA, and the Hubble SM4 ERO team.

a solution S in $\mathcal{F}$, such that

$$c(S) = OPT = \min\{c(T) \colon T \in \mathcal{F}\}.$$

That is, we want a solution with minimum cost. We could also formulate a maximization version of the optimization problem, as well, which would simply involve replacing the above "min" with "max." To keep the discussion in this section simple, however, we will typically take the view that, unless otherwise stated, our optimization goal is minimization.

The goal of an approximation algorithm is to come as close to the optimum value as possible in a reasonable amount of time. As we have been doing for this entire chapter, we take the view in this section that a reasonable amount of time is at most polynomial time.

Ideally, we would like to provide a guarantee of how close an approximation algorithm comes to the optimal value, OPT. We say that a δ-***approximation*** algorithm for a particular optimization problem is an algorithm that returns a feasible solution S (that is, $S \in \mathcal{F}$), such that

$$c(S) \leq \delta\, OPT,$$

for a minimization problem. For a maximization problem, a δ-approximation algorithm would guarantee $OPT \leq \delta\, c(S)$. Or, in general, we have

$$\delta \geq \max\{c(S)/OPT,\ OPT/c(S)\}.$$

In this chapter, we study problems for which we can construct δ-approximation algorithms for various values of δ.

18.1 The Metric Traveling Salesperson Problem

In the optimization version of the traveling salesperson problem, or TSP, we are given a weighted graph, G, such that each edge e in G has an integer weight $c(e)$, and we are asked to find a minimum-weight cycle in G that visits all the vertices in G. In this section we study approximation algorithms for a special case of TSP.

Consider a *metric* version of TSP such that the edge weights satisfy the *triangle inequality*. That is, for any three edges (u, v), (v, w), and (u, w) in G,

$$c((u, v)) + c((v, w)) \geq c((u, w)).$$

Also, suppose that every pair of vertices in G is connected by an edge, that is, G is a complete graph. This instance of TSP is called METRIC-TSP. The above properties, which hold for any distance metric, and which arise in lots of TSP applications, imply that the optimal tour of G will visit each vertex exactly once.

18.1.1 A 2-Approximation for METRIC-TSP

Our first approximation algorithm takes advantage of the above properties of G to design a very simple 2-approximation algorithm for METRIC-TSP. The algorithm has three steps. In the first step we construct a minimum spanning tree, M, of G (Section 15.1). In the second step we construct an Euler-tour traversal, E, of M, that is, a traversal of M that starts and ends at the same vertex and traverses each edge of M exactly once in each direction (Section 2.3.3). In the third step we construct a tour T from E by marching through the edges of E, but each time we have two edges (u, v) and (v, w) in E, such that v has already been visited, we replace these two edges by the edge (u, w) and continue. In essence, we are constructing T as a preorder traversal of M. This three-step algorithm clearly runs in polynomial time. (See Figure 18.3.)

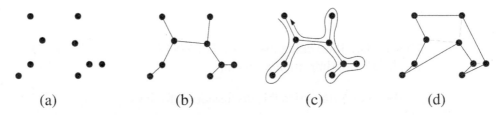

(a)   (b)   (c)   (d)

Figure 18.3: Example run of the 2-approximation algorithm for METRIC-TSP: (a) a set S of points in the plane, with Euclidean distance defining the costs of the edges (not shown); (b) the minimum spanning tree, M, for S; (c) an Euler tour, E, of M; (d) the approximate TSP tour, T.

Analysis of the 2-Approximation METRIC-TSP Algorithm

The analysis of why this algorithm achieves an approximation factor of 2 is also simple. Let us extend our notation so that $c(H)$ denotes the total weight of the edges in a subgraph H of G. Let S be a solution to METRIC-TSP, that is, an optimal TSP tour for the graph G. If we delete any edge from S, we get a path, which is, of course, also a spanning tree. Thus,

$$c(M) \le c(S).$$

We can also easily relate the cost of E to that of M, as

$$c(E) = 2c(M),$$

since the Euler tour E visits each edge of M exactly once in each direction. Finally, note that, by the triangle inequality, when we construct our tour T, each time we replace two edges (u, v) and (v, w) with the edge (u, w), we do not increase the cost of the tour. That is,

$$c(T) \le c(E).$$

Therefore, we have

$$c(T) \le 2c(S).$$

(See Figure 18.4.)

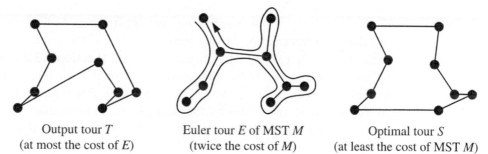

Output tour T Euler tour E of MST M Optimal tour S
(at most the cost of E)   (twice the cost of M)   (at least the cost of MST M)

Figure 18.4: Illustrating the proof that MST-based algorithm is a 2-approximation for the TSP optimization problem.

We may summarize this discussion as follows.

Theorem 18.1: *There is a 2-approximation algorithm for the METRIC-TSP optimization problem that runs in polynomial time.*

This theorem depends heavily on the fact that the cost function on the graph G satisfies the triangle inequality. In fact, without this assumption, no constant-factor approximation algorithm for the optimization version of TSP exists that runs in polynomial time, unless $P = NP$. (See Exercise C-18.1.)

18.1.2 The Christofides Approximation Algorithm

There is a somewhat more complex algorithm, which is known as the ***Christofides approximation algorithm***, that can achieve an even better approximation ratio than the above method. Like the above 2-approximation algorithm, the Christofides approximation algorithm has just a few steps that are applications of other algorithms. The most difficult step involves computing a minimum-cost ***perfect matching*** in an undirected weighted graph, H, having $2N$ vertices, that is, a set of N edges in H that has minimum total weight and such that no two edges are incident on the same vertex. This is a problem that can be solved in polynomial time, albeit using an algorithm that is somewhat complicated and thus not included in this book.

Suppose we are given an instance of METRIC-TSP specified as a complete graph G with weights on its edges satisfying the triangle inequality. The Christofides approximation algorithm is as follows (See Figure 18.5):

1. Construct a minimum spanning tree, M, for G.
2. Let W be the set of vertices of G that have odd degree in M and let H be the subgraph of G induced by the vertices in W. That is, H is the graph that has W as its vertices and all the edges from G that join such vertices. By a simple argument, we can show that the number of vertices in W is even (see Exercise R-18.12). Compute a minimum-cost perfect matching, P, in H.
3. Combine the graphs M and P to create a graph, G', but don't combine parallel edges into single edges. That is, if an edge e is in both M and P, then we create two copies of e in the combined graph, G'.
4. Create an Eulerian circuit, C, in G', which visits each edge exactly once (unlike in the 2-approximation algorithm, here the edges of G' are undirected).
5. Convert C into a tour, T, by skipping over previously visited vertices.

The running time of this algorithm is dominated by Step 2, which takes $O(n^3)$ time. Thus, although it is not as fast as the above 2-approximation algorithm, the Christofides approximation algorithm achieves a better approximation ratio.

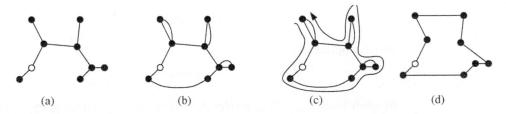

(a) (b) (c) (d)

Figure 18.5: Illustrating the Christofides approximation algorithm: (a) a minimum spanning tree, M, for G; (b) a minimum-cost perfect matching P on the vertices in W (the vertices in W are shown solid and the edges in P are shown as curved arcs); (c) an Eulerian circuit, C, of G'; (d) the approximate TSP tour, T.

Analyzing the Christofides Approximation Algorithm

To begin our analysis of the Christofides approximation algorithm, let S be an optimal solution to this instance of METRIC-TSP and let T be the tour that is produced by the Christofides approximation algorithm. Because S includes a spanning tree and M is a minimum spanning tree in G,

$$c(M) \leq c(S).$$

In addition, let R denote a solution to the traveling salesperson problem on H. Since the edges in G (and, hence, H) satisfy the triangle inequality, and all the edges of H are also in G,

$$c(R) \leq c(S).$$

That is, visiting more vertices than in the tour R cannot reduce its total cost. Consider now the cost of a perfect matching, P, of H, and how it relates to R, an optimal traveling salesperson tour of H. Number the edges of R, and ignore the last edge (which returns to the start vertex). Note that the costs of the set of odd-numbered edges and the set of even-numbered edges in R sum to $c(R)$; hence, one of these two sets has total cost at most half of that of R, that is, cost at most $c(R)/2$. In addition, the set of odd-numbered edges and the set of even-numbered edges in R are both perfect matchings; hence, the cost of P, a minimum-weight perfect matching on the edges of H, will be at most the smaller of these two. That is,

$$c(P) \leq c(R)/2.$$

Therefore,

$$c(M) + c(P) \leq c(S) + c(R)/2 \leq 3c(S)/2.$$

Since the edges in G satisfy the triangle inequality, we can only improve the cost of a tour by making shortcuts that avoid previously visited vertices. Thus,

$$c(T) \leq c(M) + c(P),$$

which implies that

$$c(T) \leq 3c(S)/2.$$

In other words, the Christofides approximation algorithm gives us the following.

Theorem 18.2: *There is a $(3/2)$-approximation algorithm for the METRIC-TSP optimization problem that runs in polynomial time.*

18.2   Approximations for Covering Problems

In this section, we describe greedy approximation algorithms for the VERTEX-COVER and SET-COVER problems (Section 17.4).

18.2.1   A 2-Approximation for VERTEX-COVER

We begin with a 2-approximation for the VERTEX-COVER problem. In the optimization version of this problem, we are given a graph G and we are asked to produce the smallest set C that is a vertex cover for G, that is, every edge in G is incident on some vertex in C.

This approximation algorithm is based on the greedy method, as mentioned above, and is rather simple. It involves picking an edge in the graph, adding both its endpoints to the cover, and then deleting this edge and its incident edges from the graph. The algorithm repeats this process until no edges are left. We give the details for this approach in Algorithm 18.6.

Algorithm VertexCoverApprox(G):
    Input: A graph G
    Output: A small vertex cover C for G

    $C \leftarrow \emptyset$
    while G still has edges **do**
        select an edge $e = (v, w)$ of G
        add vertices v and w to C
        for each edge f incident to v or w **do**
            remove f from G
    return C

        Algorithm 18.6: A 2-approximation algorithm for VERTEX-COVER.

We leave the details of how to perform this algorithm in $O(n + m)$ time as a simple exercise (R-18.1). For the analysis, first observe that each edge $e = (v, w)$ selected by the algorithm, and used to add v and w to C, must be covered in any vertex cover. That is, any vertex cover for G must contain v or w (possibly both). The approximation algorithm adds both v and w to C in such a case. When the approximation algorithm completes, there are no uncovered edges left in G, for we remove all the edges covered by the vertices v and w when we add them to C. Thus, C forms a vertex cover of G. Moreover, the size of C is at most twice that of an optimal vertex cover for G, since, for every two vertices we add to C, one of these vertices must belong to the optimal cover. Therefore, we have the following.

Theorem 18.3: *There is a 2-approximation algorithm for the VERTEX-COVER problem that runs in $O(n + m)$ time on a graph with n vertices and m edges.*

18.2.2   A Logarithmic Approximation for SET-COVER

There are some cases when achieving even a constant-factor approximation in polynomial time is difficult. In this section, we study one of the best known of such problems, the SET-COVER problem (Section 17.4). In the optimization version of this problem, we are given a collection of sets $S_1, S_2, \ldots, S_m$, whose union is a universe U of size n, and we are asked to find the smallest integer k, such that there is a subcollection of k sets $S_{i_1}, S_{i_2}, \ldots, S_{i_k}$ with

$$U = \bigcup_{i=1}^{m} S_i = \bigcup_{j=1}^{k} S_{i_j}.$$

Although it is difficult to find a constant-factor approximation algorithm that runs in polynomial time for this problem, we can design an efficient algorithm that has an approximation factor of $O(\log n)$. As with several other approximation algorithms for hard problems, this algorithm is based on the greedy method (Section 10).

A Greedy Approach

Our algorithm selects sets one at a time, each time selecting the set that has the most uncovered elements. When every element in U is covered, we are done. We give a simple pseudocode description in Algorithm 18.7.

Algorithm SetCoverApprox(S):

    Input: A collection S of sets $S_1, S_2, \ldots, S_m$ whose union is U
    Output: A small set cover C for S

    $C \leftarrow \emptyset$ // The set cover built so far
    $E \leftarrow \emptyset$ // The elements from U currently covered by C
    while $E \neq U$ **do**
        select a set S_i that has the maximum number of uncovered elements
        add S_i to C
        $E \leftarrow E \cup S_i$
    Return C.

        Algorithm 18.7: An approximation algorithm for SET-COVER.

This algorithm runs in polynomial time. (See Exercise R-18.2.)

To analyze the approximation factor of the above greedy SET-COVER algorithm, we will use an amortization argument based on a charging scheme (Section 1.4). Namely, each time our approximation algorithm selects a set S_j, we will charge the elements of S_j for its selection.

Specifically, consider the moment in our algorithm when a set S_j is added to C, and let k be the number of previously uncovered elements in S_j. We must pay a total charge of 1 to add this set to C, so we charge each previously uncovered element i of S_j a charge of

$$c(i) = 1/k.$$

Thus, the total size of our cover is equal to the total charges made. That is,

$$|C| = \sum_{i \in U} c(i).$$

To prove an approximation bound, we will consider the charges made to the elements in each subset S_j that belongs to an optimal cover, C'. So, suppose that S_j belongs to C'. Let us write $S_j = \{x_1, x_2, \ldots, x_{n_j}\}$ so that S_j's elements are listed in the order in which they are covered by our algorithm (we break ties arbitrarily). Now, consider the iteration in which x_1 is first covered. At that moment, S_j has not yet been selected; hence, whichever set is selected must have at least n_j uncovered elements. Thus, x_1 is charged at most $1/n_j$. So let us consider, then, the moment our algorithm charges an element x_l of S_j. In the worst case, we will have not yet chosen S_j (indeed, our algorithm may never choose this S_j). Whichever set is chosen in this iteration has, in the worst case, at least $n_j - l + 1$ uncovered elements; hence, x_l is charged at most $1/(n_j - l + 1)$. Therefore, the total amount charged to all the elements of S_j is at most

$$\sum_{l=1}^{n_j} \frac{1}{n_l - l + 1} = \sum_{l=1}^{n_j} \frac{1}{l},$$

which is the familiar **harmonic number**, H_{n_i}. It is well known (for example, see the Appendix) that H_{n_j} is $O(\log n_j)$. Let $c(S_j)$ denote the total charges given to all the elements of a set S_j that belongs to the optimal cover C'. Our charging scheme implies that $c(S_j)$ is $O(\log n_j)$. Thus, summing over the sets of C', we obtain

$$\sum_{S_j \in C'} c(S_j) \leq \sum_{S_j \in C'} b \log n_j$$
$$\leq b|C'| \log n,$$

for some constant $b \geq 1$. But, since C' is a set cover,

$$\sum_{i \in U} c(i) \leq \sum_{S_j \in C'} c(S_j).$$

Therefore,

$$|C| \leq b|C'| \log n.$$

This fact gives us the following result.

Theorem 18.4: *The optimization version of the* SET-COVER *problem has an* $O(\log n)$-*approximation polynomial-time algorithm for finding a cover of a collection of sets whose union is a universe of size* n.

18.3   Polynomial-Time Approximation Schemes

There are some problems for which we can construct δ-approximation algorithms
that run in polynomial time with $\delta = 1 + \epsilon$, for any fixed value $\epsilon > 0$. The running
time of such a collection of algorithms depends both on n, the size of the input,
and also on the fixed value ϵ. We refer to such a collection of algorithms as a
polynomial-time approximation scheme, or ***PTAS***. When we have a polynomial-
time approximation scheme for a given optimization problem, we can tune our
performance guarantee based on how much time we can afford to spend. Ideally,
the running time is polynomial in both n and $1/\epsilon$, in which case we have a ***fully
polynomial-time approximation scheme***.

Polynomial-time approximation schemes take advantage of a property that some
hard problems possess, namely, that they are rescalable. A problem is said to be
rescalable if an instance x of the problem can be transformed into an equivalent instance x' (that is, one with the same optimal solution) by scaling the cost function,
c. For example, TSP is rescalable. Given an instance G of TSP, we can construct an
equivalent instance G' by multiplying the distance between every pair of vertices
by a scaling factor s. The traveling salesperson tour in G' will be the same as in G,
although its cost will now be multiplied by s.

A Fully Polynomial-Time Approximation Scheme for KNAPSACK

To be more concrete, let us give a fully polynomial approximation scheme for
the optimization version of a well-known problem, KNAPSACK (Sections 10.1 and
17.5). In the optimization version of this problem, we are given a set S of items,
numbered 1 to n, together with a size constraint, s. Each item i in S is given an
integer size, s_i, and worth, w_i, and we are asked to find a subset, T, of S, such that
T maximizes the worth

$$w = \sum_{i \in T} w_i \quad \text{while satisfying} \quad \sum_{i \in T} s_i \leq s.$$

We desire a PTAS that produces a $(1 + \epsilon)$-approximation, for any given fixed constant ϵ. That is, such an algorithm should find a subset T' satisfying the size constraint such that if we define $w' = \sum_{i \in T'} w_i$, then

$$OPT \leq (1 + \epsilon)w',$$

where OPT is the optimal worth summation, taken over all possible subsets satisfying the total size constraint. To prove that this inequality holds, we will actually
prove that

$$w' \geq (1 - \epsilon/2)OPT,$$

for $0 < \epsilon < 1$. This will be sufficient, however, since, for any fixed $0 < \epsilon < 1$,

$$\frac{1}{1 - \epsilon/2} < 1 + \epsilon.$$

To derive a PTAS for KNAPSACK, we take advantage of the fact that this problem is rescalable. Suppose we are given a value of ϵ with $0 < \epsilon < 1$. Let $w_{\max}$ denote the maximum worth of any item in S. Without loss of generality, we assume that the size of each item is at most s (for an item larger than this could not fit in the knapsack). Thus, the item with worth $w_{\max}$ defines a lower bound for the optimal value. That is, $w_{\max} \le OPT$. Likewise, we can define an upper bound on the optimal solution by noting that the knapsack can at most contain all n items in S, each of which has worth at most $w_{\max}$. Thus, $OPT \le n\,w_{\max}$. To take advantage of the rescalability of KNAPSACK, we round each worth value w_i to $w_i{}'$, the nearest smaller multiple of $M = \epsilon w_{\max}/2n$. Let us denote the rounded version of S as S', and let us also use OPT' to denote the solution for this rounded version S'. Note that, by simple substitution, $OPT \le 2n^2 M/\epsilon$. Moreover, $OPT' \le OPT$, since we rounded every worth value in S down to form S'. Thus, $OPT' \le 2n^2 M/\epsilon$.

Therefore, let us turn to our solution for the rounded version S' of the KNAPSACK problem for S. Since every worth value in S' is a multiple of M, any achievable worth of a collection of items taken from S' is also a multiple of M. Moreover, there are just $N = \lceil 2n^2/\epsilon \rceil$ such multiples that need to be considered, because of the upper bound on OPT'. We can use dynamic programming to construct an efficient algorithm for finding the optimal worth for S'. In particular, let us define the parameter

$s[i, j]$ = the size of the smallest set of items in $\{1, 2, \ldots, j\}$ with worth iM.

The key insight to the design of a dynamic programming algorithm for solving the rounded KNAPSACK problem is the observation that we can write

$$s[i, j] = \min\{s[i, j-1],\ s_j + s[i - (w_j{}'/M), j-1]\},$$

for $i = 1, 2, \ldots, N$, and $j = 1, 2, \ldots, n$. (See Figure 18.8.)

The above equation for $s[i, j]$ follows from the fact that item j will either contribute or not contribute to the smallest way of achieving worth iM from the items in $\{1, 2, \ldots, j\}$. In addition, note that for the base case, $j = 0$, when no items at all are included in the knapsack, then

$$s[i, 0] = +\infty,$$

for $i = 1, 2, \ldots, N$. That is, such a size is undefined. In addition,

$$s[0, j] = 0,$$

for $j = 1, 2, \ldots, n$, since we can always achieve worth 0 by including no items in the knapsack. The optimal value is defined by

$$OPT' = \max\{iM \colon s[i, n] \le s\}.$$

This is the value that is output by our PTAS algorithm.

Analysis of the PTAS for KNAPSACK

We can easily convert the above description into a dynamic programming algorithm that computes OPT' in $O(n^3/\epsilon)$ time. Such an algorithm gives us the value of an optimal solution, but we can easily translate the dynamic programming algorithm for computing the size into one for the actual set of items.

Let us consider, then, how good an approximation OPT' is for OPT. Recall that we reduced the worth w_i of each item i by at most $M = \epsilon w_{\max}/2n$. Thus,

$$OPT' \geq OPT - \epsilon w_{\max}/2,$$

since the optimal solution can contain at most n items. Since $OPT \geq w_{\max}$, this in turn implies that

$$OPT' \geq OPT - \epsilon OPT/2 = (1 - \epsilon/2)OPT.$$

Thus, $OPT \leq (1 + \epsilon)OPT'$, which was what we wished to prove. The running time of our approximation algorithm is $O(n^3/\epsilon)$. Our scheme of designing an efficient algorithm for any given $\epsilon > 0$ gives rise to a fully polynomial approximation scheme, since the running time is polynomial in both n and $1/\epsilon$. This fact gives us the following.

Theorem 18.5: *The* KNAPSACK *optimization problem has a fully polynomial approximation scheme that achieves a $(1 + \epsilon)$-approximation factor in $O(n^3/\epsilon)$ time, where n is the number of items in the* KNAPSACK *instance and $0 < \epsilon < 1$ is a given fixed constant.*

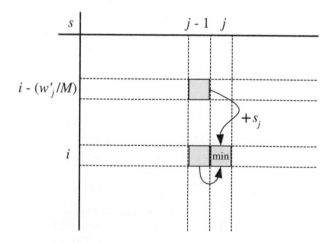

Figure 18.8: Illustration of the equation for $s[i, j]$ used in the dynamic program for the scaled version of KNAPSACK.

18.4   Backtracking and Branch-and-Bound

At this point, we know that there are many problems to be *NP*-complete. Thus, unless $P = NP$, which the majority of computer scientists believes is not true, it is impossible to solve any of these problems in polynomial time. Nevertheless, many of these problems arise in real-life applications where solutions to them need to be found, even if finding these solutions may take a long time. Thus, in this section, we address techniques for dealing with *NP*-completeness that have shown much promise in practice. These techniques allow us to design algorithms that can find solutions to hard problems, often in a reasonable amount of time. In this section, we study the methods of ***backtracking*** and ***branch-and-bound***.

18.4.1   Backtracking

The backtracking technique is a way to build an algorithm for some hard problem L. Such an algorithm searches through a large, possibly even exponential-size, set of possibilities in a systematic way. The search strategy is typically optimized to avoid symmetries in problem instances for L and to traverse the search space so as to find an "easy" solution for L if such a solution exists.

The ***backtracking*** technique takes advantage of the inherent structure that many *NP*-complete problems possess. Recall that acceptance for an instance x in a problem in *NP* can be verified in polynomial time given a polynomial-sized certificate. Oftentimes, this certificate consists of a set of "choices," such as the values assigned to a collection of Boolean variables, a subset of vertices in a graph to include in a special set, or a set of objects to include in a knapsack. Likewise, the verification for a certificate often involves a simple test of whether the certificate demonstrates a successful configuration for x, such as satisfying a formula, covering all the edges in a graph, or conforming to certain performance criteria. In such cases, we can use the ***backtracking*** algorithm, given in Algorithm 18.9, to systematically search for a solution to our problem, if such a problem exists.

The backtracking algorithm traverses through possible "search paths" to locate solutions or "dead ends." The configuration at the end of such a path consists of a pair (x, y), where x is the remaining subproblem to be solved and y is the set of choices that have been made to get to this subproblem from the original problem instance. Initially, we give the backtracking algorithm the pair $(x, \emptyset)$, where x is our original problem instance. Anytime the backtracking algorithm discovers that a configuration (x, y) cannot lead to a valid solution no matter how additional choices are made, then it cuts off all future searches from this configuration and "backtracks" to another configuration. In fact, this approach gives the backtracking algorithm its name.

Algorithm Backtrack(x):

    Input: A problem instance x for a hard problem

    Output: A solution for x or "no solution" if none exists

    $F \leftarrow \{(x, \emptyset)\}$.   // F is the "frontier" set of subproblem configurations

    while $F \neq \emptyset$ **do**

        Select from F the most "promising" configuration (x, y).

        Expand (x, y) by making a small set of additional choices.

        Let $(x_1, y_1), (x_2, y_2), \ldots, (x_k, y_k)$ be the set of new configurations.

        for each new configuration (x_i, y_i) **do**

            Perform a simple consistency check on (x_i, y_i).

            if the check returns "solution found" **then**

                return the solution derived from (x_i, y_i)

            if the check returns "dead end" **then**

                Discard the configuration (x_i, y_i).   // Backtrack

            else

                $F \leftarrow F \cup \{(x_i, y_i)\}$ // (x_i, y_i) starts a promising search path

    return "no solution"

Algorithm 18.9: The template for a backtracking algorithm.

Filling in the Details

In order to turn the backtracking strategy into an actual algorithm, we need only fill in the following details:

1. Define a way of selecting the most "promising" candidate configuration from the frontier set F.

2. Specify the way of expanding a configuration (x, y) into subproblem configurations. This expansion process should, in principle, be able to generate all feasible configurations, starting from the initial configuration, $(x, \emptyset)$.

3. Describe how to perform a simple consistency check for a configuration (x, y) that returns "solution found," "dead end," or "continue."

If F is a stack, then we get a depth-first search of the configuration space. In fact, in this case we could even use recursion to implement F automatically as a stack. Alternatively, if F is a queue, then we get a breadth-first search of the configuration space. We can also imagine other data structures to implement F, but as long as we have an intuitive notion of how to select the most "promising" configuration from F with each iteration, then we have a backtracking algorithm.

So as to make this approach more concrete, let us work through an application of the backtracking technique to the CNF-SAT problem.

A Backtracking Algorithm for CNF-SAT

Recall that in the CNF-SAT problem we are given a Boolean formula S in conjunctive normal form (CNF) and are asked whether S is satisfiable. To design a backtracking algorithm for CNF-SAT, we will systematically make tentative assignments to the variables in S and see if such assignments make S evaluate immediately to 1 or 0, or yield a new formula S' for which we could continue making tentative value assignments. Thus, a configuration in our algorithm will consist of a pair (S', y), where S' is a Boolean formula in CNF, and y is an assignment of values to Boolean variables not in S' such that making these assignments in S results in the formula S'.

To formulate our backtracking algorithm, then, we need to give the details of each of the three components to the backtracking algorithm. Given a frontier F of configurations, we make our most "promising" choice, which is the subformula S' with the smallest clause. Such a formula is the most constrained of all the formulas in F; hence, we would expect it to hit a dead end most quickly if that is indeed its destiny.

Let us consider, then, how to generate subproblems from a subformula S'. We do this by locating a smallest clause C in S', and picking a variable x_i that appears in C. We then create two new subproblems that are associated with our assigning $x_i = 1$ and $x_i = 0$, respectively.

Finally, we must say how to process S' to perform a consistency check for an assignment of a variable x_i in S'. We begin this processing by reducing any clauses containing x_i based on the assigned 0 or 1 value of x_i (depending on the choice we made). If this reduction results in a new clause with a single literal, x_j or $\overline{x_j}$, we also perform the appropriate value assignment to x_j to make this single-literal clause satisfied. We then process the resulting formula to propagate the assigned value of x_j. If this new assignment in turn results in a new single-literal clause, we repeat this process until we have no more single-literal clauses. If at any point we discover a contradiction (that is, clauses x_i and $\overline{x_i}$, or an empty clause), then we return "dead end." If we reduce the subformula S' all the way to the constant 1, then we return "solution found," along with all the variable assignments we made to reach this point. Otherwise, we derive a new subformula, S'', such that each clause has at least two literals, along with the value assignments that lead from the original formula S to S''. We call this operation the ***reduce*** operation for propagating an assignment of value to x_i in S'.

Fitting all of these pieces into the template for the backtracking algorithm results in an algorithm that solves the CNF-SAT problem in about as fast a time as we can expect. In general, the worst-case running time for this algorithm is still exponential, but the backtracking can often speed things up. Indeed, if every clause in the given formula has at most two literals, then this algorithm runs in polynomial time. (See Exercise C-17.6.)

18.4.2 Branch-and-Bound

The backtracking algorithm works for decision problems, but it is not designed for optimization problems, where, in addition to having some feasibility condition be satisfied for a certificate y associated with an instance x, we also have a cost function $f(x)$ that we wish to minimize or maximize (without loss of generality, let us assume the cost function should be minimized). Nevertheless, we can extend the backtracking algorithm to work for such optimization problems, and in so doing derive the algorithmic technique known as **branch-and-bound**.

The branch-and-bound technique has all the elements of backtracking, except that rather than simply stopping the entire search process any time a solution is found, we continue processing until the best solution is found. In addition, the algorithm has a scoring mechanism to always choose the most promising configuration to explore in each iteration.

To provide for the optimization criterion of always selecting the "most promising" configuration, we extend the three assumptions for a backtracking algorithm to add one more condition:

- For any configuration, (x, y), we assume we have a function, $lb(x, y)$, which is a lower bound on the cost of any solution derived from (x, y).

To make the branch-and-bound approach more concrete, let us consider how it can be applied to solve the optimization version of the traveling salesperson (TSP) problem. In the optimization version of this problem, we are given a graph G with a cost function $c(e)$ defined for each edge e in G, and we wish to find the smallest total-cost tour that visits every vertex in G, returning back to its starting vertex.

We can design an algorithm for TSP by computing for each edge $e = (v, w)$, the minimum-cost path that begins at v and ends at w while visiting all other vertices in G along the way. To find such a path, we apply the branch-and-bound technique. We generate the path from v to w in $G - \{e\}$ by augmenting a current path by one vertex in each loop of the branch-and-bound algorithm.

- After we have built a partial path P, starting, say, at v, we only consider augmenting P with vertices in not in P.
- We can classify a partial path P as a "dead end" if the vertices not in P are disconnected in $G - \{e\}$.
- To define the lower-bound function, lb, we can use the total cost of the edges in P plus $c(e)$. This will certainly be a lower bound for any tour that will be built from e and P.

In addition, after we have run the algorithm to completion for one edge e in G, we can use the best path found so far over all tested edges, rather than restarting the current best solution b at $+\infty$. The running time of the resulting algorithm will still be exponential in the worst case, but it will avoid a considerable amount of unnecessary computation in practice.

18.5 Exercises

Reinforcement

R-18.1 Describe in detail how to implement Algorithm 18.6 in $O(n + m)$ time on an n-vertex graph with m edges. You may use the traditional operation-count measure of running time in this case.

R-18.2 Describe the details of an efficient implementation of Algorithm 18.7 and analyze its running time.

R-18.3 Give an example of a graph G with at least 10 vertices such that the greedy 2-approximation algorithm for VERTEX-COVER given above is guaranteed to produce a suboptimal vertex cover.

R-18.4 Give a complete, weighted graph G, such that its edge weights satisfy the triangle inequality but the MST-based approximation algorithm for TSP does not find an optimal solution.

R-18.5 Give a pseudocode description of the backtracking algorithm for CNF-SAT.

R-18.6 Give a recursive pseudocode description of the backtracking algorithm, assuming the search strategy should visit configurations in a depth-first fashion.

R-18.7 Give a pseudocode description of the branch-and-bound algorithm for TSP.

R-18.8 The branch-and-bound program in Section 18.4.2, for solving the KNAPSACK problem, uses a Boolean flag to determine when an item is included in a solution or not. Show that this flag is redundant. That is, even if we remove this field, there is a way (using no additional fields) to tell if an item is included in a solution or not.

R-18.9 Suppose G is a complete undirected graph such that every edge has weight 1 or 2. Show that the weights in G satisfy the triangle inequality.

R-18.10 Suppose G is an undirected weighted graph such that G is not the complete graph but every edge in G has positive weight. Create a complete graph, H, having the same vertex set as G, such that if (v, u) is an edge in G, then (v, u) has the same weight in H as in G, and if (v, u) is not an edge in G, then (v, u) has weight in H equal to the length of a shortest path from v to u in G. Show that the edge weights in H satisfy the triangle inequality.

R-18.11 Suppose we are given the following collection of sets:

$$S_1 = \{1, 2, 3, 4, 5, 6\}, \ S_2 = \{5, 6, 8, 9\}, \ S_3 = \{1, 4, 7, 10\},$$

$$S_4 = \{2, 5, 7, 8, 11\}, \ S_5 = \{3, 6, 9, 12\}, \ S_6 = \{10, 11\}.$$

What is the optimal solution to this instance of the SET-COVER problem and what is the solution produced by the greedy algorithm?

R-18.12 Show that the number of vertices of odd degree in a tree is even.

Creativity

C-18.1 Consider the general optimization version of the TSP problem, where the underlying graph need not satisfy the triangle inequality. Show that, for any fixed value $\delta \geq 1$, there is no polynomial-time δ-approximation algorithm for the general TSP problem unless $P = NP$.

Hint: Reduce HAMILTONIAN-CYCLE to this problem by defining a cost function for a complete graph H for the n-vertex input graph G so that edges of H also in G have cost 1 but edges of H not in G have cost δn more than 1.

C-18.2 Derive an efficient backtracking algorithm for the HAMILTONIAN-CYCLE problem.

C-18.3 Derive an efficient backtracking algorithm for the KNAPSACK decision problem.

C-18.4 Derive an efficient branch-and-bound algorithm for the KNAPSACK optimization problem.

C-18.5 Derive a new lower-bound function, lb, for a branch-and-bound algorithm for solving the TSP optimization problem. Your function should always be greater than or equal to the lb function used in Section 18.4.2, but still be a valid lower-bound function. Describe an example where your lb is strictly greater than the lb function used in Section 18.4.2.

C-18.6 In the ***bottleneck traveling salesperson problem*** (***TSP***), we are given an undirected graph G with weights on its edges and asked to find a tour that visits the vertices of G exactly once and returns to the start so as to minimize the cost of the maximum-weight edge in the tour. Assuming that the weights in G satisfy the triangle inequality, design a polynomial-time 3-approximation algorithm for bottleneck TSP.

Hint: Show that it is possible to turn an Euler-tour traversal, E, of an MST for G into a tour visiting each vertex exactly once such that each edge of the tour skips at most two vertices of E.

C-18.7 In the ***Euclidean*** traveling salesperson problem, cities are points in the plane and the distance between two cities is the Euclidean distance between the points for these cities, that is, the length of the straight line joining these points. Show that an optimal solution to the Euclidean TSP is a simple polygon, that is, a connected sequence of line segments such that no two ever cross.

C-18.8 Consider the KNAPSACK problem, but now instead of implementing the PTAS algorithm given in the book, we use a greedy approach of always picking the next item that maximizes the ratio of value over weight (as in the optimal way to solve the fractional version of the KNAPSACK problem). Show that this approach does not produce a c-approximation algorithm, for any fixed value of c.

C-18.9 Consider a greedy algorithm for the VERTEX-COVER problem, where we repeatedly choose a vertex with maximum degree, add it to our cover, and then remove it and all its incident edges. Show that this algorithm does not, in general, produce a 2-approximation.

Hint: Use a bipartite graph where all the vertices on one side have the same degree.

C-18.10 In the HITTING-SET problem, we are given a set U of items, and a collection of subsets of U, $S_1, S_2, \ldots, S_m$. The problem is to find a smallest subset T of U such that T "hits" every subset S_i, that is, $T \cap S_i \neq \emptyset$, for $i = 1, \ldots, m$. Design a polynomial-time $O(\log n)$-approximation algorithm for HITTING-SET.

Applications

A-18.1 Suppose you are working for a cartography company, that is, a company that makes maps. Your job is to design a software package that can take as input the map of some region, R, and label as many of the cities of R as possible. Each of the n cities in such a region, R, is given by an (x, y) coordinate for the center of that city. Assume, for the sake of simplifying the problem, that the label, L_c, for each city, c, is a rectangle (which will contain the name of the city, c) whose lower-right corner is the (x, y)-location for c. The labels for two cities, c and d, **conflict** if L_c intersects L_d. Given your extensive algorithmic background, you realize that you can model this problem with a graph, G, where you create a vertex in G for each city and connect cities c and d with an edge if their labels conflict. Let $d = 2m/n$ be the average degree of the vertices in G, where m is the number of edges in G. Describe an $O(d)$-approximation algorithm for finding the largest number of mutually nonconflicting labels for the cities in a given region R.

A-18.2 In a synchronous optical network (SONET) ring, a collection of routers are connected with fiber-optic cables to form a single, simple cycle. A message between two routers, x and y, can then be transmitted by routing it clockwise or counter-clockwise around the ring. Given a set, M, of messages to transmit, each specified by a pair of routers (x, y), the **ring-loading problem** is to route all the messages in M so as to minimize the maximum load on any link in the ring (that joins two adjacent routers). Solving such an optimization problem is useful, since such a solution minimizes the bandwidth needed to transmit all the messages in M. Describe a 2-approximation for solving the ring-loading problem.

A-18.3 Suppose you work for a major package shipping company, FedUP, and it is your job to ship a set of n boxes from Rhode Island to California using a given collection of trucks. You know that these trucks will be weighed at various points along this route and FedUP will have to pay a penalty if any of these trucks are overweight. Thus, you would like to minimize the weight of the most heavily loaded truck. Assuming you know the integer weight of each of the n boxes, describe a simple greedy algorithm for assigning boxes to trucks and show that this algorithm has an approximation ratio of at most 2 for the problem of minimizing the weight of the most heavily loaded truck.

A-18.4 Suppose you work for a major package shipping company, FedUP, as in the previous exercise, but suppose there is a new law that requires every truck to carry no more than M pounds, even if it has room for more boxes. Now the optimization problem is to use the fewest number of trucks possible to carry the n boxes across the country such that each truck is carrying at most M pounds. Describe a simple greedy algorithm for assigning boxes to trucks and show that your algo-rithm uses a number of trucks that is within a factor of 2 of the optimal number of trucks. You may assume that no box weighs more than M pounds.

A-18.5 Suppose you are preparing an algorithm for the problem of optimally drilling the holes in an aluminum plug plate to allow it to do a spectrographic analysis of a set of galaxies. Based on your analysis of the robot drill device, you notice that the various amounts of time it takes to move between drilling holes satisfies the triangle inequality. Nevertheless, your supervisor does not want you to use the MST approximation algorithm or the Christofides approximation algorithm. Instead, your supervisor wants you to use a nearest-neighbor greedy algorithm for solving this instance of METRIC-TSP. In this greedy algorithm, one starts with city number 1 as the "current" city, and then repeatedly chooses the next city to add to the tour to be the one that is closest to the current city (then making the added city to be the "current" one). Show that your supervisor's nearest-neighbor greedy algorithm does not, in general, result in a 2-approximation algorithm for METRIC-TSP.

A-18.6 Consider the astronomy application of METRIC-TSP, as in the previous exercise, but now suppose that you have an improvement to your supervisor's nearest-neighbor idea. Your nearest-neighbor greedy algorithm works like this: you start with city number 1 and add cities one at time, always maintaining a tour, T, of the cities added so far. Given the current set of cities, C, you find the city, c, not in C that minimizes the distance to a city, d, that is in C. Then you add d to T immediately after c, add d to C, and repeat until T is a tour for all the cities. Show that your nearest-neighbor greedy approach results in a 2-approximation algorithm for METRIC-TSP.

Chapter Notes

General discussions of approximation algorithms can be found in several other books, in-cluding those by Hochbaum [101] and Papadimitriou and Steiglitz [170], as well as the chapter by Klein and Young [127]. The PTAS for KNAPSACK is modeled after a result of Ibarra and Kim [109], as presented by Klein and Young [127]. Papadimitriou and Stei-glitz attribute the 2-approximation for VERTEX-COVER to Gavril and Yannakakis. The 2-approximation algorithm for the special case of TSP is due to Rosenkrantz, Stearns, and Lewis [179]. The $O(\log n)$-approximation for SET-COVER, and its proof, follow from work of Chvátal [44], Johnson [112], and Lovász [146]. The Christofides approximation algorithm is due to Nicos Christofides [43].

The discussion of backtracking and branch-and-bound is modeled after discussions by Lewis and Papadimitriou [143] and Brassard and Bratley [37], where backtracking is intended for decision problems and branch-and-bound is for optimization problems. Nev-ertheless, our discussion is also influenced by Neapolitan and Naimipour [164], who alter-natively view backtracking as a heuristic search that uses a depth-first search of a configu-ration space and branch-and-bound as a heuristic search that uses breadth-first or best-first search with a lower-bound function to perform pruning. The technique of backtracking itself dates to early work of Golomb and Baumert [84].

Chapter

19

Randomized Algorithms

Trees with snow on branches, "Half Dome, Apple Orchard, Yosemite," 1933. Ansel Adams. U.S. government image. U.S. National Archives and Records Administration.

Contents

19.1 Generating Random Permutations 531

19.2 Stable Marriages and Coupon Collecting 534

19.3 Minimum Cuts 539

19.4 Finding Prime Numbers 546

19.5 Chernoff Bounds 551

19.6 Skip Lists 557

19.7 Exercises 563

An important feature of any single-person computer game is that it shouldn't be boring. That is, the user should have a new and distinct experience each time he or she plays the game. One way to achieve such a goal, of course, is to use randomization. That is, the execution of the algorithm shouldn't depend only on its inputs, but also on the use of a random-number generator to produce random numbers that are used to guide the execution of the algorithm. Thus, the structure of such algorithms depend on the outcomes of random events. In this context, the running time or correctness of an algorithm then becomes a random variable, which is averaged over the values of the random numbers the algorithm uses.

Because they are used extensively in computer games, cryptography, and computer simulations, methods that generate random numbers are built into most modern computers. Some methods, called ***pseudo-random-number generators***, generate random-like numbers deterministically, starting with an initial number called a ***seed***. Other methods use hardware devices to extract "true" random numbers from nature. In any case, we assume that our computer has access to numbers that are sufficiently random for our analysis, and we explore in this chapter some of the algorithms that can be designed using these tools.

A ***randomized algorithm*** is an algorithm whose behavior depends, in part, on the outcomes of random choices or the values of random bits. The main advantage of using randomization in algorithm design is that the results are often simple and efficient. In addition, there are some problems that need randomization for them to work effectively. For instance, consider the problem common in computer games involving playing cards—that of randomly shuffling a deck of cards so that all possible orderings are equally likely. This problem is surprisingly subtle, and there are even published stories of people who have been able to defeat online poker systems by exploiting the fact that those systems were not using a good card shuffling algorithm. So one of the problems that we address in this chapter on randomized algorithms is how to efficiently shuffle a deck of virtual cards. For example, an algorithm that doesn't generate all possible permutations with equal probability is to take an approach based on the riffle shuffle used by humans to shuffle cards. Thus, the shuffling methods we discuss in this chapter are quite different than this approach, but are just as fast.

We study a number of other interesting randomized algorithms in this chapter, as well, including finding prime numbers, which is important in cryptography, the coupon collector problem, which has applications to biodiversity studies, and methods for building search structures known as skip lists, using randomization. We assume throughout this chapter that the reader is familiar with the principles of basic probability covered in Section 1.2.4.

This is not the only place where we discuss randomized algorithms, however. We also have discussions of randomized algorithms in the context of hash tables in Chapter 6, random construction of binary search trees in Section 3.4, the randomized quick-sort algorithm in Section 8.2, the quick-select algorithm in Chapter 9, and a page-caching algorithm in Section 20.4.

19.1 Generating Random Permutations

As mentioned above, randomly shuffling cards is an important part of any computer gaming system that deals virtual cards. The problem of computing random permutations has many more applications than just computerized card games, however, including a host of other randomized algorithms, often as the very first step. In this section, we explore two random permutation algorithms, both of which run in linear time.

The input to the random permutation problem is a list, $X = (x_1, x_2, \ldots, x_n)$, of n elements, which could stand for playing cards or any other objects we want to randomly permute. The output is a reordering of the elements of X, done in a way so that all permutations of X are equally likely.

Both of the algorithms we discuss make use of a function, random(k), which returns an integer in the range $[0, k - 1]$ chosen uniformly and independently at random. This function is based on the use of some source of random bits. So if k is a power of 2, then we simply take $\log k$ random bits from this source and interpret them as a number in the range from 0 to $k - 1$, inclusive. Every number in this range is equally likely. If, on the other hand, k is not a power of 2, then we let K be the smallest power of 2 greater than k and we take $\log K$ random bits from this source. If interpreting these bits as a number gives us an integer in the range $[0, k - 1]$, then we take this as our output to the random(k) method. Otherwise, if we get a number that is k or larger, then we discard these bits and try again. Thus, if k is not a power of 2, then the running time of the random(k) method is itself a random variable with expected value $O(1)$. If k is a power of 2, however, then this method always runs in $O(1)$ time.

We give our first random permutation method in Algorithm 19.2. This algorithm simply chooses a random number for each element in X and sorts the elements using these values as keys. (See Figure 19.1.) If all the keys are distinct, then the resulting permutation is generated uniformly, as we show below.

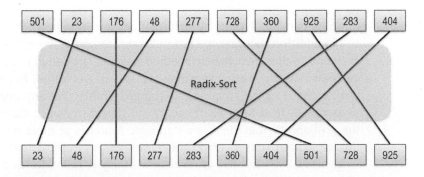

Figure 19.1: A random permutation algorithm based on sorting random numbers.

Algorithm randomSort(X):

> ***Input:*** A list, X, of n elements
>
> ***Output:*** A permutation of X so that all permutations are equally likely
>
> Let K be the smallest power of 2 greater than or equal to n^3
> **for** each element, x_i, in X **do**
> > Choose a random value, r_i, in the range $[0, K - 1]$ and associate it with x_i
>
> Sort X using the r_i values as keys via radix-sort
> **if** all the r_i values are distinct **then**
> > **return** X according to this sorted order
>
> **else**
> > Call randomSort(X)

Algorithm 19.2: A sorting-based algorithm for generating a random permutation.

Analyzing the Sorting-Based Random Permutation Algorithm

To see that every permutation is equally likely to be output by the randomSort method, note that each element, x_i, in X has an equal probability, $1/n$, of having its r_i value be the smallest. Thus, each element in X has equal probability of $1/n$ of being the first element in the permutation. Note, in addition, that because the algorithm will only terminate when all the elements are distinct, then there is exactly one element with smallest r_i value. Moreover, once we have removed this value, each remaining value, x_i, has equal probability of $1/(n - 1)$ of holding the minimum r_i value. Thus, the probability that any element from this group will be chosen second is $1/(n-1)$. Following this reasoning to its logical conclusion, this approach implies that the permutation that is output had a probability of

$$\left(\frac{1}{n}\right) \cdot \left(\frac{1}{n-1}\right) \cdots \left(\frac{1}{2}\right) \cdot \left(\frac{1}{1}\right) = \frac{1}{n!}$$

of being chosen. That is, all permutations are equally likely.

In addition, because we use radix sort to sort X by r_i values, and K is $O(n^3)$, each call to the randomSort method runs in $O(n)$ time, not counting any recursive calls that are made because a duplicate r_i value is found. In any call to this method, we choose n of the r_i values, so the probability that any one of these is the same as any other is at most $n/n^3 = 1/n^2$. Therefore, since there are n values chosen, the probability that there is a duplicate found is at most $n/n^2 = 1/n$. That is, this algorithm runs in $O(n)$ time, without any retries, with probability $1 - 1/n$. In general, we say that an event involving n items holds with ***high probability*** if it occurs with probability at least $1 - 1/n$. So the sorting-based permutation algorithms runs in $O(n)$ time with high probability.

The Fisher-Yates Shuffling Algorithm

There is another shuffling algorithm, which reduces all the uncertainty in its running time to calls of the random(k) method. Thus, if we had a way of implementing this method so that it always ran in constant time, then this second algorithm would be "almost deterministic," in that it would always succeed and it would always run in $O(n)$ time. This algorithm, which is known as the *Fisher-Yates algorithm*, assumes that the input list is given as an array; the details are given in Algorithm 19.3. (See Figure 19.4.)

Algorithm FisherYates(X):
  Input: An array, X, of n elements, indexed from position 0 to $n-1$
  Output: A permutation of X so that all permutations are equally likely

  for $k = n - 1$ **downto** 1 **do**
      Let $j \leftarrow$ random($k + 1$)   // j is a random integer in $[0, k]$
      Swap $X[k]$ and $X[j]$ // This may "swap" $X[k]$ with itself, if $j = k$
  return X

Algorithm 19.3: The Fisher-Yates algorithm for generating a random permutation.

This algorithm considers the items in the array one at time from the end and swaps each element with an element in the array from that point to the beginning. Notice that each element has an equal probability, of $1/n$, of being chosen as the last element in the array X (including the element that starts out in that position). Likewise, for the elements that remain in the first $n - 1$ positions, each of them has an equal probability, of $1/(n-1)$, of being the last element in that range. Following this reasoning to its logical conclusion implies that the permutation that is actually output by the Fisher-Yates algorithm had a probability of

$$\left(\frac{1}{n}\right) \cdot \left(\frac{1}{n-1}\right) \cdots \left(\frac{1}{2}\right) \cdot \left(\frac{1}{1}\right) = \frac{1}{n!}$$

of being the one output. That is, all permutations are equally likely. In addition, if the random(k) method runs in $O(1)$ time, then this algorithm runs in $O(n)$ time. (We revisit this issue in Section 19.5.3.)

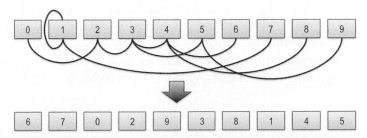

Figure 19.4: The Fisher-Yates random permutation algorithm. The arcs represent swaps, which start from 9 and go down to 1. Here, position 1 swaps with itself.

19.2   Stable Marriages and Coupon Collecting

A common question biologists often ask with respect to a given ecosystem is to determine the number of species that occupy that ecosystem. In order to get a handle on such biodiversity questions, biologists have developed various tools for sampling species. For instance, one tool that is used for this purpose is random sampling, where an ecosystem is divided into a grid, like a checkerboard, and then a careful census is prepared for a random subset of the squares in this grid. A natural issue that arises in this application, then, is to determine the right number of squares to sample in order to have a good chance of finding at least one individual from every species in the ecosystem.

One way to get a handle on this estimate is to model it as a ***coupon collector problem***, which abstracts the essence of this estimation. We imagine that there is a set, C, of n coupons and we are interested in collecting at least one of every coupon in C. We can go a ticket window once a day and request a coupon, and a clerk will choose one of the n coupons at random and give it to us. We cannot expect the clerk to remember which coupons he has given us in the past, however, so, each time he gives us a coupon, it is chosen uniformly and independently at random from among the n coupons in C. The coupon collector problem, then, is to determine the number of times we need to go to the ticket window before we have collected all n coupons. So, for instance, in the application to biodiversity estimation, each time a plant or animal is detected in a random sample is like a trip to the ticket window in the coupon collector problem.

19.2.1   Analyzing the Coupon Collector Problem

Let X be a random variable representing the number of times that we need to visit the ticket window before we get all n coupons. We can write X as

$$X = X_1 + X_2 + \cdots + X_n,$$

where X_i is the number of trips we have to make to the ticket window in order to go from having $i - 1$ distinct coupons to having i distinct coupons. So, for example, $X_1 = 1$, since we are guaranteed to get a distinct coupon in our first trip to the ticket window, and X_2 is the number of additional trips we must make to get our second distinct coupon. After we have gotten $i - 1$ distinct coupons, our chance of getting a new one in any trip to the window is

$$p_i = \frac{n - (i - 1)}{n},$$

since there are n coupons, but only $n-(i-1)$ that we don't already have at this point in time. This implies that each X_i a ***geometric random variable*** with parameter, p_i. That is, if we imagine that we have a biased coin that only comes up heads with probability p_i, then X_i is the number of times we have to flip this coin until we get it to come up heads. The expected value, $E[X_i]$, of X_i is therefore $1/p_i$.

By the linearity of expectation,

$$
\begin{aligned}
E[X] &= E[X_1] + E[X_2] + \cdots + E[X_n] \\
&= \frac{1}{p_1} + \frac{1}{p_2} + \cdots + \frac{1}{p_n} \\
&= \frac{n}{n} + \frac{n}{n-1} + \cdots + \frac{n}{1} \\
&= n \sum_{i=1}^{n} \frac{1}{i} \\
&= n H_n,
\end{aligned}
$$

where H_n is the nth harmonic number, which, as we have observed elsewhere, can be approximated as $\ln n \leq H_n \leq \ln n + 1$. In other words, the expected number of times that we need to visit the ticket window in order to get at least one instance of each of n coupons is $n H_n$, which is approximately $n \ln n$.

In some cases, such as in the biodiversity application discussed above, we would like to bound the probability that we need to make significantly more than $n \ln n$ trips to the ticket window to get all n coupons. Such a bound is known as a ***tail estimate***, since it involves bounding the end or "tail" of a probability distribution. Fortunately, in the case of the coupon collector problem, coming up with such a tail bound is not that difficult.

Let us now consider that the coupons are numbered $1, 2, \ldots, n$ and let $Y_{i,t}$ be a random variable indicating the event that coupon number i was not collected even after we have made t trips to the ticket window. Thus,

$$
\begin{aligned}
\Pr(Y_{i,t} = 1) &= \left(1 - \frac{1}{n}\right)^t \\
&\leq e^{-t/n},
\end{aligned}
$$

since $1 - x \leq e^{-x}$, for $0 < x < 1$ (see Theorem A.4). We can then bound the probability that X is more than $T = cn \ln n$, for some constant $c \geq 2$, as follows:

$$
\begin{aligned}
\Pr(X > T) &\leq \Pr\left(\sum_{i=1}^{n} Y_{i,T} \geq 1\right) \\
&\leq n \cdot \Pr(Y_{1,T} = 1) \\
&\leq n \cdot e^{-T/n} \\
&= n \cdot e^{-c \ln n} \\
&= n \cdot n^{-c} \\
&= n^{-c+1}.
\end{aligned}
$$

Thus, with high probability, we will collect all n coupons after making $cn \ln n$ trips to the ticket window, for $c \geq 2$.

19.2.2   The Stable Marriage Problem

Imagine a village consisting of n men and n women, all of whom are single, heterosexual, and interested in getting married. Every man has a list of the women ordered by his preferences, and, likewise, every woman has a list of the men ordered by her preferences. The **stable marriage problem** is to match up the men and women in a way that is **stable**. Such a matching is stable if there is no unmatched man-woman pair, (x, y), such that x and y would prefer to be married to each other than to their spouses. That is, it would be unstable if x preferred y over his wife and y preferred x over her husband. (See Figure 19.5.)

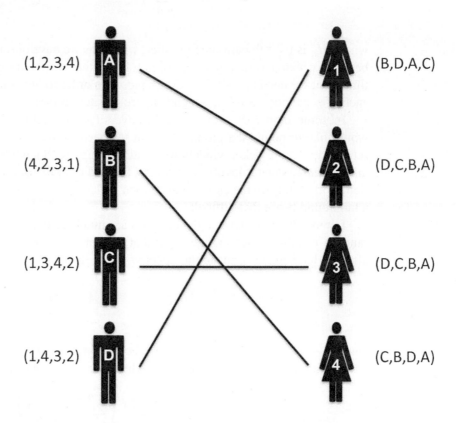

Figure 19.5: An instance of the stable marriage problem. Each man and woman is listed with his or her preference list, and the matching shown is stable. Note that even though female 2 is married to her last choice, there is no man who prefers her over his current wife.

In real life, this problem arises in the annual placement of residents in hospitals. Residents rank order the hospitals that they would like to work in, and hospitals rank the set of available residents for each of their available open slots. Then a stable "marriage" is computed between residents and available slots in hospitals.

The Proposal Algorithm

There is a simple algorithm for solving the stable marriage problem, which involves men making proposals to women in a series of rounds.

A round begins with an unmatched man making a proposal to the female highest-ranked on his list. If she is unmatched, then she accepts his proposal and the round ends. If, on the other hand, she is matched, then she accepts his proposal only if she ranks him higher than her current partner. In the case when the woman receiving the proposal is already matched, then whichever man she rejects repeats the computation for this round, making a proposal to the next woman on his list (his highest-ranked woman that he has not previously proposed to). Thus, a round continues in this way, consisting of a series of proposals and it ends when a previously unmatched woman accepts a proposal. This proposal algorithm continues performing such rounds until all the men and women are matched. (See Algorithm 19.6.)

Algorithm StableMarriage(X, Y):

> *Input:* A set, X, of n men and their prioritized lists of women in Y, and a set, Y, of n women and their prioritized lists of men in X
> *Output:* A stable marriage for X and Y
>
> **for** each man, x, in X **do**
>> Let y be x's highest-ranked woman
>> Have x propose to y
>> **while** y is matched to some man, z, such that $z \neq x$ **do**
>>> **if** y prefers x over z **then**
>>>> Match x and y
>>>> Unmatch z
>>>> Let $x \leftarrow z$
>>> Let y be x's highest-ranked woman he has not proposed to yet
>>> Have x propose to y
>> Match x and y

Algorithm 19.6: The proposal algorithm for the stable marriage problem.

To see that the matching resulting from this proposal algorithm is stable, suppose there is an unstable pair, (x, y), that are not matched by the algorithm, that is, both x and y prefer each other to the partners they end up with by following the proposal algorithm. Note that at the time x made his last proposal, to his current partner, w, he had made a proposal to every woman that he ranked higher than w. But this means that he would have made a proposal to y, which she would have accepted, because she ranks x higher than the man she ended up with. Thus, such a pair, (x, y), cannot exist.

A Worst-Case Amortized Analysis

The worst-case running time of this algorithm is $O(n^2)$. To see this fact, note that at the beginning of the algorithm, the total length of the lists of all n men is $O(n^2)$, and at each step of the algorithm, some man is using up a proposal to a woman on his list to whom he will never again propose. Thus, if we charge each entry in the list of preferences by the men 1 cyber-dollar for the work we do in having a man make a proposal, then we can pay for all the proposals using $O(n^2)$ cyber-dollars.

An Average-Case Analysis Based on Coupon Collecting

We can perform an average-case analysis of Algorithm 19.6, which has a much better performance than the worst-case bound. For the sake of this analysis, suppose the preference list for every man is an independent random permutation of the list of women. Then, each time it is a man's turn to make a proposal, he is making that proposal to a random woman he has not proposed to before.

In fact, we can simplify this analysis even further to consider a version of the algorithm where each time it is a man's turn to make a proposal, he makes his proposal to a random woman without consideration of his previous proposals. Such an algorithm is ***memoryless***, in the sense that each proposal a man makes is independent of any proposal he made earlier. Still, note that in this memoryless proposal algorithm if a man makes a proposal to a woman he has previously proposed to, she will reject his proposal, since at that point in time she will be matched to someone she prefers more than him. Thus, a bound on the running time of this memoryless algorithm gives us a bound on the original algorithm with randomly ordered preference lists, since the original version makes no more proposals than the memoryless version.

The key observation to analyze the memoryless algorithm is to focus on the women and realize that each round in this algorithm consists of a sequence of proposals to independently chosen random women until a proposal is made to an unmatched woman. That is, the memoryless algorithm is an instance of the coupon collector problem where the names of the women are the coupons. Thus, by the analysis of the coupon collector problem, the expected running time of the memoryless stable marriage algorithm is $O(n \log n)$. Therefore, we have the following theorem.

Theorem 19.1: *The expected number of proposals made in the proposal algorithm, for a set of n men and n women, is at most nH_n, assuming the preference list of each man is an independent random permutation of the list of women.*

That is, the average-case running time of the proposal algorithm for the stable marriage problem is $O(n \log n)$.

19.3   Minimum Cuts

A ***cut***, C, of a connected graph, G, is a subset of the edges of G whose removal disconnects G. That is, after removing all the edges of C, we can partition the vertices of G into two subsets, A, and B such that there are no edges between a vertex in A and a vertex in B. (See Figure 19.7.) A ***minimum cut*** of G is a cut of smallest size among all cuts of G.

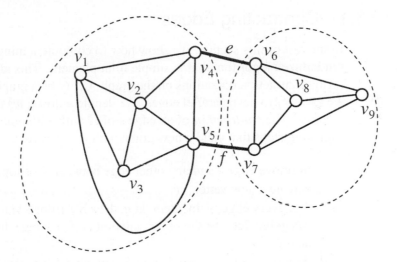

Figure 19.7: Example of a cut of a graph. The set of edges $C = \{e, f\}$, drawn with thick lines, is a cut, since removing e and f partitions the graph into two connected components. This cut is of minimum size.

In several applications, it is important to determine the size of a smallest cut of a graph. For example, in a communications network, the failures of the edges of a cut prevents the communication between the nodes on the two sides of a cut. Thus, the size of a minimum cut and the number of such cuts give an idea of the vulnerability of the network to edge failures. Small cuts are also important for the automatic classification of web content. Namely, consider a collection of web pages and model them as a graph, where vertices correspond to pages and edges to links between pages. The size of a minimum cut provides a measure of how much groups of pages have related content. Also, we can use minimum cuts to recursively partition the collection into clusters of related documents. Similar considerations can be made for minimum cuts in a social network.

As a starting point for computing minimum cuts, note that, for each vertex, v, the edges incident on v form a cut, whose size is the degree of v, $\deg(v)$, since removing all these edges separates v from the rest of the graph. Thus, the minimum degree of the vertices of a graph is an upper bound on the size of its minimum cut.

Also, recalling the notion of a biconnected graph, defined in Section 13.5, we have that a minimum cut of a biconnected graph has size at least 2.

In Section 16.1, we present a related definition of a cut in a flow network with respect to given pair of vertices, s, and t. The partition induced by such a cut has vertex s on one side and vertex t on the other size. As explored in Exercise C-19.9, one can compute a minimum cut of a graph by repeated applications of a maximum flow algorithm to a flow network derived from G.

19.3.1 Contracting Edges

In the rest of this section, we show how to compute a minimum cut by means of a randomized algorithm that is simple to implement. This algorithm repeatedly performs contraction operations on the graph. Let G be a graph with n vertices, where we allow G to have parallel edges. We denote with (v, w) any edge with endpoints v and w. The **contraction** of an edge e of G with endpoints u and v consists of the following steps that yield a new graph with $n - 1$ vertices, denoted G/e:

1. Remove edge e and any other edge between its endpoints, u and v.
2. Create a new vertex, w.
3. For every edge, f, incident on u, detach f from u and attach it to w. Formally speaking, let z be the other endpoint of f. Change the endpoints of f to be z and w.
4. For every edge, f, incident on v, detach f from v and attach it to w.

A series of contraction operations is shown in Figure 19.8. Note that a contraction may create parallel edges. Specifically, if vertices u and v have a common neighbor, z, the edges connecting z to u and v become parallel edges connecting z and w.

A contraction operation for an edge (u, v) has the important property of preserving the set of cuts that do not include any edge (u, v). This property is formally expressed by the following lemma.

Lemma 19.2: *Let G be a graph that may have parallel edges and let G/e be the graph resulting from G after contracting an edge, e, with endpoints u and v. A set, C, of edges is a cut of G/e if and only if C is a cut of G that does not contain any edge with endpoints u and v.*

Lemma 19.2 implies that the set of cuts of G/e is the same as the set of cuts of G that exclude any edge (u, v).

By Lemma 19.2, if we perform a series of contraction operations, we obtain a graph whose cuts are a subset of the cuts of the original graph. In particular, if we contract $n - 2$ edges, where n is the number of vertices of the graph, we obtain a graph with two vertices connected by parallel edges that form one of the cuts of the original graph. (See Figure 19.8.)

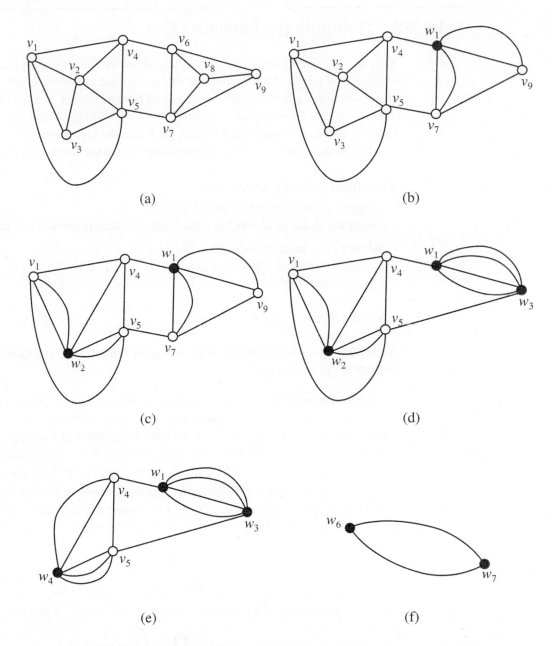

Figure 19.8: Sequence of contraction operations on a graph. (a–b) Contraction of (v_6, v_8). (b–c) Contraction of (v_2, v_3). (c–d) Contraction of (v_7, v_9). (d–e) Contraction of (v_1, w_2). (f) Final graph obtained after contracting (v_4, v_5), yielding vertex w_5, (w_4, w_5), yielding vertex w_6, and (w_1, w_2), yielding vertex w_7. The final graph has the same minimum cut as the original graph since each contraction preserves the edges of this cut.

19.3.2   Computing a Minimum Cut

Karger's algorithm for computing a minimum cut is very simple. It performs a sequence of edge contractions, selecting each time a random edge. The algorithm stops when the graph has two vertices and returns the set of edges between them. This method is summarized in Algorithm 19.9. Admittedly, the algorithm may not return a minimum cut, since, for each such cut, the algorithm may have contracted one of its edges. Nevertheless, Karger's algorithm succeeds with high probability.

Algorithm ContractGraph(G):
>   ***Input:*** An undirected graph, G, with n vertices
>   ***Output:*** A cut of G that has minimum size with probability at least $\frac{2}{n(n-1)}$
>
>   **while** G has more than 2 edges **do**
>   pick a random edge, e, of G
>   contract edge e
> $G \leftarrow G/e$
>   **return** the edges of G

Algorithm 19.9: Single iteration of Karger's randomized algorithm for finding a minimum cut of a graph.

Let us evaluate the success probability of Algorithm 19.9, that is, the probability that the algorithm returns a minimum cut. Let G be a graph with n vertices and m edges, and let C be a given minimum cut of G. We will evaluate the probability that the algorithm returns the cut C. Since G may have other minimum cuts, this probability is a lower bound on the success probability of the algorithm.

Let G_i be the graph obtained after i contractions performed by the algorithm and let m_i be the number of edges of G_i. Assume that G_{i-1} contains all the edges of C. The probability that G_i also contains all the edges of C is equal to

$$1 - \frac{k}{m_{i-1}},$$

since we contract any given edge of C with probability $1/m_{i-1}$ and C has k edges. Thus, the probability, P, that the algorithm returns cut C is given by

$$P = \prod_{i=0,\dots,n-3} \left(1 - \frac{k}{m_i}\right).$$

Since k is the size of the minimum cut of each graph G_i, we have that each vertex of G_i has degree at least k. Thus, we obtain the following lower bound on m_i, the number of edges of G_i:

$$m_i \geq \frac{k(n-i)}{2}, \quad \text{for } i = 0, 1, \dots, n-3 .$$

We can use the above inequality to derive a lower bound on P, as follows:

$$P = \prod_{i=0}^{n-3} \left(1 - \frac{k}{m_i} \right) \tag{19.1}$$

$$\geq \prod_{i=0}^{n-3} \left(1 - \frac{2k}{k(n-i)} \right) \tag{19.2}$$

$$= \prod_{i=0}^{n-3} \left(\frac{n-i-2}{n-i} \right) \tag{19.3}$$

$$= \left(\frac{n-2}{n} \right) \left(\frac{n-3}{n-1} \right) \left(\frac{n-4}{n-2} \right) \left(\frac{n-5}{n-3} \right) \cdots \left(\frac{2}{4} \right) \left(\frac{1}{3} \right) \tag{19.4}$$

$$= \frac{2}{n(n-1)} \tag{19.5}$$

$$= \frac{1}{\binom{n}{2}} \tag{19.6}$$

The above analysis shows that probability that Algorithm 19.9 returns cut C is $\Omega\left(\frac{1}{n^2}\right)$, a decreasing function that tends to 0 as n grows. However, we can boost the probability by running the algorithm multiple times. In particular, if we run the algorithm for $t\binom{n}{2}$ rounds, where t is a positive integer, we have that at least one round returns cut C with probability

$$P(t) = 1 - \left(1 - \frac{1}{\binom{n}{2}} \right)^{t\binom{n}{2}}.$$

By a well-known property (Theorem A.4) of the mathematical constant e, the base of the natural logarithm, ln, we obtain

$$P(t) \geq 1 - \frac{1}{e^t}.$$

In particular, if we choose $t = c \ln n$, where c is a constant, then we get a success probability, $1 - 1/n^c$, to obtain the cut C.

We turn now to the analysis of the running time of the algorithm. A contraction operation can be executed in $O(n)$ time. Thus, Algorithm 19.9 (ContractGraph) takes $O(n^2)$ time. We summarize our findings with the following theorem.

Theorem 19.3: *Let G be a graph with n vertices. For any positive integer constant c, we can compute a minimum cut of G with a randomized algorithm that runs in time $O(n^4 \log n)$ and has success probability $1 - 1/n^c$.*

Proof: The algorithm consists of executing Algorithm 19.9 (ContractGraph) $c\binom{n}{2} \ln n$ times and returning the smallest of the cuts obtained. ∎

19.4   Finding Prime Numbers

An integer p is **prime** if $p \geq 2$ and its only divisors are the trivial divisors 1 and p. An integer greater than 2 that is not prime is **composite**. So, for example, 5, 11, and 101 are prime, whereas 25 and 713 ($= 23 \cdot 31$) are composite. In this section, we discuss randomized ways of testing for primality and for then using these methods to find prime numbers. Such computations are useful, for example, in cryptography, which is discussed in Chapter 24.

In order to lay the groundwork for finding primes, a few words about the **modulo operator** (mod) are in order. Recall that $a \bmod n$ is the remainder of a when divided by n. That is,

$$r = a \bmod n$$

means that $r = a - \lfloor a/n \rfloor n$. In other words, there is some integer q, such that $a = qn + r$. Note, in addition, that $a \bmod n$ is always an integer in the set $\{0, 1, 2, \ldots, n-1\}$.

It is sometimes convenient to talk about **congruence** modulo n. If

$$a \bmod n = b \bmod n,$$

we say that a is **congruent** to b modulo n, which we call the **modulus**, and we write

$$a \equiv b \pmod{n}.$$

Therefore, if $a \equiv b \bmod n$, then $a - b = kn$ for some integer k.

Having laid this groundwork, we are now ready for the first theorem of this chapter, which is known as **Fermat's Little Theorem**.

Theorem 19.5 (*Fermat's Little Theorem*): *Let p be a prime, and let x be an integer such that $x \bmod p \neq 0$ and $0 < x < p$. Then*

$$x^{p-1} \equiv 1 \pmod{p}.$$

Proof: We know that, for $0 < x < p$, the set $\{1, 2, \ldots, p-1\}$ and the set $\{x \cdot 1, x \cdot 2, \ldots, x \cdot (p-1)\}$ contain exactly the same elements, when we do all arithmetic modulo p (see Exercise C-19.8). So when we multiply the elements of the sets together, we get the same value, namely,

$$1 \cdot 2 \cdots (p-1) = (p-1)!.$$

In other words,

$$(x \cdot 1) \cdot (x \cdot 2) \cdots (x \cdot (p-1)) \equiv (p-1)! \pmod{p}.$$

If we factor out the x terms, we get

$$x^{p-1}(p-1)! \equiv (p-1)! \pmod{p}.$$

Thus, because p is prime, we can cancel the term $(p-1)!$ from both sides, yielding $x^{p-1} \equiv 1 \bmod p$, which is the desired result. ∎

19.4.1 Primality Testing

Prime numbers play an important role in computations involving numbers, such as cryptographic computations, as we noted above. But how do we test whether a number is prime, particularly if it is large?

Testing all possible divisors of a number takes exponential time, so we need an alternative to the method many of us used to test for primality on grade-school Math assignments. Alternatively, Fermat's Little Theorem (Theorem 19.5) seems to suggest an efficient solution. Perhaps we can somehow use the equation

$$a^{p-1} \equiv 1 \bmod p$$

to form a test for p. That is, let us pick a number a, and raise it to the power $p - 1$. If the result is **not** 1, then the number p is definitely not prime. Otherwise, there's a chance it is. Would repeating this test for various values of a prove that p is prime? Unfortunately, the answer is "no." There is a class of numbers, called **Carmichael numbers**, that have the property that $a^{n-1} \equiv 1 \bmod n$ for all $1 \le a \le n - 1$, but n is composite. The existence of these numbers ruins such a simple way to test for primality. Example Carmichael numbers are 561 and 1105.

Independent Repetitions: A Template for Primality Testing

While the above simple test won't work, there is a related approach that will work, by making more sophisticated use of Fermat's Little Theorem. Such a probabilistic test of primality is based on the following general approach. Let n be an odd integer that we want to test for primality, and let witness(x, n) be a Boolean function of a random variable x and n with the following properties:

1. If n is prime, then witness(x, n) is always false. So if witness(x, n) is true, then n is definitely composite.
2. If n is composite, then witness(x, n) is false with probability $q < 1$.

The function witness is said to be a **compositeness witness function** with error probability q, for q bounds the probability that witness will incorrectly identify a composite number as possibly prime. By repeatedly computing witness(x, n) for independent random values of the parameter x, we can determine whether n is prime with an arbitrarily small error probability. The probability that witness(x, n) would incorrectly return "false" for k independent random x's, when n is a composite number, is q^k. A template for a probabilistic primality testing algorithm based on this observation is shown in Algorithm 19.11. This algorithm assumes we have a compositeness witness function, witness, that satisfies the two conditions above. In order to turn this template into a full-blown algorithm, we need only specify the details of how to pick random numbers, x, and compute witness(x, n), the composite witness function.

Algorithm RandomizedPrimalityTesting(n, k):
  Input: Odd integer $n \geq 2$ and confidence parameter k
  Output: An indication of whether n is composite (which is always correct) or
    prime (which is incorrect with error probability 2^{-k})
  // This method assumes we have a compositeness witness function witness(x, n)
  with error probability $q < 1$.
  $t \leftarrow \lceil k/\log_2(1/q) \rceil$
  for $i \leftarrow 1$ **to** t **do**
    $x \leftarrow$ random()
    if witness(x, n) **then**
        return "composite"
  return "prime"

Algorithm 19.11: A template for a probabilistic primality testing algorithm based
on a compositeness witness function witness(x, n). We assume that the method
random() picks a value at random from the domain of the variable x.

If the method RandomizedPrimalityTesting(n, k, witness) returns "composite," we know with certainty that n is composite. However, if the method returns
"prime," the probability that n is actually composite is no more than 2^{-k}. Indeed,
suppose that n is composite but the method returns "prime." We have that the witness function witness(x, n) has evaluated to true for t random values of x. The
probability of this event is q^t. From the relation between the confidence parameter
k, the number of iterations t, and the error probability q of the witness function
established by the first statement of the method, we have that $q^t \leq 2^{-k}$.

Given the parameter k, which is known as a **confidence parameter**, we can
make $t = \lceil k/\log_2(1/q) \rceil$ independent repetitions of our test to get force our probability of failure to be at most 2^{-k}. For instance, taking $k = 30$, forces this failure
probability to be lower than the probability that the average person will, in their
lifetime, be hit by lightning. This approach of repeating independent trials of a
randomized algorithm to force a failure probability down below a probability determined by a specified confidence parameter is a common pattern in the design of
randomized algorithms.

The Rabin-Miller Primality Testing Algorithm

We now describe the **Rabin-Miller algorithm** for primality testing. It is based on
Fermat's Little Theorem (Theorem 19.5) and on the following lemma.

Lemma 19.6: *Let p be a prime number greater than 2. If x is an element of Z_p
such that*

$$x^2 \equiv 1 \pmod{p},$$

then either $x \equiv 1 \pmod{p}$ or $x \equiv -1 \pmod{p}$.

A ***nontrivial square root of the unity*** in Z_n is an integer $1 < x < n - 1$ such that $x^2 \equiv 1 \pmod{n}$. Lemma 19.6 states that if n is prime, there are no nontrivial square roots of the unity in Z_n. The Rabin-Miller algorithm uses this fact to define the witness(x, n) function as shown below:

> **Algorithm** witness(x, n):
>   Write $n - 1$ as $2^k m$, where m is odd.
>   Compute $y \leftarrow x^m \bmod n$
>   **if** $y \equiv 1 \pmod{n}$ **then**
>   **return false**   // n is probably prime
>   **for** $i \leftarrow 1$ **to** $k - 1$ **do**
>   **if** $y \equiv -1 \pmod{n}$ **then**
>   **return false**   // n is probably prime
> $y \leftarrow y^2 \bmod n$
>   **return true**   // n is definitely composite

As we explore in an exercise (C-19.12), if the Rabin-Miller composite witness function returns **true**, then n is definitely composite. The error probability of the cases when Rabin-Miller composite witness algorithm returns **false** is provided by the following lemma, stated without proof.

Lemma 19.7: *Let n be a composite number. There are at most $(n - 1)/4$ positive values of x in Z_n such that the Rabin-Miller compositeness witness function* witness(x, n) *returns true.*

We conclude as follows:

Theorem 19.8: *Given an odd positive integer n and a parameter $k > 0$, the Rabin-Miller algorithm determines whether n is prime, with error probability 2^{-k}, by performing $O(k \log n)$ arithmetic operations.*

Finding Prime Numbers

A primality testing algorithm can be used to select a random prime in a given range, or with a prespecified number of bits. We exploit the following result from number theory, stated without proof.

Theorem 19.9: *The number, $\pi(n)$, of primes that are less than or equal to n is $\Theta(n/\ln n)$. In fact, if $n \geq 17$, then $n/\ln n < \pi(n) < 1.26 n/\ln n$.*

A consequence of Theorem 19.9 is that a random integer n is prime with probability $1/\ln n$. Thus, to find a prime with a given number b of bits, we can again use the pattern of repeated independent trials. In particular, note that if we generate a random b-bit odd number, n, then it has $\lceil \log n \rceil \geq \lceil \ln n \rceil$ bits. So n is prime with probability at least $1/b$; hence, repeating a primality test for kb such numbers gives us the following.

Theorem 19.10: *Given an integer b and a confidence parameter k, a random prime with b bits can be generated by performing $O(kb)$ primality tests, with probability at least $1 - 2^{-k}$.*

Las Vegas and Monte Carlo Algorithms

Note that in Theorem 19.10 the confidence parameter is bounding a probability that the algorithm takes longer than the stated time to run, whereas the confidence parameter in the Rabin-Miller algorithm is bounding the probability that the algorithm produces a wrong answer. These two scenarios arise so often in the context of randomized algorithms that they have names. A randomized algorithm that always succeeds in producing a correct output, but whose running time depends on random events is known as a ***Las Vegas algorithm***. A randomized algorithm that always has a deterministic running time, but whose output may be incorrect, with some probability, is known as a ***Monte Carlo algorithm***. We summarize the distinction between these two categories of randomized algorithms in Table 19.12.

	Running Time	**Correctness**
Las Vegas Algorithm	probabilistic	certain
Monte Carlo Algorithm	certain	probabilistic

Table 19.12: The difference between Las Vegas and Monte Carlo algorithms.

Note that if we have a deterministic way to test for correctness, we can always turn a Monte Carlo algorithm into a Las Vegas algorithm, as we explore in Exercise C-19.13. But without such a testing algorithm, we have no easy way of turning a Monte Carlo algorithm into a Las Vegas algorithm. Nevertheless, we do have an easy way to turn any Las Vegas algorithm into a Monte Carlo algorithm, simply by running the Las Vegas algorithm for an amount of time determined by its confidence parameter and either outputting the correct answer, if the algorithm has terminated in that time, or outputting "sorry" if it has not. Moreover, if we use a Monte Carlo algorithm as a subroutine in what would otherwise be a Las Vegas algorithm, then the resulting algorithm is Monte Carlo, using this same argument. Such is the case if we combine Theorems 19.8 and 19.10.

In addition, we say that a Monte Carlo algorithm that outputs yes-no answers has a ***one-sided error*** if, as in the Rabin-Miller algorithm, one of its outputs, "yes" or "no," is always correct. Otherwise, it has a ***two-sided error***.

19.5 Chernoff Bounds

Quite often in the analysis of randomized algorithms we are interested in proving a bound on a running time with high probability. A useful collection of tools that are frequently used to perform such analyses are the ***Chernoff bounds*** we discuss in this section. For instance, we use one in Section 6.3.3 to analyze the performance of a hash table that uses linear probing to resolve collisions.

19.5.1 Markov's Inequality

Any discussion of Chernoff bounds begins with a foundational fact of probability known as ***Markov's inequality***, which can be stated as follows.

Theorem 19.11: *Let X be a random variable such that $X \geq 0$. Then, for all $a > 0$,*

$$\Pr(X \geq a) \leq \frac{E[X]}{a}.$$

Proof: Let Y be a 0-1 indicator random variable that is 1 if $X \geq a$. Then, since $X \geq 0$,

$$Y \leq \frac{X}{a}.$$

Taking expectations of both sides, we get

$$E[Y] \leq \frac{E[X]}{a},$$

by the linearity of expectation. The theorem follows, then, by observing that

$$E[Y] = \Pr(Y = 1) = \Pr(X \geq a).$$

∎

An example application of Markov's inequality is to note that at most 10% of the U.S. population can have more than 10 times the average net worth of any American.

The bounds that can be derived directly from using Markov's inequality are not always the tightest, but they are usually simple. Moreover, another nice feature of Markov's inequality is that we don't have to know anything more about X than the fact that it is nonnegative and has expected value $E[X]$. In fact, it is sufficient for us simply to have an upper bound on $E[X]$ in order to apply Markov's inequality. For example, using Markov's inequality and Theorem 19.1, we can conclude that there is at most a 10% chance that the proposal algorithm for the stable marriage problem will make more than $10nH_n$ proposals, assuming the preference list of each man is an independent random permutation of the list of women.

19.5.2   Sums of Indicator Random Variables

Let $X = X_1 + X_2 + \cdots + X_n$ be the sum of n independent 0-1 indicator random variables, such that $X_i = 1$ with probability p_i. Using the language of probability theory, X is a random variable from the **binomial distribution**. Intuitively, X is equal to the number of heads one gets by flipping n coins such that the ith coin comes up heads with probability p_i. Define the **mean**, or expected value of X, as

$$\mu = E[X] = \sum_{i=1}^{n} p_i.$$

Then we have the following **Chernoff bound**.

Theorem 19.12: *For $\delta > 0$,*

$$\Pr(X > (1 + \delta)X) \le \left[\frac{e^{\delta}}{(1 + \delta)^{(1+\delta)}} \right]^{\mu}.$$

Proof: Applying Markov's inequality, after raising both sides of the probabilistic inequality to the power e^{λ}, for $\lambda > 0$, we get

$$
\begin{aligned}
\Pr(X > (1 + \delta)\mu) &= \Pr(e^{\lambda X} > e^{\lambda(1+\delta)\mu}) \\
&\le \frac{E[e^{\lambda X}]}{e^{\lambda(1+\delta)\mu}} \\
&= \frac{\prod_{i=1}^{n} E[e^{\lambda X_i}]}{e^{\lambda(1+\delta)\mu}},
\end{aligned}
$$

because the X_i's are mutually independent. Note that random variable $e^{\lambda X_i}$ takes on the value e^{λ} with probability p_i, and the value 1 with probability $1 - p_i$. Thus, $E[e^{\lambda X_i}] = e^{\lambda} + 1 - p_i$. So we have

$$
\begin{aligned}
\Pr(X > (1 + \delta)\mu) &\le \frac{\prod_{i=1}^{n}(e^{\lambda} + 1 - p_i)}{e^{\lambda(1+\delta)\mu}} \\
&= \frac{\prod_{i=1}^{n}(1 + p_i(e^{\lambda} - 1))}{e^{\lambda(1+\delta)\mu}}.
\end{aligned}
$$

We can use the inequality $1 + x < e^x$ for $x = p_i(e^{\lambda} - 1)$, to show

$$
\begin{aligned}
\Pr(X > (1 + \delta)\mu) &\le \frac{\prod_{i=1}^{n} e^{p_i(e^{\lambda}-1)}}{e^{\lambda(1+\delta)\mu}} \\
&= \frac{e^{\left(\sum_{i=1}^{n} p_i(e^{\lambda}-1)\right)}}{e^{\lambda(1+\delta)\mu}} \\
&= \frac{e^{(e^{\lambda}-1)\mu}}{e^{\lambda(1+\delta)\mu}}.
\end{aligned}
$$

Taking $\lambda = \ln(1 + \delta)$, which is positive for $\delta > 0$, completes the theorem.   ∎

We have the following Chernoff bound as well.

Theorem 19.13: *For $0 < \delta < 1$,*

$$\Pr(X < (1 - \delta)X) \leq \left[\frac{e^{-\delta}}{(1 - \delta)^{(1-\delta)}} \right]^{\mu}.$$

Proof: The proof is similar to that of Theorem 19.12, except that we rewrite the probability as $\Pr(e^{-\lambda X} > e^{-\lambda(1-\delta)\mu})$ and let $\lambda = \ln(1/(1 - \delta))$.   ∎

Application: Processor Load Balancing

Suppose we have a set of n processors and a set of n jobs for them to perform, but no good way of assigning jobs to processors. So we just assign jobs to processors at random. What is a good high-probability upper bound on the number of jobs assigned to any processor?

We can answer this question using a Chernoff bound. Let X be a random variable representing the number of jobs assigned to processor 1. Then X can be written as

$$X = X_1 + X_2 + \cdots X_n,$$

where X_i is the 0-1 indicator random variable that job i is assigned to processor 1. Thus, $\Pr(X_i = 1) = 1/n$ and $\mu = E[X] = 1$. Since the X_i's are clearly independent, we can apply the Chernoff bound from Theorem 19.12 to get, for any integer $m > 1$,

$$\Pr(X > m) \leq \frac{e^{m-1}}{m^m}.$$

After a bit of algebra, one can show, for

$$m \geq \frac{3 \ln n}{\ln \ln n},$$

and $n \geq 2^8$, that

$$\frac{e^{m-1}}{m^m} \leq \frac{1}{n^2}.$$

Thus, the probability that processor 1 has more than m jobs assigned to it by this random assignment is at most $1/n^2$. Therefore, the probability that any processor is assigned more than m jobs is at most $n/n^2 = 1/n$. In other words, the number of processors assigned to any processor is $O(\log n / \log \log n)$ with high probability.

19.5.3   Sums of Geometric Random Variables

Let Y be a random variable that is the sum of n independent geometric random variables with parameter p. That is,

$$Y = Y_1 + Y_2 + \cdots + Y_n,$$

where each Y_i is a number of times to flip a coin, which comes up heads with probability p, until getting an outcome of heads. Using the language of probability theory, Y is a random variable from the **negative binomial distribution**. In this case,

$$E[Y_i] = 1/p, \quad \text{for each } i = 1, 2, \ldots, n;$$

hence, $E[Y] = \alpha n$, where $\alpha = 1/p$.

The Chernoff bound for Y that we derive in this section concerns the characterization of the probability that Y exceeds its mean, which is $\alpha n = n/p$. In particular, we are interested in the probability,

$$\Pr(Y > (\alpha + t)n),$$

where $t > 0$. That is, using the coin flipping metaphor, we are interested in the probability that we have to flip a coin more than $(\alpha + t)n$ times to get n heads.

Relating the Binomial and Negative Binomial Distributions

In order to bound this probability, let us consider another random variable, X, which is the sum of $(\alpha + t)n$ independent indicator random variables, each of which is 1 with probability p. That is, X is the number of heads we get from flipping $(\alpha + t)n$ coins, each of which comes up heads with probability p. This random variable, which comes from the binomial distribution, can help us bound the above probability for Y, which comes from the negative binomial distribution, because

$$\Pr(Y > (\alpha + t)n) \;\; = \;\; \Pr(X < n).$$

In other words, the probability that it takes more than $(\alpha + t)n$ coin tosses to get n heads is equal to the probability that we get fewer than n heads in exactly $(\alpha + t)n$ coin tosses.

Note that X is the same kind of random variable we discussed in the previous subsection. Thus, we can use Theorem 19.13 to analyze it. In this case, note that if we let $\mu = E[X]$, then

$$
\begin{aligned}
\mu &= p(\alpha + t)n \\
&= p((1/p) + t)n \\
&= (1 + tp)n.
\end{aligned}
$$

We use the above fact in the following application of Theorem 19.13.

Lemma 19.14: *For $t > 0$,*

$$\Pr(Y > (\alpha + t)n) \leq e^{-tpn}(1 + tp)^n.$$

Proof: We already observed that $\Pr(Y > (\alpha + t)n) = \Pr(X < n)$, so, in order to apply Theorem 19.13, we need to bound the probability that X is less than $(1 - \delta)\mu$, where this quantity is equal to n. That is, we have

$$(1 - \delta)\mu = (1 - \delta)(1 + tp)n = n.$$

Hence,

$$1 - \delta = \frac{1}{1 + tp} \quad \text{and} \quad -\delta = \frac{-tp}{1 + tp}.$$

Thus, by Theorem 19.13,

$$\Pr(X < (1 - \delta)\mu) < \left[\frac{e^{-tp/(1+tp)}}{[1/(1 + tp)]^{1/(1+tp)}} \right]^{(1+tp)n}$$

$$= e^{-tpn}(1 + tp)^n.$$

∎

This lemma allows us to then derive the following Chernoff bound, in the spirit of Theorem 19.12.

Theorem 19.15: *Let $Y = Y_1 + Y_2 + \cdots + Y_n$ be the sum of n independent geometric random variables with parameter p. Then, for $\alpha = 1/p$ and $t \geq \alpha$,*

$$\Pr(Y > (\alpha + t)n) \leq e^{-tpn/5}.$$

Proof: By Lemma 19.14,

$$\Pr(Y > (\alpha + t)n) \leq e^{-tpn}(1 + tp)^n.$$

Unfortunately, if we use the inequality, $1 + x \leq e^x$, with $x = tp$, to bound the righthand term in the above equation, then we get a useless result. So, instead, we use a better approximation, namely, that, if $x \geq 1$, then $1 + x < e^{x/(1+1/4)}$. Thus, for $t \geq \alpha$,

$$\Pr(Y > (\alpha + t)n) \leq e^{-tpn} \cdot e^{4tpn/5}$$

$$= e^{-tpn/5}.$$

∎

A More Realistic Analysis of Fisher-Yates Random Shuffling

In the analysis given earlier for the Fisher-Yates shuffling algorithm to generate a random permutation, we assumed that the random(k) method, which returns a random integer in the range $[0, k-1]$, always runs in $O(1)$ time. If we are using a random-number generator based on the use of unbiased random bits, however, this is not a realistic assumption.

In a system based on using random bits, we would most naturally implement the random(k) method by generating $\lceil \log k \rceil$ random bits, interpreting these bits as an unsigned integer, and then repeating this operation until we got an integer in the range $[0, k-1]$. Thus, counting each iteration in such an algorithm as a "step," we could conservatively say that the random(k) method runs in 1 step with probability $1/2$, 2 steps with probability $1/2^2$, and, in general, in i steps with probability $1/2^i$. That is, its running time is a geometric random variable with parameter

$$p = \frac{1}{2}.$$

Under this more realistic assumption, the running time of the Fisher-Yates random permutation algorithm is proportional to the sum,

$$Y = Y_1 + Y_2 + \cdots Y_{n-1},$$

where each Y_i is the number of steps performed in the ith call to the random method. In other words, Y is the sum of $n-1$ independent geometric random variables with parameter $p = 1/2$, since the running times of the calls to the random(k) method are independent. Thus, focusing on the steps used in calls to this method, the expected running time of the Fisher-Yates algorithm is

$$E[Y] = 2(n-1).$$

Given this information, we can use the Chernoff bound for a sum of independent geometric random variables given in Theorem 19.15, with $\alpha = 2$, to bound the probability that the Fisher-Yates algorithm takes more than $4n$ steps as follows:

$$\Pr(Y > 4n) \le e^{-n/5}.$$

Therefore, under this more realistic analysis, the Fisher-Yates algorithm runs in $O(n)$ time with high probability.

19.6 Skip Lists

An interesting data structure for efficiently realizing the ordered set of items is the *skip list*. This data structure makes random choices in arranging the items in such a way that search and update times are logarithmic *on average*. A *skip list* S for an ordered dictionary, D, of key-value pairs consists of a series of lists $\{S_0, S_1, \ldots, S_h\}$. Each list S_i stores a subset of the items of D sorted by a nondecreasing key plus items with two special keys, denoted $-\infty$ and $+\infty$, where $-\infty$ is smaller than every possible key that can be inserted in D and $+\infty$ is larger than every possible key that can be inserted in D. In addition, the lists in S satisfy the following (see Figure 19.13):

- S_0 contains every item in D (plus special items with keys $-\infty$ and $+\infty$).
- For $i = 1, \ldots, h-1$, list S_i contains (in addition to $-\infty$ and $+\infty$) a randomly generated subset of the items in list S_{i-1}.
- S_h contains only $-\infty$ and $+\infty$.

It is customary to visualize a skip list S with list S_0 at the bottom and lists $S_1, \ldots, S_h$ above it. Also, we refer to h as the *height* of skip list S.

Intuitively, the lists are set up so that S_{i+1} contains essentially every other item in S_i. The items in S_{i+1} are chosen at random from the items in S_i by picking each item from S_i to also be in S_{i+1} with probability $1/2$. That is, in essence, we "flip a coin" for each item in S_i and place that item in S_{i+1} if the coin comes up "heads." Thus, we expect S_1 to have about $n/2$ items, S_2 to have about $n/4$ items, and, in general, S_i to have about $n/2^i$ items. In other words, we expect the height h of S to be about $\log n$. We view a skip list as a two-dimensional collection of nodes arranged horizontally into *levels* and vertically into *towers*. Each level is a list S_i and each tower contains nodes storing the same item across consecutive lists.

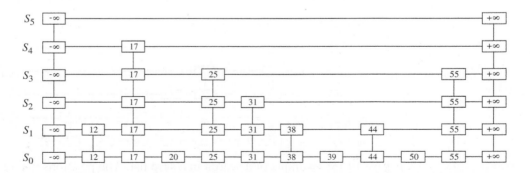

Figure 19.13: Example of a skip list.

19.6.1   Searching

The nodes in a skip list can be traversed using the following operations:

after(p): Return the node following p on the same level.
before(p): Return the node preceding p on the same level.
below(p): Return the node below p in the same tower.
above(p): Return the node above p in the same tower.

We assume that the above operations return **null** if the node requested does not exist. Searching in a skip list is based on the method shown in Algorithm 19.14.

Algorithm SkipSearch(k):

> **Input:** A search key k
> **Output:** Node in S whose item has the largest key less than or equal to k
>
> Let p be the topmost, left node of S (which should have at least 2 levels).
> **while** below(p) $\neq$ **null do**
> $p \leftarrow$ below(p)   // drop down
>   **while** key(after(p)) $\leq k$ **do**
>   Let $p \leftarrow$ after(p)   // scan forward
> **return** p.

Algorithm 19.14: Algorithm for searching in a skip list S.

Note that we begin the SkipSearch method by setting p to the topmost, left node in the skip list S, and repeating the following steps (see Figure 19.15):

1. If S.below(p) is null, then the search terminates—we are **at the bottom** and have located the largest item in S with key less than or equal to the search key k. Otherwise, we **drop down** to the next lower level in the present tower.

2. Starting at node p, we move p forward until it is at the right-most node on the present level such that key(p) $\leq k$. We call this the **scan forward** step. Note that such a node always exists, since each level contains the special keys $+\infty$ and $-\infty$. In fact, after we perform the scan forward for this level, p may remain where it started. In any case, we then repeat the previous step.

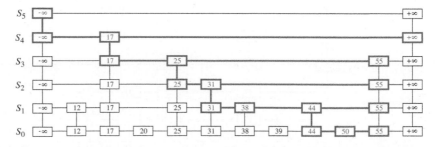

Figure 19.15: Example of a search in a skip list. The positions visited and the links traversed when searching (unsuccessfully) for key 52 are drawn with thick lines.

19.6.2 Update Operations

Given the SkipSearch method, it is easy to implement find(k)—we simply perform $p \leftarrow$ SkipSearch(k) and test whether key(p) $= k$. As it turns out, the expected running time of the SkipSearch algorithm is $O(\log n)$. We postpone this analysis, however, until after we discuss the update methods for skip lists.

Insertion

The insertion algorithm for skip lists uses randomization to decide how many nodes for the new item (k, e) should be added to the skip list. We begin the insertion of a new item (k, e) into a skip list by performing a SkipSearch(k) operation. This gives us the position p of the bottom-level item with the largest key less than or equal to k (note that p may be the node of the special item with key $-\infty$). We then insert (k, e) in this bottom-level list immediately after p. After inserting the new item at this level, we call a method random() that returns a random bit that is 1 (which stands for "heads") or 0 (which stands for "tails"), each with probability $1/2$. If the bit comes up tails, then we stop here. If the bit comes up heads, on the other hand, then we backtrack to the previous (next higher) level and insert (k, e) in this level at the appropriate position. We again generate a random bit, and if it comes up heads, we go to the next higher level and repeat. Thus, we continue to insert the new item (k, e) in lists until we finally get a flip that comes up tails. We link together all the nodes for the new item, (k, e), created in this process to create the ***tower*** for (k, e). We give the pseudocode for this insertion algorithm for a skip list S in Algorithm 19.16 and we illustrate this algorithm in Figure 19.17. Our insertion algorithm uses an operation insertAfterAbove($p, q, (k, e)$) that inserts a node storing the item (k, e) after p (on the same level as p) and above the node q, returning the node r for the new item (and setting internal references so that after, before, above, and below methods will work correctly for p, q, and r).

Algorithm SkipInsert(k, e):
    Input: Item (k, e)
    Output: None

    $p \leftarrow$ SkipSearch(k)
    $q \leftarrow$ insertAfterAbove($p,$ **null**$, (k, e)$)   // we are at the bottom level
    while random() $= 1$ **do**
        while above(p) $=$ **null do**
            $p \leftarrow$ before(p)   // scan backward
        $p \leftarrow$ above(p)   // jump up to higher level
        $q \leftarrow$ insertAfterAbove($p, q, (k, e)$)   // insert new item

Algorithm 19.16: Insertion in a skip list, assuming random() returns a random number between 0 and 1, and we never insert past the top level.

Let us begin with the expected value of the height h of S (assuming that we do not terminate insertions early). The probability that a given item is stored in a position at level i is equal to the probability of getting i consecutive heads when flipping a coin, that is, this probability is $1/2^i$. Hence, the probability, P_i, that level i has at least one item is at most $P_i \leq n/2^i$, for the probability that any one of n different events occurs is, at most, the sum of the probabilities that each occurs.

The probability that the height h of S is larger than i is equal to the probability that level i has at least one item, that is, it is no more than P_i. This means that h is larger than, say, $3 \log n$ with probability at most

$$P_{3 \log n} \leq \frac{n}{2^{3 \log n}} = \frac{n}{n^3} = \frac{1}{n^2}.$$

More generally, given a constant $c > 1$, h is larger than $c \log n$ with probability at most $1/n^{c-1}$. That is, the probability that h is smaller than or equal to $c \log n$ is at least $1 - 1/n^{c-1}$. Thus, with high probability, the height h of S is $O(\log n)$.

Consider the running time of a search in skip list S, and recall that such a search involves two nested while-loops. The inner loop performs a scan forward on a level of S as long as the next key is no greater than the search key k, and the outer loop drops down to the next level and repeats the scan forward iteration. Since the height h of S is $O(\log n)$ with high probability, the number of drop-down steps is $O(\log n)$ with high probability.

So we have yet to bound the number of scan-forward steps we make. Let n_i be the number of keys examined while scanning forward at level i. Observe that, after the key at the starting position, each additional key examined in a scan-forward at level i cannot also belong to level $i + 1$. If any of these items were on the previous level, we would have encountered them in the previous scan-forward step. Thus, the probability that any key is counted in n_i is $1/2$. Therefore, the expected value of n_i is exactly equal to the expected number of times we must flip a fair coin before it comes up heads. That is, each n_i is a geometric random variable with parameter $1/2$. Thus, $E[n_i] = 2$; hence, the expected amount of time spent scanning forward at any level i is $O(1)$. Since S has $O(\log n)$ levels with high probability, a search in S takes expected time $O(\log n)$. By a similar analysis, we can show that the expected running time of an insertion or a removal is $O(\log n)$. Moreover, by applying the Chernoff bound for a sum of independent geometric random variables, given in Theorem 19.15, we can show that searches and updates in a skip list run in $O(\log n)$ time with high probability.

Finally, let us turn to the space requirement of a skip list S. As we observed above, the expected number of items at level i is $n/2^i$, which means that the expected total number of items in S is

$$\sum_{i=0}^{h} \frac{n}{2^i} = n \sum_{i=0}^{h} \frac{1}{2^i} < 2n.$$

Hence, the expected space requirement of S is $O(n)$.

19.7 Exercises

Reinforcement

R-19.1 Give a variation of Algorithm 19.2 (randomSort) that runs in $O(n)$ time with probability $1 - 1/n^4$.

R-19.2 Suppose two teams, the Anteaters and the Bears, have a long rivalry in basketball. Suppose further that in any given game, the Anteaters will beat the Bears with probability $2/3$, independent of any other games that they play. Give a bound on the probability that, in spite of this, the Bears will win a majority of n games that they play.

R-19.3 Suppose a certain birth defect occurs independently at random with probability $p = 0.02$ in any live birth. Use a Chernoff bound to bound the probability that more than 4% of the 1 million children born in a given large city have this birth defect.

R-19.4 Suppose a builder, named Bob, wants to hammer in 20 nails into a piece of wood. Bob is very strong and can hammer down a nail in a single blow if he hits the nail square on its head. But Bob is also a little near-sighted and, in any given swing of his hammer, he only hits any given nail square on its head with probability $p = 1/3$ and misses it completely with probability $1 - p$. Derive a bound on the probability that it takes Bob more than 120 swings to hammer down all 20 nails.

R-19.5 Suppose A is an array of n bits, half of which are 0's and half of which are 1's. But the bits in A can be in any order, so that the worst-case performance of any deterministic algorithm for finding a 1 in A is $\Theta(n)$. Give a Las Vegas algorithm that finds a 1 in A in $O(\log n)$ time with high probability.

R-19.6 Give a Monte Carlo algorithm for the previous problem that examines at most $\lceil \log n \rceil$ entries in A and succeeds in finding a 1 in A with high probability.

R-19.7 Suppose that a well-known collector, Kivas Fajo, is trying to collect each of 50 coupons, as in the coupon collector problem. Derive good upper and lower bounds on the expected number of times that Kivas has to visit the ticket window to get all 50 coupons.

R-19.8 Consider the cycle graph, C_n, consisting of vertices $v_0, v_1, \ldots, v_{n-1}$ and edges $(v_i, v_{i+1 \bmod n})$, for $i = 0, \ldots, n - 1$. Clearly, the size of a minimum cut of C_n is 2. Determine the number of minimum cuts of C_n.

R-19.9 Derive the running time of Algorithm 19.10 (RecursiveContractGraph) using a recurrence relation.

R-19.10 Show that a graph with n vertices has at most $\binom{n}{2}$ minimum cuts.

R-19.11 Given a parameter, k, suppose we wish to find a number, p, that is prime with probability 2^{-k}. What is the asymptotic number of arithmetic operations needed?

R-19.12 Suppose we have a six-sided die, which we roll n times, and let X denote the number of times we role a 1.

(a) What is $E[X]$?

(b) Show that $X < n/3$ with high probability.

R-19.13 Draw an example skip list resulting from performing the following sequence of operations on the skip list in Figure 19.18: remove(38), insert(8,x), insert(24,y), remove(55). Assume the coin flips for the first insertion yield two heads followed by tails, and those for the second insertion yield three heads followed by tails.

R-19.14 Give a pseudocode description of the remove dictionary operation, assuming the dictionary is implemented by a skip-list structure.

Creativity

C-19.1 Suppose that Bob wants a constant-time method for implementing the random(k) method, which returns a random integer in the range $[0, k-1]$. Bob has a source of unbiased bits, so to implement random(k), he samples $\lceil \log k \rceil$ of these bits, interprets them as an unsigned integer, K, and returns the value $K \bmod k$. Show that Bob's algorithm does not return every integer in the range $[0, k-1]$ with equal probability.

C-19.2 Design a variation of Algorithm 19.2 (randomSort) that inserts the pairs (r_i, x_i) into a balanced tree and calls itself recursively when r_i is found to be equal to one of the previously generated random values. Give pseudocode for this variation of the algorithm and analyze its running time. Also, discuss its advantages and disadvantages with respect to the original algorithm.

C-19.3 Design a variation of Algorithm 19.2 (randomSort) that begins by generating distinct random values, r_i ($i = 1, \cdots, n$) and then sorts the pairs (r_i, x_i) . Give pseudocode for this variation of the algorithm and analyze its running time. Also, discuss its advantages and disadvantages with respect to the original algorithm.

C-19.4 Consider a modification of the Fisher-Yates random shuffling algorithm where we replace the call to random($k + 1$) with random(n), and take the for-loop down to 0, so that the algorithm now swaps each element with another element in the array, with each cell in the array having an equal likelihood of being the swap location. Show that this algorithm does not generate every permutation with equal probability.

Hint: Consider the case when $n = 3$.

C-19.5 Suppose you have a collection, S, of n distinct items and you wish to select a random sample of these items of size exactly $\lceil n^{1/2} \rceil$. Describe an efficient method for selecting such a sample so that each element in S has an equal probability of being included in the sample.

C-19.6 Suppose you have a collection, S, of n distinct items and you create a random sample, R, of S, as follows: For each x in S, select it to belong to R independently with probability $1/n^{1/2}$. Derive bounds on the probability that the number of items in R is more than $2n^{1/2}$ or less than $n^{1/2}/2$.

C-19.7 Suppose that there is a collection of $3n$ distinct coupons, n of which are colored red and $2n$ of which are colored blue. Suppose that each time you go to a ticket window to get a coupon, the clerk first randomly decides, with probability $1/2$, whether he will give you a red coupon or blue coupon and then he chooses a coupon uniformly at random from among the coupons that are that color. What is the expected number of times that you must visit the ticket window to get all $3n$ coupons?

C-19.8 Show that if we do all arithmetic modulo a prime number, p, then, for any integer $x > 0$,

$$\{ix \bmod p: \ i = 0, 1, \ldots, p-1\} = \{i: \ i = 0, 1, \ldots, p-1\}.$$

Hint: Use the fact that if p is prime, then every nonzero integer less than p has a multiplicative inverse when we do arithmetic modulo p.

C-19.9 Give an algorithm that computes a minimum cut of a graph with n vertices by $O(n)$ applications of a maximum flow algorithm to a flow network derived from G.

C-19.10 Let $P(x)$ be a probability function that satisfies the recurrence $P(i+1) \geq P(i) - \frac{1}{4}P(i)^2$, with $P(0)$ a constant. Show that $P(2\log n)$ is $\Omega\left(\frac{1}{\log n}\right)$.

C-19.11 Give a randomized algorithm that computes all minimum cuts of a graph with high probability.

C-19.12 Show that if the compositeness witness function, witness(x, n), of the Rabin-Miller algorithm returns **true**, then the number n is composite.

C-19.13 Suppose we have a Monte Carlo algorithm, A, and a deterministic algorithm, B, for testing if the output of A is correct. How can we use A and B to construct a Las Vegas algorithm? Also, if A succeeds with probability $1/2$, and both A and B run in $O(n)$ time, what is the expected running time of the Las Vegas algorithm that is produced?

C-19.14 Suppose $X_1, X_2, \ldots, X_n$ is a set of mutually independent indicator random variables, such that each X_i is 1 with some probability $p_i > 0$ and 0 otherwise. Let $X = \sum_{i=1}^{n} X_i$ be the sum of these random variables, and let μ' denote an upper bound on the mean of X, that is, $E[X] = \mu \leq \mu'$. Show that, for $\delta > 0$,

$$\Pr(X > (1+\delta)\mu') < \left[\frac{e^\delta}{(1+\delta)^{(1+\delta)}}\right]^{\mu'}.$$

C-19.15 Let $Y = Y_1 + Y_2 + \cdots + Y_n$ be the sum of n independent geometric random variables with parameter p. Show that, for $\alpha = 1/p$,

$$\Pr(Y < 0.25\,\alpha\,n) \leq 0.75^n.$$

C-19.16 Describe how to perform an operation, RangeSearch(k_1, k_2), which returns all the items with keys in the range $[k_1, k_2]$, in an ordered dictionary implemented with a skip list, and show that it runs in expected time $O(\log n + s)$, where n is the number of elements in the skip list and s is the number of items returned.

C-19.17 Show that the methods above(p) and before(p) are not actually needed to efficiently implement a dictionary using a skip list. That is, we can implement item insertion and removal in a skip list using a strictly top-down, scan-forward approach, without ever using the above or before methods.

C-19.18 Show that the randomized quick-sort algorithm runs in $O(n \log n)$ time with high probability.

Applications

A-19.1 A renowned food critic, Anton Ego, will enjoy a meal only if it is the highest-quality meal he has ever eaten up to that point in his life. Assuming that the qualities of the n meals he eats in his life are distinct and come in a random order over the course of his life, what is the expected number of times that Anton Ego will enjoy a meal in his life?

A-19.2 In the Mega Millions lottery game, a player picks five *lucky* numbers, in the range from 1 to 56, and one additional *Mega* number, in the range from 1 to 46. In order to win the jackpot, a player must match all six numbers. If there is no jackpot winner for a given drawing, then the jackpot is rolled into the next drawing. Suppose that every time a lottery ticket is sold it is chosen as an independent random pick of five lucky numbers and a Mega number. What is the expected number of Mega Millions lottery tickets that must be sold for a given drawing to guarantee with 100% certainty that there is a winner?

A-19.3 In a famous experiment, Stanley Milgram told a group of people in Kansas and Nebraska to each send a postcard to a lawyer in Boston, but they had to do it by forwarding it to someone that they knew, who had to forward it to someone that they knew, and so on. Most of the postcards that were successfully forwarded made it in 6 hops, which gave rise to the saying that everyone in America is separated by "six degrees of separation." The idea behind this experiment is also behind a technique, called *probabilistic packet marking*, for doing traceback during a distributed denial-of-service attack, where a website is bombarded by connection requests. In implementing the probabilistic packet marking strategy, a router, R, will, with some probability, $p \leq 1/2$, replace some seldom-used parts of a packet it is processing with the IP address for R, to enable tracing back the attack to the sender. It is as if, in the Milgram experiment, there is just one sender, who is mailing multiple postcards, and each person forwarding a postcard would, with probability, p, erase the return address and replace it with his own. Suppose that an attacker is sending a large number of packets in a denial-of-service attack to some recipient, and every one of the d routers in the path from the sender to the recipient is performing probabilistic packet marking.

(a) What is the probability that the router farthest from the recipient will mark a packet and this mark will survive all the way to the recipient?

(b) Derive a good upper bound on the expected number of packets that the recipient needs to collect to identify all the routers along the path from the sender to the recipient.

A-19.4 The Massachusetts state lottery game, Cash WinFall, used to have a way that anyone with enough money and time could stand a good chance of getting rich, and it is reported that an MIT computer scientist did just that. In this game, a player picks 6 numbers from the range from 1 to 46. If he matches all 6, then he could win as much as $2 million, but the odds of that payout don't justify a bet, so let us ignore the possibility of winning this jackpot. Nevertheless, there were times when matching just 5 of the 6 numbers in a $2 lottery ticket would pay $100,000. Suppose in this scenario that you were able to bet $600,000.

(a) What is the expected amount that you would win?

(b) Derive a bound on the probability that you would lose $300,000 or more in this scenario, that is, that you would have 3 or fewer of the 5 of the 6 winning tickets.

A-19.5 There is a probabilistic data structure often used for representing sets in networking and computer security applications, which is known as the **Bloom filter**. This data structure represents a set, S, using of an array, A, of m bits and a collection of k hash functions, $h_1, \ldots, h_k$. Initially, all the bits in A are 0. To add an element, x, to the set, S, we assign each of the bits, $A[h_1(x)], A[h_2(x)], \ldots, A[h_k(x)]$, to 1. To test if an element belongs to S, we check if all these bits are equal to 1. If so, then we say that x is a member of S and, if not, then we say that x is not a member of S. Note that this algorithm has a one-sided error, since it is always correct when it says that x is not in S, but there is a chance that has a **false positive**, saying that x belongs to S when really it doesn't. Assuming that each hash function maps any element, x, to k distinct random locations in A, and we have inserted $n < kn/2$ elements into S, derive a bound on the probability that a Bloom filter returns a false positive response.

A-19.6 There is a classic surprising fact from probability, known as the **birthday paradox**, which states that in a room of at least 23 people there is better than a 50-50 chance that two of them have the same birthday. This fact is surprising to some, because there are 366 possible birthdays, which is much larger than 23. While this is surprising, there is an interesting security application of the analysis that goes into the birthday paradox. Suppose a company is installing a keypad on its entry door and will be assigning each employee with an independently chosen 8-digit PIN to use when they enter the building. So there are 100 million possible PINs, but let us use n to denote this number of possible PINs and m to denote the number of employees.

(a) Imagine that we assign PINs to employees sequentially, one employee at a time. What is the probability, p_i, that the ith employee has a distinct PIN given that the $i - 1$ PINs given before are distinct?

(b) Note that the probability the PINs are all distinct is the product of the p_i's, for $i = 1, 2, \ldots, m$. Use the fact that $1 - x \leq e^{-x}$, for $0 < x < 1$, to show that this product is bounded by $e^{-m^2/2n}$.

(c) Given the above bound, how many PINs does the system need to produce so that the probability that two employees have the same PIN is at least $1/2$?

Chapter Notes

The Rabin-Miller primality testing algorithm is presented in [177]. Random shuffling is discussed by Fisher and Yates [71], Durstenfeld [59], and Knuth [131]. Arkin *et al.* [13] describe how they were able to exploit a poorly designed random shuffling algorithm to defeat online poker systems. The stable marriage problem was first studied by Gale and Shapley [78], and they present a proposal-based algorithm for solving it. Our analysis of the stable marriage problem is based on unpublished course notes by John Canny. The randomized processor load balancing application we mention for Chernoff bounds is from in a paper by Raab and Steger [176]. The randomized minimum cut algorithm based on contractions was introduced by Karger [118] and improved by Karger and Stein [120]. Skip lists were introduced by Pugh [175]. Our analysis of skip lists is a simplification of a presentation given in the book by Motwani and Raghavan [162]. In addition, there are also other more in-depth analyses of skip lists [126, 168, 172], as well as a binary-tree analogue due to Seidel and Aragon [191].

Chapter

20 B-Trees and External Memory

Columbia Supercomputer at NASA's Advanced Supercomputing Facility at Ames Research Center, 2006. U.S. government image. Credit: Trower, NASA.

Contents

20.1 External Memory 571
20.2 (2,4) Trees and B-Trees 574
20.3 External-Memory Sorting 590
20.4 Online Caching Algorithms 593
20.5 Exercises 600

There are several computer applications that must deal with a large amount of data. Examples include the analysis of scientific data sets, the processing of financial transactions, and the organization and maintenance of databases (such as telephone directories). In fact, the amount of data that must be dealt with is often too large to fit entirely in the internal memory of a computer.

In order to accommodate large data sets, computers have a *hierarchy* of different kinds of memories, which vary in terms of their size and distance from the CPU. Closest to the CPU are the internal registers that the CPU itself uses. Access to such locations is very fast, but there are relatively few such locations. At the second level in the hierarchy is the *cache* memory. This memory is considerably larger than the register set of a CPU, but accessing it takes longer (and there may even be multiple caches with progressively slower access times). At the third level in the hierarchy is the *internal memory*, which is also known as *main memory*, *core memory*, or *random access memory*. The internal memory is considerably larger than the cache memory, but also requires more time to access. Finally, at the highest level in the hierarchy is the *external memory*, which usually consists of disks, CDs, DVDs, or tapes. This memory is very large, but it is also very slow. Thus, the memory hierarchy for computers can be viewed as consisting of four levels, each of which is larger and slower than the previous level. (See Figure 20.1.)

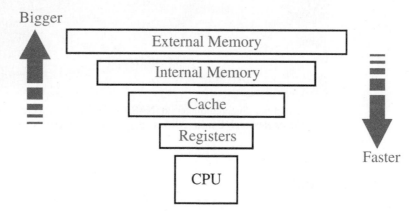

Figure 20.1: The memory hierarchy.

In most applications, however, only two levels really matter—the one that can hold all the data items in our problem and the level just below that one. Bringing data items in and out of the higher memory that can hold all items will typically be the computational bottleneck in this case. In this chapter, we focus on algorithms that accommodate this phenomenon or facilitate it, including B-trees, external-memory sorting, and online caching algorithms.

20.1 External Memory

Which two levels matter most to solving a particular problem depends on the size of that problem. For a problem that can fit entirely in main memory, the important two levels are the cache memory and the internal memory. Access times for internal memory can be as much as 10 to 100 times longer than those for cache memory. It is desirable, therefore, to be able to perform most memory accesses in cache memory. For a problem that does not fit entirely in main memory, on the other hand, the important two levels are the internal memory and the external memory. Here the differences are even more dramatic, for access times for disks, the usual general-purpose external-memory device, are typically as much as 100,000 to 1,000,000 times longer than those for internal memory.

To put this latter figure into perspective, imagine there is a student in Baltimore who wants to send a request-for-money message to his parents in Chicago. If the student sends his parents an email message, it can arrive at their home computer in about five seconds. Think of this mode of communication as corresponding to an internal-memory access by a CPU. A mode of communication, corresponding to an external-memory access that is 500,000 times slower, would be for the student to walk to Chicago and deliver his message in person, which would take about a month if he can average 20 miles per day. Thus, we should make as few accesses to external memory as possible.

Hierarchical Memory Management

Most algorithms are not designed with the memory hierarchy in mind, in spite of the great variance between access times for the different levels. Indeed, all of the algorithm analysis described in this book so far have assumed that all memory accesses are equal. This assumption might seem, at first, to be a great oversight—and one we are only addressing now in this chapter—but there are two fundamental justifications for why it is actually a reasonable assumption to make.

The first justification is that it is often necessary to assume that all memory accesses take the same amount of time, since specific device-dependent information about memory sizes is often hard to come by. In fact, information about memory size may be impossible to get. For example, a Java program that is designed to run on many different computer platforms cannot be defined in terms of a specific computer architecture configuration. We can certainly use architecture-specific information, if we have it (and we will show how to exploit such information later in this chapter). But once we have optimized our software for a certain architecture configuration, our software will no longer be device-independent. Fortunately, such optimizations are not always necessary, primarily because of the second justification for the equal-time, memory-access assumption.

The second justification for the memory-access equality assumption is that operating system designers have developed general mechanisms that allow for most memory accesses to be fast. These mechanisms are based on two important *locality-of-reference* properties that most software possesses:

- **Temporal locality**: If a program accesses a certain memory location, then it is likely to access this location again in the near future. For example, it is quite common to use the value of a counter variable in several different expressions, including one to increment the counter's value. In fact, a common adage among computer architects is that "a program spends 90 percent of its time in 10 percent of its code."
- **Spatial locality**: If a program accesses a certain memory location, then it is likely to access other locations that are near this one. For example, a program using an array is likely to access the locations of this array in a sequential or near-sequential manner.

Computer scientists and engineers have performed extensive software profiling experiments to justify the claim that most software possesses both of these kinds of locality-of-reference. For example, a for-loop used to scan through an array will exhibit both kinds of locality.

Caching and Blocking

Temporal and spatial localities have, in turn, given rise to two fundamental design choices for two-level computer memory systems (which are present in the interface between cache memory and internal memory, and also in the interface between internal memory and external memory).

The first design choice is called *virtual memory*. This concept consists of providing an address space as large as the capacity of the secondary-level memory, and of transferring into the primary-level memory, data located in the secondary level, when they are addressed. Virtual memory does not limit the programmer to the constraint of the internal memory size. The concept of bringing data into primary memory is called *caching*, and it is motivated by temporal locality. For, by bringing data into primary memory, we are hoping that it will be accessed again soon, and we will be able to quickly respond to all the requests for this data that come in the near future.

The second design choice is motivated by spatial locality. Specifically, if data stored at a secondary-level memory location l is accessed, then we bring into primary-level memory a large block of contiguous locations that include the location l. (See Figure 20.2.) This concept is known as *blocking*, and it is motivated by the expectation that other secondary-level memory locations close to l will soon be accessed. In the interface between cache memory and internal memory, such blocks are often called *cache lines*, and in the interface between internal memory and external memory, such blocks are often called *pages*.

A block on disk

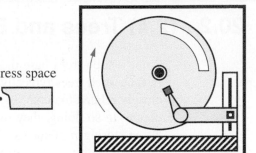

A block in the external memory address space

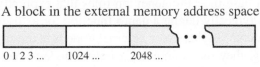

0 1 2 3 ...   1024 ...   2048 ...

Figure 20.2: Blocks in external memory.

Incidentally, blocking for disk and CD/DVD-ROM drives is also motivated by the properties of these hardware technologies. A reading arm on a disk or CD/DVD-ROM takes a relatively long time to position itself for reading a certain location, but, once the arm is positioned, it can quickly read many contiguous locations, because the medium it is reading is spinning very fast. (See Figure 20.2.) Even without this motivation, however, blocking is fully justified by the spatial locality property that most programs have.

Thus, when implemented with caching and blocking, virtual memory often allows us to perceive secondary level memory as being faster than it really is. There is still a problem, however. Primary-level memory is much smaller than secondary-level memory. Moreover, because memory systems use blocking, any program of substance will likely reach a point where it requests data from secondary-level memory, but the primary memory is already full of blocks. In order to fulfill the request and maintain our use of caching and blocking, we must remove some block from primary memory to make room for a new block from secondary memory in this case. Deciding how to do this eviction brings up a number of interesting data structure and algorithm design issues that we discuss in the remainder of this section.

A Model for External Searching

The first problem we address is that of implementing a dictionary for a large collection of items that do not fit in primary memory. Recall that a dictionary stores key-element pairs (items) subject to insertions, removals, and key-based searches. Since one of the main applications of large dictionaries is in database systems, we refer to the secondary-memory blocks as *disk blocks*. Likewise, we refer to the transfer of a block between secondary memory and primary memory as a *disk transfer*. Even though we use this terminology, the search techniques we discuss in this section apply also when the primary memory is the CPU cache and the secondary memory is the main (internal) memory. We use the disk-based viewpoint because it is concrete and also because it is more prevalent.

20.2 (2,4) Trees and B-Trees

Some search trees base their efficiency on rules that explicitly bound their depth. In fact, such trees typically define a depth function, or a "pseudo-depth" function closely related to depth, so that every external node is at the same depth or pseudo-depth. In so doing, they maintain every external node to be at depth $O(\log n)$ in a tree storing n elements. These trees are not ideally suited for external memory, however, and in such scenarios another approach is better.

20.2.1 Multi-Way Search Trees

Some bounded-depth search trees are multi-way trees, that is, trees with internal nodes that have two or more children. In this section, we describe how multi-way trees can be used as search trees, including how multi-way trees store items and how we can perform search operations in multi-way search trees. Recall that the *items* that we store in a search tree are pairs of the form (k, x), where k is the *key* and x is the element associated with the key.

Let v be a node of an ordered tree. We say that v is a *d-node* if v has d children. We define a *multi-way search tree* to be an ordered tree T that has the following properties (which are illustrated in Figure 20.3a):

- Each internal node of T has at least two children. That is, each internal node is a d-node, where $d \geq 2$.
- Each internal node of T stores a collection of items of the form (k, x), where k is a key and x is an element.
- Each d-node v of T, with children $v_1, \ldots, v_d$, stores $d - 1$ items $(k_1, x_1), \ldots, (k_{d-1}, x_{d-1})$, where $k_1 \leq \cdots \leq k_{d-1}$.
- Let us define $k_0 = -\infty$ and $k_d = +\infty$. For each item (k, x) stored at a node in the subtree of v rooted at v_i, $i = 1, \ldots, d$, we have $k_{i-1} \leq k \leq k_i$.

That is, if we think of the set of keys stored at v as including the special fictitious keys $k_0 = -\infty$ and $k_d = +\infty$, then a key k stored in the subtree of T rooted at a child node v_i must be "in between" two keys stored at v. This simple viewpoint gives rise to the rule that a node with d children stores $d - 1$ regular keys, and it also forms the basis of the algorithm for searching in a multi-way search tree.

By the above definition, the external nodes of a multi-way search do not store any items and serve only as "placeholders." Thus, we can view a binary search tree (Section 3.1.1) as a special case of a multi-way search tree. At the other extreme, a multi-way search tree may have only a single internal node storing all the items. In addition, while the external nodes could be **null**, we make the simplifying assumption here that they are actual nodes that don't store anything.

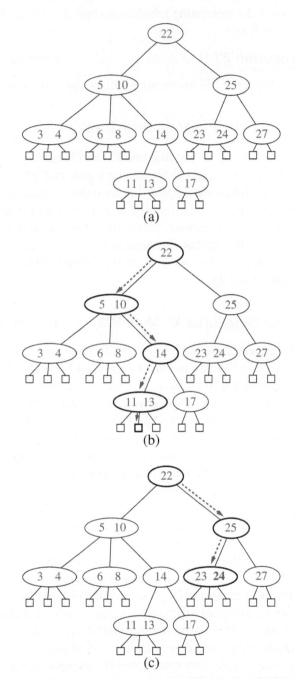

Figure 20.3: (a) A multi-way search tree T; (b) search path in T for key 12 (unsuccessful search); (c) search path in T for key 24 (successful search).

Whether internal nodes of a multi-way tree have two children or many, however, there is an interesting relationship between the number of items and the number of external nodes.

Theorem 20.1: *A multi-way search tree storing n items has $n+1$ external nodes.*

We leave the justification of this theorem as an exercise (C-4.11).

Searching in a Multi-Way Tree

Given a multi-way search tree T, searching for an element with key k is simple. We perform such a search by tracing a path in T starting at the root. (See Figure 20.3b and c.) When we are at a d-node v during this search, we compare the key k with the keys $k_1, \ldots, k_{d-1}$ stored at v. If $k = k_i$ for some i, the search is successfully completed. Otherwise, we continue the search in the child v_i of v such that $k_{i-1} < k < k_i$. (Recall that we consider $k_0 = -\infty$ and $k_d = +\infty$.) If we reach an external node, then we know that there is no item with key k in T, and the search terminates unsuccessfully.

Data Structures for Multi-Way Search Trees

In Section 2.3.4, we discussed different ways of representing general trees. Each of these representations can also be used for multi-way search trees. In fact, in using a general multi-way tree to implement a multi-way search tree, the only additional information that we need to store at each node is the set of items (including keys) associated with that node. That is, we need to store with v a reference to some container or collection object that stores the items for v.

Recall that when we use a binary tree to represent an ordered dictionary D, we simply store a reference to a single item at each internal node. In using a multi-way search tree T to represent D, we must store a reference to the ordered set of items associated with v at each internal node v of T. This reasoning may at first seem like a circular argument, since we need a representation of an ordered dictionary to represent an ordered dictionary. We can avoid any circular arguments, however, by using the ***bootstrapping*** technique, where we use a previous (less-advanced) solution to a problem to create a new (more-advanced) solution. In this case, bootstrapping consists of representing the ordered set associated with each internal node using a dictionary data structure that we have previously constructed (for example, a lookup table based on an ordered vector, as shown in Section 3.1). In particular, assuming we already have a way of implementing ordered dictionaries, we can realize a multi-way search tree by taking a tree T and storing such a dictionary at each d-node v of T.

The dictionary we store at each node v is known as a ***secondary*** or ***auxiliary*** data structure, for we are using it to support the bigger, ***primary*** data structure. We denote the dictionary stored at a node v of T as $D(v)$. The items we store in $D(v)$ will allow us to find which child node to move to next during a search operation. Specifically, for each node v of T, with children $v_1, \ldots, v_d$ and set of items, $\{(k_1, x_1), \ldots, (k_{d-1}, x_{d-1})\}$, we store in the dictionary $D(v)$ the items (k_1, x_1, v_1), (k_2, x_2, v_2), $\ldots$, $(k_{d-1}, x_{d-1}, v_{d-1})$, $(+\infty, null, v_d)$. That is, an item (k_i, x_i, v_i) of dictionary $D(v)$ has key k_i and element (x_i, v_i). Note that the last item stores the special key $+\infty$.

With the above realization of a multi-way search tree T, processing a d-node v while searching for an element of T with key k can be done by performing a search operation to find the item (k_i, x_i, v_i) in $D(v)$ with smallest key greater than or equal to k, such as in the closestElemAfter(k) operation. We distinguish two cases:

- If $k < k_i$, then we continue the search by processing child v_i. (Note that if the special key $k_d = +\infty$ is returned, then k is greater than all the keys stored at node v, and we continue the search by processing child v_d.)
- Otherwise ($k = k_i$), then the search terminates successfully.

Performance Issues for Multi-Way Search Trees

Consider the space requirement for the above realization of a multi-way search tree T storing n items. By Theorem 20.1, using any of the common realizations of ordered dictionaries (Section 6.1) for the secondary structures of the nodes of T, the overall space requirement for T is $O(n)$.

Consider next the time spent answering a search in T. The time spent at a d-node v of T during a search depends on how we realize the secondary data structure $D(v)$. If $D(v)$ is realized with a vector-based sorted sequence (that is, a lookup table), then we can process v in $O(\log d)$ time. If instead $D(v)$ is realized using an unsorted sequence (that is, a log file), then processing v takes $O(d)$ time. Let $d_{\max}$ denote the maximum number of children of any node of T, and let h denote the height of T. The search time in a multi-way search tree is either $O(h d_{\max})$ or $O(h \log d_{\max})$, depending on the specific implementation of the secondary structures at the nodes of T (the dictionaries $D(v)$). If $d_{\max}$ is a constant, the running time for performing a search is $O(h)$, irrespective of the implementation of the secondary structures.

Thus, the prime efficiency goal for a multi-way search tree is to keep the height as small as possible, that is, we want h to be a logarithmic function of n, the number of total items stored in the dictionary. A search tree with logarithmic height, such as this, is called a **balanced search tree**. Bounded-depth search trees satisfy this goal by keeping each external node at exactly the same depth level in the tree.

Next, we discuss a bounded-depth search tree that is a multi-way search tree that caps $d_{\max}$ at 4. In Section 20.2.3, we discuss a more general kind of multi-way search tree that has applications where our search tree is too large to completely fit into the internal memory of our computer.

20.2.2 (2,4) Trees

In using a multi-way search tree in practice, we desire that it be balanced, that is, have logarithmic height. The multi-way search tree we study next is fairly easy to keep balanced. It is the $(2, 4)$ tree, which is sometimes also called the 2-4 tree or 2-3-4 tree. In fact, we can maintain balance in a $(2, 4)$ tree by maintaining two simple properties (see Figure 20.4):

Size Property: Every node has at most four children.

Depth Property: All the external nodes have the same depth.

Enforcing the size property for $(2, 4)$ trees keeps the size of the nodes in the multi-way search tree constant, for it allows us to represent the dictionary $D(v)$ stored at each internal node v using a constant-sized array. The depth property, on the other hand, maintains the balance in a $(2, 4)$ tree, by forcing it to be a bounded-depth structure.

Theorem 20.2: *The height of a $(2, 4)$ tree storing n items is $\Theta(\log n)$.*

Proof: Let h be the height of a $(2, 4)$ tree T storing n items. Note that, by the size property, we can have at most 4 nodes at depth 1, at most 4^2 nodes at depth 2, and so on. Thus, the number of external nodes in T is at most 4^h. Likewise, by the depth property and the definition of a $(2, 4)$ tree, we must have at least 2 nodes at depth 1, at least 2^2 nodes at depth 2, and so on. Thus, the number of external nodes in T is at least 2^h. In addition, by Theorem 20.1, the number of external nodes in T is $n + 1$. Therefore, we obtain

$$2^h \leq n + 1 \quad \text{and} \quad n + 1 \leq 4^h.$$

Taking the logarithm in base 2 of each of the above terms, we get that

$$h \leq \log(n + 1) \quad \text{and} \quad \log(n + 1) \leq 2h,$$

which justifies our theorem.   ■

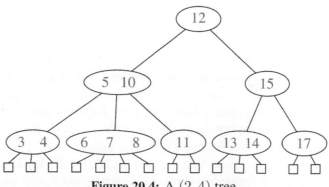

Figure 20.4: A $(2, 4)$ tree.

Insertion in a $(2,4)$ Tree

Theorem 20.2 states that the size and depth properties are sufficient for keeping a multi-way tree balanced. Maintaining these properties requires some effort after performing insertions and removals in a $(2,4)$ tree, however. In particular, to insert a new item (k, x), with key k, into a $(2,4)$ tree T, we first perform a search for k. Assuming that T has no element with key k, this search terminates unsuccessfully at an external node z. Let v be the parent of z. We insert the new item into node v and add a new child w (an external node) to v on the left of z. That is, we add item (k, x, w) to the dictionary $D(v)$.

Our insertion method preserves the depth property, since we add a new external node at the same level as existing external nodes. Nevertheless, it may violate the size property. Indeed, if a node v was previously a 4-node, then it may become a 5-node after the insertion, which causes the tree T to no longer be a $(2,4)$ tree. This type of violation of the size property is called an ***overflow*** at node v, and it must be resolved in order to restore the properties of a $(2,4)$ tree. Let $v_1, \ldots, v_5$ be the children of v, and let $k_1, \ldots, k_4$ be the keys stored at v. To remedy the overflow at node v, we perform a ***split*** operation on v as follows (see Figure 20.5):

- Replace v with two nodes v' and v'', where
  - v' is a 3-node with children v_1, v_2, v_3 storing keys k_1 and k_2
  - v'' is a 2-node with children v_4, v_5 storing key k_4.

- If v was the root of T, create a new root node u; else, let u be the parent of v.
- Insert key k_3 into u and make v' and v'' children of u, so that if v was child i of u, then v' and v'' become children i and $i+1$ of u, respectively.

We show a sequence of insertions in a $(2,4)$ tree in Figure 20.6.

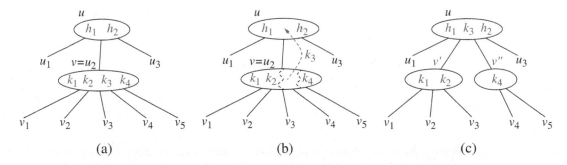

(a)   (b)   (c)

Figure 20.5: A node split: (a) overflow at a 5-node v; (b) the third key of v inserted into the parent u of v; (c) node v replaced with a 3-node v' and a 2-node v''.

A split operation affects a constant number of nodes of the tree and $O(1)$ items stored at such nodes. Thus, it can be implemented to run in $O(1)$ time.

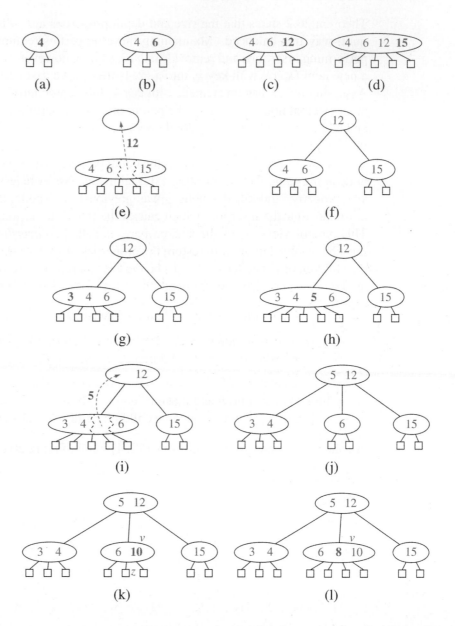

Figure 20.6: A sequence of insertions into a $(2, 4)$ tree: (a) initial tree with one item; (b) insertion of 6; (c) insertion of 12; (d) insertion of 15, which causes an overflow; (e) split, which causes the creation of a new root node; (f) after the split; (g) insertion of 3; (h) insertion of 5, which causes an overflow; (i) split; (j) after the split; (k) insertion of 10; (l) insertion of 8.

Performance of $(2, 4)$ Tree Insertion

As a consequence of a split operation on node v, a new overflow may occur at the parent u of v. If such an overflow occurs, it triggers, in turn, a split at node u. (See Figure 20.7.) A split operation either eliminates the overflow or propagates it into the parent of the current node. Indeed, this propagation can continue all the way up to the root of the search tree. But if it does propagate all the way to the root, it will finally be resolved at that point. We show such a sequence of splitting propagations in Figure 20.7.

Thus, the number of split operations is bounded by the height of the tree, which is $O(\log n)$ by Theorem 20.2. Therefore, the total time to perform an insertion in a $(2, 4)$ tree is $O(\log n)$.

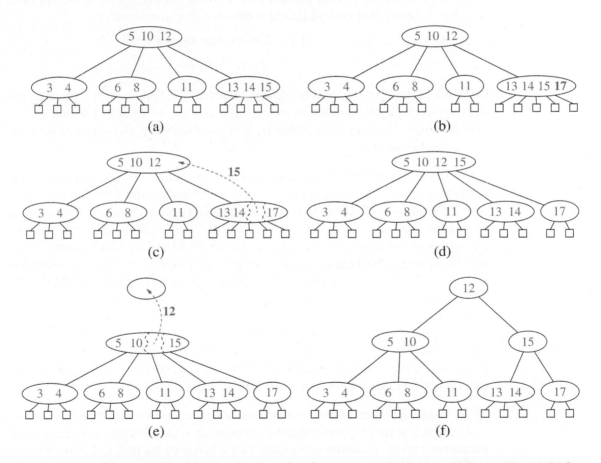

Figure 20.7: An insertion in a $(2, 4)$ tree that causes a cascading split: (a) before the insertion; (b) insertion of 17, causing an overflow; (c) a split; (d) after the split a new overflow occurs; (e) another split, creating a new root node; (f) final tree.

Removal in a $(2, 4)$ Tree

Let us now consider the removal of an item with key k from a $(2, 4)$ tree T. We begin such an operation by performing a search in T for an item with key k. Removing such an item from a $(2, 4)$ tree can always be reduced to the case where the item to be removed is stored at a node v whose children are external nodes. Suppose, for instance, that the item with key k that we wish to remove is stored in the ith item (k_i, x_i) at a node z that has only internal-node children. In this case, we swap the item (k_i, x_i) with an appropriate item that is stored at a node v with external-node children as follows (Figure 20.8d):

1. We find the right-most internal node v in the subtree rooted at the ith child of z, noting that the children of node v are all external nodes.

2. We swap the item (k_i, x_i) at z with the last item of v.

Once we ensure that the item to remove is stored at a node v with only external-node children (because either it was already at v or we swapped it into v), we simply remove the item from v (that is, from the dictionary $D(v)$) and remove the ith external node of v.

Removing an item (and a child) from a node v as described above preserves the depth property, for we always remove an external-node child from a node v with only external-node children. However, in removing such an external node we may violate the size property at v. Indeed, if v was previously a 2-node, then it becomes a 1-node with no items after the removal (Figure 20.8d and e), which is not allowed in a $(2, 4)$ tree. This type of violation of the size property is called an ***underflow*** at node v. To remedy an underflow, we check whether an immediate sibling of v is a 3-node or a 4-node. If we find such a sibling w, then we perform a ***transfer*** operation, in which we move a child of w to be a child of v, a key of w to the parent u of v and w, and a key of u to v. (See Figure 20.8b and c.) If v has only one sibling that is a 2-node, or if both immediate siblings of v are 2-nodes, then we perform a ***fusion*** operation, in which we merge v with a sibling, creating a new node v', and move a key from the parent u of v to v'. (See Figure 20.9e and f.)

A fusion operation at node v may cause a new underflow to occur at the parent u of v, which in turn triggers a transfer or fusion at u. (See Figure 20.9.) Hence, the number of fusion operations is bounded by the height of the tree, which is $O(\log n)$ by Theorem 20.2. If an underflow propagates all the way up to the root, then the root is simply deleted. (See Figure 20.9c and d.) We show a sequence of removals from a $(2, 4)$ tree in Figures 20.8 and 20.9.

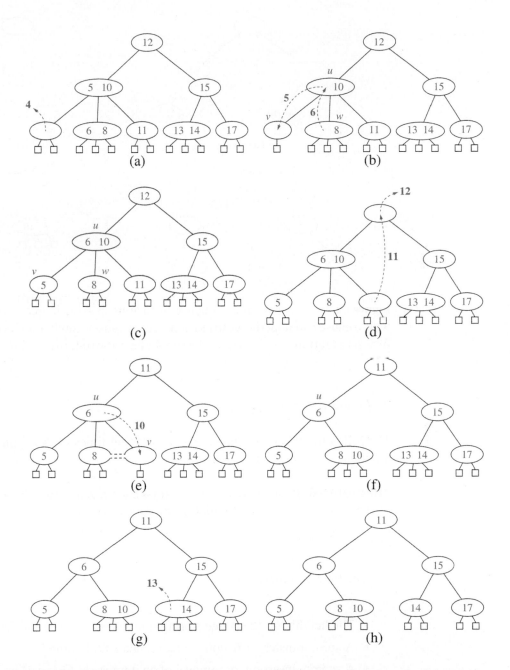

Figure 20.8: A sequence of removals from a $(2,4)$ tree: (a) removal of 4, causing an underflow; (b) a transfer operation; (c) after the transfer operation; (d) removal of 12, causing an underflow; (e) a fusion operation; (f) after the fusion operation; (g) removal of 13; (h) after removing 13.

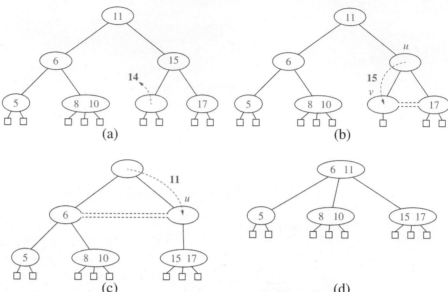

Figure 20.9: A propagating sequence of fusions in a $(2,4)$ tree: (a) removal of 14, which causes an underflow; (b) fusion, which causes another underflow; (c) second fusion operation, which causes the root to be removed; (d) final tree.

Analysis of $(2,4)$ Trees

The following theorem summarizes the running times of the main operations of a dictionary realized with a $(2,4)$ tree.

Theorem 20.3: *A $(2,4)$ tree for n key-element items uses $O(n)$ space and implements the operations of a dictionary data structure with the following running times. Finding an item, inserting an item, and removing an item each take time $O(\log n)$.*

The time complexity analysis is based on the following:

- The height of a $(2,4)$ tree storing n items is $O(\log n)$, by Theorem 20.2.
- A split, transfer, or fusion operation takes $O(1)$ time.
- A search, insertion, or removal of an item visits $O(\log n)$ nodes.

Thus, $(2,4)$ trees provide for fast dictionary search and update operations. $(2,4)$ trees also have an interesting relationship to the data structure we discuss next, which is better suited for external memory.

20.2.3 (a, b) Trees and B-Trees

Recalling the great time difference that exists between main memory accesses and disk accesses, the main goal of maintaining a dictionary in external memory is to minimize the number of disk transfers needed to perform a query or update. In fact, the difference in speed between disk and internal memory is so great that we should be willing to perform a considerable number of internal-memory accesses if they allow us to avoid a few disk transfers. Let us, therefore, analyze the performance of dictionary implementations by counting the number of disk transfers each would require to perform the standard dictionary search and update operations.

Let us first consider some external-memory inefficient dictionary implementations based on sequences. If the sequence representing a dictionary is implemented as an unsorted, doubly linked list, then insert and remove can be performed with $O(1)$ transfers each, assuming we know which block holds an item to be removed. But, in this case, searching requires $\Theta(n)$ transfers in the worst case, since each link hop we perform could access a different block. This search time can be improved to $O(n/B)$ transfers (see Exercise C-20.1), where B denotes the number of nodes of the list that can fit into a block, but this is still poor performance. We could alternately implement the sequence using a sorted array. In this case, a search performs $O(\log_2 n)$ transfers, via binary search, which is a nice improvement. But this solution requires $\Theta(n/B)$ transfers to implement an insert or remove operation in the worst case, for we may have to access all blocks to move elements up or down. Thus, sequence dictionary implementations are not efficient for external memory.

If sequence implementations are inefficient, then perhaps we should consider the logarithmic-time, internal-memory strategies that use balanced binary trees (for example, AVL trees or red-black trees) or other search structures with logarithmic average-case query and update times (for example, skip lists or splay trees). These methods store the dictionary items at the nodes of a binary tree or of a graph. In the worst case, each node accessed for a query or update in one of these structures will be in a different block. Thus, these methods all require $O(\log_2 n)$ transfers in the worst case to perform a query or update operation. This is good, but we can do better. In particular, we can perform dictionary queries and updates using only $O(\log_B n) = O(\log n / \log B)$ transfers.

The main idea for improving the external-memory performance of the dictionary implementations discussed above is that we should be willing to perform up to $O(B)$ internal-memory accesses to avoid a single disk transfer, where B denotes the size of a block. The hardware and software that drives the disk performs this many internal-memory accesses just to bring a block into internal memory, and this is only a small part of the cost of a disk transfer. Thus, $O(B)$ high-speed, internal-memory accesses are a small price to pay to avoid a time-consuming disk transfer.

(a, b) Trees

To reduce the importance of the performance difference between internal-memory accesses and external-memory accesses for searching, we can represent our dictionary using a multi-way search tree, which is a generalization of the $(2, 4)$ tree data structure to a structure known as an (a, b) tree.

Formally, an (a, b) tree is a multi-way search tree such that each node has between a and b children and stores between $a - 1$ and $b - 1$ items. The algorithms for searching, inserting, and removing elements in an (a, b) tree are straightforward generalizations of the corresponding ones for $(2, 4)$ trees. The advantage of generalizing $(2, 4)$ trees to (a, b) trees is that a generalized class of trees provides a flexible search structure, where the size of the nodes and the running time of the various dictionary operations depends on the parameters a and b. By setting the parameters a and b appropriately with respect to the size of disk blocks, we can derive a data structure that achieves good performance for external memory.

An (a, b) **tree**, where a and b are integers, such that $2 \le a \le (b + 1)/2$, is a multi-way search tree T with the following additional restrictions:

Size Property: Each internal node has at least a children, unless it is the root, and has at most b children.

Depth Property: All the external nodes have the same depth.

Theorem 20.4: *The height of an (a, b) tree storing n items is $\Omega(\log n / \log b)$ and $O(\log n / \log a)$.*

Proof: Let T be an (a, b) tree storing n elements, and let h be the height of T. We justify the theorem by establishing the following bounds on h:

$$\frac{1}{\log b} \log(n + 1) \le h \le \frac{1}{\log a} \log \frac{n + 1}{2} + 1.$$

By the size and depth properties, the number n'' of external nodes of T is at least $2a^{h-1}$ and at most b^h. By Theorem 20.1, $n'' = n + 1$. Thus,

$$2a^{h-1} \le n + 1 \le b^h.$$

Taking the logarithm in base 2 of each term, we get

$$(h - 1) \log a + 1 \le \log(n + 1) \le h \log b.$$

∎

We recall that in a multi-way search tree T, each node v of T holds a secondary structure $D(v)$, which is itself a dictionary (Section 20.2.1). If T is an (a, b) tree, then $D(v)$ stores at most b items. Let $f(b)$ denote the time for performing a search in a $D(v)$ dictionary. The search algorithm in an (a, b) tree is exactly like the one for multi-way search trees given in Section 20.2.1. Hence, searching in an (a, b) tree T with n items takes $O(\frac{f(b)}{\log a} \log n)$. Note that if b is a constant (and thus a is also), then the search time is $O(\log n)$, independent of the specific implementation of the secondary structures.

The main application of (a, b) trees is for dictionaries stored in external memory (for example, on a disk or CD/DVD-ROM). Namely, to minimize disk accesses, we select the parameters a and b so that each tree node occupies a single disk block (so that $f(b) = 1$ if we wish to simply count block transfers). Providing the right a and b values in this context gives rise to a data structure known as the B-tree, which we will describe shortly. Before we describe this structure, however, let us discuss how insertions and removals are handled in (a, b) trees.

Insertion and Removal in an (a, b) Tree

The insertion algorithm for an (a, b) tree is similar to that for a $(2, 4)$ tree. An overflow occurs when an item is inserted into a b-node v, which becomes an illegal $(b+1)$-node. (Recall that a node in a multi-way tree is a *d-node* if it has d children.) To remedy an overflow, we split node v by moving the median item of v into the parent of v and replacing v with a $\lceil (b+1)/2 \rceil$-node v' and a $\lfloor (b+1)/2 \rfloor$-node v''. We can now see the reason for requiring $a \leq (b+1)/2$ in the definition of an (a, b) tree. Note that as a consequence of the split, we need to build the secondary structures $D(v')$ and $D(v'')$.

Removing an element from an (a, b) tree is also similar to what was done for $(2, 4)$ trees. An underflow occurs when a key is removed from an a-node v, distinct from the root, which causes v to become an illegal $(a-1)$-node. To remedy an underflow, we either perform a transfer with a sibling of v that is not an a-node or we perform a fusion of v with a sibling that is an a-node. The new node w resulting from the fusion is a $(2a-1)$-node. Here, we see another reason for requiring $a \leq (b+1)/2$. Note that as a consequence of the fusion, we need to build the secondary structure $D(w)$.

Table 20.10 shows the running time of the main operations of a dictionary realized by means of an (a, b) tree T.

Method	Time
find	$O\left(\frac{f(b)}{\log a} \log n\right)$
insert	$O\left(\frac{g(b)}{\log a} \log n\right)$
remove	$O\left(\frac{g(b)}{\log a} \log n\right)$

Table 20.10: Time complexity of the main methods of a dictionary realized by an (a, b) tree. We let $f(b)$ denote the time to search a b-node and $g(b)$ the time to split or fuse a b-node. We also denote the number of elements in the dictionary with n. The space complexity is $O(n)$.

The bounds in Table 20.10 are based on the following assumptions and facts:

- The (a, b) tree T is represented using the data structure described in Section 20.2.1, and the secondary structure of the nodes of T support search in $f(b)$ time, and split and fusion operations in $g(b)$ time, for some functions $f(b)$ and $g(b)$, which can be made to be $O(1)$ in the context where we are only counting disk transfers.

- The height of an (a, b) tree storing n elements is at most $O((\log n)/(\log a))$ (Theorem 20.4).

- A search visits $O((\log n)/(\log a))$ nodes on a path between the root and an external node, and spends $f(b)$ time per node.

- A transfer operation takes $f(b)$ time.

- A split or fusion operation takes $g(b)$ time and builds a secondary structure of size $O(b)$ for the new node(s) created.

- An insertion or removal of an element visits $O((\log n)/(\log a))$ nodes on a path between the root and an external node, and spends $g(b)$ time per node.

Thus, we may summarize as follows.

Theorem 20.5: *An (a, b) tree implements an n-item dictionary to support performing insertions and removals in $O((g(b)/\log a) \log n)$ time, and performing find queries in $O((f(b)/\log a) \log n)$ time.*

B-Trees

A specialized version of the (a, b) tree data structure, which is an efficient method for maintaining a dictionary in external memory, is the data structure known as the "B-tree." (See Figure 20.11.) A *B-tree of order* d is simply an (a, b) tree with $a = \lceil d/2 \rceil$ and $b = d$. Since we discussed the standard dictionary query and update methods for (a, b) trees above, we restrict our discussion here to the analysis of the input/output (I/O) performance of B-trees.

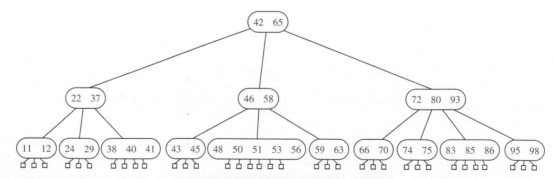

Figure 20.11: A B-tree of order 6.

Parameterizing B-trees for External Memory

The most important observation about B-trees is that we can choose d so that the d children references and the $d-1$ keys stored at a node can all fit into a single disk block. That is, we choose d so that

$$d \text{ is } \Theta(B).$$

This choice also implies that we may assume that a and b are $\Theta(B)$ in the analysis of the search and update operations on (a, b) trees. Also, recall that we are interested primarily in the number of disk transfers needed to perform various operations. Thus, the choice for d also implies that

$$f(b) = c,$$

and

$$g(b) = c,$$

for some constant $c \geq 1$, for each time we access a node to perform a search or an update operation, we need only perform a single disk transfer. That is, $f(b)$ and $g(b)$ are both $O(1)$. As we have already observed above, each search or update requires that we examine at most $O(1)$ nodes for each level of the tree. Therefore, any dictionary search or update operation on a B-tree requires only

$$
\begin{aligned}
O(\log_{\lceil d/2 \rceil} n) &= O(\log n / \log B) \\
&= O(\log_B n)
\end{aligned}
$$

disk transfers. For example, an insert operation proceeds down the B-tree to locate the node in which to insert the new item. If the node would ***overflow*** (to have $d+1$ children) because of this addition, then this node is ***split*** into two nodes that have $\lfloor (d+1)/2 \rfloor$ and $\lceil (d+1)/2 \rceil$ children, respectively. This process is then repeated at the next level up, and will continue for at most $O(\log_B n)$ levels. Likewise, in a remove operation, we remove an item from a node, and, if this results in a node ***underflow*** (to have $\lceil d/2 \rceil - 1$ children), then we either move references from a sibling node with at least $\lceil d/2 \rceil + 1$ children or we need to perform a ***fusion*** operation of this node with its sibling (and repeat this computation at the parent). As with the insert operation, this will continue up the B-tree for at most $O(\log_B n)$ levels. Thus, we have the following:

Theorem 20.6: *A B-tree with n items executes $O(\log_B n)$ disk transfers in a search or update operation, where B is the number of items that can fit in one block.*

The requirement that each internal node have at least $\lceil d/2 \rceil$ children implies that each disk block used to support a B-tree is at least half full. Analytical and experimental study of the average block usage in a B-tree is that it is closer to 67%, which is quite good.

20.3 External-Memory Sorting

In addition to data structures, such as dictionaries, that need to be implemented in external memory, there are many algorithms that must also operate on input sets that are too large to fit entirely into internal memory. In this case, the objective is to solve the algorithmic problem using as few block transfers as possible. The most classic domain for such external-memory algorithms is the sorting problem.

A Lower Bound for External-Memory Sorting

As we discussed above, there can be a big difference between an algorithm's performance in internal memory and its performance in external memory. For example, the performance of the radix-sorting algorithm is bad in external memory, yet good in internal memory. Other algorithms, such as the merge-sort algorithm, are reasonably good in both internal memory and external memory, however. The number of block transfers performed by the traditional merge-sorting algorithm is $O((n/B)\log_2 n)$, where B is the size of disk blocks. While this is much better than the $O(n)$ block transfers performed by an external version of radix sort, it is, nevertheless, not the best that is achievable for the sorting problem. In fact, we can show the following lower bound, whose proof is beyond the scope of this book.

Theorem 20.7: *Sorting n elements stored in external memory requires*

$$\Omega \left(\frac{n}{B} \cdot \frac{\log(n/B)}{\log(M/B)} \right)$$

block transfers, where M is the size of the internal memory.

The ratio M/B is the number of external-memory blocks that can fit into internal memory. Thus, this theorem is saying that the best performance we can achieve for the sorting problem is equivalent to the work of scanning through the input set (which takes $\Theta(n/B)$ transfers) at least a logarithmic number of times, where the base of this logarithm is the number of blocks that fit into internal memory. We will not formally justify this theorem, but we will show how to design an external-memory sorting algorithm whose running time comes within a constant factor of this lower bound.

Multi-way Merge-Sort

An efficient way to sort a set S of n objects in external memory amounts to a simple external-memory variation on the familiar merge-sort algorithm. The main idea behind this variation is to merge many recursively sorted lists at a time, thereby reducing the number of levels of recursion. Specifically, a high-level description of this ***multi-way merge-sort*** method is to divide S into d subsets S_1, S_2, ..., S_d of roughly equal size, recursively sort each subset S_i, and then simultaneously merge all d sorted lists into a sorted representation of S. If we can perform the merge process using only $O(n/B)$ disk transfers, then, for large enough values of n, the total number of transfers performed by this algorithm satisfies the following recurrence:

$$t(n) = d \cdot t(n/d) + cn/B,$$

for some constant $c \geq 1$. We can stop the recursion when $n \leq B$, since we can perform a single block transfer at this point, getting all of the objects into internal memory, and then sort the set with an efficient internal-memory algorithm. Thus, the stopping criterion for $t(n)$ is

$$t(n) = 1 \quad \text{if } n/B \leq 1.$$

This implies a closed-form solution that $t(n)$ is $O((n/B)\log_d(n/B))$, which is

$$O((n/B)\log(n/B)/\log d).$$

Thus, if we can choose d to be $\Theta(M/B)$, then the worst-case number of block transfers performed by this multi-way merge-sort algorithm will be within a constant factor of the lower bound given in Theorem 20.7. We choose

$$d = (1/2)M/B.$$

The only aspect of this algorithm left to specify, then, is how to perform the d-way merge using only $O(n/B)$ block transfers.

We perform the d-way merge by running a "tournament." We let T be a complete binary tree with d external nodes, and we keep T entirely in internal memory. We associate each external node i of T with a different sorted list S_i. We initialize T by reading into each external node i, the first object in S_i. This has the effect of reading into internal memory the first block of each sorted list S_i. For each internal-node parent v of two external nodes, we then compare the objects stored at v's children and we associate the smaller of the two with v. We then repeat this comparison test at the next level up in T, and the next, and so on. When we reach the root r of T, we will associate the smallest object from among all the lists with r. This completes the initialization for the d-way merge. (See Figure 20.12.)

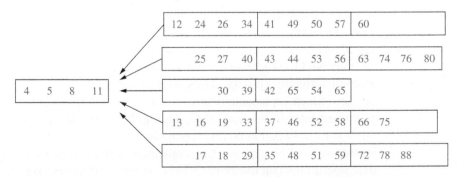

Figure 20.12: A d-way merge. We show a five-way merge with $B = 4$.

In a general step of the d-way merge, we move the object o associated with the root r of T into an array we are building for the merged list S'. We then trace down T, following the path to the external node i that o came from. We then read into i the next object in the list S_i. If o was not the last element in its block, then this next object is already in internal memory. Otherwise, we read in the next block of S_i to access this new object (if S_i is now empty, associate with the node i a pseudo-object with key $+\infty$). We then repeat the minimum computations for each of the internal nodes from i to the root of T. This again gives us the complete tree T. We then repeat this process of moving the object from the root of T to the merged list S', and rebuilding T until T is empty of objects. Each step in the merge takes $O(\log d)$ time; hence, the internal time for the d-way merge is $O(n \log d)$. The number of transfers performed in a merge is $O(n/B)$, since we scan each list S_i in order once and we write out the merged list S' once. Thus, we have the following:

Theorem 20.8: *Given an array, S, of n elements stored in external memory, we can sort S using $O((n/B)\log(n/B)/\log(M/B))$ block transfers (I/Os) and $O(n \log n)$ internal CPU time, where M is the size of the internal memory and B is the size of a block.*

Achieving "Near" Machine Independence

Using B-trees and external sorting algorithms can produce significant reductions in the number of block transfers. The most important piece of information that made such reductions possible was knowing the value of B, the size of a disk block (or cache line). This information is, of course, machine-dependent, but it is one of the few truly machine-dependent pieces of information that are needed, with one of the others being the ability to store keys continuously in arrays.

From our description of B-trees and external sorting, we might think that we also require low-level access to the external-memory device driver, but this is not strictly needed in order to achieve the claimed results to within a constant factor. In particular, in addition to knowing the block size, the only other thing we need to know is that large arrays of keys are partitioned into blocks of continuous cells. This allows us to implement the "blocks" in B-trees and our external-memory sorting algorithm as separate B-sized arrays, which we call ***pseudo-blocks***. If arrays are allocated to blocks in the natural way, any such pseudo-block will be allocated to at most two real blocks. Thus, even if we are relying on the operating system to perform block replacement (for example, using FIFO, LRU, or the Marker policy discussed later in Section 20.4), we can be sure that accessing any pseudo-block takes at most two, that is, $O(1)$, real block transfers. By using pseudo-blocks, then, instead of real blocks, we can implement a dictionary to achieve search and update operations that use only $O(\log_B n)$ block transfers. We can, therefore, design external-memory data structures and algorithms without taking complete control of the memory hierarchy from the operating system.

20.4 Online Caching Algorithms

An *online algorithm* responds to a sequence of *service requests*, each an associated *cost*. For example, a web page replacement policy maintains pages in a cache, subject to a sequence of access requests, with the cost of a web page request being zero if the page is in the cache and one if the page is outside the cache. In an *online* setting, the algorithm must completely finish responding to a service request before it can receive the next request in the sequence. If an algorithm is given the entire sequence of service requests in advance, it is said to be an *offline* algorithm. To analyze an online algorithm, we often employ a competitive analysis, where we compare a particular online algorithm A to an optimal offline algorithm, OPT. Given a particular sequence $P = (p_1, p_2, \ldots, p_n)$ of service requests, let $cost(A, P)$ denote the cost of A on P and let $cost(OPT, P)$ denote the cost of the optimal algorithm on P. The algorithm A is said to be *c-competitive* for P if

$$cost(A, P) \leq c \cdot cost(OPT, P) + b,$$

for some constant $b > 0$. If A is c-competitive for every sequence P, then we simply say that A is c-competitive, and we call c the *competitive ratio* of A. If $b = 0$, then we say that the algorithm A has a *strict* competitive ratio of c.

A well-known online problem, explained with a story, is the *ski rental problem*. Alice has decided to try out skiing, but is uncertain whether she will like it or whether she will be injured and have to stop. Each time Alice goes skiing, it costs her x dollars to "rent" the necessary skiing equipment. Suppose it costs y dollars to buy skis and the equipment that goes with them. Let us say, for the sake of the story, that y is 10 times larger than x, that is, $y = 10x$. The dilemma for Alice is to decide if and when she should buy the skiing equipment instead of renting this equipment each time she goes skiing. For example, if she buys before her first skiing trip and then decides she doesn't like skiing, then she has spent 10 times more than she should. But if she skis many times and never buys the equipment, then she will spend potentially even more than 10 times more than she should. In fact, if she skis n times, then this strategy of always "renting" will cause her to spend $n/10$ times as many dollars as she should. That is, a strategy of buying the first time has a worst-case competitive ratio of 10 and the always-rent strategy has a worst-case competitive ratio of $n/10$. Neither of these choices is good.

Fortunately, Alice has a strategy with a competitive ratio of 2. Namely, she can rent for 9 times and then buy the skiing equipment on the 10th day she skis. The worst-case scenario is that she never uses the skis she just bought. So, in this case, she spends $9x + y = 1.9y$ dollars, when she should have spent $y = 10x$; hence, this strategy has a competitive ratio of 1.9. In fact, no matter how much bigger y is than x, if Alice buys on day $\lceil y/x \rceil$, and then buys, she will have a competitive ratio of at most 2.

20.4.1   Caching Algorithms

There are several applications that must deal with revisiting information presented in pages. For instance, web page revisits have been shown to exhibit localities of reference, both in time and in space. Similarly, the way in which a CPU access disk pages tends to exhibit such localities as well. To exploit these localities of reference, it is often advantageous to store copies of such pages in a *cache* memory, so these pages can be quickly retrieved when requested again. In particular, suppose we have a cache memory that has m "slots," each of which can contain a web or disk page, depending on the application. We assume that a page can be placed in any slot of the cache. This is known as a *fully associative* cache.

As a browser executes, it requests different pages. Each time its requests such a web page l, it must determine (using a quick test) whether l is unchanged and currently contained in the cache. If l is contained in the cache, then the request can be satisfied using the cached copy. If l is not in the cache, however, the page for l is requested and transferred into the cache. If one of the m slots in the cache is available, then the new page, l is assigned to one of the empty slots. But if all the m cells of the cache are occupied, then the computer must determine which previously loaded page to evict before bringing in l to take its place. There are, of course, many different policies that can be used to determine the page to evict. Some of the better-known page replacement policies include the following (see Figure 20.13):

- **First-in, First-out (FIFO)**: Evict the page that has been in the cache the longest, that is, the page that was transferred to the cache furthest in the past.
- **Least recently used (LRU)**: Evict the page whose last request occurred furthest in the past.

In addition, we can consider a simple and purely random strategy:

- **Random**: Choose a page at random to evict from the cache.

The Random strategy is easy to implement, for it only requires a random or pseudo-random number generator. The overhead involved in implementing this policy is an $O(1)$ additional amount of work per page replacement. Moreover, there is no additional overhead for each page request, other than to determine whether a page request is in the cache or not. Still, this policy makes no attempt to take advantage of any temporal or spatial localities that a user's browsing exhibits.

The FIFO strategy is quite simple to implement, as it only requires a queue Q to store references to the pages in the cache. Pages are enqueued in Q when they are referenced by a browser, and then are brought into the cache. When a page needs to be evicted, the computer simply performs a dequeue operation on Q to determine which page to evict. Thus, this policy also requires $O(1)$ additional work per page replacement. Also, the FIFO policy incurs no additional overhead for page requests. Moreover, it tries to take some advantage of temporal locality.

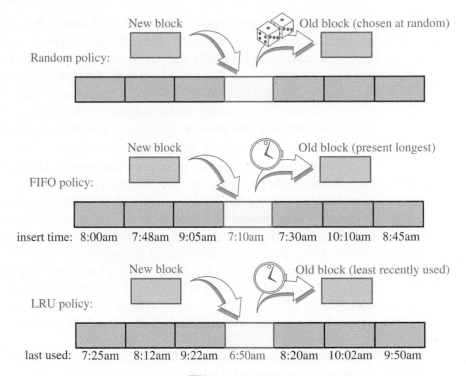

Figure 20.13: The Random, FIFO, and LRU page replacement policies.

The LRU strategy goes a step further than the FIFO strategy, which assumes that the page that has been in the cache the longest among all those present is the least likely to be requested in the near future. The LRU strategy explicitly takes advantage of temporal locality, by always evicting the page that was least recently used. From a policy point of view, this strategy is an excellent approach, but it is costly from an implementation point of view. That is, its way of optimizing temporal and spatial locality is fairly costly. Implementing the LRU strategy requires the use of a priority queue Q that supports searching for existing pages, for example, using special pointers or "locators." If Q is implemented with a sorted sequence based on a linked list, then the overhead for each page request and page replacement is $O(1)$. Whenever we insert a page in Q or update its key, the page is assigned the highest key in Q and is placed at the end of the list, which can also be done in $O(1)$ time. Even though the LRU strategy has constant-time overhead, using the above implementation, the constant factors involved, in terms of the additional time overhead and the extra space for the priority queue Q, make this policy less attractive from a practical point of view.

Since these different page replacement policies have different trade-offs between implementation difficulty and the degree to which they seem to take advantage of localities, it is natural for us to ask for some kind of comparative analysis of these methods to see which one, if any, is the best.

From a worst-case point of view, the FIFO and LRU strategies have fairly unattractive competitive behavior. For example, suppose we have a cache containing m pages, and consider the FIFO and LRU methods performing page replacement for a program that has a loop that repeatedly requests $m + 1$ pages in a cyclic order. Both the FIFO and LRU policies perform badly on such a sequence of page requests, because they perform a page replacement on every page request. Thus, from a worst-case point of view, these policies are almost the worst we can imagine—they require a page replacement on every page request.

This worst-case analysis is a little too pessimistic, however, for it focuses on each protocol's behavior for one bad sequence of page requests. An ideal analysis would be to compare these methods over all possible page-request sequences. Of course, this is impossible to do exhaustively, but there have been a great number of experimental simulations done on page-request sequences derived from real programs. The experiments have focused primarily on the Random, FIFO, and LRU policies. Based on these experimental comparisons, the ordering of policies, from best to worst, is as follows: (1) LRU, (2) FIFO, and (3) Random. In fact, LRU is significantly better than the others on typical request sequences, but it still has poor performance in the worst case, as the following theorem shows.

Theorem 20.9: *The FIFO and LRU page replacement policies for a cache with m pages have competitive ratio at least m.*

Proof: We observed above that there is a sequence $P = (p_1, p_2, \ldots, p_n)$ of page requests causing FIFO and LRU to perform a page replacement with each request—the loop of $m + 1$ requests. We compare this performance with that of the optimal offline algorithm, *OPT*, which, in the case of the page replacement problem, is to evict from the cache the page that is requested the furthest into the future. This strategy can only be implemented, of course, in the offline case, when we are given the entire sequence P in advance, unless the algorithm is "prophetic." When applied to the loop sequence, the *OPT* policy will perform a page replacement once every m requests (for it evicts the most recently referenced page each time, as this one is referenced furthest in the future). Thus, both FIFO and LRU are c-competitive on this sequence P, where

$$c = \frac{n}{n/m} = m.$$

Observe that if any portion $P' = (p_i, p_{i+1}, \ldots, p_j)$ of P makes requests to m different pages (with p_{i-1} and/or p_{j+1} not being one of them), then even the optimal algorithm must evict one page. In addition, the most number of pages the FIFO and LRU policies evict for such a portion P' is m, each time evicting a page that was referenced prior to p_i. Therefore, FIFO and LRU have a competitive ratio of m, and this is the best possible competitive ratio for these strategies in the worst case.

■

The Randomized Marker Algorithm

Even though the deterministic FIFO and LRU policies can have poor worst-case competitive ratios compared to the "prophetic" optimal algorithm, we can show that a randomized policy that attempts to simulate LRU has a good competitive ratio. Specifically, let us study the competitive ratio of a randomized strategy that tries to emulate the LRU policy. From a strategic viewpoint, this policy, which is known as the ***Marker strategy***, emulates the best aspects of the deterministic LRU policy, while using randomization to avoid the worst-case situations that are bad for the LRU strategy. The policy for Marker is as follows:

- **Marker**: Associate, with each page in the cache, a Boolean variable "marked," which is initially set to "false" for every page in the cache. If a browser requests a page that is already in the cache, that page's marked variable is set to "true." Otherwise, if a browser requests a page that is not in the cache, a random page whose marked variable is "false" is evicted and replaced with the new page, whose marked variable is immediately set to "true." If all the pages in the cache have marked variables set to "true," then all of them are reset to "false." (See Figure 20.14.)

Competitive Analysis for a Randomized Online Algorithm

Armed with the above policy definition, we would now like to perform a competitive analysis of the Marker strategy. Before we can do this analysis, however, we must first define what we mean by the competitive ratio of a randomized online algorithm. Since a randomized algorithm A, like the Marker policy, can have many different possible runs, depending upon the random choices it makes, we define such an algorithm to be *c-**competitive*** for a sequence of requests P if

$$E(cost(A, P)) \leq c \cdot cost(OPT, P) + b,$$

for some constant $b \geq 0$, where $E(cost(A, P))$ denotes the expected cost of algorithm A on the sequence P (with this expectation taken over all possible random choices for the algorithm A). If A is c-competitive for every sequence P, then we simply say that A is c-competitive, and we call c the ***competitive ratio*** for A.

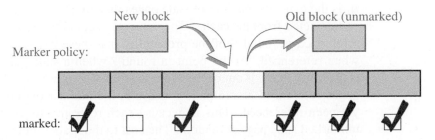

Figure 20.14: The Marker page replacement policy.

Theorem 20.10: *The Marker page policy for a cache with m pages has competitive ratio $2 \log m$.*

Proof: Let $P = (p_1, p_2, \ldots, p_n)$ be a sufficiently long sequence of page requests. The Marker policy implicitly partitions the requests in P into **rounds**. Each round begins with all the pages in the cache having "false" marked labels, and a round ends when all the pages in the cache have "true" marked labels (with the next request beginning the next round, since the policy then resets each such label to "false"). Consider the ith round in P, and call a page requested in round i **fresh** if it is not in the Marker policy's cache at the beginning of round i. Also, we refer to a page in the Marker's cache that has a false marked label **stale**. Thus, at the beginning of a round i, all the pages in the Marker policy's cache are stale. Let m_i denote the number of fresh pages referenced in the ith round, and let b_i denote the number of pages that are in the cache for the *OPT* algorithm at the beginning of round i and are not in the cache for the Marker policy at this time. Since the Marker policy has to perform a page replacement for each of the m_i requests, algorithm *OPT* must perform at least $m_i - b_i$ page replacements in round i. (See Figure 20.15.) In addition, since each of the pages in the Marker policy's cache at the end of round i are requested in round i, algorithm *OPT* must perform at least b_{i+1} page replacements in round i. Thus, the algorithm *OPT* must perform at least

$$\max\{m_i - b_i, b_{i+1}\} \geq \frac{m_i - b_i + b_{i+1}}{2}$$

page replacements in round i. Summing over all k rounds in P then, we see that algorithm *OPT* must perform at least the following number of page replacements:

$$L = \sum_{i=1}^{k} \frac{m_i - b_i + b_{i+1}}{2} = (b_{k+1} - b_1)/2 + \frac{1}{2} \sum_{i=1}^{k} m_i.$$

Next, let us consider the expected number of page replacements performed by the Marker policy.

We have already observed that the Marker policy has to perform at least m_i page replacements in round i. It may actually perform more than this, however, if it evicts stale pages that are then requested later in the round. Thus, the expected number of page replacements performed by the Marker policy is $m_i + n_i$, where n_i is the expected number of stale pages that are referenced in round i after having been evicted from the cache. The value n_i is equal to the sum, over all stale pages referenced in round i, of the probability that these pages are outside of the cache when referenced. At the point in round i when a stale page v is referenced, the probability that v is out of the cache is at most f/g, where f is the number of fresh pages referenced before page v and g is the number of stale pages that have not yet been referenced. This is because each reference to a fresh page evicts some unmarked stale page at random. The cost to the Marker policy will be highest then, if all m_i requests to fresh pages are made before any requests to stale pages. So, assuming this worst-case viewpoint, the expected number of evicted stale pages

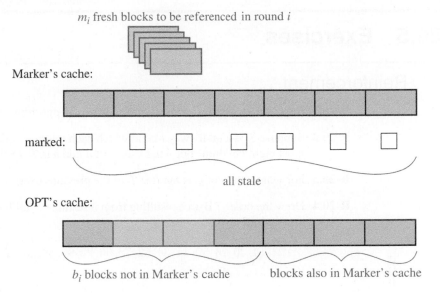

m_i fresh blocks to be referenced in round i

Marker's cache:

marked:

all stale

OPT's cache:

b_i blocks not in Marker's cache blocks also in Marker's cache

Figure 20.15: The state of Marker's cache and OPT's cache at the beginning of round i.

referenced in round i can be bounded as follows:

$$
\begin{aligned}
n_i & \leq \frac{m_i}{m} + \frac{m_i}{m-1} + \frac{m_i}{m-2} + \cdots + \frac{m_i}{m_i+1} \\
& \leq m_i \sum_{j=1}^{m} \frac{1}{j},
\end{aligned}
$$

since there are $m - m_i$ references to stale pages in round i. Noting that this summation is known as the mth harmonic number, which is denoted H_m, we have

$$
n_i \leq m_i H_m.
$$

Thus, the expected number of page replacements performed by the Marker policy is at most

$$
U = \sum_{i=1}^{k} m_i(H_m + 1) = (H_m + 1) \sum_{i=1}^{k} m_i.
$$

Therefore, the competitive ratio for the Marker policy is at most

$$
\begin{aligned}
\frac{U}{L} & = \frac{(H_m + 1) \sum_{i=1}^{k} m_i}{(1/2) \sum_{i=1}^{k} m_i} \\
& = 2(H_m + 1).
\end{aligned}
$$

Using an approximation for H_m, namely that $H_m \leq \log m$, the competitive ratio for the Marker policy is at most $2 \log m$. ∎

Thus, the competitive analysis shows that the Marker policy is fairly efficient.

20.5 Exercises

Reinforcement

R-20.1 Describe, in detail, the insertion and removal algorithms for an (a, b) tree.

R-20.2 Suppose T is a multi-way tree in which each internal node has at least five and at most eight children. For what values of a and b is T a valid (a, b) tree?

R-20.3 For what values of d is the tree T of the previous exercise an order-d B-tree?

R-20.4 Draw the order-7 B-tree resulting from inserting the following keys (in this order) into an initially empty tree T:

$$(4, 40, 23, 50, 11, 34, 62, 78, 66, 22, 90, 59, 25, 72, 64, 77, 39, 12).$$

R-20.5 Show each level of recursion in performing a four-way, external-memory merge-sort of the sequence given in the previous exercise.

R-20.6 Consider the generalization of the renter's dilemma where Alice can buy or rent her skis separate from her boots. Say that renting skis costs a dollars, whereas buying skis costs b dollars. Likewise, say that renting boots costs c dollars, whereas buying boots costs b dollars. Describe a 2-competitive online algorithm for Alice to try to minimize the costs for going skiing subject to the uncertainty of her not knowing how many times she will continue to go skiing in the future.

R-20.7 Consider an initially empty memory cache consisting of four pages. How many page misses does the LRU algorithm incur on the following page-request sequence?

$$(2, 3, 4, 1, 2, 5, 1, 3, 5, 4, 1, 2, 3)$$

R-20.8 Consider an initially empty memory cache consisting of four pages. How many page misses does the FIFO algorithm incur on the following page-request sequence?

$$(2, 3, 4, 1, 2, 5, 1, 3, 5, 4, 1, 2, 3)$$

R-20.9 Consider an initially empty memory cache consisting of four pages. How many page misses does the marker algorithm incur on the following page-request sequence: $(2, 3, 4, 1, 2, 5, 1, 3, 5, 4, 1, 2, 3)$? Show the random choices your algorithm made.

R-20.10 Consider an initially empty memory cache consisting of four pages. Construct a sequence of memory requests that would cause the marker algorithm to go through four rounds.

Creativity

C-20.1 Show how to implement a dictionary in external memory, using an unordered sequence so that insertions require only $O(1)$ transfers and searches require $O(n/B)$ transfers in the worst case, where n is the number of elements and B is the number of list nodes that can fit into a disk block.

C-20.2 Describe a modified version of the B-tree insertion algorithm so that each time we create an overflow because of a split of a node v, we redistribute keys among all of v's siblings, so that each sibling holds roughly the same number of keys (possibly cascading the split up to the parent of v). What is the minimum fraction of each block that will always be filled using this scheme?

C-20.3 Another possible external-memory dictionary implementation is to use a skip list, but to collect consecutive groups of $O(B)$ nodes, in individual blocks, on any level in the skip list. In particular, we define an ***order-*d* B-skip list*** to be such a representation of a skip-list structure, where each block contains at least $\lceil d/2 \rceil$ list nodes and at most d list nodes. Let us also choose d in this case to be the maximum number of list nodes from a level of a skip list that can fit into one block. Describe how we should modify the skip-list insertion and removal algorithms for a B-skip list so that the expected height of the structure is $O(\log n / \log B)$.

C-20.4 Suppose that instead of having the node-search function $f(d) = 1$ in an order-d B-tree T, we instead have $f(d) = \log d$. What does the asymptotic running time of performing a search in T now become?

C-20.5 Consider the page caching problem where the memory cache can hold m pages, and we are given a sequence P of n requests taken from a pool of $m + 1$ possible pages. Describe the optimal strategy for the offline algorithm and show that it causes at most $m + n/m$ page misses in total, starting from an empty cache.

C-20.6 Consider the page caching strategy based on the ***least frequently used*** (LFU) rule, where the page in the cache that has been accessed the least often is the one that is evicted when a new page is requested. If there are ties, LFU evicts the least frequently used page that has been in the cache the longest. Show that there is a sequence P of n requests that causes LFU to miss $\Omega(n)$ times for a cache of m pages, whereas the optimal algorithm will miss only $O(m)$ times.

C-20.7 Show that LRU is m-competitive for any sequence of n page requests, where m is the size of the memory cache.

C-20.8 Show that FIFO is m-competitive for any sequence of n page requests, where m is the size of the memory cache.

C-20.9 What is the expected number of block replacements performed by the Random policy on a cache of size m, for an access sequence of length n, that iteratively accesses $m + 1$ blocks in a cyclic fashion (assuming n is much larger than m)?

C-20.10 Show that the Marker algorithm is H_m-competitive when the size of the cache is m and there are $m + 1$ possible pages that can be accessed, where H_m denotes the mth Harmonic number.

Applications

A-20.1 Suppose you are processing a large number of operations in a consumer-producer process, such as a buffer for a large media stream. Describe an external-memory data structure to implement a queue so that the total number of disk transfers needed to process a sequence of n enqueue and dequeue operations is $O(n/B)$.

A-20.2 Imagine that you are trying to construct a minimum spanning tree for a large network, such as is defined by a popular social networking website. Based on using Kruskal's algorithm, the bottleneck is the maintenance of a union-find data structure. Describe how to use a B-tree to implement a union-find data structure (from Section 7.1) so that union and find operations each use at most $O(\log n/\log B)$ disk transfers each.

A-20.3 Suppose you are processing an automated course registration program. The data set in this case is a large file of N course numbers, one for each course request made by a student. Show that you can count the number of requests made for each course, using $O((N/B)\log(N/B)/\log(M/B))$ I/Os.

A-20.4 In the MapReduce framework, for performing a parallel computation, a crucial step involves an input that consists of a set of n key-value pairs, (k, v), for which we need to collect each subset of key-value pairs that have the same key, k, into a single file. Describe an efficient external-memory algorithm for constructing all such files. How many disk transfers does your algorithm perform?

A-20.5 Suppose Alice is faced with the ski rental problem, where buying skis is 20 times more expensive than renting. In this case, however, Alice notices that she has a fair coin in her pocket and is willing to consider a randomized strategy. Show that she can use her coin to come up with a strategy with an expected competitive ratio of 1.8 or better.

Chapter Notes

B-trees were invented by Bayer and McCreight [23] and Comer [47] provides a very nice overview of this structure. The books by Mehlhorn [157] and Samet [182] also discuss B-trees and their variants. Aho, Hopcroft, and Ullman [8] discuss $(2, 3)$ trees, which are similar to $(2, 4)$ trees. Arge and Vitter [12] present a weight-balanced B-tree, which has a number of nice properties. Knuth [131] has very nice discussions about external-memory sorting and searching. Aggarwal and Vitter [6] study the I/O complexity of sorting and related problems, establishing upper and lower bounds. Goodrich *et al.* [90] study the I/O complexity of several computational geometry problems. The reader interested in further study of I/O-efficient algorithms is encouraged to examine the book by Vitter [211].

The reader interested in further study of online algorithms is referred to the book by Borodin and El-Yaniv [34] or the paper by Koutsoupias and Papadimitriou [134]. The marker caching algorithm is discussed in the book by Borodin and El-Yaniv; our discussion is modeled after a similar discussion in by Motwani and Raghavan [162]. Exercises C-20.7 and C-20.8 come from Sleator and Tarjan [196].

Chapter

21

Multidimensional Searching

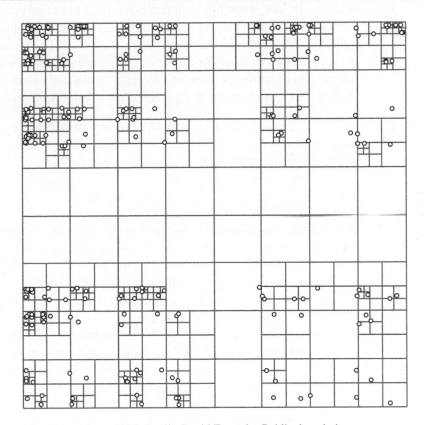

A point quadtree, 2005. Credit: David Eppstein. Public domain image.

Contents

21.1 Range Trees 605
21.2 Priority Search Trees 609
21.3 Quadtrees and k-d Trees 614
21.4 Exercises 618

We live in a multidimensional geometric world. Physical space itself is three-dimensional, for we can use three coordinates, x, y, and z, to describe points in space. Completely describing the orientation of the tip of a robot arm actually requires six dimensions, for we use three dimensions to describe the position of the tip in space, plus three more dimensions to describe the angles the tip is in (which are typically called pitch, roll, and yaw). Describing the state of an airplane in flight takes at least nine dimensions, for we need six to describe its orientation in the same manner as for the tip of a robot arm, and we need three more to describe the plane's velocity. In fact, these physical representations are considered "low-dimensional," particularly in applications in machine learning or computational biology, where 100- and 1000-dimensional spaces are not unusual. For instance, a vector describing a collection of genes or movie ratings could easily have dimensionality in this range. This chapter is therefore directed at *multidimensional searching*, which studies data structures for storing and querying multidimensional data sets.

Multi-dimensional data arise in a variety of applications, including statistics and robotics. The simplest type of multidimensional data are d-dimensional points, which can be represented by a sequence,

$$(x_0, x_1, \ldots, x_{d-1}),$$

of d numeric *coordinates*. In business applications, a d-dimensional point may represent the various attributes of a product or an employee in a database. For example, televisions in an electronics catalog would probably have different attribute values for price, screen size, weight, height, width, and depth. Multi-dimensional data can also come from scientific applications, where each point represents attributes of individual experiments or observations. For example, heavenly objects in an astronomy sky survey would probably have different attribute values for brightness (or apparent magnitude), diameter, distance, and position in the sky (which is itself two-dimensional). Thus, these applications can benefit from efficient methods for storing and searching in multidimensional data sets.

There are actually a great number of different data structures and algorithms for processing multidimensional data, and it is beyond the scope of this chapter to discuss all of them. We provide instead an introduction to some of the more interesting ones in this chapter. We begin with a discussion of *range trees*, which can store multidimensional points so as to support a special kind of query operation, called a *range-searching query*, and we also include an interesting variant of the range tree called the *priority search tree*. Finally, we discuss a class of data structures, called *partition trees*, which partition space into cells, and focus on variants known as *quadtrees* and *k-d trees*. These data structures are used, for instance, in computer graphics and computer gaming applications, where we need to find nearest neighbors to a query point or map out the trajectory of a ray through a virtual environment.

21.1 Range Trees

A natural query operation to perform on a set of multidimensional points is a *range-search query*, which is a request to retrieve all points in a multidimensional collection whose coordinates fall within given ranges. For example, a consumer wishing to buy a new television may request, from an electronic store's catalog, all units that have a screensize between 24 and 27 inches, and have a price between $200 and $400. Alternately, an astronomer interested in studying asteroids may request all heavenly objects that are at a distance between 1.5 and 10 astronomical units, have an apparent magnitude between $+1$ and $+15$, and have a diameter between 0.5 and 1,000 kilometers. The range tree data structure, which we discuss in this section, can be used to answer such queries.

Two-Dimensional Range-Search Queries

To keep the discussion simple, let us focus on two-dimensional range-searching queries. Exercise C-21.7 addresses how the corresponding two-dimensional range tree data structure can be extended to higher dimensions. A *two-dimensional dictionary* is a data structure for storing key-element items such that the key is a pair (x, y) of numbers, called the *coordinates* of the element. A two-dimensional dictionary D supports the following fundamental query operation:

findAllInRange(x_1, x_2, y_1, y_2): Return all the elements of D with coordinates (x, y) such that $x_1 \le x \le x_2$ and $y_1 \le y \le y_2$.

Operation findAllInRange is the *reporting* version of the range-searching query, because it asks for all the items satisfying the range constraints. There is also a *counting* version of the range query, in which we are simply interested in the number of items in that range. We present data structures for answering two-dimensional range queries in the remainder of this section.

Note that a two-dimensional range-search operation is directly analogous to a one-dimensional range search, which is discussed in Section 3.2. The main ideas from one-dimensional searching can inform our thoughts about how to answer a two-dimensional range-search query, but more work is needed. For instance, one way to answer is a one-dimensional range search is to use a balanced binary tree, with the keys stored in sorted order. Then we can search for the lower end of a range, x_1, and the upper end of a range, x_2, and answer the query by reporting or counting all the elements in the search tree that are between these two locations using the in-order ordering. If the points are two-dimensional, though, then this approach can only be used to report or count points in the vertical strip between the lines $x = x_1$ and $x = x_2$. Thus, for two-dimensional range searching, something more is needed.

21.1.1   Two-Dimensional Range Searching

The two-dimensional range tree is a data structure that can implement a two-dimensional dictionary. It consists of a *primary* structure, which is a balanced binary search tree T, together with a number of *auxiliary* structures. (See Figure 21.1.)

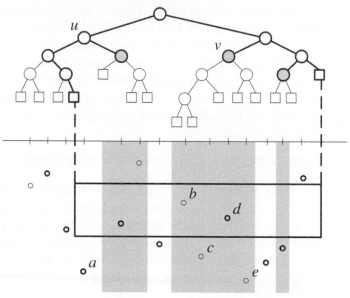

Figure 21.1: A set of items with two-dimensional keys represented by a two-dimensional range tree, and a range search on it. The primary structure T is shown. The nodes of T visited by the search algorithm are drawn with thick lines. The boundary nodes are white-filled, and the allocation nodes are gray-filled. Point a, stored at boundary node u, is outside the search range. The gray vertical strips cover the points stored at the auxiliary structures of the allocation nodes. For example, the auxiliary structure of node v stores points b, c, d, and e.

Specifically, each internal node in the primary structure T stores a reference to a related auxiliary structure. The function of the primary structure, T, is to support searching based on x-coordinates. To also support searching in terms of the y-coordinates, we use a collection of auxiliary data structures, each of which is a one-dimensional range tree that uses y-coordinates as its keys. The primary structure of T is a balanced binary search tree built using the x-coordinates of the items as the keys. An internal node v of T stores the following data:

- An item, whose coordinates are denoted by $x(v)$ and $y(v)$, and whose element is denoted by element(v).
- A one-dimensional range tree $T(v)$ that stores the same set of items as the subtree rooted at v in T (including v), but using the y-coordinates as keys.

We give the details of answering a two-dimensional range search with a range tree in Algorithm 21.2 (see also Figure 21.1).

Algorithm 2DTreeRangeSearch(x_1, x_2, y_1, y_2, v, t):

   Input: Search keys x_1, x_2, y_1, and y_2; node v in the primary structure T of a two-dimensional range tree; type t of node v

   Output: The items in the subtree rooted at v whose coordinates are in the x-range $[x_1, x_2]$ and in the y-range $[y_1, y_2]$

   if T.isExternal(v) **then**
    return $\emptyset$
   if $x_1 \leq x(v) \leq x_2$ **then**
    if $y_1 \leq y(v) \leq y_2$ **then**
        $M \leftarrow \{$element(v)$\}$
    else
        $M \leftarrow \emptyset$
    if $t = $ "left" **then**
        $L \leftarrow$ 2DTreeRangeSearch(x_1, x_2, y_1, y_2, T.leftChild(v), "left")
        $R \leftarrow$ 1DTreeRangeSearch(y_1, y_2, T.rightChild(v))
    else if $t = $ "right" **then**
        $L \leftarrow$ 1DTreeRangeSearch(y_1, y_2, T.leftChild(v))
        $R \leftarrow$ 2DTreeRangeSearch(x_1, x_2, y_1, y_2, T.rightChild(v), "right")
    else
        // $t = $ "middle"
        $L \leftarrow$ 2DTreeRangeSearch(x_1, x_2, y_1, y_2, T.leftChild(v), "left")
        $R \leftarrow$ 2DTreeRangeSearch(x_1, x_2, y_1, y_2, T.rightChild(v), "right")
   else
    $M \leftarrow \emptyset$
    if $x(v) < x_1$ **then**
        $L \leftarrow \emptyset$
        $R \leftarrow$ 2DTreeRangeSearch(x_1, x_2, y_1, y_2, T.rightChild(v), t)
    else
        // $x(v) > x_2$
        $L \leftarrow$ 2DTreeRangeSearch(x_1, x_2, y_1, y_2, T.leftChild(v), t)
        $R \leftarrow \emptyset$
   return $L \cup M \cup R$

Algorithm 21.2: A recursive method for performing a two-dimensional range search in a two-dimensional range tree. The initial method call is 2DTreeRangeSearch(x_1, x_2, y_1, y_2, T.root(), "middle"). The algorithm is called recursively on all the boundary nodes with respect to the x-range $[x_1, x_2]$. Parameter t indicates whether v is a left, middle, or right boundary node. The method, 1DTreeRangeSearch, is the same as the method, RangeQuery, given in Algorithm 3.11.

21.2.1   Constructing a Priority Search Tree

The y-coordinates of the items stored at the nodes of a priority search tree T satisfy the heap-order property (Section 5.3). That is, if u is the parent of v, then $\bar{y}(u) > \bar{y}(v)$. Also, the median x-coordinates stored at the nodes of T define a binary search tree (Section 3.1.1). These two facts motivate the term "priority search tree." Let us therefore explain how to construct a priority search tree from a set S of n two-dimensional items. We begin by sorting S by increasing x-coordinate, and then call the recursive method buildPST(S) shown in Algorithm 21.4.

Algorithm buildPST(S):

> **_Input:_** A sequence S of n two-dimensional items, sorted by x-coordinate
> **_Output:_** A priority search tree T for S

> Create an elementary binary tree T consisting of single external node v
> **if** !S.isEmpty() **then**
> > Traverse sequence S to find the item $\bar{p}$ of S with highest y-coordinate
> > Remove $\bar{p}$ from S
> > $\bar{p}(v) \leftarrow \bar{p}$
> > $\hat{p} \leftarrow S$.get($\lceil S$.size()$/2 \rceil$)
> > $\hat{x}(v) \leftarrow x(\hat{p})$
> > Split S into two subsequences, S_L and S_R, where S_L contains the items up to $\hat{p}$ (included), and S_R contains the remaining items
> > $T_L \leftarrow$ buildPST(S_L)
> > $T_R \leftarrow$ buildPST(S_R)
> > T.expandExternal(v)
> > Replace the left child of v with T_L
> > Replace the right child of v with T_R
> **return** T

>   **Algorithm 21.4:** Recursive construction of a priority search tree.

Lemma 21.3: *Given a set S of n two-dimensional items, a priority search tree for S uses $O(n)$ space, has height $O(\log n)$, and can be built in $O(n \log n)$ time.*

Proof: The $O(n)$ space requirement follows from the fact that every internal node of the priority search tree T stores a distinct item of S. The height of T follows from the halving of the number of nodes at each level. The preliminary sorting of the items of S by x-coordinate can be done in $O(n \log n)$ time using an asymptotically optimal sorting algorithm, such as heap sort or merge sort. The running time $T(n)$ of method buildPST (Algorithm 21.4) is characterized by the recurrence, $T(n) = 2T(n/2) + bn$, for some constant $b > 0$. Therefore, by the Master Theorem (11.4), $T(n)$ is $O(n \log n)$. ∎

21.2.2   Searching in a Priority Search Tree

We now show how to perform a three-sided range query findAllInRange(x_1, x_2, y_1) on a priority search tree T. We traverse down T in a fashion similar to that of a one-dimensional range search for the range $[x_1, x_2]$. One important difference, however, is that we only continue searching in the subtree of a node v if $y(v) \geq y_1$. We give the details of the algorithm for three-sided range searching in Algorithm 21.5 (PSTSearch) and we illustrate the execution of the algorithm in Figure 21.6.

Algorithm PSTSearch(x_1, x_2, y_1, v):

    Input: Three-sided range, defined by x_1, x_2, and y_1, and a node v of a priority search tree T

    Output: The items stored in the subtree rooted at v with coordinates (x, y), such that $x_1 \leq x \leq x_2$ and $y_1 \leq y$

    if $\bar{y}(v) < y_1$ **then**

        return $\emptyset$

    if $x_1 \leq \bar{x}(v) \leq x_2$ **then**

        $M \leftarrow \{\bar{p}(v)\}$ // we should output $\bar{p}(v)$

    else

        $M \leftarrow \emptyset$

    if $x_1 \leq \hat{x}(v)$ **then**

        $L \leftarrow$ PSTSearch$(x_1, x_2, y_1, T.\text{leftChild}(v))$

    else

        $L \leftarrow \emptyset$

    if $\hat{x}(v) \leq x_2$ **then**

        $R \leftarrow$ PSTSearch$(x_1, x_2, y_1, T.\text{rightChild}(v))$

    else

        $R \leftarrow \emptyset$

    return $L \cup M \cup R$

Algorithm 21.5: Three-sided range searching in a priority search tree T. The algorithm is initially called with PSTSearch$(x_1, x_2, y_1, T.\text{root}())$.

Note that we have defined three-sided ranges to have a left, right, and bottom side, and to be unbounded at the top. This restriction was made without loss of generality, however, for we could have defined our three-sided range queries using any three sides of a rectangle. The priority search tree from such an alternate definition is similar to the one defined above, but "turned on its side."

Let us analyze the running time of method PSTSearch for answering a three-sided range-search query on a priority search tree T storing a set of n items with two-dimensional keys. We denote with s the number of items reported. Since we spend $O(1)$ time for each node we visit, the running time of method PSTSearch

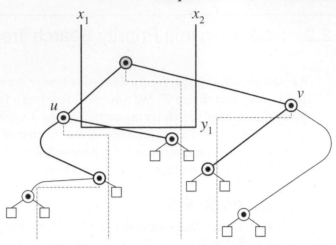

Figure 21.6: Three-sided range-searching in a priority search tree. The nodes visited are drawn with thick lines. The nodes storing reported items are gray-filled.

is proportional to the number of visited nodes.

Each node v visited by method PSTSearch is classified as follows:

- Node v is a ***boundary node*** if it is on the search path for x_1 or x_2 when viewing T as a binary search tree on the median x-coordinate stored at its nodes. The item stored at an internal boundary node may be inside or outside the three-sided range. By Lemma 21.3, the height of T is $O(\log n)$. Thus, there are $O(\log n)$ boundary nodes.
- Node v is an ***inside node*** if it is internal, it is not a boundary node, and $\bar{y}(v) \geq y_1$. The item stored at an internal node is inside the three-sided range. The number of inside nodes is no more than the number s of items reported.
- Node v is a ***terminal node*** if it is not a boundary node and, if internal, $\bar{y}(v) < y_1$. The item stored at an internal terminal node is outside the three-sided range. Each terminal node is the child of a boundary node or an inside node. Thus, the number of terminal nodes is at most twice the number of boundary nodes plus inside nodes. Thus, there are $O(\log n + s)$ terminal nodes.

Theorem 21.4: *A priority search tree T storing n items with two-dimensional keys uses $O(n)$ space and can be constructed in $O(n \log n)$ time, to answer three-sided range queries in $O(\log n + s)$ time, where s is the number of items reported.*

Of course, three-sided range queries are not as constrained as four-sided range queries, which can be answered in $O(\log^2 n + k)$ time using the range tree data structure discussed above. Still, priority search trees can be used to speed up the running time of answering standard four-sided, two-dimensional range queries. The resulting data structure, which is known as the ***priority range tree***, uses priority search trees as auxiliary structures in a way that achieves the same space bound as traditional range trees. We discuss this data structure next.

21.2.3 Priority Range Trees

Let T be a balanced binary search tree storing n items with two-dimensional keys, ordered according to their x-coordinates. We show how to augment T with priority search trees as auxiliary structures to answer (four-sided) range queries. The resulting data structure is called a ***priority range tree***.

To convert T into a priority range tree, we visit each internal node v of T other than the root and construct, as an auxiliary structure, a priority search tree $T(v)$ for the items stored in the subtree of T rooted at v. If v is a left child, $T(v)$ answers range queries for three-side ranges unbounded on the right. If v is a right child, $T(v)$ answers range queries for three-side ranges unbounded on the left. By Lemmas 21.1 and 21.3, a priority range tree uses $O(n \log n)$ space and can be constructed in $O(n \log n)$ time. The method for performing a two-dimensional range query in a priority range tree is given in Algorithm 21.7 (PSTRangeSearch).

Algorithm PSTRangeSearch(x_1, x_2, y_1, y_2, v):

  Input: Search keys x_1, x_2, y_1, and y_2; node v in the primary structure T of a priority range tree

  Output: The items in the subtree rooted at v whose coordinates are in the x-range $[x_1, x_2]$ and in the y-range $[y_1, y_2]$

  if T.isExternal(v) **then**
      return $\emptyset$
  if $x_1 \le x(v) \le x_2$ **then**
      if $y_1 \le y(v) \le y_2$ **then**
          $M \leftarrow \{\text{element}(v)\}$
      else
          $M \leftarrow \emptyset$
      $L \leftarrow$ PSTSearch($x_1, y_1, y_2, T(\text{leftChild}(v)).\text{root}()$)
      $R \leftarrow$ PSTSearch($x_2, y_1, y_2, T(\text{rightChild}(v)).\text{root}()$)
      return $L \cup M \cup R$
  else if $x(v) < x_1$ **then**
      return PSTRangeSearch($x_1, x_2, y_1, y_2, T.\text{rightChild}(v)$)
  else
      // $x_2 < x(v)$
      return PSTRangeSearch($x_1, x_2, y_1, y_2, T.\text{leftChild}(v)$)

Algorithm 21.7: Range searching in a priority range tree T. The algorithm is initially called with PSTRangeSearch($x_1, x_2, y_1, y_2, T.\text{root}()$).

Theorem 21.5: *A priority range tree T for a set of n items with two-dimensional keys uses $O(n \log n)$ space and can be constructed in $O(n \log n)$ time. Using T, a two-dimensional range-search query takes time $O(\log n + s)$, where s is the number of elements reported.*

21.3   Quadtrees and k-d Trees

Multi-dimensional data sets often come from large applications; hence, we often desire linear-space structures for storing them. A general framework for designing such linear-space structures for d-dimensional data, where the dimensionality d is assumed to be a fixed constant, is based on an approach called the partition tree.

A ***partition tree*** is a rooted tree T that has at most n external nodes, where n is the number of d-dimensional points in our given set S. Each external node of a partition tree T stores a different small subset from S. Each internal node v in a partition tree T corresponds to a region of d-dimensional space, which is then divided into some number c of different cells or regions associated with v's children. For each region R associated with a child u of v, we require that all the points in u's subtree fall inside the region R. Ideally, the c different cells for v's children should easily be distinguished using a constant number of operations.

21.3.1   Quadtrees

The first partition tree data structure we discuss is the ***quadtree***. The main application for quadtrees is for sets of points that come from images, where x- and y-coordinates are integers, because the data points come from image pixels. In addition, they exhibit their best properties if the distributions of points is fairly nonuniform, with some areas being mostly empty and others being dense.

Suppose we are given a set S of n points in the plane. In addition, let R denote a square region that contains all the points of S (for example, R could be a bounding box of a 2048×2048 image that produced the set S). The quadtree data structure is a partition tree T such that the root r of T is associated with the region R. To get to the next level in T, we subdivide R into four equal-sized squares R_1, R_2, R_3, and R_4, and we associate each square R_i with a potential child of the root r. Specifically, we create a child v_i of r, if the square R_i contains a point in S. If a square R_i contains no points of S, then we create no child of r for it. This process of refining R into the squares R_1, R_2, R_3, and R_4 is called a ***split***.

The ***quadtree*** T is defined by recursively performing a split at each child v of r if necessary. That is, each child v of r has a square region R_i associated with it, and if the region R_i for v contains more than one point of S, then we perform a split at v, subdividing R_i into four equal-sized squares and repeating the above subdivision process at v. We continue in this manner, splitting squares that contain more than one point into four subsquares, and recursing on the nonempty subsquares, until we have separated all the points of S into individual squares. We then store each point p in S at the external node of T that corresponds to the smallest square in the subdivision process that contains p. We store at each internal node, v, a concise representation of the split that we performed for v.

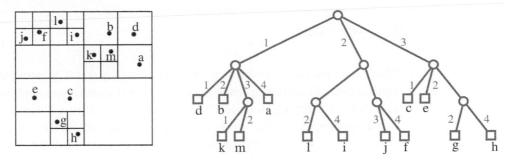

Figure 21.8: A quadtree. We illustrate an example point set and its corresponding quadtree data structure.

We illustrate an example point set and an associated quadtree in Figure 21.8. Note, however, that, contrary to the illustration, there is potentially no upper bound on the depth of a quadtree, as we have previously defined. For example, our point set S could contain two points that are very close to one another, and it may take a long sequence of splits before we separate these two points. Thus, it is customary for quadtree designers to specify some upper bound D on the depth of T. Given a set S of n points in the plane, we can construct a quadtree T for S so as to spend $O(n)$ time building each level of T. Thus, in the worst case, constructing such a depth-bounded quadtree takes $O(Dn)$ time.

Answering Range Queries with a Quadtree

One of the queries that quadtrees are often used to answer is range searching. Suppose that we are given a rectangle A aligned with the coordinate axes, and are asked to use a quadtree T to return all the points in S that are contained in A. The method for answering this query is quite simple. We start with the root r of T, and we compare the region R for r to A. If A and R do not intersect at all, then we are done—there are no points in the subtree rooted at r that fall inside A. Alternatively, if A completely contains R, then we simply enumerate all the external-node descendants of r. These are two simple cases. If instead R and A intersect, but A does not completely contain R, then we recursively perform this search on each child v of r.

In performing such a range-searching query, we can traverse the entire tree T and not produce any output in the worst case. Thus, the worst-case running time for performing a range query in a depth D quadtree, with n external nodes is $O(Dn)$. From a worst-case point of view, answering a range-searching query with a quadtree is actually worse than a brute-force search through the set S, which would take $O(n)$ time to answer a two-dimensional range query. In practice, however, the quadtree typically allows for range-searching queries to be processed faster than this.

21.3.2 k-d Trees

There is a drawback to quadtrees, which is that they do not generalize well to higher dimensions. In particular, each node in a four-dimensional analogue of a quadtree can have as many as 16 children. Each internal node in a d-dimensional quadtree can have as many as 2^d children. To overcome the out-degree drawback for storing data from dimensions higher than three, data structure designers often consider alternative partition tree structures that are binary.

Another kind of partition data structure is the k-d tree, which is similar to quadtree structure, but is binary. The k-d tree data structure is actually a family of partition tree data structures, all of which are binary partition trees for storing multidimensional data. Like the quadtree data structure, each node v in a k-d tree is associated with a rectangular region R, although in the case of k-d trees this region is not necessarily square. The difference is that when it comes time to perform a split operation for a node v in a k-d tree, it is done with a single line that is perpendicular to one of the coordinate axes. For three- or higher-dimensional data sets, this "line" is an axis-aligned hyperplane. Thus, no matter the dimensionality, a k-d tree is a binary tree, for we resolve a split by associating the part of v's region R to the "left" of the splitting line with v's left child, and associating the part of v's region R to the "right" of the splitting line with v's right child. As with the quadtree structure, we stop performing splits if the number of points in a region falls below some fixed constant threshold. (See Figure 21.9.)

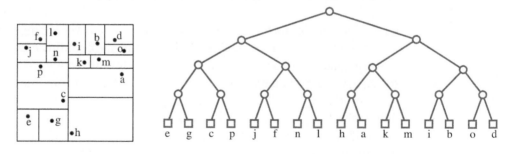

Figure 21.9: An example k-d tree.

There are two fundamentally different kinds of k-d trees, ***region-based*** k-d trees and ***point-based*** k-d trees. Region-based k-d trees are essentially binary versions of quadtrees. Each time a rectangular region R needs to be split in a region-based k-d tree, the region R is divided exactly in half by a line perpendicular to the longest side of R. If there is more than one longest side of R, then they are split in a "round-robin" fashion. On the other hand, point-based k-d trees, perform splits based on the distribution of points inside a rectangular region. The k-d tree of Figure 21.9 is point-based.

The method for splitting a rectangle R containing a subset $S' \subseteq S$ in a point-based k-d tree involves two steps. In the first step, we determine the dimension i that has the largest variation in dimension i from among those points in S'. This can be done, for example, by finding, for each dimension j, the points in S' with minimum and maximum dimension j values, and taking i to be the dimension with the largest gap between these two values. In the second step, we determine the median dimension i value from among all those points in S', and we split R with a line going through this median perpendicular to the dimension i axis. Thus, the split for R divides the set of points in S' in half, but may not divide the region R itself very evenly. Using a linear-time median-finding method (Section 9.2), this splitting step can be performed in $O(k|S'|)$ time. Therefore, the running time for building a k-d tree for a set of n points can be characterized by the following recurrence equation: $T(n) = 2T(n/2) + kn$, which is $O(kn \log n)$. Moreover, since we divide the size of the set of points associated with a node in two with each split, the height of T is $\lceil \log n \rceil$. Figure 21.9 illustrates a point-based k-d tree built using this algorithm.

The advantage of point-based k-d trees is that they are guaranteed to have nice depth and construction times. The drawback of point-based schemes is that they may give rise to "long-and-skinny" rectangular regions, which are usually considered bad for most k-d tree query methods.

Using k-d Trees for Nearest Neighbor Searching

Let us discuss how k-d trees can be used to do nearest-neighbor searching, where we are given a query point p and asked to find the point in S that is closest to p. A good way to use a k-d tree T to answer such a query is as follows. We first search down the tree T to locate the external node v with smallest rectangular region R that contains p. Any points of S that fall in R or in the region associated with v's sibling are then compared to find a current closest neighbor, q. We can then define a sphere centered at p and containing q as a current nearest-neighbor sphere, s. Given this sphere, we then perform a traversal of T (with a bottom-up traversal being preferred) to find any regions associated with external nodes of T that intersect s. If during this traversal we find a point closer than q, then we update the reference q to refer to this new point and we update the sphere s to contain this new point. We do not visit any nodes that have regions not intersecting s. When we have exhausted all possible alternatives, we output the current point q as the nearest neighbor of p. In the worst case, this method may take $O(n)$ time, but there are many different analytic and experimental analyses that suggest that the average running time is more like $O(\log n)$, using some reasonable assumptions about the distribution of points in S. In addition, there are a number of useful heuristics for speeding up this search in practice, with one of the best being the ***priority*** searching strategy, which says that we should explore subtrees of T in order of the distance of their associated regions to p.

21.4 Exercises

Reinforcement

R-21.1 What would be the worst-case space usage of a range tree, if the primary structure were not required to have $O(\log n)$ height?

R-21.2 Given a binary search tree, T, built on the x-coordinates of a set of n objects, describe an $O(n)$-time method for computing $\min_x(v)$ and $\max_x(v)$ for every node, v, in T.

R-21.3 Show that the high_y values in a priority search tree satisfy the heap-order property.

R-21.4 Argue why the algorithm for answering three-sided range-searching queries with a priority search tree is correct.

R-21.5 What is the worst-case depth of a k-d tree defined on n points in the plane? What about in higher dimensions?

R-21.6 Suppose a set S contains n two-dimensional points whose coordinates are all integers in the range $[0, N]$. What is the worst-case depth of a quadtree defined on S?

R-21.7 Draw a quadtree for the following set of points, assuming a 16×16 bounding box:

$$\{(1,2), (4,10), (14,3), (6,6), (3,15), (2,2), (3,12), (9,4), (12,14)\}.$$

R-21.8 Construct a k-d tree for the point set of Exercise R-21.7.

R-21.9 Construct a priority search tree for the point set of Exercise R-21.7.

Creativity

C-21.1 The $\min_x(v)$ and $\max_x(v)$ labels used in the two-dimensional range tree are not strictly needed. Describe an algorithm for performing a two-dimensional range-searching query in a two-dimensional range tree where each internal node of the primary structure only stores a key(v) label (which is the x-coordinate of its element). What is the running time of your method?

C-21.2 Let D be an ordered dictionary with n items implemented with a balanced search tree. Show how to implement the following method for D in time $O(\log n)$:

countAllInRange(k_1, k_2): Compute and return the number of items in D with key k such that $k_1 \leq k \leq k_2$.

Note that this method returns a single integer.

C-21.3 Give a pseudocode description of an algorithm for constructing a range tree from a set of n points in the plane in $O(n \log n)$ time.

C-21.4 Describe an efficient data structure for storing a set S of n items with ordered keys, so as to support a rankRange(a, b) method, which enumerates all the items with keys whose *rank* in S is in the range $[a, b]$, where a and b are integers in the interval $[0, n-1]$. Describe methods for object insertions and deletion, and characterize the running times for these and the rankRange method.

C-21.5 Design a static data structure (which does not support insertions and deletions) that stores a two-dimensional set S of n points and can answer, in $O(\log^2 n)$ time, queries of the form countAllInRange(a, b, c, d), which return the number of points in S with x-coordinates in the range $[a, b]$ and y-coordinates in the range $[c, d]$. What is the space used by this structure?

C-21.6 Design a data structure for answering countAllInRange queries (as defined in the previous exercise) in $O(\log n)$ time.

Hint: Think of storing auxiliary structures at each node that are "linked" to the structures at neighboring nodes.

C-21.7 Show how to extend the two-dimensional range tree so as to answer d-dimensional range-searching queries in $O(\log^d n)$ time for a set of d-dimensional points, where $d \geq 2$ is a constant.

Hint: Design a recursive data structure that builds a d-dimensional structure using $(d-1)$-dimensional structures.

C-21.8 Suppose we are given a range-searching data structure D that can answer range-searching queries for a set of n points in d-dimensional space for any fixed dimension d (like 8, 10, or 20) in time that is $O(\log^d n + k)$, where k is the number of answers. Show how to use D to answer the following queries for a set S of n rectangles in the plane:

- findAllContaining(x, y): Return an enumeration of all rectangles in S that contain the point (x, y).
- findAllIntersecting(a, b, c, d): Return an enumeration of all rectangles that intersect the rectangle with x-range $[a, b]$ and y-range $[c, d]$.

What is the running time needed to answer each of these queries?

C-21.9 Let S be a set of n intervals of the form $[a, b]$, where $a < b$. Design an efficient data structure that can answer, in $O(\log n + k)$ time, queries of the form contains(x), which asks for an enumeration of all intervals in S that contain x, where k is the number of such intervals. What is the space usage of your data structure?

C-21.10 Describe an efficient method for inserting an object into a (balanced) priority search tree. What is the running time of this method?

Applications

A-21.1 Quadtrees are often used for geometric environments defined by images, so the points involved can be normalized to be represented as pairs of fixed-precision binary numbers in the interval $[0, 1]$. Such environments also allow for quadtrees to be representable using one-dimensional search structures, as is explored in this exercise. So let (x, y) be such a point, with

$$x = 0.x_1 x_2 \ldots x_k \text{ and } y = 0.y_1 y_2 \ldots y_k,$$

in binary. Define interleave(x, y) to be the binary number, z, formed by interleaving of the binary numbers x and y, so

$$z = 0.x_1 y_1 x_2 y_2 \ldots x_k y_k,$$

in binary. Assume we have a set, S, of n such points in the plane and we have constructed a quadtree, T, for this set of points. Let Z be an array that contains the points of S in lexicographical order by the results of calling interleave on each point. Show that for any node, v, in T, the descendants of v are stored in a contiguous subarray of Z and there is no point in this subarray that is not a descendant of v in T.

A-21.2 In some computer graphics and computer gaming applications, in order to save space, we might like to store a set of two-dimensional points in a single data structure that can be used for both nearest-neighbor queries and range searching. We have already discussed above how a k-d tree can be used to answer nearest-neighbor queries with good expected-time behavior. Show that a (round-robin) k-d tree defined on n two-dimensional points can also be used to answer range-search queries in $O(\sqrt{n} + s)$ time, where s is the number of points output by the query.

A-21.3 In some applications, such as in computer vision, an input set of two-dimensional points can be assumed to be given as pairs of integers, rather than arbitrary real numbers. Suppose, then, that you are given a set of n two-dimensional points such that each coordinate is in the range $[0, 4n]$. Show that you can construct a priority search tree for this set of points in $O(n)$ time.

A-21.4 In applications involving the use of quadtrees in memory-constrained devices, such as smartphones, we often want to optimize the data structure to make it more space efficient. One obvious improvement is to take a standard quadtree, T, and replace each chain of nodes having only one child with a single edge. This gives us a data structure known as the ***compressed quadtree***. Describe an efficient method for constructing a compressed quadtree for a set of n two-dimensional points. What is the time and space complexity for your algorithm?

A-21.5 A higher-dimensional version of a quadtree is known as an ***octree***, since, in three dimensions it divides each cube into 8 subcubes and recursively constructs an octree for each nonempty subcube as a child. Suppose we are given such a three-dimensional structure, but we are only interested in two of the three dimensions, since we can only display two-dimensional images on a computer screen. Describe an efficient method for converting an octree into a quadtree defined on two of the dimensions used to construct the octree.

A-21.6 When the Sload Digital Sky Survey decided to create a data structure for storing the objects identified by their projects, they needed a method for searching for two-dimensional points that are on a sphere rather than being in a rectangle. So they started with a sphere, cut it into quarters by two perpendicular great circles going through the poles and then into eight pieces by one more cut using a great circle through the equator. This divided the sphere into eight regions that "almost" equilateral triangles. Viewing each region as a perfect equilateral triangle, describe a recursive way to subdivide each one of these triangles that results in a set of children that are also equilaterial triangles, in a fashion suggestive of a quadtree. Describe how your structure could be used to effectively answer circular range-search queries to find all the points inside a given circle on this sphere.

A-21.7 The quadtree is often used by people who never worry about its worst-case depth being high. There is a good reason for this belief, if one can assume some randomness exists for the input set of points. Use a Chernoff bound (Section 19.5) to show that the height of a quadtree defined on n points in the unit square chosen uniformly and independently at random is $O(\log n)$ with high probability.

Hint: If we divide a square into four equal-sized squares, and assign n points uniformly and independently at random to the square, consider the probability that any subsquare has more than $n/2$ of the points.

A-21.8 In computer graphics and computer gaming environments, a common heuristic is to approximate a complex two-dimensional object by a smallest enclosing rectangle whose sides are parallel to the coordinate axes, which is known as a ***bounding box***. Using this technique allows system designers to generalize range searching over points to more complex objects. So, suppose you are given a collection of n complex two-dimensional objects, together with a set of their bounding boxes,

$$\mathcal{S} = \{R_1, R_2, \ldots, R_n\}.$$

Suppose further that for some reason you have a data structure, D, that can store n four-dimensional points so as to answer four-dimensional range-search queries in $O(\log^3 n + s)$ time, where s is the number of points in the query range. Explain how you can use D to answer two-dimensional range queries for the rectangles in $\mathcal{S}$, given a query rectangle, R, would return every bounding box, R_i, in $\mathcal{S}$, such that R_i is completely contained inside R. Your query should run in $O(\log^3 n + s)$ time, where s is the number of bounding boxes that are output as being completely inside the query range, R.

A-21.9 Consider the previous exercise, but instead of explaining how to use D to answer box-containment range queries, now explain how to build an efficient data structure, D, that can store four-dimensional range queries for four-dimensional points in $O(\log^3 n + s)$ time, where s is the number of answers. What is the space complexity of your data structure, D?

Chapter Notes

Multi-dimensional search trees are discussed in books by Mehlhorn [159], Samet [181, 182], and Wood [217]. Please see these books for an extensive discussion of the history of multidimensional search trees, including various data structures for solving range queries. Priority search trees are due to McCreight [149], although Vuillemin [213] introduced this structure earlier under the name "Cartesian trees." They are also known as "treaps," as described by McCreight [149] and Seidel and Aragon [191]. Edelsbrunner [61] shows how priority search trees can be used to answer two-dimensional range queries. Arya *et al.* [15, 16] present the balanced box decomposition tree and show it can be used for approximate nearest-neighbor and range searching. The reader interested in recent developments for range-searching data structures is referred to the book chapters by Agarwal [3, 4] or the survey paper by Matouŝek [147].

Chapter

22

Computational Geometry

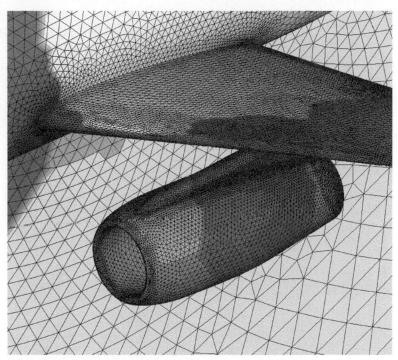

Domain decomposition for parallel processing of a wing-body-nacelle-pylon configuration. U.S. government photo. NASA.

Contents

22.1 Operations on Geometric Objects 625

22.2 Convex Hulls 630

22.3 Segment Intersection 638

22.4 Finding a Closest Pair of Points 642

22.5 Exercises 646

A common problem in robotics is to identify a trajectory from a starting point, s, to a target point, t, that avoids a certain obstacle. Among the many possible trajectories, suppose we would like to find one that is as short as possible. Let us assume that the environment is mapped out as a two-dimensional map and the obstacle is a connected region, P. We can compute a shortest trajectory for a robot to move from s to t while avoiding P with the following strategy (see Figure 22.1):

1. We determine whether the line segment $\ell = \overline{st}$ intersects P. If it does not intersect, then ℓ is the shortest trajectory avoiding P.
2. Otherwise, if $\overline{st}$ intersects P, then we compute a geometric object, H, known as the ***convex hull***, from the vertices of polygon P plus points s and t. This object can be visualized by imagining that there are two rubber bands, connecting s and t, with one touching P on the left and one touching P on the right. One of these chains would therefore be traversed by going clockwise from s to t and the other by going counterclockwise from s to t.
3. We select and return the shortest of these two polygonal chains with endpoints s and t on H.

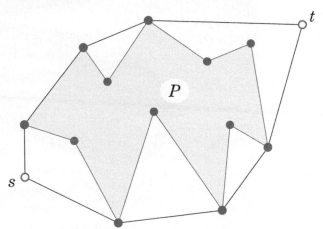

Figure 22.1: An example shortest trajectory from a point, s, to a point, t, avoiding a polygonal region, P. The shortest trajectory in this case is the clockwise chain from s to t.

Motivated by this, and other problems dealing with geometric objects, such as points, lines, and polygons, this chapter is directed at ***computational geometry***, which studies data structures and algorithms for dealing with geometric data. We include a discussion of the convex hull problem, as well as a general method for designing efficient geometric algorithms, called the ***plane-sweep*** technique. We illustrate the applicability of this technique by showing how it can be used to solve two-dimensional computational geometry problems, by reducing them to a series of one-dimensional problems. Specifically, we apply the plane-sweep technique to the computation of the intersections of a set of orthogonal line segments and to the identification of a closest pair of points from a set of points.

22.1 Operations on Geometric Objects

Geometric algorithms take geometric objects of various types as their inputs. The basic geometric objects in the plane are points, lines, segments, and polygons.

There are many ways of representing planar geometric objects. Rather than give separate detailed data structures for representing points, lines, segments, and polygons, however, which would be appropriate for a book on geometric algorithms, we instead assume we have intuitive representations for these objects. For example, a two-dimensional point could be represented by a pair of numbers, a line segment could be represented by a pair of points, a line could be represented by a linear equation, and a polygon could be represented by a circular sequence of points. Still, even with our assumption that geometric objects will have intuitive representations, we nevertheless discuss a few of the algorithmic issues related to working with geometric objects in this section.

Lines

We can represent a line l as a triple, (a, b, c), such that these values are the coefficients a, b, and c of the linear equation,

$$ax + by + c = 0,$$

associated with l. Alternatively, we may specify instead two different points, q_1 and q_2, and associate them with the line that goes through both. Given the Cartesian coordinates (x_1, y_1) of q_1 and (x_2, y_2) of q_2, such that these points have distinct x- and y-coordinates, the equation of the line l through q_1 and q_2 is given by

$$\frac{x - x_1}{x_2 - x_1} = \frac{y - y_1}{y_2 - y_1},$$

from which we derive the following:

$$
\begin{aligned}
a &= y_2 - y_1 \\
b &= x_1 - x_2 \\
c &= y_1(x_2 - x_1) - x_1(y_2 - y_1).
\end{aligned}
$$

Line Segments

A line segment s is typically represented by the pair (p, q) of points in the plane that form s's endpoints. We may also represent s by giving the line through it, together with a range of x- and y-coordinates, that restrict this line to the segment s. (Why is it insufficient to include just a range of x- or y-coordinates?)

Intersection of Two Lines

One of the most important operations that geometric objects should support is the *intersection* operation. For example, given two lines l_1 and l_2, we may want to know whether they *intersect*, that is, if they have one or more points in common. If l_1 and l_2 are represented by their equations

$$a_1x + b_1y + c_1 = 0 \quad \text{and} \quad a_2x + b_2y + c_2 = 0,$$

then l_1 and l_2 intersect if and only if one of the following two conditions is satisfied.

- The determinant

$$\begin{vmatrix} a_1 & b_1 \\ a_2 & b_2 \end{vmatrix} = a_1b_2 - a_2b_1$$

  is nonzero, which implies that the two lines intersect in exactly one point.
- There exists a positive constant k such that: $a_2 = ka_1$, $b_2 = kb_1$, and $c_2 = kc_1$, which implies that the two lines are coincident.

These tests are easily carried out in $O(1)$ time.

Intersection of Two Line Segments

Testing whether two segments s_1 and s_2 intersect, that is, if they have one or more points in common, is disappointingly more complicated, however. The reader is encouraged to think about this problem before reading on.

The first approach that might come to mind is to test whether the lines l_1 and l_2 through s_1 and s_2, respectively, intersect. We distinguish three cases:

- If l_1 and l_2 do not intersect, then we know that s_1 and s_2 also do not intersect and we return a negative answer.
- If l_1 and l_2 intersect and are coincident, we test whether the ranges of x-coordinates of s_1 and s_2 overlap, and similarly for the y-coordinates.
- Otherwise, we compute the intersection point q of l_1 and l_2. The coordinates of q are given by the solution of the system of two equations in two unknowns that are derived from the equations of lines l_1 and l_2 (which can be specified as formulas, with a little extra work). Given the intersection point q, we can then test whether point q is included both in s_1 and s_2. This can be done by checking that the x-coordinate of q lies in the range of the x-coordinates of both s_1 and s_2, and similarly for the y-coordinate of q.

This testing method is admittedly somewhat complicated. An alternative approach is based on the concept of *orientation*, which we discuss next.

Point Orientation Testing

An important geometric relationship, which arises in many geometric algorithms, and particularly for convex hull construction, is **orientation**. Given an ordered triplet (p, q, r) of points, we say that (p, q, r) makes a **left turn** and is oriented **counterclockwise** if the angle that stays on the left-hand side when going from p to q and then to r is less than π. If the angle on the right-hand side is less than π instead, then we say that (p, q, r) makes a **right turn** and is oriented **clockwise**. (See Figure 22.2.) It is possible that the angles of the left- and right-hand sides are both equal to π, in which case the three points actually do not make a turn, and we say that their orientation is **collinear**.

Given a triplet (p_1, p_2, p_3) of three points $p_1 = (x_1, y_1)$, $p_2 = (x_2, y_2)$, and $p_3 = (x_3, y_3)$, in the plane, let $\Delta(p_1, p_2, p_3)$ be the determinant defined by

$$\Delta(p_1, p_2, p_3) = \begin{vmatrix} x_1 & y_1 & 1 \\ x_2 & y_2 & 1 \\ x_3 & y_3 & 1 \end{vmatrix} = x_1 y_2 - x_2 y_1 + x_3 y_1 - x_1 y_3 + x_2 y_3 - x_3 y_2. \quad (22.1)$$

The function $\Delta(p_1, p_2, p_3)$ is often called the "signed area" function, because its absolute value is twice the area of the (possibly degenerate) triangle formed by the points p_1, p_2, and p_3. In addition, we have the following important fact relating this function to orientation testing.

Theorem 22.1: *The orientation of a triplet (p_1, p_2, p_3) of points in the plane is counterclockwise, clockwise, or collinear, depending on whether $\Delta(p_1, p_2, p_3)$ is positive, negative, or zero, respectively.*

We sketch the proof of Theorem 22.1; we leave the details as an exercise (R-22.2). In Figure 22.2, we show a triplet (p_1, p_2, p_3) of points with $x_1 < x_2 < x_3$. Clearly, this triplet makes a left turn if the slope of segment $p_2 p_3$ is greater than the slope of segment $p_1 p_2$. This is expressed by the following question:

$$\text{Is } \frac{y_3 - y_2}{x_3 - x_2} > \frac{y_2 - y_1}{x_2 - x_1} \text{ ?} \quad (22.2)$$

By the expansion of $\Delta(p_1, p_2, p_3)$ shown in 22.1, we can verify that inequality 22.2 is equivalent to $\Delta(p_1, p_2, p_3) > 0$.

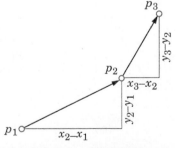

Figure 22.2: An example of a left turn. The differences between the coordinates between p_1 and p_2 and the coordinates of p_2 and p_3 are also illustrated.

In fact, there is a quick way to show the above equivalence using some facts about determinants. By a standard property of determinants, we can subtract a row from another row without changing the determinant. Hence,

$$\Delta(p_1, p_2, p_3) = \begin{vmatrix} x_1 & y_1 & 1 \\ x_2 & y_2 & 1 \\ x_3 & y_3 & 1 \end{vmatrix}$$

$$= \begin{vmatrix} x_1 & y_1 & 1 \\ (x_2 - x_1) & (y_2 - y_1) & 0 \\ (x_3 - x_2) & (y_3 - y_2) & 0 \end{vmatrix}$$

$$= (x_2 - x_1)(y_3 - y_2) - (y_2 - y_1)(x_3 - x_2).$$

Thus, testing if $\Delta(p_1, p_2, p_3) > 0$ is equivalent to answering question 22.2.

Example 22.2: *Using the notion of orientation, let us consider the problem of testing whether two line segments s_1 and s_2 intersect. Specifically, Let $s_1 = \overline{p_1 q_1}$ and $s_2 = \overline{p_2 q_2}$ be two segments in the plane. s_1 and s_2 intersect if and only if **one of** the following two conditions is verified:*

1.   (a) (p_1, q_1, p_2) *and* (p_1, q_1, q_2) *have different orientations,* **and**
     (b) (p_2, q_2, p_1) *and* (p_2, q_2, q_1) *have different orientations.*
2.   (a) (p_1, q_1, p_2), (p_1, q_1, q_2), (p_2, q_2, p_1), *and* (p_2, q_2, q_1) *are all collinear,* **and**
     (b) *the x-projections of s_1 and s_2 intersect,* **and**
     (c) *the y-projections of s_1 and s_2 intersect.*

Condition 1 is illustrated in Figure 22.3. We also show, in Table 22.4, the respective orientation of the triplets (p_1, q_1, p_2), (p_1, q_1, q_2), (p_2, q_2, p_1), and (p_2, q_2, q_1) in each of the four cases for Condition 1. A complete proof is left as an exercise (R-22.3). Note that the conditions also hold if s_1 and/or s_2 is a degenerate segment with coincident endpoints.

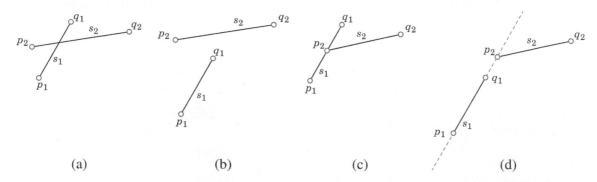

(a)   (b)   (c)   (d)

Figure 22.3: Examples illustrating four cases of Condition 1 of Example 22.2.

case	(p_1, q_1, p_2)	(p_1, q_1, q_2)	(p_2, q_2, p_1)	(p_2, q_2, q_1)	intersection?
(a)	CCW	CW	CW	CCW	yes
(b)	CCW	CW	CW	CW	no
(c)	COLL	CW	CW	CCW	yes
(d)	COLL	CW	CW	CW	no

Table 22.4: The four cases shown in Figure 22.3 for the orientations specified by Condition 1 of Example 22.2, where CCW stands for counterclockwise, CW stands for clockwise, and COLL stands for collinear.

Polygons

We can represent a polygon P by a cyclical sequence of points, called the **vertices** of P. (See Figure 22.5.) The segments between consecutive vertices of P are called the **edges** of P. Polygon P is said to be **simple**, if intersections between pairs of edges of P happen only at a common endpoint vertex. A polygon is **convex** if it is simple and all its internal angles are less than π.

Our discussion of different ways of representing points, lines, segments, and polygons is not meant to be exhaustive. It is meant simply to indicate the different ways we can implement these geometric objects.

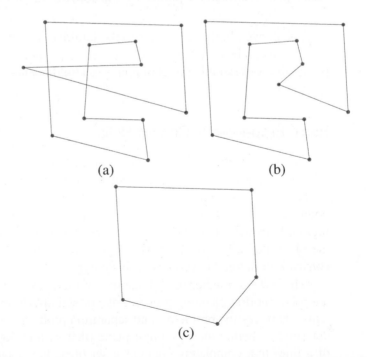

(a)   (b)

(c)

Figure 22.5: Examples of polygons: (a) intersecting, (b) simple, (c) convex.

22.2   Convex Hulls

One of the most studied geometric problems is that of computing the convex hull of a set of points. Informally speaking, the **convex hull** of a set of points in the plane is the shape taken by a rubber band that is placed "around the points" and allowed to shrink to a state of equilibrium. (See Figure 22.6.)

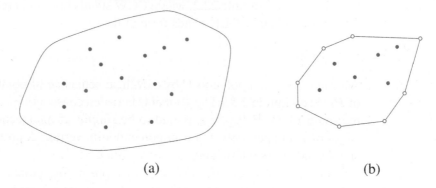

(a)   (b)

Figure 22.6: The convex hull of a set of points in the plane: (a) an example "rubber band" placed around the points; (b) the convex hull of the points.

The convex hull corresponds to the intuitive notion of a "boundary" of a set of points and can be used to approximate the shape of a complex object. Indeed, computing the convex hull of a set of points is a fundamental operation in computational geometry.

Basic Properties of Convex Hulls

We say that a region R is **convex** if any time two points p and q are in R, the entire line segment $\overline{pq}$ is also in R. The **convex hull** of a set of points S is the boundary of the smallest convex region that contains all the points of S inside it or on its boundary. The notion of "smallest" refers to either the perimeter or area of the region, both definitions being equivalent. The convex hull of a set of points S in the plane defines a convex polygon, and the points of S on the boundary of the convex hull define the vertices of this polygon.

There are a number of applications of the convex hull problem, in addition to the robot motion planning problem mentioned above, including partitioning problems, shape testing problems, and separation problems. For example, if we wish to determine whether there is a half-plane (that is, a region of the plane on one side of a line) that completely contains a set of points A but completely avoids a set of points B, it is enough to compute the convex hulls of A and B and determine whether they intersect each other.

There are many interesting geometric properties associated with convex hulls. The following theorem provides an alternate characterization of the points that are on the convex hull and of those that are not.

Theorem 22.3: *Let S be a set of planar points with convex hull H. Then*

- *A pair of points a and b of S form an edge of H if and only if all the other points of S are contained on one side of the line through a and b.*
- *A point p of S is a vertex of H if and only if there exists a line l through p, such that all the other points of S are contained in the same half-plane delimited by l (that is, they are all on the same side of l).*
- *A point p of S is not a vertex of H if and only if p is contained in the interior of a triangle formed by three other points of S or in the interior of a segment formed by two other points of S.*

The properties expressed by Theorem 22.3 are illustrated in Figure 22.7. A complete proof of them is left as an exercise (R-22.4). As a consequence of Theorem 22.3, we can immediately verify that, in any set S of points in the plane, the following *critical* points are always on the boundary of the convex hull of S:

- A point with minimum or maximum x-coordinate
- A point with minimum or maximum y-coordinate.

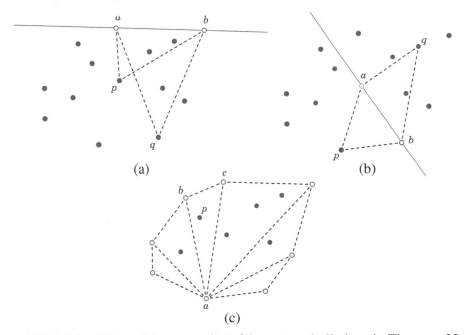

Figure 22.7: Illustration of the properties of the convex hull given in Theorem 22.3: (a) points a and b form an edge of the convex hull; (b) points a and b do not form an edge of the convex hull; (c) point p is not on the convex hull.

22.2.1   The Gift Wrapping Algorithm

Theorem 22.3 basically states that we can identify a particular point, say one with minimum y-coordinate, that provides an initial starting configuration for an algorithm that computes the convex hull. The ***gift wrapping*** algorithm for computing the convex hull of a set of points in the plane is based on just such a starting point and can be intuitively described as follows (see Figure 22.8):

1. View the points as pegs implanted in a level field, and imagine that we tie a rope to the peg corresponding to the point a with minimum y-coordinate (and minimum x-coordinate if there are ties). Call a the ***anchor point***, and note that a is a vertex of the convex hull.
2. Pull the rope to the right of the anchor point and rotate it counterclockwise until it touches another peg, which is the next vertex of the convex hull.
3. Continue rotating the rope counterclockwise, identifying a new vertex of the convex hull at each step, until the rope gets back to the anchor point.

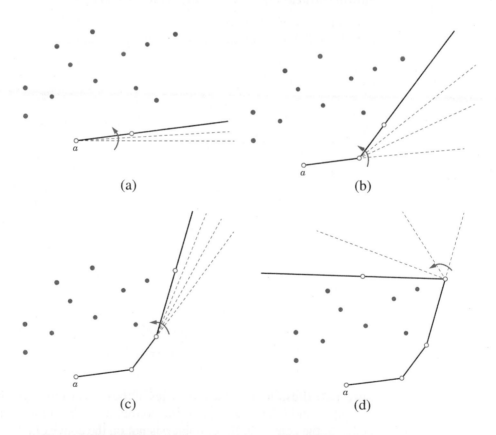

(a)   (b)

(c)   (d)

Figure 22.8: Initial four wrapping steps of the gift wrapping algorithm.

Using Orientation Testing for the Wrapping Step

Each time we rotate our "rope" around the current peg until it hits another point, we perform an operation called a ***wrapping*** step. Geometrically, a wrapping step involves starting from a given line L known to be tangent to the convex hull at the current anchor point a, and determining the line through a and another point in the set making the smallest angle with L. Implementing this wrapping step does not require trigonometric functions and angle calculations, however. Instead, we can use the following theorem, which follows from Theorem 22.3.

Theorem 22.4: *Let S be a set of points in the plane, and let a be a vertex of the convex hull, H, of S. The next vertex of H, going counterclockwise from a, is the point, p, such that triplet (a, p, q) makes a left turn with every other point q of S.*

Details of the Gift Wrapping Algorithm

We give the details in Algorithm 22.9, which starts with the set, S, of n points and a point, a, in S on the convex hull, H, of S, which could be, say, a point with minimum x-coordinate. Note that finding such a point, a, can easily be done in $O(n)$ time.

Algorithm GiftWrap(S, a):

> ***Input:*** A set, S, of points in the plane beginning with point a, such that a is on the convex hull of S
>
> ***Output:*** List H of the convex hull vertices of S in counterclockwise order

> $H \leftarrow [a]$
> **repeat**
> > Let b be the last element in H
> > Let p be a vertex in S such that $p \neq b$
> > **for** each point, q, in S, with $q \neq p$ and $q \neq b$ **do**
> > > **if** (b, p, q) forms a right turn **then**
> > > > $p \leftarrow q$
> > Add p to the end of the list H
> **until** $p = a$
> **return** H

Algorithm 22.9: The gift wrapping algorithm. Here we make the simplifying assumption that no three of the points in S are collinear.

Analysis of the Gift Wrapping Algorithm

Let us analyze the running time of the gift wrapping algorithm. Let n be the number of points of S, and let $h \leq n$ be the number of vertices of the convex hull H of S. Let $p_0, \ldots, p_{h-1}$ be the vertices of H. Finding the anchor point $a = p_0$ takes $O(n)$ time. Since with each wrapping step of the algorithm we discover a new vertex of the convex hull, the number of wrapping steps is equal to h.

Step i is a minimum-finding computation based on finding a point, p, such that every other point, q, in S forms a left turn when going from b to p to q. This step runs in $O(n)$ time, since determining the orientation of a triplet takes $O(1)$ time and we must examine all the points of S to find the smallest with respect to the orientation test. Our description assumed that no three points in S were collinear, but the above algorithm can be extended to handing this case without effecting the asymptotic performance of the algorithm. Thus, we can summarize the performance of the gift wrapping algorithm with the following theorem.

Theorem 22.5: *Given a set, S, of n points in the plane, the gift wrapping algorithm constructs a list representation of the convex hull of S in $O(nh)$ time, where h is the number of vertices on the boundary of the convex hull.*

Output Sensitivity

We note that h can be as large as n, that is, when all the points in S are vertices on the convex hull; hence, in the worst case, this algorithm runs in $O(n^2)$ time. Still, h can be as small as 3, in which case the gift wrapping algorithm would run in $O(n)$ time. Thus, there is a large difference between the best-case and worst-case performance of the gift wrapping algorithm.

This algorithm is nevertheless reasonably efficient in practice, however, for it can take advantage of the (common) situation when h, the number of hull points, is small relative to the number of input points, n. That is, this algorithm is said to be an ***output sensitive*** algorithm—an algorithm whose running time depends on the size of the output. Gift wrapping has a running time that varies between linear and quadratic, and is efficient if the convex hull has few vertices. For instance, if we choose n points uniformly and independently at random in the interior of a rectangle, then the expected number of points on their convex hull is $O(\log n)$.

We discuss in the next section an algorithm that is efficient for all hull sizes, although it is slightly more complicated.

22.2.2   The Graham Scan Algorithm

A convex hull algorithm that has an efficient running time no matter how many points are on the boundary of the convex is the ***Graham scan*** algorithm. The Graham scan algorithm for computing the convex hull H of a set P of n points in the plane consists of the following three phases:

1. We find a point a of P that is a vertex of H and call it the ***anchor point***. We can, for example, pick as our anchor point a the point in P with minimum y-coordinate (and minimum x-coordinate if there are ties).

2. We sort the remaining points of P (that is, $P - \{a\}$) radially around a, and let S be the resulting sorted list of points. (See Figure 22.10.) In the list S, the points of P appear sorted counterclockwise "by angle" with respect to the anchor point a, although no explicit computation of angles is performed.

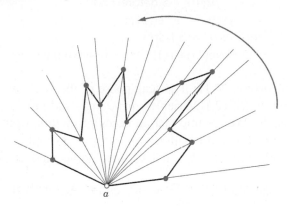

Figure 22.10: Sorting around the anchor point in the Graham scan algorithm.

3. After adding the anchor point a at the first and last position of S, we ***scan*** through the points in S in (radial) order, maintaining at each step a list H storing a convex chain "surrounding" the points scanned so far. Each time we consider new point p, we perform the following test:

   (a) If p forms a left turn with the last two points in H, or if H contains fewer than two points, then add p to the end of H.
   (b) Otherwise, remove the last point in H and repeat the test for p.

   We stop when we return to the anchor point a, at which point H stores the vertices of the convex hull of P in counterclockwise order.

   The details of the scan phase (Phase 3) are spelled out in Algorithm Scan, described in Algorithm 22.11.

Algorithm Scan(S, a):

> **Input:** A list S of points in the plane beginning with point a, such that a is on
> the convex hull of S and the remaining points of S are sorted counterclock-
> wise around a
>
> **Output:** List S with only convex hull vertices remaining
>
> S.insertLast(a)   // add a copy of a at the end of S
> $prev \leftarrow S$.first()   // so that $prev = a$ initially
> $curr \leftarrow S$.after($prev$)   // the next point is on the current convex chain
> **repeat**
>> $next \leftarrow S$.after($curr$)   // advance
>> **if** points (point($prev$), point($curr$), point($next$)) make a left turn **then**
>>> $prev \leftarrow curr$
>>
>> **else**
>>> S.remove($curr$)   // point $curr$ is not in the convex hull
>>> $prev \leftarrow S$.before($prev$)
>>
>> $curr \leftarrow S$.after($prev$)
>
> **until** $curr = S$.last()
> S.remove(S.last())   // remove the copy of a

Algorithm 22.11: The scan phase of the Graham scan convex hull algorithm. (See
Figure 22.12.) Variables *prev*, *curr*, and *next* are positions (Section 2.2.2) of the
list S. We assume that an accessor method point(pos) is defined that returns the
point stored at position *pos*. We give a simplified description of the algorithm that
works only if S has at least three points, and no three points of S are collinear.

Analysis of the Graham Scan Algorithm

Let us now analyze the running time of the Graham scan algorithm, which is illustrated in Figure 22.12. We denote the number of points in P (and S) with n. The
first phase (finding the anchor point) clearly takes $O(n)$ time. The second phase
(sorting the points around the anchor point) takes $O(n \log n)$ time provided we
use one of the asymptotically optimal sorting algorithms, such as heap-sort (Section 5.4) or merge-sort (Section 8.1). The analysis of the scan (third) phase is more
subtle. To analyze the scan phase of the Graham scan algorithm, let us look more
closely at the **repeat** loop of Algorithm 22.11. At each iteration of the loop, either
variable *next* advances forward by one position in the list S (successful **if** test), or
variable *next* stays at the same position but a point is removed from S (unsuccessful
if test). Hence, the number of iterations of the **repeat** loop is at most $2n$. Therefore,
each statement of algorithm Scan is executed at most $2n$ times. Since each statement requires the execution of $O(1)$ elementary operations in turn, algorithm Scan
takes $O(n)$ time. In conclusion, the running time of the Graham scan algorithm is
dominated by the second phase, where sorting is performed. Thus, the Graham
scan algorithm runs in $O(n \log n)$ time.

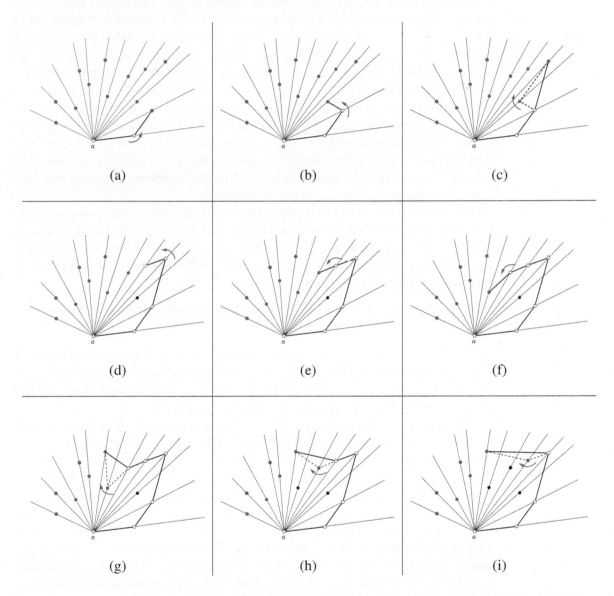

Figure 22.12: Third phase of the Graham scan algorithm (see Algorithm 22.11).

22.3 Segment Intersection

The next problem we consider is that of finding all the intersecting pairs among a set of n line segments. Of course, we could apply a brute-force algorithm to check every pair of segments to see whether they intersect. Since the number of pairs is $n(n-1)/2$, this algorithm takes $O(n^2)$ time, since we can test any pair for intersection in constant time. If all the pairs intersect, this algorithm is optimal. Still, we would like to have a faster method for the case where the number of intersecting pairs is small or there are no intersections at all. Specifically, if s is the number of intersecting pairs, we would like to have an output sensitive algorithm whose running time depends on both n and s. We shall present an algorithm that uses the plane-sweep technique and runs in $O(n \log n + s)$ time for the case when the input set of segments consists of n **orthogonal segments**, meaning that each segment in the set is either horizontal or vertical.

Before we proceed with our algorithm, we make a slight digression to review a problem discussed previously in this book. This problem is the one-dimensional range-searching problem, in which we wish to dynamically maintain a dictionary of numbers (that is, points on a number line), subject to insertions and deletions and queries of the following form:

findAllInRange(k_1, k_2): Return a list of all the elements in D with key k, such that $k_1 \le k \le k_2$.

We show in Section 3.2 how we can use any balanced binary search tree to maintain such a dictionary in order to achieve $O(\log n)$ time for insertion and removal, and $O(\log n + s)$ time for answering findAllInRange queries, where n is the number of points in the dictionary and s is the number of returned points in the range.

Let us return to the problem at hand, which is to compute all intersecting pairs of segments from a collection of n horizontal and vertical segments. The main idea of the algorithm for solving this problem is to reduce this two-dimensional problem to a collection of one-dimensional range-searching problems. In so doing, we are going to make use of a technique known as **plane sweeping**. In using this technique, we solve a static two-dimensional problem by imagining that we sweep the plane with a vertical line, L. During the sweep, we maintain various data structures for the objects that interact with L, and at various **events** we pause the sweep to update and/or query these data structures. In the case of orthogonal segment intersection, for each vertical segment v, we consider an event corresponding to a stopping of L at the vertical line $l(v)$ through v, and plunge into the "one-dimensional world" of line $l(v)$. (See Figure 22.13.) Only the vertical segment v and the intersections of horizontal segments with $l(v)$ exist in this world. In particular, segment v corresponds to an interval of $l(v)$, a horizontal segment h intersecting $l(v)$ corresponds to a point on $l(v)$, and the horizontal segments crossing v correspond to the points on $l(v)$ contained in the interval.

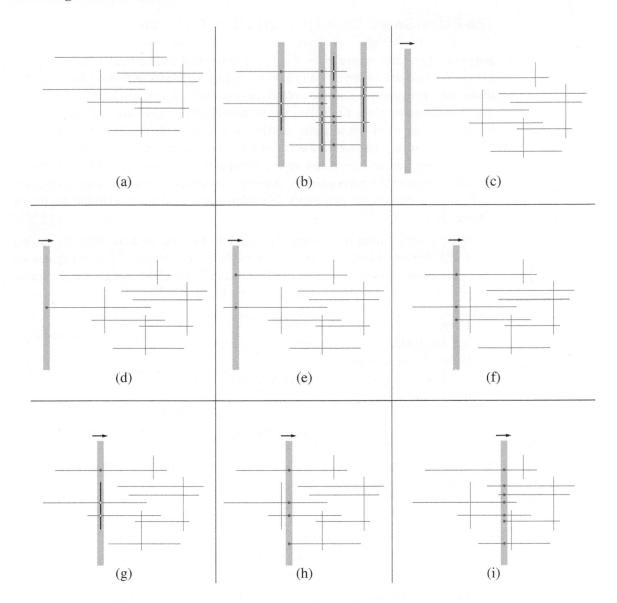

Figure 22.13: Plane sweep for orthogonal segment intersection: (a) a set of horizontal and vertical segments; (b) the collection of one-dimensional range-search problems; (c) beginning of the plane sweep (the ordered dictionary S of horizontal segments is empty); (d) the first (left-endpoint) event, causing an insertion into S; (e) the second (left-endpoint) event, causing another insertion into S; (f) the third (left-endpoint) event, causing yet another insertion into S; (g) the first vertical-segment event, causing a range search in S (two intersections reported); (h) the next (left-endpoint) event, causing an insertion into S; (i) a left-endpoint event three events later, causing an insertion into S.

The Plane-Sweep Segment Intersection Algorithm

Suppose, then, that we are given a set of n horizontal and vertical segments in the plane. We will determine all pairs of intersecting segments in this set by using the **plane sweep** technique and the collective approach suggested by the above idea. This algorithm involves simulating the sweeping of a vertical line, L, over the segments, moving from left to right, starting at a location to the left of all the input segments. During the sweep, the set of horizontal segments currently intersected by the sweep line is maintained by means of insertions into and removals from a dictionary ordered by y-coordinate. When the sweep encounters a vertical segment v, a range query on the dictionary is performed to find the horizontal segments intersecting v.

Specifically, during the sweep, we maintain an ordered dictionary, S, storing horizontal segments with their keys given by their y-coordinates. The sweep pauses at certain **events** that trigger the **actions** shown in Table 22.14, which are illustrated above in Figure 22.13. We give the details in Algorithm 22.15.

Event	Action
left endpoint of a horizontal segment h	insert h into dictionary S
right endpoint of a horizontal segment h	remove h from dictionary S
vertical segment v	perform a range search on S with selection range given by the y-coordinates of the endpoints of v

Table 22.14: Events triggering actions in the plane-sweep algorithm for orthogonal segment intersection.

Algorithm SegmentIntersect(C):
    Input: A collection, C, of horizontal and vertical line segments
    Output: All the intersecting horizontal-vertical pairs of segments in C
    Let S be an initially empty dictionary of objects ordered by y-coordinates
    Let E be a sorted listing of the segments in C by x-coordinates
    for each element, e, in E in sorted order **do**
        if e is a left endpoint of a horizontal segment, $h = ([x_1, x_2],\ y)$ **then**
            insert h into S with key y
        else if e is a right endpoint of a horizontal segment, $h = ([x_1, x_2],\ y)$ **then**
            remove h from S using the key y
        else if e is a vertical segment, $v = (x,\ [y_1, y_2])$ **then**
            Report all segments in S in the range $[y_1, y_2]$ as intersecting v

Algorithm 22.15: Orthogonal segment intersection reporting algorithm.

Analysis of the Plane-Sweep Line Intersection Algorithm

To analyze the running time of this plane-sweep algorithm, first note that we must identify all the events and sort them by x-coordinate. An event is either an endpoint of a horizontal segment or a vertical segment. Hence, the number of events is at most $2n$. When sorting the events, we compare them by x-coordinate, which takes $O(1)$ time. Using one of the asymptotically optimal sorting algorithms, such as heap-sort (Section 5.4) or merge-sort (Section 8.1), we can order the events in $O(n \log n)$ time. The operations performed on the dictionary S are insertions, removals, and range searches. Each time an operation is executed, the size of S is at most $2n$.

We can implement S as a balanced binary search tree (Chapter 4), so that insertions and deletions each take $O(\log n)$ time. As we have reviewed above, range searching in an n-element ordered dictionary can be performed in $O(\log n + s)$ time, using $O(n)$ space, where s is the number of items reported. Let us characterize, then, the running time of a range search triggered by a vertical segment v as

$$O(\log n + s(v)),$$

where $s(v)$ is the number of horizontal segments currently in the dictionary S that intersect v. Thus, indicating the set of vertical segments with V, the running time of the sweep is

$$O\left(2n \log n + \sum_{v \in V} (\log n + s(v)) \right).$$

Since the sweep goes through all the segments, the sum of $s(v)$ over all the vertical segments encountered is equal to the total number s of intersecting pairs of segments. Hence, we conclude that the sweep takes time $O(n \log n + s)$.

In summary, the complete segment intersection algorithm, outlined above, consists of the event sorting step followed by the sweep step. Sorting the events takes $O(n \log n)$ time, while sweeping takes $O(n \log n + s)$ time. Thus, the running time of the algorithm is $O(n \log n + s)$. This gives us the following.

Theorem 22.6: *Given a collection, C, of n horizontal and vertical line segments in the plane, we can report all pairs of intersecting horizontal-vertical pairs of segments in $O(n \log n + s)$ time, where s is the number of pairs.*

Thus, we have an efficient output-sensitive algorithm for orthogonal line segment intersection reporting.

22.4   Finding a Closest Pair of Points

Another geometric problem that can be solved using the plane-sweep technique involves the concept of *proximity*, which is the relationship of *distance* that exists between geometric objects. Specifically, we focus on the *closest pair* problem, which consists of finding a pair of points p and q that are at a minimum distance from each other in a set of n points. This pair is said to be a closest pair. We will use the Euclidean definition of the distance between two points a and b:

$$\text{dist}(a, b) = \sqrt{(x(a) - x(b))^2 + (y(a) - y(b))^2},$$

where $x(p)$ and $y(p)$ respectively denote the x- and y-coordinates of the point p. Applications of the closest pair problem include the verification of mechanical parts and integrated circuits, where it is important that certain separation rules between components be respected.

A straightforward "brute-force" algorithm for solving the closest pair problem is to compute the distance between every pair of points and select a pair with minimum distance. Since the number of pairs is $n(n-1)/2$, this algorithm takes $O(n^2)$ time. We can apply a more clever strategy, however.

It turns out that we can effectively apply the plane-sweep technique to the closest pair problem. We solve the closest pair problem, in this case, by imagining that we sweep the plane by a vertical line from left to right, starting at a position to the left of all n of the input points. As we sweep the line across the plane, we keep track of the closest pair seen so far, and of all those points that are "near" the sweep line. We also keep track of the distance, d, between the closest pair seen so far. In particular, as we illustrate in Figure 22.16, while sweeping through the points from left to right, we maintain the following data:

- A closest pair (a, b) among the points encountered, and the distance $d = \text{dist}(a, b)$
- An ordered dictionary S that stores the points lying in a strip of width d to the left of the sweep line and uses the y-coordinates of points as keys.

Each input point p corresponds to an event in this plane sweep. When the sweep line encounters a point p, we perform the following actions:

1. We update dictionary S by removing the points at horizontal distance greater than d from p, that is, each point r such that $x(p) - x(r) > d$.
2. We find the closest point q to the left of p by searching in dictionary S (we will say in a moment how this is done). If $\text{dist}(p, q) < d$, then we update the current closest pair and distance by setting $a \leftarrow p$, $b \leftarrow q$, and $d \leftarrow \text{dist}(p, q)$.
3. We insert p into S.

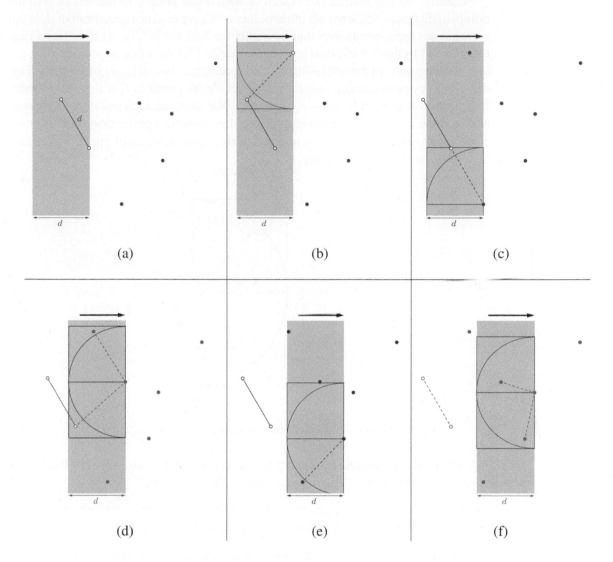

Figure 22.16: Plane sweep for the closest pair problem: (a) the first minimum distance d and closest pair (highlighted); (b) the next event (box $B(p, d)$ contains a point, but the half-circle $C(p, d)$ is empty); (c) next event ($C(p, d)$ again is empty, but a point is removed from S); (d) next event (with $C(p, d)$ again empty). The dictionary S contains the points in the gray strip of width d; (e) a point p is encountered (and a point removed from S), with $B(p, d)$ containing 1 point, but $C(p, d)$ containing none; thus, the minimum distance d and closest pair (a, b) stay the same; (f) a point p encountered with $C(p, d)$ containing 2 points (and a point is removed from S).

Clearly, we can restrict our search of the closest point q to the left of p to the points in dictionary S, since all other points will have distance greater than d. What we want are those points in S that lie within the half-circle $C(p, d)$ of radius d centered at and to the left of point p. (See Figure 22.17.) As a first approximation, we can get the points in the enclosing $d \times 2d$ rectangular box $B(p, d)$ of $C(p, d)$ (Figure 22.17) by performing a range search on S for the points in S with y-coordinates in the interval of keys $[y(p) - d, y(p) + d]$. We examine such points, one by one, and find the closest to p, denoted q. Since the operations performed on dictionary S are range searches, insertions, and removals of points, we implement S by means of an AVL tree or red-black tree.

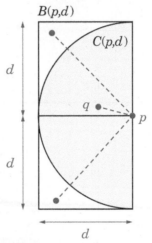

Figure 22.17: Box $B(p, d)$ and half-circle $C(p, d)$.

The following intuitive property, whose proof is left as an exercise (R-22.6), is crucial to the analysis of the running time of the algorithm.

Theorem 22.7: *A rectangle of width d and height $2d$ can contain at most six points such that any two points are at distance at least d.*

Thus, there are at most six points of S that lie in the box $B(p, d)$. So the range-search operation on S, to find the points in $B(p, d)$, takes time $O(\log n + 6)$, which is $O(\log n)$. Also, we can find the point in $B(p, d)$ closest to p in $O(1)$ time.

Before we begin the sweep, we sort the points by x-coordinate, and store them in an ordered list X. The list X is used for two purposes:

- To get the next point to be processed
- To identify the points to be removed from dictionary S.

We keep references to two positions in the list X, which we denote as firstInStrip and lastInStrip. Position lastInStrip keeps track of the new point to be inserted into S, while position firstInStrip keeps track of the left-most point in S. By advancing lastInStrip one step at a time, we find the new point to be processed. By using firstInStrip, we identify the points to be removed from S. Namely, while we have

$$x(\mathsf{point}(\mathsf{firstInStrip})) < x(\mathsf{point}(\mathsf{lastInStrip})) - d,$$

we perform operation $\mathsf{remove}(y(\mathsf{point}(\mathsf{firstInStrip})))$ on dictionary S and advance firstInStrip.

Let n be the number of input points. Our analysis of the plane-sweep algorithm for the closest pair problem is based on the following observations:

- The preliminary sorting by x-coordinate takes time $O(n \log n)$.
- Each point is inserted once and removed once from dictionary S, which has size at most n; hence, the total time for inserting and removing elements in S is $O(n \log n)$.
- By Theorem 22.7, each range query in S takes $O(\log n)$ time. We execute such a range query each time we process a new point. Thus, the total time spent for performing range queries is $O(n \log n)$.

We conclude that we can compute a closest pair in a set of n points in time $O(n \log n)$.

22.5 Exercises

Reinforcement

R-22.1 Verify that the absolute value of the function $\Delta(p_1, p_2, p_3)$ is twice the area of the triangle formed by the points p_1, p_2, and p_3 in the plane.

R-22.2 Provide a complete proof of Theorem 22.1.

R-22.3 Provide a complete proof of Example 22.2.

R-22.4 Provide a complete proof of Theorem 22.3.

R-22.5 Provide a complete proof of Theorem 22.4.

R-22.6 Provide a complete proof of Theorem 22.7.

R-22.7 Give a pseudocode description of the plane-sweep algorithm for finding a closest pair of points among a set of n points in the plane.

R-22.8 Draw as best you can the convex hull of the following set of points:

$$\{(2, 2), (4, 4), (6, 4), (8, 1), (8, 7), (9, 3), (1, 5), (5, 4)\}.$$

Creativity

C-22.1 Using the orientation test, give a pseudocode description of a method, inTriangle(p, q, r, s), which tests whether a point, p, is inside the interior of a triangle (q, r, s), assuming q, r, and s are listed in counterclockwise order.

C-22.2 Using the inTriangle(p, q, r, s) method from the previous exercise, and additional orientation tests, design a data structure that can be built for a given n-vertex convex polygon, P, to determine for any query point, p, whether p lies inside P. Your data structure should use $O(n)$ space and answer point-in-polygon queries in $O(\log n)$ time.

 Hint: Use Figure 22.7c as a guide.

C-22.3 Let S be a set of n distinct points in the plane. Say that a point $p = (x, y)$ in S is *max-max* if there is no other point $q = (x', y')$ in S such that $x < x'$ and $y < y'$. Similarly, say that a point $p = (x, y)$ in S is *max-min* if there is no other point $q = (x', y')$ in S such that $x < x'$ and $y' < y$, that $p = (x, y)$ in S is *min-max* if there is no other point $q = (x', y')$ in S such that $x' < x$ and $y < y'$, and that $p = (x, y)$ in S is *min-min* if there is no other point $q = (x', y')$ in S such that $x' < x$ and $y' < y$. Show that if a point, p, is on the convex hull of S, then it must also be a max-max, max-min, min-max, or min-min point in S.

C-22.4 Show that the expected number of points on the convex hull of a set of n points chosen uniformly and independently at random in the interior of a rectangle, R, is $O(\log n)$.

 Hint: Use the fact established in the previous exercise.

C-22.5 Design an $O(n)$-time algorithm to test whether a given n-vertex polygon is convex. You should not assume that P is simple.

C-22.6 Suppose you are given an n-vertex convex polygon, P. Describe an $O(n)$-time method for computing the area of P.

C-22.7 Say that a polygon, P, is **monotone** if any vertical line intersects the boundary of P in at most two points. Given a simple monotone polygon, P, with n vertices, show that you can find the convex hull of P in $O(n)$ time.

C-22.8 Let C be a collection of n horizontal and vertical line segments. Describe an $O(n \log n)$-time algorithm for determining whether the segments in C form a simple polygon.

C-22.9 Given a set P of n points, design an efficient algorithm for constructing a simple polygon whose vertices are the points of P.

C-22.10 Design an $O(n^2)$-time algorithm for testing whether a polygon with n vertices is simple. Assume that the polygon is given by the list of its vertices.

C-22.11 Give an example of a set of input points for which the simplified Graham scan algorithm, given in Algorithm 22.11, does not work correctly.

C-22.12 Let P be a set of n points in the plane. Modify the Graham scan algorithm to compute, for every point p of P that is not a vertex of the convex hull, either a triangle with vertices in P, or a segment with endpoints in P that contains p.

C-22.13 Suppose you are given a set S of n line segments in the plane, such that each makes a positive angle with the x-axis of either $30°$ or $60°$ (so there are only two possible slopes for the lines in S). Describe an efficient algorithm for finding all the pairs of intersecting segments in S. What is the running time of your method?

C-22.14 Suppose we are given an array, A, of n nonintersecting segments, $s_1, s_2, \ldots, s_n$, with endpoints on the lines $y = 0$ and $y = 1$, and ordered from left to right. Given a point q with $0 < y(q) < 1$, design an algorithm that in $O(\log n)$ time computes the segment s_i of A immediately to right of q, or reports that q is to the right of all the segments.

C-22.15 Describe an $O(n \log n)$-time algorithm for finding the second closest pair of points in a set, S, of n points in the plane. That is, you should return the pair, (p, q), in S, such that the only pair of points that could be closer to each other than the distance between p and q is the closest pair of points in S.

Applications

A-22.1 In several computational geometry problems involving distances defined by a set, S, of n points in the plane, it is often useful to first know what is the largest distance between a pair of points in S, which is known as the **diameter** of S. Another way to define the diameter of such a set, S, is as the largest distance between two parallel lines, L_1 and L_2, such that all the points of S are either on one of these lines or between them. Suppose, then, that your are given such a set, S. Describe an $O(n \log n)$-time algorithm for computing the diameter of S.

A-22.2 Gerrymandering is a process where voting districts are drawn to achieve various political goals, such as maximizing the number of voters from a certain party, rather than to achieve geometric goals, such as having districts drawn to have generally round or square shapes. This process often gives rise to very complicated shapes for voting districts, and it can sometimes be challenging to determine whether a giving person is inside or outside a given district, due to the ways it can wind around. Suppose, then, that you are given a voting district defined by an n-vertex simple polygon, P. Give an $O(n)$-time algorithm for testing whether a point q is inside or outside of P. You may assume that q is not on the boundary of P and that there is no vertex of P with the same x-coordinate as q.

A-22.3 Line segments and polygons are used to model geometric objects in computer graphics, video games, and computer-aided design, often in data pipelines that use the output of one program as the input to another. One complication that can arise in such scenarios is that a data format needed for the input to the second system may be missing from the output from the first. For instance, one program may output an object as an unordered set of line segments but the other may require its input to be defined by a polygon. So, suppose you are given a set, S, of n line segments, in no particular order. Describe an efficient algorithm for determining whether the segments of S form a polygon, P, and if so, give a polygonal representation for P. You may allow P to be non-simple (that is, self-intersecting), but P must be a single cyclical chain of distinct vertices connected by the segments in S. What is the running time of your algorithm?

A-22.4 In the **hidden-line elimination** problem, we would like to visualize a three-dimensional scene, described by a collection of polygons, from a particular viewing point, p, and in a particular direction. This problem is often solved by projecting the edges of the polygons in the scene onto a view plane perpendicular to the viewing direction. Then this set of segments is processed to remove the portions of edges that cannot be seen from p because they are occluded by a polygon in the scene. In order to identify visible and invisible portions of edges, it is helpful to know which pairs of line segments intersect one another. So, suppose you are given a set, S, of n line segments in the plane. Describe an algorithm to enumerate all k pairs of intersecting segments in S in $O((n + k)\log n)$ time.

Hint: Use the plane-sweep technique, including segments intersections as events. Note that you cannot know these events in advance, but it is always possible to know the next event to process as you are sweeping.

A-22.5 Computational **metrology** deals with algorithms for measuring things, such as manufactured parts, and one of the standard algorithms is to determine the flatness of an edge of a manufactured part based on a set of points that are sampled along that edge (say, by a laser range-finder or a scanning electron microscope). Since it is extremely rare for such a set of points to be perfectly collinear, we need a rigorous way of defining flatness in this context. One such way is to define the **flatness** of a set, S, of n two-dimensional points as the smallest distance between two parallel lines, L_1 and L_2, such that all the points of S are either on one of these lines or between them. This distance is known as the **width** of S. Describe an $O(n\log n)$-time algorithm for determining the width of such a set, S, of n points in the plane.

A-22.6 Suppose you are hiking in the wild country of some exotic part of the world. Naturally, an important part of your survival gear is a GPS tracking device and a digital map of the region you are hiking in, which includes the pathways of trails, rivers, and creeks, as well as obstacles like cliffs and mountains. These pathways and obstacles are described on your map by a collection, S, of n two-dimensional line segments that may intersect only at their endpoints (hence, no pair of segments in S cross). In order to locate your position on this map, however, you need to identify where your current position, (x, y), lies in reference to the segments in S. Such a query can be satisfied by imagining that we shoot a vertical ray up or down from the point, (x, y), to the first segment that it hits in S, which is known as a ***vertical ray-shooting*** query. In order to facilitate such a query, it is desirable for us to process the segments in S to define a ***trapezoidal decomposition*** of the plane. Such a decomposition is defined by shooting vertical rays up and down from every endpoint of a segment in S until it hits another segment in S or it hits the boundary of the map. In the map defined by S and these vertical rays, every face is either a trapezoid or a triangle. This partitioning allows us to then construct a data structure for answering vertical ray-shooting queries, since such a query can be answered simply by identifying the face in the trapezoidal decomposition that contains the starting point for the ray. Thus, given a set, S, of n line segments that may intersect only at their endpoints, describe an $O(n \log n)$-time algorithm for constructing a trapezoidal decomposition of S.

A-22.7 In machine learning applications, we often have some kind of condition defined over a set, S, of n points, which we would like to characterize—that is, "learn"—using some simple rule. For instance, these points could correspond to biological attributes of n medical patients and the condition could be whether a given patient tests positive for a given disease or not, and we would like to learn the correlation between these attributes and this disease. Think of the points with positive tests as painted "red," and the tests with negative tests as painted "blue." Suppose that we have a simple two-factor set of attributes; hence, we can view each patient as a two-dimensional point in the plane, which is colored as either red or blue. An ideal characterization, from a machine learning perspective, is if we can separate the points of S by a line, L, such that all the points on one side of L are red and all the points on the other side of L are blue. So suppose you are given a set, S, of n red and blue points in the plane. Describe an efficient algorithm for determining whether there is a line, L, that separates the red and blue points in S. What is the running time of your algorithm?

A-22.8 Imagine a game, Battlestrip, which involves one player laying down a set of horizontal line segments on his computer screen, and another player laying down a set of vertical segments on hers. Then the two computer screens are virtually overlaid on top of one another and the winner is the player with a single segment that intersects the most segments of his or her opponent. Your job is to determine who is the winner. So, suppose you are given a set S of n horizontal and vertical line segments in the plane. Describe an algorithm running in $O(n \log n)$ time for finding the vertical segment, v, in S that intersects the maximum number of horizontal segments in S, as well as the horizontal segment, h, in S that intersects the maximum number of vertical segments in S. (Note that there may be many more than $O(n \log n)$ pairs of intersecting horizontal and vertical line segments.)

A-22.9   Given a set S of points in the plane, define the ***Voronoi diagram*** of S to be the set of regions $V(p)$, called ***Voronoi cells***, defined, for each point p in S, as the set of all points q in the plane such that p is a closest neighbor of q in S. Such a diagram is useful in a host of different applications, including the construction of data structures to answer nearest-neighbor queries.

     a.   Show that each cell in a Voronoi diagram is convex.

     b.   Show that if p and q are a closest pair of points in the set S, then the Voronoi cells $V(p)$ and $V(q)$ touch.

     c.   Show that a point p is on the boundary of the convex hull of the set S if and only if the Voronoi cell $V(p)$ for p is unbounded.

A-22.10   Given a set S of points in the plane, define the ***Delaunay triangulation*** of S to be the set of all triangles (p, q, r) such that p, q, and r are in S and the circle defined to have these points on its boundary is empty—it contains no points of S in its interior. Such triangulations have many applications to modeling problems, as Delaunay triangulations tend to avoid "long and skinny" triangles, which are bad for modeling applications.

     a.   Show that if p and q are a closest pair of points in the set S, then p and q are joined by an edge in the Delaunay triangulation.

     b.   Show that the Voronoi cells $V(p)$ and $V(q)$, as defined in the previous exercise, share an edge in the Voronoi diagram of a point set S if and only if p and q are joined by an edge in the Delaunay triangulation of S.

Chapter Notes

The convex hull algorithm we present in this chapter is a variant of an algorithm given by Graham [91]. The plane-sweep algorithm we present for intersecting orthogonal line segments is due to Bentley and Ottmann [31]. The closest point algorithm we present combines ideas of Bentley [27] and Hinrichs *et al.* [98].

There are several excellent books for computational geometry, including books by Edelsbrunner [62], Mehlhorn [159], O'Rourke [165], Preparata and Shamos [173], Berg *et al.* [32], and handbooks edited by Goodman and O'Rourke [87], and Pach [166]. Other sources for further reading include surveys by Aurenhammer [17], Lee and Preparata [140], and book chapters by Goodrich [88], Lee [139], and Yao [218]. Also, the books by Sedgewick [188, 189] contain several chapters on computational geometry, which have some very nice figures. Indeed, the figures in Sedgewick's books have inspired many of the figures we present in this book.

Chapter

23

String Algorithms

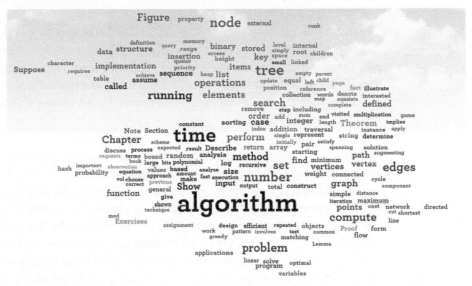

Algorithms Book Word Cloud, 2014. Word cloud produced by frequency ranking the words in this book using wordcloud.cs.arizona.edu. Used with permission.

Contents

23.1 String Operations 653

23.2 The Boyer-Moore Algorithm 656

23.3 The Knuth-Morris-Pratt Algorithm 660

23.4 Hash-Based Lexicon Matching 664

23.5 Tries 669

23.6 Exercises 680

Document processing is one of the main applications of computers. We use computers to edit documents, to search documents, to transport documents over the Internet, and to display documents on printers and computer screens. Web searching is a significant and important document processing application, and many of the key computations in all of this document processing involve character strings and string pattern matching. For example, the Internet document formats HTML and XML are primarily text formats, with added links to multimedia content. Making sense of the many terabytes of information on the Internet requires a considerable amount of text processing.

In this chapter, we study several fundamental text processing algorithms for quickly performing important operations on strings of characters. We pay particular attention to algorithms for string searching and pattern matching, since these can often be computational bottlenecks in many document processing applications. We also study some fundamental algorithmic issues involved in text processing, as well.

Not surprisingly, text processing algorithms operate primarily on inputs that use character strings as the underlying data type of the objects involved. The terminology and notation for strings, as used in this chapter, is fairly intuitive, and it turns out that representing a string as an array of characters is simple and efficient. Here, we typically think of the input size, n, as referring to the length of the strings used as inputs. So we don't spend a lot of attention discussing data structures for string representations. For instance, we can think of a string simply as an array of characters, with many string operations amounting to simple query operations on such arrays. Nevertheless, string processing often involves an interesting method for string pattern matching, and we study pattern matching algorithms in this chapter.

We also study the trie data structure, which is a tree-based structure that allows for fast searching in a collection of strings. One of the special cases of this data structure is the suffix trie, which allows for a number of interesting queries to be performed on strings.

We should also mention that there are several string problems discussed in previous chapters. For instance, we discuss an important text processing problem in Section 10.3—namely, the problem of compressing a document of text so that it fits more efficiently in storage or can be transmitted more efficiently over a network. In addition, in Section 12.5, we deal with how we can measure the similarity between two documents, based on the use of dynamic programming to solve the longest common subsequence problem. All of these problems are topics that arise often in Internet computations, such as web crawlers, search engines, document distribution, and information retrieval. We discuss, for instance, how the trie data structure can be used to implement a supporting data structure for a search engine.

23.1 String Operations

Text documents are ubiquitous in modern computing, as they are used to communicate and publish information. From the perspective of algorithm design, such documents can be viewed as simple character strings. That is, they can be abstracted as a sequence of the characters that make up their content. Performing interesting searching and processing operations on such data, therefore, requires that we have efficient methods for dealing with character strings.

At the heart of algorithms for processing text are methods for dealing with character strings. Character strings can come from a wide variety of sources, including scientific, linguistic, and Internet applications. Indeed, the following are examples of such strings:

$$P \; = \; \text{"CGTAAACTGCTTTAATCAAACGC"}$$
$$R \; = \; \text{"U.S. Lands an Astronaut on Mars!"}$$
$$S \; = \; \text{"http://www.wiley.com/college/goodrich/"}.$$

The first string, P, comes from DNA applications, the last string, S, is the URL for the website that accompanies this book, and the middle string, R, is a fictional news headline. In this section, we present some of the useful operations that are supported by string representations for processing strings.

Substrings

Several of the typical string processing operations involve breaking large strings into smaller strings. In order to be able to speak about the pieces that result from such operations, we use the term ***substring*** of an m-character string P to refer to a string of the form $P[i]P[i+1]P[i+2]\cdots P[j]$, for some $0 \le i \le j \le m-1$, that is, the string formed by the characters in P from index i to index j, inclusive. Technically, this means that a string is actually a substring of itself (taking $i = 0$ and $j = m - 1$), so if we want to rule this out as a possibility, we must restrict the definition to ***proper*** substrings, which require that either $i > 0$ or $j < m - 1$. To simplify the notation for referring to substrings, let us use $P[i..j]$ to denote the substring of P from index i to index j, inclusive. That is,

$$P[i..j] = P[i]P[i+1]\cdots P[j].$$

We use the convention that if $i > j$, then $P[i..j]$ is equal to the ***null string***, which has length 0. In addition, in order to distinguish some special kinds of substrings, let us refer to any substring of the form $P[0..i]$, for $0 \le i \le m - 1$, as a ***prefix*** of P, and any substring of the form $P[i..m - 1]$, for $0 \le i \le m - 1$, as a ***suffix*** of P. For example, if we again take P to be the string of DNA given above, then "CGTAA" is a prefix of P, "CGC" is a suffix of P, and "TTAATC" is a (proper) substring of P. Note that the null string is a prefix and a suffix of any other string.

The Pattern Matching Problem

In the classic **pattern matching** problem on strings, we are given a **text** string T of length n and a **pattern** string P of length m, and want to find whether P is a substring of T. The notion of a "match" is that there is a substring of T starting at some index i that matches P, character by character, so that

$$T[i] = P[0], \; T[i+1] = P[1], \; \ldots, \; T[i+m-1] = P[m-1].$$

That is,

$$P = T[i..i+m-1].$$

Thus, the output from a pattern matching algorithm is either an indication that the pattern P does not exist in T or the starting index in T of a substring matching P.

To allow for fairly general notions of a character string, we typically do not restrict the characters in T and P to come explicitly from a well-known character set, like the ASCII or Unicode character sets. Instead, we typically use the general symbol Σ to denote the character set, or **alphabet**, from which the characters of T and P can come. This alphabet Σ can, of course, be a subset of the ASCII or Unicode character sets, but it could also be more general and is even allowed to be infinite. Nevertheless, since most document processing algorithms are used in applications where the underlying character set is finite, we usually assume that the size of the alphabet Σ, denoted with $|\Sigma|$, is a fixed constant.

Example 23.1: *Suppose we are given the text string*

$$T = \texttt{"abacaabaccabacabaabb"}$$

and the pattern string

$$P = \texttt{"abacab"}.$$

Then P is a substring of T. Namely, $P = T[10..15]$.

Brute-Force Pattern Matching

The **brute-force** approach pattern is a technique for algorithm design when we have something we wish to search for or when we wish to optimize some function and we can afford to spend a considerable amount of time optimizing it. In applying this technique in a general situation, we typically enumerate all possible configurations of the inputs involved and pick the best of all these enumerated configurations.

In applying this technique to the **pattern matching** algorithm, we simply test all the possible placements of P relative to T. This approach, shown in Algorithm 23.1, is quite simple.

The brute-force pattern matching algorithm could not be simpler. It consists of two nested loops, with the outer loop indexing through all possible starting indices of the pattern in the text, and the inner loop indexing through each character of the

Algorithm BruteForceMatch(T, P):

    Input: Strings T (text) with n characters and P (pattern) with m characters

    Output: Starting index of the first substring of T matching P, or an indication that P is not a substring of T

    for $i \leftarrow 0$ **to** $n - m$ // for each candidate index in T **do**

        $j \leftarrow 0$

        while $(j < m$ **and** $T[i + j] = P[j])$ **do**

            $j \leftarrow j + 1$

        if $j = m$ **then**

            return i

    return "There is no substring of T matching P."

Algorithm 23.1: Brute-force pattern matching.

pattern, comparing it to its potentially corresponding character in the text. Thus, the correctness of the brute-force pattern matching algorithm follows immediately.

The running time of brute-force pattern matching in the worst case is not good, however, because, for each candidate index in T, we can perform up to m character comparisons to discover that P does not match T at the current index. Referring to Algorithm 23.1, we see that the outer for-loop is executed at most $n - m + 1$ times, and the inner loop is executed at most m times. Thus, the running time of the brute-force method is $O((n - m + 1)m)$, which is $O(nm)$. Note that, when $m = n/2$, this algorithm has quadratic running time $O(n^2)$.

In Figure 23.2 we illustrate the execution of the brute-force pattern matching algorithm on the strings T and P from Example 23.1.

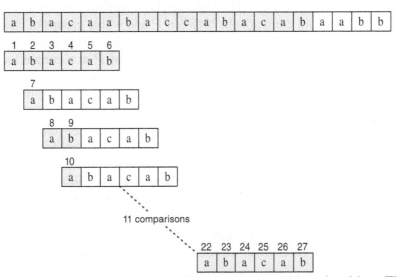

Figure 23.2: Example run of the brute-force pattern matching algorithm. The algorithm performs 27 character comparisons, indicated above with numerical labels.

Improved Analysis of the Boyer-Moore Algorithm

Indeed, the BM algorithm is often able to skip over large portions of the text. (See Figure 23.6.) There is experimental evidence that on English text, the average number of comparisons done per text character is approximately 0.24 for a five-character pattern string. The payoff is not as great for binary strings or for very short patterns, however, in which case the KMP algorithm, discussed in Section 23.3, or, for very short patterns, the brute-force algorithm, may be better.

We have actually presented a simplified version of the Boyer-Moore (BM) algorithm. The original BM algorithm achieves running time $O(n + m + |\Sigma|)$ by using an alternative shift heuristic to the partially matched text string, whenever it shifts the pattern more than the character-jump heuristic. This alternative shift heuristic is based on applying the main idea from the Knuth-Morris-Pratt pattern matching algorithm, which we discuss in the next section.

Worst-Case Improvement for String Pattern Matching

In studying the worst-case performance of the brute-force and BM pattern matching algorithms on specific instances of the problem, such as that given in Example 23.1, we should notice a major inefficiency. Specifically, we may perform many comparisons while testing a potential placement of the pattern against the text, yet if we

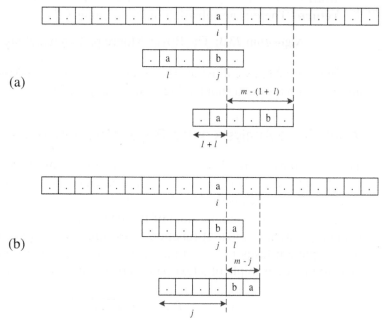

Figure 23.4: Illustration of the jump step in the BM algorithm, where l denotes $\mathsf{last}(T[i])$. We distinguish two cases: (a) $1 + l \le j$, where we shift the pattern by $j - l$ units; (b) $j < 1 + l$, where we shift the pattern by one unit.

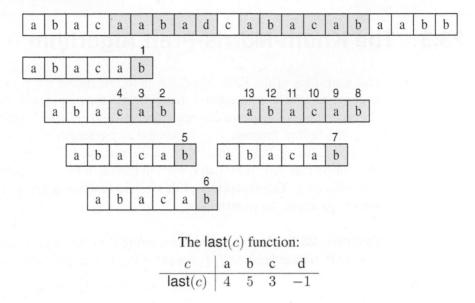

The last(c) function:

c	a	b	c	d
last(c)	4	5	3	-1

Figure 23.5: An illustration of the BM pattern matching algorithm. The algorithm performs 13 character comparisons, which are indicated with numerical labels.

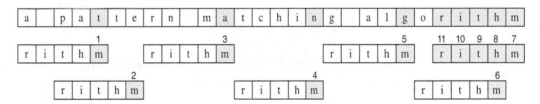

Figure 23.6: Execution of the Boyer-Moore algorithm on an English text and pattern, where a significant speedup is achieved. Note that not all text characters are examined.

discover a pattern character that does not match in the text, then we throw away all the information gained by these comparisons and start over again from scratch with the next incremental placement of the pattern.

The Knuth-Morris-Pratt (or "KMP") algorithm, which we discuss next, avoids this waste of information and, in so doing it achieves a running time of $O(n + m)$, which is optimal in the worst case. That is, in the worst case any pattern matching algorithm will have to examine all the characters of the text and all the characters of the pattern a constant number of times.

23.3   The Knuth-Morris-Pratt Algorithm

The main idea of the KMP algorithm is to preprocess the pattern string P so as to compute a *failure function* f that indicates the proper shift of P so that, to the largest extent possible, we can reuse previously performed comparisons. Specifically, the failure function $f(j)$ is defined as the length of the longest prefix of P that is a suffix of $P[1..j]$ (note that we did *not* put $P[0..j]$ here). We also use the convention that $f(0) = 0$. Later, we will discuss how to compute the failure function efficiently. The importance of this failure function is that it "encodes" repeated substrings inside the pattern itself.

Example 23.2: *Consider the pattern string $P =$ "abacab" from Example 23.1. The KMP failure function $f(j)$ for the string P is as shown in the following table:*

j	0	1	2	3	4	5
$P[j]$	a	b	a	c	a	b
$f(j)$	0	0	1	0	1	2

The KMP pattern matching algorithm, shown in Algorithm 23.7, incrementally processes the text string T comparing it to the pattern string P.

Algorithm KMPMatch(T, P):
   Input: Strings T (text) with n characters and P (pattern) with m characters
   Output: Starting index of the first substring of T matching P, or an indication that P is not a substring of T

   $f \leftarrow$ KMPFailureFunction(P)   // construct the failure function f for P
   $i \leftarrow 0$
   $j \leftarrow 0$
   while $i < n$ **do**
       if $P[j] = T[i]$ **then**
           if $j = m - 1$ **then**
               return $i - m + 1$ // a match!
           $i \leftarrow i + 1$
           $j \leftarrow j + 1$
       else if $j > 0$ // no match, but we have advanced in P **then**
           $j \leftarrow f(j - 1)$ // j indexes just after prefix of P that must match
       else
           $i \leftarrow i + 1$
   return "There is no substring of T matching P."

Algorithm 23.7: The KMP pattern matching algorithm.

Intuition Behind the KMP Algorithm

During the execution of the KMP algorithm, each time there is a match, we increment the current indices. On the other hand, if there is a mismatch and we have previously made progress in P, then we consult the failure function to determine the new index in P where we need to continue checking P against T. Otherwise (there was a mismatch and we are at the beginning of P), we simply increment the index for T (and keep the index variable for P at its beginning). We repeat this process until we find a match of P in T or the index for T reaches n, the length of T (indicating that we did not find the pattern P in T).

The main part of the KMP algorithm is the while-loop, which performs a comparison between a character in T and a character in P each iteration. Depending upon the outcome of this comparison, the algorithm either moves on to the next characters in T and P, consults the failure function for a new candidate character in P, or starts over with the next index in T. The correctness of this algorithm follows from the definition of the failure function. The skipped comparisons are actually unnecessary, for the failure function guarantees that all the ignored comparisons are redundant—they would involve comparing characters we already know match.

In Figure 23.8, we illustrate the execution of the KMP pattern matching algorithm on the same input strings as in Example 23.1. Note the use of the failure function to avoid redoing one of the comparisons between a character of the pattern and a character of the text. Also note that the algorithm performs fewer overall comparisons than the brute-force algorithm run on the same strings (Figure 23.2).

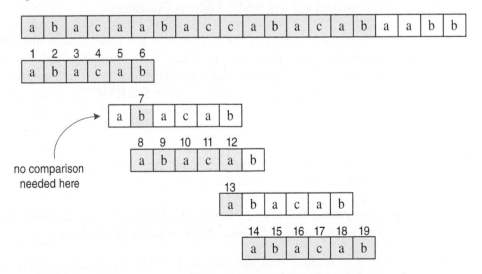

Figure 23.8: An illustration of the KMP pattern matching algorithm. The failure function f for this pattern is given in Example 23.2. The algorithm performs 19 character comparisons, which are indicated with numerical labels.

Analysis of the KMP Algorithm

Excluding the computation of the failure function, the running time of the KMP algorithm is clearly proportional to the number of iterations of the while-loop. For the sake of the analysis, let us define $k = i - j$. Intuitively, k is the total amount by which the pattern P has been shifted with respect to the text T. Note that throughout the execution of the algorithm, we have $k \leq n$. One of the following three cases occurs at each iteration of the loop.

- If $T[i] = P[j]$, then i increases by 1, and k does not change, since j also increases by 1.
- If $T[i] \neq P[j]$ and $j > 0$, then i does not change and k increases by at least 1, since in this case k changes from $i - j$ to $i - f(j-1)$, which is an addition of $j - f(j-1)$, which is positive because $f(j-1) < j$.
- If $T[i] \neq P[j]$ and $j = 0$, then i increases by 1 and k increases by 1, since j does not change.

Thus, at each iteration of the loop, either i or k increases by at least 1 (possibly both); hence, the total number of iterations of the while-loop in the KMP pattern matching algorithm is at most $2n$. Of course, achieving this bound assumes that we have already computed the failure function for P.

Constructing the KMP Failure Function

To construct the failure function used in the KMP pattern matching algorithm, we use the method shown in Algorithm 23.9. This algorithm is another example of a "bootstrapping" process quite similar to that used in the KMPMatch algorithm. We compare the pattern to itself as in the KMP algorithm. Each time we have two characters that match, we set $f(i) = j + 1$. Note that since we have $i > j$ throughout the execution of the algorithm, $f(j - 1)$ is always defined when we need to use it.

Algorithm KMPFailureFunction runs in $O(m)$ time. Its analysis is analogous to that of algorithm KMPMatch. Thus, we have the following:

Theorem 23.3: *The Knuth-Morris-Pratt algorithm performs pattern matching on a text string of length n and a pattern string of length m in $O(n + m)$ time.*

The running time analysis of the KMP algorithm may seem a little surprising at first, for it states that, in time proportional to that needed just to read the strings T and P separately, we can find the first occurrence of P in T. Also, it should be noted that the running time of the KMP algorithm does not depend on the size of the alphabet.

Algorithm KMPFailureFunction(P):

 Input: String P (pattern) with m characters

 Output: The failure function f for P, which maps j to the length of the longest prefix of P that is a suffix of $P[1..j]$

 $i \leftarrow 1$

 $j \leftarrow 0$

 $f(0) \leftarrow 0$

 while $i < m$ **do**

  if $P[j] = P[i]$ **then**

   // we have matched $j + 1$ characters

   $f(i) \leftarrow j + 1$

   $i \leftarrow i + 1$

   $j \leftarrow j + 1$

  else if $j > 0$ **then**

   // j indexes just after a prefix of P that must match

   $j \leftarrow f(j - 1)$

  else

   // we have no match here

   $f(i) \leftarrow 0$

   $i \leftarrow i + 1$

Algorithm 23.9: Computation of the failure function used in the KMP pattern matching algorithm. Note how the algorithm uses the previous values of the failure function to efficiently compute new values.

The intuition behind the worst-case efficiency of the KMP algorithm comes from our being able to get the most out of each comparison that we do, and by our not performing comparisons we know to be redundant. The KMP algorithm is best suited for strings from small-size alphabets, such as DNA sequences.

Limitations for Repeated Queries

The BM and KMP pattern matching algorithms presented above speed up the search of a pattern in a text by preprocessing the pattern (to compute the failure function in the KMP algorithm or the last function in the BM algorithm). In some applications, however, we would like to take a complementary approach, where we would consider a string searching algorithms that preprocess the text to support multiple queries. This approach is suitable for applications where a series of queries is performed on a fixed text, so that the initial cost of preprocessing the text is compensated by a speedup in each subsequent query (for example, a website that offers pattern matching in Shakespeare's *Hamlet* or a search engine that offers web pages on the *Hamlet* topic).

23.4 Hash-Based Lexicon Matching

In this section, we discuss an approach to string pattern matching that is due to Karp and Rabin and is based on hashing. The advantage of this approach is that it lets us efficiently solve a generalization of the string pattern matching problem, which we call *lexicon matching*. In this problem, we are given a set, $L = \{P_1, P_2, \ldots, P_l\}$, of l different pattern strings, and a text string, T, and we would like to find all the places in T where a pattern, P_i, is a substring. We call the set, L, the *lexicon* of strings we would like to find in T.

For example, L could be a set consisting of trademarked words for a certain company, Example.com, and T could be the text of a book published by a former employee. A lawyer for Example.com might like to search for all the instances in T where a trademarked word for Example.com is used. Alternatively, L could be a set consisting of nontrivial sentences from published articles about Shakespeare and T could be a term paper submitted by a certain student, William Fakespeare, in a Shakespeare course. The instructor for this course might wish to know whether William plagiarized any of the sentences from L in writing his term paper, T. Both of these examples are possible applications of an efficient algorithm for the lexicon matching problem.

Let $h(X)$ be a hash function that takes a character string, X, and maps it to an integer. (See Chapter 6.) Say that such a function is a *uniform hash* function for L if, for any pattern P_k in L, the number of other patterns, P_j, with $j \neq k$, such that $h(P_i) = h(P_j)$, is $O(1)$. Intuitively, we refer to h as a "uniform" hash function in this case, because it spreads the hash values for the strings in L uniformly in the range of h. Note, however, that we are not necessarily requiring that we store the patterns in L in a hash table—each hash value for a pattern in L is instead a kind of "fingerprint" for that pattern.

Let us assume, for the sake of simplicity, that all the patterns in the lexicon L are of the same length, m. (We explore a more general case in Exercise C-23.13.) The hash-based lexicon matching algorithm for L and T consists of two phases. In the first phase, we compute the hash value of each pattern in the lexicon, L, and insert this value, together with the index of the corresponding pattern, in a set, H. In the second phase, we step through the text, T, and compute the hash value of the length-m substring of T starting at that point. If we find a match with a hash value of a pattern in the lexicon L, then we do a full character-by-character comparison of the corresponding pattern and this substring of T to see if we have a confirmed substring match. (See Figure 23.10.)

We give a pseudocode description of the Karp-Rabin hash-based lexicon matching algorithm in Algorithm 23.11.

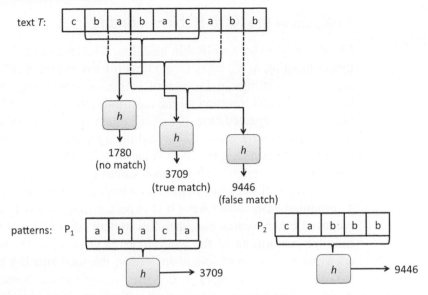

Figure 23.10: How the Karp-Rabin hash-based lexicon matching algorithm works. A hash value, $h(X)$, is computed for each length-m substring, X, of the text. If it matches the hash value of a pattern, it is then confirmed as either a true match or a false match.

Algorithm HashMatch(L, T):

    Input: A set, $L = \{P_1, \ldots, P_l\}$, of l pattern strings, each of length m, and a text string, T, of length n

    Output: Each pair, (i, k), such that a pattern, P_k, in L, appears as a substring of T starting at index i

1: Let H be an initially empty set of key-value pairs (with hash-value keys)
2: Let A be an initially empty list of integer pairs (for found matches)
3: **for** $k \leftarrow 1$ **to** l **do**
4:     Add the key-value pair, $(h(P_k), k)$, to H
5: **for** $i \leftarrow 0$ **to** $n - m$ **do**
6:     $f \leftarrow h(T[i..i + m - 1])$
7:     **for each** key-value pair, (f, k), with key f in H **do**
8:         // check P_k against $T[i..i + m - 1]$
9:         $j \leftarrow 0$
10:         **while** $j < m$ **and** $T[i + j] = P_k[j]$ **do**
11:             $j \leftarrow j + 1$
12:         **if** $j = m$ **then**
13:             Add (i, k) to A // a match at index i for P_k
14: **return** A

Algorithm 23.11: The Karp-Rabin hash-based lexicon matching algorithm.

Analysis of the Karp-Rabin Algorithm

Let us analyze the Karp-Rabin hash-based lexicon matching algorithm, assuming that computing $h(X)$ takes $O(m)$ time for any string, X, of length m. Since there are l pattern strings in L, each of length m, computing the hash values for the patterns in L and inserting all the hash-indexed pairs into H, for the patterns in L, takes $O(lm)$ expected time, if we implement H as a hash table, or $O(lm \log l)$ time if we implement H using a balanced binary search tree. Similarly, each execution of Step 6, to compute the hash value of a length-m substring of T, takes $O(m)$ time; hence, computing all the hash values for the length-m substrings in T takes $O(nm)$ time. If we implement H as a hash table, then doing each lookup for such a computed hash value takes $O(1)$ expected time, and if H is implemented with a balanced binary search tree, then this lookup takes $O(\log l)$ time. Finally, the total time for performing all the while-loops is $O(lnm)$ in the worst case, since there are l patterns, each of length m. Thus, the total running time of this algorithm is $O(lnm + (n + l) \log l) = O(lnm + l \log l)$ in the worst case. Of course, this worst-case time is no better than using the brute-force algorithm to search for every pattern in L separately.

This worst-case bound is based on the pessimistic assumption that the hash values for the patterns in L might all be identical, however. Instead, if we assume that the hash function, h, is a uniform hash function for L, then the number of collisions for any hash value, h, is $O(1)$. Under this assumption, the Karp-Rabin hash-based lexicon matching algorithm runs in $O(lm + nm)$ expected time, if H is implemented with a hash table, since the number of iterations of the **for-each** loop is $O(1)$ in each invocation in this case.

23.4.1   An Optimization for Rolling Hash Functions

Suppose the patterns in L and the text T are sufficiently diverse so that the probability that any pattern in L appears as a substring at a given location in T is at most $1/m$. This assumption is reasonable for real-world applications, for example, such as in the trademarked-words or plagiarism examples given above. Under this diversity assumption, the total time needed to perform all the tests for possible matches in the text T is expected to be $O(n(1/m)m) = O(n)$, which is optimal, since it takes $O(n)$ time just to input T itself.

Unfortunately, even under this diversity assumption, the running time for the above Karp-Rabin hash-based lexicon matching algorithm is still $\Omega(nm)$, if it takes $\Omega(m)$ time to compute the hash value of each length-m substring of the text, T (in Step 6 of Algorithm 23.11). We can eliminate this bottleneck, however, if we use a **rolling-hash function**, h, for which there exists a constant-time shift-hash function, shiftHash($h(X[i..i + m - 1])$, X, i), which takes a hash value, $h(X[i..i + m - 1])$, for the length-m substring, $X[i..i + m - 1]$, starting at index i, of a string, X, and computes the hash value, $h(X[i + 1..i + m])$, of the length-m substring,

$X[i + 1..i + m]$, starting at index $i + 1$ of X. (See Figure 23.12.)

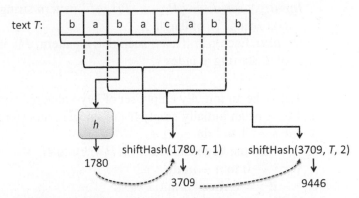

Figure 23.12: How a rolling-hash function works in the Karp-Rabin algorithm.

For example, consider polynomial-based hashing (which, as discussed in Section 6.2.2, works well for character strings) applied to length-m character strings. In this case, we have a seed value, $a > 0$, and a prime number, $p > cm$, where c is the number of characters in our alphabet, and we define the hash, $h(X[i..i+m-1])$, of a length-m substring, $X[i..i + m - 1]$, of a string, x, as follows:

$$X[i]a^{m-1} + X[i + 1]a^{m-2} + \cdots + X[i + m - 2]a + X[i + m - 1],$$

where we view each character in X as an integer in the range $[0, c - 1]$ and all arithmetic is done modulo p. We can compute this hash function using $O(m)$ arithmetic operations, by Horner's rule, as

$$X[i + m - 1] + a(X[i - m - 2] + \cdots + a(X[i + 1] + aX[i])\cdots),$$

where all arithmetic is done modulo p.

In this case, we can compute the function, shiftHash$(h(X[i..i+m-1], X, i)$, as

$$a\left(h(X[i..i + m - 1]) - X[i]a^{m-1}\right) + X[i + m],$$

which equals

$$X[i + 1]a^{m-1} + X[i + 2]a^{m-2} + \cdots + X[i + m - 1]a + X[i + m],$$

with all arithmetic done modulo p. Also, note that we can compute this shift-hash function using $O(1)$ modular arithmetic operations if we have precomputed the value of $a^{m-1} \bmod p$ and we have the hash value $h(X[i..i + m - 1])$.

We give a pseudocode description of the rolling-hash implementation of the Karp-Rabin lexicon matching algorithm in Algorithm 23.13.

Algorithm RollingHashMatch(L, T):

    Input: A set, $L = \{P_1, \ldots, P_l\}$, of l pattern strings, each of length m, and a text string, T, of length n

    Output: Each pair, (i, k), such that a pattern, P_k, in L, appears as a substring of T starting at index i

1: Let H be an initially empty set of key-value pairs (with hash-value keys)
2: Let A be an initially empty list of integer pairs (for found matches)
3: **for** $k \leftarrow 1$ **to** l **do**
4:      Add the key-value pair, $(h(P_k), k)$, to H
5: **for** $i \leftarrow 0$ **to** $n - m$ **do**
6:      **if** $i = 0$ **then**   // initial hash
7:         $f \leftarrow h(T[0..m-1])$
8:      **else**
9:         $f \leftarrow$ shiftHash(f, T, i)
10:    **for each** key-value pair, (f, k), with key f in H **do**
11:       // check P_k against $T[i..i+m-1]$
12:       $j \leftarrow 0$
13:       **while** $j < m$ **and** $T[i+j] = P_k[j]$ **do**
14:          $j \leftarrow j + 1$
15:       **if** $j = m$ **then**
16:         Add (i, k) to A // a match at index i for P_k
17: **return** A

Algorithm 23.13: A rolling-hash implementation of the Karp-Rabin lexicon matching algorithm.

Analysis of Rolling-Hash Lexicon Matching

Let us analyze this rolling-hash lexicon matching algorithm, assuming that the patterns in L and T are sufficiently diverse and the rolling-hash function, h, is chosen so that the probability that a hash value for a length-m substring of T has a match with any pattern in L is at most $1/m$. For example, in the polynomial hash function discussed above, if the prime number, p, is chosen to be larger than cm, where c is the number of characters in the alphabet, then the probability that two randomly chosen length-m character strings have the same hash value is at most $1/cm$. Under this diversity and hash-function assumption, then, the expected running time for the Karp-Rabin lexicon matching algorithm is $O(lm + n)$, assuming the set H is implemented with a hash table. This performance is due to the fact that the expected number of $O(m)$-time comparisons between a pattern P_k and a length-m substring of T is $O(n/m)$. Note that the expected running time of $O(lm + n)$ is also optimal, since it takes $O(lm + n)$ time just to read in the input strings for this problem.

23.5 Tries

A *trie* (pronounced "try") is a tree-based data structure for storing strings in order to support fast pattern matching. The main application for tries is in information retrieval. Indeed, the name "trie" comes from the word "re*trie*val." In an information retrieval application, such as a search for a certain DNA sequence in a genomic database, we are given a collection S of strings, all defined using the same alphabet.

The primary query operations that tries support are pattern matching and *prefix matching*. The latter operation involves being given a string X, and looking for all the strings in S that contain X as a prefix.

23.5.1 Standard Tries

Let S be a set of s strings from alphabet Σ, such that no string in S is a prefix of another string. A *standard trie* for S is an ordered tree T with the following properties (see Figure 23.14):

- Each node of T, except the root, is labeled with a character of Σ.

- The ordering of the children of an internal node of T is determined by a canonical ordering of the alphabet Σ.

- T has s external nodes, each associated with a string of S, such that the concatenation of the labels of the nodes on the path from the root to an external node v of T yields the string of S associated with v.

Thus, a trie T represents the strings of S with paths from the root to the external nodes of T. Note the importance of assuming that no string in S is a prefix of another string. This ensures that each string of S is uniquely associated with an external node of T. We can always satisfy this assumption by adding a special character that is not in the original alphabet Σ at the end of each string.

An internal node in a standard trie T can have anywhere between 1 and d children, where d is the size of the alphabet. There is an edge going from the root r to one of its children for each character that is first in some string in the collection S. In addition, a path from the root of T to an internal node v at depth i corresponds to an i-character prefix $X[0..i-1]$ of a string X of S. In fact, for each character c that can follow the prefix $X[0..i-1]$ in a string of the set S, there is a child of v labeled with character c. In this way, a trie concisely stores the common prefixes that exist among a set of strings.

If there are only two characters in the alphabet, then the trie is essentially a binary tree, although some internal nodes may have only one child (that is, it may be an improper binary tree). In general, if there are d characters in the alphabet, then the trie will be a multi-way tree where each internal node has between 1 and

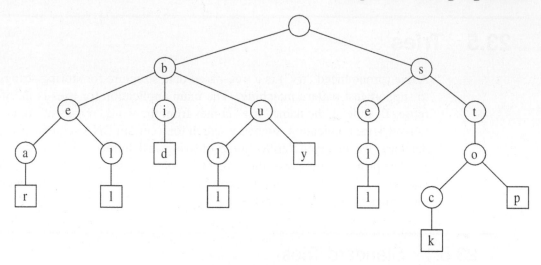

Figure 23.14: Standard trie for the strings {bear, bell, bid, bull, buy, sell, stock, stop}.

d children. In addition, there are likely to be several internal nodes in a standard trie that have fewer than d children. For example, the trie shown in Figure 23.14 has several internal nodes with only one child. We can implement a trie with a tree storing characters at its nodes.

Theorem 23.4: *A standard trie storing a collection S of s strings of total length n from an alphabet of size d has the following properties:*

- *Every internal node of T has at most d children*
- *T has s external nodes*
- *The height of T is equal to the length of the longest string in S*
- *The number of nodes of T is $O(n)$.*

The worst case for the number of nodes of a trie occurs when no two strings share a common nonempty prefix—that is, except for the root, all internal nodes have one child.

A trie T for a set S of strings can be used to implement a dictionary whose keys are the strings of S. Namely, we perform a search in T for a string X by tracing down from the root the path indicated by the characters in X. If this path can be traced and terminates at an external node, then we know X is in the dictionary. For example, in the trie in Figure 23.14, tracing the path for "bull" ends up at an external node. If the path cannot be traced or the path can be traced but terminates at an internal node, then X is not in the dictionary. In the example in Figure 23.14, the path for "bet" cannot be traced and the path for "be" ends at an internal node. Neither such word is in the dictionary. Note that in this implementation of a dictionary, single characters are compared instead of the entire string (key).

Analysis

It is easy to see that the running time of the search for a string of size m is $O(dm)$, where d is the size of the alphabet. Indeed, we visit at most $m + 1$ nodes of T and we spend $O(d)$ time at each node. For some alphabets, we may be able to improve the time spent at a node to be $O(1)$ or $O(\log d)$ by using a dictionary of characters implemented in a hash table or lookup table. However, since d is a constant in most applications, we can stick with the simple approach that takes $O(d)$ time per node visited.

Application to Word Matching

From the above discussion, it follows that we can use a trie to perform a special type of pattern matching, called ***word matching***, where we want to determine whether a given pattern matches one of the words of the text exactly. (See Figure 23.15.) Word matching differs from standard pattern matching since the pattern cannot match an arbitrary substring of the text, but only one of its words. Using a trie, word matching for a pattern of length m takes $O(dm)$ time, where d is the size of the alphabet, independent of the size of the text. If the alphabet has constant size (as is the case for text in natural languages and DNA strings), a query takes $O(m)$ time, proportional to the size of the pattern. A simple extension of this scheme supports prefix matching queries. However, arbitrary occurrences of the pattern in the text (for example, the pattern is a proper suffix of a word or spans two words) cannot be efficiently performed.

Standard Trie Construction

To construct a standard trie for a set S of strings, we can use an incremental algorithm that inserts the strings one at a time. Recall the assumption that no string of S is a prefix of another string. To insert a string X into the current trie T, we first try to trace the path associated with X in T. Since X is not already in T and no string in S is a prefix of another string, we will stop tracing the path at an ***internal*** node v of T before reaching the end of X. We then create a new chain of node descendants of v to store the remaining characters of X. The time to insert X is $O(dm)$, where m is the length of X and d is the size of the alphabet. Thus, constructing the entire trie for set S takes $O(dn)$ time, where n is the total length of the strings of S.

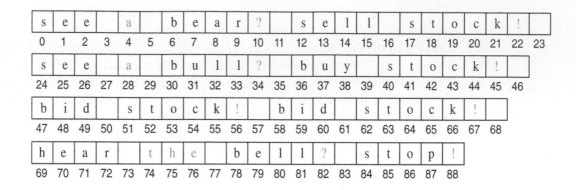

(a)

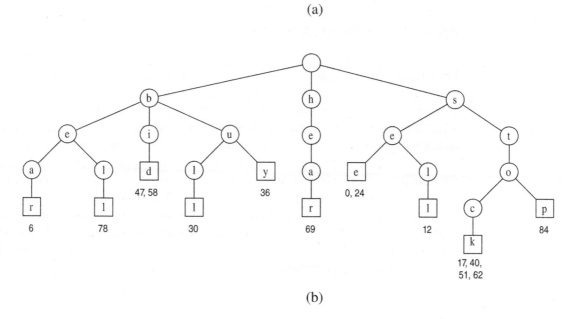

(b)

Figure 23.15: Word matching and prefix matching with a standard trie: (a) an example text that is to be searched; (b) a standard trie for the words in the text (with articles and prepositions, which are also known as *stop words*, excluded). We show external nodes augmented with indications of the corresponding word positions.

There is a potential space inefficiency in the standard trie that has prompted the development of the *compressed trie*, which is also known (for historical reasons) as the *Patricia trie*. Namely, there are potentially a lot of nodes in the standard trie that have only one child, and the existence of such nodes is a waste, for it implies that the total number of nodes in the tree could be more than the number of words in the corresponding text.

We discuss the compressed trie data structure in the next subsection.

23.5.2 Compressed Tries

A ***compressed trie*** is similar to a standard trie but it ensures that each internal node in the trie has at least two children. It enforces this rule by compressing chains of single-child nodes into individual edges. (See Figure 23.16.) Let T be a standard trie. We say that an internal node v of T is ***redundant*** if v has one child and is not the root. For example, the trie of Figure 23.14 has eight redundant nodes. Let us also say that a chain of $k \geq 2$ edges,

$$(v_0, v_1)(v_1, v_2) \cdots (v_{k-1}, v_k),$$

is ***redundant*** if

- v_i is redundant for $i = 1, \ldots, k - 1$
- v_0 and v_k are not redundant.

We can transform T into a compressed trie by replacing each redundant chain $(v_0, v_1) \cdots (v_{k-1}, v_k)$ of $k \geq 2$ edges into a single edge (v_0, v_k), relabeling v_k with the concatenation of the labels of nodes $v_1, \ldots, v_k$.

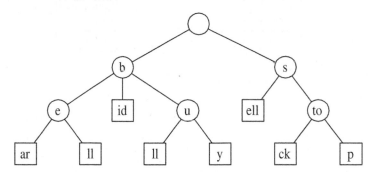

Figure 23.16: Compressed trie for the strings {bear, bell, bid, bull, buy, sell, stock, stop}. Compare this with the standard trie shown in Figure 23.14.

Thus, nodes in a compressed trie are labeled with strings, which are substrings of strings in the collection, rather than with individual characters. The advantage of a compressed trie over a standard trie is that the number of nodes of the compressed trie is proportional to the number of strings and not to their total length, as shown in the following theorem (compare with Theorem 23.4).

Theorem 23.5: *A compressed trie storing a collection S of s strings from an alphabet of size d has the following properties:*

- *Every internal node of T has at least two children and at most d children*
- *T has s external nodes*
- *The number of nodes of T is $O(s)$.*

The attentive reader may wonder whether the compression of paths provides any significant advantage, since it is offset by a corresponding expansion of the node labels. Indeed, a compressed trie is truly advantageous only when it is used as an ***auxiliary*** index structure over a collection of strings already stored in a primary structure, and is not required to actually store all the characters of the strings in the collection. Given this auxiliary structure, however, the compressed trie is indeed quite efficient.

Suppose, for example, that the collection S of strings is an array of strings $S[0]$, $S[1], \ldots, S[s-1]$. Instead of storing the label X of a node explicitly, we represent it implicitly by a triplet of integers (i, j, k), such that $X = S[i][j..k]$; that is, X is the substring of $S[i]$ consisting of the characters from the jth to the kth included. (See the example in Figure 23.17. Also compare with the standard trie of Figure 23.15.)

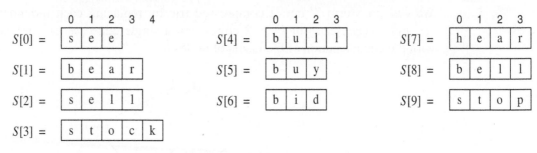

(a)

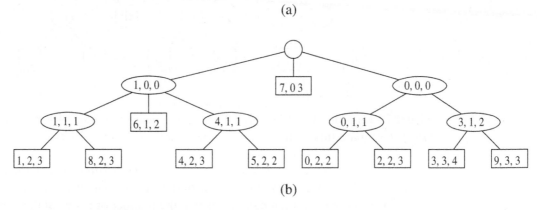

(b)

Figure 23.17: (a) Collection S of strings stored in an array. (b) Compact representation of the compressed trie for S.

This additional compression scheme allows us to reduce the total space for the trie itself from $O(n)$ for the standard trie to $O(s)$ for the compressed trie, where n is the total length of the strings in S and s is the number of strings in S. We must still store the different strings in S, of course, but we nevertheless reduce the space for the trie. In the next section, we present an application where the collection of strings can also be stored compactly.

23.5.3 Suffix Tries

One of the primary applications for tries is for the case when the strings in the collection S are all the suffixes of a string X. Such a trie is called the ***suffix trie*** (also known as a ***suffix tree*** or ***position tree***) of string X. For example, Figure 23.18a shows the suffix trie for the eight suffixes of string `"minimize"`.

For a suffix trie, the compact representation presented in the previous section can be further simplified. Namely, we can construct the trie so that the label of each vertex is a pair (i, j) indicating the string $X[i..j]$. (See Figure 23.18b.) To satisfy the rule that no suffix of X is a prefix of another suffix, we can add a special character, denoted with $, that is not in the original alphabet Σ at the end of X (and thus to every suffix). That is, if string X has length n, we build a trie for the set of n strings $X[i..n-1]$\$, for $i = 0, \ldots, n-1$.

Saving Space

Using a suffix trie allows us to save space over a standard trie by using several space compression techniques, including those used for the compressed trie. The advantage of the compact representation of tries now becomes apparent for suffix tries. Since the total length of the suffixes of a string X of length n is

$$1 + 2 + \cdots + n = \frac{n(n+1)}{2},$$

storing all the suffixes of X explicitly would take $O(n^2)$ space. Even so, the suffix trie represents these strings implicitly in $O(n)$ space, as formally stated in the following theorem.

Theorem 23.6: *The compact representation of a suffix trie T for a string X of length n uses $O(n)$ space.*

Construction

We can construct the suffix trie for a string of length n with an incremental algorithm like the one given in Section 23.5.1. This construction takes $O(dn^2)$ time because the total length of the suffixes is quadratic in n. However, the (compact) suffix trie for a string of length n can be constructed in $O(n)$ time with a specialized algorithm, different from the one for general tries. This linear-time construction algorithm is fairly complex, however, and is not reported here. Still, we can take advantage of the existence of this fast construction algorithm when we want to use a suffix trie to solve other problems.

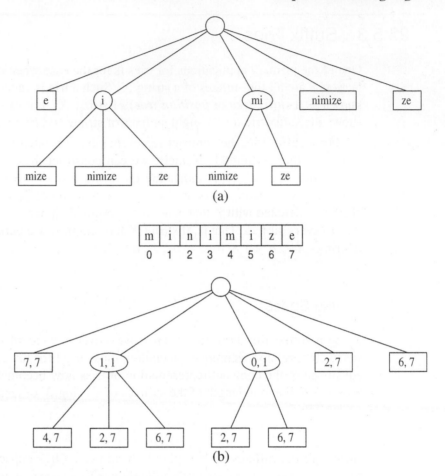

Figure 23.18: (a) Suffix trie T for the string $X = $ "minimize". (b) Compact representation of T, where pair (i, j) denotes $X[i..j]$.

Using a Suffix Trie

The suffix trie T for a string X can be used to efficiently perform pattern matching queries on text X. Namely, we can determine whether a pattern P is a substring of X by trying to trace a path associated with P in T. P is a substring of X if and only if such a path can be traced. The details of the pattern matching algorithm are given in Algorithm 23.19, which assumes the following additional property on the labels of the nodes in the compact representation of the suffix trie:

> If node v has label (i, j) and Y is the string of length y associated with the path from the root to v (included), then $X[j - y + 1..j] = Y$.

This property ensures that we can easily compute the start index of the pattern in the text when a match occurs.

Algorithm suffixTrieMatch(T, P):

   Input: Compact suffix trie T for a text X and pattern P

   Output: Starting index of a substring of X matching P or an indication that P
     is not a substring of X

   $p \leftarrow P.\text{length}()$ // length of suffix of the pattern to be matched

   $j \leftarrow 0$ // start of suffix of the pattern to be matched

   $v \leftarrow T.\text{root}()$

   repeat

      $f \leftarrow$ **true** // flag indicating that no child was successfully processed

      for each child w of v **do**

         $i \leftarrow \text{start}(w)$

         if $P[j] = T[i]$ **then**

            // process child w

            $x \leftarrow \text{end}(w) - i + 1$

            if $p \leq x$ **then**

               // suffix is shorter than or of the same length of the node label

               if $P[j..j + p - 1] = X[i..i + p - 1]$ **then**

                  return $i - j$ // match

               else

                  return "P is not a substring of X"

            else

               // suffix is longer than the node label

               if $P[j..j + x - 1] = X[i..i + x - 1]$ **then**

                  $p \leftarrow p - x$ // update suffix length

                  $j \leftarrow j + x$ // update suffix start index

                  $v \leftarrow w$

                  $f \leftarrow$ **false**

                  break out of the **for** loop

   until f or $T.\text{isExternal}(v)$

   return "P is not a substring of X"

Algorithm 23.19: Pattern matching with a suffix trie. We denote the label of a node v with $(\text{start}(v), \text{end}(v))$, that is, the pair of indices specifying the substring of the text associated with v.

Suffix Trie Properties

The correctness of algorithm suffixTrieMatch follows from the fact that we search down the trie T, matching characters of the pattern P one at a time until one of the following events occurs:

- We completely match the pattern P.
- We get a mismatch (caught by the termination of the for-loop without a breakout).
- We are left with characters of P still to be matched after processing an external node.

Let m be the size of pattern P and d be the size of the alphabet. In order to determine the running time of algorithm suffixTrieMatch, we make the following observations:

- We process at most $m + 1$ nodes of the trie.
- Each node processed has at most d children.
- At each node v processed, we perform at most one character comparison for each child w of v to determine which child of v needs to be processed next (which may possibly be improved by using a fast dictionary to index the children of v).
- We perform at most m character comparisons overall in the processed nodes.
- We spend $O(1)$ time for each character comparison.

Analysis

We conclude that algorithm suffixTrieMatch performs pattern matching queries in $O(dm)$ time (and would possibly run even faster if we used a dictionary to index children of nodes in the suffix trie). Note that the running time does not depend on the size of the text X. Also, the running time is linear in the size of the pattern, that is, it is $O(m)$, for a constant-size alphabet. Hence, suffix tries are suited for repetitive pattern matching applications, where a series of pattern matching queries is performed on a fixed text.

We summarize the results of this section in the following theorem.

Theorem 23.7: *Let X be a text string with n characters from an alphabet of size d. We can perform pattern matching queries on X in $O(dm)$ time, where m is the length of the pattern, with the suffix trie of X, which uses $O(n)$ space and can be constructed in $O(dn)$ time.*

We explore another application of tries in the next subsection.

23.5.4 Search Engines

The World Wide Web contains a huge collection of text documents (web pages). Information about these pages is gathered by a program called a ***web crawler***, which then stores this information in a special dictionary database. A web ***search engine*** allows users to retrieve relevant information from this database, thereby identifying relevant pages on the web containing given keywords. In this section, we present a simplified model of a search engine.

Inverted Files

The core information stored by a search engine is a dictionary, called an ***inverted index*** or ***inverted file***, storing key-value pairs (w, L), where w is a word and L is a collection of references to pages containing word w. The keys (words) in this dictionary are called ***index terms*** and should be a set of vocabulary entries and proper nouns as large as possible. The elements in this dictionary are called ***occurrence lists*** and should cover as many web pages as possible.

We can efficiently implement an inverted index with a data structure consisting of the following:

- An array storing the occurrence lists of the terms (in no particular order)
- A compressed trie for the set of index terms, where each external node stores the index of the occurrence list of the associated term.

The reason for storing the occurrence lists outside the trie is to keep the size of the trie data structure sufficiently small to fit in internal memory. Instead, because of their large total size, the occurrence lists have to be stored on disk.

With our data structure, a query for a single keyword is similar to a word matching query (see Section 23.5.1). Namely, we find the keyword in the trie and we return the associated occurrence list.

When multiple keywords are given and the desired output is the pages containing ***all*** the given keywords, we retrieve the occurrence list of each keyword using the trie and return their intersection. To facilitate the intersection computation, each occurrence list should be implemented with a sequence sorted by address or with a dictionary, which allows for a simple intersection algorithm similar to sorted sequence merging (Section 8.1).

In addition to the basic task of returning a list of pages containing given keywords, search engines provide an important additional service by ***ranking*** the pages returned by relevance. Devising fast and accurate ranking algorithms for search engines is a major challenge for computer researchers and electronic commerce companies.

23.6 Exercises

Reinforcement

R-23.1 How many nonempty prefixes of the string $P =$"aaabbaaa" are also suffixes of P?

R-23.2 Draw a figure illustrating the comparisons done by the brute-force pattern matching algorithm for the case when the text is "aaabaadaabaaa" and the pattern is "aabaaa".

R-23.3 Repeat the previous problem for the BM pattern matching algorithm, not counting the comparisons made to compute the last function.

R-23.4 Repeat the previous problem for the KMP pattern matching algorithm, not counting the comparisons made to compute the failure function.

R-23.5 Compute a table representing the last function used in the BM pattern matching algorithm for the pattern string

"the quick brown fox jumped over a lazy cat"

assuming the following alphabet (which starts with the space character):

$\Sigma = \{$,a,b,c,d,e,f,g,h,i,j,k,l,m,n,o,p,q,r,s,t,u,v,w,x,y,z$\}$.

R-23.6 Assuming that the characters in alphabet Σ can be enumerated and can index arrays, give an $O(m + |\Sigma|)$ time method for constructing the last function from an m-length pattern string P.

R-23.7 Compute a table representing the KMP failure function for the pattern string "cgtacgttcgtac".

R-23.8 Draw a standard trie for the following set of strings:

$\{$abab, baba, ccccc, bbaaaa, caa, bbaacc, cbcc, cbca$\}$.

R-23.9 Draw a compressed trie for the set of strings given in Exercise R-23.8.

R-23.10 Draw the compact representation of the suffix trie for the string

"minimize minime".

R-23.11 What is the longest prefix of the string "cgtacgttcgtacg" that is also a suffix of this string?

R-23.12 Give an example of an input instance for lexicon matching problem, with just a single pattern in the lexicon, L, that forces the Karp-Rabin algorithm given in Algorithm 23.11 to run in $\Omega(nm)$ time.

R-23.13 Explain why tabulation hashing, which is discussed in Section 6.2.3, is not a good candidate for use in a rolling-hash lexicon matching algorithm.

R-23.14 Describe how to compute $\mathsf{shiftHash}(h(X[i..i+m-1]), X, i)$ for the hash function, $h(X[i..i+m-1]) = X[i] + \cdots + X[i+m-1]$, where each character is viewed as an integer in the range $[0, c-1]$, with c being the size of the alphabet, and all arithmetic is done modulo a prime, p.

Creativity

C-23.1 Give an example of a text T of length n and a pattern P of length m that force the brute-force pattern matching algorithm to have a running time that is $\Omega(nm)$.

C-23.2 Give a justification of why the KMPFailureFunction method (Algorithm 23.9) runs in $O(m)$ time on a pattern of length m.

C-23.3 Show how to modify the KMP string pattern matching algorithm so as to find *every* occurrence of a pattern string P that appears as a substring in T, while still running in $O(n + m)$ time. (Be sure to catch even those matches that overlap.)

C-23.4 Let T be a text of length n, and let P be a pattern of length m. Describe an $O(n + m)$-time method for finding the longest prefix of P that is a substring of T.

C-23.5 Say that a pattern P of length m is a *circular substring* of a text T of length n if there is an index $0 \le i < m$, such that $P = T[n - m + i..n - 1] + T[0..i - 1]$, that is, if P is a substring of T or P is equal to the concatenation of a suffix of T and a prefix of T. Give an $O(n + m)$-time algorithm for determining whether P is a circular substring of T.

C-23.6 The KMP pattern matching algorithm can be modified to run faster on binary strings by redefining the failure function as

$$f(j) = \text{the largest } k < j \text{ such that } P[0..k - 2]\overline{P[k - 1]} \text{ is a suffix of } P[1..j],$$

where $overlineP[k]$ denotes the complement of the kth bit of P. Describe how to modify the KMP algorithm to be able to take advantage of this new failure function and also give a method for computing this failure function. Show that this method makes at most n comparisons between the text and the pattern (as opposed to the $2n$ comparisons needed by the standard KMP algorithm given in Section 23.3).

C-23.7 Modify the simplified BM algorithm presented in this chapter using ideas from the KMP algorithm so that it runs in $O(n + m)$ time.

C-23.8 Consider the substring pattern matching problem for a length-m pattern, P, and a length-n text, T, where one of the characters in P is a symbol, "?," which is not in the alphabet for the text. This symbol, "?," is a *wild-card* character, which matches with any character of the alphabet for the text. The pattern, P, contains exactly one "?" symbol. Show how to modify the Karp-Rabin matching algorithm for this single-pattern instance of the lexicon matching problem so that the expected running time of the resulting algorithm is $O(n + m)$.

C-23.9 Show how to perform prefix matching queries using a suffix trie.

C-23.10 Give an efficient algorithm for deleting a string from a standard trie and analyze its running time.

C-23.11 Give an efficient algorithm for deleting a string from a compressed trie and analyze its running time.

C-23.12 Describe an algorithm for constructing the compact representation of a suffix trie and analyze its running time.

C-23.13 Describe a generalized version of the Karp-Rabin lexicon matching algorithm for the case when their are k different possible pattern sizes. Characterize the running time of this algorithm in terms of n, k, and the total size, N, of all the patterns in the lexicon.

Applications

A-23.1 When a web crawler is exploring the Internet looking for content to index for a search engine, the crawler needs some way of detecting when it is visiting a copy of a website it has encountered before. Describe a way for a web crawler to store its web pages efficiently so that it can detect in $O(n)$ time whether a web page of length n has been previously encountered and, if not, add it to the collection of previously encountered web pages in $O(1)$ additional time.

A-23.2 Search engines need a fast way to detect and ignore stop words, that is, words, such as prepositions, pronouns, and articles, that are very common and carry no meaningful information content. Describe an efficient method for storing and searching a set of stop words in a way that supports stop-word identification in constant time for all constant-length stop words.

A-23.3 DNA strings are sometimes spliced into other DNA strings as a product of recombinant DNA processes. But DNA strings can be read in what would be either the forward or backward direction for a standard character string. Thus, it is useful to be able to identify prefixes and their reversals. Let T be a DNA text string of length n. Describe an $O(n)$-time method for finding the longest prefix of T that is a substring of the reversal of T.

A-23.4 Linguists are interested in studying the way in which words are constructed, with common prefixes and suffixes giving important clues to the meanings of words they are contained in. Thus, a useful tool for a linguist would be to be able to identify all the words in a given collection, W, of words, that have the same prefix, p, or suffix, s. Indeed, it is useful even to just know the number of such words in W. Describe how to build a data structure for W that can quickly answer, for any prefix, p, or suffix, s, the number of words in W that have the prefix p or suffix s. What is the performance of your method?

A-23.5 One way to mask a message, M, using a version of ***steganography***, is to insert random characters into M at pseudo-random locations so as to expand M into a larger string, C. For instance, the message,

ILOVEMOM,

could be expanded into

AMIJLONDPVGEMRPIOM.

It is an example of hiding the string, M, in plain sight, since the characters in M and C are not encrypted. As long as someone knows where the random characters where inserted, he or she can recover M from C. The challenge for law enforcement, therefore, is to prove when someone is using this technique, that is, to determine whether a string C contains a message M in this way. Thus, describe an $O(n)$-time method for detecting if a string, M, is a subsequence of a string, C, of length n.

A-23.6 Consider the previous exercise, but now suppose that the masking process first pads many random characters to form a prefix and suffix of M before adding a few random characters at various locations in the middle of M. Thus, a likely message, M, is one that is much shorter than the host string, C. Describe an $O(n^2)$-time algorithm for determining if M is a subsequence of C, and, if so, returns the shortest substring of C having M as a subsequence.

A-23.7 Suppose Bill is graduate of Slacker University, and he took a little "shortcut" when he was asked to build a software system that could take a pattern, P, of length, m, and text, T, of length, n, with both defined over the same alphabet of size d for some constant $d > 1$, and determine whether P is a substring of T. Namely, Bill's software simply returns the answer "no" whenever it is asked to determine whether a pattern P of length m is contained in a text T of length n. When confronted by his Boss about this software, Bill replied that his software system is almost always correct, that is, Bill claims that his software fails with probability that is $o(1)$ as a function of m and n. Give an asymptotic characterization of the probability that Bill's simple algorithm incorrectly determines whether P is a substring in T, assuming that all possible pattern strings of length m are equally likely. Is Bill right about his software?

A-23.8 Suppose the trustee for the estate of famous photographer, Ansel Adams, was interested in finding examples of people posting Ansel Adams photographs on their personal websites without including attributions to him. Suppose further that some of these people have tried to conceal their possible copyright infringement by cropping the image down to be a smaller size. Thus, given a candidate image, P, taken from someone's personal website, and his own photograph, T, Mr. Adams is interested in determining whether it is possible to create the image P by cropping the image T. Assuming that P and T are square images, this problem can be easily modeled as a two-dimensional version of the pattern matching problem. In ***two-dimensional pattern matching***, a pattern, P, is given as an $m \times m$ array of characters, and the text, T, is given as an $n \times n$ array of characters, and we are interested in finding a location, (i, j), such that P is a submatrix of T when shifted to the location, (i, j). That is,

$$P[k, l] = T[i + k, j + l],$$

for $k = 0, \ldots, m - 1$ and $l = 0, \ldots, m - 1$. In the context of the problem of interest for the trustee of the estate of Ansel Adams, each pixel in an image could be viewed as a character (corresponding, for example, to an 8-bit intensity value in a black-and-white image). Describe an efficient algorithm for solving this two-dimensional pattern matching problem. What are the worst-case and expected-case running times for your algorithm?

Chapter Notes

The KMP algorithm is described by Knuth, Morris, and Pratt in their journal article [132]. Boyer and Moore published their algorithm in the same year [35]. In their article, Knuth *et al.* [132] also prove that the BM algorithm runs in linear time. More recently, Cole [46] shows that the BM algorithm makes at most $3n$ character comparisons in the worst case, and this bound is tight. Hashing-based pattern matching is presented by Karp and Rabin [123]. Some of the algorithms presented in this chapter are also discussed in the book chapter by Aho [7], albeit in a more theoretical framework. The reader interested in further study of string pattern matching algorithms is referred to the book by Stephen [200] and the book chapters by Aho [7] and Crochemore and Lecroq [52].

The trie was invented by Morrison [161] and is discussed extensively in the classic book *Sorting and Searching* by Knuth [131]. The name "Patricia" is short for "Practical Algorithm to Retrieve Information Coded in Alphanumeric" [161]. McCreight [148] shows how to construct suffix tries in linear time. An introduction to the field of information retrieval, which includes a discussion of search engines for the World Wide Web, is provided in the book by Baeza-Yates and Ribeiro-Neto [20].

Chapter
24
Cryptography

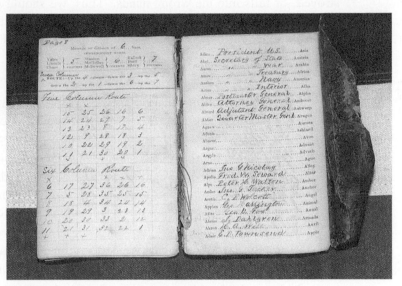

Union code book used in the U.S. Civil War. U.S. government Image. NSA.

Contents

24.1 Greatest Common Divisors (GCD) 687

24.2 Modular Arithmetic 691

24.3 Cryptographic Operations 699

24.4 The RSA Cryptosystem 703

24.5 The El Gamal Cryptosystem 706

24.6 Exercises 708

Computers today are used for a multitude of sensitive applications. Customers utilize electronic commerce to make purchases and pay their bills. Businesses use the Internet to share sensitive company documents and interact with business partners. Governments use computers to keep track of personal information about their citizens. Hospitals use databases to track patients and their billing information. And universities use networks of computers to store personal information about students and their grades. Each of us has an abundance of private and personal information that is being stored and transmitted by computers today.

Such sensitive information can be potentially damaging if it is altered, destroyed, or falls into the wrong hands. Thus, we should use powerful techniques to protect our sensitive data. In this chapter, we discuss several powerful algorithmic techniques for protecting sensitive information, so as to achieve the following goals:

- *Data integrity*: Information should not be altered without detection. For example, it is important to prevent the modification of purchase orders or other contractually binding documents transmitted electronically.

- *Authentication*: Individuals and organizations that are accessing or communicating sensitive information must be correctly identified, that is, authenticated. For example, corporations offering telecommuting arrangements to their employees should set up an authentication procedure for accessing corporate databases through the Internet.

- *Authorization*: Agents that are performing computations involving sensitive information must be authorized to perform those computations.

- *Nonrepudiation*: In transactions that imply a contract, the parties that have agreed to that contract must not have the ability of backing out of their obligations without being detected.

- *Confidentiality*: Sensitive information should be kept secret from individuals who are not authorized to see that information. That is, we must ensure that data is viewed by the sender and by the receiver, but not by unauthorized parties who can eavesdrop on the communication. For example, many email messages are meant to be confidential.

Many of the techniques we discuss in this chapter for achieving the above goals utilize *number theory*. Thus, we begin this chapter by discussing a number of important number theory concepts and algorithms. We describe the ancient, yet surprisingly efficient, Euclid's algorithm for computing greatest common divisors, as well as algorithms for computing modular exponents and inverses. We show how many of these number theory algorithms can be used in cryptographic algorithms that implement computer security services. We focus on encryption, including the popular public-key encryption schemes, RSA and El Gamal.

24.1 Greatest Common Divisors (GCD)

Many modern encryption schemes, like RSA and El Gamal, are based on viewing messages as numbers and using number-theoretic algorithms to process them. Thus, before we discuss some of these well-known encryption schemes, we should first discuss several fundamental algorithms for performing important computations involving numbers. Throughout this discussion, we assume that all variables are integers. Also, proofs of some mathematical facts are left as exercises.

24.1.1 Some Facts from Elementary Number Theory

To get us started, we need some facts from elementary number theory, including some notation and definitions. Given positive integers a and b, we use the notation

$$a|b$$

to indicate that a **divides** b, that is, b is a multiple of a. If $a|b$, then we know that there is some integer k, such that $b = ak$. The following properties of divisibility follow immediately from this definition.

Theorem 24.1: *Let a, b, and c be arbitrary integers. Then*

- *If $a|b$ and $b|c$, then $a|c$.*
- *If $a|b$ and $a|c$, then $a|(ib + jc)$, for all integers i and j.*
- *If $a|b$ and $b|a$, then $a = b$ or $a = -b$.*

Proof: See Exercise C-24.1. ∎

Recall that an integer p is **prime** if $p \geq 2$ and its only divisors are the trivial divisors 1 and p. Thus, in the case that p is prime, $d|p$ implies $d = 1$ or $d = p$. An integer greater than 2 that is not prime is **composite**. We also have the following:

Theorem 24.2 (*Fundamental Theorem of Arithmetic*): *Let $n > 1$ be an integer. Then there is a unique set of prime numbers $\{p_1, \ldots, p_k\}$ and positive integer exponents $\{e_1, \ldots, e_k\}$, such that*

$$n = p_1^{e_1} \cdots p_k^{e_k}.$$

The product $p_1^{e_1} \cdots p_k^{e_k}$ is known as the **prime decomposition** of n in this case. Theorem 24.2 and the notion of unique prime decomposition is the basis of several cryptographic schemes.

The Greatest Common Divisor (GCD)

The *greatest common divisor* of positive integers a and b, denoted $\gcd(a, b)$, is the largest integer that divides both a and b. Alternatively, we could say that $\gcd(a, b)$ is the number c, such that if $d|a$ and $d|b$, then $d|c$. If $\gcd(a, b) = 1$, we say that a and b are *relatively prime*. We extend the notion of greatest common divisor to a pair of arbitrary integers by the following two rules:

- $\gcd(a, 0) = \gcd(0, a) = a$.

- $\gcd(a, b) = \gcd(|a|, |b|)$, which takes care of negative values.

Thus, $\gcd(12, 0) = 12$, $\gcd(10\,403, 303) = 101$, and $\gcd(-12, 78) = 6$.

Relating the Modulo Operator and the GCD

The following theorem gives an alternative characterization of the greatest common divisor. Its proof makes use of the modulo operator.

Theorem 24.3: *For any positive integers a and b, $\gcd(a, b)$ is the smallest positive integer d such that $d = ia + jb$ for some integers i and j. In other words, if d is the smallest positive integer linear combination of a and b, then $d = \gcd(a, b)$.*

Proof: Suppose d is the smallest integer such that $d = ia + jb$ for integers i and j. Note that, immediately from the definition of d, any common divisor of both a and b is also a divisor of d. Thus, $d \geq \gcd(a, b)$. To complete the proof, we need to show that $d \leq \gcd(a, b)$.

Let $h = \lfloor a/d \rfloor$. That is, h is the integer such that $a \bmod d = a - hd$. Then

$$
\begin{aligned}
a \bmod d &= a - hd \\
&= a - h(ia + jb) \\
&= (1 - hi)a + (-hj)b.
\end{aligned}
$$

In other words, $a \bmod d$ is also an integer linear combination of a and b. Moreover, by the definition of the modulo operator, $a \bmod d < d$. But d is the smallest positive integer linear combination of a and b. Thus, we must conclude that $a \bmod d = 0$, which implies that $d|a$. In addition, by a similar argument, we get that $d|b$. Thus, d is a divisor of both a and b, which implies $d \leq \gcd(a, b)$.   ■

As we will show in Section 24.2, this theorem shows that the gcd function is useful for computing multiplicative modular inverses. In the next subsection, we show how to quickly compute the gcd function.

24.1.2 Euclid's GCD Algorithm

To compute the greatest common divisor of two numbers, we can use one of the oldest algorithms known, Euclid's algorithm. This algorithm is based on the following property of $\gcd(a, b)$:

Lemma 24.4: *Let a and b be two positive integers. For any integer r, we have*

$$\gcd(a, b) = \gcd(b, a - rb).$$

Proof: Let $d = \gcd(a, b)$ and $c = \gcd(b, a - rb)$. That is, d is the largest integer such that $d|a$ and $d|b$, and c is the largest integer such that $c|b$ and $c|(a - rb)$. We want to prove that $d = c$. By the definition of d, the number

$$(a - rb)/d = a/d - r(b/d)$$

is an integer. Thus, d divides both a and $a - rb$; hence, $d \leq c$.

By the definition of c, $k = b/c$ must be an integer, since $c|b$. Moreover,

$$(a - rb)/c = a/c - rk$$

must also be an integer, since $c|(a - rb)$. Thus, a/c must also be an integer, that is, $c|a$. Therefore, c divides both a and b; hence, $c \leq d$. We conclude then that $d = c$.

∎

Lemma 24.4 leads us easily to an ancient algorithm, known as Euclid's algorithm, for computing the greatest common divisor (GCD) of two numbers, shown next in Algorithm 24.1.

Algorithm EuclidGCD(a, b):

    Input: Nonnegative integers a and b
    Output: $\gcd(a, b)$

  if $b = 0$ **then**
      return a
  return EuclidGCD$(b, a \bmod b)$

        Algorithm 24.1: Euclid's GCD algorithm.

An example of the execution of Euclid's algorithm is shown in Table 24.2.

	1	2	3	4	5	6	7
a	412	260	152	108	44	20	4
b	260	152	108	44	20	4	0

Table 24.2: Example of an execution of Euclid's algorithm to compute $\gcd(412, 260) = 4$. The arguments a and b of each recursive invocation of method EuclidGCD$(412, 260)$ are shown left-to-right, with the column headings showing the level of recursion in the EuclidGCD method.

Analyzing Euclid's Algorithm

Let us analyze the running time of Euclid's GCD algorithm. The number of arithmetic operations performed by method EuclidGCD(a, b) is proportional to the number of recursive calls. So to bound the number of arithmetic operations performed by Euclid's algorithm, we need only bound the number of recursive calls. First, we observe that after the first call, the first argument is always larger than the second one. For $i > 0$, let a_i be the first argument of the ith recursive call of method EuclidGCD. Clearly, the second argument of a recursive call is equal to a_{i+1}, the first argument of the next call. Also, we have

$$a_{i+2} = a_i \bmod a_{i+1},$$

which implies that the sequence of the a_i's is strictly decreasing. We will now show that the sequence decreases quickly. Specifically, we claim that

$$a_{i+2} < \frac{1}{2}a_i.$$

To prove the claim, we distinguish two cases:

Case 1: $a_{i+1} \leq \frac{1}{2}a_i$. Since the sequence of the a_i's is strictly decreasing, we have

$$a_{i+2} < a_{i+1} \leq \frac{1}{2}a_i.$$

Case 2: $a_{i+1} > \frac{1}{2}a_i$. In this case, since $a_{i+2} = a_i \bmod a_{i+1}$, we have

$$a_{i+2} = a_i \bmod a_{i+1} = a_i - a_{i+1} < \frac{1}{2}a_i.$$

Thus, the size of the first argument to the EuclidGCD method decreases by half with every other recursive call. We may therefore summarize the above analysis as follows.

Theorem 24.5: *Let a and b be two positive integers. Euclid's algorithm computes* $\gcd(a, b)$ *by executing* $O(\log \max(a, b))$ *arithmetic operations.*

We note that the complexity bound here is based on counting arithmetic operations, which themselves can be implemented to have reasonably-fast running times as a function of their input sizes, which are defined by the number of bits of the numbers involved. Moreover, note that the numbers, a and b, are represented using $O(\log \max(a, b))$ bits. So if we let n denote the input size for Euclid's algorithm, in bits, then we can characterize its performance as using $O(n)$ arithmetic operations.

24.2 Modular Arithmetic

Let Z_n denote the set of nonnegative integers less than n:

$$Z_n = \{0, 1, \cdots, (n-1)\}.$$

The set Z_n is also called the set of ***residues*** modulo n, because if $b = a \bmod n$, b is sometimes called the ***residue*** of a modulo n. Modular arithmetic in Z_n, where operations on the elements of Z_n are performed $\bmod n$, exhibits properties similar to those of traditional arithmetic, such as the associativity, commutativity, distributivity of addition and multiplication, and the existence of identity elements 0 and 1 for addition and multiplication, respectively. Moreover, in any arithmetic expression, reducing each of its subexpressions modulo n produces the same result as computing the entire expression and then reducing that value modulo n. Also, every element x in Z_n has an ***additive inverse***, that is, for each $x \in Z_n$, there is a $y \in Z_n$ such that $x + y \bmod n = 0$. For example, the additive inverse of 5 modulo 11 is 6.

When it comes to multiplicative inverses, however, an important difference arises. Let x be an element of Z_n. A ***multiplicative inverse*** of x is an element $z^{-1} \in Z_n$ such that $xx^{-1} \equiv 1 \bmod n$. For example, the multiplicative inverse of 5 modulo 9 is 2, that is, $5^{-1} = 2$ in Z_9. As in standard arithmetic, 0 does not have a multiplicative inverse in Z_n. Interestingly, some nonzero elements also may not have a multiplicative inverse in Z_n. For example, 3 does not have a multiplicative inverse in Z_9. However, if n is prime, then every element $x \neq 0$ of Z_n has a multiplicative inverse in Z_n (1 is its own multiplicative inverse).

Theorem 24.6: *An element $x > 0$ of Z_n has a multiplicative inverse in Z_n if and only if $\gcd(x, n) = 1$ (that is, x and n have no common factors other than 1).*

Proof: Suppose that $\gcd(x, n) = 1$. By Theorem 24.3, there are integers i and j such that $ix + jn = 1$. This implies $ix \bmod n = 1$, that is, $i \bmod n$ is the multiplicative inverse of x in Z_n, which proves the "if" part of the theorem.

To prove the "only if" part, suppose, for a contradiction, that $x > 1$ divides n, and there is an element y such that $xy \equiv 1 \bmod n$. We have $xy = kn + 1$, for some integer k. Thus, we have found integers $i = y$ and $j = -k$ such that $ix + jn = 1$. By Theorem 24.3, this implies that $\gcd(x, n) = 1$, a contradiction. ∎

Recall that if $\gcd(x, n) = 1$, we say x and n are ***relatively prime*** (1 is relatively prime to all other integers). Thus, Theorem 24.6 implies that x has a multiplicative inverse in Z_n if and only if x is relatively prime to n. In addition, Theorem 24.6 implies that the sequence $0, x, 2x, 3x, \ldots, (n-1)x$ is simply a reordering of the elements of Z_n, that is, it is a permutation of the elements Z_n.

Example Multiplicative Inverses

In Table 24.3, we show the multiplicative inverses of the elements of Z_{11} as an example. When the multiplicative inverse x^{-1} of x exists in Z_n, the notation y/x in an expression taken modulo n means "$y\,x^{-1} \bmod n$."

x	0	1	2	3	4	5	6	7	8	9	10
$x^{-1} \bmod 11$		1	6	4	3	9	2	8	7	5	10

Table 24.3: Multiplicative inverses of the elements of Z_{11}.

In Table 24.4, we show the powers of the nonnull elements of Z_{11}. We observe the following interesting patterns:

- The last column of the table, with the values $x^{10} \bmod 11$ for $x = 1, \cdots, 10$, contains all ones, as given by Fermat's Little Theorem (19.5).

- In row 1, a subsequence of one element (1), is repeated ten times.

- In row 10, a subsequence of two elements, ending with 1, is repeated five times, since $10^2 \bmod 11 = 1$.

- In rows 3, 4, 5, and 9, a subsequence of five elements, ending with 1, is repeated twice.

- In each of the rows 2, 6, 7, and 8, the ten elements are all distinct.

- The lengths of the subsequences forming the rows of the table, and their number of repetitions, are the divisors of 10, that is, 1, 2, 5, and 10.

x	x^2	x^3	x^4	x^5	x^6	x^7	x^8	x^9	x^{10}
1	1	1	1	1	1	1	1	1	1
2	4	8	5	10	9	7	3	6	1
3	9	5	4	1	3	9	5	4	1
4	5	9	3	1	4	5	9	3	1
5	3	4	9	1	5	3	4	9	1
6	3	7	9	10	5	8	4	2	1
7	5	2	3	10	4	6	9	8	1
8	9	6	4	10	3	2	5	7	1
9	4	3	5	1	9	4	3	5	1
10	1	10	1	10	1	10	1	10	1

Table 24.4: Successive powers of the elements of Z_{11} modulo 11.

Euler's Totient Function

Euler's ***totient function*** of a positive integer n, denoted $\phi(n)$, is defined as the number of positive integers less than or equal to n that are relatively prime to n. That is, $\phi(n)$ is equal to the number of elements in Z_n that have multiplicative inverses in Z_n. If p is a prime, then

$$\phi(p) = p - 1.$$

Indeed, since p is prime, each of the numbers $1, 2, \ldots, p-1$ are relatively prime to it, and $\phi(p) = p - 1$.

What if n isn't a prime number? Suppose $n = pq$, where p and q are distinct primes. How many numbers are relatively prime to n? Well, initially, we observe that there are pq positive integers between 1 and n. However, q of them (including n) are multiples of p, and so they have a gcd of p with n. Similarly, there are p multiples of q (again, including n). Those multiples can't be counted in $\phi(n)$. Thus, we see that

$$\phi(n) = pq - q - (p - 1) = (p - 1)(q - 1).$$

Euler's totient function is closely related to an important subset of Z_n known as the ***multiplicative group*** for Z_n, which is denoted as Z_n^*. The set Z_n^* is defined to be the set of integers between 1 and n that are relatively prime to n. If n is prime, then Z_n^* consists of the $n - 1$ nonzero elements in Z_n, that is,

$$Z_n^* = \{1, 2, \ldots, n - 1\},$$

if n is prime. In general, Z_n^* contains $\phi(n)$ elements.

The set Z_n^* possesses several interesting properties, with one of the most important being that this set is closed under multiplication modulo n. That is, for any pair of elements a and b of Z_n^*, we have that $c = ab \bmod n$ is also in Z_n^*. Indeed, by Theorem 24.6, a and b have multiplicative inverses in Z_n. To see that Z_n^* has this closure property, let $d = a^{-1}b^{-1} \bmod n$. Clearly, $cd \bmod n = 1$, which implies that d is the multiplicative inverse of c in Z_n. Thus, again applying Theorem 24.6, we have that c is relatively prime to n, that is, $c \in Z_n^*$. In algebraic terminology, we say that Z_n^* is a ***group***, which is a shorthand way of saying that each element in Z_n^* has a multiplicative inverse and multiplication in Z_n^* is associative, has an identity, and is closed in Z_n^*.

The fact that Z_n^* has $\phi(n)$ elements and is a multiplicative group naturally leads to an extension of Fermat's Little Theorem (19.5). Recall that in Fermat's Little Theorem, the exponent is $p - 1 = \phi(p)$, since p is prime. As it turns out, a generalized form of Fermat's Little Theorem is true, too. This generalized form is presented in the following, which is known as ***Euler's Theorem***.

Euler's Theorem

Theorem 24.7 (*Euler's Theorem*): *Let n be a positive integer, and let x be an integer such that $\gcd(x, n) = 1$. Then*

$$x^{\phi(n)} \equiv 1 \pmod{n}.$$

Proof: The proof technique is similar to that of Fermat's Little Theorem. Denote the elements of set Z_n^*, the multiplicative group for Z_n, as $u_1, u_2, \ldots, u_{\phi(n)}$. By the closure property of Z_n^*,

$$Z_n^* = \{xu_i :\ i = 1, \cdots, \phi(n)\},$$

that is, multiplying elements in Z_n^* by x modulo n merely permutes the sequence $u_1, u_2, \ldots, u_{\phi(n)}$. Thus, multiplying together the elements of Z_n^*, we obtain

$$(xu_1) \cdot (xu_2) \cdots (xu_{\phi(n)}) \equiv u_1 u_2 \cdots u_{\phi(n)} \pmod{n}.$$

Again, we collect a term $x^{\phi(n)}$ on one side, giving us the congruence

$$x^{\phi(n)} (u_1 u_2 \cdots u_{\phi(n)}) \equiv u_1 u_2 \cdots u_{\phi(n)} \pmod{n}.$$

Dividing by the product of the u_i's, gives us $x^{\phi(n)} \equiv 1 \bmod n$.   ■

Theorem 24.7 gives a closed-form expression for the multiplicative inverses. Namely, if x and n are relatively prime, we can write

$$x^{-1} \equiv x^{\phi(n)-1} \pmod{n}.$$

Generators

Given a prime p and an integer a between 1 and $p-1$, the ***order*** of a is the smallest exponent $e > 1$ such that

$$a^e \equiv 1 \bmod p.$$

A ***generator*** (also called ***primitive root***) of Z_p is an element g of Z_p with order $p-1$. We use the term "generator" for such an element a, because the repeated exponentiation of a can generate all of Z_p^*. For example, as shown in Table 24.4, the generators of Z_{11} are 2, 6, 7, and 8. Generators play an important role in many computations, including several in image analysis and cryptography. The existence of generators is established by the following theorem, stated without proof.

Theorem 24.8: *If p is a prime, then set Z_p has $\phi(p-1)$ generators.*

24.2.1 Modular Exponentiation

Suppose we want to compute $30,192^{43,791} \bmod 65,301$. Multiplying $30,192$ by itself $43,791$ times and *then* taking the result modulo $65,301$ will yield unpredictable results in most programming languages due to arithmetic overflows. Thus, we should take the modulo after each multiplication, keeping the numbers in Z_n, where $n = 65,301$ is the modulus.

The Main Drawback with This Naive Approach

Unfortunately, although this "naive" exponentiation algorithm is correct, it is inefficient, for it requires $\Theta(p)$ multiplications and divisions, where p is the exponent. With large exponents, this running time would be quite slow, since it is exponential in the size of the input, which is the number of bits needed to represent the various input numbers. Fortunately, there is a better algorithm.

The Repeated Squaring Algorithm

A simple but important observation for an improved exponentiation algorithm is that squaring a number a^p is equivalent to multiplying its exponent p by two. In addition, multiplying two numbers a^p and a^q is equivalent to computing $a^{(p+q)}$. Based on these observations, we can evaluate $a^p \bmod n$ with the recursive computation, called the ***repeated squaring*** method, given in Algorithm 24.5.

Algorithm FastExponentiation(a, p, n):
> ***Input:*** Integers a, p, and n
> ***Output:*** $r = a^p \bmod n$

> **if** $p = 0$ **then**
>> **return** 1
> **if** p is even **then**
>> $t \leftarrow$ FastExponentiation($a, p/2, n$) // p is even, so $t = a^{p/2} \bmod n$
>> **return** $t^2 \bmod n$
> $t \leftarrow$ FastExponentiation($a, (p-1)/2, n$) // p is odd, so $t = a^{(p-1)/2} \bmod n$
> **return** $a(t^2 \bmod n) \bmod n$

Algorithm 24.5: Algorithm FastExponentiation for modular exponentiation using the repeated squaring method. Note that, since the modulo operator is applied after each arithmetic operation in method FastExponentiation, the size of the operands of each multiplication and modulo operation is never more than $2\lceil \log_2 n \rceil$ bits.

Analyzing the Repeated Squaring Algorithm

The main idea of this repeated squaring algorithm is to consider each bit of the exponent, p, in turn by dividing p by two until p goes to zero, squaring the current product Q_i for each such bit. In addition, if the current bit is a 1 (that is, p is odd), then we multiply in the base, a, as well.

To see why this algorithm works, define, for $i = 1, \ldots, b$,

$$Q_i = a^{q_i} \bmod n.$$

From the recursive definition of q_i, we derive the following definition of Q_i:

$$
\begin{aligned}
Q_i &= (Q_{i-1}^2 \bmod n)a^{p_{b-i}} \bmod n \quad \text{for} \quad 1 < i \le b \\
Q_1 &= a^{p_{b-1}} \bmod n.
\end{aligned}
\tag{24.1}
$$

It is easy to verify that $Q_b = a^p \bmod n$.

We show a sample execution of the repeated squaring algorithm for modular exponentiation in Table 24.6.

p	12	6	3	1	0
r	1	12	8	2	1

Table 24.6: Example of an execution of the repeated squaring algorithm for modular exponentiation. For each recursive invocation of FastExponentiation$(2, 12, 13)$, we show the second argument, p, and the output value $r = 2^p \bmod 13$.

The running time of the repeated squaring algorithm is easy to analyze. Referring to Algorithm 24.5, a constant number of arithmetic operations are performed, excluding those in the recursive call. Also, in each recursive call, the exponent p gets halved. Thus, the number of recursive calls and arithmetic operations is $O(\log p)$. We may therefore summarize as follows.

Theorem 24.9: *Let a p, and n be positive integers, with $a < n$. The repeated squaring algorithm computes $a^p \bmod n$ using $O(\log p)$ arithmetic operations.*

Since the number, p, is represented in binary using $O(\log p)$ bits, this theorem implies that the number of arithmetic operations used in the repeated squaring algorithm is linear in the input size of the exponent, p, in bits.

24.2.2 Modular Multiplicative Inverses

We turn now to the problem of computing multiplicative inverses in Z_n. First, we recall Theorem 24.6, which states that a nonnegative element x of Z_n admits an inverse if and only if $\gcd(x, n) = 1$. The proof of Theorem 24.6 actually suggests a way to compute $x^{-1} \bmod n$. Namely, we should find the integers i and j referred to by Theorem 24.3, such that

$$ix + jn = \gcd(x, n) = 1.$$

If we can find such integers i and j, we immediately obtain

$$i \equiv x^{-1} \bmod n.$$

The computation of the integers i and j referred to by Theorem 24.3 can be done with a variation of Euclid's algorithm, called **extended Euclid's algorithm**.

Revisiting Euclid's GCD Algorithm

Let a and b be positive integers, and denote with d their greatest common divisor,

$$d = \gcd(a, b).$$

Let $q = a \bmod b$ and r be the integer such that $a = rb + q$, that is,

$$q = a - rb.$$

Euclid's algorithm is based on the repeated application of the formula

$$d = \gcd(a, b) = \gcd(b, q),$$

which immediately follows from Lemma 24.4.

Suppose that the recursive call of the algorithm, with arguments b and q, also returns integers k and l, such that

$$d = kb + lq.$$

Recalling the definition of r, we have

$$d = kb + lq = kb + l(a - rb) = la + (k - lr)b.$$

Thus, we have

$$d = ia + jb, \quad \text{for } i = l \text{ and } j = k - lr.$$

This last equation suggests a method to compute the integers i and j, in addition to the GCD of a and b.

Extended Euclid's Algorithm

The resulting method, known as the extended Euclid's algorithm, is shown in Algorithm 24.7.

Algorithm ExtendedEuclidGCD(a, b):
    Input: Nonnegative integers a and b
    Output: Triplet of integers (d, i, j) such that $d = \gcd(a, b) = ia + jb$
    if $b = 0$ **then**
        return $(a, 1, 0)$
    $q \leftarrow a \bmod b$
    Let r be the integer such that $a = rb + q$
    $(d, k, l) \leftarrow$ ExtendedEuclidGCD(b, q)
    return $(d, l, k - lr)$

Algorithm 24.7: Extended Euclid's algorithm.

We present, in Table 24.8, a sample execution of this algorithm. Its analysis is analogous to that of Euclid's algorithm.

a	412	260	152	108	44	20	4
b	260	152	108	44	20	4	0
r	1	1	1	2	2	5	
i	12	-7	5	-2	1	0	1
j	-19	12	-7	5	-2	1	0

Table 24.8: Execution of ExtendedEuclidGCD(a, b), for $a = 412$ and $b = 260$, to compute (d, i, j) such that $d = \gcd(a, b) = ia + jb$. For each recursive invocation, we show the arguments a and b, variable r, and output values i and j. The output value d is always $\gcd(412, 260) = 4$.

Theorem 24.10: *Let a and b be two positive integers. The extended Euclid's algorithm for computing a triplet of integers (d, i, j) such that*

$$d = \gcd(a, b) = ia + jb,$$

executes $O(\log \max(a, b))$ arithmetic operations.

Corollary 24.11: *Let x be an element of Z_n such that $\gcd(x, n) = 1$. The multiplicative inverse of x in Z_n can be computed with $O(\log n)$ arithmetic operations.*

24.3 Cryptographic Operations

The Internet enables a growing number of useful activities, such as email, shopping, and financial transactions, to be performed electronically. However, the Internet itself is an insecure transmission network: data transmitted over Wi-Fi and other communication media travels can be observed and potentially modified enroute to its destination. A variety of cryptographic techniques have therefore been developed to support secure communication over an insecure network such as the Internet. In particular, cryptography research has developed the following useful cryptographic computations:

- *Encryption/decryption*: A message M to be transmitted, called the ***plaintext***, is transformed into an unrecognizable string of characters C, called the ***ciphertext***, before being sent over the network. This transformation is known as ***encryption***. After the ciphertext C is received, it is converted back to the plaintext M using an inverse transformation (that depends on additional secret information). This reverse transformation is called ***decryption***. An essential ingredient in encryption is that it should be computationally infeasible for an outsider to transform C back to M (without knowing the secret information possessed by the receiver).
- *Digital signatures*: The author of a message M computes a message S that is derived from M and secret information known by the author. The message S is a ***digital signature*** if another party can easily verify that only the author of M could have computed S in a reasonable amount of time.

The two techniques lead to methods for supporting the information security services discussed in the introduction:

- *Data integrity*: Computing a digital signature S of a message M not only helps us determine the author of M, it also verifies the integrity of M, for a modification to M would produce a different signature. So to perform a data integrity check we can perform a verification test that S is, in fact, a digital signature for the message M.
- *Authentication*: The above cryptographic tools can be used for authentication in two possible ways. In ***password*** authentication schemes, a user will type a user ID and password in a client application, with this combination being immediately encrypted and sent to an authenticator. If the encrypted user ID and password combination matches that in a user database, then the individual is authenticated (and the database never stores passwords in plaintext). Alternatively, an authenticator can issue a challenge to a user in the form of a random message M that the user must immediately digitally sign for authentication.

- *Authorization*: Given a scheme for authentication, we can issue authorizations by keeping lists, called *access control lists*, that are associated with sensitive data or computations that should be accessed only by authorized individuals. Alternatively, the holder of a right to sensitive data or computations can digitally sign a message C that authorizes a user to perform certain tasks. For example, the message could be of the form, "I, U.S. Corporation vice president, give person x permission to access our fourth quarter earnings data."
- *Confidentiality*: Sensitive information can be kept secret from nonauthorized agents by encrypting it.
- *Nonrepudiation*: If we make the parties negotiating a contract, M, digitally sign that message, then we can have a way of proving that they have seen and agreed to the content of the message M.

Symmetric Encryption Schemes

As mentioned above, a fundamental problem in cryptography is confidentiality, that is, sending a message from Alice to Bob so that a third party, Eve, cannot gain any information from an intercepted copy of the message. Moreover, we have observed that confidentiality can be achieved by *encryption schemes*, or *ciphers*, where the message M to be transmitted, called the *plaintext*, is *encrypted* into an unrecognizable string of characters C, called the *ciphertext*, before being sent over the network. After the ciphertext C is received, it is decrypted back to the plaintext M using an inverse transformation called *decryption*.

Secret Keys

In describing the details of an encryption scheme, we must explain all the steps needed in order to encrypt a plaintext M into a ciphertext C, and how to then decrypt that ciphertext back to M. Moreover, in order for Eve to be unable to extract M from C, there must be some secret information that is kept private from her.

In traditional cryptography, a common *secret key* k is shared by Alice and Bob, and is used to both encrypt and decrypt the message. Such schemes are also called *symmetric encryption* schemes, since k is used for both encryption and decryption and the same secret is shared by both Alice and Bob.

Substitution Ciphers

A classic example of a symmetric cipher is a *substitution cipher*, where the secret key is a permutation π of the characters of the alphabet. Encrypting plaintext M into ciphertext C consists of replacing each character x of M with character $y = \pi(x)$. Decryption can be easily performed by knowing the permutation function π.

Indeed, M is derived from C by replacing each character y of C with character $x = \pi^{-1}(y)$. The **Caesar cipher** is an early example of a substitution cipher, where each character x is replaced by character

$$y = x + k \bmod n,$$

where n is the size of the alphabet and $1 < k < n$ is the secret key. This substitution scheme is known as the "Caesar cipher," for Julius Caesar is known to have used it with $k = 3$.

Substitution ciphers are quite easy to use, but they are not secure. Indeed, the secret key can be quickly inferred using **frequency analysis**, based on the knowledge of the frequency of the various letters, or groups of consecutive letters in the text language.

Symmetric Cryptosystems

Secure and efficient symmetric ciphers do exist, and are often referred to by their acronyms, such as "3DES," "IDEA," and "AES." They perform a sequence of complex substitution and permutation transformations on the bits of the plaintext. While these systems are important in many applications, they are only mildly interesting from an algorithmic viewpoint; hence, they are out of the scope of this book. They run in time proportional to the length of the message being encrypted or decrypted. Thus, we mention that these algorithms exist and are fast, but in this book we do not discuss any of these efficient symmetric ciphers in any detail.

Public-Key Cryptosystems

A major problem with symmetric ciphers, however, is **key transfer**, or how to distribute the secret key for encryption and decryption. In 1976, Diffie and Hellman described an abstract system that would avoid these problems, the **public-key cryptosystem**. While they didn't actually publish a particular public-key system, they discussed the features of such a system. Specifically, given a message M, encryption function E, and decryption function D, the following four properties must hold:

1. $D(E(M)) = M$.
2. Both E and D are easy to compute.
3. It is computationally infeasible to derive D from E.
4. $E(D(M)) = M$.

In retrospect, these properties might seem like common sense, but they actually represent a significant innovation. The first property merely states that once a message has been encrypted, applying the decryption procedure will restore it. Property two is perhaps more obvious. In order for a cryptosystem to be practical, encryption and decryption must be computationally fast.

The third property is the start of the innovation. It means that E only goes one way; it is computationally infeasible to invert E, unless you already know D. Thus, the encryption procedure E can be made public. Any party can send a message, while only one knows how to decrypt it.

If the fourth property holds, then the mapping is one-to-one. Thus, the cryptosystem is a solution to the *digital signature* problem. Given an electronic message from Bob to Alice, how can we prove that Bob actually sent it? Bob can apply his decryption procedure to some signature message M. Any other party can then verify that Bob actually sent the message by applying the public encryption procedure E. Since only Bob knows the decryption function, only Bob can generate a signature message which can be correctly decoded by the function E.

One-Way Hash Functions

Public-key cryptosystems are often used in conjunction with a *one-way hash function*, also called a *message digest* or *fingerprint*. We provide an informal description of such a function next. A formal discussion is beyond the scope of this book.

A *one-way hash function* H maps a string (message) M of arbitrary length to an integer $d = H(M)$ with a fixed number of bits, called the *digest* of M, that satisfies the following properties:

1. Given a string M, the digest of M can be computed quickly.
2. Given the digest d of M, but not M, it is computationally infeasible to find M.

A one-way hash function is said to be *collision-resistant* if, given a string M, it is computationally infeasible to find another string M' with the same digest, and is said to be *strongly collision-resistant* if it is computationally infeasible to find two strings, M_1 and M_2, with the same digest.

Several functions believed to be strongly collision-resistant one-way hash functions have been devised. The ones currently advocated the most in practice are SHA-1, which produces a 160-bit digest, and SHA-256, which produces a 256-bit digest.

Using One-Way Hash Functions with Digital Signatures

One of the main applications of one-way hash functions is to speed up the construction of digital signatures. If we have a collision-resistant, one-way hash function, we can sign the digest of a message instead of the message itself, that is, the signature S is given by:

$$S = D(H(M)).$$

Except for small messages, hashing the message and signing the digest is faster, in practice, than signing the message directly.

24.4   The RSA Cryptosystem

Probably the most well-known public-key cryptosystem is tied to the difficulty of factoring large numbers. It is named **RSA** after its inventors, Rivest, Shamir, and Adleman. In this cryptosystem, we begin by selecting two large primes, p and q. Let $n = pq$ be their product and recall that $\phi(n) = (p-1)(q-1)$. Encryption and decryption keys e and d are selected so that

- e and $\phi(n)$ are relatively prime
- $ed \equiv 1 \pmod{\phi(n)}$.

The second condition means that d is the multiplicative inverse of $e \bmod \phi(n)$. The pair of values n and e form the public key, while d is the private key. In practice, e is chosen either randomly or as one of the following numbers: 3, 17, or $65\,537$.

The rules for encrypting and decrypting with RSA are simple. Let us assume, for simplicity, that the plaintext is an integer M, with $0 < M < n$. If M is a string, we can view it as an integer by concatenating the bits of its characters. The plaintext M is encrypted into ciphertext C with one modular exponentiation using the encryption key e as the exponent:

$$C \leftarrow M^e \bmod n \quad \text{(RSA encryption)}.$$

The decryption of ciphertext C is also performed with an exponentiation, using now the decryption key d as the exponent:

$$M \leftarrow C^d \bmod n \quad \text{(RSA decryption)}.$$

The correctness of the above encryption and decryption rules is justified by the following theorem.

Theorem 24.12: *Let p and q be two odd primes, and define $n = pq$. Let e be relatively prime with $\phi(n)$ and let d be the multiplicative inverse of e modulo $\phi(n)$. For each integer x such that $0 < x < n$,*

$$x^{ed} \equiv x \pmod{n}.$$

Proof: Let $y = x^{ed} \bmod n$. We want to prove that $y = x$. Because of the way we have selected e and d, we can write $ed = k\phi(n) + 1$, for some integer k. Thus, we have

$$y = x^{k\phi(n)+1} \bmod n.$$

We distinguish two cases.

Case 1: x does not divide n. We rewrite y as follows:

$$\begin{aligned} y &= x^{k\phi(n)+1} \bmod n \\ &= x x^{k\phi(n)} \bmod n \\ &= x(x^{\phi(n)} \bmod n)^k \bmod n. \end{aligned}$$

By Theorem 24.7 (Euler's theorem), we have $x^{\phi(n)} \bmod n = 1$, which implies $y = x \cdot 1^k \bmod n = x$.

Case 2: x divides n. Since $n = pq$, with p and q primes, x is a multiple of either p or q. Suppose x is a multiple of p, that is, $x = hp$ for some positive integer h. Clearly, x cannot be a multiple of q as well, since otherwise x would be greater than $n = pq$, a contradiction. Thus, $\gcd(x, q) = 1$ and by Theorem 24.7 (Euler's theorem), we have

$$x^{\phi(q)} \equiv 1 \pmod{q}.$$

Since $\phi(n) = \phi(p)\phi(q)$, raising both sides of the above congruence to the power of $k\phi(q)$, we obtain

$$x^{k\phi(n)} \equiv 1 \pmod{q},$$

which we rewrite as

$$x^{k\phi(n)} = 1 + iq,$$

for some integer i. Multiplying both sides of the above equality by x, and recalling that $x = hp$ and $n = pq$, we obtain

$$\begin{aligned} x^{k\phi(n)+1} &= x + xiq \\ &= x + hpiq \\ &= x + (hi)n. \end{aligned}$$

Thus, we have

$$y = x^{k\phi(n)+1} \bmod n = x.$$

In either case, we have shown that $y = x$, which concludes the proof of the theorem.

∎

The symmetry of the encryption and decryption functions implies that the RSA cryptosystem directly supports digital signatures. Indeed, a digital signature S for message M is obtained by applying the decryption function to M, that is,

$$S \leftarrow M^d \bmod n \quad \text{(RSA signature)}.$$

The verification of the digital signature S is now performed with the encryption function, that is, by checking that

$$M \equiv S^e \pmod{n} \quad \text{(RSA verification)}.$$

The Difficulty of Breaking RSA

Note that even if we know the value e, we cannot figure out d unless we know $\phi(n)$. Most cryptography researchers generally believe that breaking RSA requires that we compute $\phi(n)$ and that this requires factoring n. While there is no ***proof*** that factorization is computationally difficult, a whole series of famous mathematicians have worked on the problem over the past few hundred years. Especially if n is large ($\approx$ 200 digits), it will take a very long time to factor it. To give you an idea of the state of the art, mathematicians were quite excited when a nationwide network of computers was able to factor the ninth Fermat number, $2^{512} - 1$. This number has "only" 155 decimal digits. Barring a major breakthrough, the RSA system will remain secure. For if technology somehow advances to a point where it is feasible to factor 200-digit numbers, we need only choose an n with 300 or 400 digits.

Analysis and Setup for RSA Encryption

The running time of RSA encryption, decryption, signature, and verification is simple to analyze. Indeed, each such operation requires a constant number of modular exponentiations, which can be performed with method FastExponentiation (Algorithm 24.5).

Theorem 24.13: *Let n be the modulus used in the RSA cryptosystem. RSA encryption, decryption, signature, and verification each take $O(\log n)$ arithmetic operations.*

To set up the RSA cryptosystem, we need to generate the public and private key pair. Namely, we need to compute the private key (d, p, q) and the public key (e, n) that goes with it. This involves the following computations:

- Selection of two random primes p and q with a given number of bits. This can be accomplished by testing random integers for primality, as discussed at the end of Section 19.4.1.

- Selection of an integer e relatively prime to $\phi(n)$. This can be done by picking random primes less than $\phi(n)$ until we find one that does not divide $\phi(n)$. In practice, it is sufficient to check small primes from a list of known primes (often $e = 3$ or $e = 17$ will work).

- Computing the multiplicative inverse d of e in $Z_{\phi(n)}$. This can be done using the extended Euclid's algorithm (Corollary 24.11).

24.5   The El Gamal Cryptosystem

We have seen that the security of the RSA cryptosystem is related to the difficulty of factoring large numbers. It is possible to construct cryptosystems based on other difficult number-theoretic problems. We now consider the El Gamal cryptosystem, named after its inventor, Taher El Gamal, which is based on the difficulty of a problem called the "discrete logarithm."

The Discrete Logarithm

When we're working with the real numbers, $\log_b y$ is the value x, such that $b^x = y$. We can define an analogous discrete logarithm. Given integers b and n, with $b < n$, the **discrete logarithm** of an integer y to the base b is an integer x, such that

$$b^x \equiv y \bmod n.$$

The discrete logarithm is also called **index**, and we write

$$x = \mathrm{ind}_{b,n} y.$$

While it is quite efficient to raise numbers to large powers modulo p (recall the repeated squaring algorithm, Algorithm 24.5), the inverse computation of the discrete logarithm is much harder. The El Gamal system relies on the difficulty of this computation.

El Gamal Encryption

Let p be a prime, and g be a generator of Z_p^*. The private key x is an integer between 1 and $p - 2$. Let $y = g^x \bmod p$. The public key for El Gamal encryption is the triplet (p, g, y). If taking discrete logarithms is as difficult as it is widely believed, releasing $y = g^x \bmod p$ does not reveal x.

To encrypt a plaintext M, a random integer k relatively prime to $p - 1$ is selected, and the following pair of values is computed:

$$\begin{aligned} a &\leftarrow g^k \bmod p \\ b &\leftarrow M y^k \bmod p \end{aligned} \quad \text{(El Gamal encryption)}.$$

The ciphertext C consists of the pair (a, b) computed above.

El Gamal Decryption

The decryption of the ciphertext $C = (a, b)$ in the El Gamal scheme, to retrieve the plaintext M, is simple:

$$M \leftarrow b/a^x \bmod p \quad \text{(El Gamal decryption)}.$$

In the above expression, the "division" by a^x should be interpreted in the context of modular arithmetic, that is, b is multiplied by the inverse of a^x in Z_p. The correctness of the El Gamal encryption scheme is easy to verify. Indeed, we have

$$
\begin{aligned}
b/a^x \bmod p &= My^k(a^x)^{-1} \bmod p \\
&= Mg^{xk}(g^{kx})^{-1} \bmod p \\
&= M.
\end{aligned}
$$

Using El Gamal for Digital Signatures

A variation of the above scheme provides a digital signature. Namely, a signature for message M is a pair $S = (a, b)$ obtained by selecting a random integer k relatively prime to $p - 1$ (which, of course, equals $\phi(p)$) and computing

$$
\begin{aligned}
a &\leftarrow g^k \bmod p \\
b &\leftarrow k^{-1}(M - xa) \bmod (p-1)
\end{aligned}
\quad \text{(El Gamal signature)}.
$$

To verify a digital signature $S = (a, b)$, we check that

$$y^a a^b \equiv g^M \pmod{p} \quad \text{(El Gamal verification)}.$$

The correctness of this digital signature scheme is based on the following:

$$
\begin{aligned}
y^a a^b \bmod p &= ((g^x \bmod p)^a \bmod p)((g^k \bmod p)^{k^{-1}(M-xa) \bmod (p-1)} \bmod p) \\
&= g^{xa} g^{kk^{-1}(M-xa) \bmod (p-1)} \bmod p \\
&= g^{xa+M-xa} \bmod p \\
&= g^M \bmod p.
\end{aligned}
$$

Analysis of El Gamal Encryption

The analysis of the performance of the El Gamal cryptosystem is similar to that of RSA. Namely, we have the following.

Theorem 24.14: *Let n be the modulus used in the El Gamal cryptosystem. El Gamal encryption, decryption, signature, and verification each take $O(\log n)$ arithmetic operations.*

24.6   Exercises

Reinforcement

R-24.1 Show the execution of method EuclidGCD$(14300, 5915)$ by constructing a table similar to Table 24.2.

R-24.2 Write a nonrecursive version of Algorithm EuclidGCD.

R-24.3 What is 9^{60} mod 77?

R-24.4 Construct the multiplication table of the elements of Z_{11}, where the element in row i and column j $(0 \leq i, j \leq 10)$ is given by $i \cdot j$ mod 11.

R-24.5 Show the execution of method FastExponentiation$(5, 12, 13)$ by constructing a table similar to Table 24.6.

R-24.6 Write a nonrecursive version of Algorithm ExtendedEuclidGCD.

R-24.7 Extend Table 24.8 with two rows giving the values of ia and jb at each step of the algorithm and verify that $ia + jb = 1$.

R-24.8 Show the execution of method ExtendedEuclidGCD$(412, 113)$ by constructing a table similar to Table 24.8.

R-24.9 What are the multiplicative inverses of 113, 114, and 127 in Z_{299}.

R-24.10 Construct a table showing an example of the RSA cryptosystem with parameters $p = 17$, $q = 19$, and $e = 5$. The table should have two rows, one for the plaintext M and the other for the ciphertext C. The columns should correspond to integer values in the range $[10, 20]$ for M.

R-24.11 Show the result of an El Gamal encryption of the message $M = 8$ using $k = 4$ for the public key $(p, g, y) = (59, 2, 25)$.

Creativity

C-24.1 Prove Theorem 24.1.

C-24.2 Show the existence of additive inverses in Z_p, that is, prove that for each $x \in Z_p$, there is a $y \in Z_p$, such that $x + y$ mod $p = 0$.

C-24.3 Let p be a prime. Give an efficient alternative algorithm for computing the multiplicative inverse of an element of Z_p that is not based on the extended Euclid's algorithm. What is the running time of your algorithm?

C-24.4 Give an alternative proof of Theorem 24.6 that does not use Theorem 24.3.

C-24.5 Show how to modify Algorithm ExtendedEuclidGCD to compute the multiplicative inverse of an element in Z_n using arithmetic operations on operands with at most $2\lceil \log_2 n \rceil$ bits.

C-24.6 Suppose Alice wants to send Bob a message, M, that is the price she is willing to pay for his old bike. Here, M is just an integer in binary. She uses the RSA algorithm to encrypt M, to produce the ciphertext, C, using Bob's public key, and sends it to Bob. Unfortunately, Eve has intercepted C before it gets to Bob Explain how Eve can use Bob's public key to alter the ciphertext C to change it into C', so that if she sends C' to Bob (with Eve pretending to be Alice), then, after Bob has decrypted C', he will get a plaintext that is twice the value of M.

C-24.7 Solve the previous exercise, but use the El Gamal cryptosystem instead of RSA.

C-24.8 Suppose the primes p and q used in the RSA cryptosystem, to define $n = pq$, are in the range $[\sqrt{n} - \log n, \ \sqrt{n} + \log n]$. Explain how you can efficiently factor n using this information.

C-24.9 Why can't you use the pair $(1, n)$ as an RSA public key, even if $n = pq$, for two large primes, p and q?

Applications

A-24.1 There is a perfectly secure cipher, known as the ***one-time pad***, which is said to have been used for encrypting messages on the "hot line" between Moscow and Washington, DC, during the Cold War. In this cryptosystem, Alice and Bob each share a random bit string, K, as large as any message they might wish to communicate. The string K is the secret key. To compute a ciphertext, C, from a message, M, Alice computes

$$C = M \oplus K,$$

where "$\oplus$" denotes the bitwise exclusive-or operator. Show that Bob can decrypt the ciphertext, C, by computing $C \oplus K$. Also, show that this scheme achieves perfect confidentiality, based on the facts that each bit of the output is independent, random, and every plaintext of length $|M|$ is a possible plaintext for the ciphertext, C.

A-24.2 There are instances when it is useful to prove that a document, D, exists on a certain date. In order to facilitate such proofs, Bob collects a group of documents, $D_1, D_2, \ldots, D_n$, every day from people wanting time stamps for their documents on that day. Bob constructs a complete binary tree, T, with n leaves, of height $\lceil \log n \rceil$, with each leaf, i, associated with a document, D_i. He stores at i the result, $h_i = H(D_i)$, of a one-way hash function computed on D_i. For each internal node, v, with children x and y, he stores $h_v = H(h_x || h_y)$, where $||$ denotes concatenation. Finally, he publishes the value, h_r, for the root, r, of T in a classified advertisement in a local newspaper. How can Bob give each document owner a set of $O(\log n)$ numbers so that together with the classified advertisement, each document owner can prove the existence of his or her document on the date the ad appeared, with the confidence of the security properties of the one-way hash function, H?

A-24.3 Consider the time stamping problem from the previous exercise, but now suppose that each day that there is one document added to the set, and one document that is removed from the set, but all of the remaining documents still need to be proven to exist as a part of the set on that day. Explain how Bob can update the tree, T, in $O(\log n)$ time, to reflect these changes?

A-24.4 Suppose Alice is a U.S. spy on a 7-day trip to a faraway land and wants to prove for each day she is gone that she not been captured. She has chosen a secret random number, x, which she is keeping secret. But she did tell her CIA handler the value $y = H(H(H(H(H(H(H(x)))))))$, where H is a one-way cryptographic hash function. Unfortunately, her enemy, Eve, was able to listen in on this message; hence, Eve also knows the value of y. Explain how Alice can send a single message every day that proves she has not been captured.

A-24.5 Digital certificates are signed documents, where a respected authority verifies the binding between a person's identity information (like their name, email address, etc.) and their public key. But if that person loses the private key that goes with his or her public key, then this certification needs to be revoked. To support this service, the respected authority can keep a dictionary, D, of revoked certificates. Explain how the authority can answer any request for the revocation status for any digital certificate in $O(\log n)$ time, where n is the size of D. Also, how can the person asking this query be able to prove to a third party that the result is valid?

A-24.6 One of the main uses for public-key cryptography is that it can be used to establish a secret key for a communication session between Alice and Bob even if they have never met to share that secret key in advance. Explain how public key cryptography can be used for this purpose.

A-24.7 Suppose Bob has an RSA public key, (e, n), and that he has promised Eve that she can send him any single message, $M < n$, and he will sign M using a simple RSA signature method to compute $S = M^d \bmod n$, where d is his private RSA exponent, sending S back to Eve. What Bob doesn't know is that Eve has previously captured a ciphertext C that Alice encrypted for Bob using her plaintext, P, and Bob's RSA public key, (e, n). Eve wants to trick Bob into decrypting C for her without revealing P. So Eve asks Bob to sign the message $M = r^e C \bmod n$, where r is a random number that Eve chose to be relatively prime to n. Explain how, even though she does not know the value of d, Eve can use Bob's signature, S, on M, to discover the plaintext, P, for C.

Chapter Notes

An introduction to number theory is provided in books by Koblitz [133] and Kranakis [136]. The classic textbook on numerical algorithms is the second volume of Knuth's series on *The Art of Computer Programming* [130]. Algorithms for number theoretic problems are also presented in the books by Bressoud and Wagon [38] and by Bach and Shallit [19].

The RSA cryptosystem is named after the initials of its inventors, Rivest, Shamir, and Adleman [178]. The El Gamal cryptosystem is named after its inventor [79]. Sections 24.1 and 24.3 are based in part on an unpublished manuscript of Achter and Tamassia [1].

Chapter 25

The Fast Fourier Transform

Plate VI from Europas bekannteste Schmetterlinge. Beschreibung der wichtigsten Arten und Anleitung zur Kenntnis und zum Sammeln der Schmetterlinge und Raupen (ca. 1895), F. Nemos, Oestergaard Verlag, Berlin, 18 chromolithographische Tafeln, 160 pp. Public domain image.

Contents

25.1 Convolution 713

25.2 Primitive Roots of Unity 715

25.3 The Discrete Fourier Transform 717

25.4 The Fast Fourier Transform Algorithm 721

25.5 Exercises 727

A common computation in many cryptographic systems is the multiplication of large integers. For instance, real-world uses of the RSA cryptosystem often involve 1024-bit, 2048-bit, or even 3072-bit keys; hence, RSA encryption and decryption with such keys involves the multiplication of large integers having these bit lengths. In fact, the U.S. National Institute for Standards and Technology (NIST) has argued that to achieve a high level of security for the RSA cryptosystem one should use 15,360-bit keys. Thus, from an algorithmic viewpoint, improving the running time for integer multiplication can result in faster and more secure cryptographic protocols involving large integers.

Unfortunately, a straightforward adaptation of the standard method for multiplying integers, as taught in elementary school, results in a method for multiplying two n-bit integers that runs in $O(n^2)$ time. This can be improved to an algorithm running in $O(n^{1.585})$ time, using the divide-and-conquer Karatsuba algorithm described in Section 11.2, which is okay for moderately large integers, but multiplying the large integers used in cryptographic computations could benefit from an even faster algorithm. Interestingly, the technique we discuss in this chapter, the Fast Fourier Transform (FFT), can be used to achieve a much faster algorithm for multiplying large integers. Moreover, it turns out that the FFT has many other applications as well, including fast methods for signal processing, image processing, scientific data analysis, and the pricing of financial options.

Suppose, then, that we want to multiply two n-bit integers, $P = a_{n-1} \ldots a_1 a_0$ and $Q = b_{n-1} \ldots b_1 b_0$. Rather than attack the problem of computing $R = P \cdot Q$ directly, however, let us reduce it to a related problem—polynomial multiplication. Construct two polynomials, $p(x)$ and $q(x)$, from P and Q as follows:

$$
\begin{aligned}
p(x) &= a_0 + a_1 x + a_2 x^2 + \cdots + a_{n-1} x^{n-1} \\
q(x) &= b_0 + b_1 x + a_2 x^2 + \cdots + b_{n-1} x^{n-1},
\end{aligned}
$$

and note that $P = p(2)$ and $Q = q(2)$. Imagine, for the moment, that we had a fast algorithm to compute the polynomial

$$
r(x) = p(x) \cdot q(x).
$$

Then we could compute the integer product, $R = P \cdot Q$, by first computing the polynomial, $r(x)$, and then performing the evaluation $R \leftarrow r(2)$.

As one of the most surprising and ingenious results in algorithms, it turns out that we can compute an efficient representation for the product polynomial, $r(x)$, using $O(n \log n)$ arithmetic operations on reasonably sized numbers. Thus, using the above approach, we can design a method for multiplying two n-bit integers using $O(n \log n)$ such arithmetic operations. The FFT algorithm, which achieves this result, is based on an interesting use of the divide-and-conquer technique. We therefore devote this entire chapter to describing and analyzing this algorithm.

25.1 Convolution

A polynomial represented in **coefficient form** is described by a coefficient vector $\mathbf{a} = [a_0, a_1, \ldots, a_{n-1}]$ as follows:

$$p(x) = \sum_{i=0}^{n-1} a_i x^i.$$

The **degree** of such a polynomial is the largest index of a nonzero coefficient a_i. A coefficient vector of length n can represent polynomials of degree at most $n - 1$.

The coefficient representation is natural, in that it is simple and allows for several polynomial operations to be performed quickly. For example, given a second polynomial described using a coefficient vector $\mathbf{b} = [b_0, b_1, \ldots, b_{n-1}]$ as

$$q(x) = \sum_{i=0}^{n-1} b_i x^i,$$

we can easily add $p(x)$ and $q(x)$ component-wise to produce their sum,

$$p(x) + q(x) = \sum_{i=0}^{n-1} (a_i + b_i)x^i.$$

Likewise, the coefficient form for $p(x)$ allows us to evaluate $p(x)$ efficiently, by **Horner's rule** (Exercise C-1.14), as

$$p(x) = a_0 + x(a_1 + x(a_2 + \cdots + x(a_{n-2} + xa_{n-1}) \cdots)).$$

Thus, with the coefficient representation, we can add and evaluate degree-$(n - 1)$ polynomials using $O(n)$ arithmetic operations.

Multiplying two polynomials $p(x)$ and $q(x)$, as defined above in coefficient form, is not straightforward, however. To see the difficulty, consider $p(x) \cdot q(x)$:

$$p(x) \cdot q(x) = a_0 b_0 + (a_0 b_1 + a_1 b_0)x + (a_0 b_2 + a_1 b_1 + a_2 b_0)x^2 + \cdots + a_{n-1}b_{n-1}x^{2n-2}.$$

That is,

$$p(x) \cdot q(x) = \sum_{i=0}^{2n-2} c_i x^i,$$

where

$$c_i = \sum_{j=0}^{i} a_j b_{i-j},$$

for $i = 0, 1, \ldots, 2n - 2$. This equation defines a vector $\mathbf{c} = [c_0, c_1, \ldots, c_{2n-1}]$, which we call the **convolution** of the vectors $\mathbf{a}$ and $\mathbf{b}$. For symmetry reasons, we view the convolution as a vector of size $2n$, defining $c_{2n-1} = 0$. We denote the convolution of $\mathbf{a}$ and $\mathbf{b}$ as $\mathbf{a} * \mathbf{b}$.

Using the Interpolation Theorem for Polynomials

If we apply the definition of the convolution directly, then it will take us $\Theta(n^2)$ time to multiply the two polynomials p and q. The ***Fast Fourier Transform (FFT)*** algorithm allows us to perform this multiplication using $O(n \log n)$ arithmetic operations. The improvement of the FFT is based on an interesting observation. Namely, that another way of representing a degree-$(n-1)$ polynomial is by its value on n distinct inputs. Such a representation is unique, because of the following theorem.

Theorem 25.1 [The Interpolation Theorem for Polynomials]: *Given a set of n pairs,*

$$S = \{(x_0, y_0), (x_1, y_1), (x_2, y_2), \ldots, (x_{n-1}, y_{n-1})\},$$

such that the x_i's are all distinct, there is a unique degree-$(n-1)$ polynomial, $p(x)$, with $p(x_i) = y_i$, for $i = 0, 1, \ldots, n-1$.

Suppose, then, that we can represent a polynomial not by its coefficients, but instead by its value on a collection of different inputs. This theorem suggests an alternative method for multiplying two polynomials p and q. In particular, evaluate p and q for $2n$ different inputs $x_0, x_1, \ldots, x_{2n-1}$ and compute the representation of the product of p and q as the set

$$\{(x_0, p(x_0)q(x_0)), (x_1, p(x_1)q(x_1)), \ldots, (x_{2n-1}, p(x_{2n-1})q(x_{2n-1}))\}.$$

Such a computation would clearly require just $O(n)$ arithmetic operations, given the $2n$ input-output pairs for each of p and q.

The challenge, then, to effectively using this approach to multiply p and q is to come up quickly with $2n$ input-output pairs for p and q. Applying Horner's rule to $2n$ different inputs would require $\Theta(n^2)$ arithmetic operations, which is not asymptotically any faster than using the convolution directly. So Horner's rule is of no immediate help. Of course, we have full freedom in how we choose the set of $2n$ inputs for our polynomials. That is, we have full discretion to choose inputs that are easy to evaluate. For example, the evaluation,

$$p(0) = a_0,$$

is a simple case. But we have to choose a set of $2n$ easy inputs to evaluate p on, not just one. Fortunately, the mathematical concept we discuss next provides a convenient set of inputs that are collectively easier to use to evaluate a polynomial than applying Horner's rule $2n$ times.

25.2 Primitive Roots of Unity

One of the central ideas that allows for fast polynomial evaluation is the concept of primitive roots of unity.

Definition

A number, ω, is a ***primitive nth root of unity***, for $n \geq 2$, if it satisfies the following properties:

1. $\omega^n = 1$, that is, ω is an nth root of 1.
2. The numbers $1, \omega, \omega^2, \ldots, \omega^{n-1}$ are distinct.

Note that this definition implies that a primitive nth root of unity has a multiplicative inverse, $\omega^{-1} = \omega^{n-1}$, for

$$\omega^{-1}\omega = \omega^{n-1}\omega = \omega^n = 1.$$

Thus, we can speak in a well-defined fashion of negative exponents of ω, as well as positive ones.

A Complex Example of a Primitive Root of Unity

The notion of a primitive nth root of unity may, at first, seem like a strange definition with few examples. But it actually has several important instances.

One important example is the complex number

$$\omega = e^{2\pi i/n} = \cos(2\pi/n) + \mathbf{i}\sin(2\pi/n),$$

which is a primitive nth root of unity when we perform all our arithmetic in the complex number system, where $\mathbf{i} = \sqrt{-1}$.

An Integer Example of a Primitive Root of Unity

As another example, suppose that we have a prime number, $p = cn + 1$, for some positive integer, c. Choose x to be a multiplicative generator for the positive numbers in the finite field, Z_t, which is defined on the set of integers, $\{0, 1, 2, \ldots, t-1\}$ (see Section 24.1). That is, choose x so that the numbers, $x, x^2, \ldots, x^{t-1}$, are all distinct, modulo t. By Fermat's Little Theorem (19.5), $x^{t-1} \bmod t = 1$. Thus, the number,

$$\omega = x^c \bmod t,$$

is a primitive nth root of unity in Z_t.

Properties of Primitive Roots of Unity

Primitive nth roots of unity have a number of important properties, including the following three ones.

Lemma 25.2 (Cancellation Property): *If ω is an nth root of unity, then, for any integer $k \neq 0$, with $-n < k < n$,*

$$\sum_{j=0}^{n-1} \omega^{kj} = 0.$$

Proof: Since $\omega^k \neq 1$,

$$\sum_{j=0}^{n-1} \omega^{kj} = \frac{(\omega^k)^n - 1}{\omega^k - 1} = \frac{(\omega^n)^k - 1}{\omega^k - 1} = \frac{1^k - 1}{\omega^k - 1} = \frac{1 - 1}{\omega^k - 1} = 0.$$

∎

Lemma 25.3 (Reduction Property): *If ω is a primitive $(2n)$th root of unity, then ω^2 is a primitive nth root of unity.*

Proof: If $1, \omega, \omega^2, \ldots, \omega^{2n-1}$ are distinct, then $1, \omega^2, (\omega^2)^2, \ldots, (\omega^2)^{n-1}$ are also distinct. ∎

Lemma 25.4 (Reflective Property): *If ω is a primitive nth root of unity and n is even, then*

$$\omega^{n/2} = -1.$$

Proof: By the cancellation property, for $k = n/2$,

$$
\begin{aligned}
0 &= \sum_{j=0}^{n-1} \omega^{(n/2)j} \\
&= \omega^0 + \omega^{n/2} + \omega^n + \omega^{3n/2} + \cdots + \omega^{(n/2)(n-2)} + \omega^{(n/2)(n-1)} \\
&= \omega^0 + \omega^{n/2} + \omega^0 + \omega^{n/2} + \cdots + \omega^0 + \omega^{n/2} \\
&= (n/2)(1 + \omega^{n/2}).
\end{aligned}
$$

Thus, $0 = 1 + \omega^{n/2}$. ∎

An interesting corollary to the reflective property, which motivates its name, is the fact that if ω is a primitive nth root of unity and $n \geq 2$ is even, then

$$\omega^{k+n/2} = -\omega^k.$$

25.3 The Discrete Fourier Transform

Let us now return to the problem of evaluating a polynomial defined by a coefficient vector **a** as

$$p(x) = \sum_{i=0}^{n-1} a_i x^i,$$

for a carefully chosen set of input values. The technique we discuss in this section, called the ***Discrete Fourier Transform*** (DFT), is to evaluate $p(x)$ at the nth roots of unity, $\omega^0, \omega^1, \omega^2, \ldots, \omega^{n-1}$. Admittedly, this gives us just n input-output pairs, but we can "pad" our coefficient representation for p with 0's by setting $a_i = 0$, for $n \leq i \leq 2n-1$. This padding would let us view p as a degree-$(2n-1)$ polynomial, which would in turn let us use the primitive $(2n)$th roots of unity as inputs for a DFT for p. Thus, if we need more input-output values for p, let us assume that the coefficient vector for p has already been padded with as many 0's as necessary.

Formally, the Discrete Fourier Transform for the polynomial p represented by the coefficient vector **a** is defined as the vector **y** of values

$$y_j = p(\omega^j),$$

where ω is a primitive nth root of unity. That is,

$$y_j = \sum_{i=0}^{n-1} a_i \omega^{ij}.$$

In the language of matrices, we can alternatively think of the vector **y** of y_j values and the vector **a** as column vectors and say that

$$\mathbf{y} = F\mathbf{a},$$

where F is an $n \times n$ matrix such that $F[i, j] = \omega^{ij}$.

The Inverse Discrete Fourier Transform

Interestingly, the matrix F has an inverse, F^{-1}, so that $F^{-1}(F(\mathbf{a})) = \mathbf{a}$ for all **a**. The matrix F^{-1} allows us to define an ***inverse Discrete Fourier Transform***. If we are given a vector **y** of the values of a degree-$(n-1)$ polynomial p at the nth roots of unity, $\omega^0, \omega^1, \ldots, \omega^{n-1}$, then we can recover a coefficient vector for p by computing

$$\mathbf{a} = F^{-1}\mathbf{y}.$$

Moreover, the matrix F^{-1} has a simple form, in that $F^{-1}[i, j] = \omega^{-ij}/n$. Thus, we can recover the coefficient a_i as

$$a_i = \sum_{j=0}^{n-1} y_j \omega^{-ij}/n.$$

The following lemma justifies this claim, and is the basis of why we refer to F and F^{-1} as "transforms."

Lemma 25.5: *For any vector* $\mathbf{a}$, $F^{-1} \cdot F\mathbf{a} = \mathbf{a}$.

Proof: Let $A = F^{-1} \cdot F$. It is enough to show that $A[i, j] = 1$ if $i = j$, and $A[i, j] = 0$ if $i \neq j$. That is, $A = I$, where I is the *identity matrix*. By the definitions of F^{-1}, F, and matrix multiplication,

$$A[i, j] = \frac{1}{n} \sum_{k=0}^{n-1} \omega^{-ik} \omega^{kj}.$$

If $i = j$, then this equation reduces to

$$A[i, i] = \frac{1}{n} \sum_{k=0}^{n-1} \omega^0 = \frac{1}{n} \cdot n = 1.$$

So, consider the case when $i \neq j$, and let $m = j - i$. Then the ijth entry of A can be written as

$$A[i, j] = \frac{1}{n} \sum_{k=0}^{n-1} \omega^{mk},$$

where $-n < m < n$ and $m \neq 0$. By the cancellation property for a primitive nth root of unity, the right-hand side of the above equation reduces to 0; hence,

$$A[i, j] = 0,$$

for $i \neq j$.   ∎

Given the DFT and the inverse DFT, we can now define our approach to multiplying two polynomials p and q.

To use the discrete Fourier transform and its inverse to compute the convolution of two coefficient vectors, $\mathbf{a}$ and $\mathbf{b}$, we apply the following steps, which we illustrate in a schematic diagram, as shown in Figure 25.1.

1. Pad $\mathbf{a}$ and $\mathbf{b}$ each with n 0's and view them as column vectors to define

$$\mathbf{a}' = [a_0, a_1, \ldots, a_{n-1}, 0, 0, \ldots, 0]^T$$
$$\mathbf{b}' = [b_0, b_1, \ldots, b_{n-1}, 0, 0, \ldots, 0]^T.$$

2. Compute the Discrete Fourier Transforms $\mathbf{y} = F\mathbf{a}'$ and $\mathbf{z} = F\mathbf{b}'$.
3. Multiply the vectors $\mathbf{y}$ and $\mathbf{z}$ component-wise, defining the simple product $\mathbf{y} \cdot \mathbf{z} = F\mathbf{a}' \cdot F\mathbf{b}'$, where

$$(\mathbf{y} \cdot \mathbf{z})[i] = (F\mathbf{a}' \cdot F\mathbf{b}')[i] = F\mathbf{a}'[i] \cdot F\mathbf{b}'[i] = y_i \cdot z_i,$$

   for $i = 1, 2, \ldots, 2n - 1$.
4. Compute the inverse Discrete Fourier Transform of this simple product. That is, compute $\mathbf{c} = F^{-1}(F\mathbf{a}' \cdot F\mathbf{b}')$.

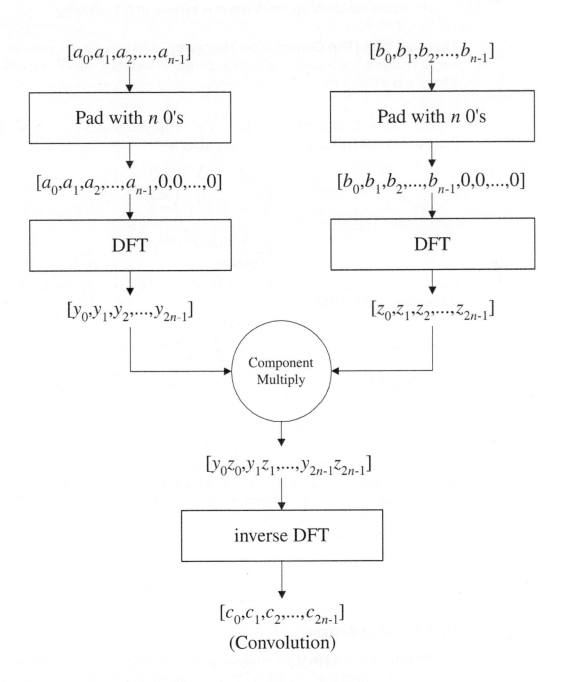

Figure 25.1: An illustration of the Convolution Theorem, to compute $\mathbf{c} = \mathbf{a} * \mathbf{b}$.

The reason the above approach works is because of the following.

Theorem 25.6 [The Convolution Theorem]: *Suppose we are given two n-length vectors $\mathbf{a}$ and $\mathbf{b}$ padded with 0's to $2n$-length vectors $\mathbf{a}'$ and $\mathbf{b}'$, respectively. Then $\mathbf{a} * \mathbf{b} = F^{-1}(F\mathbf{a}' \cdot F\mathbf{b}')$.*

Proof: We will show that $F(\mathbf{a} * \mathbf{b}) = F\mathbf{a}' \cdot F\mathbf{b}'$. So, consider $A = F\mathbf{a}' \cdot F\mathbf{b}'$. Since the second halves of $\mathbf{a}'$ and $\mathbf{b}'$ are padded with 0's,

$$
\begin{aligned}
A[i] &= \left(\sum_{j=0}^{n-1} a_j \omega^{ij} \right) \cdot \left(\sum_{k=0}^{n-1} b_k \omega^{ik} \right) \\
&= \sum_{j=0}^{n-1} \sum_{k=0}^{n-1} a_j b_k \omega^{i(j+k)},
\end{aligned}
$$

for $i = 0, 1, \ldots, 2n - 1$. Consider, next, $B = F(\mathbf{a} * \mathbf{b})$. By the definition of convolution and the DFT,

$$
B[i] = \sum_{l=0}^{2n-1} \sum_{j=0}^{2n-1} a_j b_{l-j} \omega^{il}.
$$

Substituting k for $l - j$, and changing the order of the summations, we get

$$
B[i] = \sum_{j=0}^{2n-1} \sum_{k=-j}^{2n-1-j} a_j b_k \omega^{i(j+k)}.
$$

Since b_k is undefined for $k < 0$, we can start the second summation above at $k = 0$. In addition, since $a_j = 0$ for $j > n - 1$, we can lower the upper limit in the first summation above to $n - 1$. But once we have made this substitution, note that the upper limit on the second summation above is always at least n. Thus, since $b_k = 0$ for $k > n - 1$, we may lower the upper limit on the second summation to $n - 1$. Therefore,

$$
B[i] = \sum_{j=0}^{n-1} \sum_{k=0}^{n-1} a_j b_k \omega^{i(j+k)},
$$

which proves the theorem.   ∎

We now have a method for computing the multiplication of two polynomials that involves computing two DFTs, doing a simple linear-time component-wise multiplication, and computing an inverse DFT. Thus, if we can find a fast algorithm for computing the DFT and its inverse, then we will have a fast algorithm for multiplying two polynomials. We describe such a fast algorithm, which is known as the "Fast Fourier Transform," next.

25.4 The Fast Fourier Transform Algorithm

The *Fast Fourier Transform* (FFT) algorithm computes a Discrete Fourier Transform (DFT) of an n-length vector in $O(n \log n)$ time. In the FFT algorithm, we apply the divide-and-conquer approach to polynomial evaluation by observing that if n is even, we can divide a degree-$(n-1)$ polynomial

$$p(x) = a_0 + a_1 x + a_2 x^2 + \cdots + a_{n-1} x^{n-1}$$

into two degree-$(n/2 - 1)$ polynomials

$$
\begin{aligned}
p^{\text{even}}(x) &= a_0 + a_2 x + a_4 x^2 + \cdots + a_{n-2} x^{n/2-1} \\
p^{\text{odd}}(x) &= a_1 + a_3 x + a_5 x^2 + \cdots + a_{n-1} x^{n/2-1}
\end{aligned}
$$

and noting that we can combine these two polynomials into p using the equation

$$p(x) = p^{\text{even}}(x^2) + x p^{\text{odd}}(x^2).$$

The DFT evaluates $p(x)$ at each nth root of unity, $\omega^0, \omega^1, \omega^2, \ldots, \omega^{n-1}$. Note that, by the reduction property, the values $(\omega^2)^0, \omega^2, (\omega^2)^2, (\omega^2)^3, \ldots, (\omega^2)^{n-1}$ are $(n/2)$th roots of unity. Thus, we can evaluate each of $p^{\text{even}}(x)$ and $p^{\text{odd}}(x)$ at these values, and we can reuse those same computations in evaluating $p(x)$. This observation is used in Algorithm 25.2 (FFT), which takes as input an n-length coefficient vector $\mathbf{a}$ and a primitive nth root of unity ω, where n is a power of 2.

Algorithm FFT$(\mathbf{a}, \omega)$:

    Input: An n-length coefficient vector $\mathbf{a} = [a_0, a_1, \ldots, a_{n-1}]$ and a primitive nth root of unity ω, where n is a power of 2

    Output: A vector $\mathbf{y}$ of values of the polynomial for $\mathbf{a}$ at the nth roots of unity

  if $n = 1$ **then**

    return $\mathbf{y} = \mathbf{a}$.

  $x \leftarrow \omega^0$ // x will store powers of ω, so initially $x = 1$.

  // Divide Step, which separates even and odd indices

  $\mathbf{a}^{\text{even}} \leftarrow [a_0, a_2, a_4, \ldots, a_{n-2}]$

  $\mathbf{a}^{\text{odd}} \leftarrow [a_1, a_3, a_5, \ldots, a_{n-1}]$

  // Recursive Calls, with ω^2 as $(n/2)$th root of unity, by the reduction property

  $\mathbf{y}^{\text{even}} \leftarrow$ FFT$(\mathbf{a}^{\text{even}}, \omega^2)$

  $\mathbf{y}^{\text{odd}} \leftarrow$ FFT$(\mathbf{a}^{\text{odd}}, \omega^2)$

  // Combine Step, using $x = \omega^i$

  for $i \leftarrow 0$ to $n/2 - 1$ **do**

    $y_i \leftarrow y_i^{\text{even}} + x \cdot y_i^{\text{odd}}$

    $y_{i+n/2} \leftarrow y_i^{\text{even}} - x \cdot y_i^{\text{odd}}$ // Uses reflective property

    $x \leftarrow x \cdot \omega$

  return $\mathbf{y}$

Algorithm 25.2: Recursive FFT algorithm.

The Correctness of the FFT Algorithm

The pseudocode description in Algorithm 25.2 for the FFT algorithm is deceptively simple, so let us say a few words about why it works correctly. First, note that the base case of the recursion, when $n = 1$, correctly returns a vector $\mathbf{y}$ with the one entry, $y_0 = a_0$, which is the leading and only term in the polynomial $p(x)$ in this case.

In the general case, when $n \geq 2$, we separate $\mathbf{a}$ into its even and odd instances, $\mathbf{a}^{\text{even}}$ and $\mathbf{a}^{\text{odd}}$, and recursively call the FFT using ω^2 as the $(n/2)$th root of unity. As we have already mentioned, the reduction property of a primitive nth root of unity, allows us to use ω^2 in this way. Thus, we may inductively assume that

$$\begin{aligned} y_i^{\text{even}} &= p^{\text{even}}(\omega^{2i}) \\ y_i^{\text{odd}} &= p^{\text{odd}}(\omega^{2i}). \end{aligned}$$

Let us therefore consider the for-loop that combines the values from the recursive calls. Note that in the i iteration of the loop, $x = \omega^i$. Thus, when we perform the assignment statement

$$y_i \leftarrow y_i^{\text{even}} + x y_i^{\text{odd}},$$

we have just set

$$\begin{aligned} y_i &= p^{\text{even}}((\omega^2)^i) + \omega^i \cdot p^{\text{odd}}((\omega^2)^i) \\ &= p^{\text{even}}((\omega^i)^2) + \omega^i \cdot p^{\text{odd}}((\omega^i)^2) \\ &= p(\omega^i), \end{aligned}$$

and we do this for each index $i = 0, 1, \ldots, n/2 - 1$. Similarly, when we perform the assignment statement

$$y_{i+n/2} \leftarrow y_i^{\text{even}} - x y_i^{\text{odd}},$$

we have just set

$$y_{i+n/2} = p^{\text{even}}((\omega^2)^i) - \omega^i \cdot p^{\text{odd}}((\omega^2)^i).$$

Since ω^2 is a primitive $(n/2)$th root of unity, $(\omega^2)^{n/2} = 1$. Moreover, since ω is itself a primitive nth root of unity,

$$\omega^{i+n/2} = -\omega^i,$$

by the reflection property. Thus, we can rewrite the above identity for $y_{i+n/2}$ as

$$\begin{aligned} y_{i+n/2} &= p^{\text{even}}((\omega^2)^{i+(n/2)}) - \omega^i \cdot p^{\text{odd}}((\omega^2)^{i+(n/2)}) \\ &= p^{\text{even}}((\omega^{i+(n/2)})^2) + \omega^{i+n/2} \cdot p^{\text{odd}}((\omega^{i+(n/2)})^2) \\ &= p(\omega^{i+n/2}), \end{aligned}$$

and this will hold for each $i = 0, 1, \ldots, n/2 - 1$. Thus, the vector $\mathbf{y}$ returned by the FFT algorithm will store the values of $p(x)$ at each of the nth roots of unity.

Analyzing the FFT Algorithm

The FFT algorithm follows the divide-and-conquer paradigm, dividing the original problem of size n into two subproblems of size $n/2$, which are solved recursively. We assume that each arithmetic operation performed by algorithms takes $O(1)$ time. The divide step as well as the combine step for merging the recursive solutions, each take $O(n)$ time. Thus, we can characterize the running time $T(n)$ of the FFT algorithm using the recurrence equation

$$T(n) = 2T(n/2) + bn,$$

for some constant $b > 0$. By the Master Theorem (11.4), $T(n)$ is $O(n \log n)$. Therefore, we can summarize our discussion as follows.

Theorem 25.7: *Given an n-length coefficient vector $\mathbf{a}$ defining a polynomial $p(x)$, and a primitive nth root of unity, ω, the FFT algorithm evaluates $p(x)$ at each of the nth roots of unity, ω^i, for $i = 0, 1, \ldots, n-1$, using $O(n \log n)$ arithmetic operations.*

There is also an inverse FFT algorithm, which computes the inverse DFT in $O(n \log n)$ time. The details of this algorithm are similar to those for the FFT algorithm and are left as an exercise (R-25.1). Combining these two algorithms in our approach to multiplying two polynomials $p(x)$ and $q(x)$, given their n-length coefficient vectors, we have an algorithm for computing this product using $O(n \log n)$ arithmetic operations, in the field used to define the primitive roots of unity used by the FFT algorithm.

Multiplying Big Integers

Let us revisit the problem discussed in the introduction, of multiplying two n-bit integers. Namely, suppose we are given two big integers P and J that use at most $n \geq 64$ bits each, where n is a power of 2, and we are interested in computing $R = P \cdot Q$. As mentioned earlier, we construct two polynomials, $p(x)$ and $q(x)$, from P and Q as follows:

$$
\begin{aligned}
p(x) &= a_0 + a_1 x + a_2 x^2 + \cdots + a_{n-1} x^{n-1} \\
q(x) &= b_0 + b_1 x + a_2 x^2 + \cdots + b_{n-1} x^{n-1},
\end{aligned}
$$

and note that $P = p(2)$ and $Q = q(2)$. Then we use the FFT algorithm to compute a coefficient representation of the degree-$2n$ polynomial,

$$r(x) = p(x) \cdot q(x).$$

This takes $O(n \log n)$ arithmetic operations, say, in Z_t, for a prime number, t, that can be represented using $O(\log n)$ bits. This is likely to be on the order of the word size of our computer, since it takes $O(\log n)$ bits just to represent the number n. Finally, given this representation for $r(x)$, we need to compute $r(2)$ and assign this to R.

A Divide-and-Conquer Algorithm for Evaluating $r(2)$

We can compute $r(2)$ efficiently via yet another divide-and-conquer algorithm, by noting that if $r_1(x)$ is a polynomial defined by the first n (lower-order) coefficients of $r(x)$ and $r_2(x)$ is a polynomial defined by the second n (higher-order) coefficients of $r(x)$, then

$$r(x) = r_1(x) + r_2(x) \cdot x^n.$$

Thus, we can evaluate $r(2)$ as follows:

> **if** $n = 1$ **then**
>   **return** $r(2)$
> recursively compute $R_1 \leftarrow r_1(2)$
> recursively compute $R_2 \leftarrow r_2(2)$
> Let $R_2' \leftarrow R_2 \cdot 2^n$
> **return** $R_1 + R_2'$

Note that doing the multiplication of R_2 and 2^n is not as difficult as the integer multiplication problem we are trying to solve. In particular, since we are computing $r(2)$ in binary, we can multiply $r_1(2)$ by 2^n by a left shift of the bits of $r_2(2)$ by n places. Thus, we can do the final multiplication by 2^n and addition of the resulting $O(n)$-bit numbers in $O(n)$ time. Therefore, this divide-and-conquer evaluation algorithm can be characterized by the recurrence equation,

$$T(n) = 2T(n/2) + bn,$$

for some constant $b \geq 1$; hence, the evaluation of $r(2)$ can be done in $O(n \log n)$ time. This gives us the following.

Theorem 25.8: *Given two n-bit integers P and Q, we can compute the product $R = P \cdot Q$ using $O(n \log n)$ arithmetic operations.*

Here, the arithmetic operations are done in the number system that is used to define the primitive nth roots of unity required by the FFT algorithm. For instance, if we can do all the arithmetic in Z_t, for a prime $t = cn + 1$, for a small integer constant, c, such that t can be stored in a single word on our computer, then we can perform each arithmetic operation in $O(1)$ time in the RAM model.

In some cases, we cannot assume that arithmetic involving reasonably sized words can be done in constant time, however. In such scenarios, we must pay constant time for every bit operation. In this model it is still possible to use the FFT to multiply two n-bit integers, but the details are somewhat more complicated and the running time increases to $O(n \log n \log \log n)$. We omit the details for this approach here.

Implementing the FFT Algorithm to Avoid Repeated Array Allocation

The pseudocode for the recursive FFT algorithm calls for the allocation of several new arrays, including $\mathbf{a}^{\mathrm{even}}$, $\mathbf{a}^{\mathrm{odd}}$, $\mathbf{y}^{\mathrm{even}}$, $\mathbf{y}^{\mathrm{odd}}$, and $\mathbf{y}$. Allocating all of these arrays with each recursive call could prove to be a costly amount of extra work. If it can be avoided, saving this additional allocation of arrays could significantly improve the constant factors in the running time of the FFT algorithm.

Fortunately, the structure of FFT allows us to avoid this repeated array allocation. Instead of allocating many arrays, we can use a single array, A, for the input coefficients and use a single array, Y, for the answers. The main idea that allows for this usage is that we can think of the arrays A and Y as partitioned into subarrays, each one associated with a different recursive call. We can identify these subarrays using just two variables, base, which identifies the base address of the subarray, and n, which identifies the size of the subarray. Thus, we can avoid the overhead associated with allocating lots of small arrays with each recursive call.

Having decided that we will not allocate new arrays during the FFT recursive calls, we must deal with the fact that the FFT algorithm involves performing separate computations on even and odd indices of the input array. In the pseudocode of Algorithm 25.2, we use new arrays $\mathbf{a}^{\mathrm{even}}$ and $\mathbf{a}^{\mathrm{odd}}$, but now we must use subarrays in A for these vectors. Our solution for this memory management problem is to take the current n-cell subarray in A, and divide it into two subarrays of size $n/2$. One of the subarrays will have the same base as A, while the other has base base $+ n/2$. We move the elements at even indices in A to the lower half and we move elements at odd indices in A to the upper half. In doing so, we define an interesting permutation known as the ***inverse shuffle***. This permutation gets its name from its resemblance to the inverse of the permutation we would get by cutting the array A in half and shuffling it perfectly as if it were a deck of cards. Repeating it recursively on each half gives rise to a structure known as the ***butterfly network***, because of its symmetry. (See Figure 25.3.)

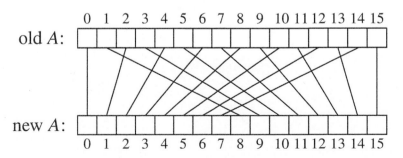

Figure 25.3: An illustration of the inverse shuffle permutation.

Avoiding Recursion

Another constant-time improvement we can make to the running of the FFT algorithm is to avoid recursion. The main challenge in such an implementation is that we have to figure out a way of performing all the inverse shuffles in the input array A. Rather than performing each inverse shuffle with each iteration, we instead perform all the inverse shuffles in advance, assuming that n, the size of the input array, is a power of two.

In order to figure out the net effect of the permutation we would get by repeated and recursive inverse shuffle operations, let us consider how the inverse shuffles move data around with each recursive call. In the first recursive call, of course, we perform an inverse shuffle on the entire array A. Note how this permutation operates at the bit level of the indices in A. It brings all elements at addresses that have a 0 as their least significant bit to the bottom half of A. Likewise, it brings all elements at addresses that have a 1 as their least significant bit to the top half of A. That is, if an element starts out at an address with b as its least significant bit, then it ends up at an address with b as its most significant bit. The least significant bit in an address is the determiner of which half of A an element winds up in. In the next level of recursion, we repeat the inverse shuffle on each half of A. Viewed again at the bit level, for $b = 0, 1$, these recursive inverse shuffles take elements originally at addresses with b as their second least significant bit, and move them to addresses that have b as their second most significant bit. Likewise, for $b = 0, 1$, the ith levels of recursion move elements originally at address with b as their ith least significant bit, to addresses with b as their ith most significant bit. Thus, if an element starts out at an address with binary representation $[b_{l-1} \ldots b_2 b_1 b_0]$, then it ends up at an address with binary representation $[b_0 b_1 b_2 \ldots b_{l-1}]$, where $l = \log_2 n$. That is, we can perform all the inverse shuffles in advance just by moving elements in A to the address that is the bit reversal of their starting address in A. To perform this permutation, we build a permutation array, reverse, in the multiply method, and then use this inside the FFT method to permute the elements in the input array A according to this permutation.

25.5 Exercises

Reinforcement

R-25.1 Describe the inverse FFT algorithm, which computes the inverse DFT in $O(n \log n)$ time. That is, show how to reverse the roles of **a** and **y** and change the assignments so that, for each output index, we have

$$a_i = \frac{1}{n} \sum_{j=1}^{n-1} y_j \omega^{-ij}.$$

R-25.2 Write the complex nth roots of unity for $n = 4$ and $n = 8$ in the form $a + bi$.

R-25.3 What is the bit-reversal permutation, reverse, for $n = 16$?

R-25.4 Show that 5 is a multiplicative generator of the positive numbers in Z_{17}.

R-25.5 Use the FFT and inverse FFT to compute the convolution of $\mathbf{a} = [1, 2, 3, 4]$ and $\mathbf{b} = [4, 3, 2, 1]$, using arithmetic in Z_{17}. Use the fact that 5 is a generator for the positive elements of Z_{17}, and show the output of each component as in Figure 25.1.

R-25.6 Use the convolution theorem to compute the product of the polynomials $p(x) = 3x^2 + 4x + 2$ and $q(x) = 2x^3 + 3x^2 + 5x + 3$, using arithmetic in Z_{17}. You may use the fact that 5 is a generator for the positive elements of Z_{17}.

R-25.7 Compute the discrete Fourier transform of the vector $[5, 4, 3, 2]$ using arithmetic modulo $17 = 2^4 + 1$. Use the fact that 5 is a generator for the positive elements in Z_{17}.

R-25.8 Compute the product of the binary numbers $(01101000)_2$ and $(10001011)_2$ using the algorithm given in the book.

R-25.9 What is the exact number of recursive calls made to compute the convolution of the vectors $[6, 2, 3, 5, 2, 5, 8, 3, 2, 6]$ and $[4, 2, 3, 2, 7, 3, 3, 9]$, using recursive definitions of the FFT and inverse FFT algorithms?

Creativity

C-25.1 Prove the following more general form of the reduction property of primitive roots of unity: For any integer $c > 0$, if ω is a primitive (cn)th root of unity, then ω^c is a primitive nth root of unity.

C-25.2 Prove that $\omega = 2^{4b/m}$ is a primitive mth root of unity when multiplication is taken modulo $(2^{2b} + 1)$, for any integer $b > 0$ that is a multiple of m.

C-25.3 Given degree-n polynomials $p(x)$ and $q(x)$, describe a method for multiplying the derivatives of $p(x)$ and $q(x)$, that is, $p'(x) \cdot q'(x)$, using $O(n \log n)$ arithmetic operations.

C-25.4 Describe a version of the FFT that works when n is a power of 3 by dividing the input vector into three subvectors, recursing on each one, and then merging the subproblem solutions. Derive a recurrence equation for the running time of this algorithm and solve this recurrence using the Master Theorem.

C-25.5 Describe a method for computing the coefficients of the polynomial,

$$P(x) = (x+1)^n,$$

in $O(n)$ time.

Applications

A-25.1 In ***Shamir secret sharing***, an administrator, Bob, chooses a secret number, s, in a finite field, Z_p, for some prime number, p. He then chooses $n-1$ more random numbers, $a_1, a_2, \ldots, a_{n-1}$, in Z_p, and uses them to define the polynomial,

$$p(x) = s + a_1 x + a_2 x^2 + \cdots + a_{n-1} x^{n-1}.$$

Then, for each of $n < p$ friends, he chooses a distinct value, x_i, and distributes $p(x_i)$ to friend number i. Argue why it is impossible for a group of $(n-1)$ friends to learn the secret s, but if all n friends cooperate, they can learn s. Also, describe a method for Bob to compute all the values, $p(x_1), p(x_2), \ldots, p(x_n)$, using $O(n^2)$ arithmetic operations in Z_p.

A-25.2 Consider the Shamir secret sharing problem from the previous exercise, but now design an algorithm for computing all the values, $p(x_1), p(x_2), \ldots, p(x_n)$, using $O(n \log^2 n)$ arithmetic operations. You may use "as a black box" an algorithm, PolyDivide, which takes two polynomials, $p(x)$ and $q(x)$, given in coefficient form, with each of them having degree at most $(n-1)$, and returns the remainder polynomial, $r(x)$,

$$r(x) = p(x) \bmod q(x),$$

in coefficient form, using $O(n \log n)$ arithmetic operations. In addition, you may use the fact that, for any point, x_i,

$$p(x_i) = p(x) \bmod (x - x_i).$$

Finally, you may use the fact that if we let

$$q_{i,j}(x) = \prod_{k=i}^{j} (x - x_k),$$

then $p(x) = p(x) \bmod q_{1,n}(x)$, and

$$p(x) \bmod q_{i,j}(x) = (p(x) \bmod q_{k,l}(x)) \bmod q_{i,j}(x),$$

for $k \le i \le j \le l$.

A-25.3 In some numerical computing applications, a desired computation is to find a polynomial that goes through a given set of points on a line, which, without loss of generality, we can assume is the x-axis. So suppose you are given a set of real numbers

$$X = \{x_0, x_1, \ldots, x_{n-1}\}.$$

Note that, by the Interpolation Theorem for Polynomials, there is a unique degree-$(n-1)$ polynomial $p(x)$, such that

$$p(x_i) = 0, \ \text{for } i = 0, 1, \ldots, n-1,$$

and these are the only 0-values for the polynomial. Design a divide-and-conquer algorithm that can construct a coefficient-form representation of this polynomial, $p(x)$, using $O(n \log^2 n)$ arithmetic operations.

A-25.4 Suppose you have a software method, Conv, that can perform the convolution of two length-n integer vectors, A and B, using the FFT algorithm described in this chapter. Suppose further that you have been asked to build a system that can take an n-bit binary "text" string, T, and an m-bit binary "pattern" string, P, for $m \le n$, and determine all the places in T where P appears as a substring. Show that in $O(n)$ time, plus the time needed for calls to the Conv method, you can solve this pattern matching problem by making two calls to the Conv function.

Hint: Note that the kth position in the convolution of two bit strings, A and B, counts the number of 1's that match among the first $k-1$ places in A with the last $k-1$ places in the reversal of B.

A-25.5 Consider a generalization of the pattern matching problem from the previous exercise, where we allow the pattern P and text T to be strings defined over an arbitrary alphabet, Σ. Show that you can still find all occurrences of P in T using two calls to the Conv method. In this case, your algorithm should run in $O(n \log |\Sigma|)$ time, plus the time needed for the calls to the Conv method.

A-25.6 Consider a further generalization of the pattern matching problem from the previous exercise, where we allow the pattern, P, to contain instances of a special "wild card" or "don't care" symbol, $\ast$, which matches any character in the alphabet, Σ. For example, with

$$P = \texttt{ab**c}$$

and

$$T = \texttt{babdfcabghci},$$

P matches T in positions 2 and 7. Show that, even in this case, you can still find all occurrences of P in T using two calls to the Conv method. In this case, your algorithm should run in $O(n \log |\Sigma|)$ time, plus the time needed for the calls to the Conv method. (Also, note that this problem cannot be solved using the efficient algorithms from Chapter 23.)

A-25.7 Suppose you are given a set, S, of n distinct number pairs, (x, y), such as in the Shamir secret sharing scheme described in Exercise A-25.1. Furthermore, assume that you have a software method, LinSolve, for solving a system of n linear equations with n unknowns. Describe how to produce a coefficient-form representation of the unique degree-$(n-1)$ polynomial that satisfies $y = p(x)$, for each (x, y) in S. Your algorithm should run in $O(n^2)$ time plus the time taken by the LinSolve method.

A-25.8 In financial and scientific data analysis applications, such as in spotting trends in stocks, we are often interested in making sense of noisy or highly fluctuating data. One method to achieve this goal is to take an average of recent values, as shown in Figure 25.4. For instance, in using a *weighted moving average*, one begins by specifying a sequence of m weights, $W = (w_0, w_1, \ldots, w_{m-1})$, with

$$\sum_{i=0}^{m-1} w_i = 1.$$

Typically, one chooses the weights so that $w_i > w_{i+1}$, for $i = 1, \ldots, n-1$, so as to give greater emphasis to recent data. Then, given a sequence of $n \geq m$ data values, $X = (x_0, x_1, \ldots, x_{n-1})$, the ith value of the weighted moving average is computed as

$$A_i = w_0 a_i + w_1 a_{i-1} + w_2 a_{i-2} + \cdots.$$

For example, if $W = (0.5, 0.3, 0.2)$ and the three most recent data values were 136, 150, 200, then the current weighted moving average would be

$$A_i = 0.5(136) + 0.3(150) + 0.2(200) = 153,$$

which is closer to 136 than it is to 200. Given the sequences W and X, as specified above, describe an efficient method for computing all the A_i values, for $i = 0, 1, \ldots, n-1$, using $O(n \log n)$ arithmetic operations.

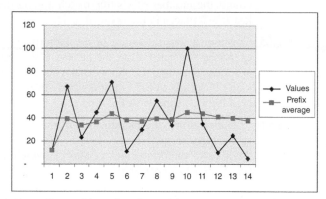

Figure 25.4: Smoothing data by taking an average of recent values.

Chapter Notes

The Fast Fourier Transform (FFT) appears in a paper by Cooley and Tukey [49]. It is also discussed in books by Aho, Hopcroft, and Ullman [8], Baase [18], and Yap [219], all of which were influential in the discussion given above. The fast integer multiplication method, running in $O(n \log n \log \log n)$ time, is due to Schönhage and Strassen [186]. For information on additional applications of the FFT, the interested reader is referred to books by Brigham [39] and Elliott and Rao [65], and the chapter by Emiris and Pan [66]. The connection between string matching and convolution begins with work by Fischer and Paterson [70]. Shamir describes a polynomial-based way to share a secret in [194].

Chapter
26

Linear Programming

Brooklyn Bridge showing painters on suspenders. By Eugene de Salgnac, October 7, 1914. From NYC Municipal Archives. Public domain image.

Contents

26.1 Formulating the Problem 734
26.2 The Simplex Method 739
26.3 Duality 746
26.4 Applications of Linear Programming 750
26.5 Exercises 753

Optimization problems are common in the real world, with many applications in business and science that involve maximizing or minimizing some goal subject to a set of given constraints. For example, we might like to maximize a profit given a certain initial investment, or we might wish to minimize the error produced by a computer simulation using a fixed number of CPUs. Thus, in such contexts, there are in general two components to such optimization problems:

- a set of constraints that must be satisfied
- an objective function to maximize or minimize subject to the given constraints.

In a business application, for instance, the constraints might include the amount of risk allowed in an investment portfolio, and in a scientific application, the constraints might be determined by the number of CPUs available to run a simulation. In either case, often the objective is to maximize profit or minimize cost.

An Example Optimization Problem

As a more detailed application, suppose that a web server company wants to buy new servers to replace outdated ones and has two options to choose from. There is a standard model which costs \$400, uses 300W of power, takes up two shelves of a server rack, and can handle 1000 hits/min. There is also a cutting-edge model, which costs \$1600, uses 500W of power, but takes up only one shelf, and can handle 2000 hits/min. With a budget of \$36,800, 44 shelves of server space and 12,200W of power, how many units of each model should the company purchase in order to maximize the number of hits it can serve every minute?

Let us introduce some variables, say x_1 and x_2, to represent the number of servers for each model. Then the number of hits per minute that can be serviced by x_1 standard servers and x_2 cutting-edge servers is

$$1000x_1 + 2000x_2.$$

Our goal is to maximize this quantity.

The number of servers the company should get is limited by three factors: the budget, which translates into

$$400x_1 + 1600x_2 \le 36800,$$

the number of shelves that can be taken up by these servers,

$$2x_1 + x_2 \le 44,$$

and the amount of power these servers can use collectively,

$$300x_1 + 500x_2 \le 12200.$$

Therefore, this optimization problem can be summarized as follows:

maximize: $\qquad z = 1000x_1 + 2000x_2$

subject to: $\qquad 400x_1 + 1600x_2 \leq 36800$

$$2x_1 + x_2 \leq 44$$

$$300x_1 + 500x_2 \leq 12200$$

$$x_1, x_2 \geq 0,$$

where the inequalities in the last line express the implicit requirement that the number of each server has to be nonnegative. Such inequalities are necessary to prevent a nonsensical solution, and they are distinguished from the other constraints in that they determine the sign of the variables. Solving optimization problems that have the above general form is known as *linear programming*, which is the topic we study in this chapter.

Linear programming encompasses a broad subclass of optimization problems, including the shortest-path problem and maximum flow, as well as fundamental applications from the realms of military, science, and business. Algorithms that solve linear programs (often abbreviated as LP) have been extensively studied in the last century. Our goal in this chapter is to understand one of these algorithms, which is still in use, called the simplex method.

Translating Problems into Linear Programs

In general, there are three steps for turning an optimization problem into a linear program, assuming such a formulation is possible:

1. Determining the variables of the problem.

2. Finding the quantity to optimize, and write it in terms of the variables.

3. Finding all the constraints on the variables and writing equations or inequalities to express these constraints.

In addition, in defining the constraints, we need to be sure to include any implicit constraints describing the range of values the variables can take and to make sure all the equations are *linear*, as in the above example. In this chapter, we discuss how to create such formulations of optimization problems.

Once we have such a formulation, we then should solve the resulting linear program, and there are several software packages available for doing this that are based on various efficient algorithms. In this chapter, we focus on a classic algorithm for solving linear programs, which is known as the *simplex method*. We also discuss an important topic known as *duality*.

26.1   Formulating the Problem

Standard Form

Recall that a function, f, is a ***linear function*** in the variables, $x_1, x_2, \ldots, x_n$, if it has the following form:

$$f(x_1, x_2, \ldots, x_n) = a_1 x_1 + a_2 x_2 + \cdots + a_n x_n = \sum_{i=1}^{n} a_i x_i,$$

for some real numbers, $a_1, a_2, \ldots, a_n$, which are called ***coefficients*** or ***weights***.

A ***linear program*** in ***standard form*** is an optimization problem with the following form:

$$\text{maximize:} \qquad\qquad z = \sum_{i \in V} c_i x_i$$

$$\text{subject to:} \qquad\qquad \sum_{j \in V} a_{ij} x_j \leq b_i \text{ for } i \in C$$

$$x_i \geq 0 \text{ for } i \in V$$

where V indexes over the set of variables and C indexes over the set of constraints. The x_i's are variables, whereas all other symbols represent fixed real numbers. The function to maximize is called the ***objective function***, and the inequalities are called ***constraints***. In particular, the inequalities $x_i \geq 0$ are called ***nonnegativity constraints***. This program is linear because both the objective and the constraints are linear functions of the variables, where an inequality is linear if there is a linear function on one side and a constant on the other side of the inequality.

As an example, the earlier linear program is reproduced below. Notice that it fits the standard form. To make this fact more explicit, we rewrite it in gray using the notation from the definition:

maximize:	$z = 1000x_1 + 2000x_2$	$z = c_1 x_1 + c_2 x_2$
subject to:	$400x_1 + 1600x_2 \leq 36800$	$a_{11}x_1 + a_{12}x_2 \leq b_1$
	$2x_1 + x_2 \leq 44$	$a_{21}x_1 + a_{22}x_2 \leq b_2$
	$300x_1 + 500x_2 \leq 12200$	$a_{31}x_1 + a_{32}x_2 \leq b_3$
	$x_1, x_2 \geq 0$	$x_1, x_2 \geq 0.$

There are two variables and three constraints, so $V = \{1, 2\}$ and $C = \{1, 2, 3\}$.

Linear programs also come in several variants of the standard form. For instance, we may want to minimize rather than maximize the objective function, the inequalities in the constraints may be expressed in terms of "greater than or equal to," or the constraints might be better expressed as equalities. Fortunately, these variants can easily be made to fit the standard form. The following table describes how this could be done.

The form ...	can also be written as ...
minimize $f(x_1, \ldots, x_n)$	maximize $-f(x_1, \ldots, x_n)$
$f(x_1, \ldots, x_n) \geq y$	$-f(x_1, \ldots, x_n) \leq -y$
$f(x_1, \ldots, x_n) = y$	$f(x_1, \ldots, x_n) \leq y$ $f(x_1, \ldots, x_n) \geq y$

For example, we can use the last two rules to rewrite $3x_1 - 2x_2 = 5$ into an equivalent form consisting of the two inequalities

$$3x_1 - 2x_2 \leq 5,$$
$$-3x_1 + 2x_2 \leq -5.$$

Matrix Notation

A linear function can be expressed as a dot product:

$$\sum_{i=1}^{n} a_i x_i = \vec{a} \cdot \vec{x}, \quad \begin{aligned} \vec{a} &= (a_1, \ldots, a_n), \\ \vec{x} &= (x_1, \ldots, x_n). \end{aligned}$$

Notice that $\vec{a}$ is a vector of numbers while $\vec{x}$ is a vector of variables. Using dot products, we can express the standard form more compactly:

$$\begin{aligned} \text{maximize:} \quad & \vec{c} \cdot \vec{x} \\ \text{subject to:} \quad & \vec{a}_1 \cdot \vec{x} \leq b_1 \\ & \vec{a}_2 \cdot \vec{x} \leq b_2 \\ & \quad \vdots \\ & \vec{a}_m \cdot \vec{x} \leq b_m. \end{aligned}$$

In fact, we can express it even more compactly, by letting A be the matrix where the ith row is vector $\vec{a}_i$. In other words, A is the $m \times n$ matrix whose ijth entry is a_{ij}. Also let $\vec{b}$ be the vector with entries b_i. If we extend the meaning of the symbol $\leq$ to row-wise inequality, we can have a more succinct description of standard form as follows:

$$\begin{aligned} \text{maximize:} \quad & \vec{c} \cdot \vec{x} \\ \text{subject to:} \quad & A\vec{x} \leq \vec{b}. \end{aligned}$$

For example, the inequalities

$$2x + z \leq 5$$
$$x - 4y - 3z \leq 1$$

can be written as

$$\begin{array}{ccc} (2, 0, 1) \cdot (x, y, z) \leq 5 & & \begin{pmatrix} 2 & 0 & 1 \\ 1 & -4 & -3 \end{pmatrix} \begin{pmatrix} x \\ y \\ z \end{pmatrix} \leq \begin{pmatrix} 5 \\ 1 \end{pmatrix}. \\ (1, -4, -3) \cdot (x, y, z) \leq 1 & \text{or} & \end{array}$$

The Geometry of Linear Programs

To understand a linear program, it helps to look at the problem from a geometric point of view. For simplicity, let us restrict ourselves to the two-dimensional case for the time being. In this case, each inequality constraint describes a half-plane, expressed as an infinite region to one side of a line. So a point that is inside all of these half-planes is a point that satisfies all the constraints. We call such a point a *feasible solution*. Now intersections of half-planes have the shape of a convex polygon (Section 22.2). So the set of all feasible solutions is a convex polygon. We call this set the *feasible region*. For example, Figure 26.1 shows the feasible region of the linear program from the web server example.

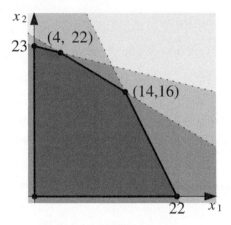

Figure 26.1: A feasible region is the intersection of half-spaces.

A region is *convex* if any two points in the region can be joined by a line segment entirely in the region (see Figure 26.2). Intuitively, if a two-dimensional shape is convex, then a person walking on its boundary, assuming it has one, would always be making left turns, or always right turns. (See, also, Section 22.2.)

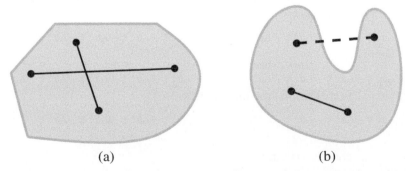

(a)   (b)

Figure 26.2: (a) In a convex set, any segment line joining two points inside the set is also inside the set. (b) In a non-convex set, there are segments joining two points in the set that are not entirely in the set.

In general, linear programs have a geometry in d dimensions where d is the number of variables. The geometric intuition is the same as in the plane but the shapes are more complex and the terminology is different. Inequality constraints in d dimensions are represented by half-spaces instead of half-planes, and their intersection forms a convex polytope instead of a convex polygon. For instance, a three-dimensional linear program could have a feasible region in the shape of a cube, pyramid, soccer ball, or any other three-dimensional convex shape with flat sides defining its boundary.

It is not enough to find just any feasible solution, of course. We are interested in one that optimizes the objective function. We refer to this feasible solution an ***optimal solution***. In the web server example, for instance, the set of points that produce a particular value, c, of the objective function is given by the equation

$$c = 1000x_1 + 2000x_2,$$

which is represented by a line. Such lines with varying values of c are all parallel, and we are interested in the one that maximizes c while still containing a feasible solution somewhere on the line. (See Figure 26.3.)

Referring to Figure 26.3, note that the slope of a line for the above objective function is always $-1/2$, regardless of the value of c. So we can imagine that, as c increases, the line sweeps the plane from the bottom left to the top right, staying parallel to itself. An optimal solution must be contained within the feasible region, which is represented by the gray region, and it must have the highest possible objective value. So the optimal solution is the point in the feasible region which is last hit by the sweeping line as it sweeps up and to the right. In this case, this point is the intersection of the lines representing the budget and power constraints,

$$400x_1 + 1600x_2 = 36800$$
$$300x_1 + 500x_2 = 12200.$$

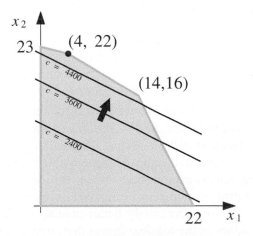

Figure 26.3: An example two-dimensional feasible region and objective function, $c = 1000x_1 + 2000x_2$. Values of the objective are represented by parallel lines.

By solving the above system of two equations in two variables, we see that the optimal solution occurs when $x_1 = 4$ and $x_2 = 22$. This example illustrates a principle that applies even to linear programs in higher dimensions—namely, that, because the feasible region is a convex polytope, an optimal solution, if one exists, always occurs on the boundary.

An optimal solution may not always be unique, however, such as when we modify the coefficients of the objective function in our example to

$$\text{maximize} \quad 1500x_1 + 2500x_2.$$

(See Figure 26.4(a).) It is also possible that the solution does not exist at all. For example, this case occurs when the feasible region is unbounded and the objective function tends to $+\infty$ as we move along a ray contained in the feasible region. (See Figure 26.4(b).)

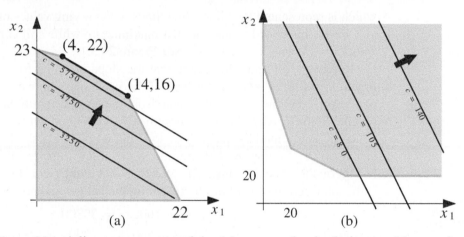

Figure 26.4: A linear program can have (a) many optimal solutions or (b) no optimal solution at all.

Finally, a linear program may not have an optimal solution simply because it has no feasible solution. This situation occurs when the constraints are so restrictive that no assignment to the variables can satisfy every constraint. Geometrically, this is the situation in which the intersection of all the half-spaces is empty.

Therefore, one algorithm to solve a linear program that has at least one optimal solution is to find all the vertices of the feasible region, and evaluate the objective function at these points. The optimal solution will be the point or points with highest objective value. This method is not particularly efficient, however, because there can be exponentially many vertices to evaluate. A better approach consists of starting at one vertex and, over several iterations, moving to a neighboring vertex with an increasingly better objective value. Thus, we can find a path on the boundary of the feasible region that starts at any vertex and ends at an optimal one. This alternative algorithm is called the simplex method, which is the algorithm we discuss next.

26.2   The Simplex Method

In this section, we describe the *simplex method*, which is an algorithm for solving linear programs that follows a path through the vertices of the feasible region that increases the objective function in a greedy fashion. Although the worst-case runtime for this algorithm is exponential, in practice the algorithm usually finishes quickly.

26.2.1   Slack Form

To solve a linear program using the simplex method, we must first rewrite the problem in a format known as *slack form*. To convert a linear program from standard form into slack form, we rewrite each of the inequality constraints as an equivalent equality constraint. This is done with the introduction of new variables, called *slack variables*, which are nonnegative and measure the difference in the original inequality. For example, to rewrite the inequality $2x - 5y \leq 28$ in slack form, we could introduce a slack variable, s, with the constraints, $s = 28 - (2x - 5y)$ and $s \geq 0$. Intuitively, variable s measures the "slack" in the inequality, that is, the amount between the lesser and greater quantities in the inequality. We perform this step for each inequality in the standard form, introducing a slack variable for each such inequality.

Formally, we say that linear program is in *slack form* if we seek to maximize a linear objective, z, subject to constraints that are either equality constraints involving a slack variable or are nonnegativity constraints, as follows:

$$\text{maximize:} \qquad z = c_* + \sum_{j \in F} c_j x_j$$

$$\text{subject to:} \qquad x_i = b_i - \sum_{j \in F} a_{ij} x_j, \quad \text{for } i \in B$$

$$x_i \geq 0 \text{ for } 1 \leq i \leq m + n.$$

The sets B and F partition the x_i variables into *basic variables* and *free variables*, respectively. That is, each equality constraint has a basic (slack) variable on the left-hand side and only free variables on the right-hand side. Thus, free variables only appear on the left-hand side of nonnegativity constraints. Taken together, the a_{ij} coefficients form a $m \times n$ matrix, A, where $n = |F|$ is the number of variables in the standard form, and $m = |B|$ is the number of constraints in the standard form. Incidentally, the minus sign in the equality constraints is needed so that the matrix A is the same in the slack form and standard form.

Example 26.1: *Below we convert the linear program in standard form (left) into a slack form (right). In this particular slack form, the basic variables are slack variables, but this is not always the case.*

maximize:	$z = x_1 + 2x_2$	maximize:	$z = x_1 + 2x_2$
subject to:	$-3x_1 + 2x_2 \le 3$	subject to:	$x_3 = 3 + 3x_1 - 2x_2$
	$x_1 + x_2 \le 2$		$x_4 = 2 - x_1 - x_2$
	$x_1 - x_2 \le 1$		$x_5 = 1 - x_1 + x_2$
	$x_1, x_2 \ge 0$		$x_1, x_2, x_3, x_4, x_5 \ge 0$

In this slack form, the free variables have indices $F = \{1, 2\}$ and the basic variables have indices $B = \{3, 4, 5\}$.

We are interested in the **basic solution** of the slack form, which means we set all the free variables to zero and let the equality constraints determine the values of the basic variables. In the above example, the basic solution is, $x_1 = x_2 = 0$, $x_3 = 3$, $x_4 = 2$, and $x_5 = 1$, or written in vector notation $\vec{x} = (0, 0, 3, 2, 1)$, and the objective function has value $z = c_* = 0$. In this case, the basic solution is a feasible solution, but this need not be the case in general.

The simplex method works by rewriting the slack form until a basic solution becomes an optimal solution. The operation we use to rewrite the slack form is called a **pivot**, which takes a free variable and a basic variable and interchanges their roles by rewriting the equality constraints and objective function. Pivoting two variables produces an equivalent slack form, meaning that it has the same feasible region and that the objective function has the same values in the feasible region.

Example 26.2: *In this example, we perform a pivot where the free variable x_1 becomes basic and the basic variable x_5 becomes free. We perform this pivot by rewriting the equality constraint with x_5 on the left-hand side so that it has x_1 on the left-hand side. Then, we substitute this new equality constraint for x_1 in the old objective function and equality constraints to obtain a new objective function and new equality constraints involving only the free variables, x_2 and x_5, on the right-hand sides.*

maximize:	$z = x_1 + 2x_2$	maximize:	$z = 1 + 3x_2 - x_5$
subject to:	$x_3 = 3 + 3x_1 - 2x_2$	subject to:	$x_3 = 6 + x_2 - x_5$
	$x_4 = 2 - x_1 - x_2$		$x_4 = 2 - 2x_2 + x_5$
	$x_5 = 1 - x_1 + x_2$		$x_1 = 1 + x_2 - x_5$
	$x_1, x_2, x_3, x_4, x_5 \ge 0$		$x_1, x_2, x_3, x_4, x_5 \ge 0$.

The basic solution of the new slack form is $(1, 0, 6, 2, 0)$ and the objective value is 1. So, as a result of the pivot, we have increased the objective value from 0 to 1. Geometrically, we have started from the vertex $(0, 0)$, where the inequalities $x_1, x_2 \ge 0$ are tight (that is, they are satisfied by equality with the right-hand side), and we have moved to the vertex $(1, 0)$ where the inequalities $x_2, x_5 \ge 0$ are tight.

The simplex method describes the procedure for performing pivots that increase the objective value to the optimal objective value. Geometrically, pivots move from a vertex of the feasible region to a neighbor that increases the objective function the most. Thus, this approach is an application of the greedy method (Chapter 10).

Lemma 26.3: *The slack form of a LP is uniquely determined by the set of free variables.*

Proof: Suppose the two slack forms below are equivalent slack forms

$$\text{maximize:} \qquad z = c_* + \sum_{j \in F} c_j x_j$$

$$\text{subject to:} \qquad x_i = b_i - \sum_{j \in F} a_{ij} x_j \text{ for } i \in B$$

$$x_i \geq 0 \text{ for } 1 \leq i \leq m + n$$

$$\text{maximize:} \qquad z = c'_* + \sum_{j \in F} c'_j x_j$$

$$\text{subject to:} \qquad x_i = b'_i - \sum_{j \in F} a'_{ij} x_j \text{ for } i \in B$$

$$x_i \geq 0 \text{ for } 1 \leq i \leq m + n$$

We aim to show that they are in fact identical, i.e., $c_* = c'_*$, $c_j = c'_j$ for all $j \in F$, $b_i = b'_i$ for all $i \in B$, and $a_{ij} = a'_{ij}$ for all $i \in B$ and $j \in F$. Consider the equality

$$0 = \left(c_* + \sum_{j \in F} c_j x_j \right) - \left(c'_* + \sum_{j \in F} c'_j x_j \right) = (c_* - c'_*) + \sum_{j \in F} (c_j - c'_j) x_j.$$

This equation must hold for all feasible (nonnegative) values of the x_j. When $x_j = 0$ for all $j \in F$, we get $0 = c_* - c'_*$, so we must have that $c_* = c'_*$. Fix $r \in F$ then let $x_r = 1$ and $x_j = 0$ for $j \in F \setminus \{r\}$. This produces the equality $0 = c_r - c'_r$, which implies $c_r = c'_r$. Since r was arbitrary, we have that $c_j = c'_j$ for all $j \in F$.

The remainder of the equalities are proved similarly, and left to Exercise C-26.14. ∎

Earlier we said we would assume that the basic solution was feasible, but what do we do when this is not the case? If we know a vertex on the feasible region, then we can find which of n inequalities are tight there and pivot the associated variable so that they are free variables. Exercise C-26.5 asks you to show that the basic solution is feasible in this new slack form. This does not however help us to find a vertex on the feasible region, however, which will wait until we develop the details for the simplex method.

26.2.2   An Extended Example

In this section, we follow the approach of the simplex method to optimize the following linear program whose feasibly region is drawn to the right. The strategy will be to perform a sequence of pivot operations, which in the end will yield a slack form that is readily optimized.

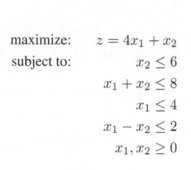

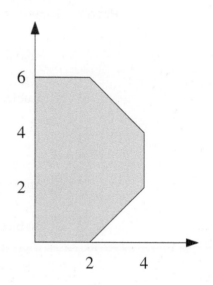

$$
\begin{aligned}
\text{maximize:} \quad & z = 4x_1 + x_2 \\
\text{subject to:} \quad & x_2 \le 6 \\
& x_1 + x_2 \le 8 \\
& x_1 \le 4 \\
& x_1 - x_2 \le 2 \\
& x_1, x_2 \ge 0
\end{aligned}
$$

First, we rewrite the linear program into the initial slack form, introducing the slack variables x_3, x_4, x_5 and x_6.

$$
\begin{aligned}
\text{maximize:} \quad & z = 4x_1 + x_2 \\
\text{subject to:} \quad & x_3 = 6 - x_2 \\
& x_4 = 8 - x_1 - x_2 \\
& x_5 = 4 - x_1 \\
& x_6 = 2 - x_1 + x_2 \\
& x_1, x_2, x_3, x_4, x_5, x_6 \ge 0
\end{aligned}
$$

Free Variables: $F = \{1, 2\}$
Basic Variables: $B = \{3, 4, 5, 6\}$
Basic Solution: $(0, 0, 6, 8, 4, 2)$
Objective Value: $c_* = 0$

Next, we look at the objective function and notice that increasing either x_1 or x_2 will increase the objective value. We choose to raise the value of x_1 as it has the largest coefficient. This greedy strategy does not necessarily improve runtime, by the way, but it is nevertheless often a useful choice in practice. While keeping x_2 fixed at zero, we increase x_1 as far as possible. The nonnegativity constraints of the basic variables impose the constraints $x_1 \le \infty$ from x_3, $x_1 \le 8$ from x_4, $x_1 \le 4$ from x_5 and $x_1 \le 2$ from x_6. The tightest of these constraints is $x_1 \le 2$. So we pivot x_1 and x_6, setting $x_1 = 2$ and $x_6 = 0$ in the basic solution. This produces a new but equivalent slack form.

maximize: $z = 8 + 5x_2 - 4x_6$

subject to: $x_1 = 2 + x_2 - x_6$

$x_3 = 6 - x_2$

$x_4 = 6 - 2x_2 + x_6$

$x_5 = 2 - x_2 + x_6$

$x_1, x_2, x_3, x_4, x_5, x_6 \geq 0$

Free Variables: $F = \{2, 6\}$

Basic Variables: $B = \{1, 3, 4, 5\}$

Basic Solution: $(2, 0, 6, 6, 2, 0)$

Objective Value: $c_* = 8$

Since the coefficient on x_6 is negative, raising it from zero will only decrease the objective function. For this reason, we keep x_6 fixed at zero and raise x_2 until we hit the first constraint. The constraints on x_2 are: $x_2 \leq \infty$, $x_2 \leq 6$, $x_2 \leq 3$, and $x_2 \leq 2$. The tightest of these constraints is $x_2 \leq 2$ coming from the basic variable x_5. So we set $x_2 = 2$ and $x_5 = 0$ by pivoting x_2 and x_5. This yields a new slack form.

maximize: $z = 18 - 5x_5 + x_6$

subject to: $x_1 = 4 - x_5$

$x_2 = 2 - x_5 + x_6$

$x_3 = 4 + +x_5 - x_6$

$x_4 = 2 + 2x_5 - x_6$

$x_1, x_2, x_3, x_4, x_5, x_6 \geq 0$

Free Variables: $F = \{5, 6\}$

Basic Variables: $B = \{1, 2, 3, 4\}$

Basic Solution: $(4, 2, 4, 2, 0, 0)$

Objective Value: $c_* - 18$

In this slack form, the coefficient of x_5 is negative. So we keep x_5 fixed at zero and increase x_6. The tightest constraint is $x_6 \leq 2$ coming from the basic variable x_4. So we pivot x_4 and x_6, yielding the next slack form.

maximize: $z = 20 - 3x_5 - x_4$

subject to: $x_1 = 4 - x_5$

$x_2 = 4 - x_4 + x_5$

$x_3 = 2 + x_4 - x_5$

$x_6 = 2 + 2x_5 - x_4$

$x_1, x_2, x_3, x_4, x_5, x_6 \geq 0$

Free Variables: $F = \{4, 5\}$

Basic Variables: $B = \{1, 2, 3, 6\}$

Basic Solution: $(4, 4, 2, 0, 0, 2)$

Objective Value: $c_* = 20$

Now something interesting has happened! Both of the variables in the objective function have negative coefficients, so increasing either of them would decrease the objective function. So we conclude that we must be at the optimum and stop. From the basic solution we see that $x_1 = 4$, $x_2 = 4$ and $c_* = 20$, which is the solution to our original problem.

26.2.3   The Simplex Algorithm

We formalize the strategy used in the previous example into Algorithm 26.5, which is commonly referred to as the *simplex method*. This version of the algorithm assumes it is given as input a slack form in which the basic solution is feasible. Earlier we showed how to produce such a slack form if we know a vertex of the feasible region, and in Exercise C-26.6 we explore how to find such a vertex.

SimplexMethod(A, b, c, c_*, F, B) :

    while there exists $j \in F$ with $c_j > 0$ **do**
        $r \leftarrow \arg\max_{j \in F} c_j$
        for $i \in B$ **do**
            $k_i \leftarrow ($ **if** $a_{ir} \neq 0$ **then** $-b_i/a_{ir}$ **else** $\infty)$
        $s \leftarrow \arg\min_{i \in B} k_i$
        if $k_s = \infty$ **then**
            return unbounded exception
        else
            Pivot x_r and x_s.
    return (A, b, c, c_*, F, B)

Algorithm 26.5: The simplex method. We assume the input is given in slack form and that the basic solution is feasible.

Analysis of the Simplex Algorithm

To analyze the running time of the simplex method, we notice that each iteration of the loop considers a different slack form of the original problem. If a slack form appears more than once while running the simplex method, then the algorithm will cycle. Since there are only $\binom{n+m}{n}$ different slack forms, one for each choice of F, we know that the algorithm will either halt in $\binom{n+m}{n}$ steps or it will cycle. We can avoid cycling, however, by having an appropriate rule for choosing among optimal pivots that don't actually change the value of the objective function, which is a phenomenon known as *degeneracy*. In practice, however, the simplex algorithm will often halt in polynomial time in any case.

    Since the simplex algorithm only works for inputs whose basic solution is feasible, we need to take into account the amount of time required to put the problem in this form. In Exercise C-26.6, we explore how to find a vertex of the feasible region by optimizing a slack form where the basic solution is feasible, taking $\binom{n+m}{n}$ time. In addition, in Exercise C-26.5, we consider how to transform a slack form into a slack form in which the basic solution is feasible given a vertex on the feasible region in time $O(mn)$. Thus, the simplex method will optimize a linear program in at most $O(\binom{n+m}{n})$ time.

Example 26.4: *Consider the following linear program, written in standard form:*

$$\text{maximize:} \quad z = x_1 + 2x_2$$
$$\text{subject to:} \quad -x_1 + x_2 \leq 3$$
$$x_1 + 3x_2 \leq 13$$
$$x_1 - x_2 \leq 1$$

To solve this linear program using the simplex method, we first we rewrite the linear program in slack form, introducing the slack variables, x_3, x_4 and x_5.

$$\text{maximize:} \quad z = x_1 + 2x_2$$
$$\text{subject to:} \quad x_3 = 3 + x_1 - x_2$$
$$x_4 = 13 - x_1 - 3x_2$$
$$x_5 = 1 - x_1 + x_2$$

We then choose to increase x_2, as it has the largest coefficient in the objective function. The most restrictive constraint is given by x_3. So we pivot x_2 and x_3, yielding the following new slack form with objective value, $c_* = 6$.

$$\text{maximize:} \quad z = 6 + 3x_1 - 2x_3$$
$$\text{subject to:} \quad x_2 = 3 + x_1 - x_3$$
$$x_4 = 4 - 4x_1 + 3x_3$$
$$x_5 = 4 - x_3$$

Next, we increase x_1, as it has the largest coefficient in the objective function. The most restrictive constraint is x_4. So we pivot x_1 and x_4, which yields the following slack form with objective value, $c_* = 9$.

$$\text{maximize:} \quad z = 9 + 0.25x_3 - 0.25x_4$$
$$\text{subject to:} \quad x_1 = 1 + 0.75x_3 - 0.25x_4$$
$$x_2 = 4 - 0.25x_3 - 0.25x_4$$
$$x_5 = 4 - x_3$$

This time, we increase x_3. Its most restrictive constraint comes from x_5. So we pivot x_3 with x_5. We get the new slack form below, with objective value, $c_* = 10$.

$$\text{maximize:} \quad z = 10 - 0.25x_4 - 0.25x_5$$
$$\text{subject to:} \quad x_1 = 4 - 0.25x_4 - 0.75x_5$$
$$x_2 = 3 - 0.25x_4 + 0.25x_5$$
$$x_3 = 4 - x_5$$

Now that all the coefficients of the objective function are negative, we see that the optimal value for this linear program is 10, with $x_1 = 4$ and $x_2 = 3$.

26.3 Duality

To prove that Algorithm 26.5 does indeed provide the correct output, we must discuss a linear program related to the original problem called the **dual**.

Suppose that our input LP has the standard form:

$$\text{maximize:} \quad z = \sum_{j \in V} c_j x_j$$

$$\text{subject to:} \quad \sum_{j \in V} a_{ij} x_j \leq b_i \text{ for } i \in C$$

$$x_j \geq 0 \text{ for } j \in V$$

It can be put into slack form as follows:

$$\text{maximize:} \quad z = \sum_{j \in F} c_j x_j$$

$$\text{subject to:} \quad x_i = b_i - \sum_{j \in F} a_{ij} x_j \text{ for } i \in B$$

$$x_j \geq 0 \text{ for } j \in F \cup B$$

Therefore, $C = B$ and $V = F$. Note that this only holds because we did the obvious transformation between the two forms. There are many more slack forms equivalent to the original standard form, such as the slack forms produced at each iteration of Algorithm 26.5, whose indexing sets B and F do not directly correspond to C and V. Nevertheless, for this section, we assume that whenever we transform the standard form into slack form, we do the obvious transformation. So we can assume that $C = B$ and $V = F$.

Given this initial LP, the **dual LP** is a minimization problem which interchanges the roles of $\vec{b}$ and $\vec{c}$ and the roles of B and F. It also introduces new variables y_i:

$$\text{minimize:} \quad z = \sum_{i \in B} b_i y_i$$

$$\text{subject to:} \quad \sum_{i \in B} a_{ij} y_i \geq c_j \text{ for } j \in F$$

$$y_i \geq 0 \text{ for } i \in B$$

When considering the original problem in relationship to its dual, we refer to the original as the **primal** LP. Note the symmetry between the primal and dual LPs written in matrix form:

	maximize: $z = \vec{c} \cdot \vec{x}$		minimize: $z = \vec{b} \cdot \vec{y}$
primal:	subject to: $A\vec{x} \leq \vec{b}$	dual:	subject to: $A^t \vec{y} \geq \vec{c}$
	$\vec{x} \geq \vec{0}$		$\vec{y} \geq \vec{0}$

When going from the standard to the slack form, we extend the set of original variables x_i (now called free) to a bigger set to include basic variables. Still, for this section, let us use $\vec{x}$ to refer to the original variables only, which are indexed by F.

Example 26.5: *Below is a primal LP written in standard form and its dual.*

maximize: $z = x_1 + 2x_2$

subject to: $-3x_1 + 2x_2 \leq 3$

$x_1 + x_2 \leq 2$

$x_1 - x_2 \leq 1$

$x_1, x_2 \geq 0$

minimize: $z = 3y_1 + 2y_2 + y_3$

subject to: $-3y_1 + y_2 + y_3 \geq 1$

$2y_1 + y_2 - y_3 \geq 2$

$y_1, y_2, y_3 \geq 0$

Note that the dual is no longer in standard form, because of the inequality constraints. It can of course be easily converted (Exercise R-26.7).

As we shall see, the solutions to the primal and dual problems are closely related. Why is that the case? Let's go back to the web server example.

Example 26.6: *Recall the primal LP representing the web server problem.*

maximize: $z = 1000x_1 + 2000x_2$

subject to: $400x_1 + 1600x_2 \leq 36800$

$2x_1 + x_2 \leq 44$

$300x_1 + 500x_2 \leq 12200$

$x_1, x_2 \geq 0$

The dual problem is:

minimize: $z = 36800y_1 + 44y_2 + 12200y_3$

subject to: $400y_1 + 2y_2 + 300y_3 \geq 1000$

$1600y_1 + y_2 + 500y_3 \geq 2000$

$y_1, y_2, y_3 \geq 0$

There is a way to interpret this dual problem. Suppose a computer manufacturer claims that it can cater to the web server company's needs, and that, by doing so, it can offer a set of web servers that will outperform the two types of servers the web server company had planned on using, while staying within its resource limits.

To do so, the computer manufacturer must assess the number of hits/min each resource can potentially produce. To outperform the first type of server, it must build a web server that can handle at least 1000 hits/min if it costs $400, occupies two shelves and uses 300W of power. This constraint corresponds to the first inequality of the dual LP. A similar explanation handles the case of the second type of servers.

The variables in this inequality represent the number of hits/min each unit of resource will contribute. For example, we can think of y_2 as the value of a single shelf measured in hits/mins, because a resource that contributes more hits/min is *likely to increase the price of the computer (this is obviously up for debate, but let us assume this is true to simplify things). Now the computer manufacturer is offering its services for profit. So it will try to minimize its own production costs given the amount of resources available. This production cost is the quantity described by the objective function of the dual LP.*

The minimum number of hits/min that the computer manufacturer can get away with offering is equal to the maximum number of hits/min its client can achieve by only using the two types of servers it had at its disposal.

Lemma 26.7: *Let $\vec{x}'$ be a feasible solution to the primal LP $(A, \vec{b}, \vec{c}, c_*, F, B)$ and let $\vec{y}'$ be a feasible solution to the dual LP. If $\vec{c} \cdot \vec{x}' = \vec{b} \cdot \vec{y}'$, then $\vec{x}'$ and $\vec{y}'$ are optimal for their respective problems.*

Proof: Any two solutions $\vec{x}$ and $\vec{y}$ that are feasible in the primal and dual problems respectively give us that

$$c_j \leq \sum_{i \in B} a_{ij} y_i \quad \text{and} \quad \sum_{j \in F} a_{ij} x_j \leq b_i.$$

Using these inequalities one at a time, we see that

$$\sum_{j \in F} c_j x_j \leq \sum_{j \in F} \sum_{i \in B} a_{ij} y_i x_j \leq \sum_{i \in B} b_i y_i.$$

So just by being feasible, we have $\vec{c} \cdot \vec{x} \leq \vec{b} \cdot \vec{y}$. In particular, $\vec{c} \cdot \vec{x} \leq \vec{b} \cdot \vec{y}'$, which means that the primal objective function cannot be larger than $\vec{b} \cdot \vec{y}'$ if we stay in the feasible region. Since this objective function achieves the value $\vec{b} \cdot \vec{y}'$ at $\vec{x}'$, this means $\vec{x}'$ is optimal for the primal problem. A similar argument shows that $\vec{y}'$ is optimal for the dual problem. ∎

We now proceed to demonstrate the correctness of Algorithm 26.5.

Theorem 26.8: *Suppose that on input LP $(A, \vec{b}, \vec{c}, 0, F, B)$, Algorithm 26.5 returns the LP $(A', \vec{x}', \vec{c}', c_*, F', B')$, then $\vec{x}'$ is optimal for the input LP.*

Proof: We show that the vector

$$\vec{y} = (y_i, i \in B) \quad \text{defined by} \quad y_i = \begin{cases} -c_i' & i \in F' \cap B \\ 0 & i \in B' \cap B \end{cases}$$

is feasible for the dual LP and $\vec{c} \cdot \vec{x}' = \vec{b} \cdot \vec{y}$ and apply the previous lemma.

The input and output LPs are equivalent, so they have the same objective function:

$$\sum_{j \in F} c_j x_j = c_* + \sum_{i \in F'} c_i' x_i \tag{26.1}$$

$$= c_* + \sum_{i \in F' \cap F} c_i' x_i + \sum_{i \in F' \cap B} c_i' x_i. \tag{26.2}$$

The split sum comes from the fact that $F' \subseteq F \cup B$. Now the last sum can be rewritten as

$$\sum_{i \in F' \cap B} -y_i \left(b_i - \sum_{j \in F} a_{ij} x_j \right),$$

by using the definitions of y_i and rewriting the slack variables, x_i, such that $i \in F' \cap B \subseteq B$, in terms of the free variables, x_k, where $k \in F$. So we get

$$\sum_{j \in F} c_j x_j = \left(c_* - \sum_{i \in B} y_i b_i \right) + \sum_{j \in F} \left(c'_j + \sum_{i \in B} a_{ij} y_i \right) x_j,$$

where we have substituted the previous expression into the one before, rearranged the order of the terms, and summed over B and F instead of $F' \cap B$ and $F' \cap F$, because $c'_j = 0$ for all $j \notin F'$. Setting the coefficients on the left-hand side and right-hand side equal for each variable x_j as well as for the constant term (see Exercise C-26.15), we have that

$$c_j = c'_j + \sum_{i \in B} a_{ij} y_i, \quad j \in F \qquad (26.3)$$

$$c_* = \sum_{i \in B} y_i b_i. \qquad (26.4)$$

Note that because $c'_j \leq 0$ for any j (this is the terminating condition of Algorithm 26.5), Equation 26.3 becomes

$$c_j \leq \sum_{i \in B} a_{ij} y_i.$$

So $\vec{y}$ is feasible for the dual problem. Also note that if we plug $\vec{x}'$ into Equation 26.1,

$$\sum_{j \in F} c_j x'_j = c_* + \sum_{i \in F'} c'_i x'_i.$$

But since $x'_i = 0$ for $i \in F'$, we have that $\vec{c} \cdot \vec{x}' = c_*$. Combined with Equation 26.4, this shows that $\vec{c} \cdot \vec{x}' = \vec{b} \cdot \vec{y}$.

Thus, we have shown that (1) $\vec{y}$ is feasible and that (2) $\vec{c} \cdot \vec{x}' = \vec{b} \cdot \vec{y}$. These are the conditions needed for Lemma 26.7, which says that $\vec{x}'$ is optimal. ∎

26.4   Applications of Linear Programming

Because linear programming has such a general formulation, it can be used to solve other algorithmic problems. In particular, if a problem can be expressed as a linear program, then we can design an algorithm to solve this problem by giving this linear program as the input to a linear program solver, such as the simplex method. In this section, we look at three familiar problems that can be reduced to linear programs.

Shortest Paths

In the shortest-path problem, for a specific source, s, and target, t, we are given a graph whose vertices represent locations, such that each edge, (u, v), has a weight, $d(u, v)$, that represents the distance between two locations, u and v. The goal is to find the shortest path between the source, s, and target, t.

We can formulate a linear program for this problem based on the setup and termination conditions for the Bellman-Ford algorithm (Section 14.3). We define for every vertex, v, a variable, d_v, which should represent the shortest distance between s and v. The initialization, $d_s = 0$, now becomes one of our constraints. To pinpoint the correct value for d_t, we use the termination condition of the Bellman-Ford algorithm—namely, that the triangle inequality holds for every edge. Recall that this is the condition that states that the shortest path from s to v should be no longer than the shortest path from s to any neighbor u of v followed by the path from u to v. We want d_t to be the largest value that satisfies these conditions, the same way the algorithm initializes $d_t = \infty$ and progressively decreases its value until all variables meet the termination condition. Thus, the corresponding linear program is the following:

$$
\begin{aligned}
\text{maximize:} \quad & d_t \\
\text{subject to:} \quad & d_s = 0 \\
& d_v \le d_u + d(u, v), \quad \text{for every edge, } (u, v)
\end{aligned}
$$

This is, of course, the variant of the shortest-paths problem that has a single source and single target. In the exercises, we explore modifications to this LP to accommodate generalizations of the shortest-path problem.

Network Flow

Recall from Chapter 16 that a flow network is a connected directed graph with a source and a sink, and in which each edge, e, has nonnegative weights called its capacity, $c(e)$.

A flow, f, is a new set of nonnegative edge weights that satisfies the following rules:

- ***The Capacity Rule:*** The flow through an edge must be less than the capacity of that edge
- ***The Conservation Rule:*** With the exception of the source and the sink, the flow into a vertex must equal the flow out of it.

The maximum flow problem is to find the maximum flow size, that is, the maximum amount of flow out of the source that satisfies the above two rules. This can be expressed with a linear program in which the variables are the edge weights, $f(e)$, the objective function is the flow size, and the constraints are given by the two rules making up the definition of a valid flow:

$$\text{maximize:} \quad \sum_{e \in E^+(s)} f(e) \qquad \text{where } s \text{ is the source}$$

$$\text{subject to:} \quad 0 \le f(e) \le c(e) \qquad \text{for all edges } e$$

$$\sum_{e \in E^-(v)} f(e) = \sum_{e \in E^+(v)} f(e) \qquad \text{for all vertices } v \text{ except for the source and the sink}$$

Here, $E^+(v)$ and $E^-(v)$ represent the set of incoming and outgoing edges of a vertex v respectively. Note that if the capacities of a flow network are integers, the simplex algorithm will produce a solution with integer edge weights.

Maximum Matching

Suppose five children have gone to a dog shelter to find a new pet. As it happens, there are exactly five dogs up for adoption. Each child has a preference for certain breeds, whereas each dog has a preference for children of a certain temperament. Figure 26.6 shows a graph in which a child and a dog who like each other are connected by an edge.

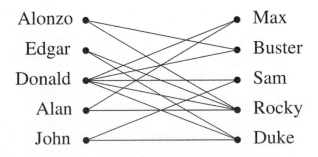

Figure 26.6: An edge connects a child and a dog who like each other.

Is there a pairing scheme in which all children and dogs will be happily matched? In other words, is there a maximum matching for the graph in Figure 26.6 equal to the number of children? In general, we can answer maximum matching questions by setting up a flow network, as done in Section 16.3, and then solving this problem using the LP given above. We create two additional vertices, a source s and a sink t. Then, we add a directed edge from the source to every child, and also an edge from every dog to the sink. Finally, we connect every child to a dog if they both like each other. We get the directed graph shown in Figure 26.7.

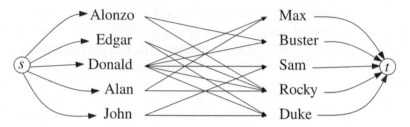

Figure 26.7: This flow network solves the bipartite matching problem.

Next, we assign a flow of 1 to each edge. Then there is a perfect matching in the original graph if and only if the maximum flow is equal to 5. Moreover, if we solve the flow network problem by converting it into an LP as we did earlier, all flows will be integers. This means that each edge can only have a flow of 0 or 1, so that we can interpret 0 as "do not pair them up" and 1 as "pair them up." Thus, we can solving the maximum matching problem using a linear program solver.

26.5 Exercises

Reinforcement

R-26.1 Recall at the beginning of the chapter we gave a linear program to help a web server company decide what server models it should purchase. Suppose that the standard server model has been replaced by a new "green" server model, which only requires $200W$ of power, costs 600, takes up one shelf in the server rack, and can handle 800 hits/min. Give a new linear program that takes into account the availability of this new model.

R-26.2 Draw the two-dimensional feasible region of the LP from Exercise R-26.1.

R-26.3 Suppose that instead of maximizing hits per minute, constraints, a web server company wants to minimize cost while maintaining a rack of standard and cutting-edge servers that can handle at least 15,000 hits per minute. Also, for the sake of redundancy, the company wants to maintain at least 10 servers in their rack. Based on these constraints, give a linear program to find the optimal server configuration. Draw the feasible region, and solve the LP geometrically.

R-26.4 In the following linear program, the objective function has a parameter, α. What values of α result in a program with no unique solution?

$$
\begin{aligned}
\text{maximize:} \quad & z = \alpha x_1 + x_2 \\
\text{subject to:} \quad & 3x_1 + 5x_2 \leq 77 \\
& 7x_1 + 2x_2 \leq 56 \\
& x_1, x_2 \geq 0.
\end{aligned}
$$

R-26.5 Solve the linear program of Exercise R-26.4, for $\alpha = 1$, using the simplex method. Show the result of each pivot.

R-26.6 For each of the regions shown in Figure 26.8, give an LP for which that region is the feasible region, or explain why no such linear program exists.

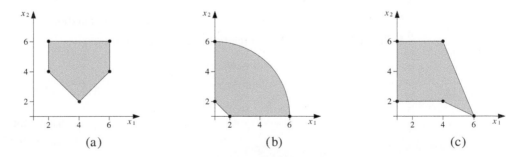

(a)   (b)   (c)

Figure 26.8: Different plausible feasible regions.

R-26.7 Convert the following linear program into standard form:

$$\text{minimize:} \quad z = 3y_1 + 2y_2 + y_3$$
$$\text{subject to:} \quad -3y_1 + y_2 + y_3 \geq 1$$
$$2y_1 + y_2 - y_3 \geq 2$$
$$y_1, y_2, y_3 \geq 0$$

R-26.8 Recall the LP for the dual of the web server problem from Example 26.6:

$$\text{minimize:} \quad z = 36800y_1 + 44y_2 + 12200y_3$$
$$\text{subject to:} \quad 400y_1 + 2y_2 + 300y_3 \geq 1000$$
$$1600y_1 + y_2 + 500y_3 \geq 2000$$
$$y_1, y_2, y_3 \geq 0$$

Convert this linear program first into standard, and then slack form.

R-26.9 Give a set of linear programming constraints that result in the feasible region shown in Figure 26.9.

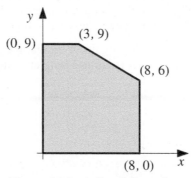

Figure 26.9: A feasible region.

R-26.10 For each vertex, $(3, 9)$ and $(8, 6)$, of the feasible region shown in Figure 26.9, give an objective function that has that vertex as the optimal solution.

R-26.11 Give an objective function for the feasible region shown in Figure 26.9, such that there are an infinite number of optimal solutions, none of which have $x = 0$ or $y = 0$. What is the value of the objective function for these solutions?

R-26.12 Formulate the dual of the linear program for the maximum flow problem.

R-26.13 What is the dual of the following linear program?

$$\text{maximize:} \quad z = x_1 + 2x_2$$
$$\text{subject to:} \quad x_1 + x_2 \leq 5$$
$$6x_1 - 3x_2 \leq 3$$
$$5x_1 \leq 24$$
$$6x_2 \leq 9$$
$$x_1, x_2 \geq 0$$

Creativity

C-26.1 Prove that there exists a linear program in two variables with exactly one feasible solution.

C-26.2 Prove that if there exists more than one optimal solution to a linear program, then there must be infinitely many optimal solutions.

C-26.3 Prove that the set of feasible solutions to a linear program with a nonempty feasible region is convex.

C-26.4 Give a linear program in three variables for which the feasible region is a tetrahedron.

C-26.5 When the simplex method was introduced, we assumed that the basic solution of the slack form was a feasible solution. Describe an algorithm that given an arbitrary slack form and a vertex on the feasible region, makes transformations to the slack form to guarantee that the basic solution is feasible.

C-26.6 Given a linear program in slack form such that the basic solution is feasible, give an algorithm to find a vertex of the feasible region by optimizing the slack form.

C-26.7 If P is a linear program, let P^* denote the dual of P, and let P^{k*} denote k application of the dual function. For example $P^{2*} = (P^*)^*$ is the dual of the dual of P. Show that for any positive integer n, $P^{2n*} = P$.

C-26.8 Show that if we allow linear programs to have strict inequalities, then there exists a linear program which is neither infeasible nor unbounded, but nevertheless does not have an optimal solution with finite objective value.

C-26.9 Prove that if there exists a point that is feasible in both a linear program and its dual, then that point is the optimal solution in both linear programs.

C-26.10 The maximum independent set (MIS) of a graph $G = (V, E)$ is the largest set of vertices $S \subseteq V$ such that for any two vertices $u, v \in S$, $(u, v) \notin E$; that is, no pair of vertices in S are neighbors. We want to create a linear program to solve the MIS problem. We create an indicator variable i_v for each vertex $v \in V$, and the sum of the i_v should denote the size of the MIS. Consider the following linear program formulation of the MIS problem:

$$\text{maximize:} \quad \sum i_v$$
$$\text{subject to:} \quad i_v \geq 0$$
$$i_v \leq 1$$
$$i_v + i_{v'} \leq 1 \text{ for } (v, v') \in E$$

What's wrong with this formulation? Give a small example graph for which the linear program does not give a reasonable answer for the size of the maximum independent set. Why doesn't the program give a reasonable answer in this case?

C-26.11 In Section 26.4, we gave a linear program to solve the shortest-path problem. What can be said about this linear program if the input graph has a negative cycle?

C-26.12 Give a linear programming formulation for the all-pairs shortest-path problem.

C-26.13 Give a linear programming formulation to find the minimum spanning tree of a graph. Recall that a spanning tree T of a graph G is a connected acyclic subgraph of G that contains every vertex of G. The minimum spanning tree of a weighted graph G is a spanning tree T of G such that the sum of the edge weights in T is minimized.

C-26.14 Finish the proof of Lemma 26.3.

C-26.15 Finish the proof of Theorem 26.8 by showing that if

$$a_0 + a_1 x_1 + a_2 x_2 + \ldots a_n x_n = b_0 + b_1 x_1 + b_2 x_2 + \ldots b_n x_n,$$

where each x_i is a real variable, then $a_i = b_i$ for $i = 0, 1, \ldots n$.

Applications

A-26.1 In geometric data compression, we are given a collection of geometric objects, such as points in the plane, and we wish to minimize the number of bits required to represent the points. Therefore, suppose that rather than express the full (x, y) coordinates of such a set of points, we encode the y-coordinates of the points using the following rudimentary data compression scheme. First, we find a line $y = ax + b$ that approximately passes through the points. Then, instead of storing the full y-coordinate of each point, we store the function $f(x) = ax + b$ and we encode y-coordinate of each point (x_i, y_i) as $\epsilon_i = f(x_i) - y_i$. Suppose you are given the following set of points:

$$\{(0, 3), (-1.8, -6.1), (-4.2, -11), (1.5, 4.8), (6.3, 19), (2.6, 9.1)\}.$$

Give a linear program that, if solved, will find the function $f(x)$ minimizing the size of the encoded points using the above compression scheme.

A-26.2 Suppose that you are preparing for the upcoming Zombie Apocalypse. The Centers for Disease Control and Prevention recommend that any Zombie Apocalypse Survival Kit should contain at least the following supplies:

- Water (1 gallon per person per day)
- Food (stock up on nonperishable items that you eat regularly)
- Medications (this includes prescription and nonprescription meds)
- Tools and Supplies (utility knife, duct tape, battery-powered radio, etc.)
- Sanitation and Hygiene (household bleach, soap, towels, etc.)
- Clothing and Bedding (a change of clothes for each family member and blankets)
- Important documents (copies of your driver's license, passport, and birth certificate, to name a few)

- First Aid supplies (although you're a goner if a zombie bites you, you can use these supplies to treat basic cuts and lacerations)

Although not officially recommended by the CDC, your kit should also include at least one self-defense item to protect yourself, your family, and your supplies from zombies and looters. In case of evacuation, each person must be able to carry their survival kit with them. Therefore, your survival kit must not weigh more than 100 lbs. In addition, you must not spend more than $500 on your kit. Your goal is to assemble a kit that maximizes your life expectancy, subject to these weight and cost constraints. Choose reasonable values for the weight and cost of each category of item, and model how each category of item might affect your life expectancy. For example, each gallon of water might increase your life expectancy by 1 day. Then solve the corresponding linear program to determine which supplies you should include in your survival kit.

A-26.3 A political candidate has hired you to advise them on how to best spend their advertising budget. The candidate wants a combination of print, radio, and television ads that maximize total impact, subject to budgetary constraints, and available airtime and print space.

type	impact per ad	cost per ad	max ads per week
radio	a	10,000	25
print	b	70,000	7
tv	c	110,000	15

Design and solve a linear program to determine the best combination of ads for the campaign.

A-26.4 A perfect pizza maximizes how great it tastes and meets your recommended daily allowance (RDA) for the three macronutrients carbohydrates, fats, and protein. Suppose that your diet should consist of 25–35% fats, 45–65% carbohydrates, and 10–35% proteins. Suppose further that your total calorie intake should be is 1800–2500 calories. Given the following pizza ingredients, assign each pizza ingredient a "taste factor" per serving that represents your personal preferences. If your favorite ingredient is not included, look up its nutritional information and add it to the list of toppings. Design a linear program choose how much of each pizza topping you should include to make a pizza that meets the above constraints and maximizes how great it tastes. Explain how you chose your objective function and constraints.

Item		Calories	Fat	Carbs	Protein	Taste
Thin Crust	(per slice)	80	0.5g	15g	0g	*
Deep Dish		160	7.5	30g	0g	*
Pizza Sauce	(1 tbsp)	8	250mg	1g	250mg	*
Mozzarella	(10 g)	27	2g	298mg	3g	*
Pepperoni		46	4g	353mg	2g	*
Sausage		17	1g	707mg	1g	*
Green Pepper		2	17mg	464mg	86mg	*
Onion		4	10mg	934mg	110mg	*
Mushroom		2	34mg	328mg	309mg	*
Olive		11	1g	524mg	95mg	*
Pineapple		5	12mg	1g	54mg	*

A-26.5 A small retail chain has three warehouses and four retail stores. Each warehouse stores a certain amount of goods, and each retail store has a demand for a certain amount of goods. In addition, for each warehouse store pair, there is a set shipping cost per unit of goods. (See Figure 26.10.) Design and solve a linear program to determine the minimum-cost shipping schedule that meets the demands of each retail store.

warehouse supply	
W_1	100
W_2	75
W_3	120

retail demand	
A	40
B	30
C	50
D	45

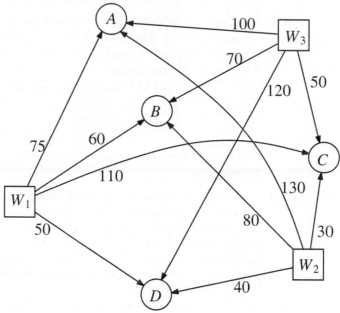

Figure 26.10: Shipping costs for warehouses and retail stores.

A-26.6 Suppose there are four power plants, which use coal, nuclear, wind, and oil, and four cities, Flat Top Mountain, Zephyrville, Cherenkov, and Iridescent Islands. The power plants and cities are connected by a directed power grid, and each link in the grid has a maximum capacity, as shown in Figure 26.11. Each city demands power with certain constraints. Flat Top Mountain demands 8 units of power, and insists that at least 5 units of this power be from the coal power plant. Zephyrville demands at least 5 units of power and insists that 4 units be generated from wind. Cherenkov demands 8 units of power and insists that 50% of its power be from nuclear power. Iridescent Islands demands at least 6 units of power but wants no more than 2 units of power from oil. Write a linear program to find the maximum flow of power that meets the demands of each city subject to the maximum capacities on the internal links in the power grid.

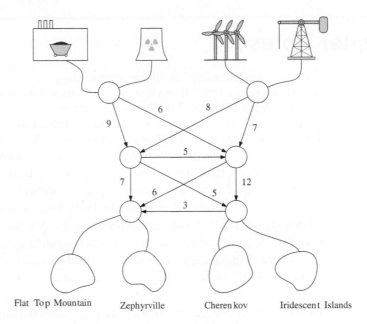

Flat Top Mountain   Zephyrville   Cherenkov   Iridescent Islands

Figure 26.11: A coal, nuclear, and wind power plant power for four cities. Power must be routed through switches in the electrical grid.

A-26.7 Suppose you are part of a trade expedition and there are 15 people in your party (including yourself). Your final destination lies across the desert, and so you must hire out camels to carry all of your party's gear for that portion of your journey. The desert can be crossed in 10 days, but it could take up to 50% longer if something goes wrong or you encounter bad weather. You need to bring the following supplies necessary for survival in the harsh desert conditions:

- Some number of 18L jugs of water. You must bring at least 2L of water per person per day spent in the desert. Bring enough water to cross the desert even if something goes wrong.

- Enough tents such that at most two people will sleep in each tent. Each tent weighs 8kg each.

- A 1kg pack of first aid supplies per ten people-days spent in the desert (for example, 5 people for 4 days would require 2 first aid packs).

- Some cases of food rations. Each case weighs 10kg and contains 12 rations. Bring at least one ration per person per day spent in the desert.

- One pack per person of personal supplies (clothing, blankets, etc.) that weigh 20kg each.

In addition, you have the following trade goods: 5 chests of spices weighing 75kg each, 5 chests of tea weighing 50 kg each, and 5 chests of silk weighing 25kg each. Each camel can carry a 300kg load after accounting for the food, water, and gear required to support the camel over the long desert journey. Design a linear program to determine the minimum number of camels required to make the journey.

Chapter Notes

The word "programming" in "linear programming" does not have the same meaning as it has in computer science. It was first used in a mathematical sense by American mathematician, George B. Dantzig [54]. Linear programming was in use prior to this by the Soviet military, thanks to Leonid Kantorovich, who invented the concept in 1939. Today, linear programming is a standard tool of operations research, and it is used to model scheduling and assignment problems, as well as routing and planning problems.

The complexity of the simplex method puzzled mathematicians for many decades. While this algorithm seemed efficient in practice, carefully constructed problem instances can produce an exponential runtime. In 1980, Leonid Khachiyan published a new LP-solving algorithm [125] with a polynomial runtime that ran slow in practice. The ellipsoid algorithm, as it was called, was nevertheless revolutionary in concept. Unlike the simplex method, the ellipsoid algorithm walks through the interior of the feasible region. Narendra Karmarkar [121] eventually improved on this idea with what is now known as the interior point method, an algorithm that is fast in practice as well as having a polynomial runtime. The discrepancy between the theoretical and practical running times of the simplex method is explained by Spielman and Teng [199], who provide a new approach to analyze an algorithm's complexity in a way that is a cross between worst-case and average case analysis.

Appendix

 A

Useful Mathematical Facts

In this appendix, we give several useful mathematical facts. We begin with some combinatorial definitions and facts.

Logarithms and Exponents

The logarithm function is defined as

$$\log_b a = c \qquad \text{if} \qquad a = b^c.$$

The following identities hold for logarithms and exponents, with $a, c > 0$:

1. $\log_b ac = \log_b a + \log_b c$
2. $\log_b a/c - \log_b a - \log_b c$
3. $\log_b a^c = c \log_b a$
4. $\log_b a = (\log_c a)/\log_c b$
5. $b^{\log_c a} = a^{\log_c b}$
6. $(b^a)^c = b^{ac}$
7. $b^a b^c = b^{a+c}$
8. $b^a/b^c = b^{a-c}$.

In addition, we have the following:

Theorem A.1: *If $a > 0$, $b > 0$, and $c > a + b$, then*

$$\log a + \log b \leq 2 \log c - 2.$$

The ***natural logarithm*** function $\ln x = \log_e x$, where $e = 2.71828\ldots$, is the value of the following progression:

$$e = 1 + \frac{1}{1!} + \frac{1}{2!} + \frac{1}{3!} + \cdots .$$

In addition,

$$e^x = 1 + \frac{x}{1!} + \frac{x^2}{2!} + \frac{x^3}{3!} + \cdots$$

$$\ln(1 + x) = x - \frac{x^2}{2!} + \frac{x^3}{3!} - \frac{x^4}{4!} + \cdots .$$

There are a number of useful inequalities relating to these functions (which derive from these definitions).

Theorem A.2: *If $x > -1$,*

$$\frac{x}{1+x} \leq \ln(1+x) \leq x.$$

Theorem A.3: *For $0 \leq x < 1$,*

$$1 + x \leq e^x \leq \frac{1}{1-x}.$$

Theorem A.4: *For any two positive real numbers x and n,*

$$\left(1 + \frac{x}{n}\right)^n \leq e^x \leq \left(1 + \frac{x}{n}\right)^{n+x/2}.$$

Integer Functions and Relations

The "floor" and "ceiling" functions are defined respectively as follows:

1. $\lfloor x \rfloor$ = the largest integer less than or equal to x.
2. $\lceil x \rceil$ = the smallest integer greater than or equal to x.

The ***modulo*** operator is defined for integers $a \geq 0$ and $b > 0$ as

$$a \bmod b = a - \left\lfloor \frac{a}{b} \right\rfloor b.$$

The ***factorial*** function is defined as

$$n! = 1 \cdot 2 \cdot 3 \cdot \cdots \cdot (n-1)n.$$

The binomial coefficient is

$$\binom{n}{k} = \frac{n!}{k!(n-k)!},$$

which is equal to the number of different ***combinations*** we can define by choosing k different items from a collection of n items (where the order does not matter). The name "binomial coefficient" derives from the ***binomial expansion***:

$$(a+b)^n = \sum_{k=0}^{n} \binom{n}{k} a^k b^{n-k}.$$

We also have the following relationships.

Theorem A.5: *If $0 \leq k \leq n$, then*

$$\left(\frac{n}{k}\right)^k \leq \binom{n}{k} \leq \frac{n^k}{k!}.$$

Theorem A.6 (Stirling's Approximation):

$$n! = \sqrt{2\pi n} \left(\frac{n}{e}\right)^n \left(1 + \frac{1}{12n} + \epsilon(n)\right),$$

where $\epsilon(n)$ is $O(1/n^2)$.

The *Fibonacci progression* is a numeric progression such that $F_0 = 0$, $F_1 = 1$, and $F_n = F_{n-1} + F_{n-2}$ for $n \geq 2$.

Theorem A.7: *If F_n is defined by the Fibonacci progression, then F_n is $\Theta(g^n)$, where $g = (1 + \sqrt{5})/2$ is the so-called* **golden ratio***.*

Summations

There are a number of useful facts about summations.

Theorem A.8: *Factoring summations:*

$$\sum_{i=1}^{n} af(i) = a \sum_{i=1}^{n} f(i),$$

provided a does not depend upon i.

Theorem A.9: *Reversing the order:*

$$\sum_{i=1}^{n} \sum_{j=1}^{m} f(i,j) = \sum_{j=1}^{m} \sum_{i=1}^{n} f(i,j).$$

One special form of summation is a *telescoping sum*:

$$\sum_{i=1}^{n} (f(i) - f(i-1)) = f(n) - f(0),$$

which often arises in the amortized analysis of a data structure or algorithm.

The following are some other facts about summations that often arise in the analysis of data structures and algorithms.

Theorem A.10:

$$\sum_{i=1}^{n} i = \frac{n(n+1)}{2}.$$

Theorem A.11:

$$\sum_{i=1}^{n} i^2 = \frac{n(n+1)(2n+1)}{6}.$$

Theorem A.12: *If $k \geq 1$ is an integer constant, then*

$$\sum_{i=1}^{n} i^k \text{ is } \Theta(n^{k+1}).$$

Another common summation is the *geometric sum*

$$\sum_{i=0}^{n} a^i,$$

for any fixed real number $0 < a \neq 1$.

Theorem A.13:

$$\sum_{i=0}^{n} a^i = \frac{1 - a^{n+1}}{1 - a}$$

for any real number $0 < a \neq 1$.

Theorem A.14:

$$\sum_{i=0}^{\infty} a^i = \frac{1}{1 - a}$$

for any real number $0 < a < 1$.

There is also a combination of the two common forms, called the ***linear exponential*** summation, which has the following expansion:

Theorem A.15: *For* $0 < a \neq 1$, *and* $n \geq 2$,

$$\sum_{i=1}^{n} i a^i = \frac{a - (n+1)a^{(n+1)} + na^{(n+2)}}{(1 - a)^2}.$$

The nth ***harmonic number*** H_n is defined as

$$H_n = \sum_{i=1}^{n} \frac{1}{i}.$$

Theorem A.16: *If* H_n *is the* nth *harmonic number, for* $n > 1$, *then* $\ln n < H_n < \ln n + 1$.

Proof: See Exercise C-3.11.   ■

Useful Mathematical Techniques

To determine whether a function is little-oh or little-omega of another, it is sometimes helpful to apply the following rule.

Theorem A.17 (L'Hôpital's Rule): *If we have* $\lim_{n \to \infty} f(n) = +\infty$ *and we have* $\lim_{n \to \infty} g(n) = +\infty$, *then* $\lim_{n \to \infty} f(n)/g(n) = \lim_{n \to \infty} f'(n)/g'(n)$, *where* $f'(n)$ *and* $g'(n)$ *denote the derivatives of* $f(n)$ *and* $g(n)$, *respectively.*

In deriving an upper or lower bound for a summation, it is often useful to ***split a summation*** as follows:

$$\sum_{i=1}^{n} f(i) = \sum_{i=1}^{j} f(i) + \sum_{i=j+1}^{n} f(i).$$

Another useful technique is to ***bound a sum by an integral***. If f is a nondecreasing function, then, assuming the following terms are defined,

$$\int_{a-1}^{b} f(x)\,dx \leq \sum_{i=a}^{b} f(i) \leq \int_{a}^{b+1} f(x)\,dx.$$

Bibliography

[1] J. D. Achter and R. Tamassia, "Selected topics in algorithms." Manuscript, 1993.

[2] G. M. Adel'son-Vel'skii and Y. M. Landis, "An algorithm for the organization of information," *Doklady Akademii Nauk SSSR*, vol. 146, pp. 263–266, 1962. English translation in *Soviet Math. Dokl.*, **3**, 1259–1262.

[3] P. K. Agarwal, "Geometric partitioning and its applications," in *Computational Geometry: Papers from the DIMACS Special Year* (J. E. Goodman, R. Pollack, and W. Steiger, eds.), American Mathematical Society, 1991.

[4] P. K. Agarwal, "Range searching," in *Handbook of Discrete and Computational Geometry* (J. E. Goodman and J. O'Rourke, eds.), ch. 31, pp. 575–598, Boca Raton, FL: CRC Press LLC, 1997.

[5] P. K. Agarwal, L. Arge, and K. Yi, "I/O-efficient batched union-find and its applications to terrain analysis," *ACM Trans. Algorithms*, vol. 7, no. 1, pp. 11:1–11:21, 2010.

[6] A. Aggarwal and J. S. Vitter, "The input/output complexity of sorting and related problems," *Comm. ACM*, vol. 31, pp. 1116–1127, 1988.

[7] A. V. Aho, "Algorithms for finding patterns in strings," in *Handbook of Theoretical Computer Science* (J. van Leeuwen, ed.), vol. A. Algorithms and Complexity, pp. 255–300, Amsterdam: Elsevier, 1990.

[8] A. V. Aho, J. E. Hopcroft, and J. D. Ullman, *The Design and Analysis of Computer Algorithms*. Reading, MA: Addison-Wesley, 1974.

[9] A. V. Aho, J. E. Hopcroft, and J. D. Ullman, *Data Structures and Algorithms*. Reading, MA: Addison-Wesley, 1983.

[10] R. K. Ahuja, T. L. Magnanti, and J. B. Orlin, *Network Flows: Theory, Algorithms, and Applications*. Englewood Cliffs, NJ: Prentice Hall, 1993.

[11] S. Alstrup, I. Li Gortz, T. Rauhe, M. Thorup, and U. Zwick, "Union-find with constant time deletions," in *Automata, Languages and Programming* (L. Caires, G. Italiano, L. Monteiro, C. Palamidessi, and M. Yung, eds.), vol. 3580 of *Lecture Notes in Computer Science*, pp. 105–105, Springer, 2005.

[12] L. Arge and J. S. Vitter, "Optimal external memory interval management," *SIAM Journal on Computing*, vol. 32, no. 6, pp. 1488–1508, 2003.

[13] B. Arkin, F. Hill, S. Marks, M. Schmid, T. J. Walls, and G. McGraw, "How we learned to cheat at online poker: A study in software security," *Developer.com: Tech Focus*, September 1999.

[14] K. Arnold and J. Gosling, *The Java Programming Language*. The Java Series, Reading, MA: Addison-Wesley, 1996.

[15] S. Arya and D. M. Mount, "Approximate range searching," *Comput. Geom. Theory Appl.*, vol. 17, pp. 135–152, 2000.

[16] S. Arya, D. M. Mount, N. S. Netanyahu, R. Silverman, and A. Wu, "An optimal algorithm for approximate nearest neighbor searching in fixed dimensions," *J. ACM*, vol. 45, pp. 891–923, 1998.

[17] F. Aurenhammer, "Voronoi diagrams: A survey of a fundamental geometric data structure," *ACM Comput. Surv.*, vol. 23, pp. 345–405, Sept. 1991.

[18] S. Baase, *Computer Algorithms: Introduction to Design and Analysis*. Reading, MA: Addison-Wesley, 2nd ed., 1988.

[19] E. Bach and J. Shallit, *Algorithmic Number Theory, Volume I: Efficient Algorithms*. MIT Press, 1996.

[20] R. Baeza-Yates and B. Ribeiro-Neto, *Modern Information Retrieval*. Reading, MA: Addison-Wesley, 1999.

[21] O. Baruvka, "O jistem problemu minimalnim," *Praca Moravske Prirodovedecke Spolecnosti*, vol. 3, pp. 37–58, 1926. (In Czech).

[22] R. Bayer, "Symmetric binary B-trees: Data structure and maintenance," *Acta Informatica*, vol. 1, no. 4, pp. 290–306, 1972.

[23] R. Bayer and McCreight, "Organization of large ordered indexes," *Acta Inform.*, vol. 1, pp. 173–189, 1972.

[24] R. Bellman, "On a routing problem," *Quarterly of Applied Mathematics*, vol. 16, no. 1, pp. 87–90, 1958.

[25] R. E. Bellman, *Dynamic Programming*. Princeton, NJ: Princeton University Press, 1957.

[26] J. Bentley, "Programming pearls: Algorithm design techniques," *Commun. ACM*, vol. 27, pp. 865–873, September 1984.

[27] J. L. Bentley, "Multidimensional divide-and-conquer," *Comm. ACM*, vol. 23, no. 4, pp. 214–229, 1980.

[28] J. L. Bentley, "Programming pearls: Writing correct programs," *Comm. ACM*, vol. 26, pp. 1040–1045, 1983.

[29] J. L. Bentley, "Programming pearls: Thanks, heaps," *Comm. ACM*, vol. 28, pp. 245–250, 1985.

[30] J. L. Bentley, D. Haken, and J. B. Saxe, "A general method for solving divide-and-conquer recurrences," *SIGACT News*, vol. 12, no. 3, pp. 36–44, 1980.

[31] J. L. Bentley and T. A. Ottmann, "Algorithms for reporting and counting geometric intersections," *IEEE Trans. Comput.*, vol. C-28, pp. 643–647, Sept. 1979.

[32] M. d. Berg, O. Cheong, M. v. Kreveld, and M. Overmars, *Computational Geometry: Algorithms and Applications*. Springer-Verlag TELOS, 3rd ed., 2008.

[33] G. Booch, *Object-Oriented Analysis and Design with Applications*. Redwood City, CA: Benjamin/Cummings, 1994.

[34] A. Borodin and R. El-Yaniv, *Online Computation and Competitive Analysis*. New York: Cambridge University Press, 1998.

[35] R. S. Boyer and J. S. Moore, "A fast string searching algorithm," *Comm. ACM*, vol. 20, no. 10, pp. 762–772, 1977.

[36] G. Brassard, "Crusade for a better notation," *SIGACT News*, vol. 17, no. 1, pp. 60–64, 1985.

[37] G. Brassard and P. Bratley, *Fundamentals of Algorithmics*. Englewood Cliffs, NJ: Prentice Hall, 1996.

[38] D. Bressoud and S. Wagon, *A Course in Computational Number Theory*. Key College Publishing, 2000.

[39] E. O. Brigham, *The Fast Fourier Transform*. Englewood Cliffs, NJ: Prentice-Hall, 1974.

[40] T. Budd, *An Introduction to Object-Oriented Programming*. Reading, MA: Addison-Wesley, 1991.

[41] S. Carlsson, "Average case results on heapsort," *BIT*, vol. 27, pp. 2–17, 1987.

[42] J. L. Carter and M. N. Wegman, "Universal classes of hash functions," *Journal of Computer and System Sciences*, vol. 18, pp. 143–54, 1979.

[43] N. Christofides, "Worst-case analysis of a new heuristic for the traveling salesman problem," in *Sympos. on New Directions and Recent Results in Algorithms and Complexity* (J. F. Traub, ed.), (New York, NY), p. 441, Academic Press, 1976.

[44] V. Chvátal, "A greedy heuristic for the set-covering problem," *Math. Oper. Res.*, vol. 4, pp. 233–235, 1979.

[45] K. L. Clarkson, "Linear programming in $O(n3^{d^2})$ time," *Inform. Process. Lett.*, vol. 22, pp. 21–24, 1986.

[46] R. Cole, "Tight bounds on the complexity of the Boyer-Moore pattern matching algorithm," *SIAM Journal on Computing*, vol. 23, no. 5, pp. 1075–1091, 1994.

[47] D. Comer, "The ubiquitous B-tree," *ACM Comput. Surv.*, vol. 11, pp. 121–137, 1979.

[48] S. Cook, "The complexity of theorem proving procedures," in *30th ACM Symp. on Theory of Computing*, pp. 151–158, 1971.

[49] J. W. Cooley and J. W. Tukey, "An algorithm for the machine calculation of complex Fourier series," *Mathematics of Computation*, vol. 19, no. 90, pp. 297–301, 1965.

[50] T. H. Cormen, C. E. Leiserson, and R. L. Rivest, *Introduction to Algorithms*. Cambridge, MA: MIT Press, 1990.

[51] T. H. Cormen, C. E. Leiserson, R. L. Rivest, and C. Stein, *Introduction to Algorithms*. Cambridge, MA: MIT Press, 2nd ed., 2001.

[52] M. Crochemore and T. Lecroq, "Pattern matching and text compression algorithms," in *The Computer Science and Engineering Handbook* (A. B. Tucker, Jr., ed.), ch. 8, pp. 162–202, CRC Press, 1997.

[53] J. Culberson and J. Munro, "Analysis of the standard deletion algorithms in exact fit domain binary search trees," *Algorithmica*, vol. 5, pp. 295–311, 1990.

[54] G. B. Dantzig, *Linear Programming and Extensions*. Princeton, NJ: Princeton University Press, 1963.

[55] G. Di Battista, P. Eades, R. Tamassia, and I. G. Tollis, *Graph Drawing: Algorithms for Geometric Representations of Graphs*. Englewood Cliffs, NJ: Prentice Hall, 1998.

[56] E. W. Dijkstra, "A note on two problems in connexion with graphs," *Numerische Mathematik*, vol. 1, pp. 269–271, 1959.

[57] M. B. Dillencourt, H. Samet, and M. Tamminen, "A general approach to connected–component labeling for arbitrary image representations," *J. ACM*, vol. 39, pp. 253–280, Apr. 1992.

[58] J. R. Driscoll, H. N. Gabow, R. Shrairaman, and R. E. Tarjan, "Relaxed heaps: An alternative to Fibonacci heaps with applications to parallel computation.," *Comm. ACM*, vol. 31, pp. 1343–1354, 1988.

[59] R. Durstenfeld, "Algorithm 235: Random permutation," *Commun. ACM*, vol. 7, p. 420, July 1964.

[60] D. Easley and J. Kleinberg, *Networks, Crowds, and Markets: Reasoning about a Highly Connected World*. Cambridge University Press, 2010.

[61] H. Edelsbrunner, "A note on dynamic range searching," *Bull. EATCS*, vol. 15, pp. 34–40, 1981.

[62] H. Edelsbrunner, *Algorithms in Combinatorial Geometry*, vol. 10 of *EATCS Monographs on Theoretical Computer Science*. Heidelberg, West Germany: Springer-Verlag, 1987.

[63] J. Edmonds, "Matroids and the greedy algorithm," *Mathematical Programming*, vol. 1, pp. 126–136, 1971.

[64] J. Edmonds and R. M. Karp, "Theoretical improvements in the algorithmic efficiency for network flow problems," *Journal of the ACM*, vol. 19, pp. 248–264, 1972.

[65] D. F. Elliott and K. R. Rao, *Fast Transform Algorithms, Analyses, and Applications*. New York: Academic Press, 1982.

[66] I. Z. Emiris and V. Y. Pan, "Applications of FFT," in *Algorithms and Theory of Computation Handbook* (M. J. Atallah, ed.), ch. 17, pp. 17–1–17–30, CRC Press, 1999.

[67] D. Eppstein, "Linear probing made easy." http://11011110.livejournal.com/232567.html.

[68] S. Even, *Graph algorithms*. Cambridge University Press, 2nd ed., 2012.

[69] R. Fagin, J. Nievergelt, N. Pippenger, and H. R. Strong, "Extendible hashing—a fast access method for dynamic files," *ACM Trans. Database Syst.*, vol. 4, pp. 315–344, Sept. 1979.

[70] M. J. Fischer and M. S. Paterson, "String-matching and other products," tech. rep., Cambridge, MA, 1974.

[71] R. Fisher, F. Yates, *et al.*, *Statistical tables for biological, agricultural and medical research*. Oliver and Boyd, Edinburgh, 3rd ed., 1949.

[72] R. W. Floyd, "Algorithm 97: Shortest path," *Comm. ACM*, vol. 5, no. 6, p. 345, 1962.

[73] R. W. Floyd, "Algorithm 245: Treesort 3," *Comm. ACM*, vol. 7, no. 12, p. 701, 1964.

[74] L. R. Ford, Jr. and D. R. Fulkerson, *Flows in Networks*. Princeton, NJ: Princeton University Press, 1962.

[75] G. N. Frederickson, "Scheduling unit-time tasks with integer release times and deadlines," *Information Processing Letters*, vol. 16, no. 4, pp. 171–173, 1983.

[76] M. L. Fredman and R. E. Tarjan, "Fibonacci heaps and their uses in improved network optimization algorithms," *J. ACM*, vol. 34, pp. 596–615, 1987.

[77] H. Gabow and R. Tarjan, "A linear time algorithm for a special case of disjoint set union," *J. Comput. Syst. Sci.*, vol. 30, pp. 209–221, 1985.

[78] D. Gale and L. Shapley, "College admissions and the stability of marriage," *The American Mathematical Monthly*, vol. 69, no. 1, pp. 9–15, 1962.

[79] T. E. Gamal, "A public key cryptosystem and a signature scheme based on discrete logarithms," *IEEE Transactions on Information Theory*, vol. IT–31, no. 4, pp. 469–472, 1985.

[80] M. R. Garey and D. S. Johnson, *Computers and Intractability: A Guide to the Theory of NP-Completeness*. New York, NY: W. H. Freeman, 1979.

[81] A. M. Gibbons, *Algorithmic Graph Theory*. Cambridge, UK: Cambridge University Press, 1985.

[82] S. S. Godbole, "On efficient computation of matrix chain products," *IEEE Transactions on Computers*, vol. C-22, no. 9, pp. 864–866, 1973.

[83] A. Goldberg and D. Robson, *Smalltalk-80: The Language*. Reading, MA: Addison-Wesley, 1989.

[84] S. Golomb and L. Baumert, "Backtrack programming," *Journal of the ACM*, vol. 12, pp. 516–524, 1965.

[85] G. H. Gonnet and R. Baeza-Yates, *Handbook of Algorithms and Data Structures in Pascal and C*. Reading, MA: Addison-Wesley, 1991.

[86] G. H. Gonnet and J. I. Munro, "Heaps on heaps," *SIAM Journal on Computing*, vol. 15, no. 4, pp. 964–971, 1986.

[87] J. E. Goodman and J. O'Rourke, eds., *Handbook of Discrete and Computational Geometry*. CRC Press LLC, 1997.

[88] M. T. Goodrich, "Parallel algorithms in geometry," in *Handbook of Discrete and Computational Geometry* (J. E. Goodman and J. O'Rourke, eds.), ch. 36, pp. 669–682, Boca Raton, FL: CRC Press LLC, 1997.

[89] M. T. Goodrich, M. Handy, B. Hudson, and R. Tamassia, "Accessing the internal organization of data structures in the JDSL library," in *Proc. Workshop on Algorithm Engineering and Experimentation* (M. T. Goodrich and C. C. McGeoch, eds.), vol. 1619 of *Lecture Notes Comput. Sci.*, pp. 124–139, Springer-Verlag, 1999.

[90] M. T. Goodrich, J.-J. Tsay, D. E. Vengroff, and J. S. Vitter, "External-memory computational geometry," in *Proc. 34th Annu. IEEE Sympos. Found. Comput. Sci.*, pp. 714–723, 1993.

[91] R. L. Graham, "An efficient algorithm for determining the convex hull of a finite planar set," *Inform. Process. Lett.*, vol. 1, pp. 132–133, 1972.

[92] R. L. Graham and P. Hell, "On the history of the minimum spanning tree problem," *Annals of the History of Computing*, vol. 7, no. 1, pp. 43–57, 1985.

[93] R. L. Graham, D. E. Knuth, and O. Patashnik, *Concrete Mathematics*. Reading, MA: Addison-Wesley, 1989.

[94] L. J. Guibas and R. Sedgewick, "A dichromatic framework for balanced trees," in *IEEE Symp. Foundations of Computer Science (FOCS)*, pp. 8–21, 1978.

[95] Y. Gurevich, "What does $O(n)$ mean?," *SIGACT News*, vol. 17, no. 4, pp. 61–63, 1986.

[96] B. Haeupler, S. Sen, and R. Tarjan, "Rank-balanced trees," in *Algorithms and Data Structures* (F. Dehne, M. Gavrilova, J. Sack, and C. Toth, eds.), vol. 5664 of *LNCS*, pp. 351–362, Springer, 2009.

[97] N. J. Higham, "The accuracy of floating point summation," *SIAM Journal on Scientific Computing*, vol. 14, no. 4, pp. 783–799, 1993.

[98] K. Hinrichs, J. Nievergelt, and P. Schorn, "Plane-sweep solves the closest pair problem elegantly," *Inform. Process. Lett.*, vol. 26, pp. 255–261, 1988.

[99] D. S. Hirchsberg, "A linear space algorithm for computing maximal common subsequences," *Comm. ACM*, vol. 18, no. 6, pp. 341–343, 1975.

[100] C. A. R. Hoare, "Quicksort," *The Computer Journal*, vol. 5, pp. 10–15, 1962.

[101] D. Hochbaum (ed.), *Approximation Algorithms for NP-Hard Problems.* Boston: PWS Publishers, 1996.

[102] J. E. Hopcroft and R. E. Tarjan, "Efficient algorithms for graph manipulation," *Comm. ACM*, vol. 16, no. 6, pp. 372–378, 1973.

[103] J. E. Hopcroft and J. D. Ullman, "Set merging algorithms," *SIAM Journal on Computing*, vol. 2, no. 4, pp. 294–303, 1979.

[104] T. C. Hu, *Combinatorial Algorithms.* Reading, MA: Addison-Wesley, 1981.

[105] T. C. Hu and M. T. Shing, "Computations of matrix chain products, part i," *SIAM Journal on Computing*, vol. 11, no. 2, pp. 362–373, 1982.

[106] T. C. Hu and M. T. Shing, "Computations of matrix chain products, part ii," *SIAM Journal on Computing*, vol. 13, no. 2, pp. 228–251, 1984.

[107] B. Huang and M. Langston, "Practical in-place merging," *Comm. ACM*, vol. 31, no. 3, pp. 348–352, 1988.

[108] D. A. Huffman, "A method for the construction of minimum-redundancy codes," *Proceedings of the IRE*, vol. 40, no. 9, pp. 1098–1101, 1952.

[109] O. H. Ibarra and C. E. Kim, "Fast approximation algorithms for the knapsack and sum of subset problems," *Journal of the ACM*, vol. 9, pp. 463–468, 1975.

[110] J. JáJá, *An Introduction to Parallel Algorithms.* Reading, MA: Addison-Wesley, 1992.

[111] V. Jarnik, "O jistem problemu minimalnim," *Praca Moravske Prirodovedecke Spolecnosti*, vol. 6, pp. 57–63, 1930. (in Czech).

[112] D. S. Johnson, "Approximation algorithms for combinatorial problems," *J. Comput. Syst. Sci.*, vol. 9, pp. 256–278, 1974.

[113] M. Johnston, "Spike: AI scheduling for NASA's Hubble Space Telescope," in *6th Conf. on Artificial Intelligence Applications*, pp. 184–190, may 1990.

[114] R. E. Jones, *Garbage Collection: Algorithms for Automatic Dynamic Memory Management.* John Wiley and Sons, 1996.

[115] M.-Y. Kao and J. Wang, "Efficient minimization of numerical summation errors," in *Automata, Languages and Programming* (K. Larsen, S. Skyum, and G. Winskel, eds.), vol. 1443 of *Lecture Notes in Computer Science*, pp. 375–386, Springer, 1998.

[116] H. Kaplan, N. Shafrir, and R. E. Tarjan, "Union-find with deletions," in *19th ACM-SIAM Symposium on Discrete Algorithms (SODA)*, pp. 19–28, 2002.

[117] A. Karatsuba and Y. Ofman, "Multiplication of multidigit numbers on automata," *Doklady Akademii Nauk SSSR*, vol. 145, pp. 293–294, 1962. (In Russian).

[118] D. R. Karger, "Global min-cuts in RNC, and other ramifications of a simple min-cut algorithm," in *Proc. ACM-SIAM Symp. on Discrete Algorithms (SODA)*, pp. 21–30, 1993.

[119] D. R. Karger, P. Klein, and R. E. Tarjan, "A randomized linear-time algorithm to find minimum spanning trees," *Journal of the ACM*, vol. 42, pp. 321–328, 1995.

[120] D. R. Karger and C. Stein, "A new approach to the minimum cut problem," *J. ACM*, vol. 43, no. 4, pp. 601–640, 1996.

[121] N. Karmarkar, "A new polynomial-time algorithm for linear programming," *Combinatorica*, vol. 4, pp. 373–395, 1984.

[122] R. Karp, "Reducibility among combinatorical problems of computer computations," in *Complexity of Computer Computations* (E. Miller and J. W. Thatcher, eds.), pp. 88–104, New York: Plenum Press, 1972.

[123] R. M. Karp and M. O. Rabin, "Efficient randomized pattern-matching algorithms," *IBM Journal of Research and Development*, vol. 31, pp. 249–260, March 1987.

[124] R. M. Karp and V. Ramachandran, "Parallel algorithms for shared memory machines," in *Handbook of Theoretical Computer Science* (J. van Leeuwen, ed.), pp. 869–941, Amsterdam: Elsevier/The MIT Press, 1990.

[125] L. G. Khachiyan, "Polynomial algorithm in linear programming," *U.S.S.R. Comput. Math. and Math. Phys.*, vol. 20, pp. 53–72, 1980.

[126] P. Kirschenhofer and H. Prodinger, "The path length of random skip lists," *Acta Informatica*, vol. 31, pp. 775–792, 1994.

[127] P. N. Klein and N. E. Young, "Approximation algorithms," in *Algorithms and Theory of Computation Handbook* (M. J. Atallah, ed.), ch. 34, pp. 34–1–34–19, CRC Press, 1999.

[128] D. E. Knuth, "Big omicron and big omega and big theta," in *SIGACT News*, vol. 8, pp. 18–24, 1976.

[129] D. E. Knuth, *Fundamental Algorithms*, vol. 1 of *The Art of Computer Programming*. Reading, MA: Addison-Wesley, 3rd ed., 1997.

[130] D. E. Knuth, *Seminumerical Algorithms*, vol. 2 of *The Art of Computer Programming*. Reading, MA: Addison-Wesley, 3rd ed., 1998.

[131] D. E. Knuth, *Sorting and Searching*, vol. 3 of *The Art of Computer Programming*. Reading, MA: Addison-Wesley, 2nd ed., 1998.

[132] D. E. Knuth, J. H. Morris, Jr., and V. R. Pratt, "Fast pattern matching in strings," *SIAM Journal on Computing*, vol. 6, no. 1, pp. 323–350, 1977.

[133] N. Koblitz, *A Course in Number Theory and Cryptography*. Springer-Verlag, 1987.

[134] E. Koutsoupias and C. H. Papadimitriou, "On the k-server conjecture," *Journal of the ACM*, vol. 42, no. 5, pp. 971–983, 1995.

[135] D. C. Kozen, *The design and analysis of algorithms*. New York: Springer-Verlag New York, Inc., 1992.

[136] E. Kranakis, *Primality and Cryptography*. John Wiley and Sons, 1986.

[137] J. B. Kruskal, Jr., "On the shortest spanning subtree of a graph and the traveling salesman problem," *Proc. Amer. Math. Soc.*, vol. 7, pp. 48–50, 1956.

[138] H. T. Kung, F. Luccio, and F. P. Preparata, "On finding the maxima of a set of vectors," *J. ACM*, vol. 22, pp. 469–476, 1975.

[139] D. T. Lee, "Computational geometry," in *The Computer Science and Engineering Handbook* (A. B. Tucker, Jr., ed.), ch. 6, pp. 111–140, CRC Press, 1997.

[140] D. T. Lee and F. P. Preparata, "Computational geometry: a survey," *IEEE Trans. Comput.*, vol. C-33, pp. 1072–1101, 1984.

[141] L. A. Levin, "Universal sorting problems," *Problemy Peredachi Informatsii*, vol. 9, no. 3, pp. 265–266, 1973. (In Russian).

[142] R. Levisse, "Some lessons drawn from the history of the binary search algorithm," *The Computer Journal*, vol. 26, pp. 154–163, 1983.

[143] H. R. Lewis and C. H. Papadimitriou, *Elements of the Theory of Computation*. Upper Saddle River, NJ: Prentice-Hall, 2nd ed., 1998.

[144] B. Liskov and J. Guttag, *Abstraction and Specification in Program Development*. Cambridge, MA/New York: The MIT Press/McGraw-Hill, 1986.

[145] W. Litwin, "Linear hashing: a new tool for file and table addressing," in *6th Int. Conf. on Very Large Data Bases (VLDB)*, (Montreal), pp. 212–223, October 1980.

[146] L. Lovász, "On the ratio of optimal integral and fractional covers," *Discrete Math.*, vol. 13, pp. 383–390, 1975.

[147] J. Matoušek, "Geometric range searching," *ACM Comput. Surv.*, vol. 26, pp. 421–461, 1994.

[148] E. M. McCreight, "A space-economical suffix tree construction algorithm," *Journal of Algorithms*, vol. 23, no. 2, pp. 262–272, 1976.

[149] E. M. McCreight, "Priority search trees," *SIAM J. Comput.*, vol. 14, no. 2, pp. 257–276, 1985.

[150] C. J. H. McDiarmid and B. A. Reed, "Building heaps fast," *Journal of Algorithms*, vol. 10, no. 3, pp. 352–365, 1989.

[151] C. C. McGeoch, "Analyzing algorithms by simulation: Variance reduction techniques and simulation speedups," *ACM Computing Surveys*, vol. 24, no. 2, pp. 195–212, 1992.

[152] C. C. McGeoch, "Toward an experimental method for algorithm simulation," *INFORMS Journal on Computing*, vol. 8, no. 1, pp. 1–15, 1996.

[153] C. C. McGeoch, D. Precup, and P. R. Cohen, "How to find the Big-Oh of your data set (and how not to)," in *Advances in Intelligent Data Analysis*, vol. 1280 of *Lecture Notes in Computer Science*, pp. 41–52, Springer-Verlag, 1997.

[154] N. Megiddo, "Linear-time algorithms for linear programming in R^3 and related problems," *SIAM J. Comput.*, vol. 12, pp. 759–776, 1983.

[155] N. Megiddo, "Linear programming in linear time when the dimension is fixed," *J. ACM*, vol. 31, pp. 114–127, 1984.

[156] K. Mehlhorn, "A best possible bound for the weighted path length of binary search trees," *SIAM Journal on Computing*, vol. 6, no. 2, pp. 235–239, 1977.

[157] K. Mehlhorn, *Data Structures and Algorithms 1: Sorting and Searching*, vol. 1 of *EATCS Monographs on Theoretical Computer Science*. Heidelberg, Germany: Springer-Verlag, 1984.

[158] K. Mehlhorn, *Data Structures and Algorithms 2: Graph Algorithms and NP-Completeness*, vol. 2 of *EATCS Monographs on Theoretical Computer Science*. Heidelberg, Germany: Springer-Verlag, 1984.

[159] K. Mehlhorn, *Data Structures and Algorithms 3: Multi-dimensional Searching and Computational Geometry*, vol. 3 of *EATCS Monographs on Theoretical Computer Science*. Heidelberg, Germany: Springer-Verlag, 1984.

[160] K. Mehlhorn and A. Tsakalidis, "Data structures," in *Handbook of Theoretical Computer Science* (J. van Leeuwen, ed.), vol. A. Algorithms and Complexity, pp. 301–341, Amsterdam: Elsevier, 1990.

[161] D. R. Morrison, "PATRICIA—practical algorithm to retrieve information coded in alphanumeric," *Journal of the ACM*, vol. 15, no. 4, pp. 514–534, 1968.

[162] R. Motwani and P. Raghavan, *Randomized Algorithms*. New York: Cambridge University Press, 1995.

[163] D. R. Musser and A. Saini, *STL Tutorial and Reference Guide: C++ Programming with the Standard Template Library*. Reading, MA: Addison-Wesley, 1996.

[164] R. Neapolitan and K. Naimipour, *Foundations of Algorithms Using C++ Pseudocode*. Boston: Jones and Bartlett Publishers, 1998.

[165] J. O'Rourke, *Computational Geometry in C*. Cambridge University Press, 1994.

[166] J. Pach, ed., *New Trends in Discrete and Computational Geometry*, vol. 10 of *Algorithms and Combinatorics*. Springer-Verlag, 1993.

[167] R. Pagh and F. Rodler, "Cuckoo hashing," *Journal of Algorithms*, vol. 52, pp. 122–144, 2004.

[168] T. Papadakis, J. I. Munro, and P. V. Poblete, "Average search and update costs in skip lists," *BIT*, vol. 32, pp. 316–332, 1992.

[169] C. H. Papadimitriou and K. Steiglitz, "Some complexity results for the traveling salesman problem," in *Proc. 8th Annu. ACM Sympos. Theory Comput.*, pp. 1–9, 1976.

[170] C. H. Papadimitriou and K. Steiglitz, *Combinatorial Optimization: Algorithms and Complexity*. Englewood Cliffs, NJ: Prentice Hall, 1982.

[171] M. Patrascu and M. Thorup, "The power of simple tabulation hashing," in *43rd ACM Symp. on Theory of Computing (STOC)*, pp. 1–10, 2011.

[172] P. V. Poblete, J. I. Munro, and T. Papadakis, "The binomial transform and its application to the analysis of skip lists," in *Proceedings of the European Symposium on Algorithms (ESA)*, pp. 554–569, 1995.

[173] F. P. Preparata and M. I. Shamos, *Computational Geometry: An Introduction*. Springer-Verlag, 3rd ed., Oct. 1990.

[174] R. C. Prim, "Shortest connection networks and some generalizations," *Bell Syst. Tech. J.*, vol. 36, pp. 1389–1401, 1957.

[175] W. Pugh, "Skip lists: a probabilistic alternative to balanced trees," *Communications of the ACM*, vol. 33, no. 6, pp. 668–676, 1990.

[176] M. Raab and A. Steger, ""balls into bins" – a simple and tight analysis," in *Randomization and Approximation Techniques in Computer Science (RANDOM)* (M. Luby, J. Rolim, and M. Serna, eds.), vol. 1518 of *LNCS*, pp. 159–170, Springer, 1998.

[177] M. O. Rabin, "A probabilistic algorithm for testing primality," *Journal of Number Theory*, vol. 12, 1980.

[178] R. L. Rivest, A. Shamir, and L. Adleman, "A method for obtaining digital signatures and public-key cryptosystems," *Communications of the ACM*, vol. 21, no. 2, pp. 120–126, 1978.

[179] D. J. Rosenkrantz, R. E. Stearns, and P. M. Lewis, "An analysis of several heuristics for the traveling salesman problem," *SIAM J. on Computing*, vol. 6, pp. 563–581, 1977.

[180] H. Sackrowitz, "Refining the point(s)-after-touchdown decision," *Chance*, vol. 13, no. 3, pp. 29–34, 2000.

[181] H. Samet, *Applications of Spatial Data Structures: Computer Graphics, Image Processing, and GIS*. Reading, MA: Addison-Wesley, 1990.

[182] H. Samet, *The Design and Analysis of Spatial Data Structures*. Reading, MA: Addison-Wesley, 1990.

[183] D. Sankoff and J. B. Kruskal, *Time Warps, String Edits, and Macromolecules: The Theory and Practice of Sequence Comparison*. Addison-Wesley, 1983.

[184] J. E. Savage, *Models of Computation: Exploring the Power of Computing*. Addison-Wesley, 1998.

[185] R. Schaffer and R. Sedgewick, "The analysis of heapsort," *Journal of Algorithms*, vol. 15, no. 1, pp. 76–100, 1993.

[186] A. Schönhage and V. Strassen, "Schnelle multiplikation grosser zahlen," *Computing*, vol. 7, pp. 281–292, 1971.

[187] B. L. Schwartz, "Possible winners in partially completed tournaments," *SIAM Review*, vol. 8, no. 3, pp. 302–308, 1966.

[188] R. Sedgewick, *Algorithms*. Reading, MA: Addison-Wesley, 1st ed., 1983.

[189] R. Sedgewick, *Algorithms in C++*. Reading, MA: Addison-Wesley, 1992.

[190] R. Sedgewick and P. Flajolet, *An Introduction to the Analysis of Algorithms*. Reading, MA: Addison-Wesley, 1996.

[191] R. Seidel and C. Aragon, "Randomized search trees," *Algorithmica*, vol. 16, no. 4-5, pp. 464–497, 1996.

[192] R. Seidel and M. Sharir, "Top-down analysis of path compression," *SIAM Journal on Computing*, vol. 34, no. 3, pp. 515–525, 2005.

[193] S. Sen and R. E. Tarjan, "Deletion without rebalancing in balanced binary trees," in *Proc. ACM-SIAM Symposium on Discrete Algorithms (SODA)*, pp. 1490–1499, 2010.

[194] A. Shamir, "How to share a secret," *Comm. of the ACM*, vol. 22(11), pp. 612–613, 1979.

[195] M. Sipser, *Introduction to the Theory of Computation*. PWS Publishing Co., 1997.

[196] D. D. Sleator and R. E. Tarjan, "Amortized efficiency of list update and paging rules," *Comm. ACM*, vol. 28, pp. 202–208, 1985.

[197] D. D. Sleator and R. E. Tarjan, "Self-adjusting binary search trees," *J. ACM*, vol. 32, no. 3, pp. 652–686, 1985.

[198] D. K. Smith, "Dynamic programming and board games: A survey," *European Journal of Operational Research*, vol. 176, no. 3, pp. 1299–1318, 2007.

[199] D. A. Spielman and S.-H. Teng, "Smoothed analysis of algorithms: Why the simplex algorithm usually takes polynomial time," *J. ACM*, vol. 51, pp. 385–463, May 2004.

[200] G. A. Stephen, *String Searching Algorithms*. World Scientific Press, 1994.

[201] H. S. Stern, "American football," in *Statistics in Sport* (J. Bennett, ed.), Arnold, 1998.

[202] V. Strassen, "Gaussian elimination is not optimal," *Numerische Mathematik*, vol. 13, pp. 354–356, 1969.

[203] R. Tamassia, ed., *Handbook of Graph Drawing and Visualization*. Chapman and Hall/CRC, 2013.

[204] R. Tarjan and U. Vishkin, "An efficient parallel biconnectivity algorithm," *SIAM J. Comput.*, vol. 14, pp. 862–874, 1985.

[205] R. E. Tarjan, "Depth first search and linear graph algorithms," *SIAM Journal on Computing*, vol. 1, no. 2, pp. 146–160, 1972.

[206] R. E. Tarjan, "A class of algorithms which require nonlinear time to maintain disjoint sets," *J. Comput. System Sci.*, vol. 18, pp. 110–127, 1979.

[207] R. E. Tarjan, *Data Structures and Network Algorithms*, vol. 44 of *CBMS-NSF Regional Conference Series in Applied Mathematics*. SIAM, 1983.

[208] R. E. Tarjan, "Amortized computational complexity," *SIAM J. Algebraic Discrete Methods*, vol. 6, no. 2, pp. 306–318, 1985.

[209] R. E. Tarjan and J. van Leeuwen, "Worst-case analysis of set union algorithms," *J. ACM*, vol. 31, pp. 245–281, Mar. 1984.

[210] J. van Leeuwen, "Graph algorithms," in *Handbook of Theoretical Computer Science* (J. van Leeuwen, ed.), vol. A. Algorithms and Complexity, pp. 525–632, Amsterdam: Elsevier, 1990.

[211] J. S. Vitter, *Algorithms and Data Structures for External Memory*. Foundations and Trends in Theoretical Computer Science, Hanover, MA: Now Publishers, 2008.

[212] J. S. Vitter and W. C. Chen, *Design and Analysis of Coalesced Hashing*. New York: Oxford University Press, 1987.

[213] J. Vuillemin, "A unifying look at data structures," *Comm. ACM*, vol. 23, pp. 229–239, 1980.

[214] S. Warshall, "A theorem on boolean matrices," *Journal of the ACM*, vol. 9, no. 1, pp. 11–12, 1962.

[215] K. Wayne, "A new property and a faster algorithm for baseball elimination," *SIAM Journal on Discrete Mathematics*, vol. 14, no. 2, pp. 223–229, 2001.

[216] J. W. J. Williams, "Algorithm 232: Heapsort," *Comm. ACM*, vol. 7, no. 6, pp. 347–348, 1964.

[217] D. Wood, *Data Structures, Algorithms, and Performance*. Reading, MA: Addison-Wesley, 1993.

[218] F. F. Yao, "Computational geometry," in *Algorithms in Complexity* (R. A. Earnshaw and B. Wyvill, eds.), pp. 345–490, Amsterdam: Elsevier, 1990.

[219] C. K. Yap, *Fundamental Problems in Algorithmic Algebra*. Oxford University Press, 1999.

δ-approximation, 510
2SAT, 491, 503
3SAT, 491, 492

(a, b) tree, 586–588
    depth property, 586
    size property, 586
accepting a string, 477
access control lists, 700
accounting method, 36–37
accumulator, 30, 33
Achter, 710
Ackermann function, 231, 232, 432
acyclic, 373
additive inverse, 691
Adel'son-Vel'skii, 154
adjacency list, 361
adjacency matrix, 361, 363
adjacent, 356
Adleman, 703
Agarwal, 239, 622
Aggarwal, 602
Aho, 88, 154, 506, 602, 684, 730
Ahuja, 396, 422, 472
algorithm, 2
algorithm analysis, 6–33
    average case, 9
    worst case, 9
alphabet, 654
Alstrup, 239
amortization, 34–41, 73, 85, 145–148, 151,
        221–235, 516–517, 662
    accounting method, 36–37
    potential function, 37–38
ancestor, 68, 372
anchor point, 632, 634–636
antisymmetric property, 157
approximation algorithms, 509–517
Aragon, 568, 622
Arge, 602
Arkin, 568
Arnold, 88
art gallery guarding, 300
Arya, 622
asymmetric relation, 356
asymptotic notation, 11–33
    big-Oh, 11–14
    big-Omega, 14
    big-Theta, 14

little-oh, 16
little-omega, 16
augmented trees, 104
augmenting cycle, 462
augmenting path, 450
Aurenhammer, 650
AVL tree, 120–124, 644
    height-balance property, 120

Baase, 730
back edge, 367, 375, 376, 393
backtracking, 365, 521–523, 528
backward induction, 338
Baeza-Yates, 114, 154, 264, 282, 684
balanced binary search tree, 116–148
balanced search tree, 577
Barůvka, 442
Barůvka's algorithm, 436–438
baseball, 352
baseball elimination, 460–461
basic solution, 740
basic variables, 739
Baumert, 528
Bayer, 154, 602
Bellman, 352, 422
Bellman-Ford algorithm, 407–409
Bentley, 114, 186, 322, 650
Berg, 650
Bertrand's Postulate, 213
BFS, *see* breadth-first search
BFS tree, 372
biconnected, 386
biconnected component, 386
big integers, 313
big-Oh notation, 11–14
big-Omega notation, 14
big-Theta notation, 14
bin packing, 153
binary encoding, 476
binary search, 91–93
binary search tree, 90, 94–100
    insertion, 97
    removal, 98–99
    rotation, 119
    trinode restructure, 119
binary space partitioning, 90
binary tree, 69, 76–82, 244
    complete, 163
    left child, 69

level, 76
  linked structure, 82
  proper, 69
  right child, 69
binomial coefficients, 347
binomial distribution, 552
binomial expansion, 762
biodiversity, 534
bipartite graph, 458
birthday paradox, 217, 567
blocking, 572
Bloom filters, 567
Booch, 88
Boolean circuit, 481
bootstrapping, 576
Borodin, 602
bottleneck, 457
bottleneck TSP, 526
boundary node, 102
bounding box, 320, 621
Boyer, 684
branch-and-bound, 524–526, 528
Brassard, 50, 528
Bratlcy, 528
breadth-first search, 370–372, 376
Brigham, 730
brute force, 654
B-tree, 588–589
bubble-sort, 183
bucket-sort, 267–268
Budd, 88
buffer, 52
butterfly network, 725

c-incremental, 503
cache, 570
cache line, 572
caching algorithms, 594–599
call-by-value, 56
Canny, 568
capacity rule, 445
Carlsson, 186
Carmichael numbers, 547
Cartesian tree, 622
Catalan number, 326
certificate, 479
character-jump heuristic, 656
Chen, 218
Chernoff bound, 108, 109, 260, 551–553
child, 68
Chomsky normal form, 348
Christofides approximation algorithm, 513
Chvátal, 528

CIRCUIT-SAT, 481, 484–486, 489
Clarkson, 282
clauses, 489
clearable table, 34
CLIQUE, 494, 502
clique, 494
clockwise, 627
closed form, 10
closest pairs, 642–645
closure, 415
CNF, *see* conjunctive normal form
CNF-SAT, 489–491, 503, 506, 522, 523
coalesced hashing, 218
coefficient form, 713
coefficients, 734
coins-in-a-line game, 334
Cole, 684
collinear, 627
collision, 193
collision resolution, 198–214
collision-resistant, 702
Comer, 602
comparator, 179
compare-exchange, 261
complement, 478
complete binary tree, 163
complexity class, 478
component design, 487
composite, 546, 687
compositeness witness function, 547
compressed quadtree, 620
computational geometry, 624–650
  closest pairs, 642–645
  convex hull, 630–636
  degeneracies, 628
  orientation, 627–629
  plane sweep, 640–645
  proximity, 642
  segment intersection, 638–641
conditional probability, 27
confidence parameter, 548
confidentiality, 686
congruence, 546
conjunctive normal form, 489, 491
connected components, 220, 221, 359, 369, 372
conservation rule, 445
constraints, 734
container, 88
contraction, 540
contradiction, 23
contrapositive, 23
convex hull, 630–636, 650

gift wrapping, 632–634
Graham scan algorithm, 635–636
convexity, 629, 630, 736
convolution, 713
Convolution Theorem, 720
Cook, 506
Cook-Levin Theorem, 484
Cooley, 730
coordinates, 605
Cormen, 239, 322, 396, 506
cost, 462
counterclockwise, 627
coupon collector problem, 534–535
Crochemore, 684
cross edge, 372, 375, 376
cryptography, 699–707
El Gamal cryptosystem, 706–707
RSA cryptosystem, 703–705
cuckoo hashing, 206–211
currency arbitrage, 422
cursor, 64
cut, 447, 539
cyber-dollar, 36
cycle, 358
directed, 358
cyptograph
public-key, 701–707

DAG, *see* directed acyclic graph
data integrity, 686, 699
data structure, 2
secondary, 576
data-oblivious, 261
decision problem, 477
decision tree, 257
decryption, 699
degeneracy, 744
degree, 356, 713
Delaunay triangulation, 650
DeMorgan's law, 23
depth, 72–73
depth-first search, 365–369
deque, 85
descendant, 68, 372
destination, 356
DFS, *see* depth-first search
DFS tree, 367
DFT, *see* Discrete Fourier Transform
Di Battista, 88
diameter, 87, 647
dictionary, 189
update operations, 560
digital signature, 699

El Gamal, 707
RSA, 704
digraph, 373
Dijkstra, 422
Dijkstra's algorithm, 400–406
Dillencourt, 239
directed acyclic graph, 382–384
directed cycle, 373
directed DFS tree, 375
discovery edge, 367, 372, 375, 376
Discrete Fourier Transform, 717–720
discrete logarithm, 706
disjunctive normal form, 490
distance, 399
divide-and-conquer, 243–245, 250–251, 305–316
DNF, *see* disjunctive normal form
DNF-DISSAT, 502
DNF-SAT, 502
d-node, 574
Doom, 90
double hashing, 204
double-entry accounting, 216
down-heap bubbling, 170, 176
dual LP, 746
Durstenfeld, 568
dynamic programming, 324–345, 377
dynamic time warping, 351

Easley, 239, 396, 422, 472
Edelsbrunner, 622, 650
edge, 355, 629
destination, 356
end vertices, 356
incident, 356
multiple, 357
origin, 356
outgoing, 356
parallel, 357
self-loop, 357
edge capacity, 445
edit distance, 347
Edmonds, 302, 472
Edmonds-Karp algorithm, 455–457
El-Yaniv, 602
Elliott, 730
El Gamal cryptosystem, 706–707
Emiris, 730
encryption schemes, 700
end vertices, 356
endpoints, 356
equivalence class, 387
equivalence relation, 387

Euclid's algorithm, 689–690
    extended, 697–698
Euler tour, 392, 395
Euler tour traversal, 79, 88
Euler's Theorem, 693
Even, 396, 422, 472
event, 26
exchange argument, 288
expected value, 27
exponent, 21
extended Euclid's algorithm, 697
external memory, 571–592, 602
external-memory algorithm, 571–592
external-memory sorting, 590–592

factorial, 762
failure function, 660
Fast Fourier Transform, 713–726, 730
feasible region, 736
feasible solution, 736
Fermat's Little Theorem, 546
FFT, *see* Fast Fourier Transform
Fibonacci progression, 763
Fibonacci sequence, 150
FIFO, 57, 592
first-in first-out, 57
Fisher, 568
Fisher-Yates algorithm, 533
Flajolet, 50
flow, *see* network flow
flow network, 445
Floyd, 186
Floyd-Warshall algorithm, 377, 396
Ford, 422
Ford-Fulkerson algorithm, 449–457
forest, 359
forward edge, 375
frame, 55
Frederickson, 239
free variables, 739
free-space optical communication, 441
Fulkerson, 472
fully polynomial-time approximation scheme,
    518
Fundamental Theorem of Arithmetic, 687
fusion, 582, 587, 589

Gabow, 239
Gale, 568
game strategies, 334–338
garbage collection, 380–381
    mark-sweep, 380
Garey, 506

Gauss, 20
Gavril, 528
GCD, *see* greatest common divisor
generator, 694
geometric random variable, 534
geometric sum, 763
Gibbons, 396, 422, 472
gift wrapping, 632–634
Godbole, 352
Golberg, 88
golden ratio, 150, 763
Golomb, 528
Gonnet, 114, 154, 186, 264, 282
Goodman, 650
Goodrich, 602, 650
googol, 15
Gosling, 88
Graham, 50, 442, 650
Graham scan algorithm, 635–636
grammar, 348
graph, 354–396, 398–422, 424–442
    acyclic, 373
    bipartite, 458
    breadth-first search, 370–372, 374–377
    connected, 359, 372
    data structures, 361–363
        adjacency list, 361–362
        adjacency matrix, 363
    dense, 378
    depth-first search, 365–369, 374–377
    digraph, 373
    directed, 355, 356, 373–384
        acyclic, 382–384
        strongly connected, 373
    mixed, 356
    reachability, 373–374, 377–378
    shortest paths, 377–378
    simple, 357
    traversal, 365–372
    undirected, 355, 356
    weighted, 398–422, 424–442
greatest common divisor, 688–690
    Euclid's algorithm, 689–690
greedy method, 284–297, 399, 400
greedy-choice, 285, 297
group, 693
guess-and-test, 308–309
Guibas, 154
Guttag, 88

Haken, 322
HAMILTONIAN-CYCLE, 499, 501, 506, 526
harmonic number, 108, 112, 517, 535, 764

hash function, 192, 204, 212, 213
    2-universal, 212
    one-way, 702
hash table, 188, 190–211
    chaining, 198
    clustering, 203
    collision resolution, 198–214
    double hashing, 204
    linear probing, 200
    open addressing, 204
    quadratic probing, 204
    secondary clustering, 204
    universal hashing, 212–214
header, 64
heap, 163–178
heap-order property, 163
heap-sort, 174–178
height, 72–73
height-balance property, 120–123
Hell, 442
Hex game, 238
hidden-line elimination, 648
high probability, 532
Hilbert, 231
Hinrichs, 650
Hirschberg, 352
Hoare, 264
Hochbaum, 528
Hopcroft, 88, 154, 239, 396, 506, 602, 730
Horner's method, 46
Horner's rule, 713
Hu, 352
Huang, 264
Huffman, 302
Huffman coding, 292–297

Ibarra, 528
identity matrix, 718
in place, 160, 162
in-degree, 356
in-place, 254, 381
incidence matrix, 496
incident, 356
incoming edges, 356
independent, 26, 28
independent set, 348, 395
INDEPENDENT-SET, 504
index, 60, *see* discrete logarithm
induction, 23–24
inorder traversal, 95, 99, 118
input size, 476
insertion-sort, 161
inside node, 102

integer multiplication, 313–314
internal memory, 570
intersection, 626
inverse shuffle, 725
inversion, 183, 260
inverted file, 242, 280
items, 189
iterative substitution, 306

JáJá, 88
Jarník, 442
Johnson, 506, 528
Johnston, 352
Jones, 396
Josephus problem, 87, 114

Kao, 264
Kaplan, 239
Karatsuba, 322
Karger, 442
Karp, 88, 472, 506
Karp-Rabin algorithm, 664, 666, 667
k-d tree, 616–617
key, 157, 189, 190, 574
key transfer, 701
Kim, 528
Klein, 442, 528
Kleinberg, 239, 396, 422, 472
KNAPSACK, 498, 504, 518–520, 525, 526, 528
knapsack problem, 286–288, 343–345
Knuth, 50, 88, 114, 154, 186, 264, 282, 396, 602, 684
Kosaraju, 396
Koutsoupias, 602
Kruskal, 352, 442
Kruskal's algorithm, 428–432
Kung, 322

L'Hôpital's Rule, 764
Landis, 154
Langston, 264
language, 477
Las Vegas algorithm, 550
last node, 163
last-in first-out, 53
LCS, *see* longest common subsequence
leaves, 68
Lecroq, 684
Lee, 650
left child, 69
left subtree, 69
left turn, 627

Leiserson, 396, 506
level, 76, 370
level numbering, 165
level order traversal, 87
Levin, 506
Levisse, 114
Lewis, 528
lexicographic, 242
lexicographical, 268
lexicon matching, 664
LIFO, 53
line, 625
line breaking, 301
linear exponential, 764
linear function, 734
linear probing, 200
linear program, 734
linear programming, 732–752
linearity of expectation, 27, 272
link components, 389
link relation, 387
linked list, 63, 64
        doubly linked, 64–66
linked structure, 82
Liskov, 88
list, 60–66
literals, 489
little-oh notation, 16
little-omega notation, 16
live objects, 380
load factor, 199, 205
local replacement, 487
locality-of-reference, 572
locator, 179–181
logarithm, 21, 761
        natural, 761
longest common subsequence, 339–342
longest common substring, 348
looking-glass heuristic, 656
lookup table, 191
loop invariant, 25
Lovász, 528
LRU, 592
Luccio, 322

machine precision, 263, 300
machine scheduling, 300
Magnanti, 396, 422, 472
making change, 349
map, 189–211
        hash table, 190–211
        skip list, 557–562
mark-sweep algorithm, 380

Marker strategy, 597
Markov's inequality, 551
master theorem, 310–312
matching, 458
matrix chain-product, 325–328
matrix closure, 415–417
matrix multiplication, 315–316
matroid theory, 302
Max-Flow, Min-Cut Theorem, 451
maxima set, 304, 317–318
maximum bipartite matching, 458–459
maximum flow, *see* network flow
maximum spanning tree, 441
maximum subarray problem, 29
maximum subarray sum, 29
maze, 223
McCreight, 602, 622, 684
McDiarmid, 186
McGeoch, 50
median, 270
Megiddo, 282
Mehlhorn, 114, 154, 396, 422, 472, 602, 622,
        650
memoization, 333, 336, 338
memory hierarchy, 570
memory management, 380, 571–573, 594–599
merge-sort, 243–249
        multi-way, 590–592
        tree, 244
mergeable heap, 151
method stack, 55–56
metric, 511
METRIC-TSP, 511–514
metrology, 281, 648
Milgram, 566
Miller, 568
minimum cut, 448, 539
minimum spanning tree, 425–438
        Barůvka's algorithm, 436–438
        Kruskal's algorithm, 428–432
        Prim-Jarnik algorithm, 433–435
minimum-cost flow, 462–468
mode, 260, 280
modular arithmetic, 58, 213, 546, 691–694,
        762
modular exponentiation, 695–696
modular multiplicative inverse, 697
modulus, 546
Monte Carlo algorithm, 550
Moore, 684
Morris, 684
Morrison, 684

Motwani, 264, 568, 602
MST, *see* minimum spanning tree
multi-objective optimization, 317
multi-way search tree, 574
multi-way tree, 574–577
multimap, 190, 216
multiplicative group, 693
multiplicative inverse, 691, 697
Munro, 186
mutually independent, 26

Naimipour, 528
natural logarithm, 761
Neapolitan, 528
nearest-neighbor query, 116
negative binomial distribution, 554
network flow, 444–472
    augmenting cycle, 462
    augmenting path, 450
    backward edge, 447
    bottleneck, 457
    capacity rule, 445
    conservation rule, 445
    cut, 447–449
    cut capacity, 448
    edge capacity, 445
    Edmonds-Karp algorithm, 455–457
    flow across a cut, 448
    flow network, 445–447
    flow value, 446
    Ford-Fulkerson algorithm, 449–457
    forward edge, 447
    Max-Flow, Min-Cut Theorem, 451
    maximum flow problem, 446, 449
    minimum cut, 448
    minimum-cost flow, 462–468
    residual capacity, 449
    residual distance, 455
    residual graph, 454
node, 63, 68, 70
    ancestor, 68
    balanced, 121
    boundary, 102
    child, 68
    descendant, 68
    external, 68
    inside, 102
    internal, 68
    outside, 102
    parent, 68
    redundant, 673
    root, 68
    sibling, 68

    size, 145
    unbalanced, 121
nonnegativity constraints, 734
nontree edge, 375, 376
NP, 478, 479
NP-completeness, 474–506
NP-hard, 483
null string, 653
number theory, 686–698

O'Rourke, 650
object-oriented design, 88
objective function, 285, 734
octree, 620
odd-even merge-sort, 261
office party problem, 350
offline-min problem, 237
Ofman, 322
one-sided error, 550
one-time pad, 709
one-way hash function, 702, 710
online algorithm, 593–599
open addressing, 200, 204
optimal binary search tree, 348
optimization problem, 329, 477
order statistic, 270
orientation, 626–628
origin, 356
Orlin, 396, 422, 472
orthogonal segments, 638
Ottmann, 650
out-degree, 356
outgoing edge, 356
output sensitive, 634, 638
outside node, 102
overflow, 579, 589

P, 478
Pach, 650
palindrome, 350
Pan, 730
Papadimitriou, 302, 528, 602
parent, 68
PARTITION, 504
partition, 221
partition tree, 614
password, 699
Patashnik, 50
path, 358
    directed, 358
    length, 399
    simple, 358
    weight, 399

path compression, 229
path length, 87
pattern matching, 653–663
    Boyer-Moore algorithm, 656–658
    brute force, 654–656
    Knuth-Morris-Pratt algorithm, 660–663
percolation theory, 224, 237
perfect matching, 513
pivot, 740
plane sweep, 640–645
point, 625
polygon, 625, 629
    convex, 629
    edges, 629
    simple, 629
    vertices, 629
polynomial, 46
polynomial-time approximation scheme, 518
polynomial-time reducible, 483
position, 63, 70
potential function, 37–38
Pratt, 684
prefix, 653
prefix code, 292
prefix sums, 31
Preparata, 322, 650
Prim, 442
Prim-Jarnik algorithm, 433–435
primality testing, 547–549
prime, 546, 687
prime decomposition, 687
primitive operations, 7–10, 36
primitive root, 694
primitive root of unity, 715
printer spooler, 59
priority queue, 157–181
priority range tree, 613–614
priority search tree, 609–612
probabilistic packet marking, 566
probability, 26–28
probability space, 26
producer-consumer model, 52
program counter, 56
proximity, 642
prune-and-search, 270–278
pseudo-blocks, 592
pseudo-polynomial-time, 345
pseudo-random-number generators, 530
pseudocode, 5–6
PTAS, *see* polynomial-time approximation scheme
public-key cryptography, 701–707
public-key cryptosystem, 701
Pugh, 568

quadratic probing, 204
quadtree, 614–615
queue, 52, 57–59
    array implementation, 57–59
quick-sort, 250–256
    tree, 251

Raab, 568
Rabin, 568
Rabin-Miller algorithm, 548
radix-sort, 268–269
Raghavan, 264, 568, 602
Ramachandran, 88
random binary search tree, 107
random permutation, 531–534
random variable, 27
random-access machine, 7
randomized algorithm, 530
randomized quick-select, 270
randomized quick-sort, 253
range query, 101
range searching
    one-dimensional, 101–103
    three-sided, 609
range tree, 605–614
range-search query, 605
rank-balanced trees, 118
Rao, 730
reachability, 373
recurrence equation, 10, 248, 305–312
recursion, 10, 56
recursion tree, 307
red-black tree, 126–129, 644
Reed, 186
reflexive property, 157
rehashing, 205
relatively prime, 688, 691
relaxation, 400, 407
repeated squaring, 695
rescalable, 518
residual capacity, 449
residual distance, 455
residual graph, 454
residue, 691
restriction, 487
restructure
    trinode, 119
Ribeiro-Neto, 684
riffle shuffle, 262
right child, 69
right subtree, 69
right turn, 627
ring-loading problem, 527

Rivest, 396, 506, 703
road network, 398
Robson, 88
rolling-hash function, 666
root, 68
root object, 380
Rosenkrantz, 528
rotation, 118, 119, 122
    double, 119
    single, 119
roundoff error, 263, 300
RSA cryptosystem, 703–705
running time, 2–4, 8–10

Sackrowitz, 352
Samet, 602, 622
sample space, 26
Sankoff, 352
SAT, 502
satisfying assignment, 481
Saxe, 322
scalability, 2
scan forward, 558
Schaffer, 186
search engine, 679
secondary clustering, 204
Sedgewick, 50, 154, 186, 650
seed, 530
segment, 625
segment intersection, 638–641
Seidel, 239, 568, 622
selection, 270–278
selection-sort, 159
self-loop, 357
sentinel, 64, 190
separate chaining, 198
separation edge, 386
separation vertex, 386
set cover, 509
SET-COVER, 494, 495, 502, 515–517, 528
Shamir, 703
Shamir secret sharing, 728
Shamos, 650
Shapley, 568
Sharir, 239
Shing, 352
shortest path, 399–417
    Bellman-Ford algorithm, 407–409
    Dijkstra's algorithm, 400–406
    matrix multiplication, 413–417
sibling, 68
simplex method, 733, 739
sink, 444, 445

ski rental problem, 593
skip list, 557–562
    analysis, 561–562
    insertion, 559
    levels, 557
    removal, 560–561
    searching, 558–559
    towers, 557
    update operations, 559–561
skyline problem, 322
slack form, 739
Sleator, 154, 602
Smith-Waterman algorithm, 350
social network, 220
sorting, 158, 243–258, 267–269
    bucket-sort, 267–268
    external-memory, 590–592
    heap-sort, 174–178
    in-place, 175, 254
    insertion-sort, 161
    lower bound, 257–258
    merge-sort, 243–249
    priority-queue, 158
    quick-sort, 250–256
    radix-sort, 268–269
    selection-sort, 159
    stable, 268
source, 444, 445
space usage, 2
spanning forest, 369, 372
spanning subgraph, 359
spanning tree, 359, 365, 367, 368, 370, 372, 425
splay tree, 139–148
split, 579, 589
stable, 268
stable marriage problem, 536–538
stack, 53–56
    array implementation, 53–54
standard form, 734
Stearns, 528
steganography, 682
Steger, 568
Steiglitz, 302, 528
Stephen, 684
Stirling's Approximation, 762
STL, 88
Stooge-sort, 320
stop words, 671, 682
Strassen's Algorithm, 315
string
    null, 653
    pattern matching, *see* pattern matching

prefix, 653
    suffix, 653
strongly collision-resistant, 702
strongly connected, 373
strongly *NP*-hard, 496
subgraph, 359
SUBGRAPH-ISOMORPHISM, 504
subproblem optimality, 326, 329
subproblem overlap, 329
subsequence, 302, 324, 339
SUBSET-SUM, 496–498, 502, 506
substring, 348, 653
subtree, 68
suffix, 653
summation, 19, 763
    geometric, 19
symmetric encryption, 700–701
symmetric relation, 355

tabulation-based hashing, 196
tail estimate, 535
tail recursion, 256
Tamassia, 88, 710
Tarjan, 50, 88, 114, 154, 239, 396, 422, 442, 472, 602
task scheduling, 289–291
telescope scheduling, 331–333, 350
telescoping sum, 35, 763
text compression, 292–297
topological ordering, 382–384
total order, 157
totient function, 693
tower, 559
traceback, 566
trailer, 64
transfer, 582
transitive closure, 374, 376
transitive property, 157
traveling salesperson problem, 480, 501
treap, 622
tree, 68–88, 359
    binary, *see* binary tree
    child node, 68
    depth, 72–73
    external node, 68
    height, 72–73
    internal node, 68
    level, 76
    linked structure, 83–84
    multi-way, 574–577
    multidimensional, 605–617
    node, 68

    ordered, 69
    parent node, 68
    root node, 68
tree edge, 375, 376
tree traversal, 74–75, 78–81
    Euler tour, 80–81
    generic, 80–81
    inorder, 79
    level order, 87
    postorder, 75, 78
    preorder, 74, 78
triangle inequality, 511
triangulation, 348
trie, 669–679
    compressed, 673
    standard, 669
trinode restructuring, 118, 122
Tsakalidis, 114, 154
TSP, 480, 501, 511, 512, 518, 524, 526, 528
Tukey, 730
two-dimensional dictionary, 605
two-dimensional pattern matching, 683
two-sided error, 550
$(2, 4)$ tree, 578–584
    depth property, 578
    size property, 578

Ullman, 88, 154, 239, 506, 602, 730
unary encoding, 476
underflow, 582, 589
uniform hash, 664
union-by-size, 229
union-find, 221–235
universal hashing, 212–214
up-heap bubbling, 168
upper envelope, 321

van Leeuwen, 396, 422, 472
verification, 479
vertex, 355
    degree, 356
    in-degree, 356
    out-degree, 356
vertex cover, 352, 471, 482
VERTEX-COVER, 482, 492–497, 499, 506, 515, 528
vertical ray-shooting, 648
virtual memory, 572
Vishkin, 88
Vitter, 218, 602
Voronoi diagram, 649
Vuillemin, 622

Wang, 264
weak AVL tree, 130–135
web crawler, 339, 365
web spider, 365
weighted moving average, 730
Williams, 186
Wood, 88, 622
word wrapping, 349

Yannakakis, 528
Yao, 650
Yap, 730
Yates, 568
Young, 528

zig, 140, 146
zig-zag, 140, 146
zig-zig, 139, 146